D0991244

THE
UNIVERSITY OF WINNIPEG
PORTAGE & BALMORAL
WINNIPEG 2. MAN. CANADA

American Political Interest Groups: Readings in Theory and Research

Edited by Betty H. Zisk
Boston University

Wadsworth Publishing Company, Inc.
Belmont, California

Wadsworth Series in American Politics

General Editor: Bernard C. Hennessy, The Pennsylvania State University

American Political Interest Groups: Readings in Theory and Research
Betty H. Zisk, Boston University

Forthcoming

The Irony of Democracy: A Concise Introduction to American Politics
Thomas R. Dye, The Florida State University, and Harmon Zeigler, The University of Oregon

Introduction To American Politics
Walter A. Rosenbaum, The University of Florida, John W. Spanier, The University of Florida, and William C. Burris, Guilford College

An Introduction to The Study of Policy-Making
Charles O. Jones, The University of Arizona

Theory and Methods of Political Science
Carl Baar, Michigan State University

L. C. Cat. Card No.: 73-80725
Printed in the United States of America

Foreword

by Harmon Zeigler

The most encouraging development in the study of interest groups is the extension of research beyond a description of the role of groups in the policy-making process. It was natural for political scientists to concern themselves with the impact of groups or policy, given the assumption of most "standard" definitions of politics. Take, for example, David Easton's "Authoritative Allocation of Values." A strict interpretation of this definition might lead one, in studying interest groups, to limit the examination to the effects of lobbyists.

However, once political scientists began a systematic examination of lobbying, some alarming (theoretically) results appeared. The political scientists found that policy makers often were largely uninfluenced by organized groups. Among those works which question the impact of interest groups, one might mention Donald Matthew's *United States Senators and Their World*, Lester Milbrath's *The Washington Lobbyists,* and Raymond Bauer, Ithiel DeSola Pool, and Lewis A. Dexter's *American Business and Public Policy*. Each of these books reached similar conclusions about the effects of lobbying. They agreed that while interest groups are involved in the legislative process, their impact is limited and sporadic.

Further research directed itself to questions that might not have been asked had not a mood of skepticism begun to develop. Rather than looking at groups as a "first cause" of policy outcome, investigators were directed toward discovering the conditions (both systemic and individual) which maximize the strength of interest groups.

Along with a new look at the policy process, there appeared a willingness to explore aspects of interest groups other than their effect (or lack thereof) upon policy. Attention was directed *internally*—towards the effects of group membership upon the individual—and *externally*—towards the functions of formal organizations for society. The collection of essays by Professor Betty H. Zisk admirably reflects these trends. Excluding the essays in Part 2 (interest group theory), there are twenty-one individual readings. Eight of these articles deal with interest groups and the political process. The remainder are concerned with the internal dynamics of organizations, characteristics of group members, and the societal functions of groups. At one time, Part 4 (interest groups and the political process) would have comprised the limits of the inquiry.

Professor Zisk has demonstrated that, with the inquiry broadened, there is a wealth of research that has emerged from the study of voluntary associations by sociologists. For instance, one of the basic tenets of group theory is the function of "overlapping affiliations" in reducing the intensity of group conflict. Yet the article by Kriesberg, published in 1949 but largely ignored by political scientists, indicates that most members of an organization are unaware of conflicting demands which develop as a consequence of multiple membership. Societal stability is more likely to be achieved by the fact that organizational membership is positively related to social class and contributes independently to efficacy or community identification (Parts 5 and 6).

In Professor Zisk's introductory comments to each section, many of the comments outlined above are linked to the readings, placing them in a coherent system of inquiry.

My emphasis on the non-policy aspects of organizations is not intended to diminish the importance of the contributions of Part 4 (interest groups and the political process) but rather to place them in the appropriate perspective. Many of the readings in this section illustrate the trend away from journalistic description toward systematic analysis. The readings most characteristic of this trend are those by Wahlke, Eulau, Buchanan, and Ferguson ("American State Legislators' Role Orientation Toward Pressure Groups") and Zisk, Eulau, and Prewitt ("City Councilmen and the Group Struggle: A Typology of Role Orientations"). Both essays are designed to test the utility of role theory in explaining the place of interest groups in the policy process. The use of one set of data (city councilmen) to extend the ideas developed from another set (state legislators) illustrates the possibilities for a kind of systematic research which was lacking in most of the earlier description of group politics.

Professor Zisk has also included essays on the comparative study of interest groups. Although several of the essays in other sections are also comparative (comparing cities or states), this section reminds us that causal theory depends upon replication and a variety of settings. Finally, the use of gaming techniques may also build a body of hypotheses which may be tested in non-experimental situations. It is appropriate to conclude the volume with a tentative statement—a game situation. Indeed, a major message of the book is that we have a great deal of work to do. In spite of the traditional preoccupation of political scientists with policy, we have not developed a reliable measure of the effects of group activity. In the laboratory, we can measure the intervention of an actor by repeating the experiment without the intervention. In the political process, we might ask what would have happened in a given situation if no group had intervened, but we cannot answer this question. Gaming does not necessarily provide an empirically valid answer, but it does make possible more logical speculation.

Eugene, Oregon H. Z.

Acknowledgments

This collection was conceived, nurtured, and brought forth as the product of a "group process." The students in my undergraduate class and graduate seminar on interest groups worked as editorial and analytical partners. I am particularly grateful to Harvey Boulay, Edward Berger, Frances Burke, and Joseph Rottenborn—all of whom combined their editorial skill with a strong measure of moral and practical support. My colleagues, Walter Clemens, Murray Levin and Allan Shank, made several contributions, not the least of which was their spirited participation in pre-testing *URBOS*. My three sons, Jonathan, Stephen, and Matthew, deserve special mention not only for their service as messengers in three plays of *URBOS* but also for their self-restraint while their mother was wrestling with deadlines (this book is dedicated, for analogous reasons, to their father). Harmon Zeigler, University of Oregon, and Norman Luttbeg, Florida State University, contributed substantial advice and critical assistance; Harmon's suggestions, over a period of several months, were indispensable. Finally, no author could hope for more congenial, or more practical, editors than Bernard Hennessy of Pennsylvania State University and Robert Gormley of Wadsworth Publishing Company. It was largely through their efforts that the group process never degenerated—in this instance—into a group struggle.

Boston

Betty H. Zisk

To Stan—
who insisted

Contents

American Political Interest Groups

The Study of American Political Interest Groups: A Framework

At bottom, group interests are the animating forces in the political process; and understanding of American politics requires a knowledge of the chief interests and of their stake in public policy. The exercise of the power of governance consists in large degree in the advancement of legitimate group objectives, in the reconciliation and mediation of conflicting group ambitions, and in the restraint of group tendencies judged to be socially destructive.
(V. O. Key, Politics, Parties and Pressure Groups).

Some American scholars might disagree with the pivotal role which V. O. Key attributes to political interest groups; others might dispute his picture of government as a mediator of group claims and a partner in furthering "legitimate group objectives." Few, however, would contend that group interests are irrelevant or unimportant.

The political interest group has been studied for several reasons. First, it is argued that such groups can act as a major link between the citizen and his government. Along with political parties and the news media, the interest group transmits the hopes and demands of individuals to their representatives. The interest group can supplement the ballot box and the indignant letter as a means of communication between the leader and the led. In a political process dominated by two broad, nonideological parties and by national elections held at fixed and relatively infrequent intervals, the role of the interest group as intermediary can assume special importance.

Second, the political interest group is viewed as a bargaining agent in the public allocation of material and human resources. Indeed, the interest group may be the only feasible medium for such bargaining. Certainly, direct consultation between public officials and those affected by their decisions is impractical in a large and complex society. Again, the political parties are too amorphous and include within their ranks too many disparate interests to act in this capacity. Spokesmen for unions, for business, for veterans, or for doctors can help to narrow the range of alternatives debated and to lay the groundwork for general acceptance of the decisions made. Prior consultation between group spokesmen and public officials does not, of course, guarantee *universal* acceptance of such decisions (nor does it invariably improve the quality of public policies), but it may bring new policies within the limits of tolerability to the majority of interested parties.

Finally, some scholars believe that the interest group—along with other "voluntary associations"—can orient the lone individual to a highly complex society.

Like a college fraternity or a Polish-American athletic society, a union, a merchants' association, or the Ku Klux Klan can furnish the individual with an opportunity to belong, to further his particular aims, and to assume a position of responsibility in society. If the individual takes advantage of this opportunity, he is less likely to feel alienated, frustrated, or lost in a mass of strangers.

A Historical Overview of Interest Group Theory and Research

We can distinguish three "eras" in the study of interest groups in America: pre-1900, the *omission* of the interest group from serious consideration; 1900-1950, the *pejorative treatment* of the interest group, despite the efforts of a few analytical pioneers; and, finally, 1950 to the present, the gradual replacement of abstract moral judgments with first-hand, precise *analysis* and *explanation.*

Interest-group theorists are prone to claim as antecedents the pluralist philosophers of Britain and the Continent (for example, Figgis and Maitland) or the rare American commentators (Madison, Calhoun, and the eloquent outsider, De Tocqueville) who discussed politics in a conflictual or sociological context. Madison's discussion of "factions," Calhoun's theory of the "concurrent majority," or De Tocqueville's observations about the American tendency to form associations have a distinctively modern tone. Their consideration of the economic and social underpinnings of political institutions and their focus on "private," as well as "legal," structures were completely outside the eighteenth- and nineteenth-century mainstream. During this period, most students of political philosophy on both sides of the Atlantic were inextricably committed to abstruse discussions of sovereignty, natural law, and other essentially formal problems.

It is not surprising that little notice was taken of interest groups in the political writings of previous centuries, since complex national organizations did not come into being until well after the Industrial Revolution. Their predecessors—guilds, workers' associations, and even the Grange—operated primarily on a local basis and showed little enduring interest in political affairs. By the last decades of the nineteenth century, however, the rising militance of organized labor brought forth counterorganization among employers; and after World War I, with the increasing nationalization of political issues, the practice of lobbying became common.

In the second era (1900 to 1950), several scholars (most notably Bentley, Herring, and Odegard[1]) argued for a serious analysis of this new phenomenon.

[1]The literature from this era will be discussed more fully below, in Section 2.

The dominant approach, however, was one of denunciation of "the interests" and of pleading for procedural reforms. Interest groups were viewed as interlopers or barriers between citizens and government. They were "irresponsible" because they were independent of popular control; they were assumed to be all-pervasive and powerful. Various remedies were suggested: regulation of campaign spending, regulation of lobbying activity, reform of parties, or establishment of mechanisms for direct democracy, such as the initiative and referendum. (This same era saw the rise of the municipal reform movement. The city-manager form of government, for example, was an effort to undermine the strength of the political "boss." Both antilobby and antiboss sentiment sprang from Populist-Progressive-reform roots.)

During this same period, interest groups were studied by some sociologists and social psychologists. Groups like the WCTU, the Townsend Plan advocates, and the various "fringe" organizations were natural subjects to those concerned with the impact of group membership on individual values. Such concerns, however, were not primarily *political;* and, like some of the early voting studies conducted by psychologists, the findings were of limited utility for building a theory of political behavior.

The third era began at about the same time as the more general "behavioral revolution" in the study of politics. (Not all of those who wrote on interest groups after 1950, however, were self-consciously behavioral in orientation.) A complete survey of the tenets of behavioralism will not be attempted, but some brief highlights are needed to provide a perspective on the studies in the volume. The behavioral approach emphasizes:

1. the need for *empirical work* (studies based on first-hand observation, participation, or interviews or on evidence from reliable records like Senate roll-call votes or census reports)
2. the need for an *interdisciplinary approach* (use of information once thought the domain of other specialties—for example, psychological motives or attitudes, social class and stratification, and the diffusion of cultural values)
3. the need for *systematic theory* (development of systems of explanation which can cover a variety of phenomena and which can be tested against the real world at concrete points; an emphasis on theory as explanation rather than on theory as moral evaluation).

There has been some disagreement in this era about the place of interest groups in the study of political behavior. Some scholars tried to make the group the center of a comprehensive theory of politics;[2] others opted for relatively modest studies, attempting to analyze interest-group organization and activity as *one part* of the American political process and social structure. There is considerable agreement, however, on the broad questions that need to be studied. These can be summarized as follows:

1. *Antecedents:* What factors shape the values, structure, and activities of interest groups?
2. *Effectors:* How do interest groups go about trying to achieve their aims?
3. *Consequences:* What impact do political interest groups have on the acts and attitudes of individual citizens? On the behavior of policy-makers?

A Framework for the Study of Interest Groups in the Political Process

This volume represents an attempt to present, in a balanced way, the available evidence on the role of interest groups in the political process. With very few exceptions, the selections included are recent reports on empirical research. Many authors concern themselves with questions of psychological motivation and social status, as well as more traditional political concerns; and most are interested in analytical rather than in normative questions.

A general summary of the antecedents, effectors, and consequences of group activity is presented in Figure 1 in the hope that it will enable the student to place the articles which follow in a meaningful framework. None of the relatively brief selections in this volume cover all facets of the interest-group process—both because of the size of such an undertaking and because of the intrinsic difficulty of some relevant questions. Taken as a whole, however, the information now available covers most topics to the middle and left of the chart; the major gaps exist in regard to the connection between interest-group activities and policy outputs.

It will be noted that from the perspective of the group itself, there are five short-range elements in the political process: group characteristics, alternative sources of influence, the targets of influence, the legal structure and general environment, and the *interactions* between the group and others (especially the target populations). In the long-range view, the element of "feedback"—the effect of policy outputs on the general environment, on the legal structure, and on the group itself—is also important.

[2]The comprehensive "group theory" approach has not been a fruitful one because the concept of "group" is not broad enough to cover the full range of relevant political phenomena unless it is broadened to the point where it becomes useless for research purposes. Group theory will be discussed at length, by several authors, in Section 2.

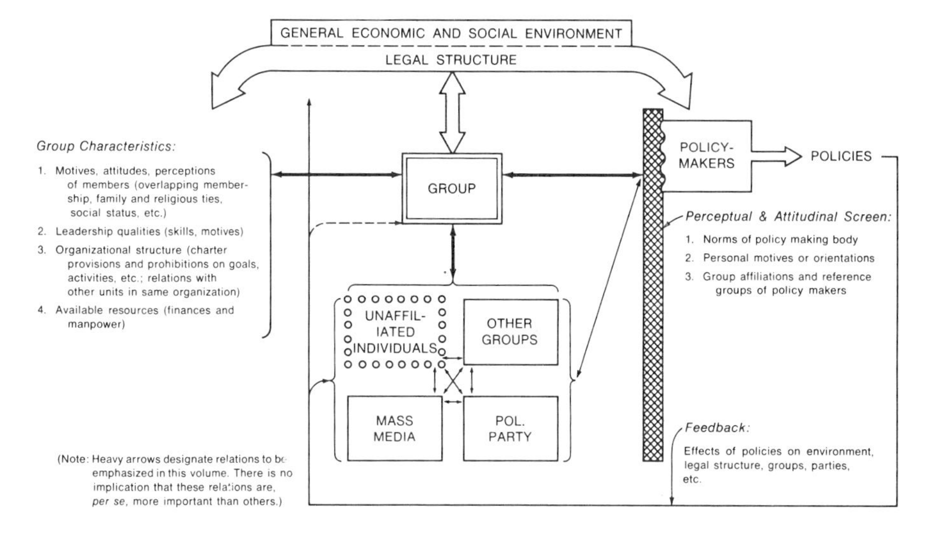

Figure 1. The Interest Group in the Political Process—
A Summary of Major Antecedents, Effectors, and
Consequences of Interest Group Activity

If this diagram is viewed in terms of our three questions, *antecedents* include group characteristics, the legal structure and general environment, and, to a degree, alternative sources of influence; *effectors* are pictured by the interaction arrows between the group and others; and *consequences* are the changes in the actions of policy-makers (or of unaffiliated individuals, the media, parties, and others), which in turn affect *policies* and, ultimately, the legal structure and general environment through "feedback." A brief discussion of each of these elements in the political process follows.

Internal characteristics. Internal characteristics may determine how effective the group is in pursuing and achieving its goals; they may also limit the tactics which the group employs. A highly unified group may be more influential, for example, than one which is fragmented, and it may also be more successful in providing a feeling of security for its members. A group which attracts ideologically oriented members may find it difficult to expand its membership beyond a "hard core." It may also lack the flexibility needed for effective bargaining. At the same time, however, such an organization probably has great tenacity in pursuing its goals over a long period of time.

Alternative sources of influence. Alternative sources of influence include political parties, the mass media, and unaffiliated individuals. These alternative sources of influence are, of course, shaped by the same factors (for example, the legal structure and the general environment) which shape the activities of the focal group.

Overlapping memberships (group members who belong to more than one organization or who belong to both an organization and a party) may be important to both the group and the society at large. If the loyalties of a significant number of group members are divided, the group may be less cohesive than organizations whose members are single-minded. At the same time, however, it is sometimes argued that overlapping memberships in a large number of groups prevent the kind of sharp cleavage or bipolarization of politics which might rend the very fabric of the society.

Targets to be influenced. There are two major targets—the official policy-maker and the unaffiliated citizen. Note the "perceptual and attitudinal screen" between the group and policy-maker. If, for example, legislative or judicial norms forbid a close relation between "disinterested" officials and lobbyists, group activities will probably be viewed with suspicion, unless they are clothed in terms of the "general interest." A similar screen may exist for individual citizens (for example, selective reading habits, cynicism, or suspicion about "the interests"). Once again, if the group can project an image of "disinterestedness," it may be more effective in reaching the general population.

The legal structure and the general environment. This category includes the available material and human resources and the competing demands on those resources; the legal and informal norms under which groups operate; and the relative social status of various groupings in the community. (Is the policy-making body chosen from a dominant religious or ethnic group which receives preferential treatment because of its position? Is there general consensus about the claims of this dominant group? Do the laws reflect this consensus?)

Interactions. The methods used by interest groups may have considerable impact on their effectiveness. Group tactics are limited, of course, by other elements in the political process: legal and informal norms (Are campaign expenditures limited? Are public hearings held? Are "interests" denounced periodically?); group characteristics (How much money is available? Will members tolerate partisan alliances? Do members and leaders possess essential political skills?); and the perceptual screens of target populations. In addition to studying these limits, however, we need to learn more about the relative effectiveness of different tactics (for example, information provision versus threats, informal versus formal contacts) and the reason for variations in tactics employed by different groups.

Feedback. This element is defined as the effect of policy outputs both on the general environment and legal structure and on the group itself. Two general categories of outputs are relevant:

1. Laws, rulings, and other enactments affect the total amount and distribution of available resources and the legal limits under which groups operate. In addition, these rulings may have considerable impact on the goals of a group. The WCTU was affected by the passage (and later repeal) of prohibition; the AMA's goals and perhaps its structure are involved in the passage or defeat of proposals for public medical aid.
2. Official debates or discussions not resulting in new enactments may have considerable effect on the political environment and direct effect on the group because they arouse hope, resignation, or despair. Defeat of civil-rights legislation may have more impact on the internal structure of the civil-rights movement than will passage of a weak bill.

It must be emphasized that Figure 1 charts the political process as if it were insulated from other political systems. This assumption is, of course, unrealistic. In dealing with a concrete political system (for instance, a local community or the United States government), external influences must be taken into account. Thus, the legal structure and general environment in a large industrial town may be affected far more by (1) state welfare laws, (2) a federal ruling on segregation, (3) the outbreak of war with its effects on manpower and resources than it is by the struggle between local groups and party organizations. Similarly, the national political process—and the efforts of national groups—cannot be understood apart from the dislocations brought about by the actions of international leaders. Appropriations for a "war on poverty," for example, are usually given short shrift during a major war; they may be treated far more sympathetically, in contrast, by a Congress facing a postwar depression.

Unanswered Questions

As mentioned above, more is now known about the antecedents and effectors of group activity than is known about the consequences. The main explanation for this state of affairs is the difference in the research complexity of the three questions; group structure and tactics can be described and analyzed without resort to the indirect reasoning that becomes necessary when the questions of influence or the long-range effects of group activities are tackled. We can compare the size or financial health of organizations, the attendance record or voting turnout at meetings, the unanimity of members, or the social status of members without much difficulty. How do we measure the success of groups in integrating the dispossessed, the lonely, or the alienated into American society? How do we demonstrate, beyond a reasonable doubt, the crucial role of a union or a civil-rights group in the passage of an appropriations bill?

"Power" has always been elusive concept in the social sciences. There are literally dozens of varying definitions of the term. Perhaps the one most relevant to the aims and methods of political interest groups is that of Bertrand Russell, who defined power as "the production of intended effects."[3] Thus, we may define the influence that A has over B in terms of the actions that B takes *which he would not have taken without A's efforts.*[4] We must now somehow separate the impact *of A's efforts from the impact* of all the other efforts made to influence B (including the impact of B's prior leanings or predispositions). The attempt to deal with this question of measuring influence, even if only indirectly, continues despite its difficulty because it is the *raison d'etre* for the study of interest groups.

There is little point in studying antecedents to political acts without some information about the effect of those acts on the "outputs" of politics, in other words, on decisions made by public officials or on the attitudes of individuals. It is in this area—the analysis of group influence on political outputs—that future work is most urgently needed. It is to be hoped that in a few decades yet another section (entitled "Policy Outputs and Feedback") can be added to a volume on this subject.

[3]Bertrand Russell, *Power: A New Social Analysis* (London: Unwin, 1962), p. 25.

[4]This definition is similar to that used by Almond and Verba, who say: "We shall roughly define the political influence of a group or individual over a governmental decision as equal to the degree to which governmental officials act to benefit that group or individual because the officials believe that they will risk some deprivation . . . if they do not so act." The definition appears on the first page of the selection from Almond and Verba's *The Civic Culture,* in Section 6 of the present volume.

Interest Group Theory

When the groups are adequately stated, everything is stated. When I say everything I mean everything. The complete description would mean the complete science in the study of social phenomena . . . (Arthur Bentley, The Process of Government).

This claim, hotly contested by later critics of "group theory," was made by the "grandfather" of group theory, Arthur Bentley, in 1908. His dogmatic tone was in part a reaction against the prevalent legalistic and moralistic approach to the study of things political—an approach which dominated American political science until shortly after World War II. While the muckraking writers of the popular press (Lincoln Steffens, Upton Sinclair, Ida Tarbell, and others) denounced "the interests" and the developing political machines of the city, the academicians, with few exceptions, continued to concentrate on the formal structure of government. Congressional-executive relations, the power of the speaker of the House, and abstract problems of natural law and sovereignty were their main interests. Bentley was urging, in essence, a shift in attention from the formal structure of government to the nitty-gritty of politics—the complex and fluid decision-making process which takes place behind the institutional facade.

Bentley's call for a focus on the group process was largely ignored for four decades. To be sure, the period between 1928 and 1950 saw some shift of attention to interest group-legislature relations through landmark studies by Peter Odegard, E. E. Schattschneider, Oliver Garceau, and a handful of other scholars.[1] Nevertheless, Bentley's central goal, his "attempt to fashion a tool,"[2] was ignored in the sense that Odegard and others contented themselves with isolated case studies rather than trying to build an empirical theory which might *explain* (rather than *describe*) a wide range of group-related phenomena. Of all the authors of this early period, Pendleton Herring perhaps came closest, in *Group Representation before Congress*, to Bentley's original goal.[3] Even his seminal work, however, remains essentially descriptive and discursive in comparison with later efforts to develop group theory.

[1]Peter H. Odegard, *Pressure Politics: The Study of the Anti-Saloon League* (Boulder, Colo.: Univ. Colorado Press, 1928); E. E. Schattschneider, *Politics, Pressures and the Tariff* (Englewood Cliffs, N. J.: Prentice-Hall, 1935); and Oliver Garceau, *The Political Life of the American Medical Association* (Cambridge, Mass.: Harvard Univ. Press, 1949).

[2]Bentley's words—on an introductory page.

[3]E. Pendleton Herring, *Group Representation before Congress* (Baltimore: Johns Hopkins Univ. Press, 1929).

It remained for Stephen Bailey (1950), Bertram Gross (1953), and especially David Truman (1951) and Earl Latham (1952) to tackle the job.[4] Bailey and Gross still concentrated on the single case—namely, the passage of the 1946 Employment Act—but *with a difference*. Bailey, in particular, took a first step toward the development of a more general theory of interest groups with his effort to handle Herring's "Four I's" (interests, institutions, individuals, and ideas) as "vectors" in a group-legislature struggle. He applied this framework, with considerable sophistication, to the legislative campaign he was studying.

In the studies of Truman and Latham, however, group theory came of age. Both men, like Bentley before them, tried to explain *all* political behavior in terms of the group. No longer content with discussing one bill, or the interplay of the grass roots, the group leaders, and the congressman in regard to one set of issues, Truman and Latham tried to cover the full range of political phenomena in terms of intra-group and intergroup relations. The questions before the contemporary student are: Did they succeed? Is the task in itself impossible? *Can* all political behavior be explained in exclusively group terms?

One theme which runs through the literature critical of group theory is its utility to the student of politics. The critics ask: What are the limitations of group theory? Does it promise more than it delivers? Is it even a practical way to handle narrow questions concerning, for example, lobbyist-legislator interactions?

An additional set of questions is raised by the critics. These questions concern the moral implications of the theory. Does such a theory push to the side all questions of "good" goals in favor of those which result from group pressures? This question is asked at two levels—and the student should attempt to distinguish each: (1) Does the political world which group theorists describe *omit* important elements of political life, such as the lone individual, values held by citizens, and the independent stance of the legislator? and (2) Does group theory *condone or rationalize* a political process which operates against individuals' best interests, public values, legislative integrity? For most modern analysts the two sets of questions are distinguishable; both should be confronted by the serious student of political behavior.

[4]Stephen K. Bailey, *Congress Makes a Law: The Story behind the Employment Act of 1946* (New York: Columbia Univ. Press, 1950); Bertram M. Gross, *The Legislative Struggle: A Study in Social Combat* (New York: McGraw-Hill, 1953); David B. Truman, *The Governmental Process* (New York: Knopf, 1951); and Earl Latham, "The Group Basis of Politics: Notes for a Theory," *American Political Science Review*, Vol. 46 (June 1952), pp. 376-97. Latham's article, which is presented in this book, is a shorter version of his theory given in *The Group Basis of Politics: A Study in Basing Point Legislation* (Ithaca, N.Y.: Cornell Univ. Press, 1952).

We begin our study of group theory with a concise article which presents the basic elements of the theory.[5] Earl Latham first distinguishes modern "analytical pluralism" (an effort to study "the structure and processes of group forms as they in fact occur") from "philosophical pluralism" as espoused by Figgis, Maitland, Laski, and others, who concerned themselves in large part with questions of social and economic reform. The distinction is crucial, particularly in light of later criticisms made by such men as Peter Odegard, Stanley Rothman, and David Smith. A primary feature of Latham and Truman's work is their effort to divorce the scientific study of the group process from an attempt to evaluate that process in terms of such norms as freedom, rationality, or the ultimate merits of the contents of legislation. Thus, Latham can define organized groups as "structures of power" which "concentrate human wit, energy and muscle for the achievement of received purposes," without inquiring too deeply into the merits of those purposes. At a later point, when describing the means by which groups deal with their environments, he predicts three major modes of adjustment (placing restraints on the environment, neutralizing it, and conciliating it), without asking about the implications of such adaptive mechanisms for "the public interest" or for those parts of the society which are as yet unorganized. Neither Latham nor Truman recognizes the existence of a "public interest" apart from the interaction of specific group interests; unorganized segments of society are conceived of as "latent" or "incipient" groups.

This lack of concern with the public interest has been heavily criticized by David G. Smith in the second article of this section. He argues that such a stance is amoral, if not immoral, in its indifference to the content of group goals, in its stress on policy as an outcome of power-relations among groups, and in its rejection of the role played by individuals *apart from* their activities in organized groups.

In this article, Smith passes an even harsher judgment on another aspect of Latham and Truman's theory—their failure to analyze and explain in detail the critical role of the official policy-maker, whether congressman or administrator. Latham's concept of "officiality" and Truman's consideration of "the rules of the game" are not adequate, argues Smith, to handle the problems created for group theorists by the "legitimacy" accorded official groups, such as Congress and administrative agencies. If group theory attempts to explain *all* political behavior, Truman and Latham's efforts to include official

[5] Latham's version of group theory is presented here because it is shorter and more concise; the student is urged, however, to dip into Professor Truman's book as well. There are several major differences in their theoretical stances—notably in their conceptions of "group" (in terms of "power" versus "shared interests") and in their handling of the concept of latency or potentiality.

policy-makers as merely political groups with "legitimate" status simply do not suffice. Group theory is weakest, argues Smith, when it attempts to deal with political outputs which are the product of long-standing policy decisions. The concept of a "group struggle" within the administration itself acknowledges the problem—and casts considerable light on the administrative process—but does not deal with it adequately in either empirical or normative terms.

This criticism of group theory is different from earlier arguments regarding amorality, antirationality, and indifference to the public interest. Here the question (and it is probably the crucial one) revolves around the adequacy of group theory as an *explanation* of the total range of political behavior. If group theory cannot adequately account for the behavior of legislators and administrators in their actions as policy-makers, then indeed Bentley's claim to explain "everything" falls short of the mark. It may account for a modest range of activity, but it does not explain why a given bill passes and another does not or why a current civil-rights bill or a poverty program without "teeth" cannot do the job.

The final article in this section, Samuel Eldersveld's survey of the current status of theory and research in the field,[6] reminds us, however, of the role which a "middle range" theory can play in aiding research. Eldersveld surveys the whole body of American interest-group literature and finds its explanatory value lacking—not because it fails to encompass the total range of the political process but because none of its advocates has provided a framework for comparative research. Eldersveld is arguing, as do most political scientists, for the development of "theory" which will enable us to predict future consequences and to explain past behavior. In essence, however, he is pleading not for a "group theory of politics" but rather for comparable standards or indices which students of the group can use in discussing and evaluating particular cases. He points out (rightly) that even the conclusions drawn from the most carefully written studies are of little help in building generalizations because the reader is never sure that the authors are focusing on comparable aspects of political behavior. In the end, Eldersveld suggests several guidelines for productive research on groups. The student will want to evaluate these suggestions in the light of his own knowledge of the field.

Formal group theory is only one possible approach to the explanation of interest-group activity. The range of alternatives is as broad as the imaginations of students of politics. Some alternative approaches are presented at a later point in this book—among them, role analysis (Wahlke *et al.*; Zisk *et al.*) and structural-functional analysis (Almond and Verba). The concept of political

[6]Written in 1958 but equally relevant today—as will be clear from a survey of the post-1958 literature included in this volume.

culture (Almond and Verba; Verba) may also be of value in explaining group behavior, particularly in a comparative context. The student of the subject is warned against a premature decision on which approach offers the most for an understanding of interest-group behavior. The approach chosen may depend on the nature of the particular problem studied.

The Group Basis of Politics: Notes for a Theory

Earl Latham

The chief social values cherished by individuals in modern society are realized through groups. These groupings may be simple in structure, unicellular, so to speak, like a juvenile gang. Or they may be intricate meshes of associated, federated, combined, consolidated, merged, or amalgamated units and subunits of organization, fitted together to perform the divided and assigned parts of a common purpose to which the components are dedicated. They may operate out of the direct public gaze like religious organizations, which tend to have a low degree of visibility. Or they may, like Congress and many other official groups, occupy the front pages for weeks at a time. National organizations are usually conspicuous; indeed, so much is this so at times that they tend to divert the eye from the great number of groups which stand at the elbow of the citizen of every small town. Everywhere groups abound, and they may be examined at close range and from afar.[1]

[1]In the small town of Amherst, Massachusetts, there are, not counting student organizations and official groups in the town government, "well more than one hundred Clubs, Lodges, Leagues, Guilds, Tribes, Granges, Unions, Chapters, Councils, Societies, Associations, Auxiliaries, Brotherhoods, and Fellowships. Their specialties or special interests, to name a few, include cards, cameras, stamps, gardens, churches, teachers, speakers, voters, horses, business, service, golf, nature, eating, fishing, gunning, parents, grandparents, ancestors, needlework, temperance, travel, and kindergarten" (William L. Doran, *University of Massachusetts Alumni Bulletin*, Vol. 31, No. 4 [December 1948], p. 4).

Earl Latham, "The Group Basis of Politics: Notes for a Theory," American Political Science Review, *Vol. 46 (1952).*

I. The Group Idea in Social Science

The literature of many disciplines agrees, as it does sometimes in little else, on the central importance of groups to an understanding of men in their relations with each other. The science of sociology, for example, devotes itself to the study of groups and groupings in society, the forms of group structure and behavior, the role of the individual in the group and his relation to it, the development of functional norms of behavior, the tendency of informal groups to sift themselves into a leadership and the led, the relation of subgroups to a central body, and so on.

But the sociologists are not alone. The instrumentalist philosophy of John Dewey rejects the abstract individual as a fictional character, and asserts that the individual has meaning only in his relations with others.[2] The psychologists, by different routes, come to the same conclusion. The Gestalt school argues that the basic forms of knowing are comprehensive collectivities, general thought forms and patterns, not atomistic particulars. Modern psychoanalytical theory, as represented by Dr. Karen Horney, rejects the earlier Freudian assumption that the singular person can be understood apart from his culture, and asserts, instead, that what were formerly regarded as innate elements of the personality are induced traits originating in the culture, the result of interpersonal, i.e., group or social, influences.[3] The concept of the group has been indispensable to those working in the combined fields of cultural anthropology and psychology.[4] The concept of the group also is basic to certain approaches to jurisprudence,[5] and it has been helpful in bringing to economics a knowledge of the human institutions through which men dig coal, make soap and battleships, create credit, and allocate the resources of production.

Commons, Veblen, Clark, Andrews, and other pioneers in the empirical study of such economic group forms as banks, corporations, granges, unions, cooperatives, railroads, brokerage houses, and exchanges did much to rectify the notion that some objective law, heedless of men, somehow filled each purse to the exact limit

[2] John Dewey, *Human Nature and Conduct: An Introduction to Social Psychology* (New York, 1922). See also Dewey's *The Public and Its Problems.*

[3] Karen Horney, *The Neurotic Personality of Our Time* (New York, 1937) and *New Ways in Psychoanalysis* (New York, 1939). For example, Sigmund Freud's *The Interpretation of Dreams*, trans. Dr. A. A. Brill (New York, 1950), describes and explains the Oedipus complex without limiting it to any culture (pp. 160-162 and 269-270). But what becomes of the Oedipus complex in a society like that of the Marquesas or the Trobriand Islands, where, anthropologists assert, it does not exist? Modern research suggests that this fundamental pattern in human behavior is a culture trait; for a discussion of the point, see Abram Kardiner, *The Individual and His Society* (New York, 1947), pp. 479 ff.

[4] Well known are the following works: Bronislaw Malinowski, *Argonauts of the Western Pacific* (New York, 1922); Ruth Benedict, *Patterns of Culture* (Boston, 1934) and *The Chrysanthemum and the Sword* (Boston, 1946); Kardiner, *The Individual and His Society*; and Ralph Linton, *The Cultural Background of Personality* (New York, 1945).

[5] As in N. S. Timasheff, *An Introduction to the Sociology of Law* (Cambridge, 1939).

justified by the contribution of its owner to the total of the goods and services of society. The economic theory of a century ago fixed the nature of the economic universe by definition and tended to derive its characteristics by deduction—an economic universe inhabited by a multiplicity of individuals in isolation, where combination was a pathological deviation. Such a *defined* (not observed) universe could not fail to work—in the realm of discourse. However, so far have we come from this view that a whole new vocabulary has been invented to explain the operations of an economic community formed of aggregations, clusters, blocs, and combinations of people and things—not individuals in isolation. Few modern writers on economics would be able to discuss their subject matter without reference to "oligopoly," "imperfect competition," "monopolistic competition," and other group phenomena in the economic community.

II. The Group Idea in Political Theory

The Utilitarians made the same assumptions about the nature of the political community that they made about the nature of the economic community. While the liberal philosophy of a John Stuart Mill rejected doctrines of natural law and right that were so familiar to the eighteenth century, it retained the feeling that the chief political problems were those that involved the singular individual on the one hand and the "state" on the other. All other and intermediate associations and groupings were dissolved, blanked, and obscured—a kind of sunken hinterland between two dominating mountainous battlements. This exaggerated individualism not only abstracted man from his social environment; it made him more sentient, more responsive to the gentle but compelling dictates of reason, more enlightened about his affairs than the facts justified. The political community seemed to possess characteristics of an Oxford debating society, policy emerging from endless debate, with reason presiding in the speaker's chair.[6]

But Utilitarian theories did not entirely dominate the field of political speculation, even in England. On the Continent and to a lesser degree in England, considerable attention was given to the works of the philosophical idealists—the school of Hegel, Fichte, and Treitschke on the Continent, and of T. H. Green, Bradley, and Bosanquet later in England. The Utilitarians virtually abolished the state, by deduction, and the philosophic idealists virtually abolished the individual, also by deduction. The first imagined the political community to be a loose coexistence of singular individuals, like marbles on a plate, held loosely together within the circumference of a common restraint but otherwise complete, unengaged, private, and unique. The second rather imagined the political

[6]This conception is fundamental to John Stuart Mill's famous essay, "On Liberty." For a discussion of the relation between Mill's view and the prevailing doctrine of free speech in the United States Supreme Court, see Earl Latham, "The Theory of the Judicial Doctrine of Freedom of Speech," in the *Journal of Politics*, Vol. 12 (November 1950), pp. 637-651.

community to resemble beads on a string, of which the separate parts by themselves were incomplete and without meaning, and which existed only to fulfill the pattern of the necklace.

The principal attack, in England at least, upon the political speculations of the philosophic idealists was made by a group of writers professing pluralist doctrines. Figgis, Maitland, G. D. H. Cole, and Laski showed that many of the assumptions of the idealist school were contrary to fact. They showed that the state does not absorb all of the loyalties of the individual in the political community, as had been asserted, but that many lesser associations, such as church, corporation, and trade union, also lay claim to the faith, attachment, devotion, and obedience of the individual, and that these claims are acknowledged by responsive behavior. The state, said the pluralists, is merely one association among a host of associations, both factually and rightfully; and far from absorbing the entire allegiance of the individual, the state must compete with conflicting group loyalties, some of which are invincible. Most people think of themselves first as members of their clubs, lodges, unions, or parishes, and only incidentally as members of the state. And since the state is merely one group among many, it is without superior right to dominate other associations. In its extreme form (in guild socialism, for example), the pluralist doctrine advocated political communities organized syndically by industries, with common affairs administered by common consent, a loose kind of confederation or working alliance.

The pluralists did useful work when they evaporated the misty figment of the state which the idealists had presented as a colossus of unity, a monolith, an absolute, a total system swallowing and assimilating all personal beliefs, attachments, obligations, and relations, endowed with some of the attributes of human personality like will, and having an autonomous and independent life and existence apart from the lives and personalitites of the members of the political community. But while this spectral personality was exorcised from the state by the pluralists, they materialized the phantasm in other bodies. The state, they said, did not have a "real" personality, separate and apart from its people; it was not a separate corpus possessing such human attributes as personality and will. What was denied to the state, however, was claimed for other associations, such as churches and trade unions. One would have thought that the arguments that caused the rejection of the real personality of the state should also have caused the rejection of the real personalities of other group associations. Or conversely, if the nonstate associations had real personalities, it was difficult to see why the state should be denied one, since it was also an association. Actually the effort, by words, to make the state disappear did not succeed, because all of the pluralist writers found it necessary to invent a normative, rule-making apparatus to represent the community interests of the constituent group associations, that is, to perform the functions of the state. What they sought to achieve was a political community based upon a federation of constituent groups to replace the consolidated lump that the idealists had been describing, authoritarian and unstriated; and in this endeavor the important insights of the pluralists were at least two. First, they pointed out the undeniable fact of the group basis of society, in both its political and its economic communities. Second, they demonstrated a few of the virtually infinite number of accommodations between the common and the universal on the one hand and the diverse and the particular on the other. These accommodations are implicit in the principle of federalism—a master principle that makes it possible to produce unities out of multiplicities of dissimilar parts, including unities as local as the organizations in the Community Fund and as universal as the United Nations.

The English pluralists did two things at the same time: they made an observation and expressed a hope. They described the group basis of society and then either erected Utopia upon this foundation or employed the insight to rationalize prejudged social and economic reforms. They intermingled wish and fact, and may indeed have been led to the second by the intensity of the first. Some support for this view is supplied by the evidence that writers like Laski, once pluralists, abandoned the doctrine and worked with more authoritarian modes of social reform, ignoring the fact when it seemed no longer to suit the hope. Perhaps for such pluralists the adjective "philosophic" may be employed, as a phrase which suggests the characteristics of system, perception, metaphysics, and value judgment which are found in their writings. The philosophic pluralists accepted the group basis of society, but failed to investigate its forms, mutations, and permutations in a scientific spirit. It has remained for others to carry forward scientific analyses of group behavior, including a number of writers on politics. The word "pluralists" may properly be applied to these investigators since they deal with the plurality of observed group forms, but they are concerned less with prejudged programs of social and economic reform than with the accurate investigation and description of the many phenomena connected with the activities of groups in society. The adjective "analytical" may be added to refer to that species of pluralist who concerns himself with the structure and processes of group forms as they in fact occur. And although analytical pluralism has characterized principal works of sociology, the term is here reserved for political writers, to distinguish them from their philosophic predecessors.

In sum the doctrine of the philosophical pluralists was systematic (although imperfectly so), conceptual, deductive, and normative. That of the many writers here called analytical pluralists was, and is, hypothetical, experimental, empirical, and descriptive. The intellectual roots of analytical pluralism are deep in the history of American thought. In a line through Peirce, James, and Dewey, the psychology has tended to be behavioristic, the philosophy pragmatic, and the metaphysics realistic rather than idealistic. This combination of intellectual elements has turned social inquiry towards process and away from static conceptualism, towards relations rather than structures, and towards consequences instead of causes. Process, relations, and consequences are not, however, the antonyms of concepts, structures, and causes. The distinctions blur, shade, and fuse. It might be more nearly correct to say, therefore, that the analytical pluralists have tended to emphasize the former while not ignoring nor neglecting the latter. Although the modern approach has much in common with the philosophy of science, fragments of pluralistic politics are to be found in the classics of American political philosophy, notably in Madison and Calhoun.

It is since Alfred Bentley in 1908 that American writers in politics have increasingly accepted the view that the group is the basic political form, although most of the literature follows Pendleton Herring's pioneer work in 1928. Studies have been made of the significance of the group in the enactment of legislation, in the conduct of party activity, in the formulation and execution of public policy, in the process of public administration, and in the protection of civil liberties. The recognition of the importance of groups to a study and an understanding of politics has drawn the attention of political scientists to the considerable amount of work done in the related social science fields on the nature of group organization, and increasingly, materials developed in these allied fields have been used in political writing and in the classroom. For example, closely relevant to politics are the studies of the structure and process of groups as simple, amorphous, and uncontrived as the street-corner gang, as remote as South Pacific islanders, and as near as Middletown. Such studies throw much light upon the contrast between the objective and subjective relationships among people in groups, the difference between the formal and the informal organization which this reflects, the imposed rule and the developed custom, the external and visible structure on the one hand and the internal and invisible network of unconscious, nonlogical personal relationships on the other, the distribution of authority and the distribution of power, the nature of leadership and the relations of leaders and followers, the importance of prestige and status anxieties, and the methods employed to develop and maintain security systems for the protection of the members of the group.

III. Organized Groups as Structures of Power

The conclusion emerges from an inspection of the literature dealing with the structure and the process of groups that, insofar as they are organized groups, they are structures of power. They are structures of power because they concentrate human wit, energy, and muscle for the achievement of received purposes. They are of the same genus, although a different species, as the state. And so we come by still another route to the insight which the philosophical pluralists demonstrated, that the state as an association (or group) is not different from other associations, like churches and trade unions. That which puts both state and nonstate associations in the same category of forms is the common factor of power. Both are associations of people for the achievement of ends common to the members, and the means of achievement is the application of the power of the association to the obstacles and hindrances which block the goal. It is true that the state and other group forms represent power in different packages, that organized groups may be regarded as systems of private government while the organs of the state represent a system of public government. However, the ubiquity of power in human relations, with its manifestations in other group forms than the state, is the reason for believing that the subject matter of politics is power, contrary to the view that its subject matter is the state, which is only one of the engines through which power is exercised. Private government is not only a legitimate but a much neglected subject of inquiry by political science.

The course of the discussion to this point may be summarized as a doctrine of the politics of plural forms. To use the phrase of John Dewey, the "doctrine of plural forms is a statement of fact: that there exists a plurality of social groupings, good, bad, and indifferent."[7] These groupings have no "real" personality; there is no derivative entity in group organization which is not people, but somehow possesses human attributes. For social groupings *are* people in connected relationships; the connected relationships do not exist apart from the people. To recognize the group basis of society and, by inclusion, the group basis of the political and other communities, is not to lose sight of the individual. Far from it—the individual is the center without which the circumference of the group could not form.

As we have seen, groups exist for the individuals who belong to them; by his membership in them the individual fulfills personal values and felt needs. To view the individual as the centerpiece of all group forms is to avoid the error of regarding society as a congeries of discrete and disconnected human particles. Recognition of the place and role of the individual in group associations also avoids the error of supposing that political processes move by a blind voluntarism in a Schopenhaueresque world. To repeat the observation with which this paper began, the whole structure of society is associational; neither disjected nor congealed, it is not a multiplicity of discontinuous persons, nor yet a solid fusion of dissolved components.

To say that the structure of the political community is associational is not to elevate other groups above the state, nor really to put them in a relationship of parity, as the philosophical pluralists did. In civil politics, some association does in fact represent the consensus by which the various groups exist in mutual relations. This is the state.[8] It establishes the norms of permissible behavior in

[7]*The Public and Its Problems*, p. 73.

[8]Although Bentley refers to the "idea of the state" as one of the "intellectual amusements of the past," he does not reject it completely but indicates that it may have some place in a complete restatement of theoretical political science. In *The Process of Government*, he was not trying to make such a comprehensive restatement but trying to describe political activity, that is, political processes (p. 263). In his later works, the subject is not referred to again. Dewey, on the other hand, is clear that state and government are not the same, that there is no archetypal state, that there could be no state without a government, that the state did not create the government, that the state is a "public," articulated and operating through representative officers. (See *The Public and Its Government*, p. 67.) For

group relations, and it enforces these norms. The fact that men have other group loyalties than the one they bear to the state does not in itself prescribe limits to the activity of the state. This activity is not confined to police functions at the margins where the intersecting and overlapping groups touch each other, because the role of the state is not limited to that of referee in the group conflict. Established as custodian of the consensus, the state helps to formulate and to promote normative goals, as well as to police the agreed rules. In the exercise of its normative functions, it may even require the abolition of groups or a radical revision of their internal structure.

Organized groups, then, are structures of power; the forms of private government differ from the forms of public government principally in that public governments possess the characteristic of officiality, which will be more fully discussed below.[9] Through usage, the word "government" has come to be associated almost exclusively with the formal official apparatus of presidents, kings, duces, fuehrers, commissars, rajahs, rasses, sachems, sagamores, legislators, councillors, commissioners, mayors, governors, ministers plenipotentiary, ambassadors, judges, and other public officeholders. But who has not heard of "office politics," "faculty politics," "union politics," and so on? These phrases are more than metaphor. They bespeak the general understanding that the phenomena of power appear in unofficial groups as well as in the formal structures of official

---

Dewey, the state is the organization of singular individuals and their relations to the officials and functionaries established to protect the perceived consequences of conjoint behaviors. The perception of such consequences creates the "public" which is the constituent power of the state. The state is not a structure but a relationship. It is an association.

[9]It is useful to distinguish groups in three senses or phases of development: incipient, conscious, and organized. The indispensable ingredient of "groupness" is consciousness of common interest and active assistance, mutually sustained, to advance and promote this interest. Where the interest exists but is not recognized by the members of the putative association, the group may be said to be incipient. Thus, all dwellers in the Caribbean may actually possess certain interests in common—economic resources, strategic position, native populations in a colonial status, exposure to the hazards of weather, and so on—which may produce a consciousness of community, as similar predisposing factors produced the Indonesian Republic. A conscious group is one in which the community sense exists but which has not become organized. An organized group is a conscious group which has established an objective and formal apparatus to promote the common interest. Habitual cooperation of the members of a group is possible without any elaborate apparatus. Mannheim, in *Man and Society in an Age of Reconstruction*, pp. 51 ff., distinguishes between substantial and functional rationality. The first is conscious, contrived, directed action which makes use of deliberate means to produce known ends, efficiently sought. Functional rationality may be likened to what is here called habitual cooperation. Wherever the objective and formal apparatus of the organized group appears in its mature manifestations, it exhibits a very similar general form and pattern. Max Weber, in *Essays in Sociology*, trans. H. H. Gerth and C. Wright Mills (New York, 1946), pp. 196 ff., discusses the phenomenon of bureaucracy, which is not limited to the institutions and behavior of public government but is universal among organized group structures. The three principal characteristics of bureaucracy are a fixed distribution of functions, a fixed distribution of authority, and a predictable procedure. By these terms, it is clear that private organizations have their bureaucracies as well as Washington and Whitehall.

agencies of the public government. We may therefore add to the subjects which are proper to political inquiry, the activities of corporation managers, trade union leaders, bishops, colonels, trade association executives, boards of directors, trustees of colleges, and other such functionaries. The vocabulary of power in public governments is a key to the understanding of the structure and processes of systems of private government also. It is in the literature of administration, perhaps, that the most notable advance has been made in recognizing the single identity of the problem of power in its public and private manifestations, one test of which is the extent to which the public bureaucracy and the private have exchanged knowledge about the ways in which the management of organizations can most efficiently and effectively be carried on. But this knowledge is not modern. John Wise, the liberal Ipswich theologian of the late seventeenth century, wrote tracts on the *government* of the Congregationalist churches in New England, which he wanted to keep democratic, as opposed to certain bureaucratic tendencies that appeared in his day. He viewed the church as an ecclesiastical polity and discussed its organization in political terms which were virtually interchangeable with the vocabulary employed for similar speculation about forms of public government.

IV. The Dynamics of Plural Forms

So far, we have been concerned with the nature of the structure of society and its principal communities, and with the composition and classification of the group forms which are basic to both. They have been held still, so to speak, while they were being viewed. But they do not in fact hold still; they are in a state of constant motion, and it is through this motion and its interactions that these groups generate the rules by which public policy is formulated and the community is to be governed. It is necessary now to consider the impulses which animate the group motion and produce these penetrating and far-reaching results.

To consider further a point which has been made, groups organize for the self-expression and security of the members which comprise them. Even when the group is a benevolent, philanthropic association devoted to the improvement of the material and spiritual fortunes of people outside its membership—a temperance or a missionary organization, for example—the work towards this goal, the activity of the organization, is a means through which the members express themselves. Satisfaction in the fulfillment of the received purposes of the group is an important element in keeping groups intact, as Barnard has shown. Indeed, if these satisfactions are not fulfilled, the group suffers loss of morale, energy, and dedication. It is for this reason that military organizations and the civil authorities to which they are responsible seek to inculcate in the soldier some sense of the general purposes for which force by arms is being employed, in an attempt to identify the soldier's personal purpose with that of the community he serves. The soldier then can fulfill his own purposes in combat, as well as those of various groups in the country whose uniform he bears.

At the same time, security is an object of every group organization if security is understood only in its elemental sense of the survival of the group itself in order to carry forward its mission. At the very least, the interest of security means the maintenance of the existence of the group. In different groups one or the other of these impulses—self-expression or security—will predominate.

Self-expression and security are sought by the group members through control of the physical and social environment which surrounds each group and in the midst of which it dwells. It is an elemental fact that environments are potentially dangerous to every group, even as homes are potentially dangerous to the members of the household, as the statistics of accidents in the home will attest. The military battalion runs the risk of being shot up. The church, new or old, runs the risk of losing its members to other and competing claims of interest and devotion. The businessman runs the risk of losing his profit or his customer to his rival. The philanthropic organization devoted to good works often regards other agencies in the same field with a venomous eye. Councils of social agencies in large cities are sometimes notorious for the rancor with which the struggle for prestige and recognition (i.e., self-expression and security) is conducted among them. Every group, large and small, must come to terms with its environment if it is to endure and to prosper.

There are three modes by which this is done. First, the environment may be made safe and predictable by putting restraints upon it. Jurisdictional fights between unions may be explained in this way. Jurisdictional fights are battles in which each claimant union seeks to make an environment for itself in the area of dispute, but to exclude its rival from this environment. On the employer side, the Mohawk Valley Formula was a pattern of actions in a planned sequence by which employers, if they followed it, could break union movements. The objective of this formula was to discredit each union and its leadership and to enlist the support of the townspeople on the side of the plant; it thus was a concerted plan to make an environment unfavorable to the success of unions. One overcomes the hostility in the environment most directly by destroying the influence which creates the hostility.

Second, the environment may be made safe and predictable by neutralizing it. In the propaganda war of giant world powers, the effort is ceaseless to neutralize the effects of propaganda with counterpropaganda so as to render the international environment favorable, or at least not hostile—that is, neutral. The Atlantic and Pacific Tea Company similarly bought a great deal of advertising space in newspapers all over the country to counteract the expectedly unfavorable impressions created by a Department of Justice action against it under the anti-trust laws. The object, among other purposes, was to make the customer-inhabited environment of the business enterprise favorable if possible, neutral at the least, concerning the merits of the charges against it.

Third, the environment may be made safe and predictable, and therefore secure, by conciliating it and making it friendly. Even where there is no manifest hostile influence, a credit of good will may be accumulated by deeds and words which reflect favorably upon the doer. It is true that concessions to a potential hostile force may work sometimes, and again they may not. In the struggle of free nations with the dictatorships, appeasement did not succeed in producing that conciliation which was hoped for it. Nonetheless, politicians are constantly at work making friends and increasing votes by performing favors of one kind or another. Friendliness towards soap is generated on the radio by endless broadcasts of simple tales of never-ending strife and frustration. And during the Second World War advertising by business enterprises was a means of cultivating and keeping good will for the products advertised, even though there was no market for them because of the wartime restrictions on production.

All of these are methods by which the environment in which groups dwell is made safe and predictable to them, and therefore secure. And because the relations of people are myriad and shifting, subject to cycles of deterioration and decay, because the environment itself changes with each passing hour, there is a ceaseless struggle on the part of groups to dominate, neutralize, or conciliate that part of their environment that presses in upon them most closely. In this struggle, there is an observable balance of influence in favor of organized groups in their dealings with the unorganized, and in favor of the best and most efficiently organized in their dealings with the less efficiently organized. Strong nations tend to take advantage of the weak, and imperial powers to take advantage of their colonies. Or, to put it another way, organization represents concentrated power, and concentrated power can exercise a dominating influence when it encounters power which is diffuse and not concentrated, and therefore weaker.

The classic struggle of farmers against business enterprise is a case in point, the latter at first being more efficiently organized, and able (before the farmer became "class conscious") to gain advantages which the farmers thought exorbitant, under conditions which the farmers found offensive. But organization begets counterorganization. The farmer organizes in the American Farm Bureau Federation or the National Grange, and uses his influence with the legislatures to write rules to his advantage. In some states of the Middle West, for example, legislation even prescribes the terms of contracts for the sale of farm equipment. But the organized farmer pays little attention to the tenant and the share-cropper, and they in turn experience an impulse to organize for their own advantage. The history of the development of farmers' organizations is instructive; the whole program of farm subsidies which has evolved in the last twenty years may be seen as an effort on the part of the farmer (organized for the purpose) to make himself independent of the vicissitudes of the business economy, that is, to take himself out of the environment which he can control only imperfectly, and to insulate himself against economic adversity.

In the constant struggle of groups to come to terms with their environments, one other phenomenon of group politics may be noted. Simple groups tend to become more complex. And the more complex they become, the greater is the tendency to centralize their control. The structure of the business community in 1950 is different from that of 1860 precisely in that relatively simple forms of business organization have become complex—have gone through federations, combinations, reorganizations, mergers, amalgamations, and consolidations in a growing tendency to rationalize the complexity and to integrate the elements in comprehensive structures. Monopolies, combinations, cartels, giant integrated enterprises are characteristic of a mature phase of the evolution of group forms. Furthermore, the history of federal administration amply shows that the tendency of simple forms of organization to become complex by combination and to develop centralized bureaucracies to cope with this complexity is to be observed among official groups as well as among the groups, like the CIO and the American Legion, which dwell outside the domain of public government.

What has been said about farmers' organizations and business enterprises supports the conclusion that the operations of the economic system lend themselves to political interpretation, that is, to analysis in terms of the struggle of economic groups to exercise power. A recent book by John Kenneth Galbraith uses political analysis to describe and explain the workings of an economy characterized no longer (if ever) by a multiplicity of small sellers without decisive market power, but by the existence of a few big firms in various industries, surrounded by a fringe of small ones.[10] Professor Galbraith does not think that the competitive model of previous economic theory is adequate to explain present-day economic activities, and for "competition" would substitute the concept of "countervailing power." Countervailing power is the development by disadvantaged sectors of the economy of resistant strength to check and balance the concentrations of private market-power represented by oligopolistic industry; and one of the functions of government is to encourage private associations to build up "countervailing power." This thesis, of course, challenges much economic thought regarded as orthodox.

The struggle of groups to survive in their environments and to carry forward the aims and interests of their members, if entirely uninhibited, would produce violence and war. Social disapproval of most of the forms of direct action, however, reduces this struggle to an effort to write the rules by which groups live with each other and according to which they compete for existence and advantage. Thus, in the development of mature institutions of collective bargaining from the raw material of unorganized workers, the time comes when violence, disorder, and force are put to one side as the normal aspect of labor relations and the conduct of negotiations occupies the energies of the leaders. In the relations of nations to each other, there has been a persistent effort to substitute diplomacy and the rule of law for war as the arbiter of the differences among national groups. As groups come to put away gross forms of coercion in their dealings

[10] John Kenneth Galbraith, *American Capitalism, The Concept of Countervailing Power* (Boston, 1952).

with each other, by equal degree the area widens within which the behavior of each is subject to codification by rules. The struggle for advantage, for benefits to the group, for the self-expression and security of its members, tends then to concentrate upon the writing of the rules. Among the forms which the rules may take are statutes, administrative orders and decrees, rules and interpretations, and court judgments.

V. The Concept of Officiality

We come then to the apparatus of the state which, through its manifold offices—legislatures, councils, agencies, departments, courts, and other forums—maintains a system of instrumentalities for the writing and enforcement of the formal rules by which the society is governed. All of these instrumentalities are themselves groups, and they possess a sense of group belonging and identification which is very strong. In what respect, then, are these groups different from the more numerous groups outside the structure of public government? In a political sense they are not different at all, but exhibit the internal social and political characteristics of group forms which are separate from the state apparatus. But there *are* differences in behavior which may be observed. The Bureau of Internal Revenue collects taxes, that is, it takes a portion of the substance of individuals and corporations—but individuals and corporations do not take a portion of the substance of the Bureau of Internal Revenue. The policeman on the corner is permitted to blow a whistle at an automobile driver and stop his travel, but the driver of the automobile is not permitted to blow a whistle at the policeman to prevent the latter from walking up and giving him a tag. Why is there this unilateral relationship between some groups and others? How does it happen that a man with a badge may give orders to men without badges, and that the reverse relationship does not prevail? The answer, of course, is that the law permits this: it establishes the difference between the badge-wearer and the others. But this answer does not go far enough. The Eighteenth Amendment was also "law" in the sense that it was on the books. For law to have force, there must be popular consent and understanding to support the law. In the example of the policeman, there is a social understanding that approves the unilateral relation between men with badges and men with boutonnieres. It is a part of the political consensus—the understood and agreed conditions of life in a civil society—that certain groups will be permitted to act like badge-wearers. The groups so privileged collectively make up the instrumentalities of the state, and such groups are distinguished from others only in their possession of the characteristic of officiality. The designation "official" is the sign which manifests that the bearer is authorized by the social understanding to exercise against all groups and individuals certain powers which they may not exercise against him. The concept of officiality, then, is the sum of the technical differences which are rooted in the social understanding as to who does what to whom; and the difference between the public and private groups is the "officiality" of the former.

What is the function in the total group struggle of the complex of official groups? What role do these groups play in the restless flux of effort on the part of groups to dominate, neutralize, or conciliate the environment in which they seek to survive? Addressing ourselves to these questions, we find that the principal function of official groups is to provide various levels of compromise in the writing of the rules, all within the body of agreed principles that forms the consensus upon which the political community rests, and that each of the three principal branches of government has a special role in performing this function.

The legislature referees the group struggle, ratifies the victories of the successful coalitions, and records the terms of the surrenders, compromises, and conquests in the form of statutes. Every statute tends to represent compromise because the very process of accommodating conflicts of group interest is one of deliberation and consent. The legislative vote on any issue thus tends to represent the composition of strength, i.e., the balance of power among the contending groups at the moment of voting. What may be called public policy is actually the equilibrium reached in the group struggle at any given moment, and it represents a balance which the contending factions of groups constantly strive to weight in their favor.[11] In this process, it is clear that blocks of groups can be defeated. In fact, they can be routed. Defeated groups do not possess a veto

[11]John Fischer, "Unwritten Rules of American Politics," *Harper's Magazine*, Vol. 197 (November 1948), pp. 27-36, expresses the thesis that Calhoun, who devised the doctrine of the concurrent majority, provides the key to an understanding of American politics today. Fischer asserts that the legislative system, especially as it functions in Congress through committees, is a modern-day institutionalization of Calhoun's concurrent majority, in which no important interest is forced to accept legislation unfavorable to it, at least in the particulars in which its interest is immediately invested. Economic interests and others also, through the groups in which they are organized, according to Fischer, then exercise a minority veto on legislation which concerns them—like the minority veto that Calhoun sought to establish for the protection of the interests of the South.

This view, however, gives too much credit to Calhoun. Far from having the key to the mysteries of American politics, Calhoun was outside the mainstream of American political thought and tendency in his own time. He was closer to Andre Vishinsky than to any American politico of our day. In fact, Calhoun could have written Vishinsky's speech of November 24, 1948, to the United Nations General Assembly's Ad Hoc Political Committee in which he said, "The veto is a powerful political tool. . . .Perhaps we use it more, but that is because we are in the minority and the veto balances power. If we were in the majority, we could make such grandiloquent gestures as offering to waive the veto on this or that." (*New York Times*, November 25, 1948).

In the functions which the American legislature performs, it is clear that no minority exercises a *veto* on legislation that affects it. Certainly no veto power is recognized in law and none is exercised in practice. The assumption that there is a minority veto, as Fischer asserts, must show that minorities can always exercise it, as they do in the United Nations Security Council, and that no minority is without it. So far as the first is concerned, what veto did businessmen interpose against the enactment of the Wagner Act of 1935? How successful have the bankers been in applying a veto to the currency reforms of the last decade? How successful were the labor unions in opposing the enactment of the restrictive features of the Taft-Hartley Act? Where were the vetoes in these and many other instances that might be cited? The answer is that they did not exist. In addition, the hypothesis of a minority veto fails to account for the failure of substantial minorities to get a hearing, let alone exercise a veto. Among these are Negroes, small businessmen, share-croppers, Okies, and so on.

on the proposals and acts that affect them. But what they do possess is the right to make new combinations of strength if they are able to do so—combinations that will support a new effort to rewrite the rules in their favor. This process of regrouping is fully in accord with the American culture pattern, which rates high in the characteristics of optimism, risk, experimentalism, change, aggressiveness, acquisitiveness, and colossal faith in man's ability to subdue and bend nature to his desire. The entire process is dynamic, not static; fluid, not fixed. Today's losers may be tomorrow's winners.

In these adjustments of group interest, the legislature does not play the part of inert cash register, ringing up the additions and withdrawals of strength; it is not a mindless balance pointing and marking the weight and distribution of power among the contending groups. Legislatures are groups also and show a sense of identity and consciousness of kind that unofficial groups must regard if they are to represent their members effectively. In fact, each of the two houses of the Congress has a conscious identity of special "house" interest, as well as a joint interest against the executive establishment. More will be said of the struggle of official groups among themselves below. At this point it may be noted that the dignity of the Congressman is an expression of his official group interest, and that it cannot be invaded lightly. Legislators have to be approached with a certain amount of deference and tact; they may be pressured, but some forms of pressure will be regarded as too gross. The Congressman, like men everywhere, comes to his position bearing in his head a cargo of ideas, principles, prejudices, programs, precepts, beliefs, slogans, and preachments. These represent his adjustment to the dominant group combination among his constituents. If he mistakes the pattern of his support or acts too independently of its desire, he loses his seat, as some Congressmen have, after one full term.

The function of the bureaucrat in the group struggle is somewhat different from that of the legislator. Administrative agencies of the regulatory kind are established to carry out the terms of the treaties that the legislators have negotiated and ratified. They are like armies of occupation left in the field to police the rule won by the victorious coalition. Thus the Transportation Act of 1920 substantially augmented the role of the Interstate Commerce Commission by vesting it with authorities acceptable to labor unions, investors, weak roads, and shippers. The Robinson-Patman Act of 1936 similarly gave to the Federal Trade Commission the authority to control the price practices on one classification of business groups in favor of another, by limiting the power of the chain stores in favor of independent merchants. The defeated coalition of groups, however, does not cease striving to wring interpretations favorable to it from the treaties that verbalize its defeats. Expensive legal talent is employed to squeeze every advantage which wit and verbal magic can twist from the cold prose of official papers; and the regulatory agencies are constantly besought and importuned to interpret their authorities in favor of the very groups for the regulation of which they were originally granted. This campaign against unfavorable rules which losing coalitions of groups address to the bureaucrats appointed to administer them is, of course, in addition to their constant effort to rewrite the rules in their favor through compliant legislators. Where the balance of power is precarious, the law will remain unsettled until the balance is made stable. This is especially true in the enforcement of the labor relations and anti-trust laws.

The function of the judge is not unlike that of the legislator and the bureaucrat, as the function of the bureaucrat is not unlike that of the legislator and the judge. The judiciary, like the civilian bureaucracy, is one of the instrumentalities for the administration of agreed rules. But the responsibility rests with the judge, more than with either the legislator or the bureaucrat, to develop a more or less homogeneous and objective pattern of rules from the many strands supplied by the statutes, administrative decrees, and causes of private clients.[12] The judiciary is a superior agency to the bureaucracy in performing this important and fateful task, and it is in this superiority that its distinguishing characteristic lies. All other distinctions (procedural mainly) between the judges and the bureaucrats are derived and secondary, not innate.

VI. The Group Struggle in Officialdom

In the small universe of official groups—small at least by comparison with the infinite group configuration outside the official domain—the same phenomena of struggle for self-expression and security take place that may be witnessed in the various nonstate communities of the society. In fact, some interesting variants are thrust into the entire political process by the existence of the official groups in what is often a state of rivalry. The Founding Fathers made sure that rivalries would occur by separating the powers of the government. It was their intention to prevent the public powers from being brought to focus in the same public authority and to endow each separated public authority with the capacity to fend off attempts by the others to invade its domain. The object of this, as Mr. Justice Brandeis said in an important case in which the rivalry of official groups was at issue, was "not to promote efficiency but to preclude the exercise of arbitrary power. The purpose was not to avoid friction, but *by means of the inevitable*

[12]Much ingenuity and resourcefulness go into the production of an objective and homogeneous pattern of law. Benjamin Cardozo, in *The Nature of the Judicial Process* (New Haven, Conn., 1925), confessed that the function of the judge is creative and original in those many interstices of the law left vacant by the statutes and administrative decrees. James M. Landis, in *The Administrative Process* (New Haven, Conn., 1938), presented a case for judicial self-restraint in the relations between the courts and the bureaucrats. In fact, the judiciary and the regulatory agencies of the quasi-judicial kind may be regarded as rival bureaucracies, with overlapping jurisdictions. The judges have been jealous for a half-century of the threat represented by the bureaucracy to their historic monopoly to say what the law is; and until recent years at least, they protected their security against this threat in their environment by dominating the danger and nullifying it on appeal.

friction incident to the distribution of government powers among three departments, to save the people from autocracy."[13]

The Congress is traditionally suspicious of the President, and historically has sought to dominate the executive establishment. The chief executive of any business enterprise is permitted to manage such staff facilities as personnel and budget, but Congress prefers to exercise these powers of the President itself. Thus when Congress set up the Tennessee Valley Authority, it reserved to itself the authority, by concurrent resolution (not subject to the veto), to remove the members of the board of directors.[14] In the Lend-Lease Act of 1941 and the Emergency Price Stabilization Act of 1942, to name only two, Congress wrote language into the statutes reserving to itself the authority to withdraw from the President the powers conveyed by those acts of legislation. And time and again Congress has sought to force from the President's subordinates the surrender of information deemed by him to be confidential.[15]

One of the prime deterrents to the development in the United States of an adequate federal civil service is the manifest hostility, relentless and unceasing, which Congressmen pour out upon officials of the executive establishment. One former official of the federal government said that it was "like being nibbled to death by ducks"; and former Secretary of the Interior Krug, when asked, at the start of the Korean War in July, 1950, whether he would return to Washington to mobilize industry as he had in the Second World War, replied that he would seek a painless death by joining the military forces this time.

It has been pointed out that overlapping but different combinations of economic groups are marshalled behind the President and Congress in this

[13]Italics supplied. The case is *Myers v. United States*, 272 U.S. 52 (1926), which involved an attempt by Congress to exercise the power which Presidents supposed they possessed to remove officials at will. The jealousy which Congress has displayed towards the chief executive is both extensive and historic. The Budget and Accounting Act of 1921 was vetoed by Wilson when it first passed Congress because Congress had reserved to itself the authority to dismiss the Comptroller-General and Wilson believed this to be unconstitutional (*Congressional Record*, 66th Cong., 2nd Sess., Vol. 59 (June 4, 1920), pp. 8609-8610). Wilson's veto was anticipated by the observation he made in his book *Congressional Government* (New York, 1925; 1st ed., 1885): "It is not often easy to see the true constitutional bearing of strictly legislative action; but it is patent even to the least observant that in the matter of appointments to office, for instance, senators have often outrun their legal rights to give or withhold their assent to appointments, by insisting upon being first consulted concerning nominations as well, and have thus made their constitutional assent dependent upon an unconstitutional control of nominations" (pp. 48-49).

[14]See *Morgan v. Tennessee Valley Authority*, 115 F (2nd) 990 (1940), certiorari denied, 312 U.S. 701 (1941), where the court held that the authority of the President to remove such directors for any cause he chose was not limited by this congressional reservation of power.

[15]See the discussion of this problem in the *New York Times*, Sept. 3, 1948, p. 5.

historic duel.[16] The rivalry between the Congress and the executive establishment would be natural and expected because of the inherent group interest of the functionaries, but the struggle is exacerbated by the support that each of the contestants is given by alliances and coalitions of groups whose interests are at stake in the outcome. Furthermore, the leverage in this content is with the Congress. As Woodrow Wilson said, "The legislature is the aggressive spirit. It is the motive power of the government. . . ."[17] Even when, as in the national elections of 1948, the Congress and its own particular and unique behavior are made an issue and a new Congress is returned, the new Congress may behave much as the old one did. The presidential power to campaign for a mandate from the people does not necessarily mean, when he gets one, that Congress will enact it.

The rivalry between the judiciary and the executive has sometimes emerged in spectacular form, as in the duel between Jefferson and Marshall and in the unsuccessful Court Plan which Roosevelt submitted to Congress in 1937; but the enduring struggle has really taken place below the surface of public events and out of the public gaze, in the silent duel waged by the judiciary against the regulatory agencies. The chief characteristic of the regulatory agency of the quasi-judicial kind is that it combines in one instrumentality the legislative, the executive and the judicial powers. It is a device invented by necessity for bringing to a focus the public powers (otherwise separated in the Constitution) for the regulation of conditions which any single one of the three traditional powers had been found inadequate to regulate.

The judges have looked at the work of these agencies with split vision and have persisted in separating the powers that necessity and the legislatures had put together. Many anomalies have resulted. At first the courts regarded rate-making as legislative in nature and not for the judges. Said the Supreme Court in the celebrated case of *Munn v. Illinois* in 1876, "For protection against abuses by legislatures the people must resort to the polls, not to the courts. . . ."[18] Eventually, however, the judges came to regard the reasonableness of rates not as a question to be decided at the polls but one to be decided in the courtrooms, that is, a judicial question; but up to the present time the rate-making process of quasi-judicial agencies is still called legislative in nature.[19] The entire

[16]See Wilfred Binkley, *The Powers of the President* (New York, 1937). Binkley's thesis is that the conservative groups have tended to support Congress and the popular and less conservative groups have tended to support the President. The Whigs and the Republicans in the main have preferred a strong Congress and a weak President, while the Democrats, in the New Freedom, New Deal, and Fair Deal versions, at least, have preferred a strong President and a weak, that is, subordinate but not docile, Congress. The alternation of strong and weak Presidents, and contrariwise, strong Presidents and strong Congresses, is the result of the shifts in the balance of power among the multifarious groups that constitute the society.

[17]*Congressional Government*, p. 36.

[18]94 U.S. 113.

[19]See *Federal Power Commission v. Hope Natural Gas Company*, 320 U.S. 591, 64 S. Ct. 281, 88 L. Ed. 333 (1944).

logomachy of words and definitions contained in the law of jurisdictional facts and evidentiary facts has developed from the concern of the judges to keep within their hands the determination of the kinds of question that historically have been decided by judges. This is understandable, perhaps; but the judges, having the last word on questions of jurisdiction, have tended to decide the close votes in their favor, as well as many that should not have been in their favor at all, and have thus moved some of the legal profession to urge that the judges retain authority in the matter in which they are expert—to wit, the law—and yield to the administrative bodies the authority to decide matters in which they are expert, such as questions of valuation.

Except where the simulacra of the judicial process were on display, the judges have tolerated a great range of unreviewed discretion in executive agencies. Thus due process is not necessarily judicial process.[20] But where the executive process appeared to rival the judicial, the judges have been stern and adamant. The Administrative Procedure Act of 1946 perpetuates the internal separation of powers within the executive agencies and thus institutionalizes and sanctifies by legislative enactment the rule that the judges had enforced by themselves.

It might be mentioned that even within the structure of official agencies in a single branch of the federal government, competition of group interests takes place. Mention has been made of the consciousness of a separate group interest in each of the two houses of Congress. Competition among the official groups in the executive establishment is both long-standing and notorious. The extended contest over unification of the military services, and the resistance of the Navy in 1949 to the curtailments enforced against it in favor of the Army and the Air Force by the Secretary of Defense, is a case in point. Many others will come to mind, as will instances which show that the states are not immune from the effects of rivalry among official groups. State departments of health, for example, are often in conflict with state departments of industry over matters that fall within the jurisdictions of both, such as the prevention and control of diseases induced by industrial occupations.

To carry analysis still a step further, we note that the subgroups of single official groups may be in competition with each other. Accordingly, committees in both the Senate and the House of Representatives frequently contest for jurisdiction over bills, parts of which fall within the competence of more than one group. In the Senate struggle in 1948-1950 over the repeal of the discriminatory tax on oleomargarine, for example, it became a matter of vital importance whether the Senate Committee on Agriculture got hold of the repealer or the Senate Committee on Finance, for the first was dominated by the farm groups opposed to repeal while the second was not. The Legislative Reorganization Act of 1946

[20]*Murray's Lessee v. Hoboken Land and Improvement Company*, 12 Howard 272 (1856).

split jurisdiction on anti-trust matters between the Senate Judiciary Committee and the Senate Committee on Interstate and Foreign Commerce, with amendments to the Clayton Act under the jurisdiction of the Judiciary Committee and amendments to the Federal Trade Commission Act under the jurisdiction of the Committee on Interstate and Foreign Commerce. The vital position which such committees hold in the legislative processes of Congress intensifies the effort of partisans in the group struggle to get their favored view before them.

There is also group tension and conflict within the structure of bureaus and divisions of single agencies and departments in the family of official executive groups. Thus within the Department of Agriculture there was once a right-left axis along which some of the bureaus tended to line. In the middle period of the New Deal, the Farm Security Administration, speaking for the small farmer, the tenant, and the sharecropper and advocating a generous lending policy, was in strife with the Farm Credit Administration, the Soil Conservation Service, and the Agricultural Adjustment Administration over the question of conversion to a defense policy, part of which involved the proposed establishment of an integrated and unified set of field services for the Department of Agriculture. In this contest, the Farm Credit Administration won over the Farm Security Administration. Within the War Department the Corps of Engineers is so powerfully entrenched, with civilian support among Congressmen interested in rivers and harbors improvements, and behind them business groups in the "improved" localities, that it was able to defy the command of the Commander-in-Chief in wartime in a dispute between the Corps and the Bureau of Reclamation over the building of dams in the Central Valley of California.

The struggle of subgroups within a department is to be found even in lower levels of administration. Divisions within bureaus may be, and often are, in contest with each other. Management improvement divisions or units of organization may and do run as rivals to finance and accounting divisions, and the personnel division or office is often the butt of bitter humor by all the others.

Attendant upon group spirit are feelings of belonging and not belonging, an acceptance of those within the group and a hostility to those outside, the fastidious sense of jurisdiction engendered by these feelings, the desire for status and prestige, the wish to be admired and to feel of account—and all of these characteristics of the behavior of people in groups are to be found where people are or have been in groups: in public government and in private enterprise, in school, college, and fraternity, in the Bank Wiring Room of the Western Electric Plant in Hawthorne, Illinois, and in the Acropolis in an earlier and more classic time. The group struggle, then, is apparent in the universe of unofficial groups and in that of official groups. Furthermore, these are not separate universes. They are one. Official groups are simply inhabitants of one pluralistic world which is an aggregation, a collection, an assemblage, a throng, a moving multitude of human clusters, a consociation of groups, a plurality of collectivities, an intersecting series of social organisms, adhering, interpenetrating, overlapping—a single universe of groups which combine, break, federate, and form constellations and coalitions of power in a flux of restless alterations.

VII. Conclusion

To some, this view of the political process may seem formless, inchoate, ambiguous, and disordered. It may be felt that little is gained in making the interaction of groups the central fact of politics without further definition and characterization of the groups that interact. But the state of the discipline is such that one is scarcely justified in being more precise. It is suggested here only that a framework exists within which political processes may be more specifically and accurately described. Galbraith's concept of the "countervailing power" is an example of the application to economic phenomena of the method advocated here. If American history could be reconsidered and rewritten in terms of the dynamics of group struggle, history would indeed provide that insight of the past leading to an understanding of the present which it frequently claims to provide, but seldom does. What is called "political history" is at present usually the life and hard times of the official functionaries of public government, when it is not the chronicles of the wars we have fought.

Some may miss in the concept under discussion the *mystique* of the law, with its authoritarian constructs, its assumption that there *must* be a supreme power, like father in the household or the Absolute, some authority which arranges disorder and judges our transgressions and supplies us in an infinite universe with a finite demesne of which we can see the walls, and feel secure. A political process which is circular, as Einsteinian space is thought to be, which bends back upon itself, in which the directions of North and South are meaningless, is an unhandy place in which to try to locate finality. However, we deceive ourselves to clothe men in gowns and call them supreme, or sovereign, or all-powerful. We sometimes deceive ourselves when we call them "Excellency," or "honorable." The celebrated finality of Supreme Court decisions, which was part of the folklore of the law before 1937, is seen in 1952 to be chimerical. Yet since 1937 the justices have only more obviously performed the function that they performed before 1937, namely, that of serving as one more level of official compromise in the never-ending march and countermarch, thrust and parry, among economic groups, enforcement agencies, legislators, and executive functionaries. The differences between the official and the unofficial groups are acknowledged, and they have been characterized; but it is the underlying similarity that strikes the eye. Both groups are points of power and compromise in a continuum of interactions.

Just as the political process described in the preceding pages may seem to some to lack the Euclidian perfection of the juristic view of the political world, others may feel that it lacks the quality of ethical sanction, that "values" are omitted, that purposive and normative elements in human conduct are neglected and ignored. But this is not so. Groups exist to fulfill the desires of those who comprise them, to achieve their choices, attain their goals—and to propagate ethical principle according to the lights of their members. If there is a multiplicity of such groups, so is there a multiplicity of ethical systems.

Finally, it may be asked, "Whatever became of the individual?" He was introduced briefly as the beneficiary of group forms and then whisked off the page. Are not individuals as well as groups important in the political process? What of a Roosevelt? What of a Gandhi? Were these not individuals, and were they not influential as political actors, and not memorable merely as the passive recipients of the fullness of group life? To this it may be said that individuals are, of course, important as political actors, when they move others to responsive behavior, or represent them, or acquire their support or tolerance. That is to say, they are significant politically in the group relations they establish and organize, or modify, or destroy.

And if it be said that these notes for a theory tell us nothing new, that we knew all of this before, the answer must indeed be the humble one suggested by the author of the *Anatomy of Melancholy*: "We can say nothing but what hath been said. Our poets steal from Homer."

Pragmatism and the Group Theory of Politics

David G. Smith

Pragmatism and the group theory of politics are closely related both historically and philosophically; and both have a continuing importance for contemporary political science.* Yet these two intellectual traditions have seldom been related

*Grants from The Rockefeller Foundation and The Carnegie Corporation helped make this study possible. I wish also to acknowledge especially the invaluable aid and criticism of my colleague, Charles E. Gilbert.

David G. Smith, "Pragmatism and the Group Theory of Politics," American Political Science Review, *Vol. 58 (1964). Reprinted with permission.*

in a systematic fashion.[1] This failure to examine both the tree and the branch—the parent tradition of pragmatism and its offshoot, group theory—has foreshortened and distorted theoretical perspective. In this article I have tried to amend this situation by relating the two traditions, setting both in a larger historical and theoretical perspective, and examining their common philosophical suppositions.

I. Common Propositions and Commitments

Among pragmatists and group theorists some have emphasized the "group," others the political "process." Despite this difference of emphasis, a broad common ground of agreement remains. Follett, Mayo, and Homans on the one side, Bentley, Dewey, and Truman on the other, used similar language, shared many interests and objectives, and agreed in philosophical approach.

One shared interest was scientific, though possibly "operationalism" or "realism" would be more descriptive terms. Dewey and Bentley both inveighed against the "spooks" and "soul-stuff" in the current theories of public life,[2] not solely, but in part because these concepts were neither pragmatically "useful" nor directly "observable." Homans made the same point more elegantly with his distinction between first-order abstractions (*e.g.*, "interaction") and second-order abstractions (*e.g.*, status). First-order abstractions are helpful and desirable because they are directly observable; second-order abstractions are not. Second-order abstractions mislead theorists because "they spare us the pain of analysis when we should not be spared."[3] How precisely to describe the point of view fortunately need not be resolved here. The broad common objective is pretty clear: to cut through the layers of abstractions and get down to the observable and therefore, presumably, the real.

The "public"—as that term was habitually used to speak of the "public interest" or to say that "the public demands"—was one of the "spooks" rejected. The point of view was anti-metaphysical and, in a sense, anti-idealist. Opinion does not descend from mind to mind, from philosopher to the farmer or the workman, as traditional political theorists often supposed. In the first place, as Dewey observed, there is not one public, but a universe of publics.[4] Also, opinion and

[1]Truman mentions the debt of group theory to pragmatism. See David B. Truman, *The Governmental Process* (New York, 1951), p. 14. The relations of these two traditions are also discussed in Bernard Crick, *The American Science of Politics* (Berkeley, 1959), pp. 91-94, and by Charles E. Gilbert, "Operative Doctrines of Representation," *American Political Science Review*, Vol. 57 (1963), pp. 604-618. For an early and important discussion of pragmatism and politics, see William Y. Elliott, *The Pragmatic Revolt in Politics* (New York, 1928). Bibliographies of recent discussions of group theory can be found in Stanley Rothman, "Systematic Political Theory," *American Political Science Review*, Vol. 54 (1960), p. 15, and Peter Loveday and Ian Campbell, *Groups in Theory and Practice* (Sydney, 1962).

[2]Arthur F. Bentley, *The Process of Government* (Chicago, 1908), p. 154; John Dewey, *The Public and Its Problems* (New York, 1927), p. 8.

[3]George C. Homans, *The Human Group* (New York, 1950), p. 12.

[4]Dewey, *op. cit.*, p. 131.

intelligence are not "diffused," they have to be communicated and "known."[5] Dewey was especially concerned about the ways in which effective communication took place, and therefore interested in the activities that went on in this process. Bentley and Follett went even farther, denying that opinion had "meaning" except as understood through "activities" or as part of "the whole social process."[6]

Pragmatists, and group theorists after them, may have substituted a will-of-the-wisp for a "spook"; but there were important insights in this approach. Much nonsense had been and continues to be talked with such language as "public" and "opinion." For practical political situations, the generation, intensities, and changes of opinion are more important than the prevalent modes of philosophy or the literary statements made by pundits at a distant remove from the actual processes of politics. To understand politics, start with people's activities in communication, their shared attitudes, and the "crossed groups" to which they belong rather than the methodology suggested by such statements as "opinion rules the world" and "the real is rational."

In rejecting received notions of public opinion, pragmatist social theory also discarded the metaphysics and epistemology that went with the concept of the "public interest." As people ordinarily used such words, Bentley, Follett and Dewey agreed, interest or interests did not *exist*, they were *generated* by activities and the activities were interpreted symbolically, that is, recognized.[7] The activities were the "objective" stuff of the interests, insofar as something tangible or objective existed, while views communicated and "known" were the subjective stuff of interest. To quote from one of the modern group theorists, ". . . from interaction in groups arise certain common habits of response which may be called norms, or shared attitudes." "The shared attitudes. . .constitute the interests."[8]

A restatement of the thesis may make the main argument stand out more sharply. Whatever, one may say, men's interests "really are," interests as they will be concretely *expressed* and specifically *understood* by those men will be a different thing. Therefore, the social scientist must get at the "stuff" and process, out of which actual political interests are immediately generated and in which they are perceived. The interest generated and expressed *in the political process* will not be a metaphysical abstraction; it will be a thing evolved in the group and the governmental process itself. As Dewey put the matter, "When. . . consequences are intellectually and emotionally appreciated, a shared interest

[5] *Ibid.*, p. 177.

[6] Bentley, *op. cit.*, p. 177; Mary Parker Follett, *Creative Experience* (London, 1924), p. 209; also, *cf.* Harold J. Laski, "Sovereignty of the State," in *Studies in the Problem of Sovereignty* (London, 1916).

[7] Bentley, *op. cit.*, p. 204; Dewey, *op. cit.*, pp. 20-22; Follett, *op. cit.*, p. 85.

[8] Truman, *op. cit.*, pp. 33, 34.

is generated and the nature of the interconnected behavior is thereby transformed."[9] The shared interest *is* itself, and not another thing.

Pragmatism was also a revolt against formalism, a restatement of the abstractions of forms and procedure in the terms of process. Law, said Bentley, is an "activity"; and as for the "system characteristics," they are "reducible to activity, just as are the laws separately considered."[10] The state, said Dewey and Follett, is a "public articulated and operating through representative officers," something "continually searched for," especially something to be "discovered experimentally."[11] Truman and Latham add to these notions the "potential groups" that enforce the "rules of the game" and the "official groups" that write and carry out the treaties;[12] but they concur as well in this substitution of *process* for juridical and political *organization.*

The political process itself is conceived in a similar way by the early pragmatists and latter-day group theorists, though pragmatism emphasized the normative while group theorists have a more positive and explanatory aim. Dewey and Follett described the process entailed in the "confronting and integrating of desires" and the outcome of "healthful functioning" or homeostasis. Bentley and Truman speak of resultants and equilibrium, and group theorists generally of the "consensus" that results from the process. In the two schools of thought is to be found much of the modern language and thought about "the group struggle" and "consensus" that are—or seem to be—so important in "The American System of Government."[13]

To this point, pragmatism and the group theory are much alike. Truman and others have carried explicit theory much farther. Applications of group theory to politics have also been enriched by studies of voting behavior, by social psychology, and the sociology of small groups. I do not believe that these developments qualify the essential propositions or philosophical commitments which group theory derived from its pragmatist heritage; hence the pertinence of further inquiry into the philosophical foundations of the two traditions.

II. What is a Public?

According to Dewey, a "public" is brought into being by the indirect consequences of action, by the perception of those consequences, and the ensuing conjoint activity. For this language, Truman's can be readily substituted:

[9]Dewey, *op. cit.*, p. 27.

[10]Bentley, *op. cit.*, p. 272.

[11]Dewey, *op. cit.*, pp. 31, 67; Follett, *op. cit.*, pp. 202, 274.

[12]Truman, *op. cit.*, pp. 159, 512-514; Earl Latham, "The Group Basis of Politics: Notes for a Theory," *American Political Science Review*, Vol. 46 (1951), pp. 390, 391.

[13]Bentley, *op. cit.*, pp. 258 and 288; Dewey, *op. cit.*, p. 27; Follett, *op. cit.*, p. 209; Truman, *op. cit.*, pp. 505 *et seq. Cf.* also, E. Pendleton Herring, *The Politics of Democracy* (New York, 1940); and Ernest S. Griffith, *The American System of Government* (New York, 1954).

tangent relations, disturbance of equilibrium, and interaction.[14] So, too, the treatment by Dewey and Follett of "communication," of the "public articulated" and of the connection of the people *in* a situation with the people that *pass on* a situation, seems to correspond closely with such constructs of group theory as "access," overlapping memberships "up-and-down-the-line," and the "two-step flow of communication."[15]

To pursue the argument of pragmatism, we can imagine a simple political process. At a busy street corner, pedestrians and motorists find that their informal, on-the-spot adjustments are no longer sufficient to regulate the flow of traffic. Enduring indirect consequences are the result–traffic congestion and accidents. Signals are installed. That which intervenes between the perceived problem and the governmental outcome is a *public*, a group of affected parties–aroused, engaged in conjoint activity, growing conscious of itself, organizing and seeking to influence officials. The terminus of the process is the *populus*, a "public organized by means of officials and material agencies," or as Follett says, "the connection of the will of the people which is in the situation with the will of the people which passes on the situation."[16]

Dewey and Follett were asserting two things. The first was that publics got going this way: that political opinion developed in this fashion. The second thesis was a normative proposition: that the metaphysics of sovereignty, the state, the "formalism" should not prevent the recognition of newly perceived indirect consequences. They were pointing to an activity, specifically a *process* which produced response and to a *duty* of officials to respond. The difficulty with pragmatism, and *a fortiori* with group theory, is the step from *public* to *populus:* in other words, why the public is a *legitimate* concern, and the *reasons* for response to it.

Pragmatism, by erecting a continuum with communication and interaction covering all terms from social and economic power to political authority, obscures this problem of legitimacy, of how to get from the public to the populus. Legitimacy is a matter of the social contract, of *determinate relations*, never of process. As a notion, it stands for modes of discrimination by which we sort out one process from another, and one "public" from another. As a political term, specifically, the referent is representation: how created and who and what are represented.

Pragmatism and group theory describe formation and communication of opinion in terms of group dynamics–of interaction within groups. One consequence is that terms like "conjoint activity" and "interaction" are made to cover all forms

[14]Dewey, *op. cit.*, p. 12 and Ch. 1 *passim*; Truman, *op. cit.*, Ch. 2.

[15]Dewey, *op. cit.*, pp. 208, 209; Follett, *op. cit.*, pp. 202, 206; Homans, *op. cit.*; and Elihu Katz, "The Two-Step Flow of Communication: An Up-to-Date Report on a Hypothesis," *Public Opinion Quarterly*, Vol. 21 (1957), p. 61.

[16]Dewey, *op. cit.*, p. 16; Follett, *op. cit.*, p. 202.

of communication: those mediated by face-to-face relations, those travelling up and down an organizational hierarchy, and those that spill unnoticed out of the mail boxes of putative opinion leaders several days of any given week. In each one of these situations, there are publics aroused and becoming conscious of themselves, increasing interaction and greater cohesion; but the publics are very different things. Some are propaganda "groups," some the association lobbyist reporting to the dues payers—others are large and formally organized publics. One ground of distinction between these publics depends upon the lines of communication involved: in one instance from the lobbyist's mimeograph machine to your mail box; in another from the desk of a staff research employee or a local officer through a series of responsible officials and committees to the membership. The channels through which communications flow differ. Also, in some instances the communications flow effectively in two ways; in others the flow is one-way and the members express their wishes mainly by "voting with their feet." The point of the latter distinction is not simply or primarily that mutuality is a good thing. The real point is that only some publics are potentially either *representative* bodies or *thought* organizations.[17]

Flows of communication are important for the group itself; they are also important in relating the group to something outside and in linking it with that something outside in a way that carries with it the stamp of legitimacy. For this purpose, *both* formal organization and *formal interaction* are needed. Forms and organization by themselves may *stand for* "thought" and representativeness; formal interaction, the official relation, provides the assurance that the forms are what they purport to be.[18]

The different ways of behaving entailed in formal and informal interaction are part of deliberation, and thus of "thought," insofar as thought is consciously evoked, stated and communicated with a deliberate organizational purpose. Thus, there are the proposals of the board, minutes of the council, resolutions of the annual conference, etc. One major group objective for such situations is to prevent interaction from producing a group with too much cohesion. Organization plus formal interaction does this, supplying thereby the *credentials* of deliberation. These credentials, important specially for elaborate associations, depend upon the integrity of those groups which organize collective thought: the boards of foundations, committees, and councils; the staff experts, lawyers and economists of trade unions; the committees and subcommittees of trade associations. Confidence in their product is related, on many occasions, to evidences of impartial and expert knowledge having been sought and considered.

The distinction between formal and informal interaction is also important for the democratic component of representation. The members interacting and the

[17]The concept of "thought organization" is borrowed from Graham Wallas.

[18]For a discussion of this point see Talcott Parsons, *Structure and Power in Modern Society* (New York, 1960), esp. Chs. 1, 2, 8.

frequency of interaction are, no doubt, related to the procedures of democracy; but they are not the same thing; and members, people, and officials do not regard them as the same thing. Few care that a lobby be "representative" or "democratic." In other cases, "democracy" and "representativeness" do matter: for trade unions, farmers' committees, cooperatives, medical and bar associations, the many "guilds" and councils of contemporary society that wield power of varying degrees of importance and are clothed with privileges or rights to be heard and consulted. Their act of resolution into a constituency to create the capacity of representation makes sense *only* as part of an attempt to establish a *legitimate* relation between the group and an outside public, or between the group and a functional scheme of rights and duties.

Finally, in accounting for the difference between a public and the populus, not only the who and how of representation is important, but *what* gets represented as well. Representation is more than a plea that many are concerned and that the many have deliberated. It is a plea that *what* they are concerned about is *entitled* to recognition; it is an attempt to establish a legitimate relation between the people that are in a situation and a functional scheme of rights and duties commonly recognized.

Consider the following dialogue:

Member: "X is a fine labor leader. He was elected a second time with an even bigger majority."

Citizen: "With the help of captive locals, goons, and bribery."

Member: "No. The boys like him. He brings home the bacon."

Citizen: "I would say the boys' reasons for liking him aren't very good ones."

Member: "Well, you people outside don't know what it was like to be a gear-buster ten years ago."

Citizen: "You're pretty well paid now, aren't you?"

Member: "Why are you complaining so much? The stuff gets there fast and for a good price, doesn't it?"

Citizen: "But I thought we were talking about whether X was a good labor leader or not."

Member "Let me ask you this: how many restaurants, warehouses, or cab companies do you think would have been organized without X?"

The dialogue, distilled from a video-tape interview with members of Hoffa's Teamsters, runs the gamut of arguments: democratic consent, group interests, functionalism, the representative quality of leadership.[19] Incidentally, it illustrates a fact given relatively little attention by pragmatism and by most group

[19]Note here the treatment by group theorists of leadership as an "affair of the group," discerning, articulating, and promoting the attitudes and interests the group shares. (Truman, *op. cit.*, p. 190; Bentley, *op. cit.*, p. 223).

theory: that many groups have power and "alternate resources"[20] of various kinds other than those directly political and that these groups are themselves subject to regulation. The dialogue also shows, more importantly for present purposes, that many groups are expected to account for the exercise of their powers not only to the state but also, in a measure, to the public. These groups are, in varying degrees, representative bodies, "thought organizations," and systems for exercising and ensuring stewardship. Members, populace, and officials expect and require something more than group egoism. The group itself earns a part of its legitimate claim for consideration by a compliance with these requisites. In fact, as the dialogue above suggests, the group is often, and expected to be, a *populus* with the connotations that term carried in its classical usage.

III. Publics and the Public

John Dewey was neither explicit nor clear in his statement of the relation between publics and the great public or the community. On the one hand, the pragmatist conception of politics had revolutionary overtones. Dewey and Follett looked at a public largely unorganized, apathetic and unaware of itself, and wanted to summon it to a successful campaign. Their views suggested ferment and conflict, opinion of intensity and a public of explosive and populistic qualities.[21] On the other hand, for Dewey, an organized public of many self-conscious, effective groups was the path toward the Great Community.[22] Also, for him, group memberships promoted contentment and political sanity. These separate views suggest both an unresolved tension and a missing term in pragmatist political theory.

A more precise examination of pragmatist theory is instructive in discovering what should be added to the account. Pragmatism closely identifies means and ends, method and outcome. The objective of this merging of concepts was to make normative theory "operational," or, as Dewey said, "instrumental." As a consequence, pragmatists tend to confuse the way in which we get to a certain political outcome with the established situation itself. The articulated public that for Dewey was the method to achieve the Great Community, becomes in pragmatist theory also the force that assures a continuing revolution and the guardian of the revolution once completed. What gets slighted in such an account is the dynamism of the new forces created by the revolution itself. The missing term in the political dialectic is the politics of established programs, as opposed to that of groups. The New State, perhaps created experimentally and pragmatically, is itself another thing than the processes that brought it into being.

[20]On the concept of alternate resources, see Robert A. Dahl, *Who Governs?* (New Haven, Conn., 1961), esp. Bk. 4; and "The Analysis of Influence in Local Communities," in C. R. Adrian, ed., *Social Science and Community Action* (Ann Arbor, Mich., 1960).

[21]Dewey, *op. cit.*, pp. 133-137; Follett, *op. cit.*, p. 242. Pluralists such as Laski also spoke of "group competing against group in a ceaseless striving for progressive expansion."

[22]Dewey, *op. cit.*, pp. 147-155.

Take the case of Dewey's Great Community as the force powering a continuing revolution. He apparently believed that the Great Community would continue to expand, giving expression to an increasing number of "publics." The proposition is *prima facie* implausible. Beneficiaries of revolutions generally become the conservators of a new *status quo* and seek to defend privileged positions as well. Truman and other group theorists have taken account of this fact and still preserved the notion of a continuing group revolution but without, in my judgment, assigning an adequate importance to the politics of the New State itself.

According to Truman, one of the reasons why American group politics remains fairly healthy—does not become "morbific"—is the ease of access to the governmental process and the readiness of political response to those that have achieved access. Another reason is the facility with which potential groups can secede from parent organizations or organize to represent a separate interest.[23] Groups tend, thus, to form and reform freely rather than become a caste or class. The theses are unexceptionable, at least to describe some activities that occur. They describe, however, only a part of the group process. In particular they do not provide an adequate account of the politics of programs.

The group revolution is, in an important way, a self-limiting one. The development and especially the growth of administrative programs supplies a major explanation. Access means influence; but often—and especially for a new group—it is valued because it leads to the establishment of new *programs* of government. Thus, for leaders and for governors there is the problem not only of adjusting the demands of many groups, but of reconciling competing and expanding programs of government. Much of the open land has already been taken up. And in the crowded area of public policy, competing and expanding programs produce costs and side-effects,[24] often increasing ones, that point to a common interest in coordination and consolidation. These same consequences also reach beyond the traditional coordination-consolidation objectives of executives and administrators, requiring new combinations of group interest and group leadership, of public and private collaboration. Some examples of such policy areas, important in recent years, are: health, education, and welfare; transportation and communications; housing and water resources; the regulation of business and labor relations. Access, influence in determining the outcomes, is one thing; but a claim for recognition and response that ignores the common good becomes increasingly difficult to entertain.

If the group revolution is self-limiting, then politics tends—according to pragmatist political philosophy and group theory—to become morbific. Access is less available given the contemporary situation of occupied ground. Here again,

[23]Truman, *op. cit.*, pp. 596 ff. Truman uses the term "morbific politics" to describe the pathology of the group process.

[24]Including not only the administrator's "dis-economies" and "externalities" but political difficulties as well.

however, the concept of a politics of programs is useful. The argument can be advanced by inquiring into changes, in recent years, within several large, cohesive groups. Among the reasons for such group developments as the dissolution of the farm bloc, for the recent quarrels within the A.M.A. and between it, the nurses, and the A.H.A., or the tensions within the labor movement, one item that stands out especially is changes in the relation between members and their professional or occupational environment. Since the professional situations are also partly a creation of the state, programs have been a major item in affecting them. As examples, one could cite developments in labor relations and labor contract administration, the increasing importance of medical research and problems of hospital administration, the independent stance of the agricultural educator and technological developments in agriculture.[25] Organizational opportunities and ease of access to government contribute to the healthy state of a pluralistic society. So does the dynamism of the welfare economy. But it should be equally obvious that the *programs* of the welfare state themselves, by modifying continually and often automatically the relations between group membership and the environment, are one of the greatest remedies for morbidity.

The New State begets a new politics, requiring particular conditions if that politics is to operate sanely and temperately. In describing the New State, Dewey and Follett presented a picture of relative contentment and social harmony because all or most could distribute their personal resources satisfactorily and achieve effective expression through a variety of group memberships. They did not explain in detail why the metamorphosis from angry group protest to social peace should occur; nor did they describe the mechanisms that would continue the state of social peace. Their omissions leave unexplained, especially, the fact that our political system *now* appears to work fairly comfortably within the extreme limits of populism and syndicalism.

Truman and other group theorists have supplied the missing concepts to connect the pre-revolutionary state with the post-revolutionary one. Truman cites as the guardians of the constitution and the defenders of the polity "the effects of overlapping memberships, particularly the vitality of membership in those potential groups based upon interests widely held throughout the society."[26] In this account, two notions may be singled out: (1) the large potential publics (including majority groups); and (2) the overlapping memberships of individual persons. Neither is, in my judgment, adequate to explain fully the defense of the "rules of the game" in the sense that most people have in mind when they use that

[25] See, for example, William J. Block, *The Separation of the Farm Bureau and the Extension Service* (Urbana, Ill., 1960); Joel Hardman and Maurice Neufeld, *The House of Labor* (New York, 1951); "The American Medical Association: Power, Purpose, and Politics in Organized Medicine," *Yale Law Journal*, Vol. 63 (1954), p. 938; A. W. Wilcox, "Hospitals and the Corporate Practice of Medicine," *Cornell Law Quarterly*, Vol. 45 (1960), p. 432.

[26] Truman, *op. cit.*, p. 535.

expression. Neither is adequate, again in my judgment, to resolve the tension between process and result in pragmatist theory.

Large, highly organized publics or groups afford one plausible example of the influence of overlapping memberships. The leaders of the larger organizations that are the major beneficiaries of the modern polity are especially subject to cross-pressures. Similarly, within these organizations, overlapping memberships operate both "up-and-down-the-line" and between the member as such and the member as citizen. This conceptual apparatus does provide one method of stating the constraints operating on leaders and members. It explains the phenomenon of group access to government, in some circumstances. Also it affords a good description of one mechanism by which the exchange between group memberships on the one hand and values and interests on the other hand is mediated. However, it supplies only two terms of the dialectic. What especially the apparatus will not serve to explain are transformations in the relations of the public and the private where the group process itself produces new indirect consequences. To meet these situations and to compete for access the group must both "think" and represent a common interest: in some measure transcend the group process.

Before considering the role of overlapping memberships among the more numerous publics, we should note two things. One is that these memberships—in terms of formal affiliations—are few.[27] If primary groups such as the family and reference groups such as an ethnic identification are included, then the average man does have a significant number of "group" memberships. These affiliations, however, represent a special class of memberships. Many or most of them are not dissolvable at will: they are part of heritage, nurture, and life situation. They represent loyalties that run especially deep.

Where memberships of the latter type are directly threatened or engaged, people are not likely to be either restrained or sober in their political expressions. One of the distinctive features of American politics since the "group revolution" is that prudent politicians often avoid the triggering of such loyalties and especially forcing constituents to choose between them. Thus, it appears that what may have been at one time a restraining mechanism has grown into a constitutional tradition. The political leaders—or many of them, at least—are not restrained by the overlapping memberships of their following, by a kind of higgling in the market with group loyalties traded against each other. Rather, they appear to have concluded a treaty or arrived at a compact of mutual

[27]About 50 percent of the population has no other formal membership than the church. Of the remainder, the largest part belong additionally only to a trade union, a farmers' organization or a fraternal lodge. Only a small percentage (and that about the same as those who would be classified as leaders in one capacity or another) belong to four or more organizations. For a citation of the relevant literature, see Rothman, *loc. cit.*, pp. 22-23.

forbearance: they agree not to engage in such practices lest the stirring up of populist or syndicalist publics erupt into destructive competition damaging to all.[28]

The compact of mutual forbearance suggests also a reason for seeking to restrict the role of majority groups and large potential publics. Tocqueville observed long ago that such groups speak out on issues like patriotism, social rights, and matters of fair play if they arouse sufficient *völkisch* sentiment. But to uphold the Fifth Amendment or academic freedom, as the Stouffer report indicates, we must look to the few and hope precisely that these issues do not arouse the wide potential groups too much or too frequently.[29] The populace usually prefers equality to liberty unless statesmen are able to find some method of reconciling these values.

At times, something like Dewey's Great Community or a majority group does become active in defense of the "rule of the game" when through leadership, communication, and an appropriate linking of symbols various kinds of publics are joined. Thus, "Ike's Budget" may be supported by economists and business leaders, and also with the aid of the President's leadership and effective use of popular similes win a large following. Similarly, following President Truman's seizure of the steel plants, the Supreme Court justices and the steel companies were supported by a large and aroused public.

In forming such a majority various types of publics may be joined or they may fuse; but the notion of a majority group or a Great Community by itself does not suggest *which* rules of the game they will defend: whether they will seek to overturn the polity or uphold it. Thus, one community arises in populist wrath when faced by a resettlement plan under Title I of the Housing Act while another defends urban renewal and the "comprehensive plan."[30] There is the political constellation aroused by "Communism, Corruption, and Korea" and that which supports free trade or the decision in *Yates et al v. United States.*[31] Either kind of alternative seems equally probable unless the standards of polity are joined by leadership to the group process.

Pragmatism, especially as represented by Dewey and Follett, was both a brilliant amendment of traditional political theory and a fairly accurate prophecy of future developments. Elaborated by group theory, it has proven to have great value for explaining and describing political behavior. As this account has tried to suggest, however, Dewey's own incomplete explanation of how matters stood between the public and the publics provides an important clue to other

[28]*Cf.* Key's discussion of the "restraining dikes" that serve to moderate populist and syndicalist opinion in the American polity. V. O. Key, Jr., *Public Opinion and American Democracy* (New York, 1960), esp. Ch. 21.

[29]Samuel A. Stouffer, *Communism, Conformity, and Civil Liberties* (New York, 1955).

[30]*Cf.* W. H. Form and D. C. Miller, *Industry, Labor, and Community* (New York, 1960).

[31]354 U. S. 298 (1957).

forces operating on the political scene. One is the cumulative power of those individuals who, at least on occasion, *do not* identify with the group process, but stand outside it for the stake–material or ideological–that they have in the New State. Another is the leadership and authority of "representative officers" who are more than group leaders and who seek answers that can reconcile the affairs of the group with the community of goods and of rights that pertain to the whole.

IV. The Public and Its Problems

As noted above, pragmatism and group theory describe those activities usually referred to as "the formation of public policy" in approximately the same ways. The objective was, largely, to avoid formalistic ideas and to talk more sensibly about what actually seemed to be happening. People–so this interpretation goes–discover what their problems are in the process of government and political activity, generating opinions or publics of varying intensities and degrees of crystallization and organization. The government or "state" itself responds not to a "brooding omnipresence" or to some facts "out there," but to the facts and desires as expressed and effectively brought home to the legislator or administrator. In particular, pragmatists wished to argue that concepts like the state, expert opinion, or the public interest were not separate things to be set over against the public and the solution of *its* problems.[32]

The word "problem" is important in most statements about the formation of policy, particularly in pragmatist political theory. The term and its uses deserve more examination than they usually receive: what is the "nature" of a problem? how is it discovered? how are the facts about a problem communicated? how is the scope of a problem defined or enlarged? and finally, what are "solutions" to problems?

What does it mean, in the formulation of policy, to say "becoming aware of a problem," or to speak of "the discovery of a problem?" "Discovery" and "problem" could mean the whole process leading up to an authoritative ratification of a "solution." But this usage robs the word of distinct meaning. Assume for the moment that discovery is restricted to that point at which a problem begins its official career. Then it is plausible to say that one way a problem is discovered is by publics "connected with," that is, having access to and interacting with officials. The agenda of decision is often scheduled this way: that is, an activity becomes a problem *now*, rather than last year or next.[33] Also, *what* is discovered, concretely, is often a matter of publics and officials interacting; *i.e.*, which problems pertaining to public health, the aged, or dependent children receive enough attention to matter.

[32]Dewey, *op. cit.*, pp. 27, 30-32, 47, 177, 207-208; Follett, *op. cit.*, pp. 28, 206.

[33]For example, in capital budgeting. *Cf.* W. H. Brown, Jr., and C. E. Gilbert, *Planning Municipal Investment: A Case Study of Philadelphia* (Philadelphia, 1961), esp. Ch. 9.

There is also another and radically different technique of discovery, one which employs officials who are in no way linked with publics or responding to them, but connected with the flow of information and the cumulated lore of administration itself. Nowadays, it is safe to say that we live in an age of the administrative state. A large part of administration is the continual flow of information, not only from publics, but in the form of financial reports, statistics, engineering surveys, and technical data and discoveries. In different words: one way problems are discovered is by administrators and elected officials, not so much responding to clienteles as reflecting upon reported data and the lore of the profession and initiating responses or possible solutions–for example, to the problems of the agricultural worker, to actual or anticipated increases in traffic loads, or actual or anticipated changes in the technology of aviation. The doctrine of administrative "expertise" is based upon the recognition of these facts. Similarly, upon these grounds and the recognition of the value of the procedures of administration, and only for these reasons, are delegations of legislative power to administrative agencies sustained. The concept "access" becomes itself intelligible only by recognizing the distinction between these two modes of discovery, for only on the assumption of alternate modes of discovery is it clear why various publics seek to have their problems recognized and solved through other channels. Neither method, in fact, makes sense without the other; they are form and matter; they are two sides of the coin.

Within the context of pragmatism or group theory, one might argue that the "facts" are chimerical and finally too elusive except when expressed through delivered political opinion and by means of access to officials. On the other hand, depending upon how important the "facts" are, "access" may not lead to influence, but the reverse. The views of officials linked to publics that have really achieved effective access are discounted. To the degree that the Interstate Commerce Commission is under the influence of the "interests," in the measure that the Federal Reserve Board is a "tool" of the Treasury, their usefulness and their political power decline. Even that *bête noir* of the public administration fraternity, the Army Corps of Engineers, and clientele agencies such as the Extension Service suffer if their reputation for professionalism and objectivity is seriously impugned.[34] For that matter, Congressmen too battle continually, in their manner, for objectivity and for the facts. They try to get behind the plausible image, to seek other sources of information, partly because of the access which many

[34]Block, *op. cit.*; Brunner and Yang, *Rural America and the Extension Service* (New York, 1949); W. R. Parks, *Soil Conservation Districts in Action* (Ames, Iowa, 1952); Arthur Maass, *Muddy Waters* (Cambridge, Mass., 1951), esp. Chs. 4, 5; also the "marasmus" controversy on the independent regulatory commissions: Samuel Huntington, "The Marasmus of the ICC," *Yale Law Journal,* Vol. 61 (1952), p. 467; C. Morgan, "A Critique of 'The Marasmus of the ICC'," *ibid.,* Vol. 62 (1953), p. 171.

groups have established.[35] If problems had only their subjective aspect, if it were impossible to establish the objective component, if access to officials were a major part in the formulation of public policy, the communication of "problems" and thereby the policy process itself would break down. Communication in government requires a knowledge of the "relevant facts" and "a consensus that there is integrity in procedures";[36] otherwise the road does not go through, the hospital or dam is not built. True, consensus and political agreement often produce results despite the "objective" nature of the problem; they can sometimes, and sometimes must, substitute for facts and a rational understanding of the nature of the problem. In other cases, they ought not to carry the day. Government is discrimination between these two situations.

To ask the next question, "In what way does the 'consensus that there is integrity in procedures' acquire the important element of conviction or certainty?" leads farther yet from the concepts of group theory and pragmatism, beyond process and even procedure, to the formal external checks placed on the process and the procedures by Congressional committees and the courts of law.[37] We can if we wish, following pragmatism, call a procedure a process and even bury the idea of a formal check on both procedure and process under the common notion of the "process" by which we solve problems.[38] To do so, however, produces theoretical confusion, and a faulty explanation of the political process itself.

Problems can also be big problems or small problems–big dams or little dams, housepainting or redevelopment. As Bentham (or Hegel, for that matter) argued, a community–its nature and its size–is partly a matter of how people define their problems, or how those problems are defined for them. Bentham's point of view has relevance here, for one difficulty with group theory and with pragmatism is the discussion of the way in which the *scope* of a problem is determined.

Once government or the governmental process is looked at from this perspective, one of the striking things about it is the enormous authority, discretion,

[35]Compare, for instance, the behavior of different committees in the House and Senate such as the Senate Committee on Banking and Currency and the House Committee on Labor and Education.

[36]Norton E. Long, "Public Policy and Administration: The Goals of Rationality and Responsibility," *Public Administration Review*, Vol. 14 (1954), p. 28.

[37]For this insight, I am indebted to Charles E. Gilbert. See his "The Framework of Administrative Responsibility," *Journal of Politics*, Vol. 21 (1959), p. 373.

[38]"Process" is central to the pragmatist description of politics, as it is to group theory. Indeed, Bentley, Follett, and Dewey have had a great deal to do with directing the attention of political scientists toward the "process" and away from organization, rules, procedure, and competence. The difficulty with the word "process" is that it tends to include, unless used carefully, not only the idea of a sequence of activities, but also (1) the procedures applied to the process, and (2) the criteria by which some things are called law and others are not. Thus, we have our casebooks. Also, there are officers who, by some rules and criteria, separate "judge-questions" from "jury-questions," and there are other officers who say that the court of first instance declared but that what they declared is not law.

and power given to officials (as opposed to publics) to control the scope of problems in the interests of equity and rationality. They decide the scope of the problem and derivatively of the public by the twin powers to determine the alternatives among which choice is made and to say who will be heard. Courts decide who has standing to sue. Administrators decide whether the hearing will be upon a segment of an air route, involve several major trunk lines, or a whole region. Committees set the propositions for a hearing and invite the witnesses. Even the political parties have varying quantities of assigned authority in nominating candidates and choosing the issues for elections. These decisions are not matters for the public; they represent a deliberate loading of the scales, partly to deal equitably ("objectively") with those who have an interest, partly to prevent "effective opinion" or access from carrying the day, and partly in order to provide deliberately for the exercise of equity, prudence, or leadership.[39]

An emphasis upon the scope of problems (the community affected by a problem), upon the "relevant facts," and upon the techniques of calculation and control that do service for "the facts" when they are unknown or unknowable corresponds to our present situation of a densely populated group universe.[40] That same situation, entailing as it does "occupied ground" in the sphere of public policy, suggests an amendment of the concept of the official as described by pragmatism and by group theory. Today's official is more than the "broker of interests," and more than an exploiter of "potential publics."

The official is only in part a broker of group interests, because brokerage is not the only way the governmental process goes on. The "broker of interests" perhaps makes sense to describe the era of "invisible government" or the present-day professional party politician. In his strictly political capacity the official may promise and bargain, when he runs for election. But he must pay off as an official, that is, by setting the government in motion or stopping it. In this respect, he can hold himself out as an entrepreneur, but he cannot be merely a broker for the simple reason that the exchange must be effected via the state, and the contract is subject to many uncertainties and implied clauses. For that matter, brokers have a way of getting replaced in this day and age by good entrepreneurs.[41]

The official today must generally be more, too, than an entrepreneur investing *in* potential publics or seeking to interact *with them*. He must for two reasons: because the group's concern is the community's concern; and because of today's situation of occupied ground and of organized and sophisticated publics. When Dewey and Follett were writing—in the heyday of Seaman Knapp, of the trade association movement, and of state labor legislation—publics needed to be taught

[39]Schattschneider has made this point forcefully. See *The Semi-Sovereign People* (New York, 1960).

[40]*Cf.* Robert A. Dahl and Charles E. Lindblom, *Politics, Economics, and Welfare* (New York, 1953), Chs. 3, 4.

[41]The conception of the politician as entrepreneur has, of course, a long history in political theory, from Weber and Schumpeter down to Robert A. Dahl.

an awareness of *their* interests, not, as the idealist formula would have it, of a good held in common. Populist and syndicalist publics can be roused, even today, but they have been pretty well exploited. The new "potential public" is not so easy to discover or to win, especially since now the official has to choose more than discover, and to justify his stand rather than contract for delivery.

The official, nowadays, is less an entrepreneur dealing in publics; he is more of a "statesman," one who links or joins the objective and subjective aspects of problems. The sanctity of the administrative state and its programs tends to impose such a role. Also, his effectiveness depends largely upon the measure in which he is able to join power with the standards of a polity: winning the support of other officials, formal agencies of government, and leaders from private life, to bring into being new communities of interest and to promote solutions to problems that these publics hold in common with others. To capitalize investments in this area the official needs the state—to get at the facts, to secure representation for interests not easily articulated, and to communicate his objectives with maximum effect. He needs the approbation and the cooperation of "representative officers," of those leaders from private life who see beyond the group process. He needs, in short, to set a style of action appropriate to the contemporary situation.

If it makes sense to speak of a polity and not merely of process, then the pragmatist conception of "solutions," or the outcome of the process, needs also to be re-examined.

To describe the outcome of the governmental process as an equilibrium, arriving at consensus, "integrating desires" or "avoiding waste" may achieve one of two objectives or both. It dispenses with "spooks" and directs inquiry away from questions of organization and procedure. It can also impart the flavor of scientific endeavor to inquiry. It conjures up the image of a stable mechanical system or a market at equilibrium. Presumably, then, one can talk about the group process as part of "political behavior" and formulate laws about it. This way of stating things, however, leaves several questions unanswered.

One problem not solved—in fact, hardly stated by Dewey or in group theory—is that of assuring a return to equilibrium. Another way of asking about this problem is, "Why do we manage to achieve a 'moving consensus' and not merely a series of unique resultants?" And still another way of putting the issue is to ask, "Why doesn't the 'game of politics' disrupt the polity?" "Consensus" might mean many things but judging from the way political scientists use the term, they seem to mean (1) widely diffused agreement on many issues; (2) low intensity of disagreement; and (3) the absence of potentially explosive publics. Pluralism and pragmatism have a lot to do with maintaining this consensus, no doubt. But so also do the amount of contentment (or apathy), the public responsibility of leaders, and the possibilities of developing special publics for particular jobs. Equally important are the procedures by which the group process is restrained and the formal checks that reinforce the sense of rationality and of due process.

By throwing away the notion of a whole–useful though that step may be up to a point–pragmatism makes explanation itself difficult.

Also, to break through the ideologies of a regime or of a period, to set men on a different footing, in different words to destroy equilibrium and establish a radically new equilibrium and consensus is part of government. For Dewey and Follett, the problem of a radically different equilibrium and how to get there presented no real difficulty. The tasks of the day for them were to establish access to government, promote experimentalism, and tear down outworn abstractions. Now, the pragmatic revolution is pretty much over, at least for the time being. And the group process, taken by itself, seems to be especially productive of conservatism and *stasis.* Sometimes it generates leadership, as a kind of antithesis to itself, for someone or some body must break the chains of custom, the outworn rights, and the dead myths. Courts do this job, so do legislatures, and so do leaders, especially those with authority of office. The American Constitution divides sovereignty. And American politics reveals in its operation the fact of that division. Still our politics shows also at times in a great act and at times in the longing for a great act, elements for which the notion of sovereignty stood, that grandfather of all the spooks on the political scene, the office and officers that existed to overcome groups and destroy customs for the sake of a new equilibrium.

V. Conclusion

One way of summarizing the argument of this article is to say that the pragmatists discarded too much of the "soul-stuff," "spooks," and formal mechanisms in their discussion of politics and government and that group theorists have followed their lead too closely. When Dewey, Bentley, and Follett were writing they said much that was important about what was happening then. Their interpretations are less important now.

Pragmatism and group theories of politics are often misleading intellectual constructs for the interpretation or description of political or governmental situations since they direct attention in principle to what men are *doing* rather than to their intentions and dilemmas as well. When intentions are included, they are interpreted with the concepts of group theory. The difficulty with this approach, however, is that government and responsibility are more than an "affair of the group" or of groups–that is to say, officials are different from leaders and representation is more than interaction.

One consequence of such an omission is that there are a good many activities of men–men in government and the political process–that group theories of politics do not explain. They explain little where the "facts" are especially important, where "rights" and due process of law or "forms" are at stake in a serious way, where leadership comes into play, or when the machinery of government is engaged extensively. From this observation follows a rather important point, that group theories have little to say about the routine of government (the administrative process) or about important changes of policy or of "rights."

Another point is that group theory fails to explain adequately the politics of programs, especially of programs that provide common or community goods and that require extensive representation and "thought."

Theorists and especially their theories ought, however, to be given their due. To say that pragmatism and group theory may seem less important—especially in understanding the politics of the 1960s—is not to say that they have been superseded. Much of our politics goes on in situations where neither a common representation, nor "style," nor "forms," nor the "facts" are especially relevant. Also, the politics of today is not that of yesterday nor necessarily that of tomorrow. Pragmatism and the group theory represent a good description of *one* kind of political action. The importance of that kind of political action varies with time and circumstances.

American Interest Groups: A Survey of Research and Some Implications for Theory and Method

Samuel J. Eldersveld

Everywhere today interest groups have become the research vogue, recognized by scholars and political analysts as critical centers of power in the political process. In his day, Lord Bryce perceived the parties as "the great moving forces" of politics;[1] today, interest groups would certainly share this status. Tentative explorations of the political group patterns in other countries have led to claims that interest groups may be more influential in the governmental process in Europe than here. Samuel Beer has recently maintained, after sketching the British pattern, that "If we had some way of measuring political power, we could quite possibly demonstrate that at the present time pressure groups are more powerful in

[1]James Bryce, *The American Commonwealth*, 1916 ed., p. 5.

Samuel Eldersveld, "American Interest Groups: A Survey of Research and Some Implications for Theory and Method," in Interest Groups on Four Continents, *ed. Henry Ehrmann (Pittsburgh: Univ. Pittsburgh Press, 1960). Reprinted with permission.*

Britain than in the U.S."[2] And Bernard Brown concludes from his survey of French groups that "Pressure groups continue to be of greater importance in France than in Great Britain or even the U.S."[3] Although these views may be open to question, the spate of "working" and "strategy" papers for orienting interest group research throughout the world has recently mushroomed to new heights. Serious scholars here and abroad are demonstrating a long-range comparative interest in such research.

The question might be parenthetically, if gently, raised at the outset, of course, as to whether all the research goals in this area are realizable. Given the apparent direction and objective of research in this field as indicated—an objective to discover, describe, and analyze regularities between and within interest group phenomena from country to country—one wonders whether the stage has been properly set for the ambitious program of research contemplated. In any field the progress of knowledge has followed five stages, from observation to the taxonomic to the structural to the dynamic to the holistic. Before ambitiously approaching the holistic stage at once, as one recent report suggests,[4] political science may have to assure itself that it has properly developed observational techniques, adequate categories for analysis, and convincing "lower level" propositions for analysis. This is not to say that we should not aim at the total process of politics. Rather, we cannot afford to ignore the requirements of knowledge and the perfection of a convincing research technology.

The widespread interest throughout social science for a careful study of interest groups is significant. Sociologists, economists, as well as political scientists are interested. The implications of this for broadening the base of our inquiry into interest groups should be readily accepted. Franz Neumann perhaps stated this need in typical fashion when he said that "the translation of economic power into social power and thence into political power becomes the crucial concern. . . ." Pressure groups, as "organizations. . .by which [social] power is translated into political power" need intensive study, he claims. And, he adds, "really sophisticated, comparative analysis is still lacking." Further, he makes the point that this process of the "translation of power" is one which "differs from country to country and from historical situation to historical situation."[5] The point is well taken. It must be re-emphasized that we must not be concerned merely with interest groups *qua* interest groups. Our aim must be to analyze them in the broad context of social and economic change, and by

[2]"Pressure Groups and Parties in Britain," *American Political Science Review*, Vol. 50 (1956), p. 3.

[3]Bernard E. Brown, "Pressure Politics in France," *The Journal of Politics*, Vol. 18 (1956), p. 718.

[4]Gabriel A. Almond, "A Comparative Study of Interest Groups and the Political Process," *American Political Science Review*, Vol. 52 (1958), p. 271.

[5]*The Democratic and the Authoritarian State* (1957), pp. 12-14.

studying their impact on the decisional process to move toward answers to questions posed by a theory of the democratic political process.

Types of American Interest Group Studies

The study of American interest groups may have some value for those interested in comparative research. The American experience may suggest certain methodological and theoretical guideposts, but it may also serve as a *caveat*. It illustrates the stages of political inquiry through which we have passed and the major questions which yet remain.

By well-nigh universal agreement the classic discussion of interest groups was presented in 1908 with Arthur F. Bentley's *The Process of Government*. Coming at a time when the insights of American scholars were rooted in the legal basis and formal structure of government and when there was an alienation from systematic theory, this original work found poor receptivity. Bentley turned from structural formalism to what he called the "raw materials" of politics, seeing these as the activities and interactions of social groups. It should be recalled that Bentley did not perceive these groups as conglomerates of unarticulated interests, but as "collectives of action," pressing, demanding, conflicting, mediating. These collectives had taken on "temporarily, or with some permanence, a fairly definite form–definite enough, at any rate, for us to handle, describe, and value in terms of other activities."[6] And, to Bentley, "the balance of the group pressures *is* the existing state of society."[7] Despite such a dynamic conception of political group process, Bentley had no influence until rediscovered within the last decade. In fact, it was not until the Twenties that any scholarly studies of pressure groups were made in the United States.

There are now at least thirty solid studies which are of relevance for an understanding of interest groups in this country. In addition there is a large body of monographic literature, journal articles, and unpublished dissertations. It is interesting to note that very little of this writing antedates the Great Depression, with the decade 1935 to 1945 being perhaps the most prolific. Since David Truman's rediscovery of Bentley and his publication in 1951 of *The Governmental Process*, studies employing systematic theory and employing empirical materials have been appearing more frequently.

Although our literature on interest groups has been generously interspersed with speculative philosophizing about the nature and importance of these groups, speculation which has been both objectively interpretive and value-oriented, the primary form of investigation has been the case study. Three major types of studies are found in our literature–the study of a single interest group; the study of interest groups as they operate in a single arena, especially the legislative

[6]Arthur F. Bentley, *The Process of Government* (new ed. 1956), p. 182.
[7]*Ibid*, pp. 258-259.

arena, over a comparatively short time-span; and the study of interest groups concerned with a particular law or policy-conflict.

Illustrative of the first type is the ground-breaking study by Peter Odegard in 1928 of the Anti-Saloon League. Odegard clearly traces the origins of this group from 1832 on, its transformation from a social movement to a national organization, the character and roles of its leadership, its complicated tactics and pressure techniques, its financial basis, and some of the counter-groups ranged against it. It is an extremely interesting description, exciting to read again even today, including rich insights into the operations of such an ideological movement a half century ago.

Many other studies which concentrate attention primarily on a single interest group exist, including Kile's study of the American Farm Bureau, Lorwin's book on the American Federation of Labor, Rutherford's work on the American Bar Association, Brady's analysis of business associations, Duffield's early study of the American Legion, and a variety of others. There are two such studies which seem to me to deserve special attention. Oliver Garceau's *The Political Life of the American Medical Association*, published in 1941, was a pioneer contribution employing relatively rigorous theory and techniques in "illuminating the always obscure relationships within these societies." He is concerned almost exclusively with the internal organization and political relationships of the AMA, exploring particularly the character and technology of the "active minority" and its problems in producing membership unity as well as in moulding public opinion generally.

The other study of this type which I would like to call to your attention is *Union Democracy*, by non-political scientist Lipset, a careful analysis of the Typographical Workers Union. This brilliant book utilizes available empirical evidence to describe and explain the internal processes of the union, especially its unique two-party system, in terms of a set of carefully developed, interrelated hypotheses. Its contribution to theory is considerable.

In the second category of studies are those which are descriptions of "lobbies" or interest groups operating in one policy arena. An early scholarly effort of this type was E. P. Herring's *Group Representation before Congress* (1929). Herring studied the lobbies of more than 100 associations, collecting much of his material by personal interview. His classification of these types of groups and his explanation of the reasons for their rise are still widely used. Furthermore, his concern with these groups as being "signs of a 'restructuralization' in human relations,"[8] although not pursued in his work, suggests a theoretical standpoint which might well motivate our research today. Studies on state legislatures, such as those of Belle Zeller (New York) and Dayton McKean (New Jersey) were further milestones in our research on the legislative arena. Both studies were gold mines of factual information and insights revealing the

[8]E. P. Herring, *Group Representation before Congress* (1929), p. xi.

decentralized and dispersed nature of interest group activities under the federal system. Two studies on the developing relationships between interest groups and the administrative process should not be overlooked: Herring's *Public Administration and the Public Interest*, and Avery Leiserson's very useful contribution to theory, *Administrative Regulation* (1942). The latter is a study which has not been given adequate recognition in my opinion. It is much more than mere description and taxonomy, being above all an attempt to generalize and hypothesize about the consequences for the "democratization of authority" of the integrative process by which interest groups have deneutralized the governmental bureaucracy.

Finally, we have had some interesting attempts to study the role of interest groups interacting with a single policy-conflict situation. Such studies have traced proposed legislation from the initial idea stage through to the stages of policy adoption and implementation. Such studies are particularly necessary in view of the complicated character of the American legislative system and the system of checks and balances. The early outstanding effort of this type was E. E. Schattschneider's *Politics, Pressures, and the Tariff* in 1935. In studying "the political behavior of economic groups in the tariff revision of 1929-1930," Schattschneider not only describes the facts of pressure group tactics carefully, but develops some interesting categories for analysis (especially categories as to the type of pressure group activity). He also attempts to test some theories implicit in the pressure group process, especially the theoretical expectations based on an economic interpretation of politics. His discussion of the bargaining process, the "process of the confrontation of official with nonofficial leaders," with particular reference to the Congressional hearing as a forum for such negotiation, is one of the earliest presentations of this interpretation.

Other studies of this type merit equal accolades, especially Stephen Bailey's *Congress Makes a Law*, a study of the passage of the Employment Act of 1946. Of particular importance in this study is the documentation of the close practical relations between the liberal-labor lobby and Congressmen in the development and execution of political strategy. Considerable light is also thrown on the nature of interest group coalitions, the circumstances which make such coalitions expedient, and their political effects.

Reference to the above studies is not meant to disparage by implication the many other solid studies which have added to our information about interest groups in the United States. I have cited here types of studies and examples of each type, with indications of only a few kinds of contributions they have made.

One type which has not been included so far is the study which employs survey research methods in order to discover the attitudes, political predispositions, and political orientations of interest group members. A significant example is *When Labor Votes*, by Arthur Kornhauser, Albert J. Mayer, and Harold L. Sheppard (1956). This survey of UAW local union members in the Detroit area was conducted with a random sample of 828 workers. It is packed with valuable data about the political interest, voting patterns, and attitudes of the members of these locals. Particularly interesting are the four basic types of UAW members, a set of categories distinguishing members on the basis of their political and union orientations. Such interpretations and predictions as the following are particularly interesting: labor union political activity will be widened and there will be "an accentuation of pressures and needs . . . toward greater political participation";[9] members will go along with the "idealism and social reform in the auto union's politics";[10] labor union members need not necessarily become more conservative politically as they become better off economically and more upwardly mobile;[11] and there is at the present no tendency among union members to prefer "individualistic" to "collective" political action alternatives.[12] This type of study has immense value for providing us with the kind of data about internal perspectives which were not realizable with studies utilizing primarily documentary and observational techniques for data-collection, supplemented by a limited number of relatively unstructured leadership interviews.

Evaluation: The Problem of Conceptualization

If one surveys this body of literature, impressive by its volume alone, one finds himself reflecting with mixed feelings. There is no question that there is here an imposing descriptive research. The case studies have uncovered important facts about the origins, formal organization, and operational techniques of pressure and interest groups. Further, there is no question but that, if one reads carefully, intermittently one picks up fugitive insights which may have relevance for a theory of interest groups. What one does not get from this reading of the literature is a clear understanding of the intrinsic nature of the interest group, the reasons for the diversity in style and tactics, or the implications of organization for interest group effectiveness. Certainly, one finds it difficult to find a real understanding of interest groups in the context of political and social change. One still asks the same basic questions concerning the role of these groups in the policy process, the political system generally, and the social order. What may be some of the reasons for such feelings of interpretative inadequacy or frustration?

One explanation is that we have not yet satisfactorily solved the problem of conceptualization, and we have not met the need to develop proper categories for analysis. There can be no question but that we have certainly striven mightily for a conceptual position, but the results have not produced clarity, in the sense of delineating the unique and distinctive character of interest groups *vis à vis* non-interest groups. Perhaps the fault or credit initially was Bentley's. He claimed that "the term 'group' will be used throughout this work in a technical sense."[13]

[9]Arthur Kornhauser *et al.*, *When Labor Votes* (1956), p. 268.
[10]*Ibid.*, p. 289.
[11]*Ibid.*, p. 278.
[12]*Ibid.*, p. 283.
[13]*Op. cit.*, p. 211.

Yet, he had no interest in combining conceptual differentiation with an exercise in taxonomy. Herring's early work did not solve the problem. The groups he studied are merely called "new agencies for the expression of opinion and for the protection of specific interests". . . which "partake of the characteristics of both the typical 'society' and the minority party."[14] Schattschneider's early study distinguished defensive-offensive, negative-positive, and primary-secondary types of interest groups. And these are the kinds of categories we used, until Truman opened up the question in 1951 again. In summarizing and codifying preceding developments in sociology, social psychology and political science, he attempts a definition, saying simply that a "political interest group" is a shared-attitude group making claims through or upon the institutions of government.[15] This is a short-hand statement which no doubt is helpful. It simplifies some previous confusion and interrelates social-psychological developments with political analysis. But it has by no means settled the age-old controversy as to the difference between interest groups and political parties. It has questionable analytical utility, and above all, does not indicate to us the conceptual categories needed for significant research. Truman's further identification of the "potential group"[16] as a collectivity of present non-interaction but possible future interaction, and the "association"[17] as a group of "tangent relations" bridging two other groups, are interesting contributions, but scarcely peculiarly adaptable to political research.

Our literature, today yet, abounds with new terminology, new attempts at definition, new indications that we are still groping for some meaningful conceptualization. Thus we speak, erroneously I feel, of "policy aspiration groups" (interest groups) and "power aspiration groups" (parties);[18] of "power groups" as contrasted to "demand groups"; of "associational" and "nonassociational" interest groups;[19] of "expressive" versus "social influence" voluntary associations;[20] of "veto groups"[21] and "peak associations"; of groups for "tangible interests" and "intangible interests."[22] It is apparent that we still need a conceptual orientation from which would emerge critical categories of political group types. There is some question, of course, as to whether these would be analytically valuable for investigating the basic relationships at issue.

[14]*Op. cit.*, pp. 2-3.

[15]David B. Truman, *The Governmental Process* (1951), p. 37.

[16]*Ibid.*, p. 36.

[17]*Ibid.*, p. 39.

[18]"Report of the Inter-University Summer Seminar on Comparative Politics, Social Science Council," *American Political Science Review*, Vol. 47 (1953), p. 649.

[19]Almond, *op. cit.*, p. 272.

[20]Arnold M. Rose, *Theory and Method in the Social Sciences* (1954), p. 52.

[21]David Riesman, "Who Has the Power?" in *Class, Status, and Power*, ed. R. Bendix and S. M. Lipset (1953), p. 154-162.

[22]Bernard C. Cohen, "Political Communication on the Japanese Peace Settlement," *The Public Opinion Quarterly*, Vol. 20 (1956), pp. 30-31.

Political science is not the only discipline confronted with this problem and challenge. Sociologists have been grappling with the distinction between group types for some time, plagued with a recognition of variations in institutional systems, but finding consensus difficult as to the basic characteristics of each. The terms are still used interchangeably. Essentially the confusion seems to arise from the use of such terms as "social movement," "organization," and "structure." Reading current sociology one discovers some confusion in the use of these terms. At most we can say that certain distinctions are being made by some writers, distinctions which, incidentally, may have some value for political scientists wrestling with the self-same problem in another context, the interest-group context. The distinctions seem to be of this order; a "social movement" is a social collective whose members voluntarily participate and for which the basic unifying factor is the psychological identification of the members with the movement. Its members normally share attitudes, values, perspectives toward the social process. But a social movement may or may not have an organization, although organizations generally stem from social movements. (Perhaps for us a case in point would be the Anti-Saloon League, a social movement which developed into an organization. Similarly, third party movements in the United States have taken on this character.) A "structure" develops within each social movement, structure meaning the social (or political) roles played by the participants in the movement. Every social movement has a "structure" or a population of roles by necessity, and these positions become critical for analysis. (For example, it is very difficult to understand the labor union movement in the United States unless one analyzes carefully the roles of men like Gompers, Lewis, Green and the Reuthers. Any amount of concentration on the bare bones of formal organization will still leave one wanting in knowledge of the movement itself.) The term "organization" is familiar to all political scientists. It develops when some of the members in the movement are designated to make decisions for the group. The development of organization is the process of delegation and distribution of power, the establishment of mechanisms of control, and the elaboration of all the apparatus of the decisional process. There are obviously various degrees of organization and types of organization. What is important to notice in the elaboration of this distinction is that every social movement has a structure but not necessarily an organization, according to the sociologist. Further, that role structure is as, if not more, important than organization. Structure precedes organization and cannot be ignored. For the study of political-social movements as interest groups this may be a critical distinction which we have overlooked.

The sociological literature has proliferated other conceptions about group types. For example, Robert Angell describes one particular type as the "struggle group," made up of persons who feel they have a common cause but with some diminution in "sense of moral community." For such groups, he says, when "the struggle becomes one between conflicting systems of ultimate values, rather than between subsidiary immediate ends or means, the element of moral community vanishes."[23] This type of group, perhaps illustrated by the White Citizens Councils in the South versus the NAACP, can be contrasted possibly to what Turner and Killian call the "control movement," "a movement devoted to dominating the . . . society . . . while leaving its value objectives flexible or undefined."[24] This distinction may have value in goal terms for understanding certain labor and business organizations, or the developing trend in such groups in the United States. The ideological "struggle group" in contrast to the expediency-oriented "control movement" is a conceptual differentiation which may have merit for the study of interest groups, over time and comparatively. The labels themselves, of course, are unimportant.

Reconceptualization of interest groups and their relation to politics in the United States involves a reexamination of the definitional components which we have almost accepted as axiomatic. The first of these deals with motivational theory and concerns our preoccupation with the term "self-interest." It is still the vogue to refer to interest groups as uniquely impelled by a body of members who are seeking to implement their "self-interest," as if this meaningfully distinguishes interest groups from other groups. The particular variant of this which has been employed is economic self-interest. James Madison in *The Federalist* is usually credited with having originated this observation. The trouble with this type of observation is that, although a beginning, it stops too soon and says very little. Yet, we have continued this tendency of characterizing these groups as sharing a self-interest, without elaborating the concept carefully for research purposes. In a recent attempt at reformulation Latham isolates two aspects of the concept—the desire for "self-expression" and the impulse to seek personal and collective "security,"[25] implying also, however, that the "chief social values cherished by individuals in modern society are realized through groups."[26] To Truman, "the shared attitudes . . . constitute the interests."[27] The assumption underlying our use of this term is that we can differentiate types of political groups on this basis, or political groups from other groups on this basis, and further that we can account for their behavior and their impact on politics in these terms. It is my opinion that we have not done so. I am particularly interested in this connection with the interpretation of Schattschneider, who applied economic determinism theory to his study of pressure groups and the tariff. His expectations were not borne out—pressure groups with equal economic stakes did not produce equal pressures and many economically affected groups were politically inert.[28] The terms "self-interest," "shared attitudes," "security," and the like are elusive and need specification and differentiation. The attempted distinction

[23]Robert C. Angell, *Integration of American Society* (1941), p. 63.

[24]Ralph A. Turner and Lewis M. Killian, *Collective Behavior* (1956), p. 361.

[25]Earl Latham, *The Group Basis of Politics* (1952), pp. 28-29.

[26]*Ibid.*, p. 1.

[27]*Op. cit.*, p. 34.

[28]E. E. Schattschneider, *Politics, Pressures, and the Tariff* (1935), pp. 162-163.

between the group which seeks to satisfy interests and the group which "propagates faiths" is also really no help.[29] These terms may have utility in the task still confronting us, namely, the development of a set of categories of goal-orientations or goal-motivations of political groups which can be useful for analytical purposes. The terms "demand" and "power" as components of the interest group conception suffer the same criticism, it seems to me. Unless one specifies the variations in power achievement status or level aspired to, and the substance, as well as the range, of demands to be expected, no categories of goal-setting which can be used will emerge.

A second area in which reconceptualization may be necessary involves the use of the term "legitimacy" to characterize political groups. One of the unfortunate circumstances surrounding the early public discussion and non-scientific literature on pressure groups was the tendency to question their propriety for the political order. They were considered, by scholars as well as muckrakers, as engaged in questionable techniques and pursuing questionable goals. They were not considered as sanctioned by the community nor as having a legitimate regime status. There is still a certain amount of thinking of this type, both in this country as well as in Europe. Lasswell and Kaplan in their recent contribution to theory, *Power and Society*, seek at one point to distinguish political parties from pressure groups as follows:

> . . . a party is an internal power group whose status has been formalized—it functions as part of the regime. There may be other internal power groups (private armies, pressure groups) whose practices are not sanctioned by the political formula. . . (The distinction between private armies, pressure groups, and parties is, of course, a matter of degree).[30]

This is an important problem in political theory, and one which can easily be argued at great length. It seems to me, however, that this position either subsumes too many of the kind of groups we call "interest groups" under the rubric "political party," or it misconceives the roles which these groups play today in the political system. Further, it implies different sets of political practices which are mutually exclusive. It is the kind of conceptual approach which is unrealistic and inhibits a holistic view of the functioning political process.

A third area for reconceptualization is in organizational theory, with particular emphasis on the use of the idea of "latency" or "potentiality" of interest groups. This raises the basic question: How wide is the term "interest group"? In the employment of the component "latency" our attention has been focused on the inclusiveness of the phenomenon, not on the problem of abstracting from group phenomena those which are uniquely relevant to political analysis. It is a

[29]Harold D. Lasswell and Abraham Kaplan, *Power and Society* (1950), p. 40.
[30]*Ibid.*, p. 170.

concept which was alien to Bentley who emphasized the group as a "collection of action" with a definite perceivable and analyzable form. While we are interested in the problem of affiliation and the processes of association as political scientists, with the members and probable "fellow-travellers" for an interest group, it seems to me that we should not be diverted in interest group research from concentration of attention to groups as structures of power. The distinction between categoric and interactional collectivities is important to make, the phenomenon of latency cannot be ignored, but these have analytical value primarily for studying such developments as the mobilization of mass support, the activation of counter-groups, and related phenomena.

"Self-interest," "legitimacy," "latency," "demand"—these, then, are not the distinguishing marks of the interest group. Perhaps *a priori* distinctions are useless to search for, and conceptual differentiation will only emerge as a concomitant to the formulation of a set of theoretical propositions about the adaptation of political groups to social and political change. Some suggestions along this line will be made shortly.

The Problem of the Identification of Relationships

American interest group research can be evaluated also from the standpoint of the isolation and testing of important theoretical relationships. Although the work has been primarily descriptive, there has been a definite undertone of interest in the development of causal theory, a searching for data which would help to explain the interrelationships between interest groups and the political process. An infinite number of research questions could, of course, be asked, but there are three major relationships which one naturally could expect such research to investigate:

1. The influence of the changes in the governmental structure, political system, and society on the nature and functioning of interest groups
2. The influence of internal organizational form and structure on internal process
3. The influence of interest groups on the policy process and institutional system

There has been a wealth of speculation in the United States in the first of these areas, particularly with reference to the impact of formal governmental organization on interest groups. It is contended that the institutional arrangements such as federalism, separation of powers and the presidency conditioned the development of a special type of two-party system which, in turn, due to its decentralized and undisciplined nature contributed to the emergence of an interest group system with peculiar characteristics. Political scientists speak quite bitterly about this sometimes. Rigorous testing of this type of proposition, of course, has not been undertaken, and in truth it would be difficult in the absence of careful comparative analysis. Very little attention in this country, on the other hand, has been devoted to demonstrating the roots of the interest group system in the social structure, and to exploring the implications of social change on interest group organization, ideology, membership, role structure, and internal process. We frequently have recognized the social basis for politics, but as yet have not perfected the tools for analysis. Herring said long ago that the interest group is "but one manifestation of a movement which reaches back to the very foundations of the social structure."[31] But beyond that generalization we have not progressed far.

The second type of relationship has been more ardently studied. Garceau's study of the AMA, Lipset's study of the Typographical Union, and earlier, Odegard's study of the Anti-Saloon League are some of the outstanding contributions in this area. Aside from these, the literature is mostly descriptive and rarely even attempts to develop a theory about the factors of internal group process. Political scientists tend to distinguish unitary from federal group forms, and then defer speculatively to Michels' law of oligarchy without rigorously testing Michels' propositions. We have discussed in intelligent terms the nature of group cohesion, the problem of overlapping and heterogeneous membership, the existence of the "active minority," and its manipulation of group machinery. Thanks to Truman we have generalized our approach to these matters, even though the data are scant. But the critical intra-group relationships which specify the conditions under which types of leadership emerge and power is exercised, the factors responsible for bureaucratic development, the effects of this on leadership ideology, and the impact of schism and factionalism on leadership and membership—these are relationships which have not been carefully explored. To a certain extent paying homage to Michels was defensible. A theoretical orientation which emphasizes that the goals and leadership of the organization are modified, expanded, or abandoned in terms of the group's changes in internal process, was and is valuable. But we have not implemented this orientation with our research. Rather, we have tended to regurgitate the oligarchical model without empirical verification, and without recognizing that certain components in the oligarchical concept and certain alleged effects of oligarchy may not be applicable to the American scene.

There are two basic questions concerning intra-group process which remain, as Lipset has pointed out: (1) What are the conditions responsible for the institutionalization of oligarchy in interest groups? (2) What are the conditions under which democratic organization and process develops and is sustained in an interest group?[32] On the latter question, Lipset's own work is the only significant contribution. He has pointed out how commonality of interest, non-stratification, ideological differences, early recognition of the legitimacy of opposition,

[31] *Op. cit.*, p. xi.

[32] S. M. Lipset, M. A. Trow, and J. S. Coleman, *Union Democracy* (1956), p. 13.

membership interests and participation were related to the development of a democratic two-party system within the ITU. Rigorous analysis of the factors leading to and sustaining oligarchy in interest groups remains to be done. We have isolated some of the important variables, but we have not tested the propositions. Some questions which need critical analysis here are: What is the extent of membership passivity in interest groups and how does this facilitate leadership control? What is the extent of overlapping membership, is its nature changing over time, and what effect does this have on group cohesion and, consequently, on the development of bureaucratization? Doesn't this tendency reduce leadership control? What are the characteristics of interest group leadership, particularly its skills, and how is this type of variable related to group cohesion, goal achievement, and perception by members of group tactics? Since even in presumably oligarchic interest groups in the United States there is recognition of the legitimacy of opposition, how does such a norm develop, what effects does it have on leadership control, how is it overcome by the elite? Does "circulation of elites" actually occur, by what process, and with what effects on leadership skill and ideology? Above all, it seems to me, there should be more emphasis on reorientation of goals, historical bases, and the nature of the changes which group processes undergo.

This is a legitimate field for investigation by the political scientist as well as the sociologist, for the nature of the group leadership, organization and process must be understood if we are to know something about the impact of these groups on the political system. It may well be that American interest groups are undergoing a transformation. The simple dichotomy of types which we assume—oligarchic and democratic—are no longer the exclusive models for research design. The changing character of social stratification, the diffusion in ideology, social equalitarianism, the acceptance of the concept of intra-group opposition, the changing nature of group membership and affiliation, as well as the power context in which these groups operate today may be inducing a third model type which should be recognized. We cannot assume the inevitability of the oligarchic model.

Here I am concerned with the primary motifs which recur in our theory of interest group influence, as well as the absence of categories for analyzing such influence. Our literature has a tendency to assume that "access" is the critical problem. "Access" is almost equated with "influence." We emphasize the "door-opening power" of group leaders, not the "decision-making power." Truman says, "The produce of effective access . . . is a governmental decision."[33] The influence relationship is a much more profound relationship than "access" implies. The influence of a political interest group, even if one wishes to look at its impact immediately only in terms of legislative votes on a given bill, is a product of such factors as: group organization, leader skill, cohesion (as Truman

[33] *Op. cit.*, p. 507.

has pointed out); its symbolic public status; its power status and bargaining potential *vis à vis* other interest groups; its "social politics" strategy, or penetration into the influence levels of the social groups not directly involved with politics; the subtlety of its manipulative tactic for the enlistment of mass support; its capacity for mobilizing political support. Although we recognize these elements from time to time (Truman's statement that group access is a function of social status),[34] we still primarily are concerned with horizontal relationships (i.e., interest groups and Congressmen, interest groups and political parties). We then feel frustrated when Bailey tells us at the end of his discussion of interest groups that "it would be difficult to prove that the direct pressures of the Lib-Lab lobby changed a single Congressional mind."[35] We need a research design to test propositions about indirect influence and vertical relationships if we are really interested in analyzing influence. Such a design must recognize assumptively the extent to which interest groups in America are inter-woven with the social, economic and cultural system.

Eventually, we need to develop categories of differential influence. There is considerable suggestion in our literature that interest groups do have differential power status. The specification of these statuses has not emerged, however. Perhaps we can hierarchize interest groups for certain periods or for certain issues into the following types:

1. Penetration into formal policy roles
2. Maintenance of close political support and referral relationships
3. Unchallengeable veto status
4. Attention, representative, and pressure relationship
5. Potential reprisal relationship
6. Rejection by power structure, agitational and resistance role

Regardless of the acceptability of these more or less off-hand distinctions, sophistication in our distinctions is necessary. There are too many hints in our literature of interest groups which indicate the inadequacy of the simple distinction between those groups with influence, in a power status, and those with no influence or minimal impact, in a pressure status.

The roles which interest groups perform in the political system and social system provide fascinating speculation, but as yet little real research. We are still not certain what the effect of interest groups is on our two-party system. A recent report suggests that American political parties "aggregate" group interests.[36] Although I am not sure what "aggregate" implies, if it means that group claims are mediated effectively within the Democratic and Republican parties, I doubt

[34] *Ibid.*, p. 265.
[35] Stephen K. Bailey, *Congress Makes a Law* (1950), p. 97.
[36] Almond, *op. cit.*, p. 275.

it. There is considerable speculative insight which leads one to the hypothesis that a more or less independent interest group system operates in large part outside the party system. Similarly, there is some theory which suggests that the interest group system has meant categorically an intensification of political competition, without looking at the counter-evidence which may imply the hypothesis that the strengthening of interest groups results in a kind of political bargaining, imperfect competition, or oligopoly. Again, the social impact of interest groups has not stimulated any significant body of theory. We have operated usually with a "conflictual" theory, that interest groups pit group against group and thereby exacerbate social relationships and promote tension. There are some, however, who have emphasized the "integrative" function of these groups in our pluralistic society. These conceptual positions have yet to be clearly spelled out and researched. The role of interest groups in the long run in distributing power, in inducing social change, and in helping the individual identify with political authority, as Rose has pointed out,[37] are ultimately the most important relationships for political analysis.

The Problem of Evidence

It remains to say briefly a few things about research technique. Much of what has already been said is methodological. Careful design and specification of the relationships to be investigated must remain as the critical area of concern for those searching for regularities in American interest group phenomena. Two observations about technique might also be made. The first relates to the problem of evidence; the second to the problem of comparability. Data-collection is a singularly trying operation when it comes to interest groups. Securing access to an interest group, interviewing its members and leaders, observing internal processes, ferreting out non-public negotiations with political parties and indirect connections with policy makers—these requirements of research procedure are hard to meet. In our investigations in the Detroit area of the political action techniques and organization of the UAW-CIO, although presumably we had maximized our rapport with the upper leadership there were still PAC coordinators who were unwilling to give us interviews. This type of problem requires a reassessment of research strategy. Related to this is the problem of the objectification of research techniques. The informal, unstructured, even casual type of interview is the type of data relied on in the past to supplement observation and documentary sources. This type of interview is considered most feasible even today. Yet, paradoxically, this is the most unsatisfactory type of data from the standpoint of scientific requirements. Unless one has highly trained and well-coordinated interviewers this type of interview process is bound to be quite subjective and unreliable. It is useful for exploration but not for proof. Our experiments in

[37]Rose, *op. cit.*, p. 51.

the past few years with a questionnaire schedule applied identically and openly with all interviewees has given us a rich body of data on political leaders and union activists. It is my feeling that there is no substitute for this if one seeks rigor, objectivity, proof. If we do not meet these requirements for knowledge, we will forever be making probabilistic statements about reality, we will be presenting "findings" which are not demonstrable and which evoke controversy. We will be forever saying "Although the evidence is weak, it appears that . . . ." A content analysis of Truman's summation of knowledge about interest groups reveals the weak evidential basis for most of our propositions. In Chapter 10, "Interest Groups and Elections," on 18 occasions the author reports the absence or negligible amount of evidence. Thus: "we know almost nothing of a systematic character about how nominations are made . . ."; "Although evidence on (the effectiveness of endorsements) is slight, it is probable . . ."; "the semi-contractual theory of contributions thrives on the dearth of evidence . . ."; "the evidence does not tell us the extent to which members' votes are 'deliverable' . . ."; etc. It must be recognized that "presumptive evidence" is not sufficient except for speculative philosophers.

The other technique problem, that of "comparability," is one that will plague us constantly as long as we rely on case studies in which there is no coordination of design. I certainly do not deplore these case studies. They have given us all the information we presently possess, and they are responsible for the few theoretical clues which we are working with. But their limitations must be apparent. I have personally tried, for example, to study side by side three studies by Odegard, Garceau, and Lipset, to see what regularities or equivalencies I could tease out of these discreet inquiries; to discover, for example, whether the form of organization determines the types of strategies utilized. I am tempted to say that these studies demonstrate that organization is unimportant and not the basic variable for an understanding of strategy. But further study reminds me that these three men went at their work with quite different assumptions, objectives, and data-collection operations. They raise different questions; they consult different bodies of data. I am not sure, therefore, whether their findings are "additive" in any real sense at all. This I feel is the real challenge for comparative research, whether within a country or among countries—the challenge to produce reliable data testing identical theoretical relationships which have emerged from a replicable design.

Interest Group Adaptations to "Fluid Politics" in America: Some Interpretations and Hypotheses

I should like to conclude with some remarks about the changing nature of interest groups in American politics. I do this not only to characterize recent developments, but also to illustrate some of the distinctions already made in this paper. These remarks attempt to reflect some of the recent speculation and investigation in this area, as well as my own observations.

It is the growing complexity and fluidity of American society, with its consequences for power distribution, which must be recognized first. The great technological changes in the U. S., accompanied by specialization, social pluralism, social mobility, and equalization of status, suggests to many an amorphous, diffuse, "open" society. In such a society, the "interconnections between the legal and social framework" are more intimate than ever before, the struggle for power is central, political group relationships are with difficulty "stabilized." Diversification of power sources means that the decision-making process is more indirect, non-public, and obscure.

This "amorphous" distribution of power in our society results in change for the governmental system, political leadership, and the political group system. Scrutiny of the governmental bureaucracy raises the question as to its "neutrality"; the legislative arena's character raises the question as to its "representativeness." Governmental decision-making is seen either as group bargaining or as stalemate. Political leadership undergoes transformations in the face of political group pluralism. The "influentials" take on new characteristics. Wealth is not as powerful as in the past.[38] There is less certainty that a "decisive ruling class," to use Riesman's term, exists. The fashionable phrase becomes the "multiple elites."[39] Although the two-party system is retained, the role of the party politician begins to be specified differently, and party-interest group interaction takes on a new pattern.

These social changes and modifications in the power context have been accompanied by new interpretations of the norms and prerequisites of the democratic political process. New popular theories are spawned about the nature of group competition, the significance of elections,[40] the role of public opinion,[41] the meaning of the "public interest,"[42] to mention only a few. Above all, the question is raised as to whether our governmental institutions are adequate to cope with these changes in the dynamics of political decision-making.[43]

If this is accepted as an apt description of developing social and political trends in America, how are interest groups adapting? What are the current

[38]Riesman, *op. cit.*, p. 162.

[39]See *The New American Right*, ed. Bell (1955), p. 178, and Riesman, *op. cit.*

[40]For example, Joseph A. Schumpeter, *Capitalism, Socialism, and Democracy* (1942), Ch. 22.

[41]Among others, see Bernard Berelson, "Democratic Theory and Public Opinion," *The Public Opinion Quarterly*, Vol. 16 (1952), pp. 313-330. Also, Walter Lippmann, *The Public Philosophy* (1955); and, for an earlier revision, Donald C. Blaisdell, *Economic Power and Political Pressures*, Temporary National Economic Committee Monograph No. 26 (1941), Chs. 1 and 2.

[42]See Glendon A. Schubert, Jr., "The Public Interest in Administrative Decision-Making," *American Political Science Review*, Vol. 51 (1957), pp. 346-368.

[43]E. P. Herring, *The Politics of Democracy* (1940), p. 107; See also House Select Committee on Lobbying Activities (81st Congress, 2nd Sess.–"Buchanan Committee") *Interim Report* (1951), pp. 3-4, 62-65.

developments in, and expectations as to the probable future of, interest group politics? In the short-hand sketch presented here it will be seen that this adaptation is not single-directional but one which can be seen often as trend and counter-trend. The propositions presented will deal with five aspects of the problem: the political action context, goal-orientations, structure, strategies, and the consequences of interest group development for the political and social order.

First, so far as the *context* is concerned, in the United States there is greater recognition today of the meaningfulness and efficacy of collective approaches to political action as compared to individualistic approaches.[44] The individual citizen working by himself despairs of effective access or influence. Our political vocabulary comes more and more to see group action as vital, even though less simple and less direct. A second general proposition is that although multiple and overlapping group membership still exists, and indeed is a major phenomenon of our time, there may be a perceptible trend towards closer group identification. The individual begins to "choose up sides," to resolve his overlapping and cross-pressures in one direction, and to decide which group is more politically representative and potent for him.[45] A third general proposition I would make is that the diffuseness of political society is gradually observable as taking on a certain order, though certainly an imperfect order. In our society the struggle for power position among groups becomes more important, and a stratification or hierarchizing of groups may be taking place over time, and with reference to particular policy issues. Earlier mention has been made of certain types of power positions which might be hypothesized. Such political stratification is inevitable and one which will be formalized over time in the image which the public as well as formal policy-makers have of the interest group complex.

So far as *goal-orientations* of interest groups are concerned, I would suggest these developments: The goals have become more than mere representation, or "articulation" of the group viewpoint. The desire is for something more than "access"; perhaps the term is "consideration." Although historically representation and access may have been the goal, the shift in objectives has led to groups concerned with ongoing political and social relationships, desiring to penetrate deeper into the political and social structure, not periodically and intermittently, but continuously and for the purpose of developing and sustaining contact and influence with the significant opinion and action leadership of the community.[46] The group perspectives are no longer merely specific and limited, but long-range and comprehensive. The basic motivation is still no doubt expediency, but an ideological-rationalizing element has been introduced in the communication of

[44]Kornhauser, *op. cit.*, p. 283.

[45]See, e.g., Martin Kriesberg, "Cross-Pressures and Attitudes," *The Public Opinion Quarterly*, Vol. 13 (1949), pp. 5-16.

[46]*Interim Report, op. cit.*, pp. 24 ff.

these perspectives to the public. Finally, while historically centered around economic self-interest (a motivation still basic today, since groups are interested in sharing in economic rewards in a prosperous society), a counter-trend has developed.[47] The trend towards social and economic equality has directed groups into setting goals concerned with the development of a "social politics," preoccupation with issues such as social equality and issues with a secondary economic importance.

Interest group *structure* is also undergoing change. There are fewer social movements and more structures of power. The interest group has become a formalized, independent action system, attempting to maximize its political strength and durability. But the old categorization of groups as oligarchic or democratic no longer seems to fit. A new type of "managerial group," highly professionalized and expert at the top stratum and attempting to maintain a body of mass support and mass membership at the lower levels, is developing.[48] Cohesion of a tightly organized membership is less the ultimate aim. Internal factionalism, present to some extent in many of our interest groups for some time, may even increase.[49] Leadership control directed at a mass public may find itself increasingly confronted with internal schism. This possibility is especially portended in the trend toward the recruitment for leadership of the professional public relations expert, on the one hand;[50] and the co-optation of nonprofessionals, on the other hand. Lobbyists with technical legal skill[51] and professional publicity experts plus coopted non-professionals (coopted for appearances of non-specialization) [are brought in] to participate in policy-planning for the group. The organizational technician gives way to the technician in bargaining and persuasion.

The *strategies* of our interest groups are of course being modified in this adaptive and adjustive process. First, it has become apparent that the indirect approaches to power may be more efficacious than the direct approaches. Manipulation replaces domination or outright demands.[52] Whereas in the past

[47]This point was discussed at considerable length at the Conference on the Comparative Study of Pressure Groups, called by Professor James K. Pollock at the University of Michigan, February 28-March 1, 1957 (report in preparation).

[48]Neumann, *op. cit.*, p. 9.

[49]Lipset, *op. cit.*, p. 407.

[50]Stanley Keller, *Professional Public Relations and Political Power* (1956).

[51]See Joseph A. Schlesinger, "Lawyers and American Politics: A Clarified View," *Midwest Journal of Political Science* (1957), p. 31; also, Lester Milbrath, "Lobbyists and Campaign Politics" (paper read at fifty-third annual meeting of the American Political Science Association, New York City, 1957), who found that three-fourths of a sample of 100 lobbyists interviewed had been trained in the law (p. 19).

[52]This distinction is made also by Morris Janowitz in "The Military Establishment as a Social System" (paper read at 1957 annual meeting of the American Sociological Association, Washington, D.C.).

emphasis was on "all or none" demands, this is now no longer overtly the case at least. Second, great emphasis is placed on the strategy of proper public presentation of demands, of selling the group and its objectives to the public, of mobilizing a long-run mass support. The objective is to picture the group in a favorable light, a task requiring important persuasive skills. But a counter-trend should not be overlooked. This is the insistence on secrecy and privacy, the determination not to be investigated, the desire to be left alone, the preference for obscurity and in a sense for irresponsibility.[53] Finally, the group strategy in relationship to other groups is one of bargaining, negotiating, coalescence, reciprocation, even combination and continued alliance.[54] Such attempts to limit competition result in less group autonomy. The negotiations necessarily take place often "out of sight" and "behind the scenes," whether with political parties or other interest groups. As a consequence, the visible relationship between interest group and party may be completely misleading. The processes of sharing expertise, intellectual resources, financial resources, personnel, as well as attitudes has become much more prevalent and important than formal organizational liaison and cooperation. This inter-group bargaining process has become much more essential today in the United States in our fluid power context. In the process, bargaining potentials gradually emerge and group goals must be modified.

What are the *consequences* for the political and social system of these developing trends? Many might be foreseen, but only a few of the most significant will be hypothesized here. In the first place, a kind of checkmate system among interest groups is materializing, especially among those in the upper strata of the group hierarchy. The tendency for groups to behave more circumspectly in terms of what they perceive they can presently achieve, and the tendency for "bargaining" indicate an awareness of the limitations on their power. Thus, open and autonomous group competition decreases in intensity. A counter-trend to this (the product of an economic or social breakdown in certain group relationships) may be the rise of radical, extremist, and even violent groups

[53]This concept of "secrecy" has of course been observed and commented on by many writers. See, particularly, Franz Neumann, *op. cit.*, pp. 9-10; also Avery Leiserson, *op. cit.*, who discusses interest group preferences for being left alone and for "irresponsibility" (p. 135). See also Oliver Garceau and Corrine Silverman, "A Pressure Group and the Pressured: A Case Report," *American Political Science Review*, Vol. 40 (1954), which reveals the "extremely low level of recognition of interest group activity" in a state legislature (p. 685); and Blaisdell, *op. cit.*, p. 7.

[54]The "bargaining" concept has been outlined well in Robert A. Dahl and Charles E. Lindblom, *Politics, Economics and Welfare* (1953), Part 4. Other specific references are as follows: Schattschneider, *op. cit.*, p. 221; Belle Zeller, *Pressure Politics in New York* (1937), pp. 230, 237-239, 249-250; Leiserson, *op. cit.*, p. 269; Herring, *Group Representation before Congress*, p. 75; Bailey, *op. cit.*, pp. 91 ff; Keller, *op. cit.*, pp. 81-211; Garceau, *The Political Life of the American Medical Association* (1941), p. 107; Brogan, *Politics in America* (1955), pp. 356, 362.

denied a demanded power position. Such groups when they emerge are likely to be social movements led by individuals, such as the fringe groups which appeared during the depression of the Thirties, or the "White Citizens Councils" in the South today. Such groups perceive themselves as rejected by the system, as operating against the system. They may become "struggle movements" which lose their sense of moral commitment to the community, although rationalizing their techniques in moral terms.

Another observed consequence is the increasing transformation of legal policy-making arenas through informal relationships with interest groups. In the long run this may mean the transformation of administration and the legislative process into an informal and functional type of representative system. Interest groups become indirectly, rather than directly, responsible for policy planning and for political support. This type of "syndicalism," while explicitly recognized and taken for granted, does not, however, become formally institutionalized. Over time this may mean either the transference of the check-mate system to the bureaucracy and legislature, a development which we already have noticed in this country on certain types of issues, or it means the alternation in power status and thus in policy control from era to era.[55]

The scope of operations of the two-party system is restricted, with these trends in interest groups. Parties lose their functions of bargaining and goal-setting, and become primarily formal agencies for the recruitment of governmental personnel. The function of the boss or party leader at the local level becomes atrophied, with primary emphasis on winning votes through an organizational machine.[56] Elections thus become primarily a contest for personality. Parties do not really "aggregate" and mediate group claims. Interest groups restrict and neutralize their capacity for leadership and policy control while maintaining indirect relationships with them. But, in all this, our chances for keeping the two-party system are maximized, because group conflict is legitimized and institutionalized outside the party arena. The "third party" is perceived as an avenue of influence only by the group rejected for the check-mate system, and this perception is an irrational miscalculation.

It is obvious from this that the rules of the political game become subtly modified. We merely develop somewhat different modes of conduct and we modify the roles of interest groups and parties in the political process. The

[55]On "bureaucratic neutrality" see particularly Reinhard Bendix, "Bureaucracy and Power Relations," in *Reader in Bureaucracy*, ed. Robert K. Merton *et al.* (1952), pp. 114-135; also Samuel P. Huntington, "The Marasmus of the ICC: The Commission, the Railroads, and the Public Interest," *Yale Law Journal*, Vol. 61 (1952), pp. 467-509. The general question of the "permeability" of the party system by interest groups has been discussed widely. A recent discussion of interest is Jean Meynaud, "Essai d'analyses de l'influence des groupes d'intérêt," *Revue Economique* (1957), pp. 217 ff.

[56]See E. P. Herring, *The Politics of Democracy*, p. 327; and Stanley Keller, *op. cit.*, p. 210.

political process may actually become less "conflictual," with interest groups assuming more of the "integrative" functions ordinarily conceived as performed by the parties—"integrative" so far as the public, group interaction, and legal policy-making are concerned.[57] We come to need interest groups more than ever in the democratic society.

These are some of the current trends and future possibilities which can be advanced about American interest groups. They suggest a frame of reference for viewing this system as interacting within the total political process and as responding to the changes in the social order. Whether this type of model is applicable to the study of interest groups in foreign countries is not for me to say. This depends of necessity on the nature of the political institutions, the character of social change, and the norms of political behavior which exist in any society. As Bacon said, "We see all governments are obscure and invisible. . . ."[58]

The American literature on interest groups is so vast (and still constantly growing) that even a selected bibliography would exceed the limitations of this volume. In addition to the works cited in the footnotes to the foregoing report the most important publications in the field will be found listed in the bibliographies of two recent standard works on the subject: David B. Truman, *The Governmental Process* (New York, 1951), pp. 537-544; and Donald C. Blaisdell, *American Democracy under Pressure* (New York, 1957), pp. 280-288.

Bibliographical Note

Group Theory

The classical statements of group theory are Arthur F. Bentley, *The Process of Government* (Cambridge, Mass.: Belknap Press of Harvard Univ. Press, 1967; 1st ed:, 1908); David B. Truman, *The Governmental Process: Political Interests and Public Opinion* (New York: Knopf, 1952); and Earl Latham, *The Group Basis of Politics* (Ithaca, N.Y.: Cornell Univ. Press, 1952). A brief and readable summary of group theory is included in Harmon Zeigler, *Interest Groups in American Society* (Englewood Cliffs, N.J.: Prentice-Hall, 1964).

Most advanced texts in American politics include a critique of group theory. The student may also wish to consult: Robert T. Golembiewski, " 'The Group

[57]A somewhat opposing interpretation to this is presented in the last chapter of *Modern Political Parties*, ed. Sigmund Neumann (Chicago, 1956). Neumann, in stressing the developing "party of social integration" (p. 404) and the relative roles of party and interest groups in "this crucial problem of national integration" (pp. 412-413), foresees a larger and more necessary role for parties.

[58]Quoted in Franz Neumann, *op. cit.*, p. 19, fn. 1.

Basis of Politics': Notes on Analysis and Development," *American Political Science Review*, Vol. 54 (December 1960), pp. 38-51; Murray S. Stedman, "The Group Interpretation of Politics," *Public Opinion Quarterly*, Vol. 17 (Summer 1953), pp. 218-229; and especially Stanley Rothman, "Systematic Political Theory: Observations on the Group Approach," *American Political Science Review*, Vol. 54 (March 1960), pp. 15-33; and David Truman's reply, "On the Invention of 'Systems,' " *American Political Science Review*, Vol. 54 (June 1960), pp. 494-495.

Alternative Frameworks

Work based on a number of alternative frameworks has been undertaken with varying degrees of theoretical explicitness. Some of the more widely discussed frameworks follow.

1. Structural-functional analysis: Harry Eckstein, *Pressure Group Politics: The Case of the British Medical Association* (Stanford, Calif.: Stanford Univ. Press, 1960); and *The Politics of the Developing Areas*, ed. Gabriel Almond and James S. Coleman (Princeton, N. J.: Princeton Univ. Press, 1960), especially the Introduction.

2. Communications theory: Lester W. Milbrath, *The Washington Lobbyists* (Chicago: Rand McNally, 1963); and "Lobbying as a Communication Process," *Public Opinion Quarterly*, Vol. 24 (Spring 1960), pp. 33-53. For a criticism of communications theory and several other approaches to interest-group activity, see Heinz Eulau, "Lobbyists: The Wasted Profession," *Public Opinion Quarterly*, Vol. 28 (Spring 1964), pp. 27-38.

3. Role analysis: John Wahlke, Heinz Eulau, William Buchanan, and LeRoy Ferguson, *The Legislative System* (New York: Wiley, 1962); articles by Wahlke *et al.* and Zisk *et al.* in the present volume; and Betty H. Zisk, *Local Interest Politics: The One-Way Street* (New York: Bobbs-Merrill, forthcoming).

4. Interaction theory: Harmon Zeigler, "How Legislators and Lobbyists Interact," paper given at annual meeting of American Political Science Association, Chicago, September 1967; and Harmon Zeigler and Michael A. Baer, *Lobbying* (Belmont, Calif.: Wadsworth, 1969).

Organizational Problems: The Leaders and the Led

To understand the political interest group, we must begin with the specific group. How is it organized? Is it "democratic"? Are group members solidly behind group projects? Does it have wide support or is it a paper tiger? Studies of such questions have probed formal organizational structure, informal interactions among group members, group cohesion—or simply the relations between the leaders and the led. Such studies are important for three reasons:

1. They may help to explain differences in the influence of competing groups.
2. They may provide answers to some basic questions about individual freedom in a bureaucratic society.
3. They may provide clues to political behavior which occurs in settings where research is prohibitively difficult or expensive.

One dominant theme in interest-group literature is the close relation between cohesion and the access which groups have to decision-makers as a major determinant of group influence.[1] Another frequently discussed topic is oligarchy. Groups such as unions and small ideological parties have argued that as fighting organizations they cannot afford the luxury of time-consuming democratic procedures. Leaders who fail to maintain a united front in a hostile bargaining situation may forfeit any hope of gaining their ends. This is the crux of the "union democracy" argument. If we take these arguments seriously, we are led to study leadership skills, homogeneity of group membership, and the formal decision-making mechanisms in the group itself.

However, some questions remain: Is cohesion as important for influence as are a host of other group attributes? What of the money or manpower available to the group, the social status of its members, the content of its goals, the extent of overlapping memberships between private and public bodies? More important, how can we measure cohesion? Is it the willingness of members to devote time to the attainment of group goals? The *speed* with which decisions are made and

[1] David Truman, *The Governmental Process* (New York: Knopf, 1952), especially pp. 159-164.

calls for action are heeded? Unanimity on major decisions? The lack of opposition slates in the election of organizational leaders?

A second set of questions concerns individual freedom. It is sometimes argued that membership in voluntary associations provides one of the few effective outlets for individual self-expression in an increasingly complex industrial society. (This is a theme to which we return in Section 5 below.) Man, as a worker, may be caught in a faceless bureaucratic web, and he may feel helpless to change public decisions through his ballot. The one way in which he can still function on a face-to-face basis as an autonomous individual, it is argued, is through his membership in secondary organizations. This contention applies to a wide range of groups—from bird-watching societies to revolutionary action groups.

But is genuine self-expression still possible in such groups? Is it a realistic goal for the group to foster? Is it possible that a member's feeling of belonging and his desire for the attainment of organizational goals are mutually exclusive objectives? And if they are incompatible, is some compromise possible?

Finally, some political institutions are very difficult to study except through formal documents and scattered voting records. The groundwork for Supreme Court decisions, congressional committee reports, and administrative recommendations is laid behind closed doors. Complex institutions like the British Parliament and the United States Congress can be analyzed by combining personal interviews and extensive observation with use of public records. But the scholar's access to legislators is limited, and such work is costly and time-consuming. It is sometimes argued, therefore, that more effort should be made to develop a comprehensive theory of organizational behavior based on common elements in a variety of institutional settings. Such a theory might logically be tested and provisionally verified in studies of readily accessible and not-too-complex organizations like unions, neighborhood associations, city councils, school boards, and state legislatures. As a next step, specific propositions could be investigated in more complex situations, and indirect methods could be used where necessary. In short, if we begin with a broad theoretical framework and attempt to test parts of such a theory in an "easy" setting, we may add to our understanding of complex or forbidden structures. This effort to develop a broad theory is of course a long-range one, and as Samuel Eldersveld pointed out in the previous section, scholars are far from agreement on even its major tenets.

A major problem in developing a broad theory concerns the *comparability* of studies of primary groups, secondary groups, and experimental groups. Is there a continuity between the behavior of members of informal face-to-face groups like the family or the work group (primary groups), of artificial laboratory or experimental groups, and of such organizations as the AMA or the AFL-CIO (secondary groups)? Even more to the point, is the local Chamber of Commerce logically comparable to the NAM? A final answer to these questions must await additional comparative studies, especially those which attempt to test experimental findings in the field or to compare national and local phenomena. In principle, however, a valid experimental finding about cohesion, consensus, oligarchy, or a host of other organizational characteristics should be relevant in a wide variety of organizational settings.

A number of existing studies are relevant to the questions posed above. Much of this work has been done by social psychologists, sociologists, and students of administrative behavior. All the relevant literature on group behavior[2] cannot be summarized here, but two sets of experiments are illustrative of the available work. One is a series of studies directed by Kurt Lewin at the University of Iowa beginning in 1935; the other is the set of "Hawthorne studies" and related work conducted by Mayo, Roethlisberger, Dickson, and others at about the same time.[3]

Lewin was interested in the influence of different styles of leadership on group structure, on individual loyalties, and on productivity. Under rigorous experimental conditions, he compared the impact of "authoritarian," "laissez-faire," and "democratic" leadership in several youth clubs on morale, unity, level of activity, and achievement of group goals. He found that in the long run democratic leadership had a positive effect on group productivity. It was greater because the members of democratically organized groups evolved into harmonious teams capable of initiating their own projects and requiring little outside supervision. Authoritarian groups, in contrast, while initially very productive, tended to disintegrate over a period of time. The level of individual interest in the group's work and the members' ability to work together dropped; overt hostility and a search for scapegoats appeared.

Mayo and his associates were interested in the productivity of factory workers. They began by studying such incentives as wages and physical working conditions. Their discovery—the *social setting* in which manual labor is performed is of crucial importance for output, and the norms of informal groups of workers govern the group's productivity—was a major breakthrough for industrial

[2]Sidney Verba provides an excellent summary of the small-group literature in *Small Groups and Political Behavior: A Study of Political Leadership* (Princeton, N.J.: Princeton Univ. Press, 1961); for other references, consult the bibliography at the end of this section.

[3]Ralph White and Ronald Lippitt, *Autocracy and Democracy* (New York: Harper, 1960) reports Lewin's work; for the Hawthorne studies, see Elton Mayo, *The Human Problems of an Industrial Civilization* (New York: Viking, 1933).

psychologists. More important for our purposes, however, are the propositions which Mayo and his associates, along with Lewin, Moreno, Whitehead, and others, contributed to the study of organizational behavior. A substantial body of experimental literature has developed, out of this early work, around the relationship between organizational structure and organizational effectiveness. It is to this relationship that most of the readings in this section are addressed.

Robert Michels, a German sociologist writing in 1911 (before Lewin and Mayo), is justly celebrated as a major figure in modern sociological analysis. The "Iron Law of Oligarchy" has been called the closest approximation to a "law" that is available to social scientists.

Michels' Law—the assertion that the need for organization leads *per se* to the domination of leaders over led (or "who says organization says oligarchy")—was based on a study of continental Socialist parties in the early years of the twentieth century. He argued that if these groups, though patently devoted to substantive democracy, could not maintain internal democracy in a procedural sense, there was little hope that *any* organization could do so. And his conclusions, after a detailed consideration of both sociological and psychological mechanisms, are pessimistic. The core of his theory is presented as the first part of this section.

Michels' methods have been strongly criticized. His choice of a select group of revolutionary organizations upon which to base statements about *all* group behavior and his focus on democratic *procedures,* while ignoring the *substance* of group goals, have come under fire. However, with very few exceptions, his findings have been confirmed by both common sense and later studies.

Seymour Lipset studied one such exception, the International Typographical Union. Lipset's work is instructive from both a methodological and a substantive viewpoint. The article is an example of a special kind of case study, "deviant-case analysis," in which the author attempts to modify or clarify existing theory through focusing on the *exceptional* instance and elaborating on the differences between the norm and the exception. Thus, Lipset concentrates on the reasons that the ITU has *not* developed an oligarchical structure in order to explain the conditions which lead to oligarchy in other groups.

The next author, Clark Kerr, argues that critics of the modern union are asking too much. Democratic procedures are to be preferred, he asserts, but those who argue that they exist only where a large number of people can participate directly in decision-making will be satisfied with nothing less than a town-meeting form of government. If, on the other hand, we are willing to accept as democratic those organizations where ultimate power is retained by the members and where leaders are "reasonably representative," most unions meet the test. The present need, in Kerr's view, is to find a contemporary substitute for the historical pressures which assured the maintenance of union democracy. He stresses as possible substitutes the need for "a new faith for the union movement" to replace the old European ideological commitments and the need for the federal government to play a positive role in protecting dissenters within the union movement. Student activists who advocate "participatory democracy" may not be satisfied with Kerr's answers; if "pure" democracy is not possible, are Kerr's alternatives an adequate substitute? What price is exacted from those who try to compromise? How much organizational democracy is possible in an industrial society?

The last two articles in this section highlight different problems. Kriesberg's study of cross-pressures was the first in a tradition of studies which assessed the effect of multiple loyalties on the politically active. Kriesberg concentrated on Catholic members of pro-Communist unions, asking how exposure to opposing views on the Soviet Union affected their political interest and activity. The question is important because it has often been argued that multiple membership serves as a kind of glue for the political system by preventing the emergence of sharp cleavages which might lead to overt civic disorders.

Finally, Luttbeg and Zeigler concentrate on another problem of considerable interest—the relation between organizational cohesion and membership consensus on organizational goals. Their study, like McClosky's work on political parties, highlights the gap between the political attitudes and perceptions of organization leaders and those of rank-and-file members. More important, perhaps, Luttbeg and Zeigler underline the fact that a degree of membership misperceptions can exist in a highly successful political interest group.

The articles included in this section cover only one segment of internal problems relevant to the study of interest-group activity. The serious student will want to consult the bibliography for further references to available research. In addition, he should bear in mind that each concept, such as oligarchy, cohesion, and cross-pressures, has been studied by a number of authors who use perspectives markedly different from those included here. To choose one example, the concept of cross-pressures has been handled by students of voting behavior in two ways. Berelson and Lazarsfeld discuss cross-pressures in terms of intrafamily or family-work conflicts over partisan loyalty (Republican wife, Democratic husband; Democratic union versus Republican neighborhood);[4] the Michigan voting

[4]Bernard Berelson, Paul F. Lazarsfeld, and W. N. McPhee, *Voting* (Chicago: Univ. Chicago Press, 1954); and Paul F. Lazarsfeld, Bernard Berelson, and Hazel Gaudet, *The People's Choice* (New York: Duell, Sloan and Pearce, 1944).

studies focus on conflicts among party, candidate and issue orientations.[5] These differences should highlight both the conceptual difficulties and the substantive promise in the available research on internal organizational relationships.

[5]Angus Campbell, Philip Converse, Warren Miller, and Donald Stokes, *The American Voter* (New York: Wiley, 1960).

The Iron Law of Oligarchy

Robert Michels

We may sum up the argument by saying that in modern party life aristocracy gladly presents itself in democratic guise, whilst the substance of democracy is permeated with aristocratic elements. On the one side we have aristocracy in a democratic form, and on the other democracy with an aristocratic content.

The democratic external form which characterizes the life of political parties may readily veil from superficial observers the tendency towards aristocracy, or rather towards oligarchy, which is inherent in all party organization. If we wish to obtain light upon this tendency, the best field of observation is offered by the intimate structure of the democratic parties, and, among these, of the socialist and revolutionary labor party. In the conservative parties, except during elections, the tendency to oligarchy manifests itself with that spontaneous vigor and clearness which corresponds with the essentially oligarchical character of these parties. But the parties which are subversive in their aims exhibit the like phenomena no less markedly. The study of the oligarchical manifestations in party life is most valuable and most decisive in its results when undertaken in relation to the revolutionary parties, for the reason that these parties, in respect of origin and of program, represent the negation of any such tendency, and have actually come into existence out of opposition thereto. Thus the appearance of oligarchical phenomena in the very bosom of the revolutionary parties is a conclusive proof of the existence of immanent oligarchical tendencies in every kind of human organization which strives for the attainment of definite ends.

In theory, the principal aim of socialist and democratic parties is the struggle against oligarchy in all its forms. The question therefore arises how we are to explain the development in such parties of the very tendencies against which they have declared war. To furnish an unprejudiced analytical answer to this question constitutes an important part of the task the author has undertaken.

In the society of today, the state of dependence that results from the existing economic and social conditions renders an ideal democracy impossible. This must be admitted without reserve. But the further question ensues, whether, and if so how far, within the contemporary social order, among the elements which are endeavoring to overthrow that order and to replace it by a new one, there may exist in the germ energies tending to approximate towards ideal democracy, to find outlet in that direction, or at least to work towards it as a necessary issue. . . .

Democracy is inconceivable without organization. A few words will suffice to demonstrate this proposition.

A class which unfurls in the face of society the banner of certain definite claims, and which aspires to the realization of a complex of ideal aims deriving from the economic functions which that class fulfils, needs an organization. Be the claims economic or be they political, organization appears the only means for the creation of a collective will. Organization, based as it is upon the principle of least effort, that is to say, upon the greatest possible economy of energy, is the weapon of the weak in their struggle with the strong.

The chances of success in any struggle will depend upon the degree to which this struggle is carried out upon a basis of solidarity between individuals whose interests are identical. In objecting, therefore, to the theories of the individualist anarchists that nothing could please the employers better than the dispersion and disaggregation of the forces of the workers, the socialists, the most fanatical of all the partisans of the idea of organization, enunciate an argument which harmonizes well with the results of scientific study of the nature of parties.

We live in a time in which the idea of cooperation has become so firmly established that even millionaires perceive the necessity of common action. It is easy to understand, then, that organization has become a vital principle of the working class, for in default of it their success is *a priori* impossible. The refusal of the worker to participate in the collective life of his class cannot fail to entail disastrous consequences. In respect of culture and of economic, physical, and physiological conditions, the proletarian is the weakest element of our society. In fact, the isolated member of the working classes is defenseless in the hands of those who are economically stronger. It is only by combination to form a structural aggregate that the proletarians can acquire the faculty of political resistance and attain to a social dignity. The importance and the influence of the working class are directly proportional to its numerical strength. But for the representation of that numerical strength organization and coordination are indispensable.

The principle of organization is an absolutely essential condition for the political struggle of the masses.

Yet this politically necessary principle of organization, while it overcomes that disorganization of forces which would be favorable to the adversary, brings other dangers in its train. We escape Scylla only to dash ourselves on Charybdis. Organization is, in fact, the source from which the conservative currents flow over the plain of democracy, occasioning there disastrous floods and rendering the plain unrecognizable. . . .

Organization implies the tendency to oligarchy. In every organization, whether it be a political party, a professional union, or any other association of the kind, the aristocratic tendency manifests itself very clearly. The mechanism of the organization, while conferring a solidity of structure, induces serious changes in the organized mass, completely inverting the respective position of the leaders and the led. As a result of organization, every party or professional union becomes divided into a minority of directors and a majority of directed.

It has been remarked that in the lower stages of civilization tyranny is dominant. Democracy cannot come into existence until there is attained a subsequent and more highly developed stage of social life. Freedoms and privileges, and among these latter the privilege of taking part in the direction of public affairs, are at first restricted to the few. Recent times have been characterized by the gradual extension of these privileges to a widening circle. This is what we know as the era of democracy. But if we pass from the sphere of the state to the sphere of party, we may observe that as democracy continues to develop, a backwash sets in. With the advance of organization, democracy tends to decline. Democratic evolution has a parabolic course. At the present time, at any rate as far as party life is concerned, democracy is in the descending phase. It may be enunciated as a general rule that the increase in the power of the leaders is directly proportional with the extension of the organization. In the various parties and labor organizations of different countries the influence of the leaders is mainly determined (apart from racial and individual grounds) by the varying development of organization. Where organization is stronger, we find that there is a lesser degree of applied democracy.

Every solidly constructed organization, whether it be a democratic state, a political party, or a league of proletarians for the resistance of economic oppression, presents a soil eminently favorable for the differentiation of organs and of functions. The more extended and the more ramified the official apparatus of the organization, the greater the number of its members, the fuller its treasury, and the more widely circulated its press, the less efficient becomes the direct control exercised by the rank and file, and the more is this control replaced by the increasing power of committees. Into all parties there insinuates itself that indirect electoral system which in public life the democratic parties fight against with all possible vigor. Yet in party life the influence of this system must be more disastrous than in the far more extensive life of the state. Even in the party congresses, which represent the party-life seven times sifted, we find that it becomes more and more general to refer all important questions to committees which debate *in camera.*

As organization develops, not only do the tasks of the administration become more difficult and more complicated, but, further, its duties become enlarged and specialized to such a degree that it is no longer possible to take them all in at a single glance. In a rapidly progressive movement, it is not only the growth in the number of duties, but also the higher quality of these, which imposes a more extensive differentiation of function. Nominally, and according to the letter of the rules, all the acts of the leaders are subject to the ever vigilant criticism of the rank and file. In theory the leader is merely an employee bound by the instruction he receives. He has to carry out the orders of the mass, of which he is no more than the executive organ. But in actual fact, as the organization increases in size, this control becomes purely fictitious. The members have to give up the idea of themselves conducting or even supervising the whole administration, and are compelled to hand these tasks over to trustworthy persons specially nominated for the purpose, to salaried officials. The rank and file must content themselves with summary reports, and with the appointment of occasional special committees of inquiry. Yet this does not derive from any special change in the rules of the organization. It is by very necessity that a simple employee gradually becomes a "leader," acquiring a freedom of action which he ought not to possess. The chief then becomes accustomed to dispatch important business on his own responsibility, and to decide various questions relating to the life of the party without any attempt to consult the rank and file. It is obvious that democratic control thus undergoes a progressive diminution, and is ultimately reduced to an infinitesimal minimum. In all the socialist parties there is a continual increase in the number of functions withdrawn from the electoral assemblies and transferred to the executive committees. In this way there is constructed a powerful and complicated edifice. The principle of division of labor coming more and more into operation, executive authority undergoes division and subdivision. There is thus constituted a rigorously defined and hierarchical bureaucracy. In the catechism of party duties, the strict observance of hierarchical rules becomes the first article. The hierarchy comes into existence as the outcome of technical conditions, and its constitution is an essential postulate of the regular functioning of the party machine.

It is indisputable that the oligarchical and bureaucratic tendency of party organization is a matter of technical and practical necessity. It is the inevitable product of the very principle of organization. Not even the most radical wing of the various socialist parties raises any objection to this retrogressive evolution, the contention being that democracy is only a form of organization and that where it ceases to be possible to harmonize democracy with organization, it is better to abandon the former than the latter. Organization, since it is the only means of attaining the ends of socialism, is considered to comprise within itself the revolutionary content of the party, and this essential content must never be sacrificed for the sake of form.

In all times, in all phases of development, in all branches of human activity, there have been leaders. It is true that certain socialists, above all the orthodox Marxists of Germany, seek to convince us that socialism knows nothing of "leaders," that the party has "employees" merely, being a democratic party, and the existence of leaders being incompatible with democracy. But a false assertion such as this cannot override a sociological law. Its only result is, in fact, to strengthen the rule of the leaders for it serves to conceal from the mass a danger which really threatens democracy.

For technical and administrative reasons, no less than for tactical reasons, a strong organization needs an equally strong leadership. As long as an organization is loosely constructed and vague in its outlines, no professional leadership can arise. The anarchists, who have a horror of all fixed organization, have no regular leaders. In the early days of German socialism, the *Vertrauensmann* (homme de confiance) continued to exercise his ordinary occupation. If he received any pay for his work for the party, the remuneration was on an extremely modest scale, and was no more than a temporary grant. His function could never be regarded by him as a regular source of income. The employee of the organization was still a simple workmate, sharing the mode of life and the social condition of his fellows. Today he has been replaced for the most part by the professional politician, *Berzirksleiter* (U.S. ward-boss), etc. The more solid the structure of an organization becomes in the course of the evolution of the modern political party, the more marked becomes the tendency to replace the emergency leader by the professional leader. Every party organization which has attained to a considerable degree of complication demands that there should be a certain number of persons who devote all their activities to the work of the party. The mass provides these by delegations, and the delegates, regularly appointed, become permanent representatives of the mass for the direction of its affairs. . . .

Political organization leads to power. But power is always conservative. In any case, the influence exercised upon the governmental machine by an energetic opposition party is necessarily slow, is subject to frequent interruptions, and is always restricted by the nature of oligarchy.

The recognition of this consideration does not exhaust our problem for we have further to examine whether the oligarchical nature of organization be not responsible for the creation of the external manifestations of oligarchical activity, whether it be not responsible for the production of an oligarchical policy. The analysis here made shows clearly that the internal policy of the party organizations is today absolutely conservative, or is on the way to become such. Yet it might happen that the external policy of these conservative organisms would be bold and revolutionary; that the anti-democratic centralization of power in the hands of a few leaders is no more than a tactical method adopted to effect the speedier overthrow of the adversary; that the oligarchs fulfil the purely provisional function of educating the masses for the revolution, and that organization is after all no more than a means employed in the service of an amplified Blanquist conception.

This development would conflict with the nature of party, with the endeavor to organize the masses upon the vastest scale imaginable. As the organization increases in size, the struggle for great principles becomes impossible. It may be noticed that in the democratic parties of today the great conflicts of view are fought out to an ever-diminishing extent in the field of ideas and with the weapons of pure theory, that they therefore degenerate more and more into personal struggles and invectives, to be settled finally upon considerations of a purely superficial character. The efforts made to cover internal dissentions with a pious veil are the inevitable outcome of organization based upon bureaucratic principles, for, since the chief aim of such an organization is to enroll the greatest possible number of members, every struggle on behalf of ideas within the limits of the organization is necessarily regarded as an obstacle to the realization of its ends, an obstacle, therefore, which must be avoided in every possible way. This tendency is reinforced by the parliamentary character of the political party. "Party organization" signifies the aspiration for the greatest number of members. "Parliamentarism" signifies the aspiration for the greatest number of votes. The principal fields of party activity are electoral agitation and direct agitation to secure new members. What, in fact, is the modern political party? It is the methodical organization of the electoral masses. The Socialist Party, as a political aggregate endeavoring simultaneously to recruit members and to recruit votes, finds here its vital interests, for every decline in membership and every loss in voting strength diminishes its political prestige. Consequently great respect must be paid, not only to new members, but also to possible adherents, to those who in Germany are termed *mitläufer,* in Italy *simpatizzanti,* in Holland *geestverwanten,* and in England *sympathizers.* To avoid alarming these individuals, who are still outside the ideal worlds of socialism or democracy, the pursuit of a policy based on strict principle is shunned, while the consideration is ignored whether the numerical increase of the organization thus effected is not likely to be gained at the expense of its quality.

The last link in the long chain of phenomena which confer a profoundly conservative character upon the intimate essence of the political party (even upon that party which boasts itself revolutionary) is found in the relationships between party and state. Generated to overthrow the centralized power of the state, starting from the idea that the working class need merely secure a sufficiently vast and solid organization in order to triumph over the organization of the state, the party of the workers has ended by acquiring a vigorous centralization of its own, based upon the same cardinal principles of authority and discipline which characterize the organization of the state. It thus becomes a governmental party, that is to say, a party which, organized itself like a government on the small scale, hopes some day to assume the reins of government upon the large scale. The revolutionary political party is a state within the state, pursuing the avowed aim of destroying the existing state in order to substitute for it a social order of a fundamentally different character. To attain this essentially political end, the party avails itself of the socialist organization, whose sole justification is found precisely in its patient but systematic preparation for the destruction of the organization of the state in its existing form. The subversive party organizes the *framework* of the social revolution. For this reason it continually endeavors to strengthen its positions, to extend its bureaucratic mechanism, to store up its energies and its funds. . . .

The party, regarded as an entity, as a piece of mechanism, is not necessarily identifiable with the totality of its members, and still less so with the class to which these belong. The party is created as a means to secure an end. Having, however, become an end in itself, endowed with aims and interests of its own, it undergoes detachment, from the teleological point of view, from the class which it represents. In a party, it is far from obvious that the interests of the masses which have combined to form the party will coincide with the interests of the bureaucracy in which the party becomes personified. The interests of the body of employees are always conservative, and in a given political situation these interests may dictate a defensive and even a reactionary policy when the interests of the working class demand a bold and aggressive policy; in other cases, although these are very rare, the rôles may be reversed. By a universally applicable social law, every organ of the collectivity, brought into existence through the need for the division of labor, creates for itself, as soon as it becomes consolidated, interests peculiar to itself. The existence of these special interests involves a necessary conflict with the interests of the collectivity. Nay, more, social strata fulfilling peculiar functions tend to become isolated, to produce organs fitted for the defense of their own peculiar interests. In the long run they tend to undergo transformation into distinct classes.

The sociological phenomena whose general characteristics have been discussed in this chapter and in preceding ones offer numerous vulnerable points to the scientific opponents of democracy. These phenomena would seem to prove beyond dispute that society cannot exist without a "dominant" or "political" class, and that the ruling class, while its elements are subject to a frequent partial renewal, nevertheless constitutes the only factor of sufficiently durable efficacy in the history of human development. According to this view, the government, or, if the phrase be preferred, the state, cannot be anything other than the organization of a minority. It is the aim of this minority to impose upon the rest of society a "legal order," which is the outcome of the exigencies of dominion and of the exploitation of the mass of helots effected by the ruling minority, and can never be truly representative of the majority. The majority is thus permanently incapable of self-government. Even when the discontent of the masses culminates in a successful attempt to deprive the bourgeoisie of power, this is after all, so Mosca contends, effected only in appearance; always and necessarily there springs from the masses a new organized minority which raises itself to the rank of a governing class. Thus the majority of human beings, in a condition of eternal tutelage, are predestined by tragic necessity to submit to the dominion of a small minority, and must be content to constitute the pedestal of an oligarchy. . . .

Reduced to its most concise expression, the fundamental sociological law of political parties (the term "political" being here used in its most comprehensive significance) may be formulated in the following terms: "It is organization which gives birth to the dominion of the elected over the electors, of the mandataries over the mandators, of the delegates over the delegators. Who says organization, says oligarchy."

Every party organization represents an oligarchical power grounded upon a democratic basis. We find everywhere electors and elected. Also we find everywhere that the power of the elected leaders over the electing masses is almost unlimited. The oligarchical structure of the building suffocates the basic democratic principle. That which *is* oppresses that which *ought to be.* For the masses, this essential difference between the reality and the ideal remains a mystery. Socialists often cherish a sincere belief that a new *elite* of politicians will keep faith better than did the old. The notion of the representation of popular interests, a notion to which the great majority of democrats, and in especial the working-class masses of the German-speaking lands, cleave with so much tenacity and confidence, is an illustion engendered by a false illumination, is an effect of mirage. In one of the most delightful pages of his analysis of modern Don Quixotism, Alphonse Daudet shows us how the "brav' commandant" Bravida, who has never quitted Tarascon, gradually comes to persuade himself, influenced by the burning southern sun, that he has been to Shanghai and has had all kinds of heroic adventures. Similarly the modern proletariat, enduringly influenced by glib-tongued persons intellectually superior to the mass, ends by believing that by flocking to the poll and entrusting its social and economic cause to a delegate, its direct participation in power will be assured.

The formation of oligarchies within the various forms of democracy is the outcome of organic necessity, and consequently affects every organization, be it socialist or even anarchist. Haller long ago noted that in every form of social life relationships of dominion and of dependence are created by Nature herself. The supremacy of the leaders in the democratic and revolutionary parties has to be taken into account in every historic situation present and to come, even though only a few and exceptional minds will be fully conscious of its existence. The mass will never rule except *in abstracto.* Consequently the question we have to discuss is not whether ideal democracy is realizable, but rather to what point and in what degree democracy is desirable, possible, and realizable at a given moment. In the problem as thus stated we recognize the fundamental problem of politics as a science. Whoever fails to perceive this must, as Sombart says, either be so blind and fanatical as not to see that the democratic current daily makes undeniable advance, or else must be so inexperienced and devoid of critical faculty as to be unable to understand that all order and all civilization must exhibit aristocratic features. The great error of socialists, an error committed in consequence of their lack of adequate psychological knowledge, is to be found in their combination of pessimism regarding the present, with rosy optimism and immeasurable confidence regarding the future. A realistic view of the mental condition of the masses shows beyond question that even if we admit the possibility of moral improvement in mankind, the human materials with whose use politicians and philosophers cannot dispense in their plans of social reconstruction are not of a character to justify excessive optimism. Within the limits of time for which human provision is possible, optimism will remain the exclusive privilege of utopian thinkers. . . .

In view of the perennial incompetence of the masses, we have to recognize the existence of two regulative principles:

1. The *ideological* tendency of democracy towards criticism and control.
2. The *effective* counter-tendency of democracy towards the creation of parties ever more complex and ever more differentiated—parties, that is to say, which are increasingly based upon the competence of the few.

To the idealist, the analysis of the forms of contemporary democracy cannot fail to be a source of bitter deceptions and profound discouragement. Those alone, perhaps, are in a position to pass a fair judgment upon democracy who, without lapsing into dilettantist sentimentalism, recognize that all scientific and human ideals have relative values. If we wish to estimate the value of democracy, we must do so in comparison with its converse, pure aristocracy. The defects inherent in democracy are obvious. It is nonetheless true that as a form of social life we must choose democracy as the least of evils. The ideal government would doubtless be that of an aristocracy of persons at once morally good and technically efficient. But where shall we discover such an aristocracy? We may find it sometimes, though very rarely, as the outcome of deliberate selection; but we shall never find it where the hereditary principle remains in operation. Thus monarchy in its pristine purity must be considered as imperfection incarnate, as the most incurable of ills; from the moral point of view it is inferior even to the most revolting of demagogic dictatorships, for the corrupt organism of the latter at least contains a healthy principle upon whose working we may continue to base hopes of social resanation. It may be said, therefore, that the more humanity comes to recognize the advantages which democracy, however imperfect, presents over aristocracy, even at its best, the less likely is it that a recognition of the defects of democracy will provoke a return to aristocracy. Apart from certain formal differences and from the qualities which can be acquired only by good education and inheritance (qualities in which aristocracy will always have the advantage over democracy—qualities which democracy either neglects altogether, or, attempting to imitate them, falsifies them to the point of caricature), the defects of democracy will be found to inhere in its inability to get rid of its aristocratic scoriae. On the other hand, nothing but a serene and frank examination of the oligarchical dangers of democracy will enable us to minimize these dangers, even though they can never be entirely avoided.

The democratic currents of history resemble successive waves. They break ever on the same shoal. They are ever renewed. This enduring spectacle is simultaneously encouraging and depressing. When democracies have gained a certain stage of development, they undergo a gradual transformation, adopting the aristocratic spirit, and in many cases also the aristocratic forms, against which at the outset they struggled so fiercely. Now new accusers arise to denounce the traitors; after an era of glorious combats and of inglorious power, they end by fusing with the old dominant class; whereupon once more they are in their turn attacked by fresh opponents who appeal to the name of democracy. It is probable that this cruel game will continue without end.

Democracy in Private Government: A Case Study of the International Typographical Union

Seymour M. Lipset

Social science has as one of its objectives the prediction of the behaviour of classes of individuals or institutions under specific structural conditions. One of the few macroscopic sets of generalizations which appears to fit the scientific criterion of predictability is the theory of organization encompassed in Robert Michels' "iron law of oligarchy."[1] The skimpy data available on the behaviour of nominally "democratic" large-scale organizations such as political parties, business corporations, trade unions and co-operatives would seem to confirm Michels' prediction that structural forces endemic in large-scale organization make control by the self-co-opting leaders of a bureaucratic hierarchy inevitable.[2]

There is, among American large-scale organizations, a clear-cut exception to Michels' generalization that oligarchic domination is inherent in the very nature of large-scale social organization. The International Typographical Union (A.F. of L.), the organization of the compositors, linotype operators and mailers in the printing industry, the oldest union in the United States, possesses an internal structure which cannot be fitted easily into a Michelsian oligarchic pattern.[3]

The democratic structure and process in the I.T.U. can be seen in the following facts. Since 1898, when the Union established the referendum system of electing international officers biennially, there have been seven changes in the

[1]Robert Michels, *Political Parties* (New York: Free Press, 1949).

[2]See Philip Selznick, "An Approach to the Theory of Bureaucracy," *American Sociological Review,* Vol. 8 (1943), pp. 47-59; Sylvia Kopald, *Rebellion in Labour Unions* (New York, 1924).

[3]While this paper deals mainly with the International Typographical Union, I do not intend to suggest that it is the only "deviant case" to Michels' "law" among American trade unions or other voluntary organizations.

Seymour M. Lipset
"Democracy in Private Government: A Case Study of the International Typographical Union,"
British Journal of Sociology,
Vol. 3 (1952), Routledge & Kegan Paul, Ltd.
Reprinted with permission.

Presidency in which incumbent officers were defeated, five of these occurring since 1920. During that same period the administration party failed to elect its complete slate for the four- to six-man executive board in eight elections out of the twenty-five which occurred. In no election since 1916 has any international official run without organized opposition. Defeated Presidential candidates have never failed to secure less than 23 per cent of the vote and have secured 35 per cent, or more, in 14 of the 16 elections since 1918. The union membership has voted in over 500 referenda since 1889 to approve or disapprove suggested union policies which have been proposed by the International Board, an annual convention, or a number of local unions. Out of the 24 referenda to increase the salary of international officials since 1900, the increase has been defeated 17 times. In this period local unions have independently put forward 27 referenda and 18 of these have passed.[4] The constitution of the union provides that any candidate for international office shall have the right to write an uncensored article presenting his views in two pre-election issues of *The Typographical Journal,* the monthly organ of the union which goes to all members.[5] Union members have the right to organize permanent or temporary union political parties, and to publish literature attacking the administration of the union.[6] This right has been exercised by groups and individuals in almost every election since 1898.

The principal continual arena of significant membership participation in the I.T.U. is found in the frequent elections and referenda which are conducted in the union. The union members do take part in choosing among the candidates running for office and the policies submitted to union referendum. The number of members voting in these elections and referenda is proportionately considerably higher than the vote in national elections in the United States: in the last five elections an average of 73 per cent of the members voted.[7] Delegates to the annual convention are also elected by secret ballot in every union print shop. Many of the larger local unions conduct their elections in a similar manner, with

[4]The data summarized above were secured from various issues of *The Typographical Journal,* the monthly organ of the I.T.U., which has been in existence since 1892.

[5]"Candidates who have received the requisite number of endorsements and who have filed their acceptance of the nomination for office sought shall be entitled to space in the April and May issues of *The Typographical Journal* for the publication of reasons and arguments in support of their candidacy, such matter to be personally prepared by the candidates, and no candidate shall issue, or sanction the issuance of, any other literature or printed matter in his behalf, unless signed by the candidate or three members in good standing. . . ." *Book of Laws of the International Typographical Union* (Indianapolis, 1948), p. 46. This clause was first adopted in 1913.

[6]Various union political groups have made use of this right for the last fifty years or more. Regular and irregular newspapers, pamphlets, and leaflets have been and are still being published attacking and supporting the incumbent administration. The official history of the union used for educating new members discusses and praises the existence of opposition groups as a normal phenomenon. See I.T.U. Bureau of Education, *Lessons in Printing,* Lesson 5 (Indianapolis, 1939), p. 4.

[7]Calculated from election returns and membership statistics published in *The Typographical Journal.*

the overwhelming majority of the membership voting. These elections and referenda present the membership with the possibility of choosing between alternative union policies.

The question must obviously be raised as to the factors related to the continued vitality of democratic institutions in the I.T.U. Here the most significant difference between the I.T.U. and other more oligarchical unions is the existence in the Typographical Union, alone among the older trade unions in North America, of two permanent rival trade union parties. These two parties, now known as the Progressives and the Independents, constitute the source of the effective checks in the union against usurpation of power by any group of leaders. The parties, or their predecessors under other names, together with occasional third parties, have contested almost every election in the union's history with virtually complete slates for every office. Since the turn of the century the two major parties have maintained permanent political organizations with their own press. At all times this institutionalized party system ensures a powerful, vocal, intelligent opposition. Regardless of which party temporarily controls the International administration, the opposition has always had a large nucleus of trained leaders—former officials of the International or incumbent officers of local unions still under opposition control—who comprise a potential alternative administration. The tendencies towards "bureaucratic conservatism" that arise within the leadership of most organizations have been checked by the existence of this permanent opposition group, which stands ready to capitalize on any fault of the administration and play up every demand which seems to have support among the members. Each party, when in opposition, has been too strong to be crushed or denied its opposition rights without destroying the union.

These parties arose out of a set of critical conditions in the early history of the union. As early as 1857, seven years after the foundation of the union, a group of members of the New York local met in Albany and formed a secret society of loyal union members to help preserve the larger organization in a period of crisis. 1857 was a year of large-scale unemployment among printers. The young union was consequently highly vulnerable to attack. Known and active unionists were fired; betrayal of a fellow worker as a member of the union often gained a man preference and a steady job.[8]

This early secret group, about which little is known, either developed into or was followed by a more formal secret organization known as the "Brotherhood of the Union of North America." Though there was a great deal of opposition to the secret societies, they continued through the latter part of the nineteenth century. Their members and leaders believed that they were serving the cause of

[8]See pamphlet, *Administration Party Was Founded in 1857* (New York, 1927). It is doubtful that the secret societies had continuity from 1857. The skimpy evidence available suggests that there was a succession of secret organizations between 1857 and the '90's when the last important one, the Wahnetas, was founded.

unionism by preventing employers' spies and lukewarm union men from influencing union policy. The name of the principal secret lodge changed at different times, presumably to preserve secrecy. The final name under which they came to be known was the Wahnetas.

These secret groups fulfilled certain definite functional needs of a weak labour union in a period in which unions were almost extra-legal. They served to protect the active union members from discrimination by employers, and kept policy control of the union in the hands of men who were willing to sacrifice to further the cause of the union. In order to carry out their objectives, the secret societies attempted to secure political control of the union and its locals, and endeavoured to place their members in jobs in important plants. They also tried to recruit foremen, who had the power to hire and fire, into the union and the secret lodges.

The Wahneta organization continued to exist after the union had become a strong, stable organization. Its members, who included the leaders of many of the locals of the International as well as of the International itself, found that a secret group served as an efficient political machine to keep control of union posts. I.T.U. members who were not members of the Wahnetas organized their own groups in the seventies and the union began to be torn apart by bitter internal conflicts. Gradually, the opposing groups developed into open factions competing for union office, the Wahnetas being known as the Administration Party, and their opponents as the Progressive Party. The Administration Party retained complete control of the International organization until the 1920's, when the Progressives finally won the major elective positions. Following a major defeat in 1928, the Administration Party broke up into conflicting factions, and the Wahneta secret organization appears to have dissolved. The individuals who belonged to the Administration Party, plus a number of dissident Progressives, however, reformed an opposition party in 1932, known as the Independent Party. Since 1932, the two parties, Progressive and Independent, have contested each International election, as well as many local elections.

The ideological differences among the various parties of the I.T.U. will be discussed in more detail elsewhere. In general, however, the split has been between greater and less militancy concerning internal trade union tactics. The Independents, and, before them, the Administration Party and the Wahnetas, have advocated conciliatory tactics in dealing with the employer or the government as the best way to advance the economic position of the membership. The Progressives, on the other hand, have been more prone to favour militant action such as strikes. Internationally, the parties took a different position to the A.F. of L.-C.I.O. controversy when it first developed in the mid-thirties. The Independents favoured supporting the A.F. of L. in its fight against the C.I.O., while the Progressives, though not favouring secession from the A.F. of L., objected to paying a special war tax to the A.F. of L. to fight the C.I.O. The Progressive President of the I.T.U., at the time, served for a while as the first secretary of the

C.I.O. Toward the end of World War II, the Progressives opposed the policy of the Independent administration in giving a no-strike pledge. Since the passage of the Taft-Hartley Act in 1947, the Progressive administration has led a number of major strikes designed to retain union gains which the Act challenges or makes illegal, and have refused to sign the non-Communist affidavits required by this law. The Independents, while also opposed to the law, have favoured a policy of trying to live within the law, and urge that union officers sign the non-Communist affidavits.

While there is probably some correlation between I.T.U. party support and external political affiliations and beliefs, there is no connection between the I.T.U. parties and non-union political groups. The old Wahneta-Administration Party, although the conservative party in the union, had a number of active Socialists in its leadership, including Max Hayes, one of the leaders of the Socialists in the A.F. of L. On the other hand, Charles Howard, the Progressive leader from 1922 to 1938, was a life-long Republican.

The parties, originally organized by men bitterly hostile to one another as a result of the early secret society fight, have become securely institutionalized in the course of the last 50 years. Since 1918 neither group has been able to win enough strength to destroy the "out" party's hopes of success in the next election. Each party continues to work between elections to present its case and win recruits both in the locals and at national conventions. The leaders on each side attempt to bring into their party any union member who seems to have leadership ability and has won a personal following. At the local level, the party leaders look for individuals who have proven themselves in their shop unit, the chapel, while at the International level, party leaders attempt to win over convention delegates from smaller locals where the party system is not strong.

Joining a party has become the accepted means of rising in the union hierarchy. Discussion with union leaders suggests that the union politicians are persons with a strong mobility drive, or with intense interest in politics in general. Printing requires a six-year apprenticeship after leaving school. Once a man has become a union printer, there are few more lucrative or secure positions open to him, and it is extremely unlikely that he will ever change his occupation. The principal means through which a typographer can rise either in income or social status is by becoming a union official. A former International Vice-President stated, "Once you are a printer, there's no other job you can get except that of a union official. . . . I had once intended to go into business for myself, but once I realized that I would always be a printer, I became interested in the possibilities of working for the union."

There is also a second group of party activists who do not seem to be motivated by the hope of gaining political office. They are individuals who have little oratorical ability or special personality characteristics which would make them good candidates. These people take part in party discussions, help spread party propaganda either by word of mouth or through literature. This group seems to be composed of people concerned with politics in general, like some of the leaders, or with a desire to be near the centre of power, to be "in on things." A knowledge of union gossip, and the sense of helping to determine party nominations and policies, are among the rewards of party activity for this group.

The actual internal membership of the two parties is unknown to any but the leaders of the parties. In New York, where the union has over 10,000 members, informants estimated that both parties together have a total of about 1,000 dues-paying members, but only about 100 active ones. In crisis situations, such as during the depression, hundreds have attended party meetings in the hope of getting the party to adopt policies which they favoured. Each party, also, has a large group of sympathizers who support it because of personal ties, tradition, sympathy with its programme, or out of an antagonism which they may have developed against one party while it was in power. The party members and sympathizers serve to keep all union members aware of important issues. The party apparatus serves also to communicate to the top leaders of the party and union the attitudes of the union members towards any union issue, and enables the leaders to adjust their policies in the direction of the prevailing opinion in the shops—a continual process dictated by the sensitivity of the party leadership to the dangers of losing the next election.

The referendum and the biennial secret election of national officers constitutes in the last analysis the basic foundation of I.T.U. democracy, *when they are combined with a vigorous opposition party system.* It is through these institutions that the members have the last word on the policies of the officialdom. An examination of the election returns suggests that this right is exercised, and that no set of leaders can afford to ignore rank and file sentiment and remain in office.

The election results cited in Table 1 suggest that neither party has the permanent loyalty of a large section of the union.

In addition to the regular and frequent turnovers in office already cited, lack of official control over the union is clearly indicated by the votes in referenda on salary increases. Since 1900 salary increases for officers have been defeated eighteen times out of twenty-six. There does not appear to be any close relationship between the electoral strength of an administration and its ability to secure a salary increase for itself. In 1916, the Wahneta administration was elected without opposition, yet in the same year the membership voted down a proposal to increase the salaries of the President and Secretary-Treasurer from $3,500 to $5,000 by almost two and one-half to one. In 1948, a year in which the Progressive slate received about 60 per cent of the vote, the members voted 33,408 to 28,361 against a salary increase. (In 1949, a proposal to pension union officers was defeated by over two to one in referendum, though the convention which proposed it was overwhelmingly Progressive.) Attempts by union leaders to receive a wage increase resemble in many ways a collective bargaining session conducted by referendum between the members and the officials. The members, in general, refuse to give their officers a raise except during periods of great prosperity. The most recent increases took place in 1919, 1929-30, 1947 and 1950, and the increases which the officers secured were proportionately less than had been received by the membership in these periods.

Table 1. Election Returns in I.T.U. from 1918 to 1950 with Proportion of Members Voting

Year	Percentage President			Percentage 1st Vice-Pres.			Percentage 2nd Vice-Pres.			Percentage Sec.-Treas.			Percentage Members Voting for President
	P	W-I	O	P	W-I	O	P	W-I	O	P	W-I	O	
1918	35.9	64.1		36.9	63.1					35.7	64.3		67.0
1920	51.3	48.7		48.0	52.0		46.7	53.3		45.4	54.6		77.8†
1922	54.3	45.7		52.0	48.0		50.1	49.9		47.6	52.4		77.1†
1924	47.7	52.3		48.5	51.5		46.8	53.2		44.7	55.3		81.4
1926	51.7	48.3		47.4	49.1	3.9	50.0	50.0†		48.3	51.7		80.5†
1928	63.9	36.1		63.4	36.6		61.4	38.6		56.5	43.5		76.6
1930	59.1	23.1	18.8	58.9	25.7	15.4	62.9	21.0	16.1	61.9	38.1		74.7
1931				49.4	50.6								64.1*†
1932	54.6	45.4		58.7	25.7	8.8	51.2	40.0	8.8	63.5	36.5		72.0
1934	57.0	43.0		64.1	35.9		59.2	25.5	15.3	65.5	34.5		69.1
1936	58.8	41.2		63.7	36.3		57.4	31.1	11.5	66.5	33.5		69.1
1938	36.8	61.2		51.2	48.8		47.2	52.8		51.8	48.2		71.5†
1940	47.8	52.2		50.9	49.1		43.3	43.8	12.8	50.2	49.8		74.8†
1942	48.2	51.8		46.3	53.7		45.3	54.7		51.0	49.0		71.4†
1944	51.7	32.6	15.7	57.0	43.0		50.3	39.3	10.5	48.5	34.7	16.8	62.1†
1946										63.1	36.9		69.2*
1946	71.7	28.9		69.0	30.6		69.0	31.0		66.3	34.7		76.0
1948	57.5	42.5		61.4	38.6		59.2	40.8		62.1	37.9		74.4
1950	55.4	44.6		53.7	46.3		58.2	41.8		57.5	47.5		79.6

**Special Election. Incumbent died in office.*
†Indicates that no party had complete control of the Executive Council.
P = Progressive.
W-I = Wahneta-Independent.
O = Other.
Source: Calculated from election returns in Typographical Journal.

It is significant to note that since 1912, every salary increase that was proposed by an International convention, except that of 1950, was defeated. The 1919, 1930 and 1946-7 increases which passed were first initiated by locals. The 1950 increase came from the floor of the convention, and was publicly opposed by the incumbent officers. Apparently the members resent a proposal for salary increases which comes from the union politicians in control of the convention.

The concern of the members to keep control over their officers can be seen in the fact that two proposals to increase the term of office from two to four years were both defeated. This proposal was defeated in 1918 by 18,649 votes to 14,611, and in 1929 by 29,400 votes to 19,967. The first proposal was made by a convention while the Wahnetas controlled the administration, and the second during a period of Progressive supremacy. In 1924, the membership voted 24,371 to 18,005 to fill vacancies among the officers by direct special election rather than by Executive Council co-optation.

The record of referenda on the most fundamental right of a self-governing body, the right to vote funds, is probably the most interesting example of the intention of the members to keep ultimate control in their own hands. The members, on a number of occasions, have refused to vote for a permanent dues increase, though there has been, of course, a secular increase in union dues. One might compare the voting record of the I.T.U. on dues increases with the historic struggles between the King and the English Parliament on the passage of appropriations. The I.T.U. members, like Parliament, will usually vote for temporary dues assessments of one year or less for a specific purpose such as a strike fund. Since 1920 four referenda to secure funds for one year or less have passed and two have been defeated. On the other hand, eight referenda proposing permanent dues increases have been defeated since 1920, while five have passed. Of these five, two were for ten cents a month increases for the maintenance of the Union Printers' Home. These votes do not reflect an unwillingness on the part of the membership to support the union, for the two most heavily supported assessments were for a 10 per cent and a 4-1/2 per cent tax on wages to support striking members. The 10 per cent assessment was passed in 1921, by a vote of 40,703 to 11,499, to support the 44 hour week strike, while the second large tax was passed, 44,829 to 21,477, in 1948 to support the many Taft-Hartley strikes of the union. The generosity of the members in supporting their fellow unionists, rather than their officers or union apparatus, can be seen from the above votes and from the fact that in 1946, the union voted by 44,539 to 11,203 to increase strike benefits from 40 to 60 per cent of the regular wage for all married men, and from 25 to 40 per cent for all single men.

Since 1900 the union has held over 250 referenda. Most of these referenda have been on constitutional changes or on assessments. There have been many votes on changing the pension system; defining the jurisdiction of the union; the question of affiliation with the A.F. of L.; adjusting the constitution to war needs; changing the date of the convention or the period of inauguration of officers; the number of days and hours which a union member may work; unemployment relief; and many other subjects which are covered in the constitution, or which a convention, Executive Council, or local finds it advisable to submit to the membership.

The extent of membership control over the officialdom can be seen in the fact that the members have defeated 29 per cent of the 83 proposals submitted by International conventions for their approval since 1920. This figure would be much higher if the non-controversial technical changes were omitted from consideration. In most organizations, union or non-union, it is assumed that the national convention of delegates, elected by the members, therefore represents the wishes of the members. It is clear from the record of contentions and referenda in the case of the I.T.U. that this assumption need not be true. A convention, in fact, usually represents the local formal leadership structure, and the leaders, even those of the small I.T.U. locals, may and frequently do have values and interests which are different from those of the members whom they represent. This gap is generally obscured by the absence of any means for the direct expression of the desires of the membership. Referenda provide such a means of expression, but only when they operate in the context of an institutionalized party system. Otherwise, as in plebiscitarian democracies, they serve to legitimize the power and decisions of a ruling group. The relation between the referenda voting and the two-party system can be seen in the fact that from 1900 to 1919, before the present system was completely institutionalized, only 16.2 per cent of the convention proposals were turned down.

The results of referenda initiated by the International Executive Council present an even more dramatic picture of membership control. Nine out of the twenty-two, or 40.9 per cent of proposals by the officials, were defeated between 1920 and 1948, compared with one out of nine, or 11.1 per cent proposed between 1900 and 1919. The defeated Executive Council proposals have included dues increases, proposals to rejoin the A.F. of L., and to postpone the annual convention.[9]

The above data suggest that a large percentage of the members of the I.T.U., though supporters at election time of one or another party, do not necessarily accept the policies of the leaders whom they support. The defeats of proposals to increase officers' salaries or to extend their term of office indicate that a certain suspicion of or at least lack of complete enthusiasm for officials exists even among the supporters of a given administration. This suspicion has made it difficult if not impossible for an incumbent administration to so amend the constitution as to perpetuate its hold on office.

Preliminary interviews with members of the union suggest the existence of two seemingly contradictory sentiments as a consequence of the two-party system. The members are critical of the motives of union "politicians," but at the same time are extremely loyal to the union—the most critical oppositionists boast that the I.T.U. is the best and most democratic union in the country. The distrust of the leaders and the loyalty to the institution appear to be related to the intense political life of the organization. Every union politician is exposed to vigorous attack at all times from the opposition. The effect of such attacks may be reflected in the fact that even supporters of a given party are suspicious of the power or income aspirations of their own leaders. On the other hand, the fact that any given administration may be defeated within two years, and that the union cannot be

[9]The above data on referenda were gathered from *The Typographical Journal* from 1900 to 1948. It is possible that I overlooked some referenda or misinterpreted the meaning of some, but the possible errors are small and would not change the general direction of the statistics.

identified with a permanent leader or group of leaders, appears to result in the members focusing their dissatisfactions on the temporary incumbent leaders rather than on the union. The prevailing sentiment among critics of a given administration seems to be: the officials are bad but the union is good. Such sentiments, once developed in a democratic society or organization, are an important part of the cluster of factors which help maintain democratic practices.

The question obviously arises, what are the significant differences between the Typographical Union and other trade unions which are related to the perpetuation of the two-party system. The officials and members of the union with whom I have discussed this problem suggest two hypotheses—one which points to the historic traditions of chapel and union democracy, going back in some cases to the seventeenth century or earlier, and another which cites the high educational level of printers compared to other crafts. Fortunately there exists a control with which to test these hypotheses—the International Pressmen's Union, an organization which was part of the Typographical Union until the start of the century. The Pressmen have the same historical traditions and institutional framework, such as chapels, as the Typographers. They work side by side in the printshops of the continent with the members of the I.T.U., and earn roughly the same wages. There is no reason to believe that the Pressmen are significantly different from the compositors and linotype operators in their personal characteristics. If the above hypotheses were true, one should expect to find the same mechanisms of democratic control operative in the Pressmen's Union.

Actually, the International Pressmen's Union is one of the most dictatorial unions in America. One administration held power in the union for over thirty years until its leaders died. Various locals of the union have been suspended for opposing the policies of the International leaders. Until the death of President George Berry in 1948, the administration was repeatedly elected without opposition, and many locals were denied the right to choose their own officers. These facts suggest that the above hypotheses do not explain the uniqueness of the I.T.U. Other hypotheses have been grouped in the following table.

Table 2

Hypotheses Adduced to Explain Party Democracy in the I.T.U.	Evidence for Not Accepting or for Rejecting Hypotheses
1. Conflict of different socio-economic groups within union accounts for democracy in the I.T.U.	The majority of the members are typesetters, except a minority of mailers and machinists. All typographers in the same location receive the same scale, yet the large and many small locals are internally divided in support of the major parties.
2. Allegiance to extra-union groups such as splits between communists and their opponents, or conflicts along ethnic and religious lines.	Majority of members are of north European or native white origin. Only a small percentage belong to ethnic minority groups. External political parties have little influence in the union.

Table 2 (Continued)

Hypotheses Adduced to Explain Party Democracy in the I.T.U.	Evidence for Not Accepting or for Rejecting Hypotheses
3. Homogeneity of membership and lack of an educated native elite as against a large mass of uneducated politically inexperienced immigrants or lower class natives.	This cannot be rejected, *but* it is also true of the Pressmen and some Railroad Brotherhoods which have not developed internal political democracy.
4. The comparatively small size of the union (87,000 members) and the large number of small locals permit direct contact with the administration. More than 4,000 local officials. This means one member of 20 has direct contacts with officials.	See 3.
5. Defeated officials and personally ambitious members tend to remain in the union and form a reservoir, larger than positions available, of persons capable and desirous of union leadership jobs.	Other skilled crafts have a low turnover because of high economic status of craft. They may not possess many former union officials but this is more a consequence of a vital political system than a determinant.
6. The stability of the union removes it from pressure towards internal unity. Thus dictatorial measures cannot be justified by leaders on the basis that the union is like an army at war.	Partially challenged by fact that many dictatorial trade unions also have stable employer relations and good conditions of work but no union democracy.
7. The great personal antagonism existing when printers were divided in secret societies is institutionalized, as a kind of permanent Civil War in the party system.	Election results show that locals voting overwhelmingly Wahneta in one election shifted to the opposition in the next and vice versa.
8. Perhaps the antagonism of small groups of union politicians is too great to permit merger of opposing groups.	Leaders in one party have shifted to the opposition and have been elected on the opposition slate.
9. Democratic mores are so ingrained that leaders abstain from using union apparatus to perpetuate themselves in power.	This is true but more likely an outcome of a democratic political life. Yet I.T.U. leaders of both sides have used the *Journal* for partisan purposes, and given patronage. In one instance a constitutional technicality was used by the incumbent to bar the opposition candidate from the ballot. Their desire to stay in power does not seem to differ from that of other union leaders.
Professor Philip Taft, in a study of the I.T.U., has suggested additional hypotheses:	
10. "In contrast to many labour unions, the I.T.U. has never experienced an influx of thousands of new members. Membership increases have been slow and steady. As a result new members are assimilated by the organization; they become aware of the Union's practices and learn its ideals."* (Taft compares the I.T.U. to the United Mine Workers who had an influx of hundreds of thousands of new members in 1933. He suggests that this influx was a large determining element in enabling Lewis to eliminate opposition.)	The comparison of I.T.U. with the United Mine Workers begs the question as there are other unions more comparable to the I.T.U. than the U.M.W. By 1930, long before the great mass influx into the U.M.W., only ten out of twenty-nine districts still had the right to elect their own officers. Moreover, Pressmen, similar to the I.T.U. in having gradual increase in membership, do not have political democracy.

Table 2 (Continued)

Hypotheses Adduced to Explain Party Democracy in the I.T.U.	Evidence for Not Accepting or for Rejecting Hypotheses
11. Bargaining is conducted primarily by the local. The international officers or representatives merely assist but do not play the dominant role as when negotiations are conducted on a regional basis.+	Again, the Pressmen and the Carpenters are composed of local bargaining units. The I.T.U., in fact, has a high degree of control through the Executive Council which approves all contracts and authorizes all strikes. Locals sometimes turn against incumbent administrations because they feel the International does not permit them to bargain as they desire.
12. "The great interest manifested by the membership in the affairs of the Union (as demonstrated by the large proportion voting in the International elections) further encourages the vitality of the democratic process."†	It may be questioned again whether a result is not taken as a cause. The elections of 1906 and 1914, in which the major posts of President and Secretary-Treasurer were uncontested, brought 54.3 and 57.9 per cent of the members to the polls while the contested elections of 1904 and 1912 resulted in participation of 72.4 and 80.2 per cent of the membership respectively.†† Interest of the members seems to be related to the two-party system, with the vote turnout being secured by the two party machines competing for power.

**Philip Taft,* op. cit., *p. 262.*
+Ibid, *pp. 262-3.*
†*Philip Taft,* op. cit., *p. 263.*
††Ibid., *p. 261.*

Conclusions

While it has not been possible to filter out a single factor which alone would account for the democratic organization of the I.T.U., preliminary research suggests that there is a unique cluster of variables making for a competition of alternative governments in the union. These factors would include: the peculiar events which initiated the two rival factions; the existence within the larger locals of a large number of private social and athletic clubs which provide independent source of power and influence, and opportunities for the training of new leadership; the fact that the union is stabilized but at the same time is subject to enough challenges to its security by the vicissitudes of the economic system and government legislation to require it to make important policy decisions upon which men may differ; the fact that it contains the large nucleus of aspiring union officials mentioned above; the smallness of the union so that there is a direct and visible link between the bottom and summits of the organization; the lack of division within the union between a sophisticated educated "elite" and an uneducated mass membership; the anti-bureaucratic values and juridical checks which developed out of the attempt to eliminate "secret society" control; and the educational and status level of printers which places them among those groups who tend to exhibit more political interest in the country as a whole.[10]

[10]The article referred to earlier, "Trade Unionism in the Printing Trades," presents in some detail the analysis of a number of structural factors which appear to be related to the high level of political democracy in the I.T.U.

The perpetuation of the party system in the I.T.U. may be explained functionally, not in terms of the union as the reference unit, but in terms of the parties themselves. Once established, they give status, privilege and power to the leaders, as well as other satisfactions to less important party activists. The parties establish and perpetuate juridical protection for themselves.

Ever since 1920 the "out" parties have always had a real possibility of returning to power within two years. Only twice in this period did the "out" party vote fall below 40 per cent. The opportunities of a return to power were considerably greater than those which could have been offered by the "in" party as inducement to end opposition. In fact, the most prominent defections have not been from the "out" to the "ins," but rather from the "ins" to the "outs."[11] Perhaps the men who deserted could not hope to secure higher positions from their own party since it was standard practice to renominate incumbents. An ambitious leader of the "ins" can often only secure a nomination to a higher post from the "out" group.

The existence of the political system within the I.T.U. suggests that the "iron law of oligarchy" as Michels presented it is not a "law." His generalizations may be qualified to include recognition of the fact that oligarchy is endemic in large-scale organization only when there is no permanent base for an opposition party system which gives the masses the opportunity to choose between alternative programmes and forces competing sets of aspiring rulers to yield to the desires of the rank and file in order to secure or maintain voting strength. Moreover, Michels only discussed those aspects of organization which in and of themselves are functional to the power position of incumbents and ignored the possibility that office has dysfunctions if an opposition exists. Decision makers create enemies as well as friends when they decide a conflict of interest. In the case of the I.T.U., as in society at large, the administration not only is negatively affected by the immediate small decisions which it must make but it may bear the brunt of the resentment against uncontrollable external situations which adversely affect the members. The three significant periods of party shift, 1920, 1938 and 1944, were times of either depression or inflation. Power in a democratic organization is not only self-perpetuating but also self-destroying, *if there is an institutional framework for mobilization of critical sentiments.*

The I.T.U. is also a deviant case to the rule that organization necessarily breeds conservatism. The "law" of organization is not conservatism but survival. Conservatism, the maintenance of an existing equilibrium, will be found, as it is frequently, when it seems to be an adequate method of keeping power. There are, however, conditions under which the problem of retaining power prescribes

[11]In 1931 Leon Rouse, former Progressive President of New York Local 6, ran as an independent after failing to obtain the vice-presidential nomination from his party. In 1936 Claude Baker, having been elected to the first vice-presidency as a Progressive, switched to the Independents while in office and headed the opposition ticket in 1938.

militancy and radicalism on the part of the power-holder. In the I.T.U. the conciliatory reaction of the Independents to restrictions of the War Labour Board during the last war was followed by their defeat. The Progressives, faced since 1947 with a similar restrictive situation as a result of the Taft-Hartley Act, have reacted by increased militancy.

Before exploring the generalizations that the unique pattern of the I.T.U. permits about the labour movement in the United States and its political structures, it is well to examine an idea which is basic in the consideration of organization. Emil Lederer in *The State of the Masses* has raised questions regarding the relationship between the varied organizations of a political society and the stability of that society. What he characterizes as the state of the masses is one in which the numerous organizations that we regard as normal and generally irrelevant to political organization have disappeared, have been destroyed or are otherwise non-existent or incorporated into the state. It is his suggestion that these organizations—labour, religious, agricultural—all have a definite function in the preservation of democracy. It is the amorphous mass, the state of the masses, the state without a multitude of internal organizations, that has high explosive potential. This concept of the state of the masses is one which deserves far more detailed examination than it has been given.

In large part, the principal source of continued power of a union administration flows from the possession of the union machinery itself. In many unions, the incumbent administration is the only legal and, in almost all unions, the only existing national organization concerned with getting and maintaining power. The formal right of free speech or secret ballot means little as an effective check on administrative power, if the union leaders have complete possession of the union administrative and field staff, union newspaper and expense account. Lazarsfeld and Merton have noted that monopolization of the channels of communication and the consequent absence of counter-propaganda is one of the basic conditions for effectiveness of propaganda in shaping attitudes and behaviour. This condition, as they note, is indigenous to the structure of totalitarian states; it is also characteristic of the one-party political structure of most labour unions. Without a continuously functioning and comparatively well-financed organization to develop issues, print and disseminate literature, and provide a rostrum for potential leaders, dissident members are at a considerable disadvantage in provoking significant opposition even under circumstances which might be expected to create membership discontent. In effect, therefore, the union which does not have any source of internal organization, except for the administration itself, is similar to the state of the masses.[12]

[12]In the larger locals of the I.T.U. large numbers of leisure-time organizations exist which have created the equivalent of an "occupational community." The factors inherent in the occupation which have led to the break-up of the "state of the masses" are discussed in S. M. Lipset and Martin Trow, *op. cit.*

These ideas should be considered in terms of the central problem of this paper, political life in private governments, especially in trade unions. An oligarchic structure which is in effect a one-party system is so common in the trade union government in America that a defender of the Soviet Union within the American labour movement has pointed to the internal structure of the trade union here as justification for the one-party system in that country.[13]

The significance of the two-party system of the International Typographical Union lies at least in part in the fact that this system is almost unique in American private associations. There are abundant examples of temporary factionalism within trade unions and other private organizations. Longstanding institutionalized opposition *parties,* however, are very largely a phenomenon of the political organization known as the state. The existence of the two-party system in the I.T.U. suggests, however, that even in the labour movement there may be sources for institutionalized opposition permitting a direct membership influence on organization policy through their power to overturn a union government. Such two-party systems existed loosely in the A.F. of L. before World War I. Also the Histadrut, or Jewish Confederation of Labour, in the new state of Israel has had continuous internal political struggles since 1920.[14]

These examples should indicate that one-party government is not inherent in the labour movement. Nevertheless, the divisions in the above examples were and are related to outside political forces—the Socialist Party in the case of the A.F. of L., and the two leading Socialist political groups in Palestine, i.e. the Mapai and the Mapam. Political divisions within the I.T.U., however, are not related to external political groups.[15] This suggests the hypothesis that the structural basis for the

[13]Harry Bridges, President of the International Longshoremen's and Warehousemen's Union, presented this argument at the 1947 convention of his union: "What is totalitarianism? *A country that has a totalitarian government operates like our union operates.* There are no political parties. People are elected to govern the country based upon their records. . . . That is totalitarianism . . . if we started to divide up and run a Republican set of officers, a Democratic set, a Communist set and something else, we could have one hell of a time . . ." (quoted in *Proceedings of the Seventh Biennial Convention, I.L.W.U., April 7-11, 1947* [San Francisco, 1947], p. 178). Bridges' statement is, of course, concealing the fact that in the U.S.S.R. and in the Longshoremen's Union political machines do exist. He is in effect saying that "we would have one hell of a time" if we had an organized opposition. Bridges believes that there is no class base for opposing political groups within the "one-class" trade union.

[14]For a more extensive discussion of this problem, see S. M. Lipset, "The Two Party System in the I.T.U.," *Labour and Nation* (Fall, 1950), pp. 33-35; S. M. Lipset and Martin Trow, *op. cit.*

[15]The fact that most dissident factions in the labour movement are tied to external radical political groups is not solely related to the proletarian orientation or composition of such parties. In most unions, opposition can only exist if organized and financed, and socialist and Communist groups are, in effect, the only existing organizational rivals of union administrative bureaucracies. The fact that, in the United States, Communist trade-union factions are able to win considerable support from obviously non- and anti-Communist workers, is evidence of the fact that organization rather than ideological appeal is often the key to Communist success in the labour movement. That is, workers who are discontented with their union officials often have no institutional alternative except the opposition Communist faction.

division of political opinion does exist within the trade union movement, but that the repressive powers inherent in the bureaucratic structure of a union are usually stronger than the factors that might sustain organized opposition.

Political divisions such as those in the A.F. of L. before 1920, and the contemporary struggles in the labour movements of other countries, may reflect as well as determine basic divisions in political outlook within unions. We know little of the structural sources of political differences *within* social classes, especially among workers. The fact remains, however, that unless restrained by totalitarian or oligarchic political machines which prevent workers from choosing between alternative union governments, men seem to divide themselves within the labour movement, as in other areas of life, between Conservatives and Liberals, between Gomperites and Socialists, between Independents and Progressives.

These differences which appear to be present within the trade union structure, and probably within other large-scale private governments as well, must be institutionalized as political parties if the members of an organization are to be able to bring their influence to bear on the summits of the structure. The incumbent leaders of a private government will usually deny that the basis for internal difference exists within their organization. Recognition that the basis for a "loyal opposition" exists within the framework of the association may mean that in the course of normal political life the incumbents, whether of the left or right, will go out of office. Convinced that they are serving the best interests of the organization and desiring to retain the only source of their power and status, leaders of labour unions use the union political apparatus to eliminate and suppress organized opposition. It may be suggested that the power of bureaucratic organization, rather than the absence of significant sources of political difference, accounts for the apparent unanimity of opinion which exists in most American unions.

The "normal" life of many American trade unions is similar to Lederer's "classless" state of the masses. The unions, without any source of power for leadership outside of the administration apparatus, is easily controlled from the top. Challenges to the incumbent administration in such monolithic organizations usually take the form of revolution, which develops into life or death struggles resembling civil wars. If one faction wins, it usually suppresses the other by force. If neither group has the strength to eliminate the other, secession may occur, with two or more unions competing as separate structures. Revolutions, however, do not occur often, and are a result of serious problems of long duration; when they do occur, they are most frequently unsuccessful. The organization, therefore, like the one-party state, may appear to be in a state of political quiescence for long intervals. If the leadership is capable and is actually satisfying the needs of large sections of the membership, it may hold power indefinitely. In such a situation, however, the problem of sources of new leadership develops.

The International Typographical Union has established and maintained a functioning party system. It suffers from the reverse malady, if it be a malady, of too many aspirants for union office. The two parties in the union are engaged in a constant search, within the locals and at International conventions, to find and recruit to their party individuals who have political leadership ability. In their struggle to win and maintain office they are also on the lookout for issues which may be popular with the rank and file. This competition for office has made the officials of the union much more militant than any other corresponding group of A.F. of L. craft union leaders.

It should be realized that there is a basic strain between the democratic values of the trade union movement and the system of internal stratification that is inherent in the structure of a large organization. Union officials have moved up in the social structure by leaving the bench. Union office necessarily involves superior income, status, and power as compared with those of ordinary members. Parsons has suggested that no system of stratification can be linked completely to an achievement pattern. That is, a certain degree of ascriptive status is unavoidable in any social system. The status system of the trade union movement necessarily cannot develop a pattern of ascriptive status. A system of stratification which is based on achievement criteria alone will subject its high status members to the need at least to legitimate or make permanent their new high position during their lifetime. The assumptions implicit in democratic trade unionism, however, require the return of union leaders to their trade upon being defeated in elections. This would be equivalent to a system of stratification in which members of the upper classes customarily moved to the bottom after a few years at the top. It is fairly obvious that such a social structure could not exist for any length of time. An elite faced with the possibility of loss of position will, therefore, make strenuous efforts to preserve its status.

The last decade has witnessed a renewed interest in the problems of bureaucratic structure, or, synonomously, large-scale organization. The emergence of the bureaucratic pattern as the dominant organizational form of a large centralized industrial society has made many people despair of the possibility of democratic control of the bureaucrats. The current interest in the work of Robert Michels, as evidenced by the fact that two of his books were republished in the last year, appears to be related to the feeling among many persons that Michels was right, that large-scale social organization is inherently non-democratic. In evaluating the potentialities of large-scale social organization, the unique structure is as important as the nine hundred and ninety-nine which take another form. In a world in which large-scale social organization is becoming synonymous with control from the top, it is important to know that in at least one large trade union, a significant measure of democracy has existed for fifty years.

I would like to acknowledge with thanks the financial assistance of the Institute of Industrial Relations of the University of California and the Social Science Research Council. The data contained in this article and in a subsequent article, "Trade Unionism in the Printing Trades," to be published elsewhere, was gathered while I was a Research Associate of the Institute of Industrial Relations or using a grant from the Social Science Research Council. Further, at the present time a survey research study of the Typographical Union is being conducted under the auspices of the Bureau of Applied Social Research of Columbia University Council on Research in the Social Sciences. I am especially indebted for aid to Robert Raschen and Grant McConnell, Research Assistants in the Institute of Industrial Relations, University of California.

Unions and Union Leaders of Their Own Choosing

Clark Kerr

If freedom is defined as the absence of external restraint, then unions reduce freedom, for they restrain the worker in many ways. They help to establish formal wage structures, seniority rosters, work schedules, pace of output, and the pattern of occupational opportunities, all of which limit his freedom of choice. They decide when he shall strike and not strike. They are—and this is one of the essentials to an understanding of unionism—disciplinary agents within society. They add to the total network of discipline already surrounding the workers through the practices and rules of the employer. They too insist upon order and obedience. It is inherent in their very existence. Two bosses now grow where only one grew before.[1]

Some loss of freedom, however, is inevitable in an effective industrial system. It will occur, more or less, whether the system is run by the employers alone, by the state alone, or even by the unions alone. Industrial society requires many rules and reasonable conformity to these rules. There must be a wage structure, a work

[1]This is not to suggest that it is not often and perhaps almost always better to have two bosses rather than one, for the union boss may help liberate the worker from the unilateral rule of the employer boss; but the worker is still subject to a web of rules, and this web tends to be more thickly woven as a result of the presence of the union.

From Clark Kerr, Unions and Union Leaders of Their Own Choosing *(Santa Barbara: Center for the Study of Democratic Institutions, 1957). Reprinted with permission.*

schedule, and so forth, no matter who operates the system. This loss of freedom is one of the prices paid by man for the many benefits in income and leisure that can flow from industrial society. The challenge is that this price not be any higher than necessary. The issue lies in the "more or less." The loss of freedom of the industrial worker will be substantial, as compared with the self-employed farmer or craftsman, but it may be less rather than more; and unions can make it either less or more.

Union Democracy—Difficulties, Detriments, Virtues

Before we can determine how the reduction of freedom may be less rather than more, three introductory observations should be made:

1. Democracy in unions is inherently difficult to achieve. A union is variously expected to be at one and the same time—as Muste[2] pointed out long ago—an army, a business, and a town meeting. Unions have usually ended up by being a business, serving the members but sometimes with those members having little more influence over the conduct of the business than stockholders have over a corporation. Unions have sometimes ended up as an army and have justified it, as Lloyd Fisher once remarked, in the terms the Communists have used to justify their "people's democracy," by reference to "capitalist encirclement." Unions have almost never ended up as a town meeting.
2. A good deal more democracy exists in unions than these comments and most outside observation would indicate. The national unions are the most visible entities and they are usually the least subject to democratic pressures. But at the local level, in many unions, there are contested elections, substantial turnover of officers, and face-to-face relations between members and leaders—here is the least entrenched bureaucracy. Particularly at the shop level, the relationship between shop stewards and workers is a responsive one. This local level is usually the most important to the workers. This is where he lives and where his grievances are handled.
3. It is sometimes argued that unions need not or even should not be democratic. Different reasons are given for this conclusion. One line of argument is that unions have become largely functionless organizations and nobody really cares whether they are democratic or not. The state guarantees full employment and social security, and the employer has been seduced by human relations. Consequently, the worker has a job—often paid above the contract rate—a pension, and a friend, perhaps even a psychiatrist; and there is nothing for the union to do. Or, it is sometimes said, unions have become quasi-governmental bureaus. They help set minimum wages and schedules of hours, and they process grievances, as government bureaus sometimes do both here and abroad. Their work is largely routine and best handled in bureaucratic fashion; and so, again, why worry about democracy? Occasionally it is also said, unions

[2]A. J. Muste, "Factional Fights in Trade Unions," in *American Labor Dynamics* (New York: Harcourt, 1928).

function best if they are removed from the pressures of democratic life. They must respond to many pressures, not those of the membership alone but also the needs of the industry, the welfare of society, the concerns of other unions. They should take a longer view of events than the current membership is likely to take, for they are organizations with a continuing life. They will be more widely responsible to society and more businesslike in their operations if they are not subject to the demands and uncertainties of active democratic participation. The conclusion to this argument is that democracy causes internal and external strife and irresponsibility.

Each of these reasons has some point to it. Unions perform less of a function than they did two decades ago; their work has become more routine as pattern-following and grievance precedents have become established; and internal democracy can cause external trouble, particularly for employers.

But the case for democracy can still be persuasive. If democracy is a superior form of government, as most of us would insist, it should be preferred in practice wherever it is possible.

Second, the workers can have a more effective voice in industry if they have an effective voice in their unions; and they are more likely to be satisfied with society if they have a sense of participation.

Third, if the unions lose their responsiveness to the interests of the workers, an opportunity is created for other organized elements, more politically motivated, to move in to represent these interests, as has happened in certain European countries.

One-Party Government—The Union Case

The overwhelming majority of all the organizations of man throughout history have been ruled by one-party governments. Most of the time in most parts of the world all organizations have been under one-party rule. In certain parts of the world at certain times in history there have been a few two-party (or multi-party) organizations; but one-party rule is the standard and well-nigh universal case. The trade union is no exception. The International Typographical Union is the single deviant specimen on a national level in the United States.

Even in the democratic United States, the corporation, the political party, the fraternal order, the religious denomination, the farm organization, the welfare group, the student government, are all one-party organizations. Only in the public area, where it is by all odds the most essential, do we have two-party government.

The neglect of the one-party model of government, in view of its significance, is astounding. The rare instances of two-party and multi-party government have attracted most of the study. Certainly two-party government, as Lipset[3] has

[3]S. M. Lipset, M. Trow, and J. Coleman, *Union Democracy* (New York: Free Press, 1956).

persuasively argued, has much to recommend it. It provides criticism of the existing government, it makes ready an alternative government if the members want it, it reduces apathy, and does much else of value. But most men all of the time, and all men some of the time, function in one-party social organizations; and so do union members.

Why are unions one-party governments? There are several reasons. Partly, it is the requirement of unity in the face of external conflict. Partly, it is the control exercised by the leaders over the mechanism of the organization. But the answer lies much deeper than the fear of the enemy and the desires of the leaders. It is that there are no continuing conflicts except over ideology, and ideological conflicts tend to split unions rather than to create two-party systems within them. Witness the separate unions in several European countries and the split-off of Communist unions in the United States. Issues over wage increases, the handling of grievances, and so forth may lead to factions and leadership rivalry but not to two-party systems on a continuing basis.

Does one-party government mean that unions are inevitably "undemocratic"? If only two-party systems are really democratic, then the answer is obviously in the affirmative. But if organizations where the supreme power is retained by the members and which are reasonably responsive[4] to membership desires may be called "democratic," even in the absence of a two-party system, then unions may be and many are "democratic."

There are dangers in any one-party government,[5] but the system may serve its members well. It is most likely to do so, however, in the long run, if it is under the proper pressures. Traditionally, this pressure on trade-union government in the United States has come from four sources, all of them, unfortunately, now

[4]There are those, of course, who would argue that the proper test of an organization is not the degree of responsiveness to the needs of those involved, but rather the degree to which the persons involved actually and directly participate in the decision-making process. For them, only town-meeting democracy is fully satisfactory; and, given the nature of industrial society, their test can be met by very few consequential organizations. It should be noted that "responsiveness" is not only a different test from "participation" but is also different from the test of "performance." "Performance," in the sense of "bringing home the bacon," may be quite exceptional without, at the same time, having much connection with "responsiveness." "Performance" refers to results; "responsiveness," to the processes which connect leadership behavior with membership desires. Performance, however, may usually be expected to be superior in the long run where responsiveness exists; and this is one of the basic tenets of democratic thought. Perhaps it should also be noted that active participation, where it is possible, is often an effective means of assuring responsiveness but by no means guarantees such responsiveness; in fact, it can serve as a technique of control. The view taken here is that performance alone is not enough and that participation, as through a two-party system, is more than can be expected under the circumstances, and, consequently, that the appropriate test is responsiveness. Responsiveness rests on a minimum degree of participation and will yield, usually, a reasonable measure of performance.

[5]Particularly if there is no judicial protection against the use of arbitrary power, as is often the case. Due process can be as important as democratic assent to the leadership.

largely of historical importance only. In the passing of these four sources of pressure lies much of our current problem.

1. When union membership was more voluntary, leaders had to be responsive to the workers to get and retain members and this was an effective check on authority. As noted earlier, union membership is now, one way or another, often compulsory, the law notwithstanding; and it is likely to become more so. Union security, with all its other advantages, and leadership responsiveness tend to move in somewhat opposite directions; the voluntary sale and the forced sale lead to different behavior in any walk of life. This is not to support voluntary membership through the compulsion of the state for it seems neither possible in many situations nor, on balance, wise.

2. When dual unionism, now largely a relic, was an active force, it had somewhat the same impact as voluntary membership. Not individuals but groups could and did shift allegiance, and this acted as a check and balance. The idea of one union in one jurisdiction, however, is so firmly embedded in American union philosophy that dual unionism can exist only sporadically and temporarily.

3. The more or less permanent faction, stopping short of a second party but hovering in the wings ready to rush out on any appropriate occasion, was a check on the leadership in many unions. The old-line Socialists served this function for many years, but the New Deal and time brought their demise. The Catholic faction continues in a few unions, but usually only in those under left-wing control; otherwise there is little basis for a Catholic faction. There are few permanent factions today and fewer still in prospect.

4. The employer, particularly the recalcitrant employer, has historically been a check and balance on the union leadership. If the two organizations—the company and the union—appealing to the same constituency are in conflict, each will criticize the other and may even stand ready to try to destroy the other. But the day of fighting the unions is largely past, at least under conditions of full employment. The separation of interests between the leaders of the two organizations is decaying because industrial peace pays. Consequently, company pressure on most unions has been greatly reduced and in some instances has entirely disappeared.

Union Democracy—The Possibilities

With union membership increasingly compulsory, dual unionism declining, the permanent faction disappearing, and company opposition more rare, is there any hope for "democracy" or leadership responsiveness to membership interests in trade unions? There still is, for there are substitutes for these historical pressures. Six such possibilities will be suggested, with particular emphasis on the sixth.

1. Membership interest. Union memberships are traditionally apathetic except in some crisis, and very little can be done about it. Compulsory strike votes proved a farce in World War II and most bargaining issues cannot properly be put to membership vote. But some experiments might be undertaken with the polling of membership opinion, with advisory referenda, and even with the use of television as a way for leaders to reach members, who will seldom come to meetings.

2. *"Professional" leaders.* Much is written about management as a profession. Perhaps union leaders might also become professional in the sense that they might be specifically trained for their jobs and might develop an "ethic" to guide their conduct—an ethic which sets boundaries to their behavior. They might, like city managers, be specifically trained for their jobs and responsible to an elected governing board.

3. *A new faith for the union movement.* Certain leaders today, in unions where the last vestiges of active democracy disappeared long ago, still serve their members well because of their adherence to the "old faith" of the union movement. But the "old faith" attracts few new followers. It was a fighting faith that grew out of evil conditions for the workers and union-busting by the employers. The conditions which gave rise to it no longer exist in the United States, although they continue to a degree in England and Germany, where the "old faith" still sets standards for union leaders. The social reformer holds himself—and is held by his environment—to a higher code of conduct than the business leader of the business union who quickly takes on the coloration of the industry with which he deals. If its ethics are high, his will be also; if they are low, so are his. The business union is a segment of the business.

What might this new faith be? It cannot be "more, more, more and now." It cannot be a vision of class conflict. It might lie, as suggested later, in the development of unions as a liberating force in industrial society; and this might carry the union leader more into the intellectual and less into the business community.

4. *Local autonomy.* Local unions, by their inherent nature, clearly can provide more opportunities for democratic participation by the members than can national unions. Consequently, the more autonomy there is at the local level, the greater the democratic life of the union movement is likely to be. The big drop in democratic participation comes in the move from the one-plant to the multi-plant local or the district union. In the one-plant local, rival leaders can get known and be effective, issues can be discussed on a face-to-face basis, and democracy can be effective. In several European countries, for example, it is the local Works Council, with substantial powers, which arouses worker interest and participation. The multi-plant unit serves the interests of the entrenched leadership in a most emphatic way. The one-plant local with real authority is the most democratic entity in the trade-union movement. Considerable constitutional reform in most unions would be prerequisite to effective single-plant locals. Among other things, the institution of the "receivership" by regional and national officials would need to be curtailed.

5. Union decertification. It is certainly desirable to continue some mechanism through which members can exercise an option in favor of another union, or of no union at all. Such an option will rarely be employed but it should be available. If it is available and is used occasionally, it can act as a minor check and balance on union leadership.

6. Discharge through rebellion. The two-party system within unions, as we have seen, is an historical oddity. The regularly contested election is a rarity. Yet union officials do get changed other than as a result of death or retirement. Union officials are, in effect, "hired" by the membership for the duration of their good behavior, as tested imprecisely by the membership. The trouble comes when they need to be "fired." The mechanism then is a contested election in which the old leader is voted out of office. For such a contested election to take place two prerequisites are necessary: *(1)* It must be possible for a faction to form and for its members to be reasonably free from retaliation through the operation of an impartial judicial process; and *(2)* there must be secret elections at appropriate intervals. Other actors must be allowed to stand in the wings and be permitted to move on stage when the audience calls them. The dissatisfied individual and the antagonistic faction must be given an opportunity.

The term "competitive discharge" might be used in the sense that the leader is subject to constant evaluation by the members and is also subject to discharge through the process of electing a competitor who is free to appear when the conditions warrant.[6] In the two-party system, the question is as to the better person; in the "competitive discharge" case, it is whether the incumbent should be fired or not.[7] Deposed union leaders usually feel—and they are right—that they have been fired, not that they have been defeated. Among other things, they almost never seek election again once they have been discharged. They are like the old bull in the buffalo herd brought to his knees by the young challenger.

[6]In one major Icelandic union, for example, this principle is explicitly recognized, rather than camouflaged. The incumbent officers are automatically reelected at each "contract reopening period" (if the stated election time may be so designated), unless a certain number of members petition for the placing of an opposition slate on the ballot, in which event a contested election is conducted. More common practice in the United States is to go through the formality of an election each time, but an opposition candidate will appear and the election will be contested usually only if the incumbent is in an unfavorable position.

[7]Such a question is most likely to be raised in an urgent fashion at the time of a "crisis" (a strike, an attack by a rival union, an unsuccessful wage negotiation, the disclosure of misuse of funds, etc.). Such crises hold within themselves the possibilities of constructive democratic action, if a minimum of democratic machinery is available; otherwise an open revolt, usually taking the form of the organization of a rival union, is the only alternative, and a very difficult one. Unfortunately, under the "competitive discharge" system an ineffective leader can retain his position much longer (i.e., until a crisis creates the condition for his downfall) than he could under the competitive election system. The machinery which is used to handle the "competitive discharge" can, of course, also be employed to handle the problem of replacement after the death of a leader.

If trade-union democracy is defined as a system of government where the supreme power is largely retained by the members and can be exercised by them in an emergency at any and all levels, then the effective right of competitive discharge, by itself, is a sufficient basis for trade-union democracy. The essential feature of a trade-union constitution is whether it guarantees this right of competitive discharge. This is the most we can reasonably expect, and it is also probably enough. . . .

The Worker, the Union, the State

The title of this paper suggests that national policy might move from the "unions of their own choosing" of the 1930's to "union leaders of their own choosing" and even, to a degree, to "union rules of their own choosing." But how is this to be accomplished? Action by the unions themselves would be most desirable and there has been a surprising amount of it during the past year. Experience here and abroad, however, suggests it will not be sufficient, that behind the good intentions of most union leaders will need to stand the power of the law, as in the case of corporations in the past.

This is a troublesome issue. The pluralist will defend the private association from the control of the state. The individual, however, also needs defense against being controlled by the private government of the trade union, and ultimately this defense can be guaranteed only by the state. If the state is to interfere in the internal life of trade unions—as it does significantly already—then it is important that this interference be wisely conceived, for the power to control is the power to destroy. Unions should in no way be destroyed as independent power centers. Clyde Summers has recently suggested[8] four guide lines for such interference and each one seems worthy of consideration: *(1)* it should be minimal, *(2)* it should be segregated from laws on other matters, *(3)* it should encourage responsible self-regulation by the unions, and *(4)* it should be enforceable.

In this discussion of the impact of unions on the freedom of the workers, six aspects of the problem were particularly emphasized: local union autonomy, a new faith for the union movement, secret elections of officers, independent judicial processes, permissive rules on entry to the union and on movement within industry, and narrow limits to union functions. Four of these areas may lend themselves properly to legislation:

1. In Australia,[9] union members can, under certain circumstances, ask the state for the conduct of secret elections of officers.

[8]"Legislating Union Democracy," paper presented to annual meeting of the Industrial Relations Research Association, September 1957. See also comments by Dunlop, *op. cit.*, and in "The Public Interest in Internal Affairs of Unions" (1957).

[9]See L. S. Merrifield, "Regulation of Union Elections in Australia," *Industrial and Labor Relations Review* (January 1957).

2. Again in Australia and to an increasing extent in the United States, union members can appeal to the courts for protection against retaliation for internal political dissent. In this connection the private external review boards of the Upholsterer's Union and the United Automobile Workers are a most interesting device, paralleling private arbitration of grievances against companies.[10]

3. Protection from discrimination in getting into a union, as well as in getting a job, is already provided in some states. Such provisions call for the open union instead of the open shop.

4. Prohibition of compulsory political contributions is now provided in both the United States and Great Britain.

Adequate legislation in these four areas would assure a reasonable degree of democracy and of individual freedom. Beyond what the law might require, many unions have provided and may provide considerably more democratic life and individual liberty. The Ethical Practices Committee of the AFL-CIO has made a substantial contribution in these directions.

The trade unions are going through a period of crisis. This crisis originates as much from self-examination by labor leaders as from the more obvious external criticisms. Out of this crisis may well come more representative government within unions and more rights for the individual worker. Since unions are an important element in our pluralistic society, their effective functioning is a contribution to the national welfare. As an element of a democratic society, they should be responsive to their members. As an element of a society founded on the significance of the individual, they should contribute to his freedom. "More, more, more and now" is no longer enough.

[10]The encouragement of the establishment of such private judicial processes better fits a pluralistic society with its independent power centers than the institution of a public labor court approach, as in Germany.

Cross-Pressures and Attitudes: A Study of the Influence of Conflicting Propaganda on Opinions regarding American-Soviet Relations

Martin Kriesberg

In recent years, organized pressure groups have increasingly concerned themselves with activities designed to influence public opinion. Public relations budgets of many organizations have been increased; groups hitherto confining their activities to informing their membership have taken to mass media; "institutional" and "ideological" advertising appear more and more frequently in newspapers and magazines. America is characterized by considerable freedom for the political propagandist and by consummate skill in promotional campaigns.

These attributes of our society raise problems in public opinion analysis which merit serious study. One such problem is the effect which conflicting propaganda has upon people's attitudes. In the face of conflicting propaganda will people's opinions be more or less moderate? Will the individual become more interested and better informed on the issue, or less so?

The following study,[1] designed to investigate these questions in connection with attitudes on American foreign policy, suggests these conclusions:

First, in an environment where people are exposed to contending propaganda regarding issues of foreign policy, relatively few individuals are aware of the conflicting interpretations to which they are exposed. Most of the people do not know that they are subjected to conflicting propaganda, and many, consciously or unconsciously, avoid continued exposure to the contradictory influences.

[1]A Social Science Research Council pre-doctoral fellowship facilitated this research; the writer is especially grateful to Dr. Samuel S. Stouffer for his invaluable criticism during the conduct of the study.

Martin Kriesberg, "Cross-Pressures and Attitudes: A Study of the Influence of Conflicting Propaganda on Opinions regarding American-Soviet Relations," Public Opinion Quarterly, *Vol. 12 (1949). Reprinted with permission.*

Second, those who remain exposed to conflicting propaganda on a foreign policy issue are more moderate in their opinions, but moderation is manifested in various ways, according to the individual's interest and information on the subject. The unconcerned and the uninformed tend to be unaware that they are exposed to conflicting influences; their attitudes tend toward uncertainty and inconsistency. The interested and the informed tend to be aware of conflicting influences and to consciously select one point of view, while rationalizing their rejection of the others. However, although these individuals give greater credence to one body of propaganda than the other, their resultant opinions are more moderate than those of people not in a conflict situation.

Third, those who remain exposed to strong cross-pressures appear to be less interested in the controversial foreign policy issue than those primarily subject to one or the other influence. The effect of conflicting propaganda upon levels of information could not be ascertained.

The Research Design

Creating a research design which would reveal the effect of conflicting influences upon attitudes is complicated by the multiplicity of variables affecting opinions. The problem is somewhat simplified by constructing a study around those determinate influences which, in a given situation, are likely to have a decided effect upon attitudes, as for instance the factor of race on opinions about anti-lynching legislation. This suggests that one might begin with a particular issue and work back to specific factors or forces which are likely to affect opinions on that issue. Then, by selecting those forces which are in conflict regarding the issue and by locating an environment in which these forces are operative, the effect of cross-pressures may more readily be ascertained.

With this approach in mind, the subject of American-Soviet relations was selected for study as one of intrinsic interest and importance and one upon which determinate forces were likely to have a decided influence. Two polar opinion groups which exercise conflicting influences on opinions about American-Soviet relations immediately came to mind: the Catholic Church and the Communist Party. Having arrived at this juncture, the problem was to locate people who were subject simultaneously to the influence of the Church and the Party.

Investigation of various geographic and social groupings led to the search for a trade union population in which Catholic and Communist influences might be evidenced.[2] Both organizations were known to participate actively in certain trade unions and, taking unequivocal stands on the subject of American-Soviet relations, both were likely to urge their views upon union members.

[2]Conceivably, the use of campus groups in experimental settings might have permitted control over more variables, but a study among men and women in a real, not artificial, setting was deemed preferable since it might permit broader generalizations.

A trade union was located which seemed to meet the research prerequisites. The probability of conflicting influences was high, since more than 65 per cent of the group were Catholics and a number of the union's local officers and rank and file admitted to Communist Party membership. Moreover, the trade union was reputed, in union circles, to be Communist led at the national level. The survey took place in an eastern city with a large Catholic population. During the period of the study, 1946, the secular press in the area tended to reenforce the Church viewpoint on American-Soviet relations. At the same time, rank and file members of the union were not only exposed to union members purveying the Party viewpoint but also to the union newspaper. This newspaper, mailed weekly to every member of the union, closely followed the line of the *Daily Worker* on the subject of American-Soviet relations.

After a population which was apparently exposed to conflicting influences had been selected, the cooperation of union officials and rank and file was solicited. In every local, cordial relations were established.

Pretest interviews were first made among members of two other trade unions and one local of the union population studied. The pilot survey was designed to test the questionnaire and the manner of interviewing to be employed. As a result of the pretest, it was decided to conduct interviews at union meetings, since interviewing the workers at home or in the shop proved to have several shortcomings. Of these, the most important for purposes of this study was that only a small proportion of those interviewed at home or at the shop came to union meetings or read their union newspaper. It appeared that people who did not come to meetings and did not read the union paper were less likely to be exposed to the Party point of view—one of the two conflicting influences.[3]

Before each meeting, the author was introduced to the membership by the local business agent or presiding officer. The author would then indicate the nature of the study and solicit cooperation. The introduction pointed out the nature of the study: a public opinion poll among working people to learn their views on foreign affairs. At the conclusion of these brief remarks, the author introduced an assistant interviewer and informed the membership that he and his assistant would pass among them soliciting interviews.[4]

Respondents were asked to accompany the interviewer to a convenient place in the rear of the meeting hall or to an adjoining room; almost none were reticent in responding. While a standard questionnaire was used, interviewers were

[3]It was important to weight the possibilities of exposure to Party propaganda since it early became evident that, compared to the Church, the Party's influence was considerably less pervasive. (Cf. p. 10.)

[4]Because of the meeting environment it was deemed advisable to utilize the help of only one assistant; the author was present at each meeting; several assistants alternated.

instructed to use probes extensively. Each local was visited several times until approximately 10 per cent of the number usually present had been interviewed. In all, 103 interviews were made from the six locals included in the analysis.[5]

Few Respondents Aware of Cross-Pressures

Perhaps the most important finding in this study of cross-pressures is the small number of individuals who evidenced awareness of conflicting influences. While all those interviewed were subject to some degree of conflicting propaganda and one-fourth could be classified as subject to "strong" cross-influences (see footnote 9) only a handful indicated that they were conscious of the contending influences.

Three probable reasons for widespread unawareness may be advanced: (1) Opinions are functional and the process of individual adjustment to conflict situations operates against acceptance of both Catholic and Communist viewpoints; (2) a large proportion of those interviewed lacked interest in issues of foreign policy and therefore both sets of propaganda were ineffectual; (3) the Communist propaganda was operative in an "inhibitive" context and even in the selective population studied was relatively weak compared to the Catholic.[6]

Opinions, like group membership, are functional; they are part of the individual's social and psychological adjustment.[7] From his earliest years the individual learns that certain opinions bring social approbation; others bring disapproval. He learns that certain opinions are approved by some people and disapproved by others. Opinions serve to rationalize social and physical environments. One individual believes that success accrues to hard work and frugality, another that it depends on luck and "drag." Both views help give meaning to a given situation, such as the individual's position in society. The body of beliefs which make up Catholicism and Communism, the cross-influences involved in this study, tend to be mutually exclusive means to comparable end satisfactions. In terms of psychological satisfaction, the two systems may be viewed as similarly authoritarian, similarly offering an integrated explanation of the individual's world, and offering similar satisfactions as a faith larger than the individual.

[5]Although the number of respondents is small and the issue upon which they were interviewed complex, the homogeneity of the population surveyed and the crystallization of opinion on the subject polled increase the reliability of the findings. Nevertheless, care should be exercised in applying the generalizations to other populations.

[6]While the relative weakness of the Communist influence may be viewed as a shortcoming of the study, it is a matter of relative strength only; the Party line was available to every respondent.

[7]See the discussion by M. B. Smith, "The Personal Setting of Public Opinions," *Public Opinion Quarterly,* Vol. 2, No. 4; also M. B. Smith, J. S. Bruner, and R. W. White, "Dynamics and Measurements of Opinion," *International Journal of Opinion and Attitude Research,* Vol. 1, No. 1 (1947); see further the studies by T. M. Newcomb, "Community Roles in Attitude Formation," *American Sociological Review* (October, 1942).

The functional nature of opinion suggests that cross-pressures are likely to be avoided.[8] Among the respondents there was a tendency to change either their beliefs or their allegiance and thereby to resolve the conflict. Catholics who most nearly reflected the opinions of the Left tended to draw away from the religious fold. Several of the men in this category remarked that while their wives or their families went to church, they did not; others reported that the Church was biased or should stay out of politics. It is also likely that a number of those interviewed, having been perturbed by the conflicting influences, had achieved a resolution of the difficulty by rejecting the subject of American-Soviet relations, as well as, or together with, the contestants.

Another means of avoiding conflicting influences, and a second factor making for relatively few cases in which cross-pressures were felt, is lack of interest in the issue involved. Apathy about foreign affairs was manifested by many respondents, and suggests that arguments presented by the Left frequently fell on non-absorbent minds; Church pronouncements on the subject probably met with similar disinterest. Therefore neither contradictions nor conflicts were perceived. Closely related to lack of interest, and perhaps causally related, is lack of information by which to evaluate arguments of either Church or Party. Inability to see the relationship between conflicting arguments or their relevance for the individual further militates against their having a serious effect upon him. This was particularly the case among women in the population studied. On the one hand, the Church had a greater influence upon their opinions than it did on the views of their menfolk. On the other hand, the women interviewed were generally members of locals where the Left influence was strongest. Despite this environment of cross-pressures, few women interviewed were conscious of conflicting influences.

A third factor making for a paucity of cross-pressure consciousness was the "inhibitive" context in which the Party line was conveyed and perceived. Despite the selective nature of the population studied, Communist propaganda was less pervasive than that of the Church. The Left influence was retarded by the status of its purveyors in relation to other sources of information. Opinions presented by most fellow workers tended to be discounted when opposed by the more widely accepted authority of Church or of secular commentators and columnists. Time and again respondents reported that none of the men in the shop or union were better informed on Russia than they. Nor did the rank and file ascribe superior knowledge to the union leadership; to most respondents, they were merely fellow workers. Moreover, ideas presented by the Church, the secular city press, and the national mass media tended to reinforce one another, thereby increasing

[8]A number of studies have been conducted illustrating the process whereby individuals avoid propaganda which conflicts with preconceived ideas. See for example M. Jahoda and E. Cooper, "Evasion of Propaganda: How Prejudiced People Respond to Anti-Prejudice Propaganda," *Journal of Psychology,* Vol. 23 (1947), pp. 15-25.

the disparity in weight between the views of the Left and of the prevailing environmental ideology.

The Left was further handicapped because its protagonists were occasionally tagged "Communist." Opinions advanced by men so labelled were discredited or derided by many of the workers interviewed. Moreover, formal discussion of Russia was usually avoided at union meetings. Where pro-Party men were in power, Communists were content to remain incognito and preferred not to raise "disruptive" issues. Where anti-Party men were in office, issues related to Russia were generally considered outside the pale of union activities.

Effect of Interest and Information on Opinions under Cross-Pressures

What were the reactions of those people who, despite the inhibitive context of Communist propaganda and the individual tendency to avoid cross-pressure situations, were subject to strong conflicting influence of Party and Church?[9] As might be expected, strong cross-pressures made for moderation of opinions but, significantly, moderateness was manifested differently according to the respondent's interest and information on American-Soviet relations. Among respondents who were unconcerned and uninformed, there was unawareness of conflict and moderateness was manifested by uncertainty and inconsistency. In the long run, these people might be expected to withdraw from both influences and to move toward general apathy on the issue.[10]

None of the respondents subject to strong cross-pressures were vehemently anti-Soviet or doctrinaire pro-Soviets.[11] This moderation was probably the result of several contributing factors. First, such cross-pressures occurred among individuals who were open to influence by both sides. When the individual dogmatically adhered to one viewpoint he was not likely to listen to propaganda for the other. Second, the individual was categorized as subject to strong cross-pressures only

[9]Twenty-three of those interviewed were classified as subject to strong cross-pressures. Catholic influence was assumed to be strong when the respondent regularly attended Church, frequently read Church publications, and was not antipathetical to Church teachings. Communist influence was assumed to be strong where the respondent regularly read the trade-union paper and regularly attended locals where at least two people interviewed in the local reported talking to a "party line" member on the subject. (A "party line" member was one whose responses to the schedule were highly similar to those who admitted Communist affiliation.) To be classified as subject to strong cross-pressure, the respondent had to meet all the above criteria.

[10]The discussion in this section is based upon the twenty-three respondents who were subject to "strong" cross-pressures at the time interviewed. It should be noted that these individuals, continuing to expose themselves to conflicting influences, might be somehow different from the others by the very fact of continued exposure. A panel study might have thrown light on the question of whether they had elected to remain exposed to contending propagandas or had not yet made a resolution of the conflict.

[11]A measure of pro- and anti-Soviet feeling was derived from answers to five questions covering various aspects of American-Soviet relations. Those whose views consistently paralleled Party members' views were categorized "pro"; those taking consistently opposite viewpoints, "anti"; and those taking neither of the polar opinions, "moderate."

if he had been exposed to considerable influence from both sides. Finally, many respondents subject to cross-pressures were worried about American-Soviet tension. For some of these, anxiety was related to a desire to see Russia in a more friendly light.

While cross-pressures tended to induce moderation, this absence of polar opinions was manifested differently according to the respondent's interest in and information on American-Soviet relations.[12] Among the more interested and informed respondents there was a recognition of the conflicting views to which they were exposed; they were aware of both Catholic and Communist ideologies. While recognizing the opposite view, they consciously accepted one in preference to the other. The positions of these respondents were frequently well structured; their views were consistent and often cogently expressed.

Among the respondents who were interested in American-Soviet relations, cross-pressures also tended to induce skepticism of information sources. For example, among informed respondents who were subject to strong cross-pressures there was a tendency to believe that both Church and union reports were slanted. For them either the secular press was a poor best choice or they trusted none of the three sources.

Among the less interested and the less well informed, moderateness was manifested by uncertainty and inconsistency. The number of "don't know" and "no opinion" responses increased in inverse proportion to the level of interest and information. Frequently respondents who were little interested and poorly informed indicated that they were uncertain of the position they took or the "correctness" of their opinion. However, they were less skeptical of the honesty of their information sources. Unfamiliar with world affairs generally, these respondents were uncritical of the information they received. They were often inconsistent in their views, reporting undigested phrases of both Party and Church ideologies. For example, they would favor international control of the atomic bomb and yet want the United States to have a preponderant voice in the UN; they would state that the Communist Party was controlled by Russia but was not a threat, or vice versa.

[12]Level of information was based upon responses to the question "Identify: Byrnes, Molotov, Bevin, Gromyko, and Bedell Smith." Owing to the small number of cases, only a two-place scale was used; respondents making fewer than 3 correct identifications were considered the less well-informed, those recognizing 3 or more correctly, the better informed.

Level of interest was based upon responses to the questions "Do you talk about world affairs, things like America's relations with Russia?" If yes, "At home? At work? At union meetings? Elsewhere?" Respondents who did not talk about world affairs or who cited only one place as the scene of conversations were classified as the less articulate and those who discussed the subject in two or more places as the more articulate.

There was a positive correlation between the two measures; those who scored high in the information measure also scored high in the articulation measure and vice versa. Accordingly, for purposes of discussion, these two measures will be considered indices of a single characteristic.

This lack of structured opinions on foreign policy issues may be contrasted to attitudes on election issues. For a great many people the social mores of their community or their group affiliation makes voting more or less mandatory. The individual is pressed to decide between alternative views in order to offer some rationalization for his vote decision.[13] However, for most people there is no equivalent social compulsion impelling decisions on foreign policy issues. It is socially acceptable to throw up one's hands at the complexities of America's international relations. While people frequently apologize for not voting, they readily admit their ignorance and indecision on foreign policy issues.

Exposure to Cross-Pressures Associated with Reduced Interest

What is the relationship between cross-pressures and information and interest? Are cross-pressures associated with increased interest owing to the suggestion of conflict which makes the issue exciting—or with reduced interest and an expedient adjustment to a difficult decision situation? While the findings are not conclusive, the evidence does suggest that continued exposure to cross-pressures and reduced interest in the issue are correlated.

The assertion that cross-pressures are associated with reduced interest is supported by responses to a question on the importance of American-Soviet policies in influencing voting behavior. Among respondents who were subject to strong cross-pressures, America's Soviet policy was a less important vote determinant than among people primarily subject to only one propaganda. This suggests that respondents subject to strong cross-pressures of Party and Church were less concerned and less interested in the issue of Soviet relations. These people also tended to be less certain of the relative importance of policy toward Russia versus domestic policy as a factor affecting their vote; a larger proportion of them answered the question with "don't know." The evidence apparently confirms Paul Lazarsfeld's finding that cross-pressures tend to reduce interest in election issues.[14]

Although people who remained exposed to cross-pressures were less concerned over U.S. policy toward Soviet Russia, they appeared to be better informed and more prone to discuss the subject than those primarily influenced by the Church. People who were primarily subject to Church influence scored lower on the information and articulation scale than those who were at the same time subject to Communist influence. Indeed, levels of information and articulation were both positively correlated with exposure to Left propaganda.

The fact that respondents who were subject to both influences made higher information scores than those who were primarily influenced by one contestant

[13]Sheldon Korchin, *Psychological Variables in the Behavior of Voters,* Harvard Ph.D. thesis (1946), argues that voting is a social experience and the vote decision is affected by the desire to find meaning in that social situation.

[14]Cf. *The People's Choice* (New York: Columbia Univ. Press, 1948).

may, however, be explained as an artifact of the criteria used in categorizing the individual as subject to strong conflicting influences. One of the criteria of strong influence by Church or Party was that the individual regularly read their respective publications, and readership of the partisan periodicals was highly correlated with wide press and periodical readership generally. Furthermore, respondents under cross-pressures tended to be more concerned with foreign affairs generally than those subject to a single preponderant influence. These factors, suggesting greater familiarity with the subject, may also explain the higher articulation scores made by respondents under strong cross-pressures over those primarily under Church influence. Since the higher information scores made by cross-pressure respondents may be an artifact, the relationship between cross-pressures and information is not illuminated by the data.

Possible Political Implications

If the findings of this study may be generalized, the political implications are noteworthy. It has been said that a prerequisite of an informed public opinion on foreign relations is "competing analyses" of the world situation and of America's role in world affairs.[15] It has also been asserted that the answer to certain evils of pressure group propaganda is more propaganda. These arguments are well taken; a multiplicity of viewpoints is essential for an enlightened public opinion. This study suggests, however, that an informed public opinion cannot be left entirely in the hands of interests competing for public acceptance of their particular views. Unless the people have a framework of information in which the arguments may be set, conflicting propaganda may lead to confusion rather than clarification, and may not be conducive to a more enlightened public opinion.

In the first place, the bulk of the people are likely to be unaware of, and unable to differentiate between, conflicting propagandas on foreign policy issues. They may assimilate views of contending interests without being aware of the source or significance of the ideas suggested. Such absorption of information would seem to contribute little toward an enlightened public opinion.

Secondly, people are prone to avoid the conflict of contending propagandas by rejecting one of the contestants or by withdrawing their attention from the contest. The study produced no conclusive evidence that exposure to conflicting opinions makes people better informed, though it presents some evidence that they become less interested in the contested issue. Moreover, if, as seems likely, the uninformed and uninterested tend to avoid the conflict situation by withdrawing attention from the issue, this point takes on special importance because so many Americans lack information and interest in the nation's foreign policies.[16]

[15]See, for example, Leonard S. Cottrell, Jr., and Sylvia Eberhart, *American Opinion on World Affairs in the Atomic Age* (Princeton, N.J.: Princeton Univ. Press, 1948), Ch. 6.

[16]*Ibid.* See also Martin Kriesberg, "Areas of Ignorance," *Public Opinion and Foreign Policy*, ed. Lester Markel (New York: Harper, 1949).

Third, although continued exposure to conflicting propaganda apparently makes for moderation of opinion, such moderation is more likely to be a manifestation of confusion and contradiction than the result of a careful weighing of the different viewpoints. Exposure to conflicting influences may not lead to further polarization of opinions, but without an underpinning of interest and basic information it may not mean a more considered opinion at any particular point on an attitude scale.

Suggestions for Further Research

The effect of cross-pressures upon political attitudes may be studied apart from omnibus national surveys on political behavior. Representative samples of national or community populations are not essential when the hypotheses to be tested are not related to such populations. Instead, small, relatively inexpensive studies may be designed around those groupings which are included in the hypotheses. However, special care is necessary to integrate the small study with related experiments and research programs in order to maximize its contribution.

A study of cross-pressures may be concerned with different levels or kinds of conflicting forces. The study reported here dealt with rather obvious influences, namely, propaganda by specific organizations. The analysis might well be carried on at other levels, e.g., cross-pressures of family group vs. friendship group, work affiliations vs. religious affiliations, personal influences vs. nonpersonal influences. Such an analysis could probably be accomplished by more intensive interviewing and by relating the respondents' opinions to those expressed by the groups with which they are associated. This information would help to establish a rough hierarchy of group influence and to throw light on the broader question of how different group affiliations affect opinion formation.

In designing research to study the influence of cross-pressures it would be profitable to use a longitudinal approach, i.e., to interview the same people over a period of time. This would facilitate an appraisal of the impact made by each body of propaganda or other source of pressure. A study over time would also aid in analyzing the metamorphosis of attitudes when subject to cross-pressures; factors which influence the direction as well as incidence of change could be explored.

To maximize the value of the research, the attitudes assayed should be related to actions such as voting, attending political rallies, or writing members of Congress. A study on action-oriented attitudes is not only more significant politically but facilitates measuring the activating or inhibiting effect of cross-pressures. Where attitudes may be channelized into socially prescribed courses of action, people are more likely to react to their cross-pressure environment in a way permitting measurement.

Political thinking and action are group phenomena, and the importance of group activities in the political life of the nation has not declined but has increased since Pendleton Herring's study stimulated research in the field of pressure groups and politics.[17] There is need for additional research in this area, particularly on pressure group influence upon the political opinions of its members and the public generally. Such studies, drawing upon the instruments and insights of psychologists and sociologists as well as political scientists, would redound to the benefit of the several disciplines.

[17]Pendleton Herring, *Group Representation before Congress* (Baltimore: Johns Hopkins Univ. Press, 1928).

Attitude Consensus and Conflict in an Interest Group: An Assessment of Cohesion

Norman R. Luttbeg
Harmon Zeigler

In America, interest groups operate within the democratic frame of reference. Like all political organizations, they are accorded more legitimacy when they can show that they are representative of the attitudes and values of a particular segment of the population. Consequently, the leaders of interest groups frequently spend a great deal of time explaining just how democratic their organizations are. If one examines the testimony of interest group leaders at state and national legislative hearings, he is likely to find that much of it is begun with an introductory statement explaining that the leadership of the testifying group is merely the voice of the membership. The personal values of the interest group leader are played down, and his function as representative (as distinguished from delegate) is exaggerated.

On the other hand, relatively few political interest groups have systematic and formalized means of ascertaining the desires of members. We know that most of the devices used to solicit member opinion are not very effective. Truman has

Norman R. Luttbeg and Harmon Zeigler, "Attitude Consensus and Conflict in an Interest Group: An Assessment of Cohesion," American Political Science Review, *Vol. 40 (1966).*

shown that the affairs of most interest groups are run on a day-to-day basis by a fraction of the total membership. The mass of the membership takes a relatively passive role with regard to the formation of public policies by the organization.[1]

Communication between leaders and followers is spasmodic and cannot provide efficient guidelines for the actions of leaders. Whether or not leadership of an organization seeks to become a manifestation of Michels' iron law of oligarchy, the realities of communication within an organization suggest that most of the communication undertaken by leaders will be with other members of the leadership clique rather than with the larger body of followers in the group.

This situation is not necessarily dysfunctional for the organization. By many criteria the leader's decision is superior to that of the average member. Leaders have more time to give to matters of special concern to the organization. The information on which they make their decisions is likely to be more extensive than that of the average member, and they are likely to be more cognizant of the long-term impact of a particular decision. Unlike the average member, however, the leader's decision is complicated by his need to consider the extra-group and intra-group impact of his various alternative decisions and actions.

In the area of extra-group considerations, he must estimate the probable responses of other actors in the political process and the effect of these responses upon the chances of achieving a desired goal, assuming that he does not possess all capabilities of realizing this goal himself. Concerning intra-group considerations he must consider how the followers will respond to a decision. Will they be aware of it? Do they care about the alternatives, and if so, how will they respond to a decision which is contrary to their desires?

Even in the absence of efficient consultative mechanisms, leaders and followers exist in a functional relationship.[2] That is to say, leaders are limited by the followers' expressed or latent values and expectations. Regardless of the efficiency of corrective mechanisms and apart from how extensive the violation of the followers' values must be before the corrective mechanism comes into play, the leader's position is less secure if he fails to satisfy the followers. If another leader is vying with him for the followers' support, the implications of failing to satisfy the followers are even more threatening. In a political interest group, the functional relationship of leaders to followers is keyed to the necessity for cohesion as a weapon in extra-group competition. The actuality or at least the appearance of unity is essential.[3]

Assuming that the leader desires to maintain an extra-group competitive position, he will therefore undertake efforts toward the fostering of intra-group cohesion.

[1]David B. Truman, *The Governmental Process* (New York: Knopf, 1951), pp. 129-139.

[2]William Haythorn *et al.*, "The Effects of Varying Combinations of Authoritarian and Equalitarian Leaders and Followers," *Journal of Abnormal and Social Psychology*, Vol. 53 (September 1956), pp. 210-219.

[3]Truman, *op. cit.*, pp. 167-187.

In a voluntary organization, one of the prime requisites for this cohesion is the extent to which the membership is satisfied with the performance of leaders.[4] There are three ways in which a leader may satisfy the desires of an organization's membership. First, he may unconsciously act consistently with their desires. For example, he may decide to act on the basis of his evaluation of extra-group factors in such a way that the membership will be entirely satisfied. Second, he may respond entirely in terms of his personal attitudes and beliefs and, because he so accurately reflects the attitudes of his membership, again satisfy their desires. Third, a leader may consciously seek to do what he believes the membership of the organization desires. His success in satisfying the membership by this effort is dependent upon the accuracy of his perceptions of their attitudes and expectations.

Research Design

In this paper we examine the latter two dynamics by which leaders can satisfy members. Our data were gathered from the membership of the Oregon Education Association. Three sets of information were collected: the beliefs and attitudes of the members of the Association, the beliefs and attitudes of the leaders of the Association, and the perception of the attitudes of the members as held by the leaders. The analysis consists of comparing these three sets of information and noting changes in their interrelationships on different attitudes. The nature of the analysis is illustrated by Figure 1.

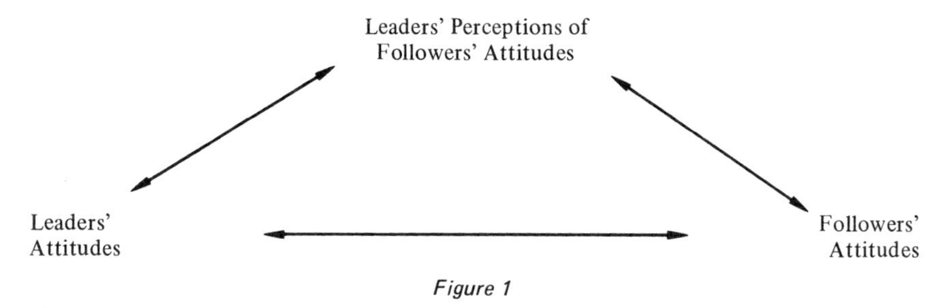

Figure 1

The sample of group members used in this study is a clustered stratified random sample of 803 high school teachers. This represents 14% of the high school teachers in Oregon.[5]

The sample of leaders includes all nine of the OEA's top administrative officials. These are the members of the executive staff, which is employed by the organization's Board of Trustees. Its official responsibility is to implement the

[4]Herbert Simon, *Administrative Behavior* (New York: Macmillan, 1957), pp. 110-122.

[5]Attitudes were assessed by personal interviews. There were 91 teachers in the original sample with whom interviews were not completed.

policies of the Representative Council, which consists of 200 representatives elected by local teachers' organizations. The Representative Council is the official policy-making body of the Association. However, both the Representative Council, which meets only once a year, and the Board of Trustees, which is supposed to deal with the specifics of the council's directives, are part-time functions. Thus, the permanent administrative staff is often forced to act in areas in which directives are vague or nonexistent. As is frequently the case in formal organizations, therefore, the permanent administrative staff has great flexibility and is a major delineator of policy.

In interviewing the leaders, we used a majority of the questions included in the teachers' interview schedule. Certain modifications in wording were made to allow for differences in organizational position. Leaders were first asked to answer the questions in terms of their own attitudes. They were then asked to take the point of view of the "average teacher" answering the same questions as they thought the "average teacher" would answer them. Only one of the leaders displayed any difficulty in assuming this attitude perspective; he had difficulty in keeping from answering questions in terms of what the teachers *should* believe rather than what he thought they actually *did* believe. The little difficulty the leaders experienced in answering these questions is evidence that the distinction between personal attitudes and the attitudes of the membership is a meaningful one for them.

These three sets of attitudes (teachers' attitudes, leaders' attitudes, and leaders' perceptions of teachers' attitudes) are studied in four attitudinal contexts. They are:

1. Mandates for organizational action
2. Expectations and satisfaction with the direction of leadership behavior
3. Abstract political values
4. Norms of teachers' political participation

The mandates for organizational action consist of two parts: expectations of behavior on the part of leaders themselves and expectations of action undertaken by teachers' organizations. In both cases, the satisfaction of the members with a particular action is dependent upon a congruence of the attitudes of the leaders with the actual attitudes of the followers.

Attitudes related to satisfaction with the direction of leadership are concerned with three of the Oregon Education Association's most strenuous activities: efforts toward salary improvement, efforts to raise teacher standards and accreditation, and efforts toward the establishment of a state sales tax with the revenues going to the public schools.

Abstract political values describe a set of attitudes, many of which are clichés often used by persons to persuade others to accept their position. They represent the basic "truths" of both the conservative and liberal points of view. A leader perceiving the membership as adhering to conservative values is ascribing conservatism to the membership and at the same time indicating that he believes an argument for action based upon these values would draw support from the membership.

The attitudes dealing with teachers' political participation concerned a broad set of politically related activities which might be undertaken by teachers in the classroom or during leisure time. The leadership's ability to satisfy members in this regard will be reflected in their efforts or lack of efforts to support teachers in trouble in their local communities for various political activities and in the formal or informal articulation of a professional ethic with respect to these activities.

Although it would be possible to analyze these data using contingency tables, the existence of 50 attitude items and three comparisons for each item would tax the reader's ability to follow the analysis. A single measure which characterizes the relationship on each comparison of attitudes is therefore required. Although numerous measures of association and correlation were considered for this purpose, we settled upon Kendall's tau chi (τ_c).[6] This measure has its faults, the principal one being that its maximum value is dependent upon the marginals of the table. Our tables frequently have marginals of 803 and 9 (the N's of our two samples). Such great differences will yield a correlation of only .044 for a perfect relationship on a 2x2 table. Since we are more interested in finding a measure to characterize the comparison of attitude distributions of leaders and followers than in using the measure as a test of statistical significance, it was decided to rely upon a new measure, τ_c over τ_c maximum.

As we are using this measure in comparing the distributions of attitudes of leaders and followers, a high correlation would indicate a strong relationship between attitudes and the person holding them. That is to say, a high correlation would indicate that leaders hold attitudes different from those of the followers. The sign of the measure will indicate the direction of this difference. Notice that a correlation of .000 indicates that leaders share the attitudes of the followers or that the two sets of attitudes compared have the same distribution.

Some may inquire of the statistical significance of the findings. There are two problems with the application of statistical significance tests to these data. First,

[6]Our data justify the use of ordinal measures of association, but there are several characteristics of our data and properties of various measures of association which complicate the choice of such a measure. First, on some of the items only two responses are possible, while others are seven-point Likert scales. Thus, any measure which is sensitive to the shape of the contingency table from which it is computed will decrease the comparability of the data across items. A measure which reaches unity when only one cell is zero is also undesirable, as instances in which the leaders are in perfect agreement while the followers differ are common in our data. Such measures would be insensitive to the degree of followers' disagreement with the leaders. The final difficulty is that some measures are sensitive to the marginals of the contingency table. No measure was discovered which did not have at least one of the characteristics. See Hubert Blalock, *Social Statistics* (New York: McGraw-Hill, 1960), p. 323; and Leo A. Goodman and William H. Kruskal, "Measures of Association for Cross Classifications," *Journal of the American Statistical Association,* Vol. 49 (December 1954), p. 750.

one of the samples is not a sample at all but the universe of the administrative leaders of the Oregon Education Association. Thus, with no sampling error contributed by the leadership sample the comparing of leaders' and followers' attitudes does not necessitate as strong a relationship to achieve statistical significance as would be normally required. In the data comparing leaders' attitudes and their perceptions of followers' attitudes, clearly no statistical significance tests are applicable because the differences are real differences for the universe of leaders. Even if the leaders did constitute a sample, their small number places an unnecessarily strict requirement on the strength of the relationship necessary to achieve statistical significance.[7] In general, therefore, greater reliance is placed upon the consistency of a relationship within an attitude area rather than on the statistical significance of any one item. However, those single-item relationships which are significant are indicated by a small "s" in the tables (the Kruskal-Wallis test is used to test statistical significance).

Findings

Leaders' perceptions of their roles. Before comparing the three sets of attitudes contained in this study, some discussion should be made of the leaders' perceptions of their roles within the organization. We refer here to the extent to which leaders believe they should act primarily in accordance with their own personal values rather than trying to reflect the desires of those whom they lead. We are asking whether leaders believe they should be delegates or representatives.[8]

Two questions were included in the leaders' interview schedule dealing with the problem of whose attitudes should be acted upon, those of the leaders or those of the followers. In one question the leaders were offered a brief dialogue between two persons, one arguing that a leader must do as the members wish and the other arguing that the leader must do what he personally believes to be correct. The leader was given the opportunity of selecting the argument which he found most satisfactory. Only one leader answered that the membership's desires should rule. Five answered that the leader should do what he personally believes to be right, although they added the comment that they thought the problem would occur very infrequently. Three of the leaders said that if this problem could not be resolved the leader should resign.

[7]David Gold, "Some Problems in Generalizing Aggregate Associations," *American Behavioral Scientist,* Vol. 8 (December 1964), p. 18.

[8]The terms "delegate" and "representative" are borrowed from the literature on the legislative process, where they are applied to the role perceptions of legislators. Heinz Eulau presents three legislative role orientations in John C. Wahlke, Heinz Eulau, William Buchanan, and LeRoy C. Ferguson, *The Legislative System* (New York: Wiley, 1962), pp. 267-268. The "trustee" of Eulau's scheme has traditionally been described as a "delegate," while the "delegate" corresponds to "representative." These roles are the extremes, with "politico" falling somewhere between them.

The second question approached the problem from a slightly different angle and achieved very dissimilar results. The leaders were asked if they felt the organization should do pretty much what the average teacher wants, what the more influential teachers want, what the school administrators want, or what they themselves want. The "pretty much" phrase in the first alternative apparently was easier to accept than the wording in the other question, as five leaders chose this alternative. Two altered the second response to indicate that they believed they should do what the "more informed" teachers wanted while two indicated that they would prefer to do what they themselves thought best.

It would seem, therefore, that the leaders accept the maxim that they should do what the followers want, but they are also jealous of their autonomy to do what they think best. There appears to be a clear internalized conflict between the representative and delegate roles. Obviously the best of all possible worlds for the leaders would be perfect consensus between them and the members. In the absence of this consensus, they appear unable to reach a clear resolution of the conflict and to find a stable definition of their roles.

The leaders' acute awareness of the problem of communication with followers is indicated by a final question. Leaders were asked what policies of the Oregon Education Association they were most dissatisfied with. Seven volunteered the answer that the greatest problem was the OEA's failure to be true to the desires of its membership. Two of the leaders who gave this response explicitly criticized the administrative structure for not administering impartially the policy decisions of the Representative Council. It appears, therefore, that the representative nature of the organization is not only meaningful to leaders but is also potentially divisive of the leadership.

Expectations concerning organizational activity. The exact nature of this potential conflict within the organization will become clearer as we proceed to the analysis of the four attitude areas. We will first consider the mandates for organizational activity.

Table 1 presents the correlations for each of the attitude comparisons for each of the questions. In this, as in the tables which follow, the first column presents the objective attitudes, the "real world," and thus measures the extent of actual conflict. The second column shows the degree to which leaders are accurate in their perceptions of followers' attitudes, while the third column measures the extent of conflict as seen by the leaders. The negative sign of the correlation means that the bottom set of attitudes is more heavily weighted in the direction of believing that leaders of the organization *should* undertake a particular action. For example, in the first column a negative sign means that leaders believe more than the followers that they or the organization should undertake a given activity. In the second column the negative sign means that the leaders perceive the followers as being more in favor of undertaking

Table 1. Comparison of the Three Attitude Sets in the Area of Mandate for Actions by Leaders, Teachers' Organizations, and the OEA

Questions	Sets of Attitudes Compared		
	Followers' Attitudes vs. Leaders' Attitudes	Followers' Attitudes vs. Leaders' Perception of Followers' Attitudes	Leaders' Attitudes vs. Leaders' Perception of Followers' Attitudes
Leaders should:			
1. Fight attacks on educational principles and methods.	−.134	−.134	.000
2. Fight against dismissal of teachers.	−.073	−.073	.000
3. Defend teachers from public attacks from getting involved in controversial issues.	−.059	−.059	.000
4. Eliminate from staff political liberals.	+.284	+.061	−.222
5. Give helping hand to school board members coming up for election.	−.317(s)	+.211	+.528
Teachers' organizations should:			
6. Endorse political candidates.	−.419(s)	+.184	+.603
7. Take sides on public issues.	−.404(s)	+.221	+.625
OEA should:			
8. Endorse candidates in school elections.	−.387(s)	+.058	+.444
9. Try to influence legislation.	.000	.000	.000

a particular action than they actually are. The positive sign in the second column means that the followers are more in favor of undertaking a particular activity than the leaders believe them to be. A negative sign in the third column means that the leaders perceive the followers as more supportive of a particular activity than the leaders are. A positive sign in the third column indicates the reverse.

The table indicates that, with the single exception of eliminating from the OEA staff people believed to be politically extreme, the leaders are more inclined to favor the involvement of the organization in each of the actions presented. This is shown by the fact that in seven of the nine cases the signs of the first column are negative. The first three of these items are the more clearly "professional" of the set. They involve the traditional academic values of freedom of expression and the protection of teachers against hostile forces in the community. These are at best *quasi*-political activities. Yet even here the followers are more restrained than the leaders. Note that on the question of eliminating political liberals from the OEA staff the followers are more in favor of such action than are the leaders. However, it is true that the greatest discrepancy between followers' and leaders' attitudes occurs on those questions involving the more purely political aspects of the organization, such as endorsing political candidates, taking sides on public issues, and taking part in the electoral activities of school board members.

With regard to these political activities, the followers are much more restrained than they are concerning more purely educational activities. Granted that the distinction between quasi-political and political is arbitrary at best, the followers do appear to make it. Thus, they are much more inclined to support the activities of the OEA if it defends teachers against public attacks than they would be if the teachers' organization endorsed political candidates.

The glaring exception to the general reluctance of the teachers to support the OEA's political activities is on the question of lobbying. Here there is nearly perfect agreement between leaders and followers. Lobbying is perceived by teachers to be an absolutely legitimate function of the organization. Teachers, therefore, are making a distinction between legislative politics and electoral politics.[9] The Association is currently engaged in a vigorous lobbying program at the state legislative level. With regard to lobbying, it is interesting to notice that not only do the attitudes of the leaders and followers converge, but also the leaders perceive that the followers support the lobbying activities. This is indicated by the zero correlation in the second and third columns.

Notice also that with regard to the first three activities (fighting attacks on educational principles and methods, fighting against the dismissal of teachers, and defending teachers from public attacks) the leaders see *more* support among the teachers than actually exists. Since the leaders overestimate the enthusiasm of followers, they see a consensus which does not hold true in the "real world." Hence the perfect correlation in the third column between the leaders' attitudes and their perceptions of teachers' attitudes is based upon faulty perceptions. This is not true with regard to the consensus about lobbying.

It is in the more purely electoral activities of the organization that discrepancies occur. Notice that on questions five, six, seven, and eight, the negative signs of the first column become positive signs in the second column. This means that, whereas leaders are more likely to want to engage in the electoral activities than are followers, the leaders perceive the followers as far more hesitant than the followers actually are. Consequently, these electoral activities can be contrasted with the professional and lobbying activities. In these professional and lobbying activities, the third column indicates that the leaders see little or no discrepancy between their point of view and the point of view of the followers, whereas the correlations on items five, six, seven, and eight in the third column indicate that the leaders see a considerable conflict between their values and those of the followers. With regard to these political activities, the leaders are correct in perceiving conflict although conflict also exists in educational activities but is missed by the leaders.

[9]Cf. Gabriel Almond and Sidney Verba, *The Civic Culture* (Boston: Little, Brown, 1965), pp. 250-251.

At this point in its organization history, the OEA is in fact more likely to engage in professional and lobbying activities than it is in electoral activities. It is these activities in which the leaders see the followers as being entirely supportive of the organization, although they are correct only with regard to lobbying. If the OEA were to increase its electoral activities, therefore, it would be engaging in practices which are less favored by the followers. However, the fact that the teachers are perceived as being more reluctant to support these activities than they actually are might result in the leaders engaging in these activities to a lesser extent than would be tolerated by the followers.

Evaluations of organizational performance. Turning from the extent to which leaders and followers are in agreement as to what the organization should do, we consider now the relationships between sets of attitudes concerning the extent of satisfaction with the actual behavior of the leaders of the organization. In Table 2 a negative sign indicates that the bottom set of attitudes is less satisfied with the performance of the teachers' organization. A positive sign indicates that the bottom set is more satisfied.

In the first analysis, we found that the leaders consistently underestimate the followers' activism. In Table 2 we find a similar tendency with several notable exceptions. On the question of the importance of the OEA's role in getting improved salaries and benefits in the past, we find a great discrepancy between leaders' and followers' attitudes: the followers are inclined to give the OEA less credit than are the leaders. However, the second column shows that the leaders' perception is accurate. Hence, they perceive followers as exhibiting more dissatisfaction with past performance than the leaders do. Leaders, intimately involved in the successes and failures of the organization, see their role as more significant than do the more passive followers. Only about one-third of the followers think that the OEA was "very important" in securing past benefits, whereas all the leaders are of this opinion.

With regard to current performance a different situation exists. The leaders are more dissatisfied with the performance of the organization and its constant fight for better salaries. Oncc again, however, they perceive more dissatisfaction among the followers than actually exists. Although accurate in their perceptions of teacher satisfaction with past performance, leaders fail in their evaluation of current satisfaction. In fact, 56% of the followers indicated that they think the OEA is doing enough about salaries. This is not exactly an overwhelming vote of confidence, but it is apparent that more satisfaction exists in reality than is perceived by the OEA leadership.

In view of the current conflict between teachers' unions and professional organizations for the loyalties of teachers, it is interesting to note that the OEA leaders are more likely to denigrate the efforts of the teachers' union than are the teachers themselves. This is indicated by the negative sign of the correlations

Table 2. Comparison of the Three Attitude Sets in the Areas of Expectations and Satisfaction with Leadership's Actions

Questions	Sets of Attitudes Compared		
	Followers' Attitudes vs. Leaders' Attitudes	Followers' Attitudes vs. Leaders' Perception of Followers' Attitudes	Leaders' Attitudes vs. Leaders' Perception of Followers' Attitudes
1. How important do you think has been the role played by the OEA in getting improved salaries and benefits?	+.556(s)	+.026	−.667
2. How about the Teachers' Union; how important do you think its role was in getting improved salaries and benefits?	−.297	−.098	+.185
3. Do you think the OEA is doing enough to improve teachers' salaries and benefits?	−.332	−.444	−.111
4. How about the Teachers' Union; is it doing enough in improving teachers' salaries and benefits?	−.396	−.396	.000
5. Do you think the OEA is doing enough in its support for higher teacher standards and accreditation to improve professional status?	−.016	−.016	.000
6. Do you think there should be a state sales tax with the revenue going to the schools?	+.253	+.364	+.111

in column one considering the role of the union in past and present efforts toward salary increases. Again column two tells us that in both of these cases leaders perceive that followers are more dissatisfied with the union than they actually are. This distinction between past and present produces some curious results in the third column, showing the extent of conflict perceived by leaders. While they exaggerate the extent of dissatisfaction on the part of followers, perhaps projecting their own desires more than an objective evaluation would indicate, they recognize that the followers are more impressed with past union performance than they (the leaders) are. Yet they persist in seeing perfect agreement between themselves and teachers concerning current union performance, an agreement which does not exist. These distortions lead the leadership to assume a "what-have-you-done-for-me-lately" attitude somewhat along the lines of old fashioned bread and butter unionism. It seems likely that these perceptions will cause them to channel more of their resources into salary increase efforts at the risk of providing less satisfactory efforts in other areas. On the other hand this risk does not appear to be very great. For example, the leaders are extremely accurate in their perceptions of teacher satisfaction with regard to support for higher professional standards and accreditation. A consensus only slightly weaker than that regarding lobbying exists here.

The final item in the table dealing with the question of state sales tax enables us to return once again to lobbying. We may well ask "Lobbying for what?" The OEA has been strongly lobbying for a state sales tax with revenues going to the public schools, but only a slight majority (53%) of the teachers agree that a state sales tax should be enacted, while more than two-thirds of the leadership favor the tax. This is apparently an elite-derived effort enjoying only weak support from the followers. In this case, however, the leaders perceive far more support than actually exists. They actually believe that followers support this effort more than the leaders do, whereas the opposite is the case. Thus, although high consensus is achieved on the legitimacy of lobbying, leaders do not show a great capability of deciding how much effort should be devoted to the pursuit of certain policies by means of lobbying. The leaders want a sales tax, perceive the followers as wanting a sales tax, and pursue this effort vigorously. It is possible that if the efforts to achieve a sales tax are continued with increased intensity, membership support might be reduced beyond the bare majority it enjoys now, and intra-group conflict may result. If this happens the perceptual errors of the leaders could prove costly.

Abstract political values. Up to this point we have been considering the explicit programs of the Oregon Education Association, and the extent to which there is a congruence between leaders' and followers' values with regard to these programs. Members of organizations, however, may have values which are not directly translatable into explicit programs but which nevertheless color the relationship between leaders and followers. The overall ideological pattern of leaders and followers is, therefore, a component in determining the extent to which leaders represent the followers' values. It is this assumption which leads us to inquire about abstract political values. The items in Table 3 are offered as important in the leaders' evaluations as to what programs might appeal to the followers and also what the nature of appeals to the membership for support on a given issue might be. On the basis of their content, the items are separated into those indicating conservatism and those indicating liberalism. The first seven questions are the conservative questions, and the last six are the liberal questions. For each group, a negative sign indicates that the bottom set of attitudes shows greater acceptance of the item.

Looking at the first column, it can readily be seen that the leaders are more likely to disagree with the conservative items and more likely to agree with the liberal items than are the followers. Furthermore, the high correlations in the third column show that the leaders believe that the followers differ greatly from them with regard to these items. Once again, however, the leaders' perceptions of teachers' attitudes tend to exaggerate the differences. In eleven of the thirteen cases, leaders perceive followers to be more conservative and less liberal than they actually are. Thus, although the OEA leaders are a biased section of the teachers with respect to their political and economic values, they tend to perceive their

Table 3. Comparison of the Attitude Sets in the Area of Orthodox Values

Questions	Sets of Attitudes Compared		
	Followers' Attitudes vs. Leaders' Attitudes	Followers' Attitudes vs. Leaders' Perception of Followers' Attitudes	Leaders' Attitudes vs. Leaders' Perception of Followers' Attitudes
Conservative			
1. The American form of government may not be perfect, but it's the best type of government yet devised by man.	−.137	+.078	+.222
2. Democracy is considered the ideal form of government by most of the world.	−.160	−.658	−.407
3. Private enterprise could do better most of the things the government is now doing.	+.365	−.171	−.568
4. The participation of the federal government in local affairs leads to undesirable federal controls.	+.564(s)	−.389	−.926
5. Communism is a total evil.	+.142	−.466	−.630
6. People of most underdeveloped countries are by nature incapable of self-government.	+.303	−.226	−.506
7. Private enterprise is the only really workable system in the modern world capable of satisfying our economic needs.	+.257	−.182	−.469
Liberal			
8. Economic and social planning by government does not necessarily lead to dictatorship.	−.326	+.125	+.444
9. Man is the maker of his own society; such events as wars and depressions could be controlled by man.	−.122	+.161	+.259
10. The growth of large corporations makes government regulation of business necessary.	−.190	+.088	+.309
11. We could increase spending for many government services without harming the nation's economy.	−.402	+.035	+.432
12. The federal government represents the needs of most people better than local government.	−.030	+.284	+.259
13. The government should increase its activities in matters of health, retirement, wages, and old-age benefits.	−.205	−.034	+.185

atypical posture as more extreme than it actually is. This discrepancy in perception is likely to influence the leaders to use more conservative appeals to the followers in urging support of particular programs than would be called for by an accurate inventory of their values.

Combined with the bread and butter perception described previously, this perceived conservatism of teachers leads the leaders into the path of heavy emphasis on salaries and other basic issues while at the same time forcing them to restrict their activities in the realm of expansion of organizational activities. If the leadership seeks to venture into untried areas which are not specifically related to educational problems, it may be hesitant to begin for fear that the programs are too liberal for the membership.

Of course, as Krech and Crutchfield point out, the degree of association between cognitive attitudes and action-orientated attitudes is not necessarily great.[10] Thus, a person holding conservative beliefs does not automatically favor conservative actions by government. To ascertain the extent to which abstract values are translatable into immediate preferences for governmental action, we administered the items from the Survey Research Center's domestic attitude scale.[11] As in the abstract value index, the leaders proved to be much more liberal than the followers. Also, the leaders saw the followers as not being as liberal as they actually are. In this case, however, the leaders are not so greatly more liberal and they do not see the followers as so greatly more conservative than they actually are. The main thrust of the conservatism scale is identical to that of the abstract political value index, but the discrepancies are not as great. It may be, therefore, that the leaders are less in danger of undercutting the cohesion of the organization should they lend its support to an explicit governmental program outside the realm of education related issues. The danger to cohesion may be not so much in the undertaking of new programs but in the appeal to followers on the basis of their perceived conservatism.

The political role of the teacher. Teachers, like the holders of any social position, have perceptions of what is permissible behavior by holders of their social position. Others who do not hold this position also have expectations. The interaction of these two expectations constitutes a role. Table 4 presents the comparisons between the three sets of attitudes with regard to norms of teachers' political participation. A negative sign indicates that the bottom set of attitudes in the comparison favors teacher participation more than does the top set of attitudes.

Here we see a remarkably consistent pattern. Leaders are, in every case save one, more supportive of actions by teachers in these areas than are the teachers. This is even true of joining a teachers' union, but it is not true of striking to secure higher salaries and other benefits. In this latter case, the teachers are slightly more likely than leaders to be willing to undertake this activity and are much more

[10] David Krech and Richard Crutchfield, *Theory and Problems of Social Psychology* (New York: McGraw-Hill, 1948), p. 251.

[11] See Angus Campbell *et al.*, *The American Voter* (New York: Wiley, 1960), pp. 194-198. V. O. Key gives the items used in this scale. See V. O. Key, Jr., *Public Opinion and American Democracy* (New York: Knopf, 1961), p. 561.

Table 4. Comparison of the Attitude Sets in the Area of the Norms of Teachers' Political Participation

Questions	Sets of Attitudes Compared		
	Followers' Attitudes vs. Leaders' Attitudes	Followers' Attitudes vs. Leaders' Perception of Followers' Attitudes	Leaders' Attitudes vs. Leaders' Perception of Followers' Attitudes
Teachers should if they want to:			
1. Join a teachers' union.	−.135	+.532(s)	+.667
2. Go on strike to secure higher salaries and other benefits.	+.067	+.317(s)	+.250
3. Join a political party organization.	−.036	+.186	+.222
4. Serve as party precinct worker in pre-election activities.	−.064	+.269	+.333
5. Publicly criticize local government officials.	−.268	+.510(s)	+.778
6. In a presidential election, outside school time, make speeches or give other services on the behalf of a candidate.	−.110	+.335(s)	+.444
7. Run for political office.	−.104	+.451(s)	+.556
8. In a presidential election, explain to class reasons for preferring one candidate.	−.055	+.279	+.333
9. Belong to the NAACP or CORE.	−.129	+.316(s)	+.444
10. Take part in a CORE or NAACP demonstration, such as public picketing.	−.112	+.460(s)	+.571
11. Allow an atheist to address the class.	−.126	+.430(s)	+.556
12. Argue in class against the censoring of literature by people who feel it is pornographic.	−.226	+.039	+.306
13. Speak out in class against the John Birch Society and groups like it.	−.153	+.180	+.333
14. Speak in favor of nationalizing the steel industry and the railroads.	−.249	+.307	+.556
15. Speak in class in favor of the Medicare program.	−.169	+.276	+.444
16. Speak in class in favor of the United Nations.	−.043	+.291	+.333
17. Allow the distribution of anticommunist literature put out by the National Association of Manufacturers.	−.254	+.191	+.444
18. Speak in class favorably about socialism.	−.105	+.229	+.333
19. Argue in class that labor unions should be more regulated or controlled by the government.	−.158	+.176	+.333
20. Allow the distribution of anticommunist literature put out by the John Birch Society.	−.443(s)	+.123	+.556

likely to be willing to strike than leaders perceive them to be. This is the single example of followers being more "activist" than leaders to achieve liberal goals. In every other case, no matter what type of action is involved, leaders are more willing to take a risk, more willing to engage in controversial activity than are followers. When we examine the leaders' perception of followers' attitudes, we find once again the consistent pattern of underevaluation of the experimental nature of teachers. Leaders perceive teachers as being unlikely to engage in these activities whereas teachers themselves, although less anxious than leaders to take part in these activities, are more willing to do so than leaders believe them to be. Thus, the teachers are more willing to join teachers' unions, political party organizations, or racial organizations than leaders believe them to be.

Conclusions

To summarize the findings of this analysis, the following points may be offered. As is true of most organizations, the leaders of the Oregon Education Association are more active than the followers. They are more liberal than the followers and they are more willing than the followers to expand the activities of the organization, but they consistently exaggerate the atypical nature of their position. They see the followers as being more conservative and restrained than they actually are. These discrepancies, both in perception and in actual attitudes, lead us to speculate as to how they came about. Is the relative activism of leaders a function of their social role, their organizational position, or their personality? It is certainly not feasible to argue that leadership positions somehow recruit more daring people. It is more feasible to seek explanations within the nature of the organization and the teaching profession. Consider, for example, the items dealing with political participation by teachers. Leaders would be subject to none of the pressures that teachers would feel from their community. Also, while teachers can recall relatively few cases in which the community made demands upon the school system for the dismissal of a teacher for engaging in controversial activity, those who can recall such incidents are of the opinion that the teachers' organization was ineffective in the defense of teachers. It is also true that the teachers look upon the local affiliates of the Oregon Education Association much more favorably than they look upon the statewide organization which employs the leaders considered in this study. In arguing for organizational position as a fundamental contributor to differential perception, we draw added support from the reaction of the leaders to the competition of the union. Leaders behave in much the same fashion as political party leaders.[12] They are more emotionally committed to the organization than are the rank and file. Hence, they find it difficult

[12]Herbert McClosky, "Consensus and Ideology in American Politics," *American Political Science Review,* Vol. 58 (June 1964), pp. 361-382.

to comprehend the problems of teaching and the restrictions traditionally imposed upon teachers by the community.

It might be useful to know something about the leaders' backgrounds. All have at one time been teachers and all have passed through some lower administrative position before achieving their present status. Most have taken graduate work, usually in educational administration. All earn in excess of ten thousand dollars per year. Thus, although they do have a teaching background, they are much more upwardly mobile than the average teacher and make more money. They are also substantially better educated. The upward mobility of the leaders of the OEA can be gleaned from the backgrounds of their fathers. Most of their fathers had less than a high school education and held low status occupations. Thus holding a position in the OEA marks more of a step up than does teaching. Perhaps, therefore, the leaders consider themselves as more sophisticated and advanced than teachers.

When we consider the fact that serving as an OEA administrator is in a sense moving beyond a teaching position, the explanation offered above becomes more plausible. Combine this with the fact that leaders have interaction with a more heterogeneous environment and their perception of teachers becomes even more understandable. Unlike the teachers, who interact mostly with teachers, students, principals, and parents, the OEA administrative staff interacts with lobbyists, legislators, state officials, and national educational officials.

As a final alternative to the explanation offered above, we considered the possibility that, whereas the leaders incorrectly perceive the political values and political role perceptions of teachers, they may base their reactions upon communication with a biased sample. There are, of course, many different shades of opinion among teachers just as there are among the general public. Is it true that the OEA leaders interact with a segment of the teaching population which is more conservative and more restrained? If this is true, then their perceptions of followers' attitudes might not be a function of their social position but might be the result of an unrepresentative sample of opinion being communicated to them. However, our evidence indicates quite clearly that there is no relationship between political conservatism and participation in organizational affairs. There is no evidence that the conservative teachers have any more interaction with OEA leaders than do the liberal teachers. Also, those teachers who take a restrained view of the political role of the teacher are no more likely to communicate with OEA leaders than are those teachers who take a more expansionist view.[13] Thus, we can say that there is no weighting of communication which comes to the attention of OEA leaders in favor of conservatism and restraint.

[13]It is true, however, that there is more interaction between leaders and small town teachers; these teachers are considerably more conservative and restrained than their big city counterparts.

Assuming, therefore, that being a leader in an organization contributes to a discrepancy between leaders' and followers' attitudes, we may inquire finally into the possibility of having a democratic interest group without frequent and carefully supervised consultative mechanisms. Can leaders be representative simply because they intuitively comprehend what is required of them? In considering this question, let us note that, with the exception of the last table, the discrepancy between leaders' attitudes and followers' attitudes is generally *greater* than the errors made by leaders in perceiving these attitudes. Thus, OEA leaders operating entirely upon their personal values would not be representative of the values of their followers. On the other hand, if they adopted a purely representative role, they would become more conservative and restrained than the teachers would prefer. Yet, with the exception of the last set of attitudes, the error would be less than would be true if followers' wishes were ignored. That is to say, if they followed their understanding of followers' values, the resulting conservatism and restraint would be closer to the actual desires of teachers than would be true if leaders used their personal values as the sole criteria of judgment. "Virtual" representation in an interest group cannot serve as a substitute for actual representation, because the position of group leader contributes to the development of attitudes which differ from those of the followers.

Bibliographical Note

Two roots of modern organizational theory and much of the literature on the internal problems of interest groups are the social psychologists' studies of small groups and the work of industrial psychologists in natural work settings. For an overview of the former, see Sidney Verba, *Small Groups and Political Behavior: A Study of Political Leadership* (Princeton, N.J.: Princeton Univ. Press, 1961); and Robert M. Golembiewski, *O & M and the Small Group* (Chicago: Rand McNally, 1962). Typical of the latter is Elton Mayo's *The Human Problems of an Industrial Civilization* (New York: Viking, 1933), reporting on the "Hawthorne studies" at Western Electric.

A recent (and retrospective) account of Lewin's early work is given in Ralph K. White and Ronald Lippitt, *Autocracy and Democracy* (New York: Harper, 1960); a feeling for Lewin's theories can be gained from Kurt Lewin, *Resolving Social Conflicts* (New York: Harper, 1948), especially from "Self-Hatred among Jews," pp. 190-200, which discusses marginality, and "Experiments in Social Space," pp. 71-83, which describes the Iowa experiments. Another excellent source for small-group studies in the Lewin tradition is *Group Dynamics: Research and Theory,* ed. Dorwin Cartwright and Alvin Zander (New York: Harper, 1960). Finally, the student may find it useful to peruse the journal *Human Relations,* published since 1947 by the Tavistock Institute in London.

The first application of Michels' theory to modern American organizations was Seymour Lipset's work, of which only a small portion has been reprinted in the present volume. For the full account, see Seymour M. Lipset, Martin A. Trow, and James S. Coleman, *Union Democracy: The Internal Politics of the International Typographical Union* (New York: Free Press, 1956). A replication of this study is reported by Leonard I. Pearlin and Henry E. Richards in "Equity: A Study of Union Democracy," in *Labor and Trade Unionism: An Interdisciplinary Reader,* ed. Walter Galenson and Seymour Lipset (New York: Wiley, 1960). For a discussion and criticism of some of Lipset's conclusions, see Paul Jacobs, "Union Democracy and the Public Good: Do They Necessarily Coincide?", *Commentary,* Vol. 25 (January 1958), pp. 68-74; and Will Herberg, "Bureaucracy and Democracy in Labor Unions," *Antioch Review*, Vol. 3 (1943), pp. 405-417.

One subject of considerable theoretical interest is the question of organizational adaptation to changing values and a changing social environment. One selection in Section 5 of the present volume—Vander Zanden's article on the Ku Klux Klan—deals with this topic. In addition, the student should consult several articles which relate adaptation to organizational cohesion and the internal values of the organization: Joseph Gusfield, "Social Structure and Moral Reform: A Study of the Women's Christian Temperance Union," *American Journal of Sociology,* Vol. 61 (November 1955); F. Stuart Chapin and John E. Tsouderos, "Formalization Observed in Ten Voluntary Organizations: Concepts, Morphology, Process," *Social Forces,* Vol. 33 (May 1955); Sheldon Messinger, "Organizational Transformation: A Case Study of a Declining Social Movement," *American Sociological Review,* Vol. 20 (February 1955); and David Sills, "Voluntary Associations: Instruments and Objects of Change," *Human Organization,* Vol. 18 (Spring 1959), pp. 17-21.

The contemporary student may be interested in several articles dealing with organizational problems in the civil-rights movement: John Orbell, "Protest Participation among Southern Negro College Students," *American Political Science Review,* Vol. 61 (June 1967), pp. 446-456; James Q. Wilson, "The Strategy of Protest: Problems of Negro Civic Action," *Journal of Conflict Resolution,* Vol. 3 (September 1961), pp. 291-303; Jack Walker, "The Functions of Disunity: Negro Leadership in a Southern City," *Journal of Negro Education,* Vol. 32 (Summer 1963), pp. 227-236; and Gerald McWorter and Robert L. Crain, "Subcommunity Gladiatorial Competition: Civil Rights Leadership as a Competitive Process," *Social Forces,* Vol. 46 (September 1967), pp. 8-21.

Interest Groups and the Political Process

Early in 1956, Senator Francis Case made a dramatic announcement to his fellow senators. He told them that he had been offered a $2,500 campaign contribution by a representative of the natural-gas lobby, at a time when natural gas was to be debated by the Senate. Because of this blatant act, he said, he had decided to oppose the Natural Gas Act that he had previously supported. During the weeks following the senator's speech, indignant statements were issued by congressmen, journalists, and private citizens, the Senate established a special committee to investigate lobbying, and the Natural Gas Act was defeated. Within a short time, however, Capitol Hill resumed its normal legislative routine.

The Case incident was unusual both because few contemporary interest groups display such a lack of subtlety in their efforts to influence congressmen and because it is one of the relatively few occasions when the details of such an act have been widely publicized. On the whole, the lobbyist-legislator relationship is a peaceful one, often characterized by reciprocal helpfulness and close relations. Most lobbying is quite open to outside scrutiny.

The episode nevertheless raises several questions that deserve serious consideration:

1. What are the methods used by most political interest groups? Whom do they approach? What means of persuasion are at their disposal?
2. What barriers exist (if any) between political interest groups and those they seek to influence? Do policy-makers vary in their attitudes and actions toward group spokesmen? If so, why?
3. How much influence do organized groups have? Do they change votes? Block the passage of legislation? Prevent impartial administration of laws already on the books? Or is their importance exaggerated by both their critics and their apologists?

The readings in this section have been organized according to the targets of group pressures—political parties, legislators at three levels of government, administrators, and the Supreme Court. Thus, most of these articles discuss group methods, group influence, and barriers to group efforts in terms of a specific institutional setting; but almost without exception, the authors provide information relevant to more than one of the three questions listed above. Only a small amount of the available literature can, of course, be presented here. The student is urged to consult the bibliographical notes for further suggestions on specific topics of interest.

Interest Groups and Political Parties

E. E. Schattschneider and Hugh Bone present sharply contrasting views of the relationship between parties and interest groups and of the role which interest groups play in political life. Schattschneider pictures the two sets of organizations as antithetical—interest-group power is exercised at the expense (and in the absence) of effective party government. Bone, in contrast, views the activities of interest groups and parties as overlapping, especially at the grass-roots level. Interest groups are important elements of electoral alliances, contributors to the party coffers, and participants in the bargaining process focused on shaping party platforms and choosing candidates. Political groups and political parties are not invariably in competition for citizen allegiance; the two institutions perform complementary functions.

Schattschneider is part of the tradition of party reformers who became vocal after World War II.[1] In his eyes, a disciplined two-party system is essential to democratic government. The citizen must be able to vote for a candidate who is fully committed to a specific party program; he should be able to vote that party and that candidate out of office if they do not fulfill their promises. And a party must be able to discipline members who fail to support the party program. In the absence of responsible parties, two "irresponsible" forces have assumed political power in America—interest groups and the local bosses. Interest groups are irresponsible by their very nature, argues Schattschneider, because they need not face public elections. Furthermore, they are not only irrelevant; they are positively harmful because they have created a government by irresponsible minorities.

Neither Bone nor Schattschneider reports on individual leaders, group members, or elected representatives. Their interest is primarily in parties or groups as total entities; their work is cast in an essentially traditional or historical mold. For this reason, while they shed some light on the techniques used by political interest groups, they are not informative about the interactions between policy-makers and group spokesmen. The next authors address themselves to this point.

One of the first studies which treated the legislator as more than a passive recipient of group pressures was Garceau and Silverman's "A Pressure Group and the

[1]Schattschneider was chairman of the American Political Science Association Committee, which issued the report "Toward a More Responsible Two-Party System," as well as author of *Party Government*, the book from which our selection is taken.

Pressured," written in 1954.[2] They found that awareness of interest-group activity varied with the way in which state legislators "structured" the session: "Policy-oriented" and "program-oriented" men were markedly more attuned to groups than others. Charles Jones made another important contribution to the problem of relations between interest groups and legislators through his study of the House Agricultural Committee.[3] He made the logical but previously ignored point that the impact of some interests may be traced to values strongly shared by congressmen, constituents, and group members rather than to overt or formal group activities.

Building on the Garceau-Silverman work, John Wahlke and his associates studied state legislators' role orientations toward political interest groups and their general perceptions of these groups. They found three major types of legislators—the Facilitator, the Neutral, and the Resistor—who differed predictably in their reactions toward political group activity. In addition to the major substantive points that legislators are not simply passive processors of group requests and that group activity will have different effects on legislators in accordance with their orientations toward "significant others" in the legislative process, the article is important for theoretical and methodological reasons. Role analysis is another approach to the study of interest groups (neither a substitute for nor a competitor to group theory) and seems particularly appropriate for analyzing the question of barriers (perceptual or attitudinal screens) which intervene between the group spokesman and the policy-maker. It can be particularly effective when used, as in this study, to explain relations between interest groups and legislators in a complex context.

The next article on groups and the legislative process (by Zisk and associates) focuses on city councilmen in nonpartisan California cities. The approach is very similar to that of Wahlke, although the specific interest-group role orientations which are developed (Pluralists, Tolerants, and Antagonists) are significantly different. Zisk *et al.* extend the Wahlke analysis to relate legislators' role orientations to legislative *behavior*. In addition, one major substantive difference emerges when state legislators and city councilmen are compared: On the whole, local officials (at least in these small California cities) are markedly less aware of, less favorably disposed toward, and less dependent upon political interest groups than are state officials.

In the next selection, Bernard Cohen studies group activities concerning the Japanese Peace Settlement made in the early 1950's. He finds two different

[2]Oliver Garceau and Corinne Silverman, "A Pressure Group and the Pressured," *American Political Science Review,* Vol. 48 (September 1954), pp. 672-691.

[3]Charles O. Jones, "Representation in Congress: The Case of the House Agricultural Committee," *American Political Science Review*, Vol. 55 (June 1961), pp. 358-367.

configurations of interests, one concentrating primarily on senators and the other on communication with the executive branch. These groupings differ in terms of strategies, relations with their own constituencies, and general outlook on the political process. His distinction between "tangible" and "intangible" interests is provocative, and, according to a related study which Cohen has published, it may help to explain congressmen's preferences for such tangible interest groups as businessmen rather than for intangible or "moral" interests like the League of Woman Voters.

These articles illustrate a new trend in the study of the effect of interest groups on the legislative process. The emphasis is now on research which is simultaneously empirical, comparative, and directed toward the building of tested theory. None of this work is as broad in scope as were earlier journalistic studies of Washington lobbies; much of it will provoke the protest "But it's only four states" (or "seventeen cities"). The only possible reply is that such work represents a modest effort to move away from reliance on folklore toward the accumulation of dependable and *precise* information. The student may want to list for himself, in parallel columns, the major findings of the studies in question and then check the list for internal consistency. After completing that task, he might refer back to Schattschneider's assertions to see if the commonly held views of the 1940s square with the information collected over the past twenty years.

Interest Groups, the Administration, and the Judiciary

The articles by Clement Vose and J. Leiper Freeman deal with the group process in the administrative and judicial branches of government. For many years, analysis of this type was inhibited by the myth of the separation of administration and adjudication from the political process. Both judges and administrators were viewed as neutral or beyond politics, the former ruling strictly in accordance with legal precedents and the latter carrying out legislative directives without the need for independent judgement. When examples of judicial or administrative "discretion" were discussed, they were invariably attributed to laws drawn up hastily or with a large degree of ambiguity. The "cure" was tightly drawn legislation or constant legislative oversight, and administrative and judicial self-restraint.[4]

Beginning about 1940, scholars like Friedrich, Selznick, Herring, and Appleby (on administration) and Dahl, Schubert, Peltason, and Schmidhauser (on the

[4]See Charles S. Hyneman, *Bureaucracy in a Democracy* (New York: Harper, 1950), especially Chapter 5, for a classic statement of this viewpoint.

courts) questioned this view.[5] They argued that neither the courts nor administrative agencies are insulated from the political process. Neither judges nor administrators can shed their past and present political attitudes, loyalties, perceptions, or predispositions; nor can concrete decisions be made in a political vacuum. No law can be passed in sufficient detail to eliminate individual judgment or individual awareness of the wishes, needs, and strengths of contending interests, individuals, and institutions.

Clement Vose's article discusses group activity vis-à-vis the courts. Interest groups perform several major functions in the judicial process: legal assistance to individual litigants, overt protest activity, and the filing of *amicus curiae* briefs on major rest cases. The informal events preceding the filing of cases may also involve group assistance to individuals. A concerned individual may first turn to a political group such as the ACLU or the NAACP for financial aid or help on strategy before the legal or formal controversy begins.[6] The general subject of interest-group activities before the courts needs considerably more research before a definitive summary is possible.

Much has been written about the relation between interest groups and administrators. Freeman, however, is interested in the pressure activities of the bureaucrats themselves rather than in the efforts of interest-group spokesmen to influence administrators. He describes the efforts of administrators to promote the interest of their own agencies and their clientele, their activity in promoting legislation, and, finally, their effort to build alliances and to gain programmatic support from members of the interested public.[7]

[5]Carl Friedrich, "Public Policy and the Nature of Administrative Responsibility," in *Public Policy, 1940* (Cambridge, Mass.: Harvard Univ. Press, 1940); Philip M. Selznick, *TVA and the Grass Roots* (Berkeley, Calif.: Univ. California Press, 1949); Pendleton Herring, *Public Administration and the Public Interest* (New York: McGraw-Hill, 1936); Paul H. Appleby, *Policy and Administration* (Tuscaloosa, Ala.: Univ. Alabama Press, 1949); Robert A. Dahl, "Decision Making in a Democracy: The Role of the Supreme Court as a National Policy-Maker," *The Journal of Public Law*, Vol. 6 (Fall 1957), pp. 279-295; Glendon Schubert, *Quantitative Analysis of Judicial Behavior* (New York: Free Press, 1959); Jack W. Peltason, *The Federal Courts in the Political Process* (New York: Doubleday, 1955); and John H. Schmidhauser, *The Supreme Court: Its Policies, Personalities and Behavior* (New York: Holt, 1960).

[6]Church organizations and groups interested in civil liberties were frequently asked for help by those involved in the witch hunts of the early 1950s. In one case, which later was settled by the Supreme Court, the victim of a "security" firing was given considerable help in finding a job and housing for his family by the Washington organization for which the author worked; this kind of informal assistance was not uncommon.

[7]For a more detailed account of administrative activity in the political process, with particular reference to the co-optation of interest groups, see Philip Selznick's landmark study, *TVA and the Grass Roots* (*op. cit.*).

Interest Groups and Protest Activity

The years since 1960 have witnessed the rise of protest and of various forms of direct action by minority groups, students, teachers, and the poor. Tactics such as strikes, marches, mass demonstrations, sit-ins, lie-ins, stall-ins, and occasional violence have supplemented traditional lobbying techniques. "Confrontation" has become the password, particularly among the have-nots.

Little of a rigorous nature has been published on this subject. Michael Lipsky's article, however, is an important first step in highlighting the strategic problems which protesting groups face in reaching various "target populations." Lipsky's extensive bibliography may guide the reader to other relevant material.

Unanswered Questions

Relations between interest groups and decision-makers have probably received more scholarly attention than any other aspect of group activity or organization. Yet after examining the wealth of studies published in the past twenty years, the observer is still troubled by some of the questions posed at the beginning of this essay. Just *how much* influence do political groups wield? *How*, precisely, do groups affect legislative, administrative, or judicial "outputs" (the substance of laws or administrative rulings)?

If we accept Almond and Verba's definition of political influence (the "degree to which government officials act to benefit that group or individual because the officials believe that they will risk some deprivation . . . if they do not so act"),[8] it is almost impossible to *demonstrate* influence. In fact, it is probably fair to say that not one study has "proved" influence in these terms. Similarly, if we attempt to demonstrate a group's impact on political outputs in strict terms, we will probably fail. (Very little research has been done on the subject, probably because of its intrinsic difficulty.)

This rather pessimistic appraisal of existing knowledge of the field is not meant to imply that there is no worthwhile information about group influence or that group influence does not exist. However, the student should be cautious in accepting unsupported assertions about the power of pressure groups; and at the same time he must make a realistic assessment of the information which is available.

[8]Gabriel Almond and Sidney Verba, *The Civic Culture* (Boston: Little, Brown, 1965), p. 136.

The Pressure Groups

E. E. Schattschneider

A political party . . . is an organization formed for the purpose of winning elections in order to get control of the directing personnel of government. Having taken possession of the principal offices, the party obtains general control of the government. The ultimate objective of the party is therefore conquest of the power to govern. The point of attack, or the method, is to nominate candidates and to support them in an election campaign. The methods and the objectives of the parties are inseparable. A pressure group, on the other hand, is an association that tries to bring about the adoption and execution of certain public policies without nominating candidates for the great offices, without fighting election campaigns, and without attempting to get complete control of government.

Parties and pressure groups differ as to method, therefore, and the method used in turn dominates the objectives of these types of political organization. In its nature the method of controlling government by nominating candidates who contest elections involves total control of the government, though it may not be perfectly successful. If a party wins an election it wins general control of the policies and activities of the government. The parties play for the supreme stakes of power. On the other hand, pressure groups are not organized to take over a government in its entirety; they seek to accomplish specific, relatively narrow tasks, to influence policy at selected points, and do not aim at winning the general power to govern. Compared with the responsibilities assumed by the parties, the function of pressure groups is extremely restricted. A pressure group may content itself with bringing about a single result, the passage of one bill, the defeat of one tax increase, the reversal of a particular executive ruling, the construction of a special bridge, or the adoption of a particular tariff rate on a special commodity, though some pressure groups sponsor policies more broadly conceived than those promoted by others. If the party is a corporation which takes possession of the ship by virtue of a mandate from the owners, the pressure group is little more than a stowaway smuggled aboard with the cargo.

Pressure Tactics

Before proceeding with the discussion of the implications of the fact that parties fight election campaigns and pressure groups avoid them, it is necessary to examine more closely the method of pressure politics. How is it possible to influence public policy without winning elections? The method of pressure politics, like all other political methods, must meet one fundamental requirement if it is to be adopted widely. It must *work easily.*

How can organized minorities or groups, unable to win elections or unwilling to make the effort to do so, induce the government to adopt the policies they advocate? Obviously a pressure group might influence policy by *creating a general opinion* in favor of the action which it advocates. This is unquestionably a legitimate method of influencing government. On the other hand, it is not an easy thing to do. The creation of a favorable opinion in a public as large as the American nation amid a welter of conflicting opinions is a formidable task well beyond the resources of most pressure groups. If these groups were restricted to general propaganda, it is certain that the number continuing in business would be restricted drastically. Pressure politics is usually conducted on a more economical plan; there would be no such thing as pressure politics if a short cut to influence had not been invented. Lobbyists long ago discovered that it is possible to get results by procedures that simply ignore the sovereign majority.

A broad program of propaganda designed to convert the public generally to the views of an organized minority is obviously one of the most legitimately democratic procedures imaginable. Under certain conditions (assume that the subject of the controversy is a great one, that the resources of the group are adequate, and that the opposition is powerful) it may be possible for an organized minority to provoke a great debate and to lay the matter before the public as the final arbiter. If the public can be convinced, it will be able to give effect to its wishes through the regular channels. As a matter of fact an enormous and incalculable quantity of discussion of this sort goes on at all times. This is the method of propaganda as distinguished from the method of pressure. Propaganda and pressure tactics may be combined by powerful organized interests and minorities, but they should not be confused.

The distinguishing mark of pressure tactics is not merely that *it does not seek to win elections* but that in addition *it does not attempt to persuade a majority.* A pressure group is not a minority becoming a majority. If this were the case there would be no difference between pressure and propaganda tactics, and there would be no special problem of pressure politics. Pressure politics is a method of short-circuiting the majority. It is the extreme case of organization to influence government with economy of effort and money, even with a great economy of public attention. It is the cheapest of political methods. Therefore pressure politics comes well within the requirement that political methods must be easy.

Defects in the Means of Popular Control

Pressure groups are able to get advantageous results with a very small outlay by taking advantage of certain deficiencies in the grand strategy of democratic government, defects in the principal means of popular control of government. The control of the government by the majority, by means of elections, by political parties, and by public opinion is not perfectly effective; these controls are powerful, even irresistible, but lack refinement. If the classical means of popular government were perfect, there would obviously be no place for government by pressure groups which are mere organized minorities without the capacity or will to become majorities. It is easy enough to speak of government by the majority or government by public opinion or party government as expressed in a general election in theory or on paper, but what in practice, on any one of ten thousand points of public policy or governmental action, is public opinion, the will of the majority, the policy of the majority party, or the verdict of the election? More often than not there is no conclusive answer. It is in this zone of doubt and confusion that the pressure group operates. In the economy of democratic government the pressure group is definitely a parasite living on the wastage of power exercised by the sovereign majority.

An examination of the principal means of popular government will show how great are the lacunae in the control of government left by them. Elections cannot be held every day. In the interval between elections, congressmen, for example, are forced to consider not merely the mandate upon which they were elected but they must also consider the *next* election. The whole constitutional system forces a congressman to wager his future on a gambler's forecast of political trends. Only those who have had the experience of being exposed periodically to the hazards of an election will know how difficult it is to guess the trend of popular opinion when it comes to some definite issue. Moreover, a modern American election is an omnibus affair out of which the elected representative of the people must distill some meaning from the greatest of uncertainties. The vote on his part makes his decision on the basis of a kind of general average of issues which cannot easily be interpreted as an intelligible rule of conduct for the guidance of his representative. An election is a confusing revelation of the will of the people.

If the mandate given in an election is vague, the idea of government by public opinion is even more indefinite. Even a superpoll of public opinion would probably create as many mysteries as it would resolve, for the polls require interpretation. The thing to be measured is too complex and too flexible for certainty. Moreover, upon most of the issues on which a member of Congress passes there is no public opinion at all—merely implications and inferences concerning public opinion. Majority opinions (on the concrete issues that must be decided in the day-by-day work of the government) are as nebulous as nearly all other general rules of public conduct—the public good, the greatest happiness of the greatest number, and justice.

Natural Advantages of Parties over Pressure Groups

Although elections, public opinion, and majority will are too vague and indefinite to furnish an effective guide to governmental policy in many specific cases, the political parties are not fatally handicapped by this condition. As general managers of politics exercising a broad power to govern, the party must interpret the vague mandate of the election and the nebulous and imponderable trends of public opinion at its own risk and enforce its decision on the government effectively. This the parties might do, and this American major parties often do *not* do. If the parties exercised the power to govern effectively, *they would shut out the pressure groups.* The fact that American parties govern only spasmodically and fitfully amid a multitude of lapses of control provides the opportunity for the cheap and easy use of pressure tactics. The role of the pressure groups in American politics is directly and intimately related to the condition of the major parties. In practice the parties, interested primarily in patronage, are not mobilized to exclude from influence pressure groups promoting special interests. The parties, as custodians of the right of the majority to govern, have never been entirely successful.

The fundamental condition necessary for the prosperity of an enormously overgrown system of pressure politics is a party system in which the parties are unable to use their great powers. The relaxation of party discipline, the weakness of the national party leadership, the preoccupation of the local bosses with patronage and their indifference to political issues arising out of public business open the way for the exercise of influence by organized minorities that do not have the will or the means of mobilizing a majority.

More specifically, a member of Congress is not required to adhere to a party line on controversial questions coming before Congress for decision. Some naive persons have supposed that the member of Congress thus freed from party discipline is able to sit in a political vacuum while making his decision on purely philosophical and moral grounds. In real life, however, the congressman must often long for the security of strong party discipline, for he escapes from the authority of the party only to fall prey to the organized special interests. It is not intelligent to compare the evils of partisanship with an idealized condition of Olympian aloofness inhabited by congressmen insulated against passion and greed. That is not the alternative. The real choice is between a strong party system on the one hand and a system of politics in which congressmen are subjected to minority pressures. The assumption made here is that party government is better than government by irresponsible organized minorities and special interests. The parties are superior because they must consider the problems of government broadly, they submit their fate to an election, and are responsible to the public. By every democratic principle the parties, as mobilizers of majorities, have claims on the public more valid and superior to those asserted by the pressure groups which merely mobilize minorities. Government by interest groups who have never dealt successfully with the majority and never have submitted themselves to the judgment of the public in an election is undemocratic and dangerous.

If a major party wins an election campaign but is unable to govern, it is the public that is frustrated and cheated. Indubitably all minorities and all interests have a right to organize and to agitate in order to persuade the majority. That is legitimate, but pressure politics is a device by which organized minorities may control public policy without persuading the public. As a matter of fact, (1) the hypertrophy of pressure politics . . . and (2) bossism . . . result from the same condition, the weakness of the national party leadership.

Under adequate national leadership the parties are incomparably stronger than the pressure groups. Proof of this proposition is to be found in the fact that the parties wage election campaigns and get the support of majorities; they are entrusted by the majority with the power to govern by the most legitimate democratic mandate imaginable. Even the largest and most powerful of pressure groups would not be so bold as to submit itself to this kind of test.

The Veterans' Bonus as an Example

The problem can be stated in terms of the behavior in recent years of the United States House of Representatives and the presidents of the United States, with reference to veterans' bonus legislation. In 1922, 1924, 1931, and 1935 the House voted to override the presidential vetoes of this legislation 258 to 54, 313 to 78, 328 to 79, and 318 to 90. That is, every president since 1920 has vetoed a bonus bill and in every instance the House has overridden the veto. The question raised by the record is, why does it seem to have been politically feasible for the president to veto bonus legislation in spite of the pressure exerted by the organized war veterans, while members of the House seem to have found it politically inadvisable to oppose this legislation, in spite of the fact that the White House and the Capitol are only a mile apart? The answer to this question ought to shed light on the nature of American politics.

There is no evidence to support the conclusion that any of the presidents who vetoed bonus legislation ever suffered politically as a result of the action. Why? In the first place, the president probably was able to make a political profit by opposing the legislation, i.e., to win more votes than he lost as a result of the veto. This is a case in which a relatively small number of veterans made a raid on the United States Treasury at the expense of the whole community. It is true that the minority was *organized* as a pressure group, while the majority was organized merely by the political parties. Nevertheless it ought to be possible for a national party leader to retain his authority under circumstances which permit him to rally an overwhelming majority of the public against the depredations of a minority. It is the business of political leaders to manage situations of this sort, and it is not immediately evident that there are any sufficient general grounds for thinking that the task is too formidable to be performed.

The presidents were able to defy the organized veterans for another reason. The veterans did not have the courage to challenge any of them in an election campaign. No major party candidate ever tried to make an issue of a presidential veto of a bonus bill and no veterans' organization ever tried to run a candidate of its own. As a result, the irate veterans have had no place to go in the election. They were given a choice between two candidates, one of whom had vetoed their bills and the other of whom refused to make a commitment to sign them. Can there by any reasonable doubt as to the outcome of the contest if the bonus had been made an issue in a presidential election? Messrs. Davis, Roosevelt, Landon, and Willkie were presented with the opportunity to make an issue of the bonus in their presidential campaigns but they did not do so. Can there be a reasonable doubt as to the result of any attempt by the American Legion to run a candidate of its own? Clearly, not even the most powerful and aggressive pressure group known to American politics is fit to be mentioned in the same breath with a major political party when it comes to the mobilization of a majority in an election campaign. In other words, the parties have the resources to defeat the pressure groups. The parties are able to get a popular mandate in an election incomparably more authoritative than anything any pressure group is able to muster. Moreover, if *both* parties refuse to make an issue of the demands of a pressure group, as they can, the pressure group is shut out. The pressure groups cannot play the parties against each other unless the parties let them do it.

The Lack of Party Discipline as an Explanation

If it is so remarkably easy for a political party to put a pressure group to rout, why do the members of the party in Congress succumb to pressure so easily? This is the nub of the question. The party in Congress is like a Mexican army; everyone in it takes care of himself. When the enemy appears he may fight, run, or parley as he thinks best. This is the kind of army that can be overwhelmed by one man assisted by a boy beating a dishpan. Congressmen succumb to pressure by organized minorities, not because the pressure groups are strong, but because congressmen see no reason for fighting at all; the party neither disciplines them nor supports them. On the one hand, a congressman is thrown upon his own resources by his party; the party makes no demands on him, does not punish him for desertion, but it also does not fight for him. On the other hand, the pressure group makes a noise like the uprising of a great mass of people, it tries to alarm him and threatens him with defeat. Because the congressman is neither punished nor protected by the party, and because in addition he is in doubt about the power of the pressure group to defeat him for re-election, he decides to play safe. This calculation reverses the normal rules of democratic government completely. Congressmen yield to the organized minorities because the majority, acting through the parties, does nothing to protect itself. All ordinary concepts of the proper relations of the majority and the minorities are thus upset. Organized special interests are able to get concessions from congressmen who find it easier and more profitable to yield than to fight, and the parties surrender to antagonists for whom they ought to feel contempt.

Some highly misleading conclusions have been drawn from the situation described in the preceding paragraphs. It has been said, for instance, that the American people are so badly divided that it is impossible to organize cohesive parties, i.e., that the special interests have disrupted the parties. The experience of American politics with the pressure groups does not support this conclusion. It is true that there is a great diversity of interests in the American nation and that modern society is complex. But this is true of other societies. The raw materials of politics, i.e., a great multiplicity of interests, is nothing new and does not prove that the community is divided by impassable barriers. It is the business of the parties to deal with situations of this sort, to discover accords among the interests. The test of the character of a political system is not that a great multiplicity of interests are found within the community, for all communities are composed of many interests, but rather what the political system makes of these raw materials. It is the task of statesmen to evolve policy amid conflicts.

In one way or another every government worthy of the name manages interests in formulating public policy. The difficulty is not that the parties have been overwhelmed by the interests, but that the political institutions for an adequate national party leadership able to deal with the situation have not been created. For want of this kind of leadership the parties are unable to take advantage of their natural superiority. Thus they let themselves be harried by pressure groups as a timid whale might be pursued by a school of minnows. The potentialities of adequate national party leadership in this connection have not yet been well explored in the United States, but it is a waste of time to talk about controlling the depredations of the pressure groups by other means. A well-centralized party system has nothing to fear from the pressure groups. On the other hand, aside from a strong party system there is no democratic way of protecting the public against the disintegrating tactics of the pressure groups.

Easy to Organize Pressure Groups

The political party having been defined as a process that grows up about elections, it follows that by virtue of that fact pressure groups are all that the parties are not. The parties, because they must get a majority, must appeal to general interests and promote accommodations and compromises among many interests, special and general. The pressure groups are relieved of this requirement. They exploit or promote special interests and go to the limit in identifying themselves with these interests. One of the first consequences of this fact is that it is possible to find excuses for organizing a great multitude of pressure groups. The effort required to organize a pressure group is infinitesimal compared with the labor and difficulty involved in the creation of a major party. This is not due only to the fact that pressure groups are small while parties are large, because some pressure groups have a very large membership. It is due primarily to the fact that *parties are mutually exclusive, whereas pressure groups are not.* That is to say it is impossible to be loyal to more than one party because all parties are in competition with each other. On the other hand, it is possible to find innumerable pressure groups with ambitions that are not in conflict. The mere fact that an individual happens to be a member of the American Association for Adult Education does not exclude him from the Anti-Saloon League of America or the National Consumers' League. Anyone so included could doubtless find thousands of organized minorities to which he might attach himself without inconsistency. There is nothing in the nature of pressure groups that tends to limit their number, as parties are restricted by the two-party system. Since pressure groups do not deal in elections and votes they are relieved of all the limitations that the nature of the election system imposes on parties. Calculations concerning numbers and politics, majorities, geographical representation, and the simplification of alternatives are irrelevant to pressure groups.

Pressure groups are likewise relieved of many of the hazards to which minor parties are subject. Since they do not nominate candidates, they do not get caught in the toils of the single-member district system which pinches the lesser parties to death. The claims of pressure groups on their membership may be much greater than those of a party, though the number of paper organizations in the field must be very great. This is possible because the pressure group assumes that all members have a *special* (i.e., intense) interest. Therefore membership in a pressure group is not like membership in a party. Finally, pressure groups, unlike parties, *are not subjected to a compulsory periodic public test of their strength in an election.* Claims as to the size, enthusiasm, and unanimity of their membership are subject to no verification by the objective public process of an election contest. The very fact that the claims are not subject to verification is one of the principal sources of the influence of pressure groups. Pressure groups, like all other political associations, are what they *must* be and *can* be under the terms of their existence. Consequently the simple fact that they do not set out to control government by winning elections has had a determinative effect upon them.

The Method of Exaggeration

The foregoing discussion indicates the answer to the question, how can pressure groups influence public policy without winning elections? First, they do so by taking advantage of the weakness of the political parties. In the second place, they have been able to wield great influence by taking a remarkable advantage of their own weakness. Since they are too feeble to fight election campaigns they avail themselves of the opportunity to make vast, unverifiable claims as to their influence, the size of their membership, the resolution and unanimity of the membership. This is the method of exaggeration. The technique is one of the oldest known to politics and has been expressed in the maxim: *Never admit that it is only you who is talking.* Political parties have immemorially used the same technique but with an extremely important variation, namely, the parties are subjected to periodic tests of strength.

In every election there is a public verification of the claims of the parties to the support of the American people. The pressure groups scrupulously avoid this test. There have been some dramatic illustrations of the deflation of pressure organizations when they have been so indiscreet as to let themselves become involved in an electoral trial of strength. Before the election of 1936 Father Coughlin had, by a strenuous campaign of ballyhoo, succeeded in building up an impression of his influence and authority so realistic and terrifying that even veterans of political warfare became alarmed. Claims that the Union for Social Justice could control millions of votes were freely made and credited. Unfortunately for his own political future, Father Coughlin allowed himself to be persuaded to put a candidate into the field—with disastrous results. Mr. Lemke was defeated so badly that the influence of the whole movement was substantially destroyed. The first rule of successful pressure politics therefore is to make a noise like the clamor of millions but never permit an investigation of the claims. Exaggeration is the life of pressure politics. The more realistically it can be done the more apt it is to worry timid congressmen, and that is enough. Congressmen become hypersensitive to all symptoms of unrest in the electorate and grow alarmed at any hostile demonstration because the parties do little to defend them.

It is precisely at this point that the relation between the pressure group and the party determines the nature of both. A strongly led party able to discipline its members and able to hold its lines on controversial questions will be able to defy the guerilla tactics of the pressure groups. The whole assumption of this statement is that the number of votes that can be delivered by a pressure group is likely to be very small; that the pressure group is putting up a stupendous bluff. It follows that, if the party is able to force its congressmen to fight against pressures, they are extremely likely to win. Pressure groups are rarely organized to deliver votes; they are rarely able to conduct an active campaign in the electorate. In the great majority of cases a little courage and resolution will suffice to put to rout any pressure group. To force pressure groups into the electoral campaign to show how many votes they can deliver is to force them also to try to persuade the public generally and to drive them out of a favored position. That is, an indolent, weakly led party will let the pressure groups win without a showdown, cheaply, without forcing them to conduct an expensive campaign in the general electorate.

The strategy of pressure politics can be made difficult if we produce another kind of party system. A strong party can do much more than merely force its members in Congress to resist pressures. It can take aggressive measures to support congressmen on the firing line and can combat pressure tactics. The strong party can take the offensive by defining *public* issues on grounds calculated to appeal to large segments of the electorate so strongly that it need not fear the raids by organized minorities. If the demands of the special interest become intolerable, the party can counterattack by taking the issue to the public, nearly always with great advantage to its own cause. The enmity of a few selfish minorities and special interests is generally an asset to any party. To single out a pressure group for attack is to annihilate it.

The second technique of pressure politics is one of the inevitable results of political organization. A well-organized and well-staffed pressure group is able to get much information not easily available to people generally. It can maintain an office in Washington and employ agents who have access to Congress and the executive departments and agencies of the government. It can follow the movements of hostile interests, movements usually concealed from the public. On the basis of information so collected, an organized special interest is able to rally its supporters and to apply pressure when and where it can be employed most advantageously. A good intelligence service is therefore the basis of effective pressure tactics.

It is a significant characteristic of American pressure groups that no clear philosophy of their public responsibilities has been developed. Aside from periodic gestures of irritation at groups which have succeeded in annoying the public, and some halfhearted and futile attempts at regulation, pressure groups have been allowed to ply their traffic without restraint and without guidance, in a condition of almost complete and irresponsible freedom. It cannot be said that there is anything like a coherent body of opinion as to what ought to be done about them. Any attempt to regulate pressure groups or to restrain their most pernicious activities is certain to prove difficult becuase this form of politics is based upon the greatest rights in the decalogue of American civil liberties: the right of free association, the right of petition, the right of freedom of speech and agitation, and so on. To regulate pressure politics by suppressing these great liberties is to cure the disease by killing the patient. The consequence of an almost complete absence of attempts to define the proper role of pressure groups in American politics, plus the absence of any systematic investigation of the claims of pressure groups to represent their constituencies, has fostered abuses and has produced a condition in which it has been impossible for the government to make the best possible use of interest groups for the guidance and enlightenment of public policy. The fact that these groups exercise valuable rights, that they may be useful and may even be necessary but are also pernicious, constitutes a challenge to students of politics to reconsider their ideas on the subject.

The Right to Be Heard

In attempting to define the proper place of pressure groups in American politics a clear distinction should be made between *pressure* and the right to be heard. The right to be heard is intimately associated with a battery of highly valued restrictions on arbitrary government and is closely related to the idea of government by consent. It is not unlikely that there will be a great extension of this right in the future development of democratic government. At the present time this right is clearly established only in judicial proceedings and in certain administrative proceedings where it is required by due process of law. It seems likely, however, that in the future the government will develop procedures giving it an opportunity to inform itself by hearing the testimony of interested groups before it acts in an increasing variety of cases. Voluntary associations of special interest minorities have a valuable contribution to make at this point. There is, however, a very great difference between giving a minority the right to be heard, to offer information, and to protest, on the one hand, and the tactics of "pressure," on the other.

It will probably never be possible to divorce hearing from pressure perfectly, though we have gone a long way in the judicial process in accomplishing this very thing. However, it is important that the government, i.e., administrators and congressmen, should not be intimidated but rather should be conscious of the strong public support of the political parties. An adequate national party leadership devoted to the protection of the great public interests in government will provide the conditions under which the expansion of organized contacts between the government and the nation may be carried out safely. We ought not to conclude that congressmen adequately supported by strong national parties and therefore not easily intimidated by the threats of special interest groups will be less just than the timid men who now inhabit the halls of Congress. The minorities have a right to be heard; they do not have the right to govern. The power to govern must be reserved to the majority acting through the political parties. It is not oppressive to distinguish between the valid and useful right of organized minorities to be heard and unreasonable claims of these minorities to power.

Once the supremacy of the parties over the organized special interests has been established, it should be possible also to require that petitioners identify themselves and give proper evidence of their representative authority. The fact that congressional committees now permit the representatives of special interests to appear before them without showing their credentials is a mark of the timidity of Congress when confronted by the pressure groups. Insistence on the right of Congress to know precisely who it is that appears before its committees and the insistence on the right to audit the representative claims of the pressure groups should go a long way toward the deflation of the abusive tactics of these groups. Pendleton Herring has already demonstrated sufficiently that the executive departments will be able to resist improper pressures if Congress is able to do so.[1] At all points the problem of the management of pressures is a problem of the political parties.

[1]Pendleton Herring, *Public Administration and the Public Interest* (New York: McGraw-Hill, 1936).

Political Parties and Pressure Group Politics

Hugh A. Bone

Political interest groups and political parties share political power and influence in running American politics. Their interests, objectives, and techniques overlap in so many ways that they appear indistinguishable at times. Nevertheless, most students of government see a pressure group as "issue or policy oriented," and a political party as "election or personality oriented." A party is seen as primarily motivated toward capturing and operating the government; the interest group's motivation is to shape public policy.

These observations on differences undoubtedly contain a large grain of truth. But a party which controls the government is expected to shape policy and to assume responsibility for it. If a pressure group wishes to shape policy to its interests it can hardly ignore the necessity for electing persons sympathetic to its views. Parties and private groups both seek access to government and must perforce have contacts and relationships with each other. Both afford channels by which the citizen may participate in the control of his government. Both complement and supplement each other. There is a constant two-way process of influence and relationship from interest group to party and from party to interest group.

Although many persons are active in a party and in a pressure group, the professional bureaucracies of the two have usually remained separate. The same is true of the leadership. A state or county chairman is seldom the president of a chamber of commerce or of a labor union. But the leadership, active workers, and enthusiastic supporters of parties and groups have so much in common that they remain in touch with each other much of the time. Major opportunities for contacts are afforded by nomination, campaigns, campaign finance, party programming, and infiltration.

Nonpartisan and Partisan Elections

In the United States some 800,000 public offices are filled by election. A considerable number of local officers such as clerks, councilmen, judges, treasurers, park and education board members are nonpartisan. Party intrusions into these elections are usually denounced and may actually hurt the candidacy of the ones

Hugh A. Bone, "Political Parties and Pressure Group Politics," Annals of the American Academy of Political and Social Science, *Vol. 319 (1958). Reprinted with permission.*

receiving party support. In nonpartisan elections, therefore, the support of interest groups is often of paramount importance and eagerly sought. Because a nonpartisan nominee lacks the organizational and financial backing of a political party, interest groups have an excellent chance to influence the outcome of these elections and may aid candidates without being charged as being pro-Republican or pro-Democratic. The campaign of a candidate for the nonpartisan office of state superintendent of public instruction in Washington State was directed almost exclusively from the office of an educational association whose membership was largely composed of teachers, school directors, and persons vitally concerned with curriculum and financial support of the schools.

In a number of large cities, citizens groups publicly rate the various candidates for local offices. Recommendations are eagerly sought by candidates for nonpartisan offices, and they are usually willing to appear before the "candidate committees" of the civic groups in the hope that they will receive favorable comment. Newspapers often carry the statements on candidates prepared by the associations so that the influence of the association carries far beyond its limited membership. In the absence of a party label, a number of voters are guided by the endorsements—or lack of them—given by a municipal league to candidates for nonpartisan offices.

Private interest groups are no less concerned with numerous other state and local offices where a partisan ballot is used. Insurance and land commissioners, sanitary engineers, port officials, and so on often run as Republicans or Democrats but, for various reasons, receive little more than nominal help from the party organization. These officials have the power to make decisions which vitally affect certain private groups, and it becomes understandable that the latter should take an active part in securing the election of officials whose rulings and orders may influence their membership. The multiplicity of offices and the long ballot are confusing to the voter. This situation plays into the hands of pressure groups and also makes it imperative for them to take an interest in who is elected to administer the diverse state functions.

Nominations

In addition to its mixture of nonpartisan and partisan elections, the American electoral system has another feature which has encouraged political activity on the part of numerous interest groups—the direct primary system of nominations. In parts of the United States the party organizations are forbidden by law or party rules to endorse a candidate where there is a contest in the primary. In many other places it is customary for the parties to remain neutral in the primaries. Those entering the primary, therefore, cannot hope to receive financial or other help from either the national or the local party committees. Under the circumstances the nominee must finance his own primary campaign or seek help from personal friends—neither of which may be sufficient. Hopefuls are likely to find pressure groups ready to assist them in the primaries provided the latter feel the prospective nominee will be friendly to their cause. It stands to reason that those candidates who appear to have some chance of winning the primary will receive more help than those less likely to capture the nomination. Occasionally, however, an interest group will support a candidate even though he has little chance of winning. This is done because the group wishes to use the primary campaign as a forum for criticizing an incumbent or championing certain issues. Labor unions have done this on occasion where anti- or non-union views appear to predominate. In this sense the primary campaign is run as an "educational" program rather than as a potentially successful electoral venture.

Interest groups of diverse objectives often co-operate in getting persons registered. The officials or special committees of interest groups may decide to make endorsements among the candidates in the primary. Where there are contests in both party primaries, interest groups sometimes make an endorsement in each, but it is more likely that approval will be given to only one candidate. Endorsements are made known to the membership through the channels of the press and more particularly in the official newspaper or magazine of the organization. Some of these publications carry information on all candidates, but the material is presented in such a way as to show favoritism for one of them. Candidates may be invited to speak before a meeting of the group and given access to the pages of the journal to present views of interest to the membership. Literature on the primaries is often distributed to the members and a door-bell ringing or telephone corps is used to get out the vote on primary day. Activities by interest groups on behalf of candidates have undoubtedly swelled the numbers of persons participating in the primaries.

Nominations for President and Vice-President are made at party conventions. Over half the delegates in the national convention are selected by conventions in the states. In some states party conventions also designate certain candidates for public office. Where an interest group feels that the nominees of the convention may have views strongly for or against something it stands for, the group becomes vitally concerned with the choice of delegates and may seek either to have some of its own members chosen to the convention or to influence the selection. Delegates also adopt the party's platform, a matter in which the interest groups are most interested.

Prior to the 1952 convention, it was clear that Governor Stevenson's opposition to state ownership of submerged offshore lands was of concern to oil interests especially in the South. Delegates were made aware of this "liability." Delegates are likewise urged by private groups to ascertain the views of potential nominees on civil rights, labor, agriculture, and a host of other issues. Delegates are likely to be deluged with letters and telegrams expressing views on candidates as well as platform proposals. Many of these are inspired by interests back home.

Influential members of interest groups are often present in the convention city and seek meetings with chairmen of the state delegations, potential candidates, and powerful leaders within the party. The late Senator Alben Barkley went to the 1952 Democratic National Convention confident of the support of organized labor for the Presidential nomination. He relates that, on the eve of the opening of the convention,

> a little group of labor men, purporting to speak for the AFL and CIO, but acting, so far as anyone has been able to learn, with no mandate from their respective organizations, gave out an announcement that "organized labor" could not support me because of my age. This, so far as my candidacy was concerned, was a kiss of death.[1]

In 1948 a group of physicians were especially active in defeating Harold Stassen's bid for the nomination and aiding the cause of Governor Dewey. Every delegate to the Republican National Convention received a printed circular from the Oregon Physicians Fighting Political Medicine, on a letterhead containing the names of prominent past presidents in medical societies, urging that he cast his vote for Dewey in order to forestall "socialized medicine." The Oregon physicians were instrumental in defeating Stassen in that state's Presidential primary.

No complete study has been made of the interest group background of delegates to the national conventions but the state by state analysis of the selection of delegates to the 1952 conventions shows that many groups did try to get representation.[2] It was not unusual for an official in the Chamber of Commerce, a farm organization, or a county medical society to be found among the state delegations in 1952. In a number of instances labor unions paid the expenses of delegates to the national convention and a number of other interests were alleged to have defrayed some of the expense of certain delegates.

National conventions are dominated by certain powerful political leaders such as governors, senators, congressmen, and local party chairmen. The majority of delegates are persons with a record of active partisan politics. For this reason pressure groups find they must operate most of the time off the convention floor. But the leaders of the private groups maintain contacts during conventions with the influential delegates, and hotel lobbies in the convention city teem with representatives of private groups.

General Elections

The activities of pressure groups in a general election differ only in emphasis and detail from that of the primary. Perhaps most important is that in the general election the group must work out its relationship and modus operandi with the party organization. Three alternatives are possible. First the pressure group may develop its own campaign organization paralleling to some extent the precinct

[1]*That Reminds Me* (New York: Doubleday, 1954), p. 236.

[2]See the five volume work by Paul T. David, Malcolm Moos, and Ralph M. Goldman, *Presidential Nominating Politics in 1952* (Baltimore: Johns Hopkins Press, 1954).

and other organization of the party. The group remains quite independent from the party. Labor unions have done this on numerous occasions. Party leaders are not invariably enthusiastic about this. They feel that the campaign run by the pressure groups may be too amateurish and operate at cross purposes with the strategy of the party. If the candidate wins, the pressure group may ask for patronage or certain concessions.

A second alternative is for the interest group to operate closely with the party organization with the campaign direction largely in the hands of the latter. In this instance the pressure group furnishes personnel to the party headquarters, providing doorbell ringers and speakers as requested by the party chairmen and campaign managers. It co-operates with and in general takes its orders from the party. This arrangement appeals to the party leaders.

A third arrangement is a combination of the two with the interest groups maintaining considerable autonomy, but working closely with the party and perhaps providing direct assistance to the party headquarters. Which of these three alternatives is to be followed is determined by expediency, local conditions, the leadership of the party and the interest group and, of course, the preference of the candidate. Pressure groups are usually less interested in the entire ticket and prefer to concentrate on certain candidacies. What often takes place in practice then is more a pressure group-candidate relationship than a pressure group-party relationship.

The alleged successes of interest groups in primary and general elections may perhaps belong in the category in which Mark Twain once placed reports on his death—as highly exaggerated. Voting behavior is not likely to be explained exclusively by the activities or lack of them of pressure groups. Endorsement of a candidate by one group is frequently offset by endorsement of his opponent by another. Reliable data, moreover, is scanty. In 1946 California Republicans made an effective issue of the CIO-supported candidates for Congress, labeling them "package" candidates. In this election only 73 Political Action Committee-endorsed candidates out of 318 in House contests won. Yet in the 1948 election Labor's League for Political Education saw 172 of its "friends" elected to Congress and 106 of its "enemies" retired. With the support of the American Federation of Labor and Congress of Industrial Organizations Adlai Stevenson was unable to win either in 1952 or in 1956. Interest-group support may be important and significant but not necessarily determinative.

A recurrent theme of this volume is the desire of pressure groups to gain access to government. A highly important method of access is through the public elected official. It follows then that the pressure group must function in one way or another in campaigns. Campaigns bring the pressure group in direct contact with the candidate and/or his managers and party officials. In the long run these relationships are more important than the precise degree to which the group contributes to the election itself.

Campaign Finance

One of the most important developments in recent years is the increasingly large role of nonparty groups in the financing of campaigns. With the cost of campaigns increasing, parties and candidates are looking for additional sources of revenue and also agencies through which money can be expended without exceeding the 3 million dollars limitation imposed by the Hatch Act for one committee. Corporations and labor unions are forbidden by law from making direct contributions to political campaigns. These various laws, often referred to collectively as corrupt practices legislation, have not kept political-interest groups from giving donations but made them somewhat more circumspect. There are several ways by which groups may raise funds for candidates and still remain within the law.

The first is to form a "political action committee" illustrated by the Machinists Non-Partisan Political League, the United Automobile Workers-CIO Political Action Committee, and the AFL-CIO Committee on Political Education (COPE). Political funds are raised and expended separately from the treasuries of the labor unions. By this device labor unions may assist candidates without violating the law. In the off-year of 1957, thirteen labor organizations comparable to those above spent $243,000 or 5 per cent of the total reported to the Clerk of the House of Representatives in that year.

The now defunct Peoples Committee to Defend Life Insurance and Savings offered an analagous opportunity for insurance executives and stockholders to contribute to campaigns. "Healing arts committees" have provided a channel for doctors, nurses, dentists, and pharmacists to contribute to campaigns.

A host of "citizens" and "volunteers" groups crop up all over the nation during campaigns. Many of these political groups are not as broadly constituted as were the Citizens for Eisenhower-Nixon and Volunteers for Stevenson. A careful analysis of some of these local groups will often reveal important economic interests as dominant in both the leadership and finance of the organizations. In only a relatively few instances is a title used (except for labor) which clearly identifies the interest group involved. Examples of these in 1956 were the Indiana Farm Research Committee (Republican), Timber Farmers for Stevenson-Kefauver, Conservationists for Stevenson-Kefauver, and the National Business Council for Stevenson-Kefauver.

By creating separate political committees, the organizations themselves remain officially neutral in partisan politics. This is less offensive to those members who do not believe that campaigns should be financed out of the organization's treasury or who may hold political views at variance with the majority of the membership.

Governmental investigation committees. The United States House and Senate usually create special campaign investigating committees for every biennial election. Over the years they have amassed much data on sources of revenue in political campaigns. A Subcommittee of the Senate Rules and Administration Committee made an extraordinarily comprehensive study of the 1956 general election and estimated that 33 million dollars was spent by the parties and private organizations participating in the campaigns for federal office.[3] Large sums of money are never reported and the committee's figures must be regarded as understating rather than providing a full picture of campaign finance. A few of the committee's findings, however, deserve citation.

Labor organizations reported contributions to various candidates totaling $1,078,000; all but $4,000 went to Democratic candidates. This is in addition to the $941,000 spent directly by the political action committees. Expenditures reported by miscellaneous interest groups included Christian Nationalist Crusade, $38,000; Americans for Democratic Action, $57,000; and the National Committee for an Effective Congress, $17,000.

A special study was made of the amount of money contributed by officials of the 225 largest corporations in the United States and/or their wives to parties or other campaign groups. The figures included only contributions of $500 or more. It was found that $3,029,000 was contributed to the Republicans and $111,000 to the Democrats. Officials of manufacturing corporations contributed $1,830,000; commercial banks, $536,000; transportation companies, $360,000; life insurance companies, $186,000; and the public utilities, $71,200. The active and graduate members of the Department of Commerce's Business Advisory Council contributed over a quarter of a million dollars.

The contributions of oil interests to campaigns have been widely publicized for many years. Officials of the American Petroleum Institute reported contributions exceeding $171,000 in 1956. The offer of a $2,500 campaign contribution to Senator Francis Case by the oil and natural-gas interests set off a Congressional investigation and resulted in a Presidential veto of a measure to exempt natural gas from federal regulation. In his veto message President Eisenhower took cognizance of alleged "bribes" and attempts through campaign donations to influence Senate votes. He said:

> a body of evidence has accumulated indicating that private persons, apparently representing only a very small segment of a great and vital industry, have been seeking to further their own interests by highly questionable activities. These include efforts I deem to be so arrogant and so much in defiance of acceptable standards of propriety as to risk creating doubt among the American people concerning the integrity of governmental processes.[4]

[3]A useful summary and analysis of the committee's findings will be found in the *Congressional Quarterly Weekly Report*, Vol. 15 (February 8 and 22, 1957). See also the *Final Report of the Special Committee to Investigate Political Activities, Lobbying and Campaign Contributions*, U.S. Senate, 85th Congress, 1st Sess., May 31, 1957.

[4]*Washington Post and Times Herald*, February 18, 1956.

In many large cities the parties have prepared a list of business executives who regularly give campaign donations. The head of a corporation has at times solicited funds for a party or a candidate from his junior executives. The head of a large advertising agency sent a three-page letter to his top 125 executives calling for contributions to re-elect Eisenhower "to preserve this climate of business confidence" and pointed out that "business uncertainty might follow his defeat."[5] He suggested a scale of giving as follows:

Pre-tax Income	Contribution
$ 5,000	$ 25
10,000	75
25,000	375
50,000	1,000
100,000	3,000
Over 100,000	3½ per cent

Interest groups are heavy donors to state and local parties and candidates. There are several states which require no statement of campaign expenditures and others which require only statements of spending in a direct primary. As a result the public generally has less knowledge of the role played by groups in financing local elections than for federal offices.

Platform Influencing

The fact that party platforms are usually ambiguous and general has not kept the pressure groups from trying to influence them. National party platforms are drafted by the national convention's committee on resolutions composed of one person from each state delegation. The committee members even before they arrive in the convention city receive communications and personal requests from interest groups on diverse planks and proposals. A preliminary draft is prepared by a group appointed by the national committee, and this group is also the recipient of requests from certain interests.

After the resolutions committee is convened, it is often divided into subcommittees according to subject matter such as foreign policy, civil rights, veterans, and agriculture. The subcommittees then hold public hearings. Witnesses distribute copies of their prepared addresses to the committee members, answer questions, and elaborate upon their statements. Edward F. Cooke found that seventy spokesmen for interest groups submitted briefs and oral arguments before the Republican resolutions committee in 1952.

[5]*New York Times*, June 12, 1956. For an illuminating article on business contributions, see "How to Give Money to Politicians," *Fortune* (May 1956), pp. 113-117, 237-245.

> Upon conclusion of the open hearings [he writes], the subcommittees went into executive session in order to draft a specific recommendation for their respective policy areas. In their deliberations the members were aided by the digest of platform suggestions, the written briefs of the interest groups, copies of previous platform planks, and expert assistance from staff technicians drawn from Republican Congressional and party offices in Washington, some of whom had sat in on the public hearings.[6]

Party platform formation on the state and county level also affords the pressure group an opportunity both for publicity and influence. It is not unusual for the local press to record a state party platform as "strongly pro-labor," "a victory for the conservatives" or "a bid for the minorities vote," thus suggesting victories for dominant factors and interests.

The making of a party platform is a way by which a political party can build a coalition of supporting interest groups. Platform drafters can remind an interest group that it was "heard" and point to a plank or clause contributed by a group. At the same time a pressure group can remind officeholders of platform pledges.

Infiltration

Infiltration of the party organizations by members of interest groups is not unusual. The reverse also takes place though it is less publicized and obvious. A former party chairman in metropolitan Seattle made it a studied policy to encourage his precinct committeemen to join pressure groups and to become active as well in philanthropic and cultural societies. The chairman felt that his workers would have many opportunities to bring the "gospel" to the various nonparty groups and thereby build up favorable sentiment for the party among those who were perhaps unresponsive to partisan publicity. The chairman pointed out to would-be candidates that one of the best ways to become known was to be active in civic improvement and various other private groups.

In 1956 the Republican National Committee created a special labor division to counteract the tendency of union labor to vote Democratic. One of its projects was to try to locate members of unions who were sympathetic to the Republican cause and who might be willing to take a position in the local party organization. These persons could be used to pass out literature at union meetings. During Presidential campaigns it is customary for both national headquarters to create special interest divisions such as farm, veterans, Negro, and national resources.

If a party is able to have some of its members active in nonparty groups, other values may be realized. Party members can help to engineer invitations to

[6]"Drafting the 1952 Platforms," *Western Political Quarterly*, Vol. 9 (September 1956), p. 701.

party candidates and officials to speak to the group. The minorities division of the national committees have their members in nationalities societies; they notify the office of important dates so that the national chairman or some other prominent person may send appropriate congratulations. Additional members of the group may be won over and recruited for party activity. Active partisans can serve as a source of intelligence on views, attitudes, and sentiments of the pressure groups on public policies and candidates. Political parties have the perennial problem of raising money, and prospective donors may be found in the membership of the pressure group.

As parties desire to broaden their strength and support among interest groups, the latter wish to extend their influence within the party organization. In most parts of the nation, party organization is loose, making it relatively easy for members of interest groups to become active members of parties. Willing and eager persons soon have opportunities for positions in the precinct, district, and county party organizations or in party clubs. This in turn affords the opportunity to attend party conventions, participate in campaigns, draft resolutions and, at times, to run for public office.

It is unusual, however, for wholesale infiltration to take place. There have been times nonetheless when a nonparty group has, by design, set about to capture control of the party organization. The Non-Partisan League in North Dakota employed the tactics of infiltration rather than third-party politics. League nominees were placed in the Republican primaries and were successful in capturing the Republican State Committee. By 1918 the Republican party, platform, and state government were taken over completely by the League and much of its legislative program was enacted.

Michigan provides another success story of interest group infiltration. The state has been traditionally Republican and there was no permanent Democratic organization until the New Deal. In 1948 the CIO-PAC observed that "progressives" in the Democratic party leadership were outnumbered by "reactionaries," but that the Democrats afforded the best channel for supporting the interests of Michigan labor and liberalism. Accordingly the PAC advised all CIO members "to become active precinct, ward, county, and congressional district workers and attempt to become delegates to Democratic conventions."[7] The CIO built a coalition with certain ethnic, liberal, and other labor groups and captured control of the state Democratic committee. It did this by training and electing precinct captains and taking control of the party conventions. The coalition, therefore, was able to have a noticeable influence on both primary and convention nominations.

The CIO coalition brought about many changes in the Democratic party. One of these was the emphasis upon state party platforms. The platforms were

[7]A detailed account of the Michigan story will be found in Fay Calkins, *The CIO and the Democratic Party* (Chicago: Univ. Chicago Press, 1952), Ch. 6.

oriented toward specific liberal, social programs, and potential candidates were evaluated in terms of their attitude toward the platform. Governor G. Mennen Williams has continuously stressed these issues in his campaigns and in his inaugural addresses. The coalition continued to govern the selection of party officers, eject the conservative Old Guard, and appoint liberals to policy-determining patronage jobs. Labor people compose about one-third of the party offices today.

Advantages and liabilities of infiltration. Infiltration has certain advantages for an interest group. Miss Calkins notes that in a rural Republican area in Northern Illinois:

> . . . a Democratic label was bad enough, but a PAC label was impossible. From its internal position, PAC could call its man Goldman a Democrat. It could get local lawyers to run on a Democratic ballot who would not think of associating themselves with a third party or an independent labor group. It could tap the support of other community groups which would have been very suspicious of labor operating alone. Under the party cover PAC was less vulnerable to newspaper attack as a special interest group.[8]

An internal party relationship gives a pressure group a chance to breathe vigor and life into a party and to strengthen its organizational base. It helps to further its legislative program and to inform the other officials of the party about the needs of the group.

There are also potential liabilities to the internal party relationships both for the party and the interest group. The interest group may find that its activity within a party may heighten factionalism within its own ranks. The Teamsters Union in Michigan fought the liberal coalition and some of its membership went over to the rival party. In very few organizations are all of the members Republicans or Democrats, and the minority is likely to resent the partisan activities of the majority. Control of a party requires financial resources, sustained effort, and other activities. It is not easy to keep up the activity necessary to control the party year in and year out and may divert energies of the group's leadership away from problems of internal group organization and program.

Party politics require concessions and compromises which may be unpalatable to many members of the group. Charges of betrayal and "double-crossing" are not unusual. If the interest group fails to elect candidates or to obtain programs from the party it has infiltrated, some of the membership is bound to become disgruntled and to request that the efforts to control the political party be abandoned. Nevertheless, infiltration is a tempting tactic for it gives the group a chance to influence nominations and platforms from the inside rather than from outside the organization.

[8] *Ibid.*, p. 99.

Conclusion

The nature of the American political system provides pressure groups many opportunities to influence political parties and their candidates at all levels of government. Federalism and separation of powers have caused a decentralization of party organization with congressmen looking more to their own congressional and senatorial campaign committees than to the national committees. The direct primary system has removed from the party organization itself the historic function of designation. The cost of running for office is rapidly increasing so that many candidates must look outside of the party for assistance. Added to this complex picture is the high degree of voter independence and a large number of nonpartisan offices.

All of these factors have tended to make candidates more dependent upon nonparty sources for money, votes, and services. Party leaders have seen potential voters brought together in thousands of economic, political, social, and ethnic associations. If they can deal with the leaders of these groups, it may be easier and more effective than dealing with them as isolated individuals.

If parties have become dependent upon pressure groups, the reverse is also true. As Donald Blaisdell has pointed out:

> The organization which the parties set up and maintain for the purpose of gaining control over the governing personnel is thus the vehicle by which interests are able to share power with the titular leaders. As a means of gaining the power of governing, party structure and organization serve not only the leaders nominally in official and party positions but also the pressure groups.[9]

Pressure groups at times have tried to operate through the channels of minor parties. The abolitionists and "dry" forces were active at times through third parties. Organized labor, though divided, achieved some limited successes in New York State through the American Labor and Liberal parties. Agrarian malcontents used the Greenback, Populist, and Farmer-Labor parties to further their ends. But the pressure groups found that third parties seldom gave them the desired access to government. With a few exceptions, pressure groups today regard the influencing of the two major parties the better strategy and tactic.

Persons who become influential and active both in a party and a group become valuable members to both because of the access to each. They become aware of the problems of each and understand the limitations and strengths. Members of interest groups who become active partisans learn what a party can and cannot do and what its potential is likely to be. Similarly a party member who joins a pressure group comes to know its viewpoints and demands. An

[9]*American Democracy under Pressure* (New York: Ronald, 1957), p. 144.

infiltrator in time may serve as a valuable mediator and interpreter. As Ivan Hinderaker has stated:

> as the infiltrator becomes more active in party affairs, he gains an education in the realities of party politics, and in his party role his pressure group loyalties must take second position behind his party loyalty. Though he still works for his pressure group objectives, now he begins to understand why the broad-based major party cannot accede to his pressure group's every demand.[10]

Pressure groups serve society in many useful and valuable ways. They provide a type of political self-expression, formulate policies and seek their fulfillment, provide public officials with information, and help to define the public interest. At the same time the pressure group must be watched so that it does not subvert the public interest. Political parties have the function of accommodating the demands of private interests into the larger public interests. Our major parties are combinations of great interests, but they are also an entity apart from any one pressure group. The interests of the American society and of the interest group itself are best served when a pressure group makes no permanent identification with either major party. Each can best make its contribution to politics by remaining separate. But the realities of American politics make it necessary for them to have close contact with each other.

[10]*Party Politics* (New York: Holt, 1956), p. 66.

American State Legislators' Role Orientations toward Pressure Groups

John C. Wahlke
William Buchanan
Heinz Eulau
LeRoy C. Ferguson

I

In modern pluralistic political systems, the legislature is a central forum where organized interest groups articulate and express their views and press for public action favorable to their concerns. Indeed, the free representation of interests crucially affects the legitimacy of modern democratic legislatures. If interest groups were removed or prevented from influencing legislative action, the authority of the legislature would be put in jeopardy and its decisions would be found unacceptable. Yet in spite of the critical importance of the relationship between interest groups and law-making institutions, research offers surprisingly little theoretical explanation and few cumulative or comparative empirical data about this phase of the representative process. [1]

Most case studies of pressure groups do little more than describe the qualities, properties or activities of some of the pressuring groups, taking for granted

[1] Samuel J. Eldersveld, "American Interest Groups: A Survey of Research and Some Implications for Theory and Method," *Interest Groups on Four Continents*, ed. Henry W. Ehrmann (Pittsburgh, 1958), pp. 173-196; Oliver Garceau, "Interest Group Theory in Political Research," *Annals of the American Academy of Political and Social Science*, Vol. 319 (1958), pp. 104-112.

For discussion of some of the general problems of research, theory and conception, see also Gabriel A. Almond, "A Comparative Study of Interest Groups and the Political Process," *American Political Science Review*, Vol. 52 (1958), pp. 270-282; Alfred de Grazia, "The Nature and Prospects of Political Interest Groups," *Annals of the American Academy of Political and Social Science*, Vol. 319 (1958), pp. 113-122; W. J. M. Mackenzie, "Pressure Groups: The 'Conceptual Framework,'" *Political Studies*, Vol. 3 (1955), pp. 247-252.

John C. Wahlke, William Buchanan, Heinz Eulau, and LeRoy C. Ferguson, "American State Legislators' Role Orientations toward Pressure Groups," Journal of Politics, *Vol. 22 (1960). Reprinted with permission.*

the persons they press upon.[2] Such studies tend to be preoccupied with assessing the relative power of the various groups active in some particular situation and to neglect other kinds of questions political science ought to be considering: What sort of *system* is it within which groups act and become represented? How do institutional structures of this sort come into being? How do they change, or why do they not change? How does the system or structure itself facilitate or hinder performance of the representative function in the governmental process?

Questions like these direct attention to the official actors in the political process—in this case, to the activities and behavior of legislators. For, after all, the legislature is describable as an institutionalized group only insofar as relevant behaviors of legislators follow certain predictable patterns. A too-simple "group approach" to the legislative process implies an unrealistic conception of legislators' behavior and of the resultant character of the legislative process. The public policy decisions of legislatures cannot realistically be visualized as simple mathematical resultants of a given number of "pressures," each of measurable direction and strength, impingeing on passively reacting legislators.[3]

Role theory provides a more appropriate and useful model. While it is not possible to develop the point exhaustively here, a few observations should be made.[4] First of all, it seems obvious that legislators' *perceptions* of pressure groups—or of any other factor, for that matter—will vitally affect the part played by that factor in the legislative process.[5] More particularly, legislators'

[2]Henry W. Ehrmann, *op. cit.*, the most extensive work considering pressure groups in a trans-system context, contains a series of studies of particular countries, but not broader comparison or analysis.

Among the most noteworthy of those few studies which do deal extensively with the behavior of pressured legislators are Oliver Garceau and Corinne Silverman, "A Pressure Group and the Pressured: A Case Report," *American Political Science Review*, Vol. 48 (1954), pp. 672-691; John Millett, "The Role of an Interest Group Leader in the House of Commons," *Western Political Quarterly*, Vol. 9 (1956), pp. 915-926; and V. O. Key, "The Veterans and the House of Representatives: A Study of a Pressure Group and Electoral Mortality," *The Journal of Politics*, Vol. 5 (1943), pp. 27-40.

[3]This is one of the main criticisms voiced, for example, by Peter Odegard, "A Group Basis of Politics: A New Name for an Ancient Myth," *Western Political Quarterly*, Vol. 11 (1958), pp. 689-702. See also Robert M. MacIver's criticism of Bentley in *The Web of Government* (New York, 1947), pp. 220-221. Of course, both the criticized and the critics readily admit, if pointedly asked, that "The politician-legislator is not equivalent to the steel ball in a pinball game, bumping passively from post to post down an inclined plane. He is a human being, involved in a variety of relationships with other human beings. In his role as legislator his accessibility to various groups is affected by the whole series of relationships that define him as a person" (David B. Truman, *The Governmental Process* [New York, 1951], pp. 332-333). The question is not one of recognizing such a basic postulate but of incorporating it in research and explanation.

[4]An admirable, research-oriented discussion of role theory, including a review of the relevant literature, which uses "role" and related terms in much the way they are used in this research, can be found in Neal Gross, Ward S. Mason, and Alexander W. MacEachern, *Explorations in Role Analysis* (New York, 1968), pp. 3-75, 244-257, 281-318.

[5]The point is forcibly demonstrated by Corinne Silverman, "The Legislator's View of the Legislative Process," *Public Opinion Quarterly*, Vol. 18 (1954), pp. 180-190.

perceptions of what constitutes legitimate or desirable or harmful activity by pressure groups or other factors, as well as their perceptions of the supposedly objective "facts" about such activity, are not random or idiosyncratic opinions held independently by each legislator individually, but are opinions intimately associated with what Truman has called the "influence of office"[6] and Latham has called "officiality."[7] Membership in the legislature constitutes a *status or position* in society. This means that people in the society *expect* certain behaviors by incumbents of that position. Legislators have similar expectations toward each other, and they all have expectations with respect to other classes of actors they encounter in doing their legislative business. The key concept to refer to these patterns of behavior associated with a given position or status in the expectations and orientations of people is *role.*

From the abstract and general principles of role theory we take the working hypothesis that legislators' conceptions of their role as legislators will be a crucial factor governing their legislative behavior and thereby affecting the access, influence or power of all groups, as well as differentiating among groups.[8] General role theory suggests that legislators' role conceptions constitute a determining factor in pressure politics at least as important as the number, size, strategy, skill or other characteristics of pressure groups themselves, the individual group affiliations and identifications of legislators, or the peculiarities of personality and personal whim of those legislators. These role conceptions can usefully be made the focal point of comparative and analytical study.

Such an approach, it should be emphasized, does not "contradict" group-focussed (or other) conceptions of pressure politics. Rather, it complements and carries them forward by linking them potentially to more general concepts and more general bodies of theory. Every hypothesis about a relation between group characteristic and group influence plainly rests upon assumptions about the behavior of the legislators supposedly reacting to the group pressures. For example, the belief that a group will have more influence if its lobbyists follow certain tactical principles rests upon assertions, sometimes quite explicit, about how

[6]Truman, *op. cit.,* pp. 346-350.

[7]Earl Latham, *The Group Basis of Politics* (Ithaca, N. Y., 1952), pp. 33-40.

[8]This proposition is in Truman's discussion of the influence of office and Latham's discussion of officiality. It is more directly suggested in Huitt's discussion of the way in which legislators' differing conceptions of their roles *pro* or *con* interest groups lead them to bring "competing versions of the facts" to their discussions of conflicting group demands (Ralph K. Huitt, "The Congressional Committee: A Case Study," *American Political Science Review,* Vol. 48 [1954], p. 350). It is the basis for empirical research in one very important instance (Garceau and Silverman, *op. cit.*), which differentiates faction-oriented, policy-oriented, program-oriented and non-generalizers' conceptions of the appropriate mode of behavior for legislators, although not formally utilizing role theory or role concepts to do so.

legislators will react to lobbyists acting in accordance with these principles.[9] Research which tests the behavioral assumptions of group-focussed (or other) studies against the observed behavior of legislators is essential to validation of any propositions linking group power and influence to group characteristics of any sort (or any other independent variable).

II

Among the questions asked of some 474 legislators in four states during the 1957 legislative sessions[10] were several which make it possible to explore legislators' role orientations toward pressure groups and their agents.

1. A typology of role orientations toward pressure groups. Several cautionary remarks should be made here. We are concerned with the functioning of the legislative *institution* in general, rather than with unique historical events or outcomes in the states studied. Similarly, the concern here is not with the *particular* group affiliations and identifications of individual legislators or their relative friendship or hostility toward specific groups but rather with their orientations toward pressure groups as a *generic* class of "significant others." The typology which follows has been constructed and used to suit this ultimate theoretical concern. Furthermore, rather than attempt, at this early stage of research using the role concept, to discover and describe in exhaustive detail the innumerable behaviors which add up (in the legislators' expectations) to the prevailing role conceptions relevant to pressure groups in the four state systems, attention has been restricted to what seem the most obvious areas of role orientation.

Political scientists are familiar with the doctrinal disagreement about the value of pressure politics. One view holds, as did Rousseau, that expression and promotion of conflicting private interests is inimical to discovery and promotion of the public interest; an opposing view, that of many "pluralist" theorists, holds that what is called "the public interest" is never more than the harmonization of

[9]Bertram Gross (*The Legislative Struggle* [New York, 1953], pp. 302-303) quotes the following rules set for N.A.M. lobbyists: "Avoid demagoguery before a Committee. It is resented." "Get directly to the facts. Committees are not much interested in long discussions about the trends of the time." "Don't assume a superior attitude." An often-cited rule of lobbying tactics in America, to "build up a bloc of votes in Congress to be backed with appeals from home at the psychological moment" (Stuart Chase, *Democracy under Pressure* [New York, 1945], pp. 24-26), likewise rests obviously upon assumptions about the motivations and behavior of congressmen.

[10]94% of the California, 100% of the New Jersey, 94% of the Ohio, and 91% of the Tennessee legislature were interviewed, using a fixed schedule of questions. Interviews averaged about an hour and a half in length. For other findings of the study see the authors' "The Political Socialization of American State Legislators," *Midwest Journal of Political Science*, Vol. 3 (1959), pp. 188-206; "The Role of the Representative: Some Empirical Observations on the Theory of Representation of Edmund Burke," *American Political Science Review*, Vol. 53 (1959), pp. 742-756; "The Legislator as Specialist," *Western Political Quarterly* (forthcoming).

just such partial and private interests and that organized interest groups, therefore, play an indispensable part in defining and legislating in the public interest. Legislators' views on the subject likewise differ widely. Some agree with the member who said, "Hell! We wouldn't have a government if there were no interest groups. It would be a form of anarchy if groups and parties didn't do their job." Or, as another said, when asked about the desirability of having the individual citizen participate in government directly, rather than through interest groups, "How's he going to do it 'directly'? You have to organize or go into an organization to do anything." But others agree with the legislator who said, in response to the same question, "Stop there (after the word 'directly') and you've got the whole story about our citizens and what they should do." Many legislators share the suspicion of interest groups in general expressed by the member who said, "I've heard of them all my life, but I didn't aim to fool with that, and I don't know nothing about it."

It seems obvious that a legislator's reaction to the activities of pressure groups and lobbyists will vary according to such differences in evaluation of pressure politics. Legislators' generalized attitudes of friendliness, neutrality or hostility to

Table 1. Attitude of State Legislators toward Pressure Politics

Question	Attitude*				
	Friendly ⟷ Hostile				
	1	2	3	4	5
1. Would you say that, on the whole, the legislature would work [better or worse] if there were no interest groups or lobbies trying to influence legislation? (N = 452)	41%	34%	12%	7%	6% = 100%
2. [Do you agree that] the job of the legislator is to work out compromises among conflicting interests? (N = 462)	31%	42%	2%	12%	13% = 100%
3. [Do you agree that] lobbyists and special interests have entirely too much influence in American state legislatures? (N = 464)	26%	34%	1%	22%	17% = 100%
4. [Do you agree that] under our form of government, every individual should take an interest in government directly, not through interest-group organizations? (N = 458)	19%	24%	3%	19%	35% = 100%

**Response categories to Question 1 were "much worse," "somewhat worse," "about the same," "somewhat better," and "much better"; to Questions 2-4, "agree," "tend to agree," "undecided," "tend to disagree," and "disagree." The most friendly responses are (1) "much worse," (2) "agree," (3) "disagree," and (4) "disagree."*

pressure politics were therefore measured by a four-item Likert scale utilizing replies to the questions shown in Table 1. Their attitudes were found to vary as indicated in that table.[11]

It likewise seems obvious that legislators' reactions to pressure groups or lobbyists will vary with their different degrees of knowledge or awareness of group activity. The legislator who knows what the Municipal League is, what it wants, who speaks for it and when, will react differently to cues from the League than the legislator who never heard of it and doesn't identify anyone as its spokesman. Legislators' awareness of lobbying activities was therefore measured by asking them to identify a list of lobbyists more or less active in their state legislatures during the time of interviewing.[12]

It is almost universally assumed that one important factor determining the representativeness, legitimacy and authority of any given legislature is the extent and manner of its taking into account the demands of significant interest groups in its social environment. This, in turn, is no more than a reflection of the behavior of the legislators. Some members, by their behavior toward lobbyists and

[11]The scale was constructed by awarding 4 points for the most friendly answer to a question, 3 points for the next most friendly, 2 points if undecided, 1 point if on the unfriendly side of "undecided" and 0 for the most unfriendly response. Averaging the four question-scores gives a scale-score. The power of each question to discriminate between respondents of high and low tolerance is more than sufficient, as shown by the values of Discriminatory Power obtained when the high and low *thirds* are used (actually, top 32% and bottom 35%)–a much more stringent requirement for a satisfactory scale than the usual one of at least 1.0 D.P. between upper and lower *quartiles.*

	Question Number			
	1	2	3	4
Mean score of upper 1/3	3.5	3.4	3.2	2.6
Mean score of lower 1/3	2.2	1.9	1.2	0.7
Discriminatory power	1.3	1.5	2.0	1.9

[12]The exact wording of the question was, "Here are the names of some persons that people have told us are connected with various interest groups and lobbies. Could you tell me who each of them is or what he does?" A respondent was credited with a "correct" answer if he identified the organizational tie, the general type of interest represented, or some particular legislative measure of concern for each lobbyist listed. Names on the list had been selected to include lobbyists of varying degrees of presumed familiarity. To obtain a more precise measure, scores were weighted to give greater credit for identifying lesser-known than for identifying universally-known lobbyists.

Unlike the tolerance scores, the awareness scores cannot be compared directly across state lines, since there is no way of comparing the recognition-value of lobbyists in different systems. But corresponding quintile groups can be so compared.

Garceau and Silverman (*op. cit.*) measured several other dimensions of awareness–ability to identify selected pressure groups, and ability to recognize more than one issue on which selected groups had been active. Pre-tests indicated that the single measure based on lobbyist-recognition produced awareness scores correlating very closely with those obtained by more complex measures; the simple unidimensional measure was therefore used here.

other group representational agents or activity, will serve to accommodate the demands of organized interest groups in the legislative process.[13] Others will serve to resist consideration or accommodation of these demands in any form. And still others, presumably attuned to other persons or factors, will play a neutral role toward such group demands.

Assuming, then, that any given legislator's behavior in this respect will depend to a considerable extent upon his general affective orientation toward pressure politics as a mode of political activity and his awareness of such activity when it occurs around him,[14] one can construct the following very simple typology of legislator's role orientations toward pressure groups:

Facilitators: Have a friendly attitude toward group activity *and* relatively much knowledge about it.

Resisters: Have a hostile attitude toward group activity *and* relatively much knowledge about it.

Neutrals: Either (1) Have no strong attitude of favor or disfavor with respect to group activity (regardless of their knowledge of it),
Or (2) Have very little knowledge about it (regardless of their friendliness or hostility toward it),
Or (3) Both (1) and (2).

By the measures of tolerance and awareness already described each of the legislators interviewed was classified under one of these three headings. They are distributed in the four states as shown in Table 2.

[13]"Accommodation" does not mean "accession," although that is, of course, one form accommodation may take. Accommodation here means conscious consideration. The assumption is that persons voicing demands will far more likely accept decisions as authoritative, even if their demands are *not* accepted, if they believe the decision-makers have given them explicit consideration than if they have not. This proposition is strongly implied in J. D. Stewart's discussion of "consultation" as the characteristic form of relationship between a group and a governmental organ (*British Pressure Groups* [Oxford, 1958], pp. 3-27).

[14]These two dimensions are suggested not only in numerous general social-psychological discussions of role- and self-concepts, but also by two of the very few empirical and analytical studies of group politics. Garceau and Silverman (*op. cit.*, pp. 685 ff.) report as the "most striking fact" discovered in their Vermont study "the extremely low level of recognition of interest group activity," and suggest that differences in legislative behavior toward groups as well as legislators' ideas about appropriate behavior toward them are associated with different levels of information about groups. Samuel H. Beer, in his analysis of operative theories of interest representation in Britain ("The Representation of Interests in British Government: A Historical Perspective," *American Political Science Review,* Vol. 51 [1957], pp. 613-650), suggests a number of respects in which legislators' different conceptions of the appropriate place of interest groups (described as Old Tory, Old Whig, Liberal, Radical, and Collectivist theories) imply different conceptions of how legislators should behave toward such groups or their agents. Beer singles out for special attention one facet of the legislator-group role-relationship—that involving the activity of the legislator as agent of a group (the "interested M. P.").

Table 2. Distribution of Role-Orientations toward Pressure Groups in Four State Legislatures

Role Orientation	California N = 97	New Jersey N = 78	Ohio N = 157	Tennessee N = 116	Total N = 448
Facilitators	38%	41%	43%	23%	37%
Neutrals	42	32	35	37	37
Resisters	20	27	22	40	26
	100%	100%	100%	100%	100%

The reasons given by legislators for their varying opinions about groups further describe the differences among them. When legislators were asked why they thought the legislature would work better or worse in the absence of pressure group activity, most of their responses could be coded into a comparatively few categories. These have been arranged in the order of decreasing friendliness toward group activity in Table 3. When respondents made more than one comment, only the most favorable (highest in the table) was coded. The table shows that almost two-thirds of the Facilitators think the legislature could not get along without pressure group activity, whereas a substantial number of Resisters (40%) expressed much less favorable opinions. The differences are of extreme statistical significance.[15]

Table 3. Attitude Differences among Facilitators, Neutrals and Resisters as Shown by Their Appraisals of Pressure-Group Activity

Most Favorable Opinion Expressed	Role Orientation*		
	Facilitator N = 124	Neutral N = 105	Resister N = 76
1. Groups are indispensable.	63%	39%	14%
2. Group activity is in general good, though certain "bad practices" of groups are undesirable.	23	41	46
3. Other less favorable opinions: *e.g.*, group activity may be objectionable but one ought not interfere with the democratic right to be heard; group influence is overrated, it is not an important factor; group activity is a wholly disruptive force which ought to be eliminated.	14	20	40
	100%	100%	100%

**Total is only 305 because some legislators failed to give reasons when answering the question and others expressed appraisals not codable in these categories.*

[15] $\chi^2 = 50.48$, D.F. = 4, $p < 0.001$; the differences are consistent in all four states.

In spite of these very striking and consistent differences, however, it should not be overlooked that even the Resisters express fairly tolerant appraisals of group activity, some 60% venturing opinions (numbers 1 and 2 in Table 3) which are quite favorable. We must, in other words, recognize the fact that pressure politics has become rather widely accepted among legislators in American states.

Legislators' differences in perception of groups are not simple quantitative differences of more or less, as the initial measure of lobbyist-recognition might suggest. In responding to a question asking them to name the most powerful groups in their own state, 56% of the Facilitators but only 36% of the Resisters named only or mainly *specific organizations* or lobbyists; similarly, only 36% of the Facilitators but 58% of the Resisters referred to *broad interest aggregations* ("labor," "farmers," *etc.*). In other words, Facilitators, significantly more than either Neutrals or Resisters, tend to see groups and group activities in concrete and specific terms.[16] That Facilitators are more alert to perceive groups and group cues is strikingly indicated by the fact that, even though interviewers sought, by probing, to have all respondents uniformly name six groups in response to the question, Facilitators nevertheless named significantly more groups than either Neutrals or Resisters.[17]

Table 4. Facilitators Think More Groups Worth Listening to Than Do Neutrals or Resisters

Number of Groups Named	Role Orientation		
	Facilitators N = 141	Neutrals N = 134	Resisters N = 108
0-1	11%	17%	20%
2-3	24	34	37
4 or more	29	27	23
"All are worth listening to"*	36	22	20
	100%	100%	100%
Mean number of groups named	4.17	3.50	3.35

**This response counted only if no more precise answer given (i.e., no group named).*

[16] Complete data not shown. The differences are statistically significant: $X^2 = 14.9$, D.F. = 4, $0.01 > p > .001$; the direction of difference is the same in all four states. The question was asked in the following form: "You hear a lot these days about the power of interest groups and lobbies in state politics. What would you say are the most powerful groups of this kind here in [state]?"

[17] 62% of the Facilitators named 5 or more groups, compared with 57% of the Resisters and 45% of the Neutrals. If Facilitators are compared with Neutrals and Resisters, $X^2 = 8.91$, D.F. = 1, $0.01 > p > 0.001$; the differences are consistently in the same direction in all four states.

Some of the grosser behavioral characteristics of the three types of legislator being described can also be explored. To begin with, assuming the validity of the role-orientation typology, one should expect to find Facilitators more ready than either Neutrals or Resisters to listen to the exhortations of pressure groups. This hypothesis is supported by the finding (see Table 4) that Facilitators named significantly more groups than did either Neutrals or Resisters when asked the question,

> We've been told that there are always some groups whose advice ought to be considered, whether they happen to be powerful or not. Would you name some of these groups here in [state]?[18]

Not only do Facilitators think more groups are worth listening to than do Neutrals or Resisters; they apparently tend also to give more weight to what they hear from group representatives. At least on the problem of school needs, which was selected as a typical issue, when legislators were asked to rate the influence of several factors–committee recommendations, advice of party leaders, views of constituents, etc.–on their own thinking, Facilitators attributed more importance to the "views of interest groups or lobbies" than did Neutrals or Resisters (see Table 5).[19] Finally, the data provide internal evidence that at least two of the legislative behaviors one would expect to find associated with the accommodation of group interest and demands do indeed appear more characteristic of Facilitators than of Neutrals or Resisters. Tables 6 and 7 show the former to be more ready to use, or at least to admit to using, the aid of lobbyists both in drafting bills and in lining up support for bills.[20]

There is ample justification, then, for the conclusion that there are significant differences among legislators in their role orientations toward pressure groups and group agents. It is not just that they differ in tolerance and awareness of group activity–that, indeed, was assumed in constructing the typology of Facilitators, Neutrals and Resisters. The point is, important tendencies toward

[18] X^2 for the table = 15.96, D.F. = 6, $0.02 > p > 0.01$; X^2 for Facilitators compared with Resisters = 11.86, D.F. = 3, $0.01 > p > 0.001$; X^2 for Facilitators compared with Neutrals and Resisters together = 14.88, D.F. = 3, $0.01 > p > 0.001$. Again, the differences are consistently in the same direction within each state, except that Tennessee Resisters name somewhat more groups than Tennessee Neutrals (mean of 3.74 as against mean of 3.35). This finding, like the one just preceding, was wholly unanticipated, since interviewers sought to elicit a uniform number of groups from all respondents.

[19] X^2 = 23.40, D.F. = 2, $p < 0.001$; the differences are consistent within each state.

[20] The questions asked were, "[Do you agree to the statements], I get valuable help in drafting bills from interest groups or their agents" (Table 6), and "Interest groups or their agents give me valuable help in lining up support for my bills" (Table 7). For Table 6, comparing Facilitators with Neutrals and Resisters, X^2 = 4.71, D.F. = 1, $0.05 > p > 0.02$; for Table 7, X^2 = 10.03, D.F. = 2, $0.01 > p > 0.001$. The differences are consistent within all four states, except that, in Table 7, New Jersey Resisters agree in greater proportions than do Facilitators, although New Jersey Neutrals agree much less.

Table 5. Facilitators Rate Importance of Pressure Groups on Own Views of "School Needs" Problem Higher Than Do Neutrals or Resisters

Importance Attributed to Views of Pressure Groups	Role Orientation		
	Facilitators N = 146	Neutrals N = 137	Resisters N = 101
Very important or important	70%	57%	40%
Not very or not at all important	30	43	60
	100%	100%	100%

Table 6. More Facilitators Than Neutrals or Resisters Agree Lobbyists Give Them Valuable Help in Drafting Bills

Answer to Statement That Lobbyists Give Valuable Help in Bill-Drafting	Role Orientation		
	Facilitators N = 163	Neutrals N = 160	Resisters N = 120
Agree or tend to agree	63%	52%	52%
Tend to disagree or disagree	37	48	48
	100%	100%	100%

Table 7. More Facilitators Than Neutrals or Resisters Agree Lobbyists Give Them Valuable Help in Lining Up Support for the Legislator's Own Bills

Answer to Statement That Lobbyists Give Valuable Help in Lining Up Support	Role Orientation		
	Facilitators N = 159	Neutrals N = 157	Resisters N = 115
Agree or tend to agree	78%	67%	61%
Tend to disagree or disagree	22	33	39
	100%	100%	100%

different patterns of behavior are associated with these basic differences in affect and cognition. The patterns are sharper for the Facilitators and Resisters, since they are attuned, favorably or unfavorably, to group behavior, and perceive, understand and react in characteristic fashion. The Neutrals, a category consisting of those who apparently fail to perceive, understand or formulate a coherent standard for judging groups in general, demonstrate, as one might expect, a more erratic, less distinct and consistent pattern. It is possible that each individual Neutral, at his own level of awareness or concern, behaves toward some or all group representatives in a manner that could be characterized as "role behavior," but that these patterns cancel each other out in the statistical treatment of responses. In any case, Facilitators are more likely to be aware of the nature of group demands and respond to them; Resisters to be aware of them but deliberately fail to respond; Neutrals to respond or resist, but for assorted other reasons, without caring or without knowing that a demand has been made by a group. It should be clear that these role categories do no more than classify one aspect of legislators' attitudes and behavior: they are not fixed categories of types-of-person, nor will they by any means describe all aspects of legislators' behavior. They are constructs, devised to help us explore further the working of the legislative system and, ultimately, the larger political system.

2. Demographic and ecological correlates of role orientation toward pressure groups. "Explanation" of the differences in role orientation described above was not an objective of this study, but the data nevertheless do suggest several comments on this problem. One would naturally expect that a variable defined generally in terms of cognition and affect, as role orientation has been defined here, would be closely related to respondents' education. If, as many educators say, education liberates the mind, eliminates excessive faith in the dogmatic truth of simple ideas, and provides increasing factual understanding of the social and physical world, then legislators with much education (and therefore greater knowledge and greater acceptance of group diversity) will more often be Facilitators than Resisters and those with comparatively little education will more often be Neutrals than either Facilitators or Resisters. As between the latter two types, less-educated persons will more often be Resisters than Facilitators. The data shown in Table 8 are consistent with all these hypotheses and are statistically significant.[21]

Table 8. More-Educated Legislators Tend More to Be Facilitators and Less to Be Either Neutrals or Resisters Than Do the Less-Educated Legislators

Role Orientation	Level of Education	
	Less Than Completed College (N = 201)	At Least Completed College (N = 247)
Facilitators	26%	45%
Neutrals	44	31
Resisters	30	24
	100%	100%

[21] $\chi^2 = 16.64$, D.F. = 2, $p < 0.001$. Non-college includes some legislators who acquired law-school degrees without attending college beforehand, as well as some who had various non-college postgraduate work after high school (business school, night school, etc.). There are some intra-state departures from the pattern: California non-college-educated legislators are less likely to be Resisters than are college-educated and are more likely to be Facilitators, and college-educated Tennessee legislators are less likely to be Facilitators than to be either Neutrals or Resisters.

Role orientation is hardly a simple reflex function of education, however. It has already been shown (above, Table 2) that the four states studied differ significantly in the distribution of role-orientation types. Such differences among the states persist even if we compare only groups of comparable educational background. As Table 9 shows, there is, on the whole, at least as much variation from state to state *within* each educational level as there is *between educational levels* within any given state.[22] This suggests that "political culture"[23] is a significant variable differentiating the states' modes and styles of pressure politics. Quite possibly, norms and expectations peculiar to each state system are transmitted and circulated more or less generally among the population of that system, so that legislators, like citizens or occupants of other roles in the system, have acquired some role orientations and potential responses appropriate to their own specific legislature and state political system before they come actually to play their roles.

Some very oblique justification for such a line of reasoning is provided by the fact that role orientation is not significantly related to any of the demographic variables often discussed in behavioral research.[24] Socio-economic status, by almost any index chosen, fails to exhibit such correlation: legislators with low, medium or high income fall in all three role-orientation categories with equal

Table 9. Inter-State Differences in Friendliness toward Pressure Politics Are as Great as Differences between Legislators of Different Educational Backgrounds

	Mean Score for Friendliness toward Pressure Politics*				
Legislator's Education	California N = 106	New Jersey N = 79	Ohio N = 160	Tennessee N = 117	Inter-State Range
Less than college	2.65	3.17	3.09	3.76	1.11
At least college	2.51	2.52	2.32	3.24	0.92
Intra-state, inter-level range	0.14	0.65	0.77	0.52	

**Scores represent quintile groups, score 1 being the most friendly, score 5 the least, on the scale described above.*

[22]Inter-state differences are greater than intra-state, inter-level differences when California or Tennessee is compared with either New Jersey or Ohio, but inter-level differences are slightly greater than inter-state differences when Ohio or New Jersey is compared with either of the other two states. It must be remembered that the knowledge dimension of role-orientation was normalized in the four states; for this reason the discussion here is directed toward the affective dimension, degree of friendliness (see above, note 12).

[23]For discussion of the concept of "political culture" see Gabriel A. Almond, "Comparative Political Systems," *The Journal of Politics*, Vol. 18 (1956), pp. 391-409.

[24]For a general discussion of these variables see *Legislative Behavior*, ed. John C. Wahlke and Heinz Eulau (New York, 1959), pp. 239-272.

probability.[25] Neither their type of occupation nor their occupational status appears significantly associated with legislators' role orientation.[26] The urban-or-rural character of their county-of-residence is likewise unrelated to role orientation, as is urban-or-rural character of the places where legislators were brought up. Nor do the data show a relation between legislators' religious affiliations and their role orientations toward pressure groups. The one familiar demographic variable which does emerge significantly related to role orientation is that discussed above—education. And education, it has already been shown, fails to account for inter-state differences.

These findings hardly "prove" the suitability of "political culture" as a basic concept for the analysis of political systems, let alone prove that role-orientation is determined by such a cultural variable. But they do strongly suggest that, because the norms and expectations constituting roles in a political system are by no means wholly or directly dependent on social class, communal type, or similar supposedly controlling variables, efforts should be made to describe any political system in such a way as to include political culture variables in the basic structural description.

3. Interest inclinations and role orientation. Students of the legislative process usually assume there is a relationship between legislators' personal convictions or group sympathies and their actions as legislators. In order to inquire into this relationship, legislators were classified as pro-business, pro-labor or economic neutrals. The process of classification (too complex to display here fully) involved three main steps: (1) all interest groups mentioned were classified as economic or other-than-economic, and all economic-interest groups then classified as either business, labor or agricultural; (2) each legislator's pattern of reference to each group separately was then classified as either favorable, neutral or unfavorable;[27] and, finally, (3) each legislator's interest inclination was determined on the basis

[25]Data not shown. Income-level measured by responses to the question, "Now, including your legislative salary, into which of these four income groups would you say your total annual income falls—(1) less than $5000, (2) $5000 to $10000, (3) $10000 to $20000, or (4) over $20000?"

[26]Data not shown. Types of occupation include Manufacturing, Construction, Mining, Transportation, Communication, Utilities, Wholesale or Retail Trade, Financial, Real Estate, Other Professions, Religion, Labor, Public Service, Housewives, Miscellaneous. Occupational statuses include Managers, Proprietors and Officials; Professional and Technical; Clerical, Sales; Craftsmen, Foremen and Skilled Labor; Farmers and Farm Managers; Housewives.

[27]A group or interest could be named in three possible contexts during the interview: (1) *group power*: Was a group named in response to the question, "What would you say are the most powerful [interest groups or lobbies] here in [state]?" (2) *worth of group*: Was it named in response to the question, "Would you name some [interest groups or lobbies] here in [state] whose advice ought to be considered, whether or not they are particularly powerful?" (3) *hostility to group*: Did respondent express hostility toward this same group at any time during the interview? (Interviewers recorded such volunteered indications, and they were coded for all respondents and all groups.) Reference to a group in context 2 only or in both 1 and 2 were considered *favorable* references; those in context 1 only, or in both

of his pattern of favor, disfavor or neutrality toward the three classes of economic interest.[28]

The question is, how do such interest inclinations affect the role orientations of legislators toward interest-group activity in general? The most obvious hypothesis is that individuals who are committed to any particular interest (business, labor, *etc.*) will be less likely than individuals not so committed to look favorably upon the assertion of demands by other groups or interests, especially if those others are conflicting interests. On the other hand, because the nature of their assertion of their own interests calls attention to the group-basis of those interests, the more committed legislators will not likely be especially resistant to group activity in the abstract. From this we can infer that economic neutrals will tend more than will pro-business or pro-labor legislators to be Facilitators and tend less to be Resisters. Table 10 shows this hypothesis is significantly supported.[29]

One other feature of Table 10 deserves comment: whereas pro-business legislators tend more to be Neutrals or Facilitators than to be Resisters, pro-labor legislators tend above all to be Resisters. This suggests but by no means proves that American pro-labor legislators are more ideologically doctrinaire and less tolerant of pluralistic diversity than are pro-business legislators. One possible

Table 10. Legislators Who Are Ideologically Neutral, Where Economic Interests Are Concerned, Are More Likely Than Legislators Committed to Either Business or Labor to Manifest Role Orientation of Facilitator

Role	Economic-Interest Inclination		
	Pro-Business N = 239	Neutral N = 130	Pro-Labor N = 51
Facilitator	34%	49%	26%
Neutral	36	33	33
Resister	30	18	41
	100%	100%	100%

2 and 3 (an essentially ambivalent response), or in all three contexts (also ambivalent) were considered *neutral*; and references in context 3 only or in both 1 and 3 were considered *unfavorable*.

[28]The classification exhausts the logically possible combinations of favorable-neutral-or-unfavorable references to business-labor-or-agricultural interests. "Pro-agricultural" inclinations were combined with "pro-business" while "anti-agricultural" were included with "pro-labor," since neither category contained sufficient cases for analysis, and since it seemed reasonable to assume that most contemporary interest cleavages of the sort relevant to a "conservative-liberal" distinction involve primarily the conflict between business and labor and that in most such conflicts agricultural interests side with business interests.

[29]When economic neutrals are compared with pro-business and pro-labor groups combined, $X^2 = 13.13$, D.F. = 2, $.01 > p > .001$; the differences in all states are consistent.

explanation is that labor-union officials or members, and presumably other persons who see the world as they do, are likely to see arrayed against them only one main group antagonist (the employer, or an association of employers), to be faced with only one, if any, competing labor organization, and, at least until recently, to feel little need to sell themselves to any consumer interest or organization. The businessman or person viewing the world as he does, on the other hand, is more likely to be exposed to a multiplicity of groups—not just antagonistic labor and target consumer groups and interests, but competing groups identical in kind with his own immediate business organization. It need hardly be emphasized, of course, that all such reasoning is at this stage highly speculative.

4. The political entailment of role orientation. General role theory holds that roles in any system are to a considerable extent engendered by the very system itself in which the roles occur.[30] Roles, in other words, are functionally specific to the system in which they are played. For example, the role of "buyer" in a market system calls for the complementary role of "seller." On such grounds one can very generally postulate that role orientations toward pressure groups are related to the functions of the political system in general, and more closely, to the functions of the legislative sub-system in particular.

Political scientists distinguish between the different functions of legislature, executive, administration and judiciary *vis-a-vis* pressure groups. As Earl Latham has said,

> The legislature referees the group struggle, ratifies the victories of the successful coalitions, and records the terms of the surrenders, compromises, and conquests in the form of statutes. . . . The function of the bureaucrat in the group struggle is somewhat different from that of the legislator. Administrative agencies of the regulatory kind are established to carry out the terms of the treaties that the legislators have negotiated and ratified. . . . The function of the judge is not unlike that of the bureaucrat.[31]

Even those who deny vehemently the adequacy of this view as a *complete* account of the governmental process generally admit that, insofar as *any* agency of government has the legitimate function of basing its decisions to *any* extent upon the expressed demands of organized interest groups, that function belongs more properly to legislative than to executive, administrative or judicial agencies.

If this is so and if, as it is reasonable to assume, commitment to legislative purpose increases with increasing service in the legislature, then legislators with most tenure should tend more than those with little tenure to be Facilitators. Table 11 shows that, except for Tennessee Resisters, this is indeed the

[30] See especially S. F. Nadel, *The Theory of Social Structure* (New York, 1951), pp. 57 *ff.*
[31] *Op. cit.*, pp. 35, 38, 39.

Table 11. Legislators with the Most Legislative Service Tend Most to Be Facilitators and Least to Be Neutrals

Role Orientation	Median Number Years' Legislative Service Prior to 1957			
	California N = 99	New Jersey N = 79	Ohio N = 155	Tennessee N = 115
Facilitators	7.3	5.6	6.2	2.2
Neutrals	4.8	2.5	4.4	2.1
Resisters	5.3	3.8	4.6	2.4

case.[32] By the same reasoning, persons who have been active in legislative office should be more inclined to Facilitative and less to Resistant role orientations than those active in non-legislative offices. This is borne out by Table 12. The table also seems to show that persons who had *no* previous governmental experience are still more likely than are those with legislative experience to be Facilitators. But the differences here, in contrast to the differences between persons with legislative and persons with executive or administrative experience, are not statistically significant,[33] and this apparent tendency is also counterbalanced by a correspondingly greater tendency for persons with no previous governmental experience, when compared with persons having prior legislative experience, to be Resisters.

Table 12. Experience in the Legislature Inclines Legislators toward Facilitator Role Orientation and away from Resister Role Orientation More Than Does Experience in Executive or Administrative Office

Role Orientation	Office Held prior to Entry to State Legislature*		
	Executive or Administrative (But Not Legislative) Office N = 84	Legislative (But Not Executive or Administrative) Office N = 105	No Previous Office N = 202
Facilitators	24%	36%	41%
Neutrals	39	43	34
Resisters	37	21	25
	100%	100%	100%

**At all levels of government—state, federal, local.*

[32]If the groups are dichotomized into those having less and those having more than the median number of years' legislative tenure in their legislature, then $X^2 = 6.14$, D.F. = 2, $.05 > p > .02$.

[33]Comparing those with executive-administrative experience and those with legislative experience, and only with respect to the Facilitator and Resister categories, $X^2 = 7.37$, D.F. = 1, $.01 > p > .001$. Comparing those with legislative experience (prior to state legislature) and those with no previous experience, $X^2 = 2.39$, D.F. = 2, $.50 > p > .30$. Comparing them only with respect to Neutral as against both other categories combined, $X^2 = 1.19$, D.F. = 1, $.30 > p > .20$.

5. Role orientation and the legislative system. It seems reasonable to suppose that the number and pervasiveness of groups in American political processes are so great that no legislator can hope to operate in disregard of them. The individual legislator can work effectively and can feel he is working effectively as a legislator only if he makes his peace with the world of pressure groups. In other words, other things being equal, the Facilitator will probably be a more effective legislator, and will feel hinself to be so, than will the Neutral or the Resister.

A crude measure of legislators' effectiveness is provided by their responses to the following question:

> We've been told that every legislature has its unofficial rules of the game—certain things members must do and things they must not do if they want the respect and cooperation of fellow-members. What are some of these things—these rules-of-the-game—that a member must observe . . . ?

On the assumption that the more effective legislators are award of a greater number and a greater diversity of "rules of the game," one can hypothesize that Facilitators will outrank Neutrals and Resisters in both these respects. In fact, Facilitators averaged naming 4.13 rules when answering, as compared with 3.88 for Resisters and 2.53 for Neutrals. That they likewise named rules in greater diversity is shown in Table 13.[34] It is worth noting that the Neutrals rank lower than either Facilitators or Resisters in both measures.

It can likewise be shown (see Table 14) that significantly more Facilitators *feel* themselves to be effective legislators than do the other two types. [35] But whereas Neutrals rank lowest of the three types in effectiveness, Resisters rank lowest in *sense* of effectiveness.

[34]For Table 13, $X^2 = 11.49$, D.F. = 2, $.01 > p > .001$; in both cases the differences are consistent in all four states, except that Tennessee Resisters name slightly more rules than do Tennessee Facilitators. These differences are *not* merely reflections of legislators' differing educational backgrounds. In both cases (number and diversity of rules named), they are significantly greater among Facilitators, Neutrals and Resisters of the same educational level than are the differences between legislators of different educational levels (data not shown).

[35]$X^2 = 13.64$, D.F. = 4, $.01 > p > .001$. Tennessee Resisters have a higher efficacy sense than do Tennessee Facilitators, but they also outrank the latter in *low* efficacy sense. Efficacy sense was measured by a Guttman-type scale based on the following questions: "[Do you agree or disagree that] (1)There is so little time during a session to study all the bills that sometimes I don't know what I'm voting for or against; (2) Many of the bills are so detailed and technical that I have trouble understanding them all; (3) So many groups want so many different things that it is often difficult to know what stand to take; and (4) My district includes so many different kinds of people that I often don't know just what the people there want me to do." The results are not biased by the inclusion of the item number (3) dealing specifically with pressure groups.

Table 13. Facilitators Name (and Presumably, Therefore, Are Aware of) a Greater Diversity of "Rules of the Game"

Number of Categories* in Which Rules Were Named	Role Orientation		
	Facilitators N = 162	Neutrals N = 160	Resisters N = 119
Two or less	46%	64%	51%
Three or more	54	36	49
	100%	100%	100%

***The categories include rules (1) regarding predictability of behavior, (2) regarding restraint or canalization of conflict, (3) expediting legislative business, promoting group cohesion or solidarity, (4) which are tactical, primarily for the benefit of individual members, and (5) which are "personal qualities" rather than rules.**

Table 14. Facilitators Have Highest and Resisters Have Lowest Efficacy Sense

Efficacy Sense	Role Orientation		
	Facilitators N = 164	Neutrals N = 163	Resisters N = 119
High	43%	31%	29%
Medium	38	46	36
Low	19	23	35
	100%	100%	100%

Another way to look at the problem of legislators' relative effectiveness is to consider other legislators' perceptions and judgments of them. It seems reasonable to assume that those most esteemed by their colleagues will have at least greater potential for influence or effectiveness than their less esteemed colleagues. On this assumption, an index of potential effectiveness was constructed from the replies by respondents in each house to three questions regarding the fellow members they considered to be "personal friends," "experts" in some legislative subject-matter field, and "respected for following the rules of the game." Ranking the members with respect to the number of mentions each received differentiates between those who stand out in the eyes of their fellows and those who are lost in the shuffle or (in a few instances) disliked or distrusted. This ranking of a member, be it noted, is entirely independent of his own responses to the questions, since it is a composite view of the member as seen by his colleagues. Table 15 shows that Facilitators do, in fact, rate higher with their colleagues than do Resisters and Neutrals.[36]

[36] $\chi^2 = 5.20$, D.F. = 2, p = just over .05. The tendency is the same in every chamber in all four states, except the Tennessee House, where Resisters are the top-rated group. If the Tennessee House is eliminated from the table, the percentage of Facilitators in the top half is increased to 55%.

Table 15. Facilitators Are Rated Higher Than Resisters or Neutrals by Their Colleagues (Composite Ratings as "Friend," "Respected," and "Expert")

Rating	Role Orientation		
	Facilitators N = 163	Neutrals N = 164	Resisters N = 120
Top half*	53%	40%	47%
Bottom half*	47	60	53
	100%	100%	100%

**These "halves" are approximate, since tie scores made it impossible to divide some chambers exactly. Standards differed slightly between chambers with the internal distribution, but all in the top half were named by one or more members in each of the three categories, and their mentions in all three categories total six or more. None of those in the bottom half had more than eight mentions in all.*

III

6. Conclusions. Several important, though tentative, conclusions are suggested by the above findings. Perhaps the most important is that the group struggle is mediated in the legislature primarily by legislators who are relatively *least* committed as advocates or agents to particular conflicting interests and who are rather conciliators among them (Section 3 above). The emerging picture of the Facilitative legislator who is above or outside of group conflicts even while he more or less consciously defines his official role to include the accommodation of group demands adds a new dimension to the conception of government ordinarily guiding study of pressure groups. At the same time, the detection of Resisters and Neutrals warns against a too simple view of the legislative struggle as a struggle between elementary group demands. There is evidence, if such is required, that a legislature cannot forge public policy out of the raw material of naked group interests alone. Resisters are to be found in all legislatures who do not want to base public policy on such demands; even Facilitators, by standing above most groups, indicate their refusal to recognize the views of any particular groups as specially pregnant with the public interest.

On the other hand, pressure groups occupy too prominent a place in American society to permit a legislator seriously to think of doing his legislative job in complete disregard of them. What is more, the legislative function seems clearly to include the function of harmonizing and integrating group demands, so that incumbency in legislative office itself serves to shape legislators' role orientations so as to promote the group-conciliating function (see Section 4), and the effective performance of individual legislators, probably the effective performance of the legislative system itself, depends to some extent upon legislators' acquiring such orientations (Section 5).

The findings also emphasize the "autonomy" of the legislative sub-system and of the larger political system. While the differences among the four states in distribution of legislators' role orientations appear superficially to follow interstate differences in general educational level, economic status and urban-rural character of the general population, the failure of corresponding demographic characteristics of legislators to correlate with their role orientations (see Section 2) warns us against accepting such correlations as "explanations." The fact that the Tennessee legislature is a far more informal and less "professional" legislature than those of California, New Jersey and Ohio is as important as, and is by no means directly the result of, the fact that the Tennessee population is more rural, poorer and less well educated. Whatever the causal mechanism linking such sociological variables to legislative behavior, it seems necessary to visualize a "political culture" intervening between to give to the legislative and political system of each state a characteristic structure which is more immediately significant in determining what gets done there than is the sociological composition of the population or the day-to-day specifics of pressure-group activity.

The most general conclusion, therefore, is that political science can profitably re-direct its attention to basic questions of institutional structure, mechanics and process. These questions can be properly answered by further rigorous attention to the behavior of political actors, the ultimate data for all political investigation.

City Councilmen and the Group Struggle: A Typology of Role Orientations

Betty H. Zisk
Heinz Eulau
Kenneth Prewitt

The activities of American interest groups have only recently become a subject for systematic inquiry—in contrast to the spate of earlier descriptive case studies. As a result, there has been remarkably little cumulative knowledge about the components of group influence on policy outcomes. This hiatus is unfortunate in light of the claims which have been made about the role that interest groups

Betty H. Zisk, Heinz Eulau, and Kenneth Prewitt, "City Councilmen and the Group Struggle: A Typology of Role Orientations," Journal of Politics, *Vol. 27 (1965).*

play in a democracy. It has been argued that associational activity is at least as important as the vote in providing a vehicle for civic participation. It is assumed, furthermore, that the whole process of claims-presentation and the way in which claims are processed by policy-makers carries implications for the legitimacy of public decisions. A specification of the conditions for group "success" thus seems crucial for understanding or evaluating the political process. Yet the *measurement* of interest group "success" is, in itself, difficult to achieve.

It is not our purpose to enter into the debate over the merits or shortcomings of the "group approach" to political behavior. We prefer to consider the question of group influence as one which can be approached from a variety of perspectives. We would argue, however, that those who undertake research which covers only a segment of the range of relevant variables—and our own study is so limited—must specify that range.

Group influence might be accounted for in terms of two general propositions:

1. The predispositions of policy-makers act as filters through which interest group efforts to influence policy outcomes must pass. The accessibility of public officials to groups, and the degree to which they accommodate group requests, depends in part on these predispositions.
2. Given the predispositions of policy-makers not only toward interest groups but toward "significant others" in the political system (e.g., political parties, administrators, legislators), the influence of specific groups will vary with internal group organization, tactical and leadership skills, and other characteristics of the groups themselves.

Our own theoretical concerns—particularly our interest in the consequences of the interest group-legislator relationship for the adaptability of the political system—lead us to focus on the first of these two hypotheses. This study analyzes the perceptions, attitudes and behavior of legislators (in this case city councilmen) toward group spokesmen and toward interest group activity in general. We do not believe this study (or the theoretical and empirical work to which it is indebted) is incompatible with the substantial body of research related to the second proposition. The two statements are, in our view, not contradictory but complementary.

We realize, of course, that our findings in local communities cannot automatically be generalized to other political units. The problem of inference—in this case from political systems where contacts are intimate and informal to systems where they are discontinuous and formalized—remains one of the many dilemmas for students of political behavior. It is in part because of this difficulty that we utilize some notions borrowed from role theory and systems analysis. Role theory enables us to handle and to relate systematically the cultural, social and psychological variables (e.g., community norms, reference groups of legislators, perceptions and attitudes toward others in the political system) which may be relevant to interest group-legislator relations. It serves to relate individual acts to institutions, since each role presupposes one or more counter-roles played with some degree of regularity. Institutions, in this scheme, are viewed as interlocking sets of roles. But, most important, we use the concepts of role and role system as functional constructs, rather than relying on conventional categories like "city councils" or "state legislatures," in order to solve, in part, the problem of inference from one level of analysis to another.[1]

If we make two assumptions:

1. that actors in all political systems will behave at least partially in accordance with the expectations of others, and
2. that the tasks that political systems must perform (in order to continue to function as systems) will require that certain roles be taken by individuals in some structure that is part of the system,

we are probably justified in inferring that the patterns found in city councils will have their *functional* equivalent in state or national bodies.

This, then, is a study of the predispositions of elected officials in twenty-two small political systems toward spokesmen for interest groups and toward others who make claims on the system. It represents an attempt to answer one broad question: how do these role orientations affect the relations between legislators and interest groups?

I. Research Design and Construction of a Typology of Role Orientations

This preliminary work has been undertaken as part of a five-year study of all incumbent councilmen in the 73 cities of the San Francisco Bay Area. Structured interviews have been completed with 123 incumbents of twenty-three city councils; 112 councilmen from twenty-two cities answered the series of questions concerning interest groups, and it is on their responses that this report is based.

These cities do not constitute a random sample of either California cities or the hypothetical universe of American non-partisan cities. We selected the cities to be studied without the certainty that we have taken into account all relevant variables. The choice was in fact governed largely by research convenience.

[1]Our ability to make generic statements depends on our handling the data at a level of abstraction which will pinpoint both similarities and differences between the small systems we are studying and the universe of macro-politics. The role theory-systems analysis approach is one of several possible analytical frameworks which might provide such an inferential link; decision-making, communications, and group theory are others. For a discussion of some of the problems in regard to the last two, see Heinz Eulau, "Lobbyists: The Wasted Profession," *Public Opinion Quarterly*, Vol. 28 (1964), pp. 27-38.

The full interview, covering a wide range of subjects, lasted in some cases as long as five hours. The portion dealing with interest groups and related topics consisted of seventeen open-ended questions and two check-lists.[2]

The main analytical tool used for the study of councilman-interest group relations was a typology of respondents' role orientations toward interest groups. This typology was constructed on the basis of three variables: councilmen's attitudes toward interest groups, the number of influential groups perceived, and the perceived bases of group influence. The typology was then used to account for some of the differences in both the willingness of councilmen to accommodate group requests and their own reliance on such groups.[3]

Respondents were asked two questions about their attitudes toward, and accessibility to, groups in the community: "How do you feel about efforts of groups to make their views known to you and seek your support?" and "Do you feel that, in general, you should make it easy for them to contact you, or should you try to avoid them?" While very few councilmen stated that they "avoid" group contacts, a broad range of opinions about community group activities were expressed. These opinions can be divided into three categories: esteem, neutrality, and rejection.

[2]The average interview lasted two and one-half hours; the interest group section constitutes about 20% of the total. The fact that the questions in this section came near the end of the interview accounts, in large part, for the drop in the number of respondents. We are not employing statistical tests of significance in connection with our analysis for a number of reasons. At this time, we wish to be free to move both inductively and deductively between our data and the theory. We prefer to present a series of theoretically linked hypotheses, no one table standing alone, and then allow our readers to decide whether the data will support the inferences made. A test of significance for any one table is thus not meaningful. In interpreting the data, however, we are led by elementary caution to adopt one ground rule: In no instance do we view a difference of less than 10% as anything but chance. It will be noted that in six of our eight analytical tables, including the two where the number of respondents falls below 96, the difference between Pluralists and Antagonists exceeds 20%. Our reasons for not anticipating much difference between Tolerants and Antagonists are discussed elsewhere in this paper.

[3]This approach rests on one premise—that knowledge of an actor's role orientation (his own expectations of the kind of behavior he ought to exhibit in carrying out his duties) can serve as a valid basis for inference about his role behavior. Thus we will attempt to make statements connecting the councilman-interest group relationship to policy outputs by our analytical focus on the connection between the interest-group role orientation and the purposive orientation of councilmen. Such a procedure requires an assumption of at least a minimal "strain toward consistency" on the part of a councilman in regard to his perceptions, attitudes, and behavior, at least *vis-à-vis* any one part of the political system. We do not believe, however, that the possible discrepancy between orientations and behavior is necessarily as great as the possibility of a discrepancy between the reports of either scientific observers or the press (via observation at council meetings and the like) and the meaning of the acts observed to the councilmen themselves. Indeed, because our own interest is in the implications of differing predispositions for the councilman-interest group relationship, and particularly in light of the difficulty in observing this relationship, we believe that the present observational perspective is especially appropriate.

Some councilmen seem to value group activity *per se*. They comment on the utility of groups in providing information, mobilizing community support, or in serving as advocates for differing points of view. Examples of this kind of statement are:

> I think they should be given every opportunity to contact me. I feel that more, and not less, participation is essential, and that groups are as important, possibly more important, than individuals. When groups have decided on a position one can assume that the membership of the group has participated and thus a substantial number of people have the same position on the issue. I feel this is valuable. We have to get people to agree.
>
> From my legal training, I welcome any disagreement. It's the only way the truth really comes out—the truth will emerge from intelligent opposition.

In contrast, other councilmen express reservations or answer in more neutral terms:

> Sure, they can come and present their view. I listen as long as they are arguing for what's best for the city.
>
> I'll listen to anyone who'll buy the coffee.
>
> I think one should hear all sides; everyone has a right to speak his piece. I may not agree with them, but I won't avoid them.

This second type of councilman seems to make himself available to group spokesmen because, presumably, he has accepted community standards with respect to the group's "right to a hearing." The distinction is thus between those who see groups and/or competition between groups as having potential utility for the council, the councilman, or the community, and those who are willing to listen mainly because it is expected of them.

Finally, a small group of respondents reject the idea that consideration of group claims is worthwhile. Many of these respondents say that they "avoid" group contacts whenever possible. For example:

> I don't think groups should contact councilmen. They should take their problems directly to the city—to the staff or to the whole council. I don't trust points of view formed by small groups without open hearings and the other side being represented. I must be a little special in this.

Table 1 shows the distribution of these responses.

Distinguishing councilmen solely on the basis of their attitudes toward group approaches will not enable us to predict their behavior toward these groups. Variations in the salience of groups and group activity must also be taken into account. The policy-maker must at least be aware of a potential ally or enemy within the political system to be motivated to interact with him, or to adjust

*Table 1. Respondents' Attitudes toward Groups**

Attitude	Respondents	
Groups are esteemed, are perceived as useful	48	(43%)
Groups are described in neutral terms; "They have a right to be heard"	49	(44%)
Groups are resisted	15	(13%)
	112	(100%)

**Attitudes are coded from responses to two open-ended questions: "How do you feel about efforts of groups to make their views known to you and seek your support?" and "Do you feel that, in general, you should make it easy for them to contact you, or should you try to avoid them?"*

behavior to his expectations. This is equally true whether the behavioral adjustment is based on positive or negative affect. The extent of a councilman's perception of interest groups, as indicated by the number of influential groups he names, can serve as a first approximation of the salience of groups for him.

Table 2 presents the relevant information. It can be seen that the perceived intensity of group life in these twenty-two Bay Area cities is low. The median number of groups seen as influential is 2.4. More than a third of the respondents perceive either one or no groups as active before the council in their community; not more than 14% name as many as five influential groups. In constructing our typology, we made the simple distinction between those councilmen who: (1) name one group or none, and (2) name two groups or more.

We chose this cut-off point in order to accommodate (1) differences in the way that councilmen interpret the word "influential" and (2) variations among council cities in the complexity of the group universe. If we had set it above the median number of groups named, we might have included some councilmen who are quite aware of the limited amount of group activity that takes place in their communities among those councilmen who live in more complex communities

*Table 2. Perception of Influential Groups**

Number of Groups Named as "Influential"	Respondents		Cumulative Per Cent
None	18	(16%)	16%
One	26	(23%)	39%
Two	22	(19%)	58%
Three	14	(12%)	70%
Four	19	(16%)	86%
Five or more	16	(14%)	100%
	115	(100%)	

**The question: "Speaking of groups or organizations here in (city) which are active and sometimes appear before the Council—which would you say are the most influential?"*

but are less perceptive.[4] Furthermore, the councilman who names only one "influential" group probably differs in important respects from those who name two or more. He may be mentioning his major reference group (e.g., a union local from which he takes some of his cues) without being aware of the activities of other organizations in the community.

It is difficult to predict the relationship between councilmen's attitudes toward, and perceptions of, groups. A problem arises from the phrasing of the question that asked respondents to name "influential" groups. The word "influential" sometimes evoked an emotional response from councilmen. If a councilman dislikes several dominant groups in his community, he may deny that influential groups exist. This seems particularly likely if he is defensive about his views. For example:

> Nobody is influential. There are a couple here that are suspect from the start . . . interests that are of necessity working for their own gains and ends. Their arguments shouldn't be considered as having weight unless they are valid for the city as a whole. I don't give a damn about any organization as such, especially if it has an axe to grind.

In general, however, we would expect that a favorable attitude and high perceptions would go together, while either negative or neutral attitudes will probably be associated with limited awareness. Table 3 supports this expectation. It can be seen that almost half of those who esteem groups, in comparison with only one-fifth of those who reject or are neutral toward groups, name four or more "influential" groups. Similarly, about half of those who reject groups or are neutral perceive no groups or one. In contrast, only 23% of those who esteem groups fail to name at least two groups as influential.

Perception is not, by itself, an adequate measure of the salience of group life in the community. It does not distinguish between councilmen who perceive groups as (actual or potential) interest articulators and councilmen who are unaware of the capacity of groups to perform this input function. We assume that those who perceive structures performing such functions *as groups* will act in a different manner from those who perceive groups as nothing more than a number of people with certain desirable or undesirable traits. Thus, we need to include in our typology a variable based on this distinction.

[4]In one of the 22 cities, all five incumbents stated that only one organization which concerned itself with council affairs was in existence. There is no reason to doubt this statement, since the community in question excludes all commercial or industrial activity and is one of the smallest in the study. We could not set the criteria for salience of groups so low as to take this situation into account—but the cut-off point of two groups seems reasonable in light of the inclusion of several other primarily (although not wholly) residential communities in the study.

Table 3. Number of Influential Groups Perceived in Relation to Attitude toward Groups (Number of Respondents = 112)

Number of Influential Groups Perceived	Attitude toward Groups					
	Esteems		Neutral		Rejects	
0-1	11	(23%)	24	(49%)	7	(56%)
2-3	16	(33%)	15	(31%)	4	(22%)
4 or more	21	(44%)	10	(20%)	4	(22%)
	48	(100%)	49	(100%)	15	(100%)

Councilmen can be separated into two categories on the basis of their answers to the question: "What would you say makes these groups so influential –what are the reasons for their influence?" Some respondents confine their answers to group influence-by-respect; others mention objective strength (e.g., voting power, wealth) and/or "stake in society" as bases for influence. Respondents are divided into two categories:

1. Those who attribute group influence to respect, if his discussion of group influence is limited to respect variables–honesty, intelligence, common sense, etc. E.g., "It has a respected name." "They're objective about government affairs and they're nonpartisan."
2. Those who attribute group influence to objective strength (size, voting power, wealth) and/or "stake in society" as components of group influence. E.g., "It developed in the past election as a solid deliverer of votes. It's better to be for it than against it." "They have a vested interest in the community and play an important part in its functioning."

It should be noted that, by our definition, while the councilman who attributes group influence to respect does not mention either of the other two bases for influence, the councilman who attributes influence to objective strength and/or perceived stake may also have responded in terms of respect variables.

The distribution of reasons given for group influence is reported in Table 4. It can be seen that more than twice as many respondents mention "respect" characteristics as either of the other two bases.[5] As is probably the case with councilmen who perceive only one or no groups, we would expect a councilman who confines his responses to this category to adopt an orientation that is either

[5]Of the 87 councilmen whose answers could be classified on this question, 34 answered in terms of only respect characteristics, in comparison with 14 councilmen who confined themselves to either of the other two categories. The remaining 39 respondents gave responses which fitted under at least two categories.

*Table 4. Perceived Bases of Group Influence**
(Number of Respondents = 87)

Basis of Influence	Respondents Mentioning Basis†
Objective strength (size, voting power, wealth)	27 (31%)
Stake in society	32 (37%)
"Respect" characteristics (honesty, intelligence, common sense, etc.)	73 (84%)

**The question: "What would you say makes these groups so influential—what are the reasons for their influence?"*

†Percentages total more than 100 because of multiple responses.

neutral toward or indifferent to groups. Those who attribute group influence to objective strength or perceived stake are probably, in contrast, either more negative or more favorably inclined to group activity.[6]

We have thus developed two criteria for the salience of the group universe for councilmen, and one indicator of their attitude both toward group activity and toward the utility of interest articulation for the local political system.[7]

[6]Because the number of reasons given by councilmen for group influence varies directly with the number of groups named, and, as we have already shown, the number of groups named is related to respondents' attitudes toward groups, the relationship between group attitude and bases of group influence, using total respondents as a base, follows the pattern shown in Table 3: those who esteem groups are more likely than others to attribute group influence to all three bases. If, however, we compute the percentages on a base of only those respondents who perceive groups, the following relationship emerges: there is no difference in the relative frequency of councilmen whose attitudes differ in regard to "objective strength"; those who esteem and those who reject groups are more likely than the neutrals to mention stake in society (40%, 44%, and 31% respectively); while those who are neutral are more likely than others to mention respect characteristics (94% in comparison with 77% of the esteemers and 78% of the rejectors).

[7]These indicators were chosen on the basis of theoretical considerations. Our original plan, in developing a typology of role orientations, had been to combine perceptual indicators with responses to a direct question concerning respondents' self-expectations: "Do you feel that, in general, you should make it easy for them [groups] to contact you or should you try to avoid them?" As mentioned in the text, very few councilmen stated that they try to avoid group contacts, and, at the same time, a broad range of attitudes toward group activity was expressed in these responses. Once the decision was made to seek another indicator for underlying attitudes or self-expectations, both because of the skewed distribution of responses (which would render analysis very difficult) and the fact that it did not enable us to take into account varying reasons for accessibility, the three indicators which we now utilize were chosen.

While respondents' *attitudes* toward groups in fact correlate quite highly with several of our dependent variables (e.g., seeking group support), we included the perceptual indicators in our typology because so much of the small group literature, the voting studies, and the

Using these three variables, we can distinguish three types of councilmen:

1. *Pluralists:* those who esteem groups, who perceive many groups and who attribute group influence to objective strength or perceived stake;
2. *Tolerants:* (1) those who are neutral toward groups and who perceive one or no groups, regardless of perceived bases of group influence, or those who are neutral, perceive many groups, and attribute group influence to respect; (2) those who esteem or reject groups but who perceive few groups and attribute group influence to respect;
3. *Antagonists:* (1) those who reject groups and attribute group influence to objective strength or perceived stake, regardless of level of perception; (2) those who are neutral toward groups, perceive many groups, and attribute group influence to objective strength or perceived stake.[8]

---

like stress the importance of the *salience* of "significant others" for determining behavior toward those "others."

This typology is similar, but not identical, to the one utilized by Wahlke *et al., (op. cit.,* pp. 313-316, 469-470). These authors employed two different measures for salience–one a composite index based on degree of specificity of groups named (e.g., "American Farm Bureau Federation" versus "farm groups") the other an "awareness" index based on ability to identify a list of specific lobbyists. Neither of these devices seems appropriate for the local setting, since it is likely that degree of specificity and ability to identify group spokesmen will be widespread, without providing the necessary clue to salience of groups *qua* groups. In addition, it is believed that the use of an indicator for perceived bases of group influence will tap an additional dimension which may be inappropriate for state legislators, but seems highly relevant for the present group of respondents.

[8]It will be noted that the only relevant factor in distinguishing Pluralists from Antagonists is attitude. Put another way, all councilmen who are both high perceivers and who attribute group influence to objective strength or stake in society are either Pluralists or Antagonists, depending on their attitudes; all others fall into the residual category of Tolerants.

The decision to equate neutral and rejecting attitudes among councilmen who rank high on both perceptual and sophistication dimension– that is, to classify both categories as Antagonists–is based on two assumptions:

1. Given the relatively widespread democratic norm that all individuals and groups have "a right to be heard," adherence to this norm may be stated by those whose *de facto* orientations are less favorable to group activity than the norm requires.
2. A high degree of perception and sophistication is likely to be accompanied by high affect, which in turn will be manifest in role behavior. The highly aware are unlikely to take the relatively passive role which we would predict for those we have termed Tolerants.

We are, in effect, making two distinctions–one based on respondents' *awareness* of the group universe, the other on *attitudes* toward those groups. Other things being equal, we would expect sharply contrasting orientations and behavior between polar opposites on both dimensions. It is difficult to predict, however, the relative "weight" of these two (attitudinal and perceptual) dimensions. In some instances, "unawareness" and hostility may be functionally equivalent. Thus the behavior of Tolerants and Antagonists may be, for all practical purposes, indistinguishable. In other cases (e.g., in terms of *perceptual* responses), the Antagonist may resemble the Pluralist more closely than he does the Tolerant. We may

In general, we expect Pluralists to be most likely to interact frequently with spokesmen for interest groups; to put forth most effort to accommodate group requests; to be most likely to seek group support for their own proposals. We anticipate that Pluralists will serve as a link between the council and those who seek to articulate interests for segments of the community. We expect the Antagonists to interact very little with group spokesmen, to be unaccommodating, and to make little effort to seek group support for council projects. The Tolerants, as disinterested neutrals—unlikely to modify their behavior in response to group activity—will probably fall in an intermediate position.

Yet rejection coupled with a high degree of awareness of community groups may be functionally equivalent—as far as *behavior* toward the groups themselves is concerned—to neutrality and low awareness. The Tolerant accepts the group's "right to a hearing"—but because the group does not loom large in his perceptual world, he is unlikely to spend much effort in either seeking advice from groups or in assisting them beyond the level of lip service. Many Antagonists would like to avoid group contacts, but they may be forced, in the relatively intimate political system of the community, to maintain at least minimal contact, and even occasionally to accept group support for their views on controversial issues. We believe that the distinction between the two types of role orientations is theoretically meaningful—and that the differences between Tolerants and Antagonists in regard to both affect toward and awareness of groups may imply differing orientations in regard to other role sectors (e.g., "purposive roles"—orientations taken with regard to policy outputs). We thus feel justified in treating the two types separately at this point even though we suspect that for all practical purposes, their interactions with groups may be very similar.

II. Perceptions and Attitudes of Councilmen Toward Interest Groups

The typology of interest group role orientations was designed to discriminate between councilmen with markedly different conceptions of the local political process. We plan to use it as an explanatory device, capable of accounting for attitudinal and behavioral differences among councilmen.

Two "acid tests" can be devised to check the validity and the utility of the typology. The first concerns the kind of group activity that is perceived as "influential." The second hinges on what might be termed the respondent's notion of "legitimacy" in interest group activities.

Given the high visibility of groups and individuals alike in these relatively small political systems, most councilmen are likely to perceive *some* group

---

find this happening, for example, when Antagonists respond to questions which do not arouse much affective content (e.g., in regard to group support for specific programs; concerning group participation in elections).

activity, regardless of whether they characterize it as "influential." The crucial question becomes one of the kind of group which is perceived. Economic groups (e.g., merchants' and realtors' associations, unions) are probably more likely than civic associations (e.g., service clubs, women's clubs, neighborhood improvement associations) to concentrate the bulk of their energies on interest articulation. The councilman who conceives of the political system as interest-based is therefore more likely than others to be aware of these economic groups. Conversely, the councilman who is either tolerant of or antagonistic to this conception of the function of interest groups in the political system is less likely to see interest articulation as a basis for group influence. He is more likely to be unaware of economic groups. Such a councilman may stress the impartiality or lack of a "selfish" viewpoint of a community organization as a reason for its influence. He thus is likely to be most aware of more apolitical (e.g., civic) organizations.

It can be seen from Table 5 that our data tend to confirm these expectations. Almost half of the Pluralists, in contrast to about a quarter of the Tolerants and Antagonists, name economic organizations as influential. In contrast, there is considerably less difference between the proportion of the three types of councilmen naming civic or reform groups. In other words, almost all councilmen are aware of groups that are *not* primarily interest articulators, but it is only the Pluralists who tend, in fairly large numbers, to perceive those that concentrate on interest articulation. Respondents' awareness of the emphasis that economic groups place on interest articulation is shown in comments like these:

> We have to consider the union's view. They own property here and sponsor cooperative housing projects.
>
> The realtors have a direct interest in the city's decisions.

*Table 5. Relation between Interest Group Role Orientation and Kind of Groups Perceived**

	Interest Group Role Orientation			
Groups Perceived	Pluralist (N = 24)	Tolerant (N = 48)	Antagonist (N = 24)	Total (N = 96)†
Economic (merchants, realtors, unions, etc.)	11 (46%)	10 (22%)	6 (25%)	27 (28%)
Civic (service clubs, citizens' commissions, improvement associations)	24 (100%)	43 (90%)	23 (96%)	90 (94%)
Taxpayers associations and reform groups	5 (21%)	10 (22%)	5 (21%)	20 (21%)

**The question: "Speaking of groups or organizations here in (city) which are active and sometimes appear before the council—which would you say are the most influential?"*

†*Responses total more than 100% because of multiple percentages. Tabulation includes only those respondents who named at least one group.*

The same respondent went on to say:

> Pressure groups are probably more important in local government than they are nationally or in the state, because they're right here. You see them and they see you, and what you do affects them. It's not like in Washington, where half the time a businessman doesn't really know what the result will be for him.

The contrasting response, made by Pluralists as well as others, in regard to civic organizations, is illustrated by these comments:

> It's composed of a lot of intelligent people, not rabble rousers. It always has good intentions and is capable of expressing itself in the shortest possible time.
> They always have a representative at every one of our meetings.

Some of the responses to the question concerning group influence intimate that councilmen view certain activities—e.g., "rabble rousing"—as detrimental to group efforts to influence public policy. Two questions, placed near the end of the series concerning interest group activities, touch more directly on this point. The first asked: "Are there any groups here which are consistently critical of the council? Which groups or organizations seem to be critical?" Given Antagonist awareness and sophistication *vis-à-vis* the group universe, we should expect more Antagonists and Tolerants to perceive critical groups. We might also anticipate a similar difference between both Antagonists and Tolerants, on the one hand, and Pluralists, on the other, since those who value groups activities probably see claims-presentation as a routine part of the political process itself, not as a disruptive or "critical" activity.

The councilmen do not conform to these expectations. We note, in Table 6, that Tolerants are markedly more aware than other councilmen of "consistently critical" groups—and the Antagonists are the *least* likely to name such groups. How can we account for this pattern of responses? It seems reasonable to attribute the difference in part to respondents' interpretations of the term "consistently critical." The Pluralists may be the only type of respondents who make a clear distinction between critical and other groups. Neither Tolerants nor Antagonists consider group claims essential or desirable for the political system. The Tolerants are perhaps more aware than the Antagonists of the *content* of group claims, because they believe that groups should be given a hearing. Since they find little value in these group claims, many of them are likely to view groups as "critical"—i.e., demanding or dissatisfied. The Antagonists, on the other hand, seem to have insulated themselves from the content of such claims. Thus, they may fail to perceive any group as uniquely more critical than others. If all three of these

*Table 6. Relation between Role Orientation and Perception of "Consistently Critical" Groups**

Perception of Critical Groups	Interest Group Role Orientation		
	Pluralist	Tolerant	Antagonist
Critical groups are perceived	8 (36%)	29 (57%)	7 (29%)
Critical groups are not perceived	14 (64%)	22 (43%)	17 (71%)
	22 (100%)	51 (100%)	24 (100%)

**The question: "Are there any groups here which are consistently critical of the council? Which groups or organizations seem to be critical?"*

assumptions are correct (that Pluralists can distinguish between critical and other groups; that Tolerants are likely to see groups as critical; than Antagonists are not likely to see much difference among any of these organizations), we would expect the pattern of responses in Table 6.

Two statements about critical groups, made by Tolerants, illustrate the point that Tolerants see claims *per se* as critical:

> The PTA always want things their way. This disrupts the council. The Chamber of Commerce would like to run things. The council doesn't favor growth of the tourist industry. They don't agree—they're for business. They represent a small-town business point of view.

In contrast, those Pluralists and Antagonists who named critical groups were likely to give reasons less closely related to claims or public issues *per se*:

> This neighborhood association is really a personal vehicle. The president of the group has gotten considerable publicity and is now running for the council.
>
> This group is critical because of the tax controversy a year ago. A personal feud still exists.

This point, in regard to differences between councilmen's notions of what constitutes "consistent criticism," is closely related to the second "acid test." Immediately preceding the question about critical groups, councilmen were asked: "What kind of activity weakens a group's ability to influence the city council?" Responses to this question can be divided into two categories: answers disapproving of specific group characteristics, and answers opposing the whole idea of a group struggle. Examples of the first type of response (into which 61% of the answers were classified) are:

If they aren't honest, if they lack integrity.
Being consistently obstructionist in their attitude. Having a griping approach.

Examples in the second category, answers opposing group pressure as such, are:

If they try to put the pressure on, by numbers or threats of reprisal.
Or if they have a totally selfish nature.
A special interest working against the general will.
When it becomes evident that they have self-interest, that they have placed particular monetary gain beyond what would benefit the community as a whole.

Clearly the councilman's concept of legitimacy, in regard to group activity, is implicit in these responses. The second type of statement appears to be based on a Rousseau-like belief that men (and groups) must achieve their ends by foregoing "self" and seeking, instead, for a common good. In contrast, those who believe that a conflict of interests *leads,* through compromise, to a common good (i.e., the Madisonian tradition) would be unlikely to make such statements.

It follows from the considerations that went into the typology of group role orientations that both Antagonists and Tolerants will be more likely than Pluralists to criticize group activity in terms of their distrust of the group struggle. Antagonists (like Pluralists) seem to be highly aware of group activity but (unlike Pluralists) reject the concept of interest-based politics. Tolerants, while generally neutral or unaware of group activity, are likely, insofar as awareness does exist, to view claims-presentation as threatening.

The pattern of responses in Table 7 seems to confirm these expectations. Less than one-quarter of the answers given by Pluralists fall into the category of opposition to group pressures, in contrast to 40% of the answers given by Antagonists and 46% of the Tolerant responses. This finding, together with those reported in the two preceding tables, provides considerable justification for the

Table 7. Relation of Interest Group Role Orientations to Perception of What Undermines Group Influence (by Total Responses)*

	Interest Group Role Orientation		
Response	Pluralist	Tolerant	Antagonist
Anti-group-struggle answers	8 (24%)	31 (46%)	14 (40%)
Anti-group-traits answers	25 (76%)	36 (54%)	21 (60%)
	33 (100%)	67 (100%)	35 (100%)

**The question: "What type of activity weakens a group's ability to influence the city council?"*

conclusion that our indicators measure what they were intended to measure—different conceptions of the political process. This distinction is of considerable importance for both methodological and theoretical reasons. On the one hand, because our typology appears to have consistent discriminatory power, we can now move with some confidence to an examination of responses more directly related to councilmen's role *behavior*. By the same token, these contrasting political conceptions of councilmen imply markedly different relations between councilmen and group spokesmen. Differing relations in turn will have consequences, presumably, for both the content of political decisions and the stability of the political system itself. It is to these role relations that we now turn.

III. Role Behavior of Councilmen toward Interest Groups

Insofar as a political actor views his decision-making tasks as including the effort to accommodate community interests, we would expect him to depend on interest group spokesmen both because they can provide needed information to him,[9] and because they may help to mobilize community support behind his proposals. In contrast, we expect those who reject or are neutral toward such groups to find little value in group performance of these functions.

Table 8 shows this to be the case in regard to the first group function, providing information. Councilmen were asked to rate six potential information sources; of the four shown, organizations in the community rank third. (Because 100% of the respondents rated the city manager as "very important" or "important," and more than 90% accorded the same value to other councilmen, responses to these sources are not shown.) As we expected, the Pluralists value community organizations more than do their fellow legislators.

A quite important feature of the responses shown in Table 8 is the consistency of the attitudes of each type of councilman toward all four sources. In each case it is the Pluralists who find a given source most valuable. It appears that the group role orientation taps a broad, and internally consistent, syndrome of attitudes that is related to the kind of inputs councilmen believe appropriate for the political process. We have inferred, from the kind of criticisms made of group activities (Table 7), that many Tolerants and Antagonists advocate a direct search for the "good of the community"; in contrast, Pluralists seem more likely to take for granted the necessity for compromise between conflicting demands. The perceived value of extra-council structures varies, of course, with the view held. Group activity is an integral part of a balancing-of-interests and disruptive in a search for a direct consensus.

[9]David Truman, *op. cit.*, pp. 333-334, cites interest group ability to fill legislators' need for information (both on technical matters and concerning the political consequences of alternative policies) as one of the major determinants of group access.

Table 8. Relation of Interest Group Role Orientations to Perceived Importance of Information Sources * *(by Percentage of Those Rating Source "Very Important" or "Important")*

Information Source	Interest Group Role Orientation			
	Pluralist	Tolerant	Antagonist	Total
Organizations in the community (N = 68)†	56%	49%	33%	47%
People in the community (N = 105)	83%	64%	58%	67%
People at council meetings (N = 104)	67%	58%	60%	61%
Newspaper (N = 105)	50%	42%	42%	45%

**The question: "We are wondering from whom you think you get the* best *information about city affairs. Could you rank these items as to their importance: city manager or other city officials; other councilmen; people at council meetings; organizations in the community; people in the community or my neighborhood; the newspaper." Respondents were handed a check-list on which they were asked to designate each source as "very important," "important," "not very important" or "not important at all."*

†The number of respondents is small on this item because it was not included in the 1962 interview schedule.

A similar conclusion can be drawn from Table 9, which shows responses to the question: "Before a council decision is made, do you ever seek support from any of the groups you have mentioned?" It can be seen that the "group struggle," in the sense of a dynamic process of alliance-formation between legislators and private groups, is almost nonexistent in these cities. We have already found that less than one-half of these councilmen consider groups as valuable information sources. We now note that just over one-quarter seek group help. Yet we cannot dismiss the finding as simply indicative of a lack of

Table 9. Relation of Group Role Orientation to Role Behavior: Respondents' Seeking Group Support for Their Own Proposals * *(1963 and 1964 Respondents Only)*

Whether Respondent Seeks Group Support	Interest Group Role Orientation			
	Pluralist	Tolerant	Antagonist	Total
Seeks support	10 (59%)	6 (15%)	3 (20%)	19 (27%)
Doesn't seek support	7 (41%)	33 (85%)	12 (80%)	52 (73%)
	17 (100%)	39 (100%)	15 (100%)	71 (100%)

**This question was not a part of the 1962 interview schedule. It reads: "Before a Council decision is made, do you ever seek support from any of the groups you have mentioned?"*

group activity in these communities, since some of our respondents do perceive and do rely on such groups. Again, a majority of the Pluralists–in contrast to less than a fifth of the other councilmen–solicit group aid.

This last contrast between the Pluralists and other councilmen is another of the consistent series of differences that we have reported. The Pluralist is strikingly more aware of, accommodating to, and dependent upon a particular set of actors outside of the council–interest group spokesmen–than are his fellow incumbents. The Pluralist seems to be the only councilman who consistently attempts to draw group spokesmen into the policy-making process. There is very little difference between the Tolerants and Antagonists–in fact, the Antagonists are slightly more likely than the more neutral Tolerants (20% of the Antagonists, 15% of the Tolerants) to seek group support for their own projects. Apparently our earlier speculation that, in terms of role behavior *vis-à-vis* groups, the two types of orientations may be functionally equivalent is borne out in this case. The indifference (or hostility) of these councilmen to the potential role that group spokesmen might play, as advisors or allies, is in marked contrast to the behavior ascribed to state and national legislators by most students of the "group struggle."

That it is the role orientations of councilmen, and not demographic characteristics (or some other feature) of the population in these cities, that underlie these results is evidenced by the distribution of role orientations across the cities. There is at least one Tolerant on every council, there is at least one Antagonist on 76% (17) of the councils, and there is at least one Pluralist on 59% (13) of the councils. There are ten councils on which all three orientations are present; there are only two councils where only one (the Tolerant) orientation exists.[10] It should be noted that respondents from the same city show remarkably little similarity in their perceptions of, and behavior toward, groups. Thus five Pluralists from five cities are considerably more alike in terms of their tendency to seek group support than are five respondents from the same council.

[10]We have examined most of our dependent variables in considerable detail on a city-by-city basis. There appears to be a slightly higher incidence of the Pluralist orientation (and the accompanying tendency for more groups to be perceived and used as allies) in upper-income residential suburbs, in contrast to the industrial cities. The differences which we have reported in this paper, however, do not wash out when controls for differing demographic characteristics of council cities are introduced. Pluralists tend to behave as Pluralists (or not) regardless of the character of their cities; similar statements can be made concerning the attitudes and behavior of Tolerants and Antagonists.

When, for example, we examine the relation between the socio-economic status of the population in council cities and the proportion of councilmen who seek group support, we find only a small difference: 25% of the councilmen in high-SES cities seek group support; 32% in low-SES cities do so. Similarly, when the industrial complexity of the city is used as an independent variable, only a small difference emerges.

It is our view that while there is undoubtedly a relationship between the global characteristics of council cities and the roles which councilmen play *vis-à-vis* groups in those

The community context within which a councilman operates probably structures interest group-councilmen relations. Similarly, the characteristics and tactics of the interest groups themselves are almost certainly relevant to these relations. A councilman cannot call for help from union leaders in a community where no union exists. Few councilmen are likely to turn for information to a group that has been found to misrepresent questions of fact. Nevertheless, the pattern of responses that we have found indicates that, within these limits, councilmen feel free to welcome or ignore those groups that are interested and active. In short, our data seem to indicate that the councilman's private conception of the desirability and/or propriety of the process of claims-presentation is a major determinant of his behavior, and thus indirectly of the character of the group life in his community.

The relationship between group role orientations and what we might call antecedent variables will be discussed in a forthcoming report. Similarly, we shall give separate treatment to the pattern of relations between these councilmen and potential interest articulators other than groups. That subject must be considered in the context of councilmen's general attitudes toward their constituents, their legislative style, and their orientations toward legislative outputs. We must anticipate our findings, however, if we are to have any assurance that role orientations toward interest groups are *general* in nature and useful as predictors of councilmen's orientations toward other parts of the political system. Thus we shall devote brief attention, in conclusion, to councilmen's relations with one other set of interest articulators.

We can envision at least three other sources of advice and support for councilmen–the city staff, the press, and prominent individuals in the community. It is possible that these sources, along with interest groups, are viewed by councilmen as mutually exclusive alternatives. Thus, those who value groups may not value individual activity because individuals do not often aggregate as well as articulate interests. Similarly, those who resent group "pressure tactics" –particularly through private contacts–may feel less irritated by the more public efforts of the newspaper editor to influence community affairs. Nevertheless, we would expect some continuity in the behavior of councilmen toward these two extra-council sources of information, if the interest group role orientation hinges on an orientation toward claims-presentation itself rather than

cities, there are also several other variables which are associated with role orientations–and thus with role behavior. We might mention, for example, legal arrangements (e.g., size of council, whether a committee system exists), bloc patterns, personal characteristics (amount of education). Thus any direct link between only *one* antecedent or contextual variable and respondents' behavior toward groups is likely to be weak. A more promising approach, in contrast, necessitates two series of questions: first, what orientations are likely to account for the behavior we wish to explain, and second, what general conditions are likely to give rise to different orientations?

toward the character of the claims-presenter. A consideration of respondents' perceptions of and reliance upon community influentials may help to examine this expectation.

Table 10 shows a marked relationship between councilmen's role orientations and the number of individuals they name as "influential" on city decisions. About three-quarters of the Pluralists, in contrast to one-third of the Tolerants and 40% of the Antagonists, name at least four "influential" individuals. Conversely, less than 10% of the Pluralists, in contrast to almost a quarter of the Antagonists and more than one-third of the Tolerants, state flatly that there are no influential individuals in the city.

*Table 10. Relation between Interest Group Orientation and Perception of Community Influentials**

Number of Influentials Named	Interest Group Role Orientation		
	Pluralist	Tolerant	Antagonist
"There are none here"	2 (9%)	18 (35%)	6 (24%)
1-3 individuals named	4 (18%)	17 (33%)	9 (36%)
4 or more named	16 (73%)	17 (33%)	10 (40%)
	22 (100%)	52 (101%)	25 (100%)

**The question: "Are there any persons who are particularly influential here—I mean people whose voices are really important in decisions affecting the city? Who are they?"*

Respondents were asked whether they seek the advice or support of these influential individuals on problems confronting the council. This question, it will be noted, is analogous to one concerning the reliance of councilmen on groups (see Table 9). If group role orientations are predictive of general behavior patterns toward those who make claims on the political system, we would expect Pluralists to be most eager for this support. An examination of Table 11 shows that this is the case.

The most striking difference, in both Tables 10 and 11, is the greater awareness of the Pluralists of this source of private influence. Pluralists are both more aware of individual influence and more likely than other councilmen to turn to such individuals for help. (Of course, the opposite pattern could hardly occur—i.e., non-awareness and seeking of help—but there is no necessity for seeking of help to follow from awareness.) This general pattern of responses supports our view that the interest group role orientation implies a general orientation toward the local political process.

We may also note that the Antagonists are slightly more aware of, and dependent upon, those influential individuals than are the Tolerants. This finding—if not spurious— may be attributable to Antagonists' generally greater

*Table 11. Relation between Interest Group Role Orientation and Seeking of Advice or Support from Community Influentials**

Whether Seeks Advice or Support	Interest Group Role Orientation		
	Pluralist	Tolerant	Antagonist
Seeks advice or support	17 (77%)	21 (45%)	13 (54%)
Doesn't seek advice or support	5 (23%)	26 (55%)	11 (46%)
	22 (100%)	47 (100%)	24 (100%)

**The question: "Of the important people you mentioned, are there any whose judgment you particularly trust and whose advice you might generally want to seek? Who are they?"*

awareness of the group universe and varying bases for group influence. On the other hand, it is possible that some of those who reject group activity in general do not object to *individual* effort at "influence." Perhaps the activities of the latter are not perceived as pressures on the council, or the councilman himself.

The inferences can be supported by comments of the respondents. We may note, first, that the reasons given for individual influence are similar to those given about groups. Thus the typical Pluralist mentions the value of the advice and information given by individuals. For example, one Pluralist said, in regard to two businessmen, a realtor, and a member of the local planning commission:

> These are all spokesmen for different parts of the community. They are all people I use as sounding boards. I have no one person or group that I use to steer me—instead, I've developed a checklist of about eighteen people that I consult regularly, depending on the nature of the problem.

Another said:

> I go to different people: a man at the Labor Temple on personnel questions, a friend at the university on administrative problems. We all have our own sources of advice.

Another aspect of individual influence stressed by several Pluralists, and by almost all of the Antagonists who perceived and sought help from influentials, was the ability of these individuals to mobilize community support. For example, one Antagonist commented, in regard to both the local postmaster and the newspaper editor:

> I think that these are probably people who can help me get something through if I can convince *them* it would be good for the community.

Another Antagonist, who named several individuals, but reported his reliance on only one—a party official at the county level—put it bluntly:

> The people who are important to a councilman are those who can and will influence other people during elections.

In marked contrast, most Tolerants emphasize what we have earlier called "respect" characteristics. For example:

> I've known him all my life—I trust him implicitly.
> He's really concerned about the welfare of the people—he's not just interested in what the city can do for him.

This essentially a-political viewpoint, which occupies such a prominent place in Tolerants' statements, seems related to their tendency to approach the tasks of legislators in terms of vague general principles. In contrast, the more pragmatic approach of the Pluralist might be characterized as that of seeking answers for which, first and foremost, support and ultimate community acceptance can readily be found.

IV. Conclusion

We have analyzed some aspects of interest group "influence" on political decision-makers by a study of the role orientations of 112 city councilmen in twenty-two cities of the San Francisco Bay Area. Our analysis has been guided by one general hypothesis: that the behavior of elected officials toward those who attempt to influence policy outcomes is related to their general predispositions toward the process of interest articulation. In accordance with this proposition, we have classified councilmen on the basis of responses to three questions. One of these relates to their attitude toward interest group activity. The others tap both the basis for, and the extent of, their awareness of group influence.

We have seen that most councilmen do not view interest group activities as indispensable to the political system. About three-quarters of our respondents are either neutral or negative toward such groups. They do not encourage group approaches, and they do not turn to such groups for help. It appears that the "group struggle" in local political systems (at least in these twenty-two cities) takes place largely on a one-way street upon which relatively little traffic is noticed or invited by those who dwell at the upper end.

It does not appear to matter greatly, in terms of the behavior we are describing, whether the councilman is neutral and relatively unaware, or hostile and highly aware, of the groups. *Unless groups are both salient and valued*, the political actor in the local community makes little effort to modify his behavior on their behalf.

At the same time, we have isolated, by means of the typology of interest group role orientations, a select group of councilmen whose attitudes and behavior are in sharp contrast to the majority of our respondents. These councilmen—the Pluralists—constitute about a quarter of our respondents. They are not only considerably more receptive and accommodating to community organizations—they are more likely to make legislative allies of such groups. In contrast, Tolerants and Antagonists are either neutral or hostile toward group activities. They do not value groups as either information sources or mobilizers of community support, and, on the whole, they do not seek group help.

These general predispositions, which we have characterized as interest group role orientations, appear to rest on yet more basic orientations toward the local political process. We have described them as representing two hypothetical extremes: some councilmen see politics as a bargaining process, while others view it as a direct search for the common good. The first viewpoint is the tacit assumption of many students of the political process; the second, ironically, seems to be more widespread among political practitioners, at least in the local political systems that we have studied. Given the finding that three-quarters of our respondents espouse the latter view, the adequacy of the "group struggle" model as an explanatory device is called into question. The question then arises: what difference (in terms of policy outputs) do these contrasting approaches on the part of incumbents make?

Presumably the content of policy decisions advocated by officials who view "extra-council" demands as irrelevant or disruptive will differ from decisions that are made by those who attempt to take such demands into account. In addition, we might expect corresponding differences in both the adaptability and the stability of the political systems in question. If interest articulators and the general public are aware of their own exclusion from serious consideration (and this is an empirical question) they may call into question the legitimacy of public decisions. On the other hand, where major priority is given, by policy-makers, to the mediation of group claims at the possible expense of achieving efficient or practical solutions for community problems, the system may fail to adapt itself to a changing environment.

These questions are beyond the scope of our present discussion. We shall present further evidence for our interpretation and undertake a more extensive substantive analysis in two forthcoming reports on the antecedents and consequences of interest group role orientations. For the present, we shall rest our case on the internal consistency of councilmen's perceptions, attitudes, and behavior toward groups. The analogous pattern of responses concerning another set of potential interest articulators—community "influentials"—adds further weight to our view that the interest group role orientation is of a general enough nature to enable us to predict some aspects of councilmen's predispositions and behavior toward other parts of the political system as well.

We would not argue that legislators' role orientations are the only relevant factors in accounting for group "influence," or in assessing the far more crucial consequences of the way in which both latent and expressed claims are taken into account in a political system. We have found considerable evidence, however, for the importance of these "filters" through which group demands must pass.

Political Communication on the Japanese Peace Settlement

Bernard C. Cohen

Political relations, like other human relations, are frequently made more difficult because of selective processes of perception and evaluation which stand like screens between individuals and filter intended meanings out of their communications to one another.[1] A further distortion may be introduced into political relationships if political entities are regularly exposed to divergent kinds of communication. In the case of the Japanese peace settlement, members of the Executive and the Congress received somewhat different images of "public opinion" on the treaty, because different groups and individuals communicated different things to them at different times.[2] Let us consider, first, how communications on the settlement differed at their points of origin, and then how they differed at their points of reception on the governmental level.

[1]This article is from a chapter in *Political Process and Foreign Policy: The Making of the Japanese Peace Settlement* (Princeton, N.J.: Princeton Univ. Press, 1957). I have had the able assistance of Margaret Brown Cram, and am grateful to Gabriel A. Almond and David B. Truman for their advice.

[2]This pattern of political communication is based on a detailed canvass of the sources of evident and acknowledged interest in the peace settlement, as well as of those groups that customarily take part in discussions of foreign policy problems but no trace of which could be easily discovered on this particular issue. Information was gathered from the Department of State's files on the Japanese peace settlement, from the published records of

Bernard C. Cohen, "Political Communication on the Japanese Peace Settlement," Public Opinion Quarterly, *Vol. 20 (1956). Reprinted with permission.*

How, then, did the interest and opinion groups who were concerned with the Japanese peace settlement actually become involved in the political process on that foreign policy issue?[3] At the most general level, we can say that different kinds of organizations became involved in different ways, partly because they visualized the process, and their own roles in relation to it, in special and distinctive terms. More specifically, the leaders of these groups seem to have differed, among other things, in the way they viewed their own political roles, and in what they regarded as the most effective and proper points of access to the political process. And these differences, in turn, seem to be related to differences in the character of group memberships or constituencies, and in the kinds of responsibility that group leaders bear toward their constituencies.

This brief summary suggests that the customary approach to political interest groups, which treats them all as having the single function of trying to shape public policy according to well-defined special purposes, is quite oversimplified. Actually, when one looks at the different ways in which they behave, they display a rather complex set of functions. The articulate leadership group acts as a multidirectional conveyor belt, carrying information and opinions upward to policy-makers, and downward or across to colleagues, constituents, or citizens in an effort to create a "public opinion" for which it might again be a sounding board upward. Particular organizations or types of organizations specialize at different times in particular aspects of the "conveyor" relationship; but collectively the articulate public both leads and follows, formulates and persuades. It *is* "public opinion," it *represents* "public opinion," and it *creates* "public opinion."

The kinds of political behavior engaged in by specific groups among the articulate public seem to be partly traceable to some rather stable factors which are internal to the groups, and which are mostly unaffected by kaleidoscopic changes in policy issue or political alignment. These internal factors provide two relatively simple but useful ways to differentiate the various types of organizations that were part of the process of reaching a Japanese peace settlement. One

---

Senate hearings and debates, from newspapers, and from personal correspondence with officials in about fifty political interest groups. No one, of course, can maintain that the picture thus drawn is absolutely complete; there is, however, good cause to believe that it is reasonably comprehensive, and that no organizations of major consequence in American public life, nor any public sources that have left an impression on policy itself, have escaped the net.

[3]The participation of individuals has of necessity been omitted from the following analysis. This exclusion does not impute any lack of significance to the participation of private citizens; rather it simply recognizes that the universe of such individuals has not been explored or sampled sufficiently in this case to warrant our making even the most tentative statements or hypotheses about them. Later on, however, we shall consider the participation of individuals from a different vantage point (see footnote 7).

of these, the character of the membership, is perhaps less strategic than the other, the kinds of interests served by the organization. Let us look at some of the variations in political behavior that seem to grow out of, or at least attend on, these differences.

Character of the Membership

Political interest groups may, in the first instance, be differentiated by the size and diversity of their memberships. On the one hand, there are large organizations, mostly on the national level, with heterogeneous memberships; and, on the other, there are relatively small groups, some on the national but more on the local level, with a considerable degree of homogeneity in their membership.

The veterans' associations, labor unions, business associations, religious groups, and women's organizations that participated in the peace settlement generally represented the first of these two membership types. For the most part, these organizations draw their constituents from across the nation, and from groups of people who attach a tremendous variety of values and a wide range of importance to the work of the organizations. Inescapably, this imposes certain restraints on the freedom of action of leaders of such groups, causing them to forge some kind of operational consensus within their organizations before they can confront a policy with a position.[4]

Quite a different situation exists with respect to the second of these membership types, that is, groups with small and relatively homogeneous constituencies. The Japanese treaty met this type in the ethnic groups, the financial associations, and the regional and local business and labor organizations, the prosperity of whose members was linked to the fate of a single commodity, fish. These are not what might be called "open-ended" groups; the number of people to whom they appeal is small, and the degree of intimacy and agreement on values among their constituents is rather large. Under these conditions, the leaders of the groups are to a considerable extent freed from the constraints that hem in their counterparts in large organizations. Where the latter must work to establish a consensus, the former can generally achieve it more easily, and can turn their energies more rapidly and completely to its implementation at the public policy level.

Organizations with large and relatively diversified memberships cast most of their communications on the peace settlement in the form of statements and articles, and aimed most of them in the direction of their own members and a wider, mass media-reading, general public. A quite opposite course was taken by

[4]Even when the consensus thus established is limited to an active elite, it still requires time, political acumen, and at least the appearance of democratic procedure. Cf. William C. Hamilton, *The Development of Foreign Policy Attitudes in Certain American Pressure Groups*, unpublished Ph.D. dissertation, Yale University, 1955.

those groups with small and relatively homogeneous constituencies. The leaders of these groups, not having to undergo a long drawn-out process of reaching a formal agreement among their members, devoted most of their efforts to communicating to people in the Executive and Legislative branches of the government; and in the process they employed more direct and private methods of communication, such as letters, telephone calls, or face-to-face contacts.

Character of the Interests Served

Political interest groups may be differentiated not only by the size and diversity of their memberships, but, more significantly, by the character of the interests they serve and by the attendant relationships between a group's leadership and the mass of its members. On the one hand, there are organizations that serve specific and relatively tangible interests, and whose leaders stand in a representative relationship to their constituents; and, on the other hand, there are organizations that cater to more general and intangible interests, and whose leaders stand in an educational and exemplary relationship to their members and, hopefully, to a wider public.

Veterans', labor, business, ethnic, and financial groups, and the fishing industry's combination of business and labor organizations, were the groups involved in the treaty settlement whose interests in policy are more or less specific and tangible. These groups have a continuing interest in certain rather clearly defined policy preserves, and are traditionally sensitive and alert to any moves which affect their position with respect to those areas. Many of these interests are economic, but financial gain or loss is not the sole criterion of "tangible interest." Veterans' groups, for example, include military policy among their greatest concerns, though it has no direct connection with the well-being of veterans as such.

Ideological and pacifist groups, religious bodies, and women's organizations, on the other hand, were the treaty-involved groups that served general and intangible, frequently moral, interests. There are few organizationally inspired limits to the policy concerns of these organizations; they scan the entire range of public policy, in a radar-like effort to spot areas or problems that seem to impinge on their general or traditional conceptions of right or wrong and to offer opportunities for public restatement of those concepts.

Organizations of the latter type, with intangible interests, seem to cast their leadership in an educational role vis-à-vis the general membership. Women's organizations, for example, are often quite explicit about their educational purposes, and about the informational dividends that will accrue to the attentive member. And religious groups inplicitly suggest the same thing when they seek to develop among their congregations a public opinion on the vital issues of the times.

Groups with more specific interests impose a different sort of task upon their leaders. These men have the responsibility of representing the policy views of their constituents to government officials. They are cast in the role of spokesman, but for some of them, particularly in business and labor organizations, that role is a complicated one, because along with specific interests their groups also have massive memberships, with attendant internal differences of opinion. In other words, these men are caught in a small conflict of roles; as leaders of groups with tangible interests they face away from their constituents and toward the policy-maker, and as leaders of groups with massive memberships they have to face their constituents until they can agree on a policy position. Sometimes the differences cannot be resolved; the National Association of Manufacturers, for example, counting as members people who stand on all sides of the foreign trade question, is sometimes unable to reach a group decision on what to do about American foreign economic policy. Immobilization of this sort is not the rule; but to avoid it there is need for some process of formalizing the views of the constituents, a process in which the democratic element is clearly visible to the rank-and-file membership, to the public at large, and to the government official who may want to test the representative character of a group's leadership before evaluating its testimony on policy issues.

Most of the actual differences in the political communication of organizations on the issue of the peace settlement seem to be related in some way to these differences in the character of their interests. There are areas, to be sure, where these differences work in the same direction as differences in the character of their memberships, each reinforcing the other. This is the case, for example, with religious and women's groups, both of which have large and diversified memberships, and serve intangible interests; and it is the case with financial groups and the fishing organizations, which have small and homogeneous memberships and serve highly specific interests. Yet the character of the interest seems to be the more basic of these two sets of criteria, accounting for most of the differences in behavior that comprise the pattern of political communication on foreign policy issues.

Differences in the Methods Employed

The methods of communication employed by political interest groups have been recorded for present purposes under six headings: articles, statements, letters, telegrams, telephone calls, and face-to-face contacts. Letters and face-to-face contacts were the media most often employed by individual participants, official and private; organized groups, however, relied most extensively upon articles and statements.

The groups with the most specific interests, those which were caught up in some of the concrete details of the settlement, used the greater number of available methods to communicate their views. The fishing industry, including both labor and management groups, seems to have been the only kind of organization to employ all six methods; it was closely followed by business groups, who were the only type of organization to use five methods. Four different types of organizations employed four methods of communication, and three of these types–religious, ideological, and pacifist–serve generalized and intangible rather than specific interests.

The choice of methods also reflected the kinds of relationships that the leaders of "tangible" and "intangible" groups hold toward their members. Ideological, pacifist, religious, and women's organizations, intangible groups whose leaders feel an educational responsibility toward their members, relied more heavily on interpretive, descriptive, and explanatory articles than on any other type of communication. These four types of organizations together accounted for a large majority of the articles that were written by political interest groups on the subject of the peace settlement. On the other hand, veterans' associations, business groups, and labor unions, which have relatively specific areas of interest and diverse memberships and whose leadership has a representational responsibility, placed greater emphasis on formally approved statements of organizational position than on any other type of communication. These three kinds of organizations were responsible for a majority of all the group statements on the peace settlement.

Differences in the Timing of Communications

There are some striking differences among organizations in the timing of their communications on the treaty. Organizations serving specific and relatively tangible interests started communicating at an early date, and kept it up more or less regularly as the treaty-making process unfolded. Organizations serving more general and intangible interests, however, were somewhat slower to react. These groups sent out most of their messages late in the process, when policy substance had already hardened.

Tangible interest groups, like business, financial, veterans', and commodity (fishing) organizations, had done most of their communicating by the end of July, 1951, when the treaty draft had been completed and invitations to the Conference at San Francisco were being delivered. Religious, ideological, pacifist, and women's organizations, however, satisfied their more general (but not necessarily less intense) interests in the months after July, 1951, when the opportunities and possibilities for altering the treaty documents were fewer and more restricted. A specific comparison may reveal these differences more clearly. Business groups and labor unions, together with the fishing industry's combination of the two, contributed more than half of the communications on the settlement coming from organized groups during the period January-March, 1951, when the peace settlement was still in the negotiating and drafting stages. During the same three months of the following year, however, after the terms had been generally agreed to, and when the documents, with only a few points of difference remaining, were going through the process of securing Congressional consent, fully half of the communications from organized groups came from the pacifist and other ideological groups.

Differences in the Audiences for Communications

Four audiences, or objects of communication, have been distinguished in order to establish meaningful differences in the political communication of organized groups. Two audiences, the Executive and the Legislative, are on the governmental level; each includes the full range of offices and individuals that make up its branch of government. The non-governmental audience has also been divided into two parts, which are termed "constituent public" and "general public." "Constituent public" consists almost wholly of the members of organized interest groups, while "general public" refers to an undifferentiated, generally mass, audience.

If we look, first of all, at the two audience levels, the governmental and the non-governmental, we will find some supporting evidence for the earlier hypotheses that groups with tangible interests and with homogeneous constituents both tend to direct communications toward policy-makers, and that groups with intangible interests and with diverse memberships both tend to direct their communications toward those members rather than toward policy-makers. Business, ethnic, financial, and commodity organizations directed most of their communications on the Japanese peace settlement to the governmental level. All four of these types of organizations have tangible interests, and all but the business groups have homogeneous constituencies. And labor, religious, pacifist, ideological, and veterans' groups aimed most of their communications at the non-governmental level. All five of these have heterogeneous constituencies, and three of them have intangible interests.

The differences that exist *between* Executive and Legislative audiences, and *between* constituent and general publics, however, are the more significant elements in this pattern of communication. For here the lines of governmental and non-governmental are crossed in a curious and unexpected way. On the governmental level, groups with tangible interests, such as business, labor, financial, commodity, and veterans' organizations, favored the Executive with their communications. Intangible interest groups, specifically the religious, pacifist, ideological and women's organizations, on the other hand, communicated mostly to the Congress. On the non-governmental level, the intangible interest groups communicated for the most part to their own constituents, while the organizations with specific interests were found communicating to an undifferentiated, mass audience.

These findings offer an insight into two quite different kinds of orientation toward the subject of political access, and specifically toward the question of what were seen in this case as the most effective and the most proper channels for communicating political preference. On the one hand, groups with highly specific interests seemed to regard the Executive as the place where their communication would have the most effect; these direct operations were backstopped, so to speak, by communication to a general audience, perhaps partially designed to make the specific interest resemble a general one. Organizations with intangible interests, on the other hand, apparently viewed the Congress as the logical governmental audience for their communication, which most frequently consisted of the expression of value preferences. This direction of communication was paired, however, not with publicity-oriented communication to a general audience, as one might expect from organizations with exemplary purposes, but rather with a concentration on their own constituents; this emphasis on communication to constituent publics may have stemmed in part from their educative responsibilities, and in part from the feeling that they had to combine value messages to Congress with some evidence that the values in the messages were shared by their constituents.

A factor of great importance affecting this subject of access to the Executive and the Congress seems to be the character of the governmental process on the issue involved. In the case of the Japanese peace settlement, the Executive had a comparatively free hand both constitutionally and politically, and thus it was the focal point for pressures from groups with specific and special interests to further. In cases in which the powers of Congress may be formally greater than those of the Executive, their respective positions may be reversed. In the case of the periodic renewals of the Reciprocal Trade Agreements Act, for example, where the crucial power of decision lies with the Congress, the weight of specific interests seems to have come down on that branch.[5]

A further point on the subject of different orientations to the Executive and the Legislative branches of government bears mention. Among organized groups, but not necessarily among private individuals, there was no substantial difference in the number of communications on the Japanese peace settlement that were sent to the Executive and the number sent to the Congress. There was a difference in the methods employed in the sending of these messages, however; many more face-to-face contacts were made with the Legislature than with the Executive. This suggests that among political interest groups as a whole, without differentiation as to type, Congress is seen as of substantial importance along with the Executive in matters of foreign policy. Perhaps more important,

[5]Cf., e.g., J. Robert Barlow and Robert T. Holt, *The Reciprocal Trade Agreements Act of 1949: A Case Study*, unpublished paper prepared for the Graduate Research Seminar of the Woodrow Wilson School of Public and International Affairs, Princeton University, May 1954; see also the preliminary findings of the study by the Center for International Studies at M.I.T. concerning the impact of business communications on foreign economic policy-making in the United States, as reported by Ithiel de Sola Pool in his paper *Some Aspects of Political Behavior in International Relations*, prepared for the 51st annual meeting of the American Political Science Association, September 1955.

it suggests also that Congress is seen as more directly approachable than the Executive, particularly by those groups which for one reason or another are unsympathetic to the policy proposals emanating from the Executive branch.[6]

These data on differences in the choice of audiences give added weight to some recent hypotheses about the political effectiveness of groups that might be described as having general and intangible interests. The findings just presented support the view that groups with a heavily value-laden interest in public policy have a small impact on the opinions of others, partly because most of their efforts are spent in communicating to their own constituents, to people, that is, who are already predisposed to share the values of their group's leaders.

The Pattern as Seen by Congress and the Executive

Thus far we have looked at the pattern of political communication from the points where the communication originates, asking ourselves how the articulate political interest groups became a part of the political process on the Japanese peace settlement. Now we shall look at the pattern from the other end of the telescope, so to speak, from the points where the communication is received. We shall focus our attention on the governmental level in the political process, and ask how the Executive and the Legislative branches were reached by the various types of articulate public participation.[7] As a general hypothesis, it seems that different elements in the political process come into contact with different parts of the articulate public, and hence they feel the impact of that "public" in different ways. Members of the Congress and members of the Executive Branch did not always have before them the same image of the articulate public's reaction to the course of policy on this issue. These differences in exposure were by no means the chief causes of difference in interpretation or argumentation as between the two branches of government; yet they may have worked in this direction by helping to stoke some fires of disagreement that already existed.

[6]A similar difference in approachability is discernible even where groups with specific interests put the major emphasis on the Congress. Pool, *op. cit.*, reports, for example, that active protectionist businessmen were more likely than low-tariff activists to approach Congressmen directly.

[7]In the first part of this article, communications from private individuals were excluded because not enough information was available to make accurate generalizations about the pattern of that particular source of communication at the point of its origin. In the part that follows, however, dealing with the Executive and the Congress, communications from private individuals will be reintroduced. All of these messages are not available, to be sure, but enough of them are known to indicate that the pattern of political communication, at the point of its reception at the government level, would be distorted more by excluding the available private communications than by including them.

Volume and Composition

One thing that was common to the communications milieus of both the Executive and the Congress was the impression of general public indifference or apathy to the problem of the Japanese peace settlement. We can only mention here the low volume of mail to the White House and the Department of State on this issue, and the small number of private witnesses at the Senate hearings. The volume of letters coming to the offices of Senators cannot have been very large, either, to judge by the complaints of some of the Congressmen. Senator Dirksen, for example, represented himself as astonished and upset by the brief attention given to the treaty by the American people; the day before the Senate voted to ratify, he remarked in the course of debate: "I doubt whether there is a Senator who has received from his constituency as much as 100 pieces of mail on this treaty. My own mail on the subject is limited to about a dozen letters. . . . probably those would not have been forthcoming . . . [had I not] blanketed the air lanes of my State with an informal discussion of this subject."[8]

Though low in volume, the composition of this body of communication differed as between the two branches of government. Communications from citizens and from organized groups to the Executive came mostly in the form of letters; members of Congress, however, confronted a more diversified system of communication. They received more letters than any other form of communication, but these were augmented by greater numbers of formal statements of organizational position, and of face-to-face contacts, than were made to the Executive. Such diversification in the methods of communication that reach Congress is facilitated by the organization and practices of the Legislative branch, and is probably present on most policy issues that attract any public attention whatever. This undoubtedly contributes to a sentiment that lurks in the shadows of many Congressional debates, that members of the Legislature have a more "accurate" or "realistic" system of assessing the opinion of the articulate public than is possessed by the Executive.

Source and Subject Matter

In the case of the Japanese treaty, the box score of organizations and individuals favoring and disapproving the documents of settlement differs according to whether one reads it from Capitol Hill or from the Executive offices. In the first place, the totals were quite different. The Legislature received many more, perhaps twice as many, avowed judgments of approval or disapproval than the Executive received.

These separate bodies of appraisal, each of different size, were also quite different in their balance of favorable and unfavorable valuations. Judgments

[8]*Congressional Record*, Vol. 98, No. 45 (March 19, 1952), p. 2540.

reaching the Executive from individuals and organized groups were evenly divided, with about as many sources upholding the plans for the settlement as attacking them. The "balancing-off" process was not as easy for members of the Congress, for a greater number of negative than positive assessments reached their ears. Put somewhat differently, members of Congress heard more favorable judgments than the Executive heard, but at the same time the legislators were at the receiving end of an even larger number of unfavorable estimations of the settlement.

While Members of Congress were hearing explicit summary judgments about the settlement as a whole, members of the Executive branch were receiving comments, criticisms, and pieces of advice on discrete and often technical aspects of the peace settlement–communications which avoided any explicit appreciation of the whole policy. In some cases, the Executive could reason that small advice and limited criticism implied approval of the larger issue, but there were just as many cases where the final opinion remained in doubt.

More evidence that the Executive and the Congress did not share the same world of communication is found by looking at the specific subject matter that was brought to the attention of each. The Executive heard more about rearmament, fisheries, claims, and the Japanese economy than about any other subjects. Only two of these topics were among the most important ones reaching Congressmen; the latter heard more about rearmament, preservation of sovereignty, territorial questions, and the Japanese economy than about any other subjects.

These differences in exposure to subject matter can be approached from another angle. Congress, then, heard considerably more than did the Executive branch about Nationalist China, reparations, preservation of sovereignty, territorial questions, and about how the treaty aided Communism. In fact, nearly the whole of the sovereignty topic was aimed at the Congress. The Executive, on the other hand, heard more than the Congress about fisheries, claims, and about how necessary it was to have a treaty and how good this particular treaty was. Thus, while the Executive was getting more of a mixture of general praise and specific comments about particular clauses of the settlement, Congress was hearing the roster of ultra-conservative objections to it. Nationalist China, for example, was seen as betrayed because it was not invited to sign the treaty at San Francisco; and Japan was viewed as owing billions in reparations to Communist China because of the wording of the treaty. The conservatism of the communication reaching the Congress clearly distinguishes it from the messages going to the Executive. One might even describe the differences that existed between the two worlds of communication in these terms: the Executive confronted a discussion of how the settlement would affect the future of Japanese-American relations, while the Congress was exposed to a discussion of how the settlement would affect the power of Communists and others to alter both the international and national political and social *status quo*.

The Executive branch of the government is not wholly dependent, for its knowledge of articulate opinion, on the messages that come to it. It has techniques of its own, which are not matched by the Congress, of gathering information on the policy ideas that circulate between leaders and constituents of political interest groups. Insofar as the Executive was exposed to these ideas, however, its view of articulate public opinion was at even greater variance with that held by members of the Congress. For there was hardly any trace of the ultraconservative ideological attacks on the treaty among the communications directed toward interest group constituencies. Even further, these groups were being extensively told what the Executive itself was hearing, and was indeed glad to hear—that the peace treaty with Japan was a good one.

Conclusion

The case of the Japanese peace settlement suggests, then, that different types of interest groups approach the political arena in varying ways, and that the pattern of their political communication on any issue reflects these different orientations toward key elements in the political process. As a result of these differences in communications behavior, members of the Executive branch and members of Congress were differently exposed to ideas on the Japanese peace settlement. The consequences of differential exposure will vary, no doubt, from case to case, according to the calculations of the political strength reflected in public sentiment that each branch makes. In this instance, however, the consequences were not especially serious, since it was clear to almost everyone concerned in both branches that the treaty was, at the least, a bone of very little contention, and at best highly popular, and further that the governmental policy-makers had wide discretion vis-à-vis public opinion. But, while not of overriding importance, the effect of these different exposures was still great enough to put Mr. Dulles to some work to moderate their impact. In his efforts to enlarge the area of agreement on the peace settlement, even as the treaty-making process approached the decisive ratification stage, Mr. Dulles sought to overcome the possible adverse consequences of these different exposures. And in the ratification debate itself one can see the effort of the settlement's supporters to counteract the stream of conservative nationalist communication that had been focused on the Congress.

Interest Groups, Judicial Review, and Local Government

Clement E. Vose

Past scholarship on judicial review of state and local government has been high on structure, power, and policy and low on process. The classic work of Dillon, McQuillin and McBain proved the power of courts in limiting municipal rule against state policy, and state action in many fields against federal constitutional limitations.[1] Rhyne has shown, in an up-to-date treatise, that judge-made doctrines continue to govern state and local practice.[2] The inferior position of these governmental units to both state and federal courts has long been illustrated in law school casebooks on municipal corporations and explained in political science texts on state and local government.

The importance of courts is well understood; the ways in which these passive instruments of government are stimulated to action is not. My attention to the details of litigation sponsored by organized interest groups flows from a central assumption that the important thing about appellate courts in the American system is that these courts govern by making policy. They may do this by deciding what is constitutional or unconstitutional and they may do it by the interpretation of statutes, administrative rules and regulations, the decisions of lower courts and so on. To say that courts are important in American government is to speak the obvious. But emphasis on their importance because of their policy-making function is not always the starting point in the textbook treatment of the judiciary. If it were, I believe there would be more attention to the ways cases are brought and to identifying

[1]John F. Dillon, *Commentaries on the Law of Municipal Corporations,* 5th ed. (Boston: Little, Brown, 1911), 5 vols.; Eugene McQuillin, *A Treatise on the Law of Municipal Corporations,* 2d ed. (Chicago: Callaghan, 1945), 7 vols.; Howard Lee McBain, *The Law and Practice of Municipal Home Rule* (New York: Macmillan, 1916).

[2]Charles Rhyne, *Municipal Law* (Washington: NIMLO, 1957).

Clement E. Vose, "Interest Groups, Judicial Review, and Local Government," Western Political Quarterly, *Vol. 19 (March 1966). Reprinted by permission of the University of Utah, copyright owners.*

the true parties in such cases. Political scientists have not sufficiently moved off the dime of constitutional doctrine to describe the real gold of politics in the judicial process. This article looks at litigation conducted by action organizations and points to the importance of group agitation for judicial review of state and municipal public policy.

The Legitimacy of Interest Groups in Court Cases

The Supreme Court of the United States in 1963 vindicated the right of the most successful litigating organization of the day, the National Association for the Advancement of Colored People, to pursue its goals through the courts. In *NAACP* v. *Button,*[3] the Court recognized the extent of group sponsorship of litigation and certified it against state legislation that aimed to severely limit cases brought by organizations. This was, of course, one way for a state government to protect its policies against judicial review. The failure of Virginia and other southern states to stop organizations from litigating further legitimized judicial review and recognized the right of organizations to seek redress in the judicial forum. This is what Mr. Justice Brennan said for the Supreme Court:

> . . . In the context of NAACP objectives, litigation is not a technique of resolving private differences; it is a means for achieving the lawful objectives of equality of treatment by all government, federal, state and local, for the members of the Negro community in this country. It is thus a form of political expression. Groups which find themselves unable to achieve their objectives through the ballot frequently turn to the courts. Just as it was true of the opponents of New Deal legislation during the 1930's, for example, no less is it true of the Negro minority today. And under the conditions of modern government, litigation may well be the sole practicable avenue open to a minority to petition for redress of grievances.
>
> The NAACP is not a conventional political party; but the litigation it assists, while serving to vindicate the legal rights of members of the American Negro community, at the same time and perhaps more importantly, makes possible the distinctive contribution of a minority group to the ideas and beliefs of our society. For such a group, association for litigation may be the most effective form of political association.[4]

[3]371 U.S. 451 (1963).
[4]*Ibid.*, at 425.

Academic categories of state and local government on the one hand and civil rights and civil liberties on the other have not kept organized interest groups from action. These are the propositions that link them together: (1) For some thirty years the Supreme Court has been nationalizing the constitutional rights of individuals. (2) In hundreds of decisions dealing with freedom of expression and religion, rights of defendants and rights of racial minorities against segregation and discrimination, the Supreme Court has spelled out new constitutional doctrine. (3) The bulk of these cases have questioned state and municipal public policy with the result that many, many state statutes, municipal ordinances, and other forms of state action have been invalidated. (4) National organizations have participated in practically 100 per cent of these cases by providing financial or legal assistance, by appearing as *amicus curiae,* or by giving strategic advice.[5]

The most active organizations include the following: the National Association for the Advancement of Colored People, the American Civil Liberties Union, the Commission on Law and Social Action of the American Jewish Congress, the American Committee for Protection of the Foreign Born, the Emergency Civil Liberties Committee, the Watchtower Bible and Tract Society (Jehovah's Witnesses), American Jewish Committee, Japanese American Citizens League, Congress of Racial Equality, and Protestants and Other Americans United for the Separation of Church and State. Attorneys employed by these and other organizations provide the expertise that continuous attention to a problem brings to practitioners. Their persuasive powers are applied to the courts in long series of cases which spread over many years. That this has, at least, sometimes been true may be seen by looking briefly at some of the most celebrated Supreme Court reviews of state and local government policy in civil rights and liberties.

The School Segregation cases of 1954 and 1955 were themselves the product of litigation sponsored by the NAACP Legal Defense and Education Fund.[6] These five cases had been preceded by some fifty favorable Supreme Court decisions extending over the previous thirty years. Those decisions have been followed by a steady stream of litigation which has seen NAACP lawyers in an average of ten appearances a year in the Supreme Court. The Association has also participated in numerous cases in the lower federal courts. Certainly some 90 per cent of this vast litigation has put in question a

[5]For a survey of the activity of organizations in the major cases of recent years, see "Comment, 'The South's Amended Barratry Laws: An Attempt to End Group Pressure through the Courts,' " 72 *Yale L. J.* 1613-45 (Summer 1963). The great changes in the legal status of Negroes are explained in Jack Greenberg, *Race Relations and American Law* (New York: Columbia Univ. Press, 1959).

[6]*Brown* v. *Board of Education,* 347 U.S. 483 (1954), 349 U.S. 294 (1955).

policy adopted by Southern states and municipalities. Much of it has dealt with the segregation of school pupils but, of course, local school arrangements are public policy.

The Flag Salute cases of 1940 and 1943[7] as well as the Prayer cases of 1961 and 1963[8] dealt also with public school policy and resulted in the invalidation of local law by the Supreme Court. Manwaring has shown that the flag salute question had stood unanswered for years because no organization would challenge the practice in the Courts. The Jehovah's Witnesses did so in the 1930's and after several tries gained review in the Supreme Court. They were finally successful in 1943 in having the obligatory flag salute for public school students invalidated.[9]

Individuals who conscientiously opposed the recitation of prayers in public school were parties to the recent cases on this question. This was necessary to establish standing as a party in the cases. But despite the national prominence of some successful parties in these cases—one thinks back to Mrs. Vashti McCollum as well as to Mrs. [Madalyn] Murray, perhaps America's two most prominent lady atheists—organized interest groups have not been far behind the scenes. *Amicus curiae* briefs were filed in the most recent prayer cases by the American Humanist Association, the American Ethical Union, the Synagogue Council of America and the National Community Relations Advisory Council, and the American Jewish Committee and Anti-Defamation League of B'nai B'rith.

The extent of interest group activity in litigation is certainly not yet realized. Nor has the data so far collected been accommodated to a political theory of democracy. This article focuses on cases which define the limits of state and local governmental power and insists that group activity in the litigation is both widespread and legitimate. The large number of cases sponsored by organizations is a function of the power of courts to act. This authority of the judiciary was beautifully set forth by Norman Williams, Jr., ten years ago, as follows:

> The main premises of American constitutional law represent a codification and institutionalization of the primary values of a democratic society—equality of opportunity and equality of treatment, freedom of thought and considerable freedom of action, and fairness. Under the

[7]*Minersville School District* v. *Gobitis,* 310 U.S. 586 (1940); *West Virginia State Board of Education* v. *Barnette,* 319 U.S. 624 (1943).

[8]*Engle* v. *Vitale,* 370 U.S. 421 (1962). *Abington Township School District* v. *Schempp* and *Murray* v. *Curlett,* 374 U.S. 203 (1963).

[9]For a thorough review of methods of litigation used by The Witnesses, see David Manwaring, *Render unto Caesar* (Chicago: Univ. Chicago Press, 1962).

> American system, a more or less independent mechanism of judicial review is established to provide an independent check on whether specific governmental decisions conform to these standards. While controversy has often raged about judicial action in other areas, *it has always been recognized that it is an essential part of the judicial function to watch over the parochial and exclusionist attitudes and policies of local governments, and to see to it that these do not run counter to national policy and the general welfare.*[10]

But courts are passive instruments of control and must be moved to decision by a party controverting government policy. The performance of this function has often been fulfilled by organized interest groups.

Interests opposed to each other in litigation are ordinarily not readily identifiable in the court reports. The parties are named and their counsel are listed but the parties are often there to give legal standing to the wider interests supporting a litigation. And the attorneys are representatives of those interests, often on a full-time basis. Little has been written on the function of interest groups in litigation. The current collection of examples will suggest something further about the variety of the phenomenon and show that group activity is not limited to celebrated cases on civil rights. Rather, litigation is a flow of pressure group activity that is old, common, and essential to the judicial review of the most controversial policies of municipal government.

Public School Cases

Public education is important as a budget item and as a political issue in American communities. Many organizations have drawn the judiciary into the consideration of various aspects of local school affairs. Racial segregation was outlawed in cases initiated in this way and we are now well through the first decade of follow-up litigation to bring practice into conformity with constitutional doctrine. Court tests of school activities offensive to different religions have come up frequently in the past twenty years.

In 1933, well before this spate of cases on race and religion, an authority on the legal basis of school organization and administration wrote that "the relation of the school to civil society, on the one hand, and to the individual, on the other, is nowhere so well defined as in the great body of decisions rendered by the highest of our state and federal courts."[11] Since then,

[10] "Planning Law and Democratic Living," *Law and Contemporary Problems,* Vol. 20 (1955), p. 317.

[11] Newton Edwards, *The Courts and the Public Schools* (Chicago: Univ. Chicago Press, 1933; 1955).

outside control of education has advanced as an activist judiciary has applied new tests to local practices. Of course, there is disagreement over whether these decisions are different from those in the first part of the century which Justice Holmes condemned because they prevented "the making of social experiments that an important part of the community desires, in the insulated chambers afforded by the several States."[12] Edward S. Corwin believed that these issues are alike. After the decision in the McCollum case in 1948 outlawing released time practices in the public schools of Champaign, Illinois, Corwin said: "In my opinion the Court would act wisely to make it clear at the first opportunity that it does not aspire to become, as Justice Jackson puts it, 'a super board of education for every school district in the nation.' "[13] Whatever one's view may be there can be no denying that court decisions are having important ramifications in the educational life of American communities.

Interest Groups in Zoning Cases

The interest group approach follows the tradition of legal realism and emphasizes the political impulses behind litigation and the political results of judicial decisions rather than the arguments, reasoning and doctrines of law in cases. We are interested in the effect of judicial decisions on the distribution of power in communities. Take as an example the recent cases testing the authority of local zoning boards. In *Senior* v. *New Canaan Zoning Commission*[14] the Connecticut Supreme Court of Errors, in 1959, held constitutional the upgrading of lots in a residential semi-rural zone from two to four acre minimums. The decision met with mixed reaction throughout Fairfield County. The Court noted in its opinion that "the town of New Canaan, as of the 1950 census, had the highest per capita income of any town, village, or city in the United States."[15] It was not surprising to learn that the First Selectman of New Canaan described the ruling as beneficial. "It is good for the town to keep its prestige in a major suit of this kind," he said. There was general agreement that "the decision strengthened the power of zoning boards to decide the character of their communities." More recently *House and Home* has said that the U.S. Supreme Court's refusal to hear the arguments in the New Canaan Case "is seen as strengthening the power of

[12]*Truax* v. *Corrigan,* 257 U.S. 312, 344 (1921) (dissenting opinion).

[13]Edward S. Corwin, "The Supreme Court as a National School Board," *Law and Contemporary Problems,* Vol. 14 (Winter 1949), p. 22. The quotation of Justice Jackson is from *McCollum* v. *Board of Education,* 333 U.S. 203 (1948) (dissenting opinion).

[14]*Senior* v. *New Canaan Zoning Commission,* 146 Conn. 531, 153 A.2d 415 (1959); appeal dismissed, 80 S. Ct. 1083 (1960).

[15]*The New York Times,* July 5, 1959, p. 58.

zoning boards generally."[16] Civic groups in other communities were encouraged to fight further for similar zoning for minimum lot area. It was also recognized that such zoning worked hardships on lower-income groups and believed by some that it prevented an orderly population growth. The effect of the Court decision upholding four-acre minimum lots was also said to be an increase in price of existing two-acre lots which were comparatively scarce. Quite certainly the courts which considered this case dealt with legal issues that touched not only the distribution of power within one community but in many similar suburban places and in central cities, as well. This was true for the Court of Common Pleas which, in the first instance, declared the zoning ordinance unconstitutional. It was also true for the Connecticut Supreme Court of Errors which reversed that decision and the United States Supreme Court which, on May 21, 1960, dismissed the appeal.[17]

The pressures for and against acreage, or snob, zoning (called "Ivy League socialism" by Dean Jefferson Fordham of the University of Pennsylvania Law School)[18] came to the surface in a case brought by a construction company against Easttown Township, a main-line suburb of Philadelphia.[19] There a 1940 ordinance provided that a minimum lot area in an "A" residential district should be one acre, with a minimum frontage of 150 feet. The court test was begun when the applicant sought to build a dwelling on a site slightly less than a half-acre, with a frontage of 100 feet. The Easttown Township Board of Adjustment refused to grant a variance and this decision was supported by the Chester County Court of Common Pleas. The Supreme Court of Pennsylvania first reversed the lower court, by a vote of 6 to 1, on June 28, 1957, then granted a rehearing, vacated its order, and in a final order, on May 27, 1958, reversed itself by a 4 to 3 vote, and ruled the order of the Board of Adjustment to be valid. By the time the case reached reargument the defense of acreage zoning by Easttown Township and its Devon Citizens Association was supported by the *amici curiae* briefs of Lower Merion Township, Willistown Township, the Pennsylvania Local Government Conference, the Pennsylvania Planning Association, and George Wharton Pepper, Esquire, a well-known citizen of Easttown. The opposing position of the Bilbar Construction Company was supported in briefs *amici curiae* by the Home

[16]*House and Home,* July 1960, p. 41.

[17]The appeal was dismissed "for want of a substantial federal question," 80 S. Ct. 1083 (1960).

[18]*House and Home,* July 1960, p. 59.

[19]*Bilbar Construction Company* v. *Easttown Township Board of Adjustment,* 393 Pa. 62, 141 A.2d 851 (1958).

Builders Association of Philadelphia and the Home Life Insurance Company.[20]

In stressing the organizations in a case there is danger of neglecting other important considerations. This is the problem of any interpretation built around a single approach. But the objective is understanding, not a complete explanation that would satisfy all social scientists and lawyers at once. Very important new doctrine may be found in the Easttown Township decision when the Pennsylvania Supreme Court ruled that the regulation need only have a substantial or reasonable relation to health, safety, morals, or the general welfare. This seemingly went against Dillon's rule in holding that the presumption of constitutionality of an ordinance is as strong as that attending an act of the legislature.[21] With this and other decisions the importance of doctrine is assumed but the interest group environment in which these cases are decided is stressed.

Few major zoning disputes have been carried to the U. S. Supreme Court since the original case of *Euclid* v. *Ambler Realty Co.* was decided in 1926.[22] The Village of Euclid had as counsel a young man named James Metzenbaum who has said: "It has been my understanding that the railroads, the industrial plants and the realtors (*then* afraid of zoning; now strong champions of zoning) paid the large fee to Mr. Newton D. Baker."[23] There is little question but what zoning cases are rife with organized interests.[24]

The National Institute of Municipal Law Officers

In exploring the group nature of the litigation which gives rise to judicial decisions affecting municipal governments I shall first describe the side of government and, perhaps underplaying the role of the attorney for a municipality, tell of some organizations which stand behind him. Here is the defense of municipal power and the policies favored by the majority. Considering the values of local rule it is heartening to see that this defense is often well made. Then I shall identify groups which have lost out in municipal decisions and

[20]David Craig, "Zoning," *U. of Pitt. L. Rev.*, Vol. 20 (1958), p. 278.

[21]Theodore O. Rogers and others, *Zoning for Minimum Lot Area* (Philadelphia: Univ. Villanova Press, 1959). See John M. Anderson, "Book Review," *Notre Dame Law*, Vol. 34 (1959), p. 603.

[22]*Euclid* v. *Ambler Realty Co.*, 272 U.S. 365 (1926). See James Metzenbaum, *The Law of Zoning* (New York: Baker, Voorhis, 1956), 3 vols.; editorial, *New York Times*, February 11, 1956.

[23]Interview of James Metzenbaum, Cleveland, Ohio, May 15, 1955; letters of James Metzenbaum to author, September 22, 1955, and October 13, 1955.

[24]For valuable analyses of the important cases in this field, see the annual reviews of Norman Williams, Jr., "Recent Decisions in Planning Law," *American Institute of Planners Journal*, Vol. 27 (May 1961), p. 159; *ibid.*, Vol. 28 (May 1962), p. 132; *ibid.*, Vol. 29 (May 1963), p. 127; *ibid.*, Vol. 30 (May 1964).

turn to the courts for relief. Considering that many of their cases are brought to protect citizen rights it is impressive that these groups bring zeal, skill, and money to litigation. Thus the place of courts in municipal power struggles will be reached indirectly.

Although the defense of actions by municipal corporations is formally in the hands of their chief legal officer, titled variously corporation counsel, law director, or city, town, village, borough or county attorney, this work has been aided since 1935 by the National Institute of Municipal Law Officers. Known by its initials, NIMLO was an offshoot of the United States Conference of Mayors though always an independent organization. Its headquarters are in Washington where a full-time legal staff is maintained under Charles S. Rhyne, who has served as director since 1939. Its members are 1,200 American municipalities which rely on NIMLO as a collection center for their varied legal experience. A description by NIMLO shows it to be supported entirely by the annual membership fees paid by member cities. Interestingly, this tells that "information collected and on file in the Washington Office is never used by, nor made available to, any person other than an attorney for a NIMLO member so that there is no possibility that this material will be employed against the cities which have collected it."[25]

NIMLO represents a kind of perfect expression of a paradoxical development –the nationalization of municipal law. It aids the busy municipal attorney "who needs the strength flowing from joint support of many municipalities in instances where the protest of a single municipality would be ineffective." Or, put another way by NIMLO, "furnishes an effective agency through which municipal attorneys can take joint cooperative action on Federal legislation and on any other matter of nationwide consequence to municipalities on matters in Washington, D.C., with great effectiveness." NIMLO offers many services but two activities may be identified as directly shaping the legal position of municipalities: drafting model ordinances and defending them by briefs in the Supreme Court of the United States.[26]

The very idea of model state constitutions and legislation, model city charters and ordinances has not been much explored. The phenomenon is very well known and accepted, for on its face it is easy to understand as necessary in a nation of fifty states and thousands of lesser governmental units. Yet the folklore

[25]The quotation is from a leaflet published by the National Institute of Municipal Law Officers, 839 17th Street, N.W., Washington 6, D.C. I am indebted to Mr. Brice W. Rhyne for information about NIMLO. Interview, Washington, D.C., March 25, 1960.

[26]The most important publication is Charles S. Rhyne, *Municipal Law* (Washington: NIMLO, 1957), said to be the only one-volume treatise on municipal law published since 1910. Regularly issued publications include *NIMLO, Municipal Law Review, NIMLO Model Ordinance Service, Municipal Ordinance Review, Municipal Law Court Decisions,* and the *Municipal Law Journal.*

of American government must yield a bit when it is realized that much modern local legislation has been drafted in Washington! At any rate, the *NIMLO Model Ordinance Service* is followed closely by most municipal law officers in advising local councils in the enactment of local legislation. The *Service* is in a loose-leaf binder to facilitate constant revision and supplementation and "each model ordinance has tried and proven provisions with citations to the special studies or leading court decisions upon which it is based." And it may be truly said that "many of these model ordinances have already been adopted by hundreds of municipalities."

If a "test case" is one whose outcome will affect interests beyond those of the parties in the dispute then NIMLO's frequent interest in municipal ordinance litigation is to be expected. In the bulk of instances cases involving model ordinances are settled at the state level and are prepared by the law officers of member municipalities. For example, in 1950 the NIMLO Model Sound Truck Ordinance, which had been adopted by the City of Allentown, Pennsylvania, was upheld by the Pennsylvania Superior Court.[27] The case for sustaining the ordinance was made by the city solicitor of Allentown. The lower court's holding was affirmed by the State Supreme Court and an appeal from this dismissed by the United States Supreme Court. When cases involving member municipalities come before the Supreme Court, NIMLO may take action in two ways. The organization may provide assistance to the city law officer in charge of the case by making suggestions on the brief or on the approach to the oral argument. On occasion Charles S. Rhyne, Director of NIMLO, may join as a joint author of a brief for a municipality.

The second form of NIMLO support in court cases is by *amici curiae* briefs, an activity which seems to be flourishing nowadays.[28] At least most of NIMLO's *amici* briefs have been in cases during the last three terms of the Supreme Court. There are nine cases which NIMLO has entered in this way. Of these, seven have supported city efforts to obtain lower gas and utility rates and two have involved municipal inspection practices.[29]

[27]*Commonwealth* v. *Guess*, 168 Pa. Super. 22, 76 A.2d 500 (1950), *affirmed* without opinion, 368 Pa. 290, 81 A.2d 553 (1912), *appeal dismissed*, 342 U.S. 912 (1952). See Rhyne, *Municipal Law*, p. 471, n. 28.

[28]See Samuel Krislov, "The Amicus Curiae Brief: From Friendship to Advocacy," *Yale L.J.*, Vol. 72 (April 1963), p. 694.

[29]Among cases in which NIMLO has filed a brief as *amicus curiae* are the following: *Frank* v. *Maryland*, 359 U.S. 360 (1959); *City of Detroit* v. *Murray Corporation*, 355 U.S. 489 (1958); *Phillips Petroleum* v. *Wisconsin*, 347 U.S. 672 (1954); *District of Columbia* v. *Little*, 338 U.S. 866 (1949), in support of the petition for certiorari, and at 339 U.S. 1 (1950), on the merits; *Oklahoma Natural Gas Co.* v. *Federal Power Commission*, 358 U.S. 877 (1958), in support of petition for certiorari; *United Gas Pipe Line Co.* v. *Memphis Light, Gas & Water*, 355 U.S. 938 (1958), in opposition to certiorari, 358 U.S. 103 (1958), on the merits; *Smith* v. *California*, 80 S. Ct. 399 (1960), in support of rehearing.

NIMLO, as a kind of semi-governmental institution, acts with decorum and restraint in its work of ordinance design and defense. But, occasionally, an ally in extending and justifying municipal power may beseech the courts to act right by supporting a pet policy aim. A current example may be seen in criticisms of courts by supporters of urban renewal and slum clearance programs in American cities. In 1960 the *Cleveland Plain Dealer* addressed the courts editorially in this tone: "Frankly, we think the municipal judges who now try these cases have not given enough thought to the cancer which slums and rank overcrowding have created in this city. In our view, there consistently are too many postponements and too many suspended fines. . . . This wrist-slapping business must be stopped, for what's the use of hiring new inspectors and putting through a stricter housing code if the court doesn't follow up the good work?"[30] This point of view was applied to courts in other cities in the spring of 1960 by the National Association of Housing and Redevelopment which criticized judicial leniency in Cincinnati, Dayton, and St. Louis.[31] In those cities courts rejected evidence of violations obtained during inspections without search warrants. On June 20, 1960, a 4-to-4 tie vote in the United States Supreme Court let stand the arrest of a Dayton homeowner for refusing to admit a housing inspector without a warrant.[32] The defense of the Dayton ordinance permitting such inspections was led by Charles Rhyne in cooperation with the city attorney and NIMLO filed an *amicus curiae* brief in support, also. However, the tie vote has no force or precedent, so this particular problem is not yet ended.

NIMLO protects local law in the courts as a matter of routine and as a primary obligation. There are other organizations, established to serve the interests of local government, which participate in law suits only occasionally. Thus, the United States Conference of Mayors has been involved in only one case since its founding in 1934. As an organization of mayors of approximately 300 cities with a population of 50,000 or more the Conference in 1957 filed a brief *amicus curiae* supporting a petition by Mayor Hartsfield of Atlanta requesting the Supreme Court of the United States to consider the constitutionality of the Georgia County Unit Primary.[33] This brief contended that this system "represents a systematic discrimination against, and continuous debasement of, the political voice and

[30]Quoted in *Journal of Housing*, Vol. 17 (May 1960), pp. 187-188.

[31]*Ibid.* The position of the National Association of Housing and Redevelopment was widely reported. See *The New York Times*, July 10, 1960, p. 43; *Milwaukee Journal*, August 21, 1960.

[32]*Ohio ex rel. Eaton* v. *Price, Chief of Police*, 80 S. Ct. 1465 (1960).

[33]*Hartsfield* v. *Sloan*, 357 U. S. 916 (1958). This information was obtained through a visit to the offices of the United States Conference of Mayors, 1707 H Street, N.W., Washington 6, D.C. See the pamphlet *The United States Conference of Mayors: Its History, Organization, Activities, and Services* (Washington, 1953).

position of municipalities and their citizens." And, "State Governments controlled by self-perpetuating rural minorities systematically discriminate against the interests of municipalities and their citizens." The Conference therefore entered its brief in order to place the Georgia County Unit Primary "in the larger context of urban underrepresentation." However, the Supreme Court denied review. It is fair to conclude that the United States Conference of Mayors ordinarily finds better expression of its goals than through litigation.

In contrast, the state leagues of municipalities act much more like NIMLO for, among many activities, they prepare codes of model ordinances appropriate in a single state and especially for smaller communities. These organizations also represent the interests of their member municipalities before state legislatures, administrative agencies and courts. In a typical state, for instance, the League of Wisconsin Municipalities filed eight *amici curiae* briefs in state supreme court cases during the past decade.[34] Ordinarily the preamble of such briefs explains that "the disposition of the matter before the court is of vital concern to all Wisconsin cities and villages." It is this judgment that the executive committee of the League applies in authorizing that a brief be submitted on behalf of its members. In Wisconsin the cities and villages which are members now number 492. State municipal leagues often decide whether to file briefs in cases partly on their view of the competence of the municipal corporation attorney for it continues to be a great irony of our judicial process that great principles affecting many interests not heard in a lawsuit may rise or fall in a quietly pursued litigation. The organizations that support the work of city law officers are understandable developments in this system of lawmaking.

Thus far I have assumed that municipal corporations have enough in common to join together in common defense when there are law suits questioning their powers, policies, and procedures. This view is supported by the program of the American Municipal Association, the national organization of the various state municipal leagues, which speaks of "the national municipal policy" which guides their activities. But while there are broad areas of agreement the differences in the size, location, financial condition and outlook among American communities are surely reflected in these organizations. Accordingly, the larger cities in a state are frequently at odds with the public position of their municipal league. And, no doubt, the American Municipal Association does not feel as strongly about the need for reapportionment as does the United States Conference of Mayors. Certainly the litigation in which these groups are active reflects their different constituencies and outlooks.

[34]This information is based, in part, on an interview with Mr. Robert D. Sundby, Legal Counsel, League of Wisconsin Municipalities, 30 East Johnson Street, Madison, Wisconsin, August 17, 1960.

Turning to the single municipality and its attorney one finds some well-established differences. Litigation for a large city is proportionately much greater than for a smaller place though rate of growth is a factor of importance. Tax and liability cases bulk large in this work while annexation and related issues show up in the legal business of a growing place. While national and state organizations of government officials often contribute to the defense of municipal corporations in the courts, municipal law officers do not depend solely on this support. Political scientists should give attention to this office and the political factors which condition its conduct.

To the extent that local government policy is set by organized interests in a locality then the defense of that policy in the courts is also a defense of those interests. There are many instances where this private interest is given ample chance to speak officially in support of the policy. In *Dean Milk Co.* v. *Madison*,[35] the city of Madison was represented throughout the litigation by the city attorney and an attorney for the Madison Milk Producers Association, as well. In *Zorach* v. *Clauson*,[36] the city of New York was represented by its own counsel and by an *amicus* brief by a city-wide committee of Protestants, Catholics, and Jews which favored released time from the schools for religious instruction. When the Borough of Rutherford, New Jersey, wished to defend distribution of Bibles in the public schools it accepted the support of the Gideons International as intervenor to defend the policy in the courts and carry the costs.[37]

The frequent judicial defeat of states and municipalities a generation ago was attributed by Justice Brandeis to inferior public counsel. He felt over and over again that attorneys representing private interests were abler men than those representing cities and states. It is hard to make a comparison today. No doubt the organizations of public officials, especially the National Institute of Municipal Law Officers, the state leagues of municipalities, and the National Association of Attorneys General, have provided vital skill in support of individual public law officers in crucial legal tests. Private supporters also volunteer legal aid to governments in court cases. Abler men, larger staffs and bigger budgets today enable cities to defend themselves in the courts to balance adversary proceedings which tend to be lopsided when superior private counsel is employed.

American Trial Lawyers Association—Formerly National Association of Claimants' Counsel of America

Strong feelings of aggrieved parties, the devotion of able attorneys and associations of persons similarly situated go together in many of the best known actions

[35]*Dean Milk Co.* v. *Madison*, 340 U.S. 349 (1950).

[36]*Zorach* v. *Clauson*, 343 U.S. 306 (1952).

[37]*Tudor* v. *Gideons International*, 14 N. J. 31, 100 A2d 857 (1953), *certiorari denied*, 348 U.S. 816 (1954).

against state and local government in recent years. In the city of New York, and elsewhere increasingly, a substantial part of the cost of operating the law department is due to the defense against "sidewalk injury cases." In 1959 the *NIMLO Municipal Law Review* reported that perhaps the most important problem of the municipal attorney is the question of tort liability. The report said: "This [condition] appears to be particularly true when consideration is given to the number of claims being presented, the large amounts now being awarded in damages, often the lack of funds with which to pay the same, the inability to secure adequate, if any, public liability insurance, and the removal by the courts and legislatures in various states of the municipalities' immunity from tort liability when acting in a governmental capacity."[38] The assault on the doctrine of municipal immunity from tort liability has been led by the National Association of Claimants' Counsel of America. The 7,500 members of this nation-wide bar association, known as NACCA, are no doubt, the most zealous, hardest working, best paid lawyers in the country. NACCA was founded in 1946. The National Association of Claimants' Counsel of America is made up of "attorneys specializing in the representation of injured persons."[39] Through national and regional conferences, reports and the *NACCA Law Journal*, the organization has stimulated and applauded a sensational trend toward bigger and better damage suits.[40] In 1965 the organization was renamed the American Trial Lawyers Association.

The opposing interests caught up by this trend were pointed up by the reaction of NACCA and NIMLO attorneys to the lifting of municipal immunity from tort liability by the Supreme Court of Florida in 1957 in the case of *Hargrove v. Town of Cocoa Beach*.[41] This was an action by a widow against the municipality for damage for the alleged wrongful death of her husband who died of smoke suffocation in an unattended jail. (The court report says the "husband was incarcerated in the town jail while in a helpless condition because of excessive intoxication.") The trial judge dismissed the complaint on the theory that the town was immune to liability for this type of tort. On appeal, the Florida Supreme Court reversed and receded from its prior decisions holding a municipal corporation immune from liability for the torts of police officers. Positively, the court held "that when an individual suffers a direct, personal injury proximately caused by the negligence of a municipal employee while acting

[38]Comment of William E. Collins, Corporation Counsel, Rockford, Illinois, *NIMLO Municipal L. Rev.*, Vol. 22 (1959), pp. 357-358.

[39]*Encyclopedia of Associations*, 3rd ed.,: Vol. 1, *National Organizations of the United States* (Detroit: Gale Research Co., 1961), p. 266.

[40]Litigation is not the only form of activity for this organization. See the argument for juries by its President, Jacob D. Fuchsberg, "A Brief for the Jury in Civil Cases," *New York Times Magazine*, March 1, 1964, p. 34.

[41]96 So. 2d 130 (1957).

within the scope of his employment, the injured individual is entitled to redress for the wrong done."[42] The court reasoned that the immunity doctrine was inappropriate in a modern, urban democracy where the city "is in substantial measure a large business institution." In departing from the rule of municipal immunity, the Florida Supreme Court explained that its conclusion had "not been hastily formulated" and added: "The matter was thoroughly briefed and argued by counsel for the parties. At the invitation of the Court, the Florida League of Municipalities filed briefs and through counsel ably presented the matter *amicus curiae*."[43]

At the next annual convention of the National Institute of Municipal Law Officers, the city attorney of Pensacola reported that this opinion was most alarming and there was general concern that such judgments could "financially cripple any city or village at any time."[44] The Pensacola city attorney's comments were uttered with some humor and, while it may be unfair to take them at face value, a quotation will reveal something of the spirit of one official faced with the prospect of damage suits in the future.[45]

> . . . on leaving my home in Pensacola the other day I picked up a newspaper and read that in Miami a circuit court jury had returned a verdict in the sum of $23,000.00 because a man's arm was broken while he was being arrested. Of course, that's Miami. (Laughter.)
> . . . We look with a great deal of fear and trepidation to the decision in the *Hargrove* case in Florida, particularly so in the Miami area where the verdicts are so fantastic. I hope that the Northern part of Florida where the real Southerners of Florida live that they will be much more practical in their verdicts in the event that we have such a thoughtless officer on our police department as to break a man's arm when he is drunk. (Applause.)

In contrast, a note in the *NACCA Law Journal* praised the decision of the Supreme Court of Florida in the Hargrove case as "commendably repudiating the indefensible rule of municipal immunity from tort liability."[46] Municipalities were described by the claimant's compensation attorneys as "one of the best loss-distributing units of society." The note said simply, but in emotion-charged words, that the immunity rule was "barefaced injustice." The NACCA position may be summed up as follows: "It is better that the losses due to the

[42] *Ibid.*, pp. 133-134.

[43] *Ibid.*, p. 136.

[44] Comment of F. Churchill Mellen, City Attorney, Pensacola, Florida, *NIMLO Municipal L. Rev.*, Vol. 22 (1958), p. 450.

[45] *Ibid.*, p. 452.

[46] Case note by Thomas F. Lambert, Jr., *NACCA L. J.*, Vol. 20 (November 1957), p. 241.

torts of city employees should fall upon the cities and for the latter to bear the cost of such casualties than upon the innocent victim of 'official' torts. Such losses should be regarded as the social cost of administering government, spread over the citizenry by the tax device, rather than have the cities partially subsidized by the coerced contributions of their victims."[47] This view appears to be gaining popular and judicial acceptance. Without straining its implications too greatly one can see the obligations of local government and the tax burden growing through this judicial change of heart brought about, at least in part, by the zealousness of NACCA, henceforth to be known as the American Trial Lawyers Association.

Court Rules and Interest Group Access

Among all litigants those who challenge municipal action perhaps have the easiest path. In conformity with "Dillon's rule," the powers possessed by municipalities are ordinarily interpreted in a restrictive way by the courts.[48] The troubles of municipal corporations are increased by the procedures of state courts which make them far easier marks than federal courts. Friendly suits are common. Advisory opinions are rendered in many states. The declaratory judgment is more fully developed. Class actions are permitted more readily. The rules for *amicus curiae* and intervenors are less stringent. Above all, the "taxpayer's suit" stands as a symbol of the many procedures by which state courts have been brought to exert such power over local government. This device led Sayre and Kaufman, in their study of New York City, to conclude that courts "offer nongovernmental groups in the city a chance to influence officials in the other branches indirectly when they cannot do so directly."[49]

"Taxpayers' suits" satisfy the jurisdictional requirement that plaintiffs have standing to sue.[50] Normally, this requirement means that the plaintiff must sustain specific personal injury before he is allowed to go to court. However,

[47]*Ibid.*, pp. 236-237.

[48]"Dillon's Rule" was originally expressed as follows: "It is a general and undisputed proposition of law that a municipal corporation possesses and can exercise the following powers, and no others: First, those granted in express words; second, those necessarily or fairly implied in or incident to the powers expressly granted; third, those essential to the accomplishment of the declared objects and purposes of the corporation—not simply convenient, but indispensable. Any fair, reasonable, substantial doubt concerning the existence of power is resolved by the courts against the corporation, and the power is denied." Dillon, *op. cit.*, I, p. 448.

[49]Wallace S. Sayre and Herbert Kaufman, *Governing New York City: Politics in the Metropolis* (New York: Russell Sage Foundation, 1960), p. 496.

[50]This section of my paper is drawn largely from "Comment, 'Taxpayers' Suits: A Survey and a Summary'," *Yale L. J.*, Vol. 69 (April 1960), pp. 895-924.

municipal action in virtually every state may be tested under this relaxation of the "standing" doctrine where a plaintiff's status as a taxpayer "has been held sufficient to allow damage to him which is shared equally with all members of the public to form a judicially cognizable issue."[51] A taxpayer's suit has been defined as "a representative class action in equity, brought on behalf of all taxpayers against officials of the governmental unit challenged."[52] In practice, the word "taxpayer" has been treated so loosely that a group of persons wishing to question governmental action in the courts need only find the money and a nominal plaintiff to do so. This is why "taxpayers' suits" have functionally become "citizens' suits."[53]

A *Yale Law Journal* survey shows that the objectives sought by plaintiff-taxpayers have varied widely with the following in order of importance:[54] (1) challenges to the use of the eminent domain power in connection with slum clearance, housing, highways, airport, and other public works projects; (2) attacks on the constitutionality of various methods of bond financing used by municipalities to circumvent limitations on indebtedness; (3) cases questioning the granting of franchises or licenses which represent public approval of privately owned but publicly used facilities; (4) efforts to withhold salary payments to civil servants who hold office in violation of statutory standards; (5) challenges to sales or donations of the public domain to private parties; (6) cases to achieve civil liberties objectives such as the prevention of expenditures for illegal methods of law enforcement or expenditures which would violate the separation of church and state; (7) suits to reapportion election or judicial districts.

Taxpayers' suits were first allowed by American courts just prior to the Civil War but did not reach a great volume until the end of the nineteenth century. Then in the Populist and Progressive periods a number of devices of democratic intent were fashioned to cope with entrenched officials and vested interests. In this connection the taxpayer's suit should be linked with the initiative, referendum, and recall as a symbol of the era. In this century the taxpayer's suit has been one of the chief weapons in the arsenal of the good government movement. The editor of the Madison, Wisconsin, *Capital Times*, whose roots are deep in the LaFollette movement, in 1960 established a special fund of $10,000 to be used, as he said, "in the protection of the public domain which is being raided periodically by private interests at the expense of the public interest."[55] He said that this fund would allow his newspaper "to start a taxpayer's suit where we believe that the state's lakes, rivers, streams, forests and parks are being taken over by

[51] *Ibid.*, p. 898.
[52] *Ibid.*, p. 906.
[53] *Ibid.*
[54] *Ibid.*, pp. 907-908.
[55] Madison, Wisconsin, *Capital Times*, February 22, 1960, p. 1.

private interests for private profit."[56] Similarly, the Citizens Union of the City of New York, described as "probably the most widely known and influential organization among the city's multitude of non-governmental groups,"[57] and with origins before 1900 in the good government reform movement, has begun numerous taxpayers' actions throughout its history. Its activity in the courts has also taken other forms and has varied with the character of the local government. During the administrations of Mayors John F. Hylan (1918-25) and James J. Walker (1926-32) the Citizens Union brought some nineteen lawsuits to restrain illegal expenditures of public funds and was successful in about twelve. The present counsel of the Citizens Union said recently that in the last few years he had "brought some half dozen suits to restrain various governmental actions which we believed to be illegal. In addition, the Citizens Union occasionally intervenes, by leave of the court, as *amicus curiae* or friend of the court, in suits brought by others."[58] This use of taxpayers' suits by one newspaper and one civic organization is indicative of practices throughout the country.

The situation created by this easy access to the courts has been described by the *Yale Law Journal* in the following way:

> . . . Such litigation allows the courts, within the framework of traditional notions of "standing," to add to the controls over public officials inherent in the elective process the judicial scrutiny of the statutory and constitutional validity of their acts. Taxpayers' suits also extend the uniquely American concept of judicial review to legislative action by allowing minorities ineffective at the ballot box to invalidate statutes or ordinances on constitutional grounds. . . . Taxpayers' suits thus create an army of potential private attorneys general acting on whatever private incentives may induce them to spend the time and money to bring a taxpayer's suit. . . . And since group financing of such litigation is not infrequent, taxpayers' suits also mobilize various voluntary associations seeking private, economic, or social objectives to further law enforcement and prevention of corruption in government.[59]

The objections to the widespread use of taxpayers' suits are numerous. Even when unsuccessful the delay occasioned by such actions "may unduly obstruct

[56] *Ibid.*

[57] Sayre and Kaufman, *Governing New York City*; see note 36, above.

[58] Letter of Samuel D. Smoleff to author, July 7, 1960. Citizens Union cases include the following: *Childs* v. *Moses,* 290 N. Y. 828, 50 N.E. 2d 235; *Bergerman* v. *Murphy,* 303 N. Y. 762, 103 N. E. 2d 545; *Bergerman* v. *Gerosa,* 3 N. Y. 2d 855, 166 N. Y. Supp. 2d 306; *Bergerman* v. *Byrnes,* 305 N. Y. 811, 113 N. E. 2d 557; *Bergerman* v. *Wagner,* 2 N. Y. 2d 908, 161 N.Y. Supp. 2d 434.

[59] "Comment," *op. cit.*, p. 904.

the completion of public projects."[60] These suits may harass officials and immobilize local government thereby inhibiting progressive community action. But most important of all, "taxpayers' suits may push the concept of judicial review of legislative and executive action too far."[61] The common complaints about judicial review merit repeating:

> By calling upon the courts to sit in judgment of decisions taken by the political branches of government, when no one is sufficiently injured thereby to have standing as an individual, taxpayer litigation may undermine the independence and prestige of the judiciary, impairing its ability to perform more traditional judicial functions. Since the courts are not designed, as are the political branches, to harmonize divergent views within the community and take action in accordance with the broadest possible consensus, such reviews may exceed their proper function. Moreover, placing the courts in the role of a "super legislature" may encourage irresponsibility and lack of creativity on the part of the political branches because they will be aware that decisions taken by them are always subject to judicial reversal.[62]

This would suggest that the concept of judicial review, which is usually thought of merely in terms of Supreme Court review of acts of Congress and of state legislatures, deserves consideration from the viewpoint of the government of communities, as well. The vast array of state and federal courts which may review the actions of community governments means that the scope of local power is always open to challenge by litigating interest groups.

[60] *Ibid.*
[61] *Ibid.*, p. 910.
[62] *Ibid.*

The Bureaucracy in Pressure Politics

J. Leiper Freeman

It is not a novel statement that we live in a society of "organization men," but we have yet to comprehend adequately the implications of this fact. Today's bureaucratic world is a reality within which the vast majority of Americans are enmeshed. Large, complex, specialized, hierarchical organizations are means of achieving the mass production, communications, services, regulation, and destruction possible in modern society. These bureaucracies are both public and private, large and small, demanding and lenient; but in any case they are the dominating form of social organization in America today.

Although bureaucracies are primarily regarded as organizations which execute policies assigned to them by society, they must also be reckoned with as sources of influence upon social policies. The nature of this influence is basically twofold. First, members of bureaucracies can give shape to stated policies through the exercise of choice and judgment in administering them. Second, in attempting to affect the objectives and working conditions which society will authorize for their organizations, members of bureaucracies necessarily engage in pressure politics.

It is with this second aspect of bureaucratic behavior that this article is chiefly concerned. Furthermore, it is confined to pressure politics engaged in by governmental, as opposed to private, bureaucracies and to pressure politics aimed at influencing official governmental policies.

Public bureaucracies—national, state and local—today employ about one-eighth of the labor force of the United States. About 3 million of these members of public bureaucracies are in the armed forces; slightly more than 2.2 million are civilian employees of the federal government; more than 1.1 million are classroom teachers in the public schools; about 3.5 million are otherwise employed by the state and local governments. If these bureaucrats, numbering between 9 and 10 million, formed one large group sharing a common identity, they would constitute a force in pressure politics to defy the imagination. But

J. Leiper Freeman, "The Bureaucracy in Pressure Politics," Annals of the American Academy of Political and Social Science, *Vol. 319 (1958). Reprinted with permission.*

public bureaucrats are divided into many bureaucracies by levels of government, by special functions, by special technologies, by differing clienteles, and by territories. The result is a patchwork of official organizations devoted to limited, specialized interests.

Bureaucracies as Pressure Groups

Since a public bureaucracy is concerned with special and limited aspects of public policy, to a degree it resembles the ordinary private pressure group. It is a congregating place for individuals concerned with the same subjects. Some of these interested individuals become members of the administrative agency while others join groups which look to that organization as a rallying point, and the agency takes a leading part in representing their interests. In this representative process perhaps the bureaucracy's most important function is to promote the idea that its special area of concern is important—be it education, air power, or mental health. The bureaucracy also promotes special solutions to policy problems in its area. Finally, it promotes objectives which are of particular interest to its members *as bureaucrats.* These are matters such as their working conditions, status, and compensation, as well as the maintenance and survival of their organization.

A public bureaucracy, as part of the official government, is subject to some controls over its pressure politics which do not apply to private groups. There are laws at the federal level to restrict the public relations and legislative activities of bureaucrats. Federal agencies are forbidden by an act passed in 1913 to use public funds to compensate "any publicity expert unless explicitly appropriated for that purpose."[1] Another act, passed in 1919, provides that appropriations shall not be used, unless explicitly authorized by Congress, "directly or indirectly to pay for any personal service, advertisement, telegram, telephone, letter, printed or written matter, or other device, intended or designed to influence in any manner a Member of Congress, to favor or oppose, by vote or otherwise, any legislation or appropriation by Congress, whether before or after the introduction of any bill or resolution proposing such legislation or appropriation. . . ."[2]

These general restrictions, however, have served mainly as policy statements to be used as threats against agency officials rather than as bases for actual cases. "Publicity experts" have not been hired, but "information," "education," and "publication" officers have been employed in good quantity.[3] Although these

[1] 38 Stat. L. 212.

[2] 41 Stat. L. 68.

[3] James L. McCamy, *Government Publicity* (Chicago: Univ. Chicago Press, 1939), p. 7; V. O. Key, Jr., *Politics, Parties, and Pressure Groups* (New York: Crowell, 1952), pp. 731-732.

publicists have often been flayed in the halls of Congress, no cases have arisen in which they have been held as violators of the law. Furthermore, despite the prohibitions against spending public funds to influence a member of Congress, there has remained a great latitude for legislative activity by public administrators. The expectations of Congressmen in this regard were well summarized by Representative Frank Buchanan in his committee's investigation of bureaucratic lobbying in 1950:

> . . . It is equally necessary for the executive branch of Government to be able to make its views known to Congress on all matters in which it has responsibilities, duties, and opinions. The executive agencies have a definite requirement to express views to Congress, to make suggestions, to request needed legislation, to draft proposed bills or amendments, and so on. And there is, of course, the power centered in the executive branch to overrule by veto any action of Congress which is not supported by a clear two-thirds majority of both Houses.[4]

Chief Executive Controls

It is safe to conclude that such statutory restrictions are not important limitations upon administrative propagandizing and lobbying in the federal government, and they are even less so in state and local governments where laws governing political activities of bureaucrats are generally less numerous and less stringent. Instead, more meaningful controls over bureaucratic pressure politics are to be found in the powers of the Chief Executive.

At all levels of government today there is a tendency toward giving the Chief Executive more effective authority over finance, organization, and personnel to help him control the actions of administrative agencies. These sanctions do not necessarily remove bureaucrats from the arena of pressure politics, but they tend to channel their activities along lines amenable to the Chief Executive. The stronger these sanctions are—as in the case of the city manager or strong mayor form of municipal executive, or the strong governorship, or the Presidency—the smaller the relative autonomy allowed bureaucrats in legislative and public relations.

In the federal government, the Bureau of the Budget and the provisions of the Budgeting and Accounting Act of 1921 aid the President in establishing central control over tendencies toward agency autonomy in seeking appropriations. Executive departments and bureaus are prohibited from seeking amounts larger than those requested for them in the President's budget when they appear

[4]United States Congress, House, Select Committee on Lobbying Activities, *Legislative Activities of Executive Agencies,* Hearings, 61st Cong., 2nd Sess., Part 10 (Washington, 1950).

before appropriations committees of Congress. Nevertheless, there have been instances in which questioning by committee members has brought into the record a bureau's original requests which perhaps the Budget Bureau had eliminated or curtailed. This device for circumventing the prescribed budget procedure is probably welcomed by an administrator, with friendly committee members and sympathetic interest groups doing the prodding. Yet, on the whole, the executive budget is a significant means of co-ordinating administrative requests for funds.

In proposals for legislation, the Bureau of the Budget is also of some help to the President since it has the power to require that agencies' legislative requests should be submitted to it to determine whether they are "in accord with the program of the President." This does not prevent an agency from submitting proposals to Congress which are not "in accord," but it is supposed to enable Congress to know whether measures are consonant with the President's program when it takes action on them. There is no clear agreement among persons who have studied the effectiveness of this procedure, but the most recent evaluation indicates that in recent years it has become somewhat more effective in curbing autonomous action by the various agencies.

The organizational status of a bureaucracy in the executive hierarchy determines to some degree the autonomy its members will have in their public and legislative relations. The more independently an agency is located in the structure of executive authority, the less formal power the Chief Executive can exercise over its political activities as well as on its administration of the laws. Thus, independent commissions and government corporations may enjoy some measure of independence from central direction of their political entrepreneurship which is not available to regular departments.

Personnel and Schedule C. Under the kind of government most often found in the United States, with a popularly elected Chief Executive having constitutional authority separate from the legislative branch, the President needs and usually has a coterie of political appointees. They serve both as political directors of the agencies and as leaders of the bureaucracies in their attempts to promote policies in their special spheres of interest.

The federal government under the Eisenhower administration enlarged the number of offices in this category by creating the so-called Schedule C positions for policy-making personnel in order to give the Republicans a larger crew of high-echelon officials. The major rationale for this enlargement was that the huge bureaucracies inherited from the previous administration, largely protected by Civil Service status, would otherwise be so intractable that the new administration would not be able to curb their autonomous tendencies. The results of this measure are not yet clear, although it has led to the removal of certain posts at the bureau-chief level from merit system status and into the creation of a number of new assistant secretaries and administrative assistants, who are patronage appointees. They compose an enlarged group of party representatives engaged in legislative liaison, public relations, and policy development at higher levels of the administration. They may have also reduced the political leeway of officials at lower levels.

Bureaucratic Autonomy

Despite the restrictions which may be placed upon bureaucracies because they are part of the government, they still have considerable autonomy within the executive structure to engage in pressure politics. They enjoy certain advantages by being in the official family which help to offset the restrictions placed upon them. One advantage is the fact that they are expected by legislators to make recommendations to the legislative body on a continuing, legitimate basis. Furthermore, they may have the blessings of the Chief Executive in their legislative operations and consequently can speak with considerable force as the administration's specialists.

When Representative Buchanan voiced the thought that bureaucrats should "make their views known" to Congress, he was speaking with restraint. Virtually no piece of legislation of any consequence reaches any advanced stage of the legislative process without at least one administrative agency making some statement concerning it. On many bills, the chances are great that the proposal originated in an executive agency. Furthermore, in the highly decisive stage of the legislative process—committee hearings—officials from the administration are invariably among the most regular and most crucial witnesses. Legislators at all levels of government, despite their defensiveness toward bureaucracy, like to hear from the bureaucrats most intimately concerned when making up their minds about proposed legislation, and the bureaucrats oblige them energetically.

The various bureaucracies are also expected by the Chief Executive and top leaders of the administration to carry a good deal of the burden of legislative leadership for the executive branch in their own special areas. This aspect of lobbying by administrative agencies is sometimes overlooked or unduly subordinated by students of the subject because of a preoccupation with the desirability of integrated executive leadership. In reality the Chief Executive cannot personally get involved in every legislative skirmish without tending to reduce his effectiveness and dissipating his resources for political leadership. On lesser matters and indeed on many that are of considerable importance, the bureaucracies are depended upon by the top level of the executive branch to work out the proposals, to secure their introduction, to mobilize support from the public and elsewhere, and to negotiate with the committees and the leaders of the legislative branch to secure favorable action.

General Legislative Liaison

Administrative agencies do not wait until a specific proposal is to be urged upon the legislature to cultivate harmonious relations with legislators. A continuous process of legislative liaison is maintained. This may be found at all levels of government and at all tiers of administration within these levels, although it is most marked at the higher echelons of federal administration. In the federal government, the growth of this process is reflected in recent institutional developments in which the major agencies have appointed high ranking officials with sizeable staffs to spend their full time on it. Every bureau is also equipped to consider requests from Congressmen and to furnish them information speedily. In the field offices, major headquarters follow the same pattern.

Accommodating legislative requests and inquiries where legitimately possible serves to keep agencies in the good graces of legislators and opens the way for suggestions and requests from administrators in return. Field officials usually work with Representatives and Senators from their own area. In Washington, where the liaison machinery is more elaborate and more concerned with agency-wide problems, particular attention is focused upon Congressional leaders and members of key committees.

While a good part of this activity is precautionary in that it is intended to keep legislators from becoming annoyed with an agency, it is also part of the agency's attempt to "cast bread upon the waters," to maintain a reservoir of good will, and to keep the solons aware of the important work the agency is doing.

At the state and local levels, legislative liaison has not become as highly organized and institutionalized as it has at the national level, but the essential ingredients are the same.

Strategy with Committees

Because so much of the meaningful work of legislative bodies is done in committees rather than in the full assemblies, the relations of spokesmen for the bureaucracies with committee members specializing in given policy areas are crucial aspects of administrative pressure politics. Committee members and agency officials who work together on common problems can build up the kind of understanding which maximizes the effect of agency opinions upon committee decisions. Committee recommendations in turn have a primary effect upon the content of laws passed by the parent body. Committee hearings therefore are not merely means by which legislative groups exert control over bureaucracies they are also critical opportunities for bureaucrats to influence legislation.

In general, committee members need information on policy questions, and administrative officials are in a position to have a vast store of it to present. This information, derived from the elaborate network of a bureaucracy, is a source of power. By presenting it strategically, leaders from the bureaucracy can use hearings to good advantage. Since hearings are usually covered by the press, the information presented may not only make a direct impression upon the committee members but also furnish ammunition to the agency's friends among the public.

Using higher-echelon support. Leaders of a bureaucracy who appear before legislators to advocate any new laws or changes in policy which their agency desires usually try to enlist the support of others. In many instances one of the most helpful sources of support is the Chief Executive or others in the higher echelons of the administration. Many things that an agency desires are not regarded as being of vital importance to the top leaders of the administration, even though the Chief Executive and his advisors may have nothing against their passage. If, however, the bureau chief and department officials seeking the legislation can secure from the Chief Executive a statement to the legislative committee, or a comment to the press, or a paragraph in a speech favorable to their proposal, they may very well enhance its possibilities of adoption.

The effectiveness of this action is, of course, related to the state of the Chief Executive's popularity and prestige with the legislators. If the bureaucrats decide that the Chief Executive would in a given instance be more of an albatross than a guardian angel, they will naturally hope that he will not associate himself with their legislative project in any way.

The use of higher-echelon support is also available to bureaucrats as a defense against unwanted legislation. Their advice is given much weight in questions regarding the use of the Chief Executive's veto power on legislation falling within their special spheres of competence.

Mobilizing employee support. One of the great reservoirs of political strength available to agency leaders in certain kinds of legislative activities lies in their organization's employees. This is naturally more true of the larger organizations since elected officials tend to be impressed by numbers. In the federal government, the Post Office Department (with over 500,000 employees) is a good example of an agency which tends to profit appreciably from employee support.

There is no particular evidence, however, that employees are necessarily helpful to their agency leaders on *all* legislative matters. Detailed studies of municipal department heads' legislative strategies show that they are not inclined to view their employees as important sources of support in dealing with the city council except on matters such as salaries, job conditions, and the like.[5] The

[5]Based on interviews and observations in the "Bay City" project, conducted at the Harvard Graduate School of Education under a grant from the W. K. Kellogg Foundation. "Bay City" is a pseudonym for a Massachusetts city of nearly 50,000 population where a series of related research inquiries was conducted on local decision making during the period

reason is that public employee organizations tend to concentrate their efforts on their interests as bureaucrats, often relegating larger policy questions to a secondary position. For this reason, agency leaders are often faced with the problem of tying employee benefits to other policy objectives and thereby evoking a maximum effort by the mass of the bureaucrats in their organizations to influence the legislative body.

At the federal level, a recent example of the linking of employee interests with broader policy objectives was seen in the fight waged by the Post Office Department to secure a modernization of the postal service and the most comprehensive revision of postage rates in over twenty years. Within the postal service, postmasters and postal employees were convinced that new buildings and equipment and increases in salaries were not to be obtained without the revision, and they contributed to the effort to obtain it. Legislative representatives from state and national organizations of postmasters conferred with the legislators. Organizations of postal employees lobbied and propagandized for it heavily.

The employees of the Brooklyn Post Office paid for a full-page advertisement in *The New York Times* to reprint an article by Senator Olin D. Johnston, Chairman of the Senate Committee on Post Office and Civil Service, which in general advocated modernization of the service and increasing the postage rates. Readers were urged to clip the article and mail it to their Senators.[6]

Mobilizing clientele support. Employees are, after all, not always the most appropriate pleaders in behalf of a bureaucracy in the legislative arena. Legislators are inclined to regard employees as pleading their own cases and therefore may discount their contentions. Consequently, administrative leaders seek to have their proposals endorsed by private groups who carry weight with legislators.

The easiest groups of this type for most agencies to mobilize are the so-called clientele groups. In many instances they are highly organized and easily identified. The Veterans Administration counts heavily on the American Legion and to a lesser extent on other veterans organizations to support its recommendations to Congress. In fact, it seldom tends to make a recommendation to Congress that is not reasonably acceptable to these organizations, so strong is their partnership in all pressure politics dealing with veterans affairs.

The pattern is similar with many other agencies and their clienteles such as the Commerce Department and business organizations; the Labor Department and the unions; and the Agriculture Department and the Farm Bureau, the Grange, and other farmer organizations. These other groups do not, however,

---

1952-55 by a professional staff consisting chiefly of Peter H. Rossi, Alice S. Rossi, James M. Shipton, and the present writer.

[6]*The New York Times,* February 18, 1958, p. 13.

always show the same degree of collaboration as that evinced by the Veterans Administration and its customers.

In fact, many of the difficulties attending Secretary Ezra Benson's efforts to convince Congress that his department's recommendations are the answer to the farm problems of the United States are related to an estrangement between the present leadership of the Department of Agriculture and significant portions of its clientele. Agency leaders who fail to maintain the confidence of their patrons are apt to lose the most crucial element of their support in legislative relations. Groups that are not in the clientele of an agency are more difficult to encourage to take as much interest and exert as much effort in the agency's behalf.

Other group support. Bureaucracies welcome and at times aid the organization of groups to serve as their sponsors. These groups are not necessarily composed of steady customers of an agency, but they are made up of people who for various reasons are interested in its aims and its existence. Some of these groups are completely unofficial in nature; but many are given some official recognition in the agency's operations, rendering them quasi-public in character. By elaborating their administrative structure, public bureaucracies at all levels of American government have enlisted the participation of interested and often influential citizens in their business to give them advice and sometimes even to help them set and administer policies. In turn, the bureaucracies expect and usually receive support for their legislative objectives.

Among the many groups of this type to be found at the federal level are, for example, the various reserve officer associations of the military branches, or the very exclusive advisory committee of the Commerce Department, or any of the many other advisory committees in other units. Over the years the Agriculture Department has built up one of the most complex systems of citizen participation in administration at the local level that could be imagined. Some of its major programs are handled at the county level by committees elected by farmers and working in conjunction with full-time paid employees of the Department. In this way, for example, the Agricultural Stabilization and Conservation Service enlists sponsors composed of local farm leaders in county after county across the nation.

In local governments, outstanding examples of sponsor groups are to be found in Parent-Teacher Associations or in "Friends of the Library." And at a more official and formal level they may be found in the plethora of boards and commissions which are officially charged with setting policies for various municipal agencies.

The way in which board sponsorship works to an administrator's advantage was observed a few years ago in a New England city. The head of the library board was the woman with the most prestige in town, and the librarian was regarded as her protégée. These two ladies got the board chairman's husband to agree to buy a bookmobile for the public library if the city would agree to maintain it. Then the City Council was presented with this proposition at a meeting in which the library board was well represented and virtually able to make the matter one in which the Council would appear cheap if it refused. The Council, seeing that it had little choice, voted the funds to maintain the bookmobile and, of course, to furnish a driver.

Pressure by administrative decision. Bureaucrats can often generate pressure upon legislators through the exercise of their legitimate discretion in the course of conducting the public's business. One of the most recent and most widely argued examples was furnished by Postmaster General Arthur Summerfield. He gave orders to curtail mail deliveries one day a week last year when Congress was showing reluctance to appropriate some funds which Mr. Summerfield said were necessary to prevent deficiencies in his agency. Despite outraged cries, Congress gave Mr. Summerfield the money. After all, people wanted their mail on Saturdays.

Looking again at the municipal level, the Water Commissioner of a New England city used his administrative powers to help arouse public support and pressure upon the Council for a bond issue to expand the water supply—a measure which certain industries in the city favored. Although it was a hot and dry summer, the Commissioner helped the drought along for some people by diverting water to the country club from a main which served many residences in a high part of the city. When the residents on this main could not draw bath water, not knowing that their water was being siphoned off to the golfers' showers, they were even more emphatic than the Water Commissioner and his industrialist supporters that the water supply needed expansion. Eventually the Council voted the bonds.

General Publicity Activities

The ultimate aim of bureaucratic publicity is in large measure to create a climate of opinion which will be favorable to its objectives. Some of an agency's publicity is necessary to the administrative process of making more acceptable to the public the things it has already been assigned to do. But the cultivation of favorable public images also may serve to build up support for legislation which the agency desires but does not have, and it is difficult to separate one function of bureaucratic publicity from the other.

The many books and articles written about the exploits of the Federal Bureau of Investigation agents, the continuous, favorable publicity accorded to Mr. J. Edgar Hoover, and the speeches and writings of Mr. Hoover himself all help to make the jobs which are assigned to the FBI easier to accomplish. Yet this publicity also makes the agency more successful in its relations with Congress, for Congressmen are sensitive to the image maintained among the public at large.

Of course, the FBI is unusually fortunate in comparison with other federal bureaus in the nature and extent of its publicity, but many administrative units get a good deal of coverage on a fairly steady basis. There are abundant opportunities for members of the higher echelons of the bureaucracy not only to release news through regular channels and to talk to reporters, but also to make addresses, write articles, and in other ways create publicity for their organizations. Furthermore, in the field offices, regional press coverage is generally well maintained, especially for the larger agencies, and this substantially supplements the publicity emanating from Washington. Since nine-tenths of federal employees are not in Washington, there is immense opportunity for publicity to be generated at local levels, where it can often affect the constituents of Congressmen most directly.

There is also usually a network of friendly media especially interested in the subjects dealt with by an agency and willing to help carry the propaganda battle. Some of these are "trade" publications, which, combined with official publications and reports, give bureaucracies ample outlets to reach the most interested audiences. Due to the limited nature of general public interest in most public problems, it is frequently more important to reach the highly concerned portion of the public than to try to publicize in general.

Bureaucrats can become victims of their own overzealous publicity tactics. Legislators are capable of being very sensitive to what they regard as improper administrative propagandizing, especially if it encroaches on their domains. It does not help administrative leaders and the agencies they represent to become branded as propagandists. The kinds of retribution they suffer in such instances vary from oratorical chastisement in the legislative halls to denial of the very objects which they seek to have the legislators bestow—funds and authority.

Protest as a Political Resource

Michael Lipsky

The frequent resort to protest activity by relatively powerless groups in recent American politics suggests that protest represents an important aspect of minority group and low income group politics.[1] At the same time that Negro civil rights strategists have recognized the problem of using protest as a meaningful political instrument,[2] groups associated with the "war on poverty" have increasingly received publicity for protest activity. Saul Alinsky's Industrial Areas Foundation, for example, continues to receive invitations to help organize low income communities because of its ability to mobilize poor people around the tactic of protest.[3] The riots which dominated urban affairs in the summer of 1967 appear not to have diminished the dependence of some groups on protest as a mode of political activity.

[1]"Relatively powerless groups" may be defined as those groups which, relatively speaking, are lacking in conventional political resources. For the purpose of community studies, Robert Dahl has compiled a useful comprehensive list. See Dahl, "The Analysis of Influence in Local Communities," *Social Science and Community Action*, Charles R. Adrian, ed. (East Lansing, Mich., 1960), p. 32. The difficulty in studying such groups is that relative powerlessness only becomes apparent under certain conditions. Extremely powerless groups not only lack political resources, but are also characterized by a minimal sense of political efficacy upon which in part successful political organization depends. For reviews of the literature linking orientations of political efficacy to socioeconomic status, see Robert Lane, *Political Life* (New York, 1959), Ch. 16; and Lester Milbrath, *Political Participation* (Chicago, 1965), Ch. 5. Further, to the extent that group cohesion is recognized as a necessary requisite for organized political action, then extremely powerless groups, lacking cohesion, will not even appear for observation. Hence the necessity of selecting for intensive study a protest movement where there can be some confidence that observable processes and results can be analyzed. Thus, if one conceives of a continuum on which political groups are placed according to their relative command of resources, the focus of this essay is on those groups which are near, but not at, the pole of powerlessness.

[2]See, e.g., Bayard Rustin, "From Protest to Politics: The Future of the Civil Rights Movement," *Commentary* (February 1965), pp. 25-31; and Stokely Carmichael, "Toward Black Liberation," *The Massachusetts Review*, Autumn 1966.

[3]On Alinsky's philosophy of community organization, see his *Reveille for Radicals* (Chicago, 1945); and Charles Silberman, *Crisis in Black and White* (New York, 1964), Ch. 10.

Michael Lipsky, "Protest as a Political Resource," American Political Science Review, *Vol. 62 (December 1968).*

This article provides a theoretical perspective on protest activity as a political resource. The discussion is concentrated on the limitations inherent in protest which occur because of the need of protest leaders to appeal to four constituencies at the same time. As the concept of protest is developed here, it will be argued that protest leaders must nurture and sustain an organization comprised of people with whom they may or may not share common values. They must articulate goals and choose strategies so as to maximize their public exposure through communications media. They must maximize the impact of third parties in the political conflict. Finally, they must try to maximize chances of success among those capable of granting goals. The tensions inherent in manipulating these four constituencies at the same time form the basis of this discussion of protest as a political process. It is intended to place aspects of the civil rights movement in a framework which suggests links between protest organizations and the general political processes in which such organizations operate.

I

Protest activity as it has been adopted by elements of the civil rights movement and others has not been studied extensively by social scientists. Some of the most suggestive writings have been done as case studies of protest movements in single Southern cities. [4] These works generally lack a framework or theoretical focus which would encourage generalization from the cases. More systematic efforts have been attempted in approaching the dynamics of biracial committees in the South,[5] and comprehensively assessing the efficacy of Negro political involvement in Durham, N.C. and Philadelphia, Pa.[6] In their excellent assessment of Negro politics in the South, Matthews and Prothro have presented a thorough profile of Southern Negro students and their participation in civil rights activities.[7] Protest is also discussed in passing in recent explorations of the social-psychological

[4]See, e.g., Jack L. Walker, "Protest and Negotiation: A Case Study of Negro Leadership in Atlanta, Georgia," *Midwest Journal of Political Science*, Vol. 7 (May 1963), pp. 99-124; Jack L. Walker, *Sit-Ins in Atlanta: A Study in the Negro Protest*, Eagleton Institute Case Studies, No. 34 (New York, 1964); John Ehle, *The Free Men* (New York, 1965) (Chapel Hill); Daniel C. Thompson, *The Negro Leadership Class* (Englewood Cliffs, N.J., 1963) (New Orleans); M. Elaine Burgess, *Negro Leadership in a Southern City* (Chapel Hill, N.C., 1962) (Durham).

[5]Lewis Killian and Charles Grigg, *Racial Crisis in America: Leadership in Conflict* (Englewood Cliffs, N.J., 1964).

[6]William Keech, "The Negro Vote as a Political Resource: The Case of Durham," unpublished Ph.D. dissertation, University of Wisconsin, 1966; and John H. Strange, "The Negro in Philadelphia Politics 1963-65," unpublished Ph.D. dissertation, Princeton University, 1966.

[7]Donald Matthews and James Prothro, *Negroes and the New Southern Politics* (New York, 1966). Considerable insight on these data is provided in John Orbell, "Protest Participation among Southern Negro College Students," *American Political Science Review*, Vol. 61 (June 1967), pp. 446-456.

dimensions of Negro ghetto politics[8] and the still highly suggestive, although pre-1960's, work on Negro political leadership by James Q. Wilson.[9] These and other less systematic works on contemporary Negro politics,[10] for all of their intuitive insights and valuable documentation, offer no theoretical formulations which encourage conceptualization about the interaction between recent Negro political activity and the political process.

Heretofore the best attempt to place Negro protest activity in a framework which would generate additional insights has been that of James Q. Wilson.[11] Wilson has suggested that protest activity be conceived as a problem of bargaining in which the basic problem is that Negro groups lack political resources to exchange. Wilson called this "the problem of the powerless."[12]

While many of Wilson's insights remain valid, his approach is limited in applicability because it defines protest in terms of mass action or response and as utilizing exclusively negative inducements in the bargaining process. Negative inducements are defined as inducements which are not absolutely preferred but are preferred over alternative possibilities.[13] Yet it might be argued that protest designed to appeal to groups which oppose suffering and exploitation, for example, might be offering positive inducements in bargaining. A few Negro students sitting at a lunch counter might be engaged in what would be called protest, and by their actions might be trying to appeal to other groups in the system with positive inducements. Additionally, Wilson's concentration on Negro civic action, and his exclusive interest in exploring the protest process to explain Negro civic action, tend to obscure comparison with protest activity which does not necessarily arise within the Negro community.

Assuming a somewhat different focus, protest activity is defined as a mode of political action oriented toward objection to one or more policies or conditions, characterized by showmanship or display of an unconventional nature, and undertaken to obtain rewards from political or economic systems while working within the systems. The "problem of the powerless" in protest activity is to activate "third parties" to enter the implicit or explicit bargaining arena in ways favorable to the protesters. This is one of the few ways in which they can "create" bargaining resources. It is intuitively unconvincing to suggest that

[8]Kenneth Clark, *Dark Ghetto* (New York, 1965).

[9]*Negro Politics* (New York, 1960).

[10]A complete list would be voluminous. See, e.g., Nat Hentoff, *The New Equality* (new York, 1964); and Arthur Waskow, *From Race Riot to Sit-In* (New York, 1966).

[11]"The Strategy of Protest: Problems of Negro Civic Action," *Journal of Conflict Resolution*, Vol. 3 (September 1961), pp. 291-303. The reader will recognize the author's debt to this highly suggestive article, not least Wilson's recognition of the utility of the bargaining framework for examining protest activity.

[12]*Ibid.*, p. 291.

[13]See *Ibid.*, pp. 291-292.

fifteen people sitting uninvited in the Mayor's office have the power to move City Hall. A better formulation would suggest that the people sitting-in may be able to appeal to a wider public to which the city administration is sensitive. Thus in successful protest activity the reference publics of protest targets may be conceived as explicitly or implicitly reacting to protest in such a way that target groups or individuals respond in ways favorable to the protesters.[14]

It should be emphasized that the focus here is on protest by relatively powerless groups. Illustrations can be summoned, for example, of activity designated as "protest" involving high status pressure groups or hundreds of thousands of peope. While such instances may share some of the characteristics of protest activity, they may not represent examples of developing political resources by relatively powerless groups because the protesting groups may already command political resources by virtue of status, numbers or cohesion.

It is appropriate also to distinguish between the relatively restricted use of the concept of protest adopted here and closely related political strategies which are often designated as "protest" in popular usage. Where groups already possess sufficient resources with which to bargain, as in the case of some economic boycotts and labor strikes, they may be said to engage in "direct confrontation."[15] Similarly, protest which represents efforts to "activate reference publics" should be distinguished from "alliance formation," where third parties are induced to join the conflict, but where the value orientations of third parties are sufficiently similar to those of the protesting group that concerted or coordinated action is possible. Alliance formation is particularly desirable for relatively powerless groups if they seek to join the decision-making process as participants.

The distinction between activating reference publics and alliance formation is made on the assumption that where goal orientations among protest groups and the reference publics of target groups are similar, the political dynamics of petitioning target groups are different than when such goal orientations are relatively divergent. Clearly the more similar the goal orientations, the greater the likelihood of protest success, other things being equal. This discussion is intended to highlight, however, those instances where goal orientations of reference publics depart significantly, in direction or intensity, from the goals of protest groups.

[14]See E. E. Schattschneider's discussion of expanding the scope of the conflict, *The Semisovereign People* (New York, 1960). Another way in which bargaining resources may be "created" is to increase the relative cohesion of groups, or to increase the perception of group solidarity as a precondition to greater cohesion. This appears to be the primary goal of political activity which is generally designated "community organization." Negro activists appear to recognize the utility of this strategy in their advocacy of "black power." In some instances protest activity may be designed in part to accomplish this goal in addition to activating reference publics.

[15]For an example of "direct confrontation," one might study the three-month Negro boycott of white merchants in Natchez, Miss., which resulted in capitulation to boycott demands by city government leaders. See *The New York Times*, December 4, 1965, p. 1.

Say that to protest some situation, A would like to enter a bargaining situation with B. But A has nothing which B wants, and thus cannot bargain. A then attempts to create political resources by activating other groups to enter the conflict. A then organizes to take action against B with respect to certain goals. *Information concerning these goals must be conveyed through communications media* (C, D, and E) to F, G, and H, which are B's *reference publics.* In response to the reactions of F, G, and H, or in anticipation of their reactions, B responds, *in some way*, to the protesters' demands. This formulation requires the conceptualization of protest activity when undertaken to create bargaining resources as a political process which requires communication and is characterized by a multiplicity of constituencies for protest leadership.

A schematic representation of the process of protest as utilized by relatively powerless groups is presented in Figure 1. In contrast to a simplistic pressure group model which would posit a direct relationship between pressure group and pressured, the following discussion is guided by the assumption (derived from observation) that protest is a highly indirect process in which communications media and the reference publics of protest targets play critical roles. It is also a process characterized by reciprocal relations, in which protest leaders frame strategies according to their perception of the needs of (many) other actors.

In this view protest constituents limit the options of protest leaders at the same time that the protest leader influences their perception of the strategies and rhetoric which they will support. Protest activity is filtered through the communications media in influencing the perceptions of the reference publics of protest targets. To the extent that the influence of reference publics is supportive of protest goals, target groups will dispense symbolic or material rewards. Material rewards are communicated directly to protest constituents. Symbolic rewards are communicated in part to protest constituents, but primarily are communicated to the reference publics of target groups, who provide the major stimuli for public policy pronouncements.

The study of protest as adopted by relatively powerless groups should provide insights into the structure and behavior of groups involved in civil rights politics and associated with the "war on poverty." It should direct attention toward the ways in which administrative agencies respond to "crises." Additionally, the study of protest as a political resource should influence some general conceptualizations of American political pluralism. Robert Dahl, for example, describes the "normal American political process" as

> one in which there is a high probability that an active and legitimate group in the population can make itself heard effectively at some crucial stage in the process of decision.[16]

[16]*A Preface to Democratic Theory* (Chicago, 1956), pp. 145-146.

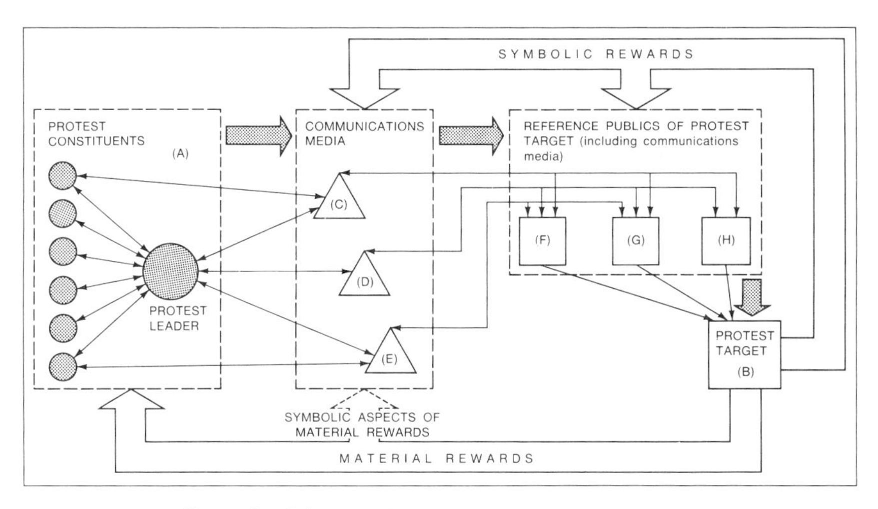

Figure 1. Schematic Representation of the Process of Protest by Relatively Powerless Groups

Although he agrees that control over decisions is unevenly divided in the population, Dahl writes:

> When I say that a group is heard "effectively" I mean more than the simple fact that it makes a noise; I mean that one or more officials are not only ready to listen to the noise, but expect to suffer in some significant way if they do not placate the group, its leaders, or its most vociferous members. To satisfy the group may require one or more of a great variety of actions by the responsive leader: pressure for substantive policies, appointments, graft, respect, expression of the appropriate emotions, or the right combination of reciprocal noises.[17]

These statements, which in some ways resemble Truman's discussion of the power of "potential groups,"[18] can be illuminated by the study of protest activity in three ways. First, what are the probabilities that relatively powerless groups can make themselves heard effectively? In what ways will such groups be heard or "steadily appeased"?[19] Concentration on the process of protest activity may reveal the extent to which, and the conditions under which, relatively powerless groups are likely to prove effective. Protest undertaken to obstruct

[17] *Ibid.*

[18] *The Governmental Process* (New York, 1951), p. 104.

[19] See Dahl, *A Preface to Democratic Theory*, p. 146.

policy decisions, for example, may enjoy greater success probabilities than protest undertaken in an effort to evoke constructive policy innovations.[20]

Second, does it make sense to suggest that all groups which make noises will receive responses from public officials? Perhaps the groups which make noises do not have to be satisfied at all, but it is other groups which receive assurances or recognition. Third, what are the probabilities that groups which make noises will receive tangible rewards, rather than symbolic assurances?[21] Dahl lumps these rewards together in the same paragraph, but dispensation of tangible rewards clearly has a different impact upon groups than the dispensation of symbolic rewards. Dahl is undoubtedly correct when he suggests that the relative fluidity of American politics is a critical characteristic of the American political system.[22] But he is less precise and less convincing when it comes to analyzing the extent to which the system is indeed responsive to the relatively powerless groups of the "average citizen."[23]

The following sections are an attempt to demonstrate the utility of the conceptualization of the protest process presented above. This will be done by exploring the problems encountered and the strains generated by protest leaders in interacting with four constituencies. It will be useful to concentrate attention on the maintenance and enhancement needs not only of the large formal organizations which dominate city politics,[24] but also of the ad hoc protest groups which engage them in civic controversy. It will also prove rewarding to examine the role requirements of individuals in leadership positions as they perceive the problems of constituency manipulation. In concluding remarks some implications of

[20]Observations that all groups can influence public policy at some stage of the political process are frequently made about the role of "veto groups" in American politics. See *ibid.*, pp. 104ff. See also David Riesman, *The Lonely Crowd* (New Haven, Conn., 1950), pp. 211ff., for an earlier discussion of veto-group politics. Yet protest should be evaluated when it is adopted to obtain assertive as well as defensive goals.

[21]See Murray Edelman, *The Symbolic Uses of Politics* (Urbana, Ill., 1964), Ch. 2.

[22]See Dahl, *Who Governs?* (New Haven, Conn., 1961), pp. 305ff.

[23]In a recent formulation, Dahl reiterates the theme of wide dispersion of influence. "More than other systems, [democracies] . . . try to disperse influence widely to their citizens by means of the suffrage, elections, freedom of speech, press, and assembly, the right of opponents to criticize the conduct of government, the right to organize political parties, and in other ways" (*Pluralist Democracy in the United States* [Chicago, 1967], p. 373). Here, however, he concentrates more on the availability of options to all groups in the system, rather than on the relative probabilities that all groups in fact have access to the political process. See pp. 372ff.

[24]See Edward Banfield, *Political Influence* (New York, 1961), p. 263. The analysis of organizational incentive structure which heavily influences Banfield's formulation is Chester Barnard, *The Functions of the Executive* (Cambridge, Mass., 1938).

the study of protest for the pluralist description of American politics will be suggested.[25]

II

Protest leadership and organizational base. The organizational maintenance needs of relatively powerless, low income, ad hoc protest groups center around the tension generated by the need for leadership to offer symbolic and intangible inducements to protest participation when immediate, material rewards cannot be anticipated, and the need to provide at least the promise of material rewards for protest participation. Protest leaders must try to evoke responses from other actors in the political process, at the same time that they pay attention to participant organizational needs. Thus relatively deprived groups in the political system not only receive symbolic reassurance while material rewards from the system are withheld,[26] but protest leaders have a stake in perpetuating the notion that relatively powerless groups retain political efficacy despite what in many cases is obvious evidence to the contrary.

The tension embraced by protest leaders over the nature of inducements toward protest participation accounts in part for the style adopted and goals selected by protest leaders. Groups which seek psychological gratification from politics, but cannot or do not anticipate material political rewards, may be attracted to militant protest leaders. To these groups, angry rhetoric may prove a desirable quality in the short run. Where groups depend upon the political system for tangible benefits, or where participation in the system provides intangible benefits, moderate leadership is likely to prevail. Wilson has observed similar tendencies among Negro leaders of large, formal organizations.[27] It is no less true for leadership of protest groups. Groups whose members derive tangible satisfactions from political participation will not condone leaders who are stubborn in compromise or appear to question the foundations of the system. This coincides with Truman's observation:

> Violation of the 'rules of the game' normally will weaken a group's cohesion, reduce its status in the community, and expose it to the claims of other groups.[28]

[25] In the following attempt to develop the implications of this conceptualization of protest activity, I have drawn upon extensive field observations and bibliographical research. Undoubtedly, however, individual assertions, while representing my best judgment concerning the available evidence, in the future may require modification as the result of further empirical research.

[26] As Edelman suggests, cited previously.

[27] *Negro Politics*, p. 290.

[28] *The Governmental Process*, p. 513.

On the other hand, the cohesion of relatively powerless groups may be strengthened by militant, ideological leadership which questions the rules of the game and challenges their legitimacy.

Cohesion is particularly important when protest leaders bargain directly with target groups. In that situation, leaders' ability to control protest constituents and guarantee their behavior represents a bargaining strength.[29] For this reason Wilson stressed the bargaining difficulties of Negro leaders who cannot guarantee constituent behavior, and pointed out the significance of the strategy of projecting the image of group solidarity when the reality of cohesion is a fiction.[30] Cohesion is less significant at other times. Divided leadership may prove productive by bargaining in tandem,[31] or by minimizing strain among groups in the protest process. Further, community divisions may prove less detrimental to protest aims when strong third parties have entered the dispute originally generated by protest organizations.

The intangible rewards of assuming certain postures toward the political system may not be sufficient to sustain an organizational base. It may be necessary to renew constantly the intangible rewards of participation. And to the extent that people participate in order to achieve tangible benefits, their interest in a protest organization may depend upon the organization's relative material success. Protest leaders may have to tailor their style to present participants with tangible successes, or with the appearance of success. Leaders may have to define the issues with concern for increasing their ability to sustain organizations. The potential for protest among protest group members may have to be manipulated by leadership if the group is to be sustained.[32]

The participants in protest organizations limit the flexibility of protest leadership. This obtains for two reasons. They restrict public actions by leaders who

[29]But cf. Thomas Schelling's discussion of "binding oneself," *The Strategy of Conflict* (Cambridge, Mass., 1960), pp. 22ff.

[30]"The Strategy of Protest," p. 297.

[31]This is suggested by Wilson, "The Strategy of Protest," p. 298; St. Clair Drake and Horace Cayton, *Black Metropolis*, rev. ed. (New York, 1962), p. 731; and Walker, "Protest and Negotiation," p. 122. Authors who argue that divided leadership is dysfunctional have been Clark, p. 156; and Tilman Cothran, "The Negro Protest against Segregation in the South," *The Annals*, Vol. 357 (January 1965), p. 72.

[32]This observation is confirmed by a student of the Southern civil rights movement:

> Negroes demand of protest leaders constant progress. The combination of long-standing discontent and a new-found belief in the possibility of change produces a constant state of tension and aggressiveness in the Negro community. But this discontent is vague and diffuse, not specific; the masses do not define the issues around which action shall revolve. This the leader must do.

Lewis Killian, "Leadership in the Desegregation Crises: An Institutional Analysis," in *Intergroup Relations and Leadership*, ed. Muzafer Sherif (New York, 1962), p. 159.

must continue to solicit active participant support, and they place restraints on the kinds of activities which can be considered appropriate for protest purposes. Poor participants cannot commonly be asked to engage in protest requiring air transportation. Participants may have anxieties related to their environment or historical situation which discourages engagement in some activities. They may be afraid of job losses, beatings by the police, or summary evictions. Negro protest in the Deep South has been inhibited by realistic expectations of retribution.[33] Protests over slum housing conditions are undermined by tenants who expect landlord retaliation for engaging in tenant organizing activity.[34] Political or ethical mores may conflict with a proposed course of action, diminishing participation.[35]

On the other hand, to the extent that fears are real, or that the larger community perceives protest participants as subject to these fears, protest may actually be strengthened. Communications media and potential allies will consider more soberly the complaints of people who are understood to be placing themselves in jeopardy. When young children and their parents made the arduous bus trip from Mississippi to Washington, D.C. to protest the jeopardizing of Head Start funds, the courage and expense represented by their effort created a respect and visibility for their position which might not have been achieved by local protest efforts.[36]

Protest activity may be undertaken by organizations with established relationship patterns, behavior norms, and role expectations. These organizations are likely to have greater access to other groups in the political system, and a demonstrated capacity to maintain themselves. Other protest groups, however, may be ad hoc arrangements without demonstrated internal or external relationship patterns. These groups will have different organizational problems, in response to which it is necessary to engage in different kinds of protest activity.

[33]Significantly, Southern Negro students who actively participated in the early phases of the sit-in movement "tended to be unusually optimistic about race relations and tolerant of whites [when compared with inactive Negro students]. They not only *were* better off, objectively speaking, than other Negroes but *felt* better off." Matthews and Prothro, *op. cit.*, p. 424.

[34]This is particularly the case in cities such as Washington, D.C., where landlord-tenant laws offer little protection against retaliatory eviction. See, e.g., Robert Schoshinski, "Remedies of the Indigent Tenant: Proposal for Change," *Georgetown Law Journal*, Vol. 54 (Winter 1966), pp. 541ff.

[35]Wilson regarded this as a chief reason for lack of protest activity in 1961. He wrote: ". . . some of the goals now being sought by Negroes are least applicable to those groups of Negroes most suited to protest action. Protest action involving such tactics as mass meetings, picketing, boycotts, and strikes rarely find enthusiastic participants among upper-income and higher status individuals" ("The Strategy of Protest," p. 296).

[36]See *The New York Times*, February 12, 1966, p. 56.

The scarcity of organizational resources also places limits upon the ability of relatively powerless groups to maintain the foundations upon which protest organizations develop. Relatively powerless groups, to engage in political activity of any kind, must command at least some resources. This is not tautological. Referring again to a continuum on which political groups are placed according to their relative command of resources, one may draw a line somewhere along the continuum representing a "threshold of civic group political participation." Clearly some groups along the continuum will possess some political resources (enough, say, to emerge for inspection) but not enough to exercise influence in civic affairs. Relatively powerless groups, to be influential, must cross the "threshold" to engage in politics. Although the availability of group resources is a critical consideration at all stages of the protest process, it is particularly important in explaining why some groups seem to "surface" with sufficient strength to command attention. The following discussion of some critical organizational resources should illuminate this point.

Skilled professionals frequently must be available to protest organizations. Lawyers, for example, play extremely important roles in enabling protest groups to utilize the judicial process and avail themselves of adequate preparation of court cases. Organizational reputation may depend upon a combination of ability to threaten the conventional political system and of exercising statutory rights in court. Availability of lawyers depends upon ability to pay fees and/or the attractiveness to lawyers of participation in protest group activity. Volunteer professional assistance may not prove adequate. One night a week volunteered by an aspiring politician in a housing clinic cannot satisfy the needs of a chaotic political movement.[37] The need for skilled professionals is not restricted to lawyers. For example, a group seeking to protest an urban renewal policy might require the services of architects and city planners in order to present a viable alternative to a city proposal.

Financial resources not only purchase legal assistance, but enable relatively powerless groups to conduct a minimum program of political activities. To the extent that constituents are unable or unwilling to pay even small membership dues, then financing the cost of mimeographing flyers, purchasing supplies, maintaining telephone service, paying rent, and meeting a modest payroll become major organizational problems. And to the extent that group finances are supplied by outside individual contributions or government or foundation grants,

[37]On housing clinic services provided by political clubs, see James Q. Wilson, *The Amateur Democrat: Club Politics in Three Cities* (Chicago, 1962), pp. 63-64, 176. On the need for lawyers among low income people, see, e.g., *The Extension of Legal Services to the Poor*, Conference Proceedings (Washington, D.C., n.d.), esp. pp. 51-60; and "Neighborhood Law Offices: The New Wave in Legal Services for the Poor," *Harvard Law Review*, Vol. 80 (February 1967), pp. 805-850.

the long-term options of the group are sharply constrained by the necessity of orienting group goals and tactics to anticipate the potential objections of financial supporters.

Some dependence upon even minimal financial resources can be waived if organizations evoke passionate support from constituents. Secretarial help and block organizers will come forward to work without compensation if they support the cause of neighborhood organizations or gain intangible benefits based upon association with the group. Protest organizations may also depend upon skilled non-professionals, such as college students, whose access to people and political and economic institutions often assists protest groups in cutting across income lines to seek support. Experience with ad hoc political groups, however, suggests that this assistance is sporadic and undependable. Transient assistance is particularly typical of skilled, educated, and employable volunteers whose abilities can be applied widely. The die-hards of ad hoc political groups are often those people who have no place else to go, nothing else to do.

Constituent support will be affected by the nature of the protest target and whether protest activity is directed toward defensive or assertive goals. Obstructing specific public policies may be easier than successfully recommending constructive policy changes. Orientations toward defensive goals may require less constituent energy, and less command over resources of money, expertise and status.[38]

III

Protest leadership and communications media. The communications media are extremely powerful in city politics. In granting or withholding publicity, in determining what information most people will have on most issues, and what alternatives they will consider in response to issues, the media truly, as Norton Long has put it, "set . . . the civic agenda."[39] To the extent that successful protest activity depends upon appealing to, and/or threatening, other groups in the community, the communications media set the limits of protest action. If protest tactics are not considered significant by the media, or if newspapers and television reporters or editors decide to overlook protest tactics, protest organizations will not succeed. Like the tree falling unheard in the forest, there is no protest unless protest is perceived and projected.

A number of writers have noticed that the success of protest activity seems directly related to the amount of publicity it receives outside the immediate

[38]An illustration of low income group protest organization mobilized for veto purposes is provided by Dahl in "The Case of the Metal Houses." See *Who Governs?*, pp. 192ff.

[39]Norton Long, "The Local Community as an Ecology of Games," in Long, *The Polity*, ed. Charles Press (Chicago, 1962), p. 153. See pp. 152-154. See also Roscoe C. Martin, Frank J. Munger, *et al., Decisions in Syracuse: A Metropolitan Action Study* (New York, 1965) (originally published 1961), pp. 326-327.

arena in which protest takes place. This view has not been stated systematically, but hints can be found in many sources. In the literature on civil rights politics, the relevance of publicity represents one of the few hypotheses available concerning the dynamics of successful protest activity.[40]

When protest tactics do receive coverage in the communications media, the way in which they are presented will influence all other actors in the system, including the protesters themselves. Conformity to standards of newsworthiness in political style, and knowledge of the prejudices and desires of the individuals who determine media coverage in political skills, represent crucial determinants of leadership effectiveness.

The organizational behavior of newspapers can partly be understood by examining the maintenance and enhancement needs which direct them toward projects of civic betterment and impressions of accomplishment.[41] But insight may also be gained by analyzing the role requirements of reporters, editors, and others who determine newspaper policy. Reporters, for example, are frequently motivated by the desire to contribute to civic affairs by their "objective" reporting of significant events; by the premium they place on accuracy; and by the credit which they receive for sensationalism and "scoops."

These requirements may be difficult to accommodate at the same time. Reporters demand newsworthiness of their subjects in the short run, but also require reliability and verifiability in the longer run. Factual accuracy may dampen newsworthiness. Sensationalism, attractive to some newspaper editors, may be inconsistent with reliable, verifiable narration of events. Newspapers at first may be attracted to sensationalism, and later demand verifiability in the interests of community harmony (and adherence to professional journalistic standards).

Most big city newspapers have reporters whose assignments permit them to cover aspects of city politics with some regularity. These reporters, whose "beats" may consist of "civil rights" or "poverty," sometimes develop close relationships with their news subjects. These relationships may develop symbiotic overtones because of the mutuality of interest between the reporter and the news subject. Reporters require fresh information on protest developments, while protest leaders have a vital interest in obtaining as much press coverage as possible.

[40]See, e.g., Thompson, *op. cit.*, p. 134 *passim*; Martin Oppenheimer, "The Southern Student Movement: Year I," *Journal of Negro Education*, Vol. 33 (Fall 1964), p. 397; Cothran, *op. cit.*, p. 72; Pauli Murray, "Protest against the Legal Status of the Negro," *The Annals*, Vol. 357 (January 1965), p. 63; Allan P. Sindler, "Protest against the Political Status of the Negroes," *The Annals*, Vol. 357 (January 1965), p. 50.

[41]See Banfield, *op. cit.*, p. 275.

Inflated reports of protest success may be understood in part by examining this relationship between reporter and protest leader. Both have role oriented interests in projecting images of protest strength and threat. In circumstances of great excitement, when competition from other news media representatives is high, a reporter may find that he is less governed by the role requirement of verification and reliability than he is by his editor's demand for "scoops" and news with high audience appeal.[42]

On the other hand, the demands of the media may conflict with the needs of protest group maintenance. Consider the leader whose constituents are attracted solely by pragmatic statements not exceeding what they consider political "good taste." He is constrained from making militant demands which would isolate him from constituents. This constraint may cost him appeal in the press.[43] However, the leader whose organizing appeal requires militant rhetoric may obtain eager press coverage only to find that his inflammatory statements lead to alienation of potential allies and exclusion from the explicit bargaining process.[44]

News media do not report events in the same way. Television may select for broadcast only thirty seconds of a half-hour news conference. This coverage will probably focus on immediate events, without background or explanatory material. Newspapers may give more complete accounts of the same event. The most complete account may appear in the weekly edition of a neighborhood or ethnic newspaper. Differential coverage by news media, and differential news media habits in the general population,[45] are significant factors in permitting protest leaders to juggle conflicting demands of groups in the protest process.

[42]For a case study of the interaction between protest leaders and newspaper reporters, see Michael Lipsky, "Rent Strikes in New York City: Protest Politics and the Power of the Poor," (unpublished Ph.D. dissertation, Princeton University, 1967), pp. 139-149. Bernard Cohen has analyzed the impact of the press on foreign policy from the perspective of reporters' role requirements; see his *The Press and Foreign Policy* (Princeton, N.J., 1963), esp. Chs. 2-3.

[43]An example of a protest conducted by middle-class women engaged in pragmatic protest over salvaging park space is provided in John B. Keeley, *Moses on the Green,* Inter-University Case Program, No. 45 (Univ. of Ala., 1959).

[44]This was the complaint of Floyd McKissick, National Director of the Congress of Racial Equality, when he charged that ". . . there are only two kinds of statements a black man can make and expect that the white press will report. . . . First . . . is an attack on another black man. . . . The second is a statement that sounds radical, violent, extreme–the verbal equivalent of a riot. . . . [T] he Negro is being rewarded by the public media only if he turns on another Negro and uses his tongue as a switchblade, or only if he sounds outlandish, extremist or psychotic." Statement at the Convention of the American Society of Newspaper Editors, April 20, 1967, Washington, D.C., as reported in *The New York Times,* April 21, 1967, p. 22. See also the remarks of journalist Ted Poston, *ibid.*, April 26, 1965, p. 26.

[45]Matthews and Prothro found, for example, that in their South-wide Negro population sample, 38 percent read Negro-oriented magazines and 17 percent read newspapers written

Similar tensions exist in the leader's relationships with protest targets. Ideological postures may gain press coverage and constituency approval, but may alienate target groups with whom it would be desirable to bargain explicitly. Exclusion from the councils of decision-making may have important consequences, since the results of target group deliberations may satisfy activated reference publics without responding to protest goals. If activated reference publics are required to increase the bargaining position of the protest group, protest efforts thereafter will have diminished chances of success.

IV

Protest leadership and "third parties." The argument here has been that the essence of political protest consists of activating third parties to participate in controversy in ways favorable to protest goals. In previous sections we have attempted to analyze some of the tensions which result from protest leaders' attempts to activate reference publics of protest targets at the same time that they must retain the interest and support of protest organization participants. This phenomenon is in evidence when Negro leaders, recognized as such by public officials, find their support eroded in the Negro community because they have engaged in explicit bargaining situations with politicians. Negro leaders are thus faced with the dilemma that when they behave like other ethnic group representatives they are faced with loss of support from those whose intense activism has been aroused in the Negro community, yet whose support is vital if they are to remain credible as leaders to public officials.

The tensions resulting from conflicting maintenance needs of protest organizations and activated third parties present difficulties for protest leaders. One way in which these tensions can be minimized is by dividing leadership responsibilities. If more than one group is engaged in protest activity, protest leaders can, in effect, divide up public roles so as to reduce as much as possible the gap between the implicit demands of different groups for appropriate rhetoric, and what in fact is said. Thus divided leadership may perform the latent function of minimizing tensions among elements in the protest process by permitting different groups to listen selectively to protest spokesmen.[46]

Another way in which strain among different groups can be minimized is through successful public relations. Minimization of strain may depend upon ambiguity of action or statement, deception, or upon effective inter-group communication. Failure to clarify meaning, or falsification, may increase protest effectiveness. Effective intragroup communication may increase the likelihood that protest constituents will "understand" that ambiguous or false public

---

for Negroes. These media treat news of interest to Negroes more completely and sympathetically than do the general media. See pp. 248ff.

[46]See footnote 31 above.

statements have "special meaning" and need not be taken seriously. The Machiavellian circle is complete when we observe that although lying may be prudent, the appearance of integrity and forthrightness is desirable for public relations, since these values are widely shared.

It has been observed that "[t]he militant displays an unwillingness to perform those administrative tasks which are necessary to operate an organization. Probably the skills of the agitator and the skills of the administrator . . . are not incompatible, but few men can do both well."[47] These skills may or may not be incompatible as personality traits, but they indeed represent conflicting role demands on protest leadership. When a protest leader exhausts time and energy conducting frequent press conferences, arranging for politicians and celebrities to appear at rallies, delivering speeches to sympathetic local groups, college symposia and other forums, constantly picketing for publicity and generally making "contacts," he is unable to pursue the direction of office routine, clerical tasks, research and analysis, and other chores.

The difficulty of delegating routine tasks is probably directly related to the skill levels and previous administrative experiences of group members. In addition, to the extent that involvement in protest organizations is a function of rewards received or expected by individuals because of the excitement or entertainment value of participation, then the difficulties of delegating routine, relatively uninteresting chores to group members will be increased. Yet attention to such details affects the perception of protest groups by organizations whose support or assistance may be desired in the future. These considerations add to the protest leader's problem of risking alienation of protest participants because of potentially unpopular cooperation with the "power structure."

In the protest paradigm developed here, "third parties" refers both to the reference publics of target groups and, more narrowly, to the interest groups whose regular interaction with protest targets tends to develop into patterns of influence.[48] We have already discussed some of the problems associated with activating the reference publics of target groups. In discussing the constraints placed upon protest, attention may be focused upon the likelihood that groups seeking to create political resources through protest will be included in the explicit bargaining process with other pressure groups. For protest groups, these constraints are those which occur because of class and political style, status, and organizational resources.

The established civic groups most likely to be concerned with the problems raised by relatively powerless groups are those devoted to service in the public

[47]Wilson, *Negro Politics,* p. 225.

[48]See Wallace Sayre and Herbert Kaufman, *Governing New York City* (New York, 1960), pp. 257ff. Also see Banfield, *op. cit.*, p. 267.

welfare and those "liberally" oriented groups whose potential constituents are either drawn from the same class as the protest groups (such as some trade unions), or whose potential constituents are attracted to policies which appear to serve the interest of the lower class or minority groups (such as some reform political clubs).[49] These civic groups have frequently cultivated clientele relationships with city agencies over long periods. Their efforts have been reciprocated by agency officials anxious to develop constituencies to support and defend agency administrative and budgetary policies. In addition, clientele groups are expected to endorse and legitimize agency aggrandizement. These relationships have been developed by agency officials and civic groups for mutual benefit, and cannot be destroyed, abridged or avoided without cost.

Protest groups may well be able to raise the saliency of issues on the civic agenda through utilization of communications media and successful appeals or threats to wider publics, but admission to policy-making councils is frequently barred because of the angry, militant rhetorical style adopted by protest leaders. People in power do not like to sit down with rogues. Protest leaders are likely to have phrased demands in ways unacceptable to lawyers and other civic activists whose cautious attitude toward public policy may reflect not only their good intentions but their concern for property rights, due process, pragmatic legislating or judicial precedent.

Relatively powerless groups lack participation of individuals with high status whose endorsement of specific proposals lends them increased legitimacy. Good causes may always attract the support of high status individuals. But such individuals' willingness to devote time toward promotion of specific proposals is less likely than the one-shot endorsements which these people distribute more readily.

Similarly, protest organizations often lack the resources on which entry into the policy-making process depends. These resources include maintenance of a staff with expertise and experience in the policy area. This expertise may be in the areas of the law, planning and architecture, proposal writing, accounting, educational policy, federal grantsmanship or publicity. Combining experience with expertise is one way to create status on issue areas. The dispensing of information by interest groups has been widely noted as a major source of influence. Over time the experts develop status in their areas of competence somewhat independent of the influence which adheres to them as information-providers. Groups which cannot or do not engage lawyers to assist in proposing legislation, and do not engage in collecting reliable data, cannot participate in policy deliberations or consult in these matters. Protest oriented groups, whose primary talents are

[49]See Wilson, *The Amateur Democrat,* previously cited. These groups are most likely to be characterized by broad scope of political interest and frequent intervention in politics. See Sayre and Kaufman, *op. cit.*, p. 79.

in dramatizing issues, cannot credibly attempt to present data considered "objective" or suggestions considered "responsible" by public officials. Few can be convincing as both advocate and arbiter at the same time.

V

Protest leadership and target groups. The probability of protest success may be approached by examining the maintenance needs of organizations likely to be designated as target groups.[50] For the sake of clarity, and because protest activity increasingly is directed toward government, I shall refer in the following paragraphs exclusively to government agencies at the municipal level. The assumption is retained, however, that the following generalizations are applicable to other potential target groups.

Some of the constraints placed on protest leadership in influencing target groups have already been mentioned in preceding sections. The lack of status and resources that inhibits protest groups from participating in policy-making conferences, for example, also helps prevent explicit bargaining between protest leaders and city officials. The strain between rhetoric which appeals to protest participants and public statements to which communications media and "third parties" respond favorably also exists with reference to target groups.

Yet there is a distinguishing feature of the maintenance needs and strategies of city agencies which specifically constrains protest organizations. This is the agency director's need to protect "the jurisdiction and income of his organization [by] . . . [m]anipulation of the external environment."[51] In so doing he may satisfy his reference groups without responding to protest group demands. At least six tactics are available to protest targets who are motivated to respond in some way to protest activity but seek primarily to satisfy their reference publics. These tactics may be employed whether or not target groups are "sincere" in responding to protest demands.

1. Target groups may dispense symbolic satisfactions. Appearances of activity and commitment to problems substitute for, or supplement, resource allocations and policy innovations which would constitute tangible responses to pro-

[50]Another approach, persuasively presented by Wilson, concentrates on protest success as a function of the relative unity and vulnerability of targets. See "The Strategy of Protest," pp. 293ff. This insight helps explain, for example, why protest against housing segregation commonly takes the form of action directed against government (a unified target) rather than against individual homeowners (who present a dispersed target). One problem with this approach is that it tends to obscure the possibility that targets, as collections of individuals, may be divided in evaluation of and sympathy for protest demands. Indeed, city agency administrators under some circumstances act as partisans in protest conflicts. As such, they frequently appear ambivalent toward protest goals: sympathetic to the ends while concerned that the means employed in protest do not reflect negatively on their agencies.

[51]Sayre and Kaufman, *op. cit.*, p. 253.

test activity. If symbolic responses supplement tangible pay-offs, they are frequently coincidental, rather than intimately linked, to projection of response by protest targets. Typical in city politics of the symbolic response is the ribbon cutting, street corner ceremony or the walking tour press conference. These occasions are utilized not only to build agency constituencies,[52] but to satisfy agency reference publics that attention is being directed to problems of civic concern. In this sense publicist tactics may be seen as defensive maneuvers. Symbolic aspects of the actions of public officials can also be recognized in the commissioning of expensive studies and the rhetorical flourishes with which "massive attacks," "comprehensive programs," and "coordinated planning" are frequently promoted.

City agencies establish distinct apparatus and procedures for dealing with crises which may be provoked by protest groups. Housing-related departments in New York City may be cited for illustration. It is usually the case in these agencies that the Commissioner or a chief deputy, a press secretary and one or two other officials devote whatever time is necessary to collect information, determine policy and respond quickly to reports of "crises." This is functional for tenants, who, if they can generate enough concern, may be able to obtain short-cuts through lengthy agency procedures. It is also functional for officials who want to project images of action rather than merely receiving complaints. Concentrating attention on the maintenance needs of city politicians during protest crises suggests that pronouncements of public officials serve purposes independent of their dedication to alleviation of slum conditions.[53]

Independent of dispensation of tangible benefits to protest groups, public officials continue to respond primarily to their own reference publics. Murray Edelman has suggested that

> Tangible resources and benefits are frequently not distributed to unorganized political group interests as promised in regulatory statutes and the propaganda attending their enactment.[54]

His analysis may be supplemented by suggesting that symbolic dispensations may not only serve to reassure unorganized political group interests, but may also contribute to reducing the anxiety level of organized interests and wider publics which are only tangentially involved in the issues.

[52]See *ibid.*, pp. 253ff.

[53]See Lipsky, *op. cit.*, Chs. 5-6. The appearance of responsiveness may be given by city officials *in anticipation* of protest activity. This seems to have been the strategy of Mayor Richard Daley in his reaction to the announcement of Martin Luther King's plans to focus civil rights efforts on Chicago. See *The New York Times*, February 1, 1966, p. 11.

[54]Edelman, *op. cit.*, p. 23.

2. Target groups may dispense token material satisfactions. When city agencies respond, with much publicity, to cases brought to their attention representing examples of the needs dramatized by protest organizations, they may appear to respond to protest demands while in fact only responding on a case basis, instead of a general basis. For the protesters served by agencies in this fashion it is of considerable advantage that agencies can be influenced by protest action. Yet it should not be ignored that in handling the "crisis" cases, public officials give the appearance of response to their reference publics, while mitigating demands for an expensive, complex *general* assault on problems represented by the cases to which responses are given. Token responses, whether or not accompanied by more general responses, are particularly attractive to reporters and television news directors, who are able to dramatize individual cases convincingly, but who may be unable to "capture" the essence of general deprivation or of general efforts to alleviate conditions of deprivation.

3. Target groups may organize and innovate internally in order to blunt the impetus of protest efforts. This tactic is closely related to No. 2 (above). If target groups can act constructively in the worst cases, they will then be able to pre-empt protest efforts by responding to the cases which best dramatize protest demands. Alternatively, they may designate all efforts which jeopardize agency reputations as "worst" cases, and devote extensive resources to these cases. In some ways extraordinary city efforts are precisely consistent with protest goals. At the same time extraordinary efforts in the most heavily dramatized cases or the most extreme cases effectively wear down the "cutting-edges" of protest efforts.

Many New York City agencies develop informal "crisis" arrangements not only to project publicity, as previously indicated, but to mobilize energies toward solving "crisis" cases. They may also develop policy innovations which allow them to respond more quickly to "crisis" situations. These innovations may be important to some city residents, for whom the problems of dealing with city bureaucracies can prove insurmountable. It might be said, indeed, that the goals of protest are to influence city agencies to handle every case with the same resources that characterize their dispatch of "crisis" cases.[55]

But such policies would demand major revenue inputs. This kind of qualitative policy change is difficult to achieve. Meanwhile, internal reallocation of resources only means that routine services must be neglected so that the "crisis" programs can be enhanced. If all cases are expedited, as in a typical "crisis" response, then none can be. Thus for purposes of general solutions, "crisis" resolving can be self-defeating unless accompanied by significantly greater resource allocation. It is not self-defeating, however, to the extent that the

[55]See Lipsky, *op. cit.*, pp. 156, 249ff.

organizational goals of city agencies are to serve a clientele while minimizing negative publicity concerning agency vigilance and responsiveness.

4. Target groups may appear to be constrained in their ability to grant protest goals.[56] This may be directed toward making the protesters appear to be unreasonable in their demands, or to be well-meaning individuals who "just don't understand how complex running a city really is." Target groups may extend sympathy but claim that they lack resources, a mandate from constituents, and/or authority to respond to protest demands. Target groups may also evade protest demands by arguing that "If-I-give-it-to-you-I-have-to-give-it-to-everyone."

The tactic of appearing constrained is particularly effective with established civic groups because there is an undeniable element of truth to it. Everyone knows that cities are financially undernourished. Established civic groups expend great energies lobbying for higher levels of funding for their pet city agencies. Thus they recognize the validity of this constraint when posed by city officials. But it is not inconsistent to point out that funds for specific, relatively inexpensive programs, or for the expansion of existing programs, can often be found if pressure is increased. While constraints on city government flexibility may be extensive, they are not absolute. Protest targets nonetheless attempt to diminish the impact of protest demands by claiming relative impotence.

5. Target groups may use their extensive resources to discredit protest leaders and organizations. Utilizing their excellent access to the press, public officials may state or imply that leaders are unreliable, ineffective as leaders ("they don't really have the people behind them"), guilty of criminal behavior, potentially guilty of such behavior, or are some shade of "left-wing." Any of these allegations may serve to diminish the appeal of protest groups to potentially sympathetic third parties. City officials, in their frequent social and informal business interaction with leaders of established civic groups, may also communicate derogatory information concerning protest groups. Discrediting of protest groups may be undertaken by some city officials while others appear (perhaps authentically) to remain sympathetic to protest demands. These tactics may be engaged in by public officials whether or not there is any validity to the allegations.

6. Target groups may postpone action. The effect of postponement, if accompanied by symbolic assurances, is to remove immediate pressure and delay specific commitments to a future date. This familiar tactic is particularly effective in dealing with protest groups because of their inherent instability. Protest groups are usually comprised of individuals whose intense political activity cannot be sustained except in rare circumstances. Further, to the extent that protest depends upon activating reference publics through strategies which have some

[56]On the strategy of appearing constrained, see Schelling, *op. cit.*, pp. 22ff.

"shock" value, it becomes increasingly difficult to activate these groups. Additionally, protest activity is inherently unstable because of the strains placed upon protest leaders who must attempt to manage four constituencies (as described herein).

The most frequent method of postponing action is to commit a subject to "study." For the many reasons elaborated in these paragraphs, it is not likely that ad hoc protest groups will be around to review the recommendations which emerge from study. The greater the expertise and the greater the status of the group making the study, the less will protest groups be able to influence whatever policy emerges. Protest groups lack the skills and resource personnel to challenge expert recommendations effectively.

Sometimes surveys and special research are undertaken in part to evade immediate pressures. Sometimes not. Research efforts are particularly necessary to secure the support of established civic groups, which place high priority on orderly procedure and policy emerging from independent analysis. Yet it must be recognized that postponing policy commitments has a distinct impact on the nature of the pressures focused on policy-makers.

VI

In this analysis I have agreed with James Q. Wilson that protest is correctly conceived as a strategy utilized by relatively powerless groups in order to increase their bargaining ability. As such, I have argued, it is successful to the extent that the reference publics of protest targets can be activated to enter the conflict in ways favorable to protest goals. I have suggested a model of the protest process which may assist in ordering data and indicating the salience for research of a number of aspects of protest. These include the critical role of communications media, the differential impact of material and symbolic rewards on "feedback" in protest activity, and the reciprocal relationships of actors in the protest process.

An estimation of the limits to protest efficacy, I have argued further, can be gained by recognizing the problems encountered by protest leaders who somehow must balance the conflicting maintenance needs of four groups in the protest process. This approach transcends a focus devoted primarily to characterization of group goals and targets, by suggesting that even in an environment which is relatively favorable to specific protest goals, the tensions which must be embraced by protest leadership may ultimately overwhelm protest activity.

At the outset of this essay, it was held that conceptualizing the American political system as "slack" or "fluid," in the manner of Robert Dahl, appears inadequate because of (1) a vagueness centering on the likelihood that any group can make itself heard; (2) a possible confusion as to which groups tend to receive satisfaction from the rewards dispensed by public officials; and (3) a lumping together as equally relevant rewards which are tangible and those which are symbolic. To the extent that protest is engaged in by relatively powerless groups which must create resources with which to bargain, the analysis here suggests a number of reservations concerning the pluralist conceptualization of the "fluidity" of the American political system.

Relatively powerless groups cannot use protest with a high probability of success. They lack organizational resources, by definition. But even to create bargaining resources through activating third parties, some resources are necessary to sustain organization. More importantly, relatively powerless protest groups are constrained by the unresolvable conflicts which are forced upon protest leaders who must appeal simultaneously to four constituencies which place upon them antithetical demands.

When public officials recognize the legitimacy of protest activity, they may not direct public policy toward protest groups at all. Rather, public officials are likely to aim responses at the reference publics from which they originally take their cues. Edelman has suggested that regulatory policy in practice often consists of reassuring mass publics while at the same time dispensing specific, tangible values to narrow interest groups. It is suggested here that symbolic reassurances are dispensed as much to wide, potentially concerned publics which are not directly affected by regulatory policy, as they are to wide publics comprised of the downtrodden and the deprived, in whose name policy is often written.

Complementing Edelman, it is proposed here that in the process of protest symbolic reassurances are dispensed in large measure because these are the public policy outcomes and actions desired by the constituencies to which public officials are most responsive. Satisfying these wider publics, city officials can avoid pressures toward other policies placed upon them by protest organizations.

Not only should there be some doubt as to which groups receive the symbolic recognitions which Dahl describes, but in failing to distinguish between the kinds of rewards dispensed to groups in the political system, Dahl avoids a fundamental question. It is literally fundamental because the kinds of rewards which can be obtained from politics, one might hypothesize, will have an impact upon the realistic appraisal of the efficacy of political activity. If among the groups least capable of organizing for political activity there is a history of organizing for protest, and if that activity, once engaged in, is rewarded primarily by the dispensation of symbolic gestures without perceptible changes in material conditions, then rational behavior might lead to expressions of apathy and lack of interest in politics or a rejection of conventional political channels as a meaningful arena of activity. In this sense this discussion of protest politics is consistent with Kenneth Clark's observations that the image of power, unaccompanied by material and observable rewards, leads to impressions of helplessness and reinforces political apathy in the ghetto.[57]

[57]Clark, *op. cit.*, pp. 154ff.

Recent commentary by political scientists and others regarding riots in American cities seems to focus in part on the extent to which relatively deprived groups may seek redress of legitimate grievances. Future research should continue assessment of the relationship between riots and the conditions under which access to the political system has been limited. In such research assessment of the ways in which access to public officials is obtained by relatively powerless groups through the protest process might be one important research focus.

The instability of protest activity outlined in this article also should inform contemporary political strategies. If the arguments presented here have been persuasive, civil rights leaders who insist that protest activity is a shallow foundation on which to seek long-term, concrete gains may be judged essentially correct. But the arguments concerning the fickleness of the white liberal, or the ease of changing discriminatory laws relative to changing discriminatory institutions, only in part explain the instability of protest movements. An explanation which derives its strength from analysis of the political process suggests concentration on the problems of managing protest constituencies. Accordingly, Alinsky is probably on soundest ground when he prescribes protest for the purpose of building organization. Ultimately, relatively powerless groups in most instances cannot depend upon activating other actors in the political process. Long-run success will depend upon the acquisition of stable political resources which do not rely for their use on third parties.

Bibliographical Note

The literature on this subject is voluminous, and only a few representative examples can be cited here. Some of the classics are discussed in the introduction to this section and in the introduction to Section 2, on group theory.

Parties and Elections

Dozens of studies about the voting behavior of members of categoric and formal groups are in print; work on unions is perhaps the most common. The following are representative: Nicholas A. Masters, "The Politics of Union Endorsement of Candidates in the Detroit Area," *Midwest Journal of Political Science*, Vol. 1 (August 1957), pp. 136-150; Arthur Kornhauser, A. L. Sheppard, and A. J. Mayer, *When Labor Votes* (New York: University Books, 1956); James Q. Wilson, *The Amateur Democrat* (Chicago: Univ. Chicago Press, 1962); Lawrence Fuchs, "American Jews and the Presidential Vote," *American Political Science Review*, Vol. 49 (June 1955); V. O. Key, Jr., "The Veterans and the House of Representatives: A Study of a Pressure Group and Electoral Morality," *Journal of Politics*, Vol. 5 (February 1943), pp. 27-40.

Groups and the Legislature

A number of excellent case studies focus on the legislative activity of specific groups or on group activity in regard to particular issues. These include: Bertram Gross, *The Legislative Struggle: A Study in Social Conflict* (New York: McGraw-Hill, 1953); Stephen K. Bailey, *Congress Makes a Law: The Story behind the Employment Act of 1946* (New York: Columbia Univ. Press, 1950); Oliver Garceau, *The Political Life of the American Medical Association* (Cambridge, Mass.: Harvard Univ. Press, 1941); Charles M. Hardin, *The Politics of Agriculture: Soil Conservation and the Struggle for Power in Rural America* (New York: Free Press, 1952); Raymond Bauer, Ithiel de Sola Pool, and Lewis A. Dexter, *American Business and the Politics of Foreign Trade* (New York: Atherton Press, 1963); and Harry Eckstein, *Pressure Group Politics: The Case of the British Medical Association* (Stanford, Calif.: Stanford Univ. Press, 1960).

Studies of somewhat wider theoretical and methodological interest include: Lester W. Milbrath, *The Washington Lobbyists* (Chicago: Rand McNally, 1963); David Truman, *The Governmental Process* (New York: Knopf, 1951); Oliver Garceau and Corinne Silverman, "A Pressure Group and the Pressured," *American Political Science Review*, Vol. 48 (September 1954), pp. 672-691; Charles O. Jones, "Representation in Congress: The Case of the House Agricultural Committee," *American Political Science Review*, Vol. 55 (June 1961), pp. 358-367; Bernard C. Cohen, "Political Communication on the Japanese Peace Settlement," *Public Opinion Quarterly*, Vol. 20 (Spring 1956), pp. 27-38; and Donald R. Matthews, *U. S. Senators and Their World* (Chapel Hill, N.C.: Univ. North Carolina Press, 1960), Ch. 8.

Interest Groups, Administrators, and the Judiciary

The literature on group-administrator relations is a rich one; in contrast, not much work has been done on groups and the courts. See Philip M. Selznick, *TVA and the Grass Roots* (Berkeley, Calif.: Univ. California Press, 1949); Merle Fainsod, "Some Reflections on the Nature of the Regulatory Process," in *Public Policy, 1940*, ed. C. J. Friedrich and Edward S. Mason (Cambridge, Mass.: Harvard Univ. Press, 1940), pp. 299-320.

Several case studies published by the Inter-University Case Program (Bobbs-Merrill, New York) are relevant, including Maass, "The Kings River Project"; Stratton and Sirotkin, "The Echo Park Controversy"; Foss, "The Grazing Fee Dilemma"; and Marshall and Zisk, "The Federal-State Struggle for Offshore Oil."

On groups and the courts, Robert Dahl, "Decision-Making in a Democracy: The Supreme Court as a National Policy-Maker," *Journal of Public Law*, Vol. 6 (Fall 1957); and Clement E. Vose, "Litigation as a Form of Pressure Group Activity," *Annals*, Vol. 319 (September 1958), pp. 20-31, are cited most frequently.

An excellent summary of the literature discussing the normative implications of lobbying is found in Lewis A. Bayles, "Are Pressure Groups Threatening American Democracy?", *The Midwest Quarterly*, Vol. 2 (October 1960), pp. 49-60.

Groups and the Legal Structure

Robert A. Horn, *Groups and the Constitution* (Stanford, Calif.: Stanford Univ. Press, 1956) provides an excellent summary of constitutional theory and relevant Supreme Court cases. The text of the Legislative Reorganization Act of 1946, Title III, Regulation of Lobbying Act (Sections 301-311) and the text of the Supreme Court decision upholding its constitutionality are reprinted in Congressional Quarterly News Service, *Legislators and the Lobbyists* (Washington, D.C.: Congressional Quarterly, 1966). The student may also want to consult the *Final Report of the Senate Special Committee to Investigate Political Activities, Lobbying, and Campaign Contributions* (Senate Report 395, 85th Congress, 1st Sess.).

The following articles are also highly relevant: Lewis A. Froman, Jr., "Some Effects of Interest Group Strength in State Politics," *American Political Science Review*, Vol. 60 (December 1966), pp. 952-962, which relates amendment procedures and length of state constitutions to interest group strength; Robert Salisbury, "St. Louis Politics: Relationships among Interests, Parties and Governmental Structure," *Western Political Quarterly*, Vol. 13 (June 1960), pp. 498-507; and Charles S. Liebman, "Electorates, Interest Groups and Local Government Policy," *American Behavioral Scientist*, Vol. 5 (January 1961), pp. 8-11.

5

Interest Groups and the Individual

The plight of modern man, lonely and helpless in an impersonal and fragmented society, has been dramatized and deplored by a generation of poets, philosophers, and political theorists. The theme is at least as old as Matthew Arnold; in recent years, however, it has reached a crescendo among students, academicians, and apologists for organized groups. It is the latter aspect of the discussion which is the concern of this section.

Theories of alienation in a "mass society" have been ably summarized by William Kornhauser.[1] He sees two major problems arising from the loss of social solidarity and of the stratification of preindustrial society: (1) a feeling of individual isolation and a sense of individual powerlessness and (2) a lack of buffers between political elites and masses who can be mobilized by demagogues promising easy answers to mass frustration.

At this point, the group enters the discussion. Kornhauser and others assert that membership in groups may help individuals to overcome their sense of powerlessness. Groups may integrate social isolates into at least one part of society; group membership may make them less responsive to irrational and simplistic appeals of mass leaders.

There is no need to debate the existence of a problem—whether that problem is labeled alienation, powerlessness, or general disenchantment with society at large. We need not agree that America is becoming a mass society to recognize the presence of large numbers of individuals who *feel* isolated, helpless, and frustrated or to note the rise of mass protest and mob violence in some areas of political life. The point which concerns us, however, is the claim that social organizations and political interest groups provide adequate outlets for individual action. We need to know the answers to these questions:

[1]William Kornhauser, *The Politics of Mass Society* (New York: Free Press, 1959).

1. How many and what kinds of individuals are involved in associational activity?
2. Do formal organizations play the part assigned to them—do they decrease individuals' sense of powerlessness?
3. Do formal organizations integrate individuals into the larger society, or do they foster the establishment of distinctive, separate, and potentially divisive subcultures in that society?

Charles Wright and Herbert Hyman's analysis of national-survey data shows that only a minority of Americans belong to organized groups. Even more important, the likelihood of individual participation is *lowest* among low-status people—those with little education, low incomes, or unskilled jobs. Thus, the very segments of the population which might benefit most from organizational support as an antidote to individual powerlessness are those which do not take advantage of the opportunity. Group membership appears to be a predominantly middle-class and upper-class luxury.

Wright and Hyman do not attempt a detailed explanation of their findings. However, it seems reasonable to assume that there is probably a dual tendency at work. High-status individuals are likely to come from homes with participant parents. They may have been educated by teachers for whom political participation was also the norm. They have probably entered adult life with a set of expectations concerning their citizenship responsibilities and capabilities which differs markedly from that of their contemporaries from disadvantaged backgrounds.[2] In addition, it is likely that most formal organizations (with a few exceptions like unions) are oriented toward the middle class, and, without intending to, middle-class participants may alienate potential lower-status members. James Q. Wilson has discussed the problem at some length in regard to the failure of Democratic Reform clubs to attract lower-income and immigrant members in New York.[3] Workers and their wives, with limited energy for leisure-time pursuits, have not found an evening's discussion of U. N. membership for Communist China or a factional battle requiring a detailed knowledge of Robert's Rules of Order either relevant or relaxing.

[2]All the voting studies and surveys of civic participation show a marked difference between high-status and low-status people. See, for example, Morris Janowitz and Dwaine Marvick, *Competitive Pressure and Democratic Consent* (Ann Arbor, Mich.: Institute of Public Administration, University of Michigan, 1956); or the selection from Almond and Verba's *The Civic Culture,* reprinted in the next section of this book.

[3]James Q. Wilson, *The Amateur Democrat* (Chicago: Univ. Chicago Press, 1962).

Wright and Hyman's main point—the impact of socioeconomic status on individual participation—has been confirmed by several later studies. Almond and Verba found in a crossnational survey[4] that level of education is a major determinant of level of political activity, not only in the United States but in Britain, Germany, Italy, and Mexico. The trend was consistent for acts ranging from discussions and voting on national elections to participation in partisan and interest-group activity. Bennett Berger made an intensive study of auto workers in California who had moved from a larger city to a small working-class suburb.[5] He found that the relatively apolitical, nonparticipant patterns of working-class life were carried from the urban to the suburban setting; the men and women he studied were totally unlike William Whyte's middle-class "organization man in suburbia."[6] It seems clear that the De Tocquevilles, the Sinclair Lewises, and the William Whytes who have pictured America as a nation of joiners based their observations on a rather select (although influential) portion of the population.

It should be noted, however, that several later studies report a markedly higher rate of participation in voluntary associations than did Wright and Hyman. Almond and Verba[7] found, for example, that 57 percent of the Americans in their sample belong to at least one organization, in contrast to the 36 percent reported by Wright and Hyman in Table 1 of the article which follows. The question used by Almond and Verba included union membership and in fact listed a wide variety of groups, including athletic clubs, fraternal groups, and charitable, civic, and religious organizations. The study reported by Wright and Hyman, in contrast, was simple and nonexplicit—and *excluded* unions. It also focused on "groups or organizations in the community here," thus excluding, by implication, national organizations. The problem in reconciling these differences, as Wright and Hyman themselves recognize, is not one of accuracy but of comparability. Those who conduct surveys have long realized that if you ask different questions, you get different answers. Unfortunately, there has been no general agreement on which form of the question is most useful in the study of interest groups.

Melvin Seeman discusses the second question listed above—the relationship between group membership and individual powerlessness. He finds that organization members feel more powerful as individuals than do nonmembers and that

[4]See Section 6 below.

[5]Bennett M. Berger, *Working Class Suburb: A Study of Auto Workers in Suburbia* (Berkeley, Calif.: Univ. California Press, 1960); Herbert J. Gans reports similar results in a recent study, *The Levittowners* (New York: Pantheon Books, 1967).

[6]William H. Whyte, Jr., *The Organization Man* (New York: Simon and Schuster, 1956).

[7]*Op. cit.* (Little, Brown edition), p. 246.

members of formal groups are generally better informed than nonmembers. He attributes these results to group success in teaching relevant skills to members. Seeman's article and the next study by Putnam provide excellent examples of theory-building analysis; they attempt much more than a simple correlation of empirical phenomena such as group membership and lack of powerlessness. Both men are trying to develop empirical generalizations about universal social mechanisms and individual characteristics. They are interested in *how* individuals come to behave as they do or to hold particular kinds of attitudes.

Robert Putnam discusses the local group as an integrating force in local community. He attempts to explain an often observed phenomenon, the disproportionate advantage of majority views in the community. (Most undecided voters in a predominantly Republican community vote Republican, while most undecided votes go to the Democrats in a heavily Democratic area.) He finds a very close relationship between individual membership in community groups and agreement with dominant community values. This relationship holds for both primary-group and secondary-group members, and it increases as level of activity in organizations or number of organization memberships goes up. Thus, officers in local groups or those who are members of several groups are even more likely to agree with majority views than are the rank-and-file members of one group.

The Putnam and Seeman articles seem to show that the claims made for organizations as reducers of powerlessness and as agents of social integration have considerable justification, if it is remembered that the population under observation (the joiners) is not drawn in equal proportion from all segments of society.

What becomes of the lower-status individuals who are not attracted to "mainstream" organizations? James Vander Zanden's study of the Ku Klux Klan provides some insight into one such organization which has been successful in attracting the normal nonjoiner. The majority of Klan members studied[8] are anxious about their status and frustrated at a lack of opportunity for personal advancement. Because they have internalized the American success ethos but lack a socially acceptable outlet for achieving their goals, they have turned to a spare-time organizational outlet for their frustrations. The Klan's endorsement of white superiority and superpatriotism enables the Klansman to affirm his own superior position in relation to the Negro. It also provides him with an explanation for his troubles—namely a scapegoat (the Negro and his Northern allies).

[8]An admittedly, but unavoidably, biased sample of 153 Klan members. General membership lists of such groups as the Klan or the John Birch Society are not available to the public or to the interested scholar.

The Klan (and, in all likelihood, other "anti" groups of both the right and left—the Birch Society, White Citizens' Councils, and probably the Communist party) seem to perform one major service for those who reject mainstream organizations: they foster an increase in personal efficacy and a diminution of personal anxieties. Their role is thus a constructive one from the point of view of the member. At the same time, their role is anything but an integrative one in terms of the larger society, given their highly conspiratorial focus, their obsession with secrecy, their search for scapegoats, and, above all, their lack of a positive program.

Therefore, the tasks which organized groups are alleged to perform for the individual-in-society (as distinguished, at least analytically, from the individual-as-political-man, discussed in Section 4) are not uniformly successful. Mainstream organizational membership does serve to reduce powerlessness and to integrate high-status individuals into the political and social systems. Those who begin from a relatively advantageous position may have joined groups *because* of their initially higher sense of personal efficacy, which is then increased through group membership. In the meantime, the low-status or status-anxious individual will probably remain outside of this mainstream of organizational activity as an isolated individual, as a joiner of "anti" or "fringe" groups, or as an occasional participant in mass-protest activities.

Voluntary Association Memberships of American Adults: Evidence from National Sample Surveys

Charles R. Wright
Herbert H. Hyman

Introduction

Several recent studies have demonstrated the need for a thorough reappraisal of the commonly held belief that Americans are a nation of joiners. For example, Komarovsky[1] and Axelrod[2] have provided evidence for urban dwellers, to whom such behavior has been especially attributed, that membership in a large number of associations is not characteristic of many Americans and is far from universally distributed throughout the various segments of the population.

Unfortunately, most investigators of the problem have had to work within serious limitations imposed by the nature of their data. In some instances, the sampling procedures available to the investigator could not provide adequate data.[3] In other instances, while the researcher was fortunate enough to have access to representative samples, the findings relate to such circumscribed and limited universes as small local communities, a single metropolis, or one social class within a particular city.[4] What has been missing in the literature is evidence

[1]Mirra Komarovsky, "The Voluntary Associations of Urban Dwellers," *American Sociological Review,* Vol. 11 (December 1946), pp. 686-698.

[2]Morris Axelrod, "Urban Structure and Social Participation," *American Sociological Review,* Vol. 21 (February 1956), pp. 13-18.

[3]For example, Komarovsky's study was based on responses of persons contacted at places of employment or other organizational meetings, hence not purporting to be a representative sample of New York adults. *Op. cit.*

[4]For example, see the following studies: Scott Greer, "Urbanism Reconsidered: A Comparative Study of Local Areas in a Metropolis," *American Sociological Review,* Vol. 21

Charles R. Wright and Herbert H. Hyman, "Voluntary Association Membership in American Adults: Evidence from National Sample Surveys," American Sociological Review, Vol. 23 (1958). Reprinted with permission of the American Sociological Association and the authors.

of the voluntary association memberships of Americans in general and of important sub-groups within the nation, derived from adequate sampling of the general population. The present paper provides data that partially meet this need.

More specifically, the paper presents evidence bearing on the following problems: (1) the pattern of membership in voluntary associations of adult Americans in general, and of specific sub-groups, such as racial and religious minorities; (2) some correlates of membership which might be considered determinants, for example, socio-economic status, urban or rural residence; and (3) some of the correlates of membership which might be considered consequences of significance to theories about such functions of voluntary association membership for society as interest in politics, voting, and charitable activity.

Method and Data

Solutions of these problems are provided by secondary analysis of recent survey data, where the universes studied often approximate the national adult population and where the samples have been drawn through probability designs. Through good fortune, a number of nationwide and local surveys conducted by the National Opinion Research Center[5] have contained one or more questions on voluntary association memberships. These items provide substantial information on the actual magnitude and pattern of voluntary association membership of the American people and of sub-groups within the general population. Secondary analysis of these surveys can also provide evidence about numerous sociological determinants of membership, which have figured in past speculative discussions but have seldom been supported by much empirical data, for example, the effect of urbanization upon membership. In addition, the surveys often contain data on possible determinants of membership which have rarely been treated, either speculatively or empirically, in past writings. Thus data are available on various situational factors which might facilitate or impede membership and participation, such as parenthood, residential mobility, travel time to work, and the like.

(February 1956), pp. 19-25; Wendell Bell and Maryanne T. Force, "Urban Neighborhood Types and Participation in Formal Associations," *American Sociological Review,* Vol. 21 (February 1956), pp. 25-34; Herbert Goldhamer, "Some Factors Affecting Participation in Voluntary Associations," unpublished Ph.D. dissertation (microfilmed), University of Chicago, 1942; Morris Axelrod, *op. cit.;* Floyd Dotson, "Patterns of Voluntary Association among Urban Working-Class Families," *American Sociological Review,* Vol. 16 (October 1951), pp. 687-693; Mirra Komarovsky, *op. cit.* Thus Greer's study used two census tracts within Los Angeles; Bell and Force employed four tracts within San Francisco; Goldhamer's study is confined to Chicago; Axelrod's to Detroit; Dotson's to New Haven; and Komarovsky's to New York City.

[5]The authors wish to acknowledge their indebtedness to NORC and to its director, Clyde Hart, who made the data available for secondary analysis, and to Jack Feldman, who provided many special tabulations.

For many of these latter analyses, it is necessary to consult sample surveys which were conducted on local rather than national populations, but here too all the inquiries have the merit of being based on large samples drawn by a probability design. Therefore, though limited to the cities or counties involved, they still constitute reliable evidence concerning hypotheses based on representative sampling. Finally, by secondary analysis tabulation of voluntary association membership is possible, not only by hypothesized determinants, but also by the customary questions asked in such surveys about attitudes, opinions, interests, conduct, and so on. In this manner, some empirical perspective can be obtained on the fundamental question of the functions of organizational membership for citizens in a democratic society.

Admittedly there are serious limitations to such secondary analysis. Foremost among these is the reliance put upon questions not primarily designed for the study of voluntary association memberships. Since data on such memberships were only incidental to the primary purposes of the surveys, the questioning in this area is not as thorough as would be desired. Furthermore, the wording of questions about membership varies from study to study, hence complicating the analysis. Nevertheless, we believe that these inherent limitations of secondary analysis are more than offset by the gains which have been outlined above.

The bulk of the analysis to be presented is based on two national probability samples of the adult, non-institutionalized population of the United States, over 21 years of age. The first sample contains 2,809 men and women, and the second 2,379. The studies were conducted in the years 1953 and 1955. In addition to the national data, findings on voluntary association membership were available for representative samples from NORC studies of the following localities: a large metropolitan area (New York metropolitan area represented by a probability sample of 1,053 cases drawn in 1951); a medium sized Western metropolis (Denver represented by a probability sample of 920 cases obtained in the spring of 1949); a small city and surrounding county (Findley and Hancock County, Ohio, represented by 535 cases drawn in May, 1952). The local findings on magnitude of membership and its social distribution are not presented in detail, although, where confirmation or contradiction occurs, some brief reference will be made. They will be used to examine hypotheses about particular variables, however, which are not demonstrable on a national scale.

Findings

Memberships of Americans. Data from the national surveys confirm the conclusions drawn by previous researchers based on local studies, which showed that a sizeable group of Americans are not members of any voluntary associations and that only a minority belong to more than one such organization. Table 1 presents data from two surveys, one of which inquired about the

Table 1. Membership in Voluntary Associations for Two National Cross-Sections of American Adults, 1953 and 1955

Number of Voluntary Associations	Percentage of *Families* Whose Members Belong to Organizations as Indicated (1953)*	Percentage of *Adults* Who Were Themselves Members of the Organizations as Indicated (1955)†
None	47	64
One	31	20
Two	12	9
Three	5	4
Four or more	4	3
Unknown	1	0
	100%	100%
Total	(2,809)	(2,379)

**"Does anyone in the family belong to any sort of club, lodge, fraternal order, or union with ten or more members in it?" If* yes, *"What organization? Any other?" (Source: NORC Survey 335.)*

†*Union membership is* not *included in these data because the interviewing on organizational membership during this part of the survey concerned associations other than union. The question was, "Do you happen to belong to any groups or organizations in the community here?" If* yes, *"Which ones? Any other?" (Source: NORC Survey 367.)*

voluntary association membership of *any* member of the family, the other survey pertained to activities of the respondent himself. Calculated either way, voluntary association membership is not a major characteristic of Americans. Nearly half of the families (47 per cent) and almost two-thirds of the respondents (64 per cent) belong to no voluntary associations. About a third of the families (31 per cent) and a fifth of the respondents belong to only one such organization. Only about a fifth of the families (21 per cent) and a sixth of the respondents (16 per cent) belong to two or more organizations. These findings hardly warrant the impression that Americans are a nation of joiners.[6]

[6]To some extent, the open-ended form of the questions in the national studies might have reduced the proportion of memberships reported insofar as respondent recall might be faulty. There is some indication, however, that the impact of question format was not great in this instance. In the Denver study, a card listing several types of organizations was handed to the respondent before he reported memberships. Under these conditions, 36 per cent of the Denverites reported that they belonged to no organizations, including unions. In the 1953 national survey, which used an open-ended question, 39 per cent of the urbanites living in large cities (1,000,000 or more) and 42 per cent of those living in any sizeable city (50,000 or more) reported no organizational memberships, including unions, for anyone in their family.

Obviously, primary research on voluntary association membership would require more and different questioning in this area, including check lists of organizations, investigation of the meaning of "belonging" to the respondent, etc. The data used in the current secondary analysis, however, were obtained from studies in which information on membership was

Data on the types of organizations to which Americans belong are also revealing. In the 1953 survey, which contained an account of organizations to which any family member belonged, only two (unions and fraternal or secret societies) have relatively large memberships, 23 per cent and 19 per cent respectively. Next in order are neighborhood-ethnic-special interest groups (8 per cent), veterans' organizations (7 per cent), civic organizations (5 per cent), church sponsored organizations (3 per cent), youth organizations (2 per cent), and professional and learned societies (2 per cent). These findings provide national perspective on the data recorded by former studies of local populations, such as the Detroit Area Study, in which unions and fraternal organizations also accounted for more of the citizens' voluntary memberships than any other type of association.[7]

Racial and religious subgroups. Table 2 presents figures on the membership patterns for two types of subgroups within American society: racial and religious. Comparison of Negro and white respondents shows that voluntary association membership is somewhat more characteristic of whites than Negroes. Less than half (46 per cent) of the white families and 63 per cent of the white respondents belong to no associations in contrast to 60 per cent of the Negro families and 73 per cent of the Negro adults. And nearly a quarter (23 per cent) of the white families belong to two or more organizations in contrast to only 11 per cent of the Negro families.

Differences in rates of membership also distinguish the major religious subgroups of the population. Whether measured on a family or individual basis, the highest rate of membership is found among the Jews. On a family basis, the next highest participants in voluntary associations are the Catholics (56 per cent), and the least active are the Protestants (51 per cent). Data on individual memberships, however, are different, with a higher percentage of Protestants than Catholics belonging to any organizations.

Interesting comparisons with national data on memberships of religious subgroups are available from the local studies of New York City and Denver. In both cities the ordering of memberships agrees with the national sample on

---

only incidental to the primary purposes of the surveys, for which the open-ended questions sufficed. Confidence in the interpretation of the findings as indicative of low membership among Americans is increased through the use of data from *several* national and local surveys, which support one another, in general, despite variations in the wording of questions.

Of course, this is not to dispute the fact that, from a *comparative* point of view, Americans may be more prone to such membership than other national groups. Such a mode of analysis is illustrated, for example, by Arnold Rose, *Theory and Method in the Social Sciences* (Minneapolis: Univ. Minnesota Press, 1954), pp. 72-115.

[7] Axelrod, *op. cit.* Also see *A Social Profile of Detroit: 1952.* A report of the Detroit Area Study (Ann Arbor: Univ. Michigan Press, 1952), pp. 13-19.

Table 2. Voluntary Association Memberships of Racial and Religious Subgroups Based on National Samples

(A) Family Data (1953)	Per Cent of Families Whose Members Belong to:			
	No Organization	One	Two or More	N (100%)
Race*				
Negro	60	29	11	279
White	46	31	23	2,472
Religion†				
Jewish	31	37	32	99
Catholic	44	34	22	579
Protestant	49	30	21	1,992

(Source: NORC Survey 335.)

(B) Respondent Data (1955)	Per Cent of Respondents Who Belong to:			
	No Organization	One	Two or More	N (100%)
Race‡				
Negro	73	18	9	229
White	63	20	17	2,139
Religion‡				
Jewish	45	25	30	71
Protestant	63	20	17	1,701
Catholic	69	17	14	519

**Figures exclude 58 cases of other races or of unknown race.*
†Figures exclude 139 cases who report some other religion or none at all.
‡Figures exclude 11 cases of other races.
‡Figures exclude 88 cases who report some other religion or none at all.
(Source: NORC Survey 367.)

individual memberships: the rate of membership is highest for Jews, next for Protestants and lowest for Catholics. In New York, 64 per cent of the Jewish respondents reported membership in at least one voluntary association, 54 per cent of the Protestants and 37 per cent of the Catholics. In Denver, the membership rates were 77 per cent for Jews, 65 per cent for Protestants and 55 per cent for Catholics. Thus the Catholic membership rates in these urban settings appear lower than those of the Jews and Protestants, as in the 1955 national survey.[8]

[8]These findings are consistent with those reported by Bell and Force, *op. cit.*, from their study in San Francisco during 1953. They not only found that Protestants were more likely than Catholics to belong to formal associations but also that the relationship persisted even when economic level was controlled.

Social stratification and membership. On the local level, several studies have demonstrated a relationship between the social status of the respondent, as measured by a variety of indices, and membership in voluntary associations.[9] These studies generally agree that there is an increase in the percentage of memberships in formal associations the higher the status of the respondents. The magnitude of the difference in membership between classes varies considerably, however, from study to study. For example, Komarovsky found that 60 per cent of working class men in her sample of New Yorkers belonged to no voluntary association in contrast to only 53 per cent of white collar workers. Similarly Dotson's study of families in New Haven reported that 70 per cent of the working class adults in his sample belonged to no organizations. On the other hand, Bell and Force in a recent study of San Francisco report that even in low status neighborhoods about three-quarters of the men belong to at least one formal group.

Data from the national samples support the correlation between social status and membership. Table 3 presents data on the membership of the 1955 sample classified by five indices of social status: family income, education of respondent, interviewer's rating of family's level of living, occupation of head of household, and home ownership. Whichever index of status is used, an appreciably higher percentage of persons in higher status positions belong to voluntary associations than do persons of lower status. For example, fully 76 per cent of the respondents whose family income falls below 2,000 dollars do not belong to any organizations in contrast to only 48 per cent of those whose income is 7,500 dollars or more. Furthermore, there is an increase in the percentage of persons who belong to *several* organizations as social status increases. For example, only 7 per cent of the lowest income group belong to two or more associations in contrast to 30 per cent of the highest income group. Similar findings are obtained from inspection of the data on education, level of living, occupation, and home ownership, as examination of Table 3 reveals.[10]

One set of findings warrant special mention. The pattern of voluntary association membership among different occupational levels indicates even less participation among blue collar workers than had been noted in previous local studies. For example, from 68 to 87 per cent of the blue collar workers belong

[9]See, for example, Komarovsky, *op. cit.*; Dotson, *op. cit.*; and Bell and Force, *op. cit.*

[10]Data from the 1953 sample on family participation in voluntary associations generally corroborated the findings presented above and hence are not reproduced here. In addition, several of the local studies contain data in support of the relationships described. For example, home ownership data were available in Denver and provided an opportunity to examine the influence of this factor within an urban setting. Here, as on the national level, home owners were more likely to be members than were renters, 67 per cent versus 59 per cent respectively. And in New York, families employing domestic help were more likely to be members than those without help, 73 per cent versus 45 per cent.

*Table 3. Indices of Stratification and Voluntary Association Membership, 1955**

	Per Cent Who Belong to:			
	No Organization	One Organization	Two or More	No. of Cases (100%)
A. Income level				
Under $2,000	76	17	7	385
2,000–2,999	71	17	12	304
3,000–3,999	71	18	11	379
4,000–4,999	65	21	14	450
5,000–7,499	57	22	21	524
7,500 and over	48	22	30	328
B. Education				
0–6 years	83	12	5	348
7–8 years	73	17	10	522
9–11 years	67	20	13	495
12 years	57	23	20	610
1–3 yrs. of college	46	24	30	232
4 yrs. college or more	39	25	36	170
C. Level of living (Interviewer's rating)				
Very low	92	7	1	125
Below average	81	14	5	580
Average	61	22	17	1,318
Above average	43	25	32	288
Very high	18	18	64	44
D. Occupation				
Professional	47	24	29	259
Prop., mgrs., officials	47	24	29	294
Farm owners	58	28	14	265
Clerical and sales	59	21	20	240
Skilled labor	68	19	13	447
Semi-skilled labor	77	14	9	492
Service	73	18	9	142
Non-farm labor	79	16	5	155
Farm labor	87	13	0	54
Retired, unemployed	77	11	12	35
E. Home ownership				
Owns home	57	22	21	1,407
Rents	75	16	9	968

**Data exclude union membership.*
(Source: NORC Survey 367.)

to no organizations (not counting union membership), in contrast to 59 per cent of the white collar workers and 47 per cent of the businessmen and professionals. The higher rate of voluntary association membership among businessmen and professionals is clearly documented by the national data, which show that 29 per cent of the members of these two occupational categories belong to two or more organizations, in contrast with only 5 to 13 per cent of the blue collar workers. These data extend to the national level a relationship noted by Komarovsky in her New York study, namely that it is only in the business and professional classes that the majority is formally organized.

Urbanization and voluntary association membership. Voluntary associations customarily have been identified as characteristic of the urban way of life, and membership in such associations has been assumed to be more common for city residents than rural people. Recent observers, however, have noted that the spread of urbanization in America is reducing such differences between city and country. Williams, for example, has noted that "Formally organized special-interest associations are most highly developed in urban areas, but have increasingly pervaded the open country as well." Nevertheless, we have lacked specific information on the differential rates of voluntary association membership of residents of various sized communities. A breakdown of national survey data provides considerable information on this question.

From the 1953 national survey it is possible to determine the number of associational affiliations of family members living in counties of varying degrees of urbanization, taking the size of the largest city in the county as a crude index of its degree of urbanism. Three types of counties can be examined: (1) highly urbanized counties, those with at least one city of 50,000 population or more; (2) moderately urbanized, with at least one city of 10,000 to 50,000 population; and (3) least urbanized, having no city of 10,000 or more. Examination of the memberships of residents of these three types of counties reveals that only 57 per cent of the families who live in highly urbanized counties have members in at least one voluntary association, 53 per cent of those in moderately urbanized counties, and 41 per cent of those living in the least urbanized or predominantly rural counties. Thus some correlation appears between the degree of urbanization and voluntary association membership, although the difference between the most urban and least urban counties is not great.

But the type of county is only a crude index of the social atmosphere within which the citizen lives. Within each county, for example, there are areas of more *and* less urban nature. Therefore a finer breakdown is desirable in order to determine more precisely the relationship between urbanism and membership in voluntary associations. Table 4 presents data on membership according to urban, rural non-farm, and rural farm residences within each type of county.

Several interesting findings emerge. First, it appears that, with one exception (rural farm residents in moderately urbanized counties) the relationship between urbanization of county and membership in voluntary associations persists. That is, more of the residents of highly urbanized counties belong to organizations than do persons living in similar types of neighborhoods but in less urbanized

Table 4. Urbanism and Voluntary Association Membership, 1953

Per Cent of Families Whose Members Belong to:	Place of Residence								
	Metropolitan Counties (with City of 50,000 or More)			Other Urbanized Counties (with City of 10-50,000)			Primarily Rural Counties (Have No Town of 10,000)		
	Urban Residence	Rural Non-Farm	Rural Farm	Urban	RNF	RF	Urban	RNF	RF
No organization	42	40	67	46	46	53	54	52	70
One organization	33	37	21	36	34	28	27	24	21
Two or more organizations	25	23	12	18	20	19	19	24	9
Total	100%	100%	100%	100%	100%	100%	100%	100%	100%
Cases	1,394	193	48	294	115	134	110	264	252

(Source: NORC Survey 335.)

counties. For example, only 42 per cent of the urbanites in highly urbanized counties belong to no organization, in contrast with 46 per cent of the urbanites in moderately urbanized counties, and 54 per cent in the least urbanized.

Secondly, within each type of county, rural farm residence is more closely associated with non-membership than is either rural non-farm or urban residence. For example, within highly urbanized counties 67 per cent of the rural farm residents belong to no voluntary association, in contrast to only 40 per cent of the rural non-farm residents and 42 per cent of the urbanites.[11]

Third, there is *no* appreciable difference between the membership rates of urbanites and rural non-farm residents within any type of county. This finding, in connection with the second, suggests an interesting hypothesis about the spread of urbanism into American suburban and rural areas. If the countryside were becoming urbanized then one might expect that rural-urban differences would be minimal in counties which contained large cities and maximal in counties still rural. Such is not the case, at least with respect to voluntary association membership. True, the urban pattern of membership prevails in rural non-farm areas but it does not extend to rural farms. Furthermore, an anomaly

[11]The higher incidence of organizational membership among urban residents in contrast with their rural neighbors also was evident in the Hancock County, Ohio, survey. In this survey a distinction was made between the residents of a small town (Findley, pop. approximately 24,000) and persons in the surrounding county. Fifty-six per cent of the Findley townspeople belonged to some voluntary association, in contrast to 49 per cent of the ruralites. For a recent summary of some surveys on rural memberships see Raymond Payne, "Some Comparisons of Participation in Rural Mississippi, Kentucky, Ohio, Illinois, and New York," *Rural Sociology*, Vol. 18 (June 1953), pp. 171-172.

(requiring further substantiation) appears in that rural farm persons living in *moderately* urbanized counties resemble their urban and rural non-farm neighbors more than do ruralites in either highly urbanized or heavily rural counties. Perhaps this finding means that rural-urban differences in general are polarized—being greatest in both highly urban and highly rural counties and least in partially urbanized areas.

Some situational determinants of membership. In this section some data from the Denver survey are examined to clarify certain situational factors which might be presumed to affect urban participation in voluntary associations. Specifically, data are presented on the effect of length of residence in the community, length of residence at the same address, type of residence (for example, single family dwelling versus apartment), travel time to work, and family status (for example, single, married with children or without children). The presumed influence of such factors is illustrated by the hypothesis that long-time residents in the community or in the neighborhood are more likely to be involved in formal organizations. Or, persons living in apartments might be expected to participate less in voluntary associations than those living in single family dwellings. Persons who spend less time commuting to work, it may be argued, should have more time to devote to organizations and therefore should show a higher incidence of membership. Similarly, single men and women, who are unencumbered by children, might have more spare time and hence be more apt to belong to voluntary groups. Table 5 presents data which fail to support several of these arguments.

None of the residential factors shows a systematic relationship with the incidence of affiliation with voluntary associations. For example, persons born in Denver are hardly more likely to belong to voluntary associations than those who have arrived recently.[12] Apartment dwellers are slightly more likely to be voluntary association members than persons renting houses. Commuters who spend more than 45 minutes getting to work are about as likely to belong to organizations as are those people who have to travel only 25 minutes or less.

[12]These data are consistent with those obtained in Hancock County, Ohio, where 51 per cent of the persons who had resided in the county for 20 years or more were members of voluntary associations, 57 per cent of the 10-19 year residents were members, 58 per cent of the 5-8 year residents, and 57 per cent of the persons living there less than five years. The survey was conducted in May 1952. On the other hand, Zimmer, in a study of married men in a mid-western community of 20,000, found that membership in formal organizations increased directly with length of time in the community. Zimmer's relationship persisted within age, occupational, and educational control categories. See Basil Zimmer, "Participation of Migrants in Urban Structures," *American Sociological Review*, Vol. 20 (April 1955), pp. 218-224. And a recent study in Spokane, Washington, indicates a relationship between mobility and voluntary association membership; see Howard Freeman, Edwin Novak, and Leo Reeder, "Correlates of Membership in Voluntary Associations," *American Sociological Review*, Vol. 22 (October 1957), pp. 528-533.

Table 5. Some Situational Determinants of Voluntary Association Membership: Evidence from Denver Survey

	Percentage of Each Type Who Belong to Voluntary Associations	No. of Cases in Base
A. Residential history		
Born in Denver or lived there at least 20 yrs.	65	504
Lived in Denver less than 20 years	62	404
Lived in Denver at present address over 20 years	63	200
Lived at present address for 5 to 20 years	67	346
Lived at present address less than 5 years	60	358
B. Residential mobility		
Moved to Denver from place of under 2,500 population	61	272
Moved from place of 2,500 to 25,000 population	60	205
Moved from place larger than 25,000	64	281
C. Type of residence		
Single family house, rented	57	81
Multiple family dwelling, rented	59	165
Apartment building, rented	60	117
Owned, all types of dwelling	67	512
D. Travel time to work		
45 minutes or more daily	60	81
35-44 minutes	70	185
30-34 minutes	64	256
25-29 minutes	66	192
Less than 25 minutes	57	205
E. Family status		
Men: Not married	66	79
Married, no children under 18 yrs. old	74	182
Married, with children under 18 yrs. old	82	162
Women: Not married	51	149
Married, no children under 18 yrs. old	53	174
Married, with children under 18 yrs. old	56	174

(Source: Denver Community Survey, NORC-12B.)

Only two of these situational factors–home ownership and family status–seem related to voluntary association membership. Home ownership as a determinant of membership, as brought out above, is related to social stratification. The data on family status show that married persons are more likely to be members of organizations than single persons; and that men and women with children are more likely to be members than childless couples. One might hypothesize that children–and perhaps the expectation of children–draw adults into participation in the voluntary associations in the urban community. This finding corroborates that of Janowitz in his study of Chicago residents in which he notes that neighborhood involvement often centers around activities connected with the rearing of children in a metropolis. As Janowitz remarks, on the neighborhood level, "children are not only the best neighbors in the community but they lead their parents to neighborhood community participation and orientation."[13]

Civic involvement of voluntary association membership. In this final section, data from the Denver Survey are presented which demonstrate psychological and behavioral differences between citizens who are members and those who are not members of formal organizations. Admittedly the data do not indicate that such differences can be attributed solely to the respondents' patterns of associational membership. Clearly several factors already established as correlates of membership (for example, high socio-economic status, occupation, place of residence) may also account for differences in political interest, voting and charitable acts of members and non-members. The authors feel, however, that comparison of members and non-members without controlling these associated factors is proper insofar as the purpose is solely to *describe* the differences between persons who are or are not members of voluntary associations, regardless of the ultimate causes of such differences.[14] Hence Table 6 presents simple comparisons between the formally organized and unorganized, concerning their interest in political topics, voting records, and contributions to charity.

Several measures of interest in public affairs (including presidential elections, unemployment, labor relations, minority problems, public schools, and city planning) indicate that persons belonging to voluntary associations are more concerned with such topics than are non-members. For example, fully 84 per cent of the Denverites who belonged to any voluntary association said they took a great deal of interest in presidential elections, in contrast with only 73 per cent

[13]Morris Janowitz, *The Community Press in an Urban Setting* (New York: Free Press, 1952), p. 124. Janowitz's remark is made in connection with family structure as a determinant of readership of the community press, but its import extends to other forms of involvement in community activities.

[14]For a discussion of the differential demands of descriptive vs. explanatory analysis, see Herbert Hyman, *Survey Design and Analysis: Principles, Cases and Procedures* (New York: Free Press, 1955), especially pp. 121-124.

Table 6. Political Interests and Behavior Associated with Voluntary Association Membership: Evidence from Denver Survey, 1949

	Persons Who Were Members of:	
	No Organizations	One or More Organizations
A. Per cent who said they take "a great deal" of interest in:		
Presidential elections	73	84
Unemployment in the U.S.	53	57
The Denver public schools	33	50
City planning in Denver	31	50
Labor relations	31	45
The situation of Denver Negroes	23	35
B. Per cent who voted in each of the following elections:		
1944 Presidential	36	40
1946 Congressional	27	36
1947 City charter	15	24
1948 Primary	24	34
C. Per cent who report making a contribution to the Community Chest in Denver	56%	72%
Total cases	335	585

(Source: Denver Community Survey, NORC-12B.)

of the non-members. And members were more likely than non-members to be interested in city planning, 50 per cent to 31 per cent respectively.

Political interest is backed by participation in the political process, insofar as participation is measured by voting. Data on behavior in four elections—the 1944 Presidential, 1946 Congressional, 1947 City Charter, and 1948 Primary—indicate in every instance a greater percentage of voting among Denverites who were members of voluntary associations than among non-members.

Finally, in the non-political sphere of community life, charity, 72 per cent of the persons belonging to associations reported having made a contribution to the Community Chest in Denver, in contrast to 56 per cent of the non-members.

Thus three separate measures—interest in social issues, voting, and support of community charities—show that voluntary association participants are more involved civically than the non-members. Further research might fruitfully be addressed to such questions as the following: (1) to what extent does the citizen's interest in public affairs lead him to join voluntary associations; (2) to what extent do the voluntary associations contribute to their members' interest in public affairs; (3) to what extent is membership in one or more voluntary associations functional for the citizen who has a great deal of interest in public affairs. Questions of this order, however, fall beyond the scope of this secondary analysis.[15]

Summary

A secondary analysis of two national and several local surveys provides evidence on the topics: the pattern of membership in voluntary associations of Americans in general and of such specific subgroups as class and religion; some possible determinants of membership, for example, socio-economic status; and certain correlates of membership which relate to civic participation, for example, interest in public issues and voting.

The major findings are listed below in abbreviated form. In each case, the major source of data, that is, national or local survey, is indicated in parentheses. Subject to the qualifications noted above, the major findings are:

1. Voluntary association membership is not characteristic of the majority of Americans (National).
2. A relatively small percentage of Americans belong to two or more voluntary associations (National).
3. Membership is more characteristic of the white than Negro population (National).
4. Membership is more characteristic of Jewish than Protestant persons, and of Protestant than Catholics (National).
5. Membership is directly related to socio-economic status, as measured by level of income, occupation, home ownership, interviewer's rating of level of living, and education (National).
6. Membership is more characteristic of urban and rural non-farm residents than of rural farm residents (National).
7. Membership does not appear to be related to a variety of situational factors, for example, length of residence in the community, length of residence at the same address, type of dwelling unit, commuting time to work (Denver).
8. Membership is related to family status, being higher for couples with children than without (Denver).

[15]For examples of earlier theoretical and empirical work on the functions of voluntary association membership, see Rose, *op. cit.;* and Bernard Barber, "Participation and Mass Apathy in Associations," in *Studies in Leadership: Leadership and Democratic Action,* ed. Alvin Gouldner (New York: Harper, 1950), pp. 477-504.

9. Membership is accompanied by a greater interest in such public affairs as unemployment problems, city planning, and public schools (Denver).

10. Membership is associated with voting in Presidential, Congressional and local elections (Denver).

11. Membership is associated with support for local charities (Denver).

Alienation, Membership, and Political Knowledge: A Comparative Study

Melvin Seeman

This paper documents the compatibility between two major lines of theorizing in social psychology: on the sociological side, the theory of mass society, and in psychology, learning theory. My thesis is that the mass society tradition is not so far removed from learning theory as it might seem, and that the union of these seemingly divergent interests provides a useful framework for analyzing the problem of developing an informed public in modern society. The elaboration of this thesis calls first for some comment on the essentials of the two theories involved here—mass society theory and Rotter's social learning theory[1] —and then for a presentation of empirical work on powerlessness and political information that reflects this joint interest.

A Theoretical Frame

The central theme in mass theory is that the destruction of the old community has separated the individual from binding social ties, and that the consequences of such separation can be both personally devastating and destructive of democratic values. But a theme is not yet a theory, and we need to specify how the mass society viewpoint provides the ingredients of a useful theory. In brief, it

[1] Julian B. Rotter, *Social Learning and Clinical Psychology* (New York: Prentice-Hall, 1954).

Melvin Seeman, "Alienation, Membership and Political Knowledge: A Comparative Study," Public Opinion Quarterly, *Vol. 30 (1966). Reprinted with permission.*

becomes a theory by combining (1) an historically oriented account of contemporary social structure, (2) assertions about the *psychological effects* of that structure, and (3) predictions about the resulting *individual behavior.* Alienation is the crucial intervening variable: it is produced by the social structure and, in turn, produces distinctive behavior.

Each of these three elements in the theory can readily be summarized. The *social structural* features that constitute the independent variables are standard ones, for example, the decline of kinship as a criterion of social position and the concomitant rise of anonymity and impersonality, and the development of secularized social forms (bureaucracy, mechanization, etc.). The *alienation* that the theory predicates as a derivative of these conditions takes several forms, and it has elsewhere been suggested[2] that there are at least five distinguishable varieties of alienation—statable in the language of social learning theory—that are regularly invoked (including, for example, powerlessness, normlessness, and the idea of "self-estrangement"). The gamut of *behaviors* that constitute the dependent variables in mass theory includes political passivity, participation in millenarian social movements, intergroup prejudice, and the like.[3]

Two aspects of this theoretical model are most crucial here. First, the model embodies a structure-alienation-behavior sequence, and requires that two main questions be tested: whether the structural conditions have the alienative effects, and whether alienation has the specified consequences. Second, given the emphasis upon personal alienation as an intervening variable, some version of psychological theory is necessarily implicated in the propositions of mass society theory.

The version I have found most useful is Rotter's social learning theory. This theory, which uses both expectancy and reinforcement constructs, holds principally that behavior is a function of (1) the expectancy, or probability held by an individual, that a particular behavior will, in a given situation, have a successful outcome, and (2) the value of that outcome—i.e., the preference (or "reinforcement value") that the individual assigns to the reward or goal in question.

It is this theory which served as the basis for clarifying the alternative meanings of alienation in mass society theory (see note 2). We are here concerned with only one of these meanings: alienation as powerlessness (i.e. the expectancy or probability held by the individual that his own behavior cannot determine the

[2]Melvin Seeman, "On the Meaning of Alienation," *American Sociological Review,* Vol. 24 (1959), pp. 783-791.

[3]This tripartite ordering of mass theory is not made explicit in the literature on mass society; it is a distillation from that literature—cf., for example, Hannah Arendt, *The Origins of Totalitarianism* (New York: Harcourt, 1951); Leon Bramson, *The Political Context of Sociology* (Princeton, N.J.: Princeton Univ. Press, 1961); Erich Fromm, *The Sane Society* (New York: Holt, 1955).

occurrence of the outcomes he seeks). Interestingly enough, in Rotter's theory we find an important corollary to powerlessness–namely, the idea of "internal" vs. "external" control of reinforcements. This distinction points to differences (among persons or situations) in the degree to which success or failure is attributable to external factors (e.g. luck, chance, or powerful others), as against success or failure that is seen as the outcome of one's personal skills or characteristics.

Rotter and his co-workers have argued that the paradigm employed in most studies of animal and human learning has unwittingly been one that stresses "external" control (e.g., the subject's success is readily attributable to experimenter control). Social learning theory would predict, however, that when the individual's expectancies for internal control are made relevant, the learning patterns will differ markedly. A number of recent studies have shown that this is indeed the case. In these studies, the same task performed under varied instructions (designed to produce "internal" and "external" orientations), and different tasks designed to simulate "skill" vs. "luck" conditions, have yielded striking differences in learning and extinction patterns. What is most important for present purposes, these studies suggest that the individual learns less from his experience in the situation that is conceived to be chance-controlled.[4]

It is commonplace for mass theorists similarly to argue that the bureaucratized and isolated individual in contemporary society becomes convinced of his own powerlessness and, as a result, turns his attention away from control-relevant learning; he becomes apathetic and uninformed in political affairs and generally inattentive to knowledge that bears importantly upon his performance. Thus, mass society theory and social learning theory agree in proposing that those who differ in powerlessness should also differ in their learning; for both theories, this proposition occupies a central position in its argument. The logic that ties powerlessness to low knowledge acquisition is one that, as a fundamental generalization in both theories, ought to apply cross-culturally and to a wide range of behavior-relevant information. The present study is one of a series of investigations aimed at examining the alienation problem within this theoretical

[4]See (among others) Julian B. Rotter, Shephard Liverant, and Douglas P. Crowne, " The Growth and Extinction of Expectancies in Chance-Controlled and Skilled Tasks," *Journal of Psychology,* Vol. 52 (1959), pp. 161-177. The idea of powerlessness refers to the individual's attributions regarding causality and the locus of control; hence, it is not only relevant to Rotter's theory, but is prominent in other psychological theorizing–e.g., in Heider's well-known work on "phenomenal causality" or in Thibaut and Kelley's discussion of "fate control"; cf. Fritz Heider, *The Psychology of Interpersonal Relations* (New York: Wiley, 1958); John W. Thibaut and Harold H. Kelley, *The Social Psychology of Groups* (New York: Wiley, 1959).

context. Taken together, these studies are conceived simultaneously as explorations in the logic and limits of mass society theory, and as extensions of the laboratory studies on learning.

Alienation and Knowledge in Sweden

The present Swedish study was conceived as a replication and extension of investigations carried out in the United States—studies which bear upon both the structural sources of powerlessness and its consequences for learning.

One U.S. study was designed to test whether, as predicted, members of a work-based formal organization (a union, business, or professional association) exhibit less powerlessness than nonmembers. Given the prominence of unstabilizing features in the portrait of mass society (e.g. high mobility, increased scale, and specialization), it is not surprising that one of the recurrent themes in the theory concerns the organizational ties that must mediate between the isolated, potentially powerless individual and the centers of decision (e.g., the state and the corporation). This prediction that membership and a sense of mastery are related was borne out in a questionnaire study of some 450 workers in Columbus, Ohio, the high powerlessness of the unorganized workers being sustained when the appropriate controls (for age, income, etc.) were applied. The evidence also suggested that the powerlessness effect was a reasonably specific one, since a generalized measure of disaffection (Srole's anomia scale) did not yield the same differences between the organized and unorganized workers.

A second pair of studies in the United States sought to show that powerlessness (whether structurally generated or not) is related to poor knowledge in control-relevant domains of information. In a hospital setting, it was shown that tuberculosis patients who are high in powerlessness know less about health matters than their (matched) unalienated counterparts. And in a reformatory study, inmates who were relatively high in powerlessness learned less when exposed to parole-relevant information.

These findings clearly bear on the credibility of the alienation theme in mass society theory, but the demonstration remained provisional on at least three counts. There was, of course, the need for comparative data, particularly regarding membership effects (which might well reflect a uniquely American phenomenon). There was, further, the need to bring all three elements of the organization-powerlessness-knowledge sequence into a single study, so that the structural and the learning correlates of powerlessness could be jointly considered. Finally, attention needed to be given to a domain of knowledge that is not so specialized as health or corrections, and one that is regularly implicated in the literature on mass society—namely, politics and international affairs.

The present study was designed to fulfill these needs, and was carried out by interview (in Swedish) with a sample of the male work force in Malmö. This is the third largest city in Sweden, with a population of roughly 240,000 and a concentration on commercial and seaport occupations. A random sample of males between the ages of twenty and seventy-nine years was drawn from the official register maintained by the Swedish authorities. A total of 558 workers were interviewed (and an additional 115 were unobtainable, of which only 37 were refusals, the remainder being persons who were seriously ill, had moved to an unknown address, etc.). The retired workers have been excluded from the analysis.

The interview contained questions on three major variables:

1. Powerlessness: The individual's expectancy for control was measured by means of a forced-choice scale that has been variously called the I-E (internal-external control) or powerlessness scale. The items offer the person a choice between an expression of mastery and of powerlessness, as in the examples which follow:[5]

1. ___ Many times I feel that I have little influence over the things that happen to me.
   ___ I do not believe that chance and luck are very important in my life.
2. ___ Becoming a success is a matter of hard work; luck has little or nothing to do with it.
   ___ Getting a job depends mainly on being in the right place at the right time.

Fifteen items were used, essentially the same questions as those in the U.S. study (concentrating heavily on the political-economic issues of war, inflation, jobs, national prestige, control over pressure groups, etc.).

2. Organization membership: In addition to mere membership in a work organization, evidence was gathered on (a) the respondent's degree of participation in the work organization and (b) his involvement in other-than-work organizations.

3. Political knowledge: A sixteen-item information test was prepared and pre-tested, dealing with both Swedish politics and international affairs (e.g., "Sweden's foreign minister at the present time is Osten Unden"; "Switzerland is a member of the European Economic Community"). The respondent was instructed not to guess, and three alternatives were provided: true, false, don't

[5]This test is largely the work of the late Professor Shephard Liverant and his colleagues (formerly at Ohio State University), Julian B. Rotter, and Douglas P. Crowne. The scale has been thoroughly pre-tested, item-analyzed, and compared with criterion measures–much of this material being reported in dissertations completed at Ohio State and in the related work cited here. As noted in these works, the reliabilities have been generally satisfactory: for example, in an early version with a sample of college males, the test-retest coefficient, over a one-week interval, was .93; the Guttman reproducibility coefficient in the American community study was .87; and a factor analysis on the Swedish sample yielded a clear general factor for fifteen powerlessness items.

know. The individual's score was the number of correct answers. The Kuder-Richardson reliability estimate was .73 for this knowledge test.

Since the thesis under review holds that organization membership is associated with both powerlessness and knowledge, these data are presented together in Table 1. The data are presented independently for the manual and nonmanual workers, classified into three groups: (1) unorganized (i.e., not a member of a work organization); (2) organization member (but never an official); and (3) officials (those who are members of a work organization and hold or have held office in it). The main interest is in the comparison between the members and the unorganized, the officials having been separated because they represent a group whose exposure to mastery experience in the organization makes them distinctive.

Table 1. Mean Scores (and Standard Deviations) on Powerlessness and Political Knowledge, for Organized and Unorganized Workers in Sweden

	Manual Workers			Nonmanual Workers		
	Unorganized (N = 25)	Members (N = 231)	Officers (N = 45)	Unorganized (N = 76)	Members (N = 86)	Officers (N = 18)
Powerlessness	6.08 (3.2)	4.87 (2.8)	4.56* (2.9)	6.01 (3.1)	4.83 (2.5)	4.50* (2.9)
Political knowledge	5.60 (3.4)	6.55 (3.2)	7.27 (2.9)	8.16 (3.7)	9.78 (3.5)	10.44† (3.2)

**Significant at the .05 level (two-tailed test).*
†Significant at the .01 level (two-tailed test).
Note: *The differences among the four triads (e.g., manual workers across three organization categories) were tested through a one-way analysis of variance. The differences in political knowledge among manual workers are significant at the .05 level using a one-tailed t-test (with "members" and "officers" combined).*

Two points are noteworthy in these data. First, in all four of the comparisons across organization categories, the differences are consistently and significantly as predicted: high powerlessness and low political knowledge are found among the unorganized workers. Second, in all four comparisons there is a relatively small and predictable difference between officials and members.

These results are clearly congruent with the learning and mass society thesis to which they are addressed, but we need to establish the controls and explore the details that can make the demonstration both more firm and more illuminating. The most crucial control, since we are dealing with knowledge as a major variable, is education. As in the American results, neither education nor the other standard controls eliminate these trends in the Swedish data.

This can be shown in several ways, but two forms of control will illustrate the point. First, the partial *r's* were computed between alienation and political knowledge, with various background variables controlled, and these show no change resulting from the partialing process. For example, the zero-order *r's* between powerlessness and knowledge were −.21 for the manual workers ($N = 302$) and −.15 for the nonmanuals ($N = 182$), both *r's* being significant beyond the .01 level, and the respective partials with education controlled were −.21 and −.12. The same pattern holds with income, occupational prestige, age, and mobility controlled. Second, Table 2 retains the distinction between members and nonmembers, and shows their alienation and knowledge scores with education controlled. Although the *N*'s in this breakdown become rather small and disproportionate, the data show a reasonable consistency. All four of the political knowledge comparisons go as predicted; and three of the four powerlessness comparisons also show substantial differences in the predicted direction. In the group that has comparable *N*'s for the unorganized and organized (low education, nonmanuals), the powerlessness difference (6.39 vs. 4.57) is significant at the .01 level ($t = 3.31$; two-tailed test), and the knowledge difference approximates significance using a one-tailed test ($t = 1.53$). The import of Table 2 is that the alienation and knowledge relationship, both in itself and as it bears on organization membership, is not an artifact of educational differences.

Table 2. Mean Scores on Powerlessness and Political Knowledge, with Education Controlled, for Organized and Unorganized Workers in Sweden

	Manual Workers		Nonmanual Workers	
	Unorganized	Organized	Unorganized	Organized
Low education:				
Powerlessness	5.86	4.89	6.39	4.57
Knowledge	5.52	6.43	7.50	8.51
	($N = 21$)	($N = 236$)	($N = 56$)	($N = 53$)
High education:				
Powerlessness	8.25	4.13	4.82	4.96
Knowledge	6.25	8.40	9.73	11.26
	($N = 5$)	($N = 40$)	($N = 22$)	($N = 50$)

Note: *The organized category includes those who were "members and officers." The education distribution was dichotomized at the median for each work group.*

We have seen that those who have been officers in a work organization are lowest in powerlessness and highest in political knowledge. The implication (both in these data and in the theory) is that involvement in the life of the organization (as against mere formal membership) produces low alienation and greater information. That implication can be explored without invoking the special circumstances associated with office holding by focusing upon organization members only (ignoring both the nonmembers and the officials) and comparing the more engaged and less engaged members. Though one would not necessarily expect a close tie between degree of participation and level of alienation (or knowledge), it is reasonable to suppose that, on the whole, the more involved members will show less alienation (and perhaps greater political knowledge as well).

Three indicators of involvement in the organization were obtained: (1) frequency of attendance at meetings (scored on a four-point scale ranging from "never attend" to "attend frequently and have been to a meeting within the past year"); (2) the importance of the organization to the respondent (rated by him on a three-point scale); and (3) the perceived influence that members have on organizational affairs (again using a three-point scale). These three indices are rather different and were not scalable; hence they have not been combined into a single measure of involvement. Their association with alienation and political knowledge is presented in Table 3. These data are consistent with the previous comparison of the organized and unorganized workers. There is a modest but consistently negative relation between involvement in the organization and powerlessness; and, for the manual workers, involvement and political knowledge go together as well.

Table 3. Correlation of Three Indices of Organizational Involvement with Powerlessness and Political Knowledge, for Manual and Nonmanual Workers in Sweden

	Manual Workers (*N* = 231)		Nonmanual Workers (*N* = 86)	
Involvement Index	Powerlessness	Knowledge	Powerlessness	Knowledge
Attendance at meetings	−.17*	.17*	−.10	.01
Importance of membership	−.11	.05	−.15	.00
Perceived member influence	−.12	.16*	−.20*	.01

*Significant at the .05 level of confidence.

Note: *Those who were not organization members and those who were "members and officers" were excluded from these calculations.*

The interview was also designed to generate evidence bearing on the process that is assumed to be producing these results—i.e. to test the assumption that those who are high in powerlessness are less *interested* in the control-relevant material that is available for learning. We predicted that expressed political interest and actual political knowledge would be positively correlated, and that high powerlessness would go with low interest. Thus, interest is seen as a determinant of knowledge, and it is presumed that the poor knowledge among the alienated is mediated by their low interest in political information.

The respondents were asked (at the outset of the interview) to indicate how interested they were in various kinds of activities, including the two activities that are especially pertinent here, discussion of politics and keeping up with international affairs. The data in Table 4 show that those who express greater interest do, in fact, know more about politics. What is more important, those who are high in powerlessness are less interested in political activities; and this, taken together with their low knowledge, is consistent with the theoretical argument at stake: those who are low in expectancy for control are not interested in and do not absorb control-relevant learning.

Table 4. Correlation of Expressed Interest in Discussion of Politics and in International Affairs with Powerlessness and Political Knowledge, for Manual and Nonmanual Workers in Sweden

	Manual Workers (*N* = 302)		Nonmanual Workers (*N* = 182)	
Indication of Interest	Powerlessness	Knowledge	Powerlessness	Knowledge
Discussion of politics	−.22*	.43*	−.15†	.34*
Keeping up with international affairs	−.22*	.52*	−.13	.43*

*Significant at or beyond the .01 level of confidence.
†Significant at the .05 level of confidence.

Can this argument regarding interest be traced back to the structural variable of organization? The answer is that it can, for Table 5 shows the expected differences in interest between the unorganized and organized workers. The latter express significantly greater interest in political affairs. Furthermore, the data do not reflect a *generalized* withdrawal of interest on the part of the alienated workers. When relatively less control-relevant affairs are being rated (e.g. the worker's interest in local events or in discussing his work), the organizational differences are considerably muted. The data of Table 5 make a reasonable case for the view that these differences in interest are not simple differences in rating habits between the organized and unorganized workers, or generalized differences in their readiness to be engaged or express interest. The fact of organization makes no consistent difference in the interest expressed in non-political matters. These findings support the view that we are not describing

Table 5. Mean Level of Expressed Interest in Politically Relevant Events and in Nonpolitical Events, for Organized and Unorganized Workers in Sweden

	Manual Workers			Nonmanual Workers		
Event	Unor-ganized *(N = 25)*	Organized *(N = 276)*	Mean Difference	Unor-ganized *(N = 76)*	Organized *(N = 103)*	Mean Difference
Political:						
Discussion of politics	1.92	2.43	+.51*	2.19	2.63	+.44*
International affairs	2.58	2.83	+.25	3.12	3.41	+.29
Nonpolitical:						
Discuss my work	3.23	3.12	−.11	3.05	3.20	+.15
Read about local events	3.25	3.29	+.04	3.26	3.51	+.25

**Mean differences (between organized and unorganized) significant at the .05 level of confidence. A positive sign indicates higher interest on the part of the organized workers.*

simply a generalized disaffection or disengagement that is characteristic of those who are unorganized and alienated, but rather a more specific powerlessness phenomenon that is theoretically clear and empirically traceable.

The learning theory outlined earlier, however, makes a distinction between expectancy and value; thus far, we have been emphasizing the expectancy side, since the idea of alienation (or powerlessness) is here defined in terms of expectancies for control. The question is: Can attention to the variable of "reward value" illuminate matters further? The earlier reformatory study suggested that it could. In that case, both control-relevant knowledge (concerning parole matters) and noncontrol knowledge (descriptive information about the reformatory) were made available for learning, with the prediction that the more alienated inmates would show differential learning of the control-relevant information (and no differences in learning of the reformatory-centered material). This prediction was borne out, but again this is a difference between those who vary in their *expectancies* for control.

The inmates were also classified into two groups differing in their relative *valuation* of the events at stake—i.e. in their apparent dedication to the conventional norms of the prison authorities and the parole apparatus. A rough behavioral index of commitment to conventional values was obtained from the reformatory records concerning "merit earnings" (money and/or time "points" earned by the inmate's demonstration of his dedication to rehabilitation goals). The essential prediction was that the alienation-knowledge relationship would be greater among those who place high value on the conventional goals: i.e., motivation to learn was seen as being dependent not only upon *expectancies* for control of one's outcomes, but also upon the *value* one places upon the outcomes to which the learning is relevant. Thus, one's expectancies for control ought to be less critical for learning where the material to be learned is not considered important from the outset. The data conformed to the predicted pattern: among the conventional inmates, the correlation between alienation and learning of parole information was –.40; while among the unconventional inmates (i.e. those who had no merit earnings, and hence were presumably uncommitted to conventional norms and rehabilitation goals), an *r* of –.16 was obtained.

Although, in the Swedish case, we did not have a comparable behavioral index of value differences, a question bearing on such differences was included in the interview. The respondent was asked whether he agreed or disagreed (on a five-point Likert scale) with the statement: "Actually, the basic decisions on political and social questions should be made by the specialists and experts." The question was especially designed for the Swedish situation, for it is a society that makes rather heavy use of experts in its conduct of government (e.g. considerable weight is assigned to expert-based committee reports on social problems). Respondents who opt for specialist control are expressing, we presume, a relatively low valuation of personal control in political affairs as compared with those who reject the experts as the basic decision makers. As expected, "expert orientation" is high in the Swedish sample: 56 per cent agreed with the statement, and there was no difference between manuals and nonmanuals in this respect. Interestingly enough, in view of the independence postulated in Rotter's social learning theory, this index of "value on control" does not correlate highly with the index of "expectancy for control" (powerlessness), the *r* being .19 for the total sample ($N = 488$), although the values and the expectancies involved are both socio-political in nature.

Our interest in this (admittedly crude) value index is a dual one. First, it allows us to examine the relation between alienation and knowledge for those who value personal control as against those who are more willing to "let the experts decide." Among the latter, one might expect (as in the reformatory case) to find that the powerlessness-knowledge relationship is attenuated–i.e., expectancy for control may be less significant as a determinant of knowledge among those who reject the importance of control. Second, we are interested in knowing whether the *value* commitment about control tells as much, or more, about knowledge acquisition as does the individual's *expectancy* for control; and whether the distinction between expectancy and value bears meaningfully on the fact of organizational membership.

These interests are reflected in Tables 6 and 7. Table 6 shows the correlations between alienation and political knowledge for those who are "expert-oriented"

Table 6. Correlations between Powerlessness and Political Knowledge among Workers Who Are Expert-Oriented and Those Not Expert-Oriented, for Manual and Nonmanual Workers in Sweden

	Manual Workers	Nonmanual Workers
Expert-oriented	−.16* *(N = 167)*	−.11 *(N = 107)*
Not expert-oriented	−.28† *(N = 135)*	−.09 *(N = 75)*

*Significant at the .05 level of confidence.
†Significant at the .01 level of confidence.
Note: *The "expert-oriented" were those who either "strongly agreed" or "agreed" with the statement that basic decisions should be made by experts, in contrast to those who were undecided or disagreed.*

Table 7. Correlation, and Mean-Scores, of Political Knowledge with Powerlessness (Expectancy) and Expert Orientation (Value), for Organized and Unorganized Workers in Sweden

	Manual		Nonmanual	
Measure	Unorganized *(N = 25)*	Organized *(N = 276)*	Unorganized *(N = 76)*	Organized *(N = 103)*
Correlations:				
Powerlessness-knowledge	−.11	−.22*	−.13	−.07
Expert orientation - knowledge	−.14	−.07	−.07	−.37*
Mean scores:				
Powerlessness	6.08	4.82*	6.01	4.77*
Expert orientation	3.50	3.58	3.98	3.39*

*Correlation, or mean difference, significant at the .01 level.
Note: *The "organized" category includes those who were "members and officers."*

and those who are not. The difference in the degree of correlation is not significant for either the manual workers or the nonmanuals; although for the manuals the correlation is higher, as it should be, among the "not expert-oriented" (−.28). Whether a more behavioral index of "value on control" would produce sharper differences, as in the reformatory study, remains an open question.

Does the expectancy measure (powerlessness) tell more about political awareness than the value index? The answer, provided in Table 7, appears to be that it depends upon whether one is speaking of the manual workers or the nonmanuals. For organized nonmanuals, it is the value placed on expert control that correlates most highly with information (–.37), with the expert-oriented being low in political knowledge, while among the organized manuals it is the expectancy measure that is more closely related to knowledge (–.22). The mean scores presented in Table 7 seem generally to conform to this pattern: for the manuals, there are clear differences in powerlessness between the organized and unorganized, but expert orientations do not differ, while among the nonmanual workers, there is a significant difference which places the unorganized nonmanuals relatively high in their reliance on experts. It would seem, although these data cannot demonstrate the point, that organization can be functionally important for knowledge by affecting one's *expectations* for control or one's commitment to the *value* of control; and the latter effect seems to occur more clearly among the nonmanual workers. The implication, in any event, is that organization "works differently" for the two groups.[6]

Conclusion

These results in a Swedish setting successfully repeat and extend the findings in the United States. They repeat the observation that the individual's sense of powerlessness is bound up with his organizational membership, and they extend that observation by showing that political awareness is related to alienation and membership as well. These results must be taken in the context of the theoretical view proposed at the outset of the present paper. For, if that theory is correct, the connection between organization and membership should hold cross-culturally, and the connection between powerlessness and learning should hold in a variety of institutional contexts with a variety of control-relevant information. The present evidence from Sweden, about politics rather than health information or parole knowledge, conforms to this theoretical requirement.

Furthermore, it should be possible to show, as survey procedures cannot, that we are in fact dealing with *learning* that is dependent in some important degree upon the individual's established expectancy for control.[7] In the reformatory study, the design was calculated to demonstrate that it is "learning" that is involved, not the reverse (for example, a sense of powerlessness generated

[6]The provisional character of the value index employed here does not justify extensive documentation. It may be noted that a series of further analyses, not presented here, produced data that generally conform with the evidence and the interpretation given. For example, a series of second-order partial correlations indicate that, among the manual workers, powerlessness is significantly related to knowledge when expert orientation and education are controlled ($r = -.20$), while among the nonmanuals it is the expert-orientation index that maintains its predictive power (when powerlessness and education are controlled ($r = -.22$).

[7]Obviously, the implication that organization membership *leads* to high powerlessness cannot be demonstrated with the present data. For an effort to examine this causal imputation in the structure-alienation-behavior model of mass society, see Neal and Seeman, *op. cit.*

by the lack of knowledge), and that this learning effect of alienation is relatively specific. The alienated reformatory inmates did *not* differ on all kinds of learning, but most particularly differed in their unresponsiveness to knowledge that implied control over one's life outcomes (in this case, the manageable features of parole). Where nonparole (and merely descriptive, noncontrol) reformatory information was involved, no differences in learning between alienation groups were found.

Taken together, these studies make a reasonably strong case for the conclusion that the construct that has been variously called powerlessness, alienation, or expectancy for control is important in the learning process and is related to organization membership. The demonstration gains significance because the construct involved is a central term in both social learning and mass society theory. Thus, these studies constitute, in effect, an essay in mutuality of interest. They bear upon the credibility of the alienation thesis that features so prominently in mass society theory; at the same time, they are extensions from social learning theory, establishing the fact that the learning principle at stake (emphasizing the importance of perceived "internal control" for learning) is operative not only in the laboratory or with simulated tasks, but among people who are exposed to a variety of control-relevant information that bears upon their everyday life. To put it briefly, these studies show how the two seemingly unrelated theories actually involve related propositions about knowledge processes.

Furthermore, as one might expect in a theoretically based approach, the demonstration reveals both generality of application and specificity of prediction. The principles involved, for example, are shown to hold cross-culturally and to hold across varied learning situations (health, politics, and reformatory knowledge). Yet we are not, apparently, making predictions about *any* knowledge or *any* interest, or *any* disaffection—as the negative evidence on anomia, on non-parole learning, and on nonpolitical interest in the Swedish case attest.

Perhaps the most significant feature of the demonstration presented here lies not in what it accomplishes, but in what it promises. These studies are essentially relatively controlled tests of propositions that can be found in various forms, and in various degrees of explicitness, in the sociological literature describing the mass society. The tie between alienation and knowledge (and, more generally, the structure-alienation-behavior model) is found in a vast literature concerned with contemporary public response: mass movements, ethnic hostility, mass communication, and the like. This literature on alienation engages a powerful array of humanistic values—not only powerlessness and mastery, but also (when one includes the alternative meanings of alienation) normlessness and trust, meaninglessness and understanding, self-estrangement and integrity. The promise is that our assertions regarding these important matters can be made amenable to rigorous test, and that in the process we will discover the value and the means of integrating our disparate social psychologies—symbolically speaking, the social psychology of the laboratory and of institutional studies; the social psychology of learning theory and of mass society.

Political Attitudes and the Local Community

Robert D. Putnam

Politicians and political scientists alike have long recognized the impact of the local political environment on the attitudes and behavior of community residents. V.O. Key demonstrated in a variety of contexts the striking persistence of distinctive community political traditions. The extensive discussion of the "suburban conversion" hypothesis has turned in part on the question of the influence of the local community on partisan attitudes. A number of studies of voting behavior have shown that majority views in a community have a disproportionate advantage in gaining and holding adherents. There is, in short, good reason to suspect that the local community has a significant influence on social attitudes and political behavior. Why is this so? How does the Republican "atmosphere" in Elmira affect the votes of individual Elmirans? How are community political traditions maintained through decades of changing community composition? Why does the minority party in a community fail to mobilize many of the voters who are predisposed toward it? What explanation of these sorts of community influence seems most adequate?—this is the question to be examined in this paper.[1]

[1]This paper was originally prepared for a seminar led by Professor Robert E. Lane. The data used are from the 1952 and 1960 national electoral surveys conducted by the Survey Research Center of the University of Michigan and made available through the Inter-University Consortium for Political Research. I want to thank Professor Lane, Professor Hayward Alker, Jr., the staff of ICPR, and Rosemary Putnam for their help in the preparation of this report. Naturally, I alone am responsible for any remaining errors.

Robert D. Putnam, "Political Attitudes and the Local Community," American Political Science Review, *Vol. 60 (1966). Reprinted with permission.*

Alternative Explanations

There are at least three important theoretical alternatives. The first and simplest proposal rests on two empirical assumptions. Let us assume that the intensity of each party's campaign activities in any community is a function of that party's electoral strength in that community. Let us asume, that is, that the majority party is apt to campaign more actively. Let us also assume that these campaign activities have a significant influence on individual voting decisions. On these assumptions, we would expect the majority party in a given area to gain disproportionately from uncommitted voters, as a result of that party's greater organizational activity. In other words, the influence of the community majority on residents' attitudes would operate through the activity of the majority party organization. I shall term this the "party activity" theory of community influence.

Angus Campbell has proposed a second explanation of community influence, in terms of motivated conformity to perceived community norms. Using the model for group influence developed in *The American Voter,* Campbell indicates two crucial factors in the community influence process: "community identification" and (perceived) community standards. Just as trade union influence depends on the closeness of the member's attachment to the union (his "identification" with the union) and on the clarity and acceptability of union norms on political issues, so, Campbell argues, community influence depends on identification with the local community and on the clarity and acceptability of community political standards. This is an attractively simple explanatory model, drawing substantially on reference-group theory. Motivated conformity to perceived community norms is, then, a second possible explanation of community influence.

A final explanation, which I shall call the "social interaction" theory, suggests that community influence is mediated primarily through the numerous personal contacts among members of a community. Such social interaction within the community would, on the whole, tend to support political attitudes commonly held by community members, and to undermine "deviant" views. The extensive literature on personal influence spells out in greater detail the social and psychological processes assumed by this theory. Whereas Campbell's theory emphasizes a resident's psychological attachment to his community, the social interaction theory emphasizes the resident's social involvement in the community. Obviously, we would expect these two factors—psychological attachment and social involvement—to be related, but they are distinct, both logically and (it will turn out) empirically. Campbell's theory asserts that the "community" itself is a significant reference group for many voters, whereas the social interaction theory implies that voters can be influenced by their community environment even if they are not motivated to conform to community norms, indeed, even if they are unaware that such norms exist. All that is necessary according to this latter theory is that the voters be involved in social interaction within the community, and that they be subject to personal influence in these daily, face-to-face contacts.

Each of these three theories has considerable plausibility. The present study will tentatively assess the adequacy of each as an explanation of the relationship between the community political environment and the attitudes and behavior of members of the community.

Research Design

As a crude indicator of one complex set of political attitudes presumably subject to community influence, I shall here use the reported presidential vote of the non-Southern respondents in the Survey Research Center's 1952 national survey.[2] Obviously, "community environment" could be defined at any number of levels, ranging from the state down to the precinct. It seems reasonable to expect more noticeable effects of community influence, the more localized the operational definition of "community environment." In this study exigencies of the data available force us to use the county as our operational "community" unit. This definition is consistent with previous work on this problem, such as that by Key, by Miller, and by Campbell and his associates. In defining the county as the environmental unit, I am not assuming that it is itself a "community" in the sociological sense. Like these other investigators, I assume that for a national sample of voters the partisan complexion of their counties will be a relatively good indicator of the partisan complexion of their more immediate community environment.

The political complexion of a given county is indicated by the Democratic percentage of the two-party vote for President in 1952.[3] The 62 counties represented are then classified into four levels of partisan dominance, from most Republican (18%-29% Democratic) to most Democratic (50%-62% Democratic). Note that this is an ordinal continuum of relative partisan dominance, so that in 1952 the "moderately Democratic" counties were in fact only 40%-49% Democratic. The rationale for using this relative ordinal continuum is given by Miller.

Before going into a detailed discussion of the findings, I want to illustrate the mode of analysis to be used. Table 1a displays for the entire sample the simple relationship between community political environment and reported

[2]Non-voters have been excluded from the entire analysis, as their inclusion would have complicated it immensely. Southern respondents have been excluded, since preliminary analysis of data from Southern respondents gave some reason to doubt that the nature of the community influence process is quite the same in that region as in the rest of the country. The entire study has, wherever possible, been replication, except those involving primary and secondary group membership. It was impossible to replicate these latter findings, since the 1960 survey did not include the relevant questions.

[3]Data from *America Votes,* ed. Richard M. Scammon (New York: Macmillan, 1956), Vol. 1.

vote of respondent. Obviously, this table reveals merely a fairly close relationship between the partisan proportions characteristic of certain counties and the partisan proportions characteristic of samples drawn from those counties. Within the limits of sampling error, we must (logically "must") expect the positive association shown here. Beside the table is shown Kendall's *tau c* characterizing the correlation between the two variables.[4] Roughly speaking, this statistic can be interpreted as a measure of the gradient in the percentage of Democratic votes among *respondents* as we move from strongly Republican to strongly Democratic *counties,* here the gradient 28%–32%–44%–49%.

Table 1b shows this same environment-vote relationship separately for two sub-groups of the total sample, the first sub-table for respondents who rank high on an index of social integration, the second, for respondents who rank low on this index. (This index of "social integration" is based on responses to questions dealing with home-ownership, intent to remain in the local community, and membership in various secondary associations. The index is used merely for illustrative purposes here; each of its components will be examined individually later in the paper.) Consider the *relative* sizes of the *taus* for the two sub-tables. Clearly, the relationship between individual vote and county environment is much stronger for well-integrated respondents than for their poorly-integrated counterparts, for the *tau* for respondents "high" on this index is .25, while the *tau* for respondents "low" on the index is .07. Stated somewhat differently, the partisan distribution of the votes of poorly-integrated respondents is much less sensitive to differences in the community political environment than is the comparable distribution for well-integrated respondents. It is also true that respondents with low social integration are in general more likely to vote Democratic than are respondents with high social integration, but this fact does not vitiate the crucial observation that respondents with high social integration are apparently more susceptible to community influence than are respondents with low social integration.[5]

The present analysis will focus primarily on comparisons of the strengths of the environment-vote relationship (as measured by *tau c*) in various categories of respondents. There is no straight-forward test for the statistical significance of

[4]Kendall's *tau c* is a widely used measure of the correlation between two ordinal-scale variables. It ranges between 0 (which indicates no correlation at all) and ± 1.0 (which indicates perfect correlation), and thus is very roughly (*not* mathematically) equivalent to the more familiar Pearsonian *r*, which is used in connection with ratio-scale variables. See Hubert M. Blalock, *Social Statistics* (New York: McGraw-Hill, 1960), pp. 317-324; and Maurice G. Kendall, *Rank Correlation Methods* (London: C. Griffin, 1955), Chs. 1 and 3.

[5]Note that a high positive *tau* for a given table does not mean that respondents represented in that table are concentrated in extreme one party areas; it means that the direction of their vote is highly dependent on their political enviroment. Hence, it is illegitimate to argue that this evidence of community influence is artifactual on the grounds that integrated respondents tend to be Republican and that most counties were Republican in 1952.

Table 1. Community Influence and "Social Integration"

	County Environment, in Terms of Democratic % of Two-Party Vote for President, 1952				Kendall's *tau c*
	18%–29%	30%–39%	40%–49%	50%–62%	
Table 1a:					
Total sample	28%* (134)	32% (300)	44% (280)	49% (252)	.18 (N = 966)
Table 1b:					
R's "high" on "social integration" index	18% (33)	28% (78)	41% (63)	50% (64)	.25 (N = 238)
R's "low" on "social integration" index	46% (13)	52% (25)	48% (27)	58% (26)	.07 (N = 91)

**Entries are percentage Democratic votes among respondents in the indicated category. Below each percentage is given the base on which it has been calculated, i.e., the total number of respondents in the indicated category.*

differences between *taus*. Fortunately, however, most of the differences which will concern us are quite clear-cut and the patterns of findings are consistent. In Table 1b, for example, it seems fairly clear that there is an important difference with respect to sensitivity to the community political environment between respondents of low social integration and those of high integration.

The "Party Activity" Theory

The simplest explanation of the tendency for the majority party in a community to pick up more than its "fair share" of the uncommitted votes refers to the differential strengths of the party organizations. All our respondents were asked whether or not they had been contacted by party workers during the campaign. In our analysis we shall use the extent of this party contact as our indicator of party organizational strength. (The overall level of such personal contact by the parties is rather low. Only about 14% of all respondents reported being contacted by a representative of either party.) The first and crucial assumption of the "party activity" explanation of community influence is that campaign activity is disproportionately undertaken by the majority party in each area. Table 2 shows that there is at the county level virtually no such disproportionate concentration of party activity. The correlation between party electoral strength and the extent of personal contact by the party organizations is virtually nil. Thus, this first, crucial assumption of the "party activity" theory is disconfirmed.

There is further evidence which casts doubt on this theory. If community influence depends on party activity, then those respondents who have been personally contacted by some party representative will show greater sensitivity to the community political environment than those who have not. Table 3 shows,

Table 2. Incidence of Party Organizational Contact as Related to County Environment

	County Environment, in Terms of Democratic % of Two-Party Vote for President, 1952			
	18%–29%	30%–39%	40%–49%	50%–62%
Number of R's contacted by Democrats	5	17	24	35
Number of R's contacted by Republicans	2	23	33	33
Total contacts	7	40	57	68

Kendall's *tau c* for this relationship = .04

Table 3. Community Influence and Party Contact

	County Environment, in Terms of Democratic % of Two-Party Vote for President, 1952				Kendall's *tau c*
	18%–29%	30%–39%	40%–49%	50%–62%	
R's contacted by one or both parties	43%* (7)	38% (39)	30% (46)	49% (53)	.10 (N = 145)
R's contacted by neither party	28% (127)	31% (260)	47% (234)	49% (197)	.19 (N = 818)

**Entries are percentage Democratic votes among respondents in the indicated category. Below each percentage is given the base on which it has been calculated, i.e., the total number of respondents in the indicated category.*

however, that, if anything, the opposite relationship obtains. While we cannot explain this anomalous finding without further information about the types of people reached by party organizations, it is clear that the "party activity" theory of community influence is inadequate.

The "Community Identification" Theory

According to Campbell's theory of community influence, one crucial variable in the influence process is "community identification"—the sense of attachment and commitment to the local community. Since we have no direct and unambiguous measures of this variable in the data available, we must use a variety of indirect indicators to test the theory. Gresham Sykes in an investigation of the "differential distribution of community knowledge" found that several social attributes were closely associated with knowledge about local politics and government. Homeowners, parents with children in local schools, and long-time local residents were all, according to Sykes, especially apt to be oriented toward the local community, and hence to be more knowledgeable about community affairs.[6] It is reasonable to suppose that such individuals would have greater "community identification" in Campbell's sense, and thus, if his theory is correct, that they would be more susceptible to community influence.

Sykes found a positive relationship between home-ownership and "localism." One might expect homeowners to tend to be more strongly identified with the local community than non-owners, and, according to Campbell's theory, to be relatively more sensitive to the community political environment. Surprisingly, however, our data in Table 4a suggest a contrary finding: homeowners are, if anything, less sensitive to the political community than non-owners, though the difference between *taus* of .13 and .21 is probably not significant. Parents of school-children are also, according to Sykes, more apt to be "locals." If so, however, this "localism" does not result in a greater susceptibility to community influence, as is shown in Table 4b. Finally, if community identification is to some extent a function of length of residence, and if community influence depends significantly on community identification, then we would expect respondents who have lived in their present community for some time to be much more sensitive to this political environment than relative newcomers would be. The slight difference between *taus* of .12 for newcomers and .18 for long-time residents, shown in Table 4c, though in the predicted direction, indicates a very weak relationship at best.[7]

Another item which seems very closely related to "community identification" tapped the respondent's feelings of having "settled down to stay" in his community. Individuals who feel they have "settled down to stay" should also feel greater community identification than those who are not so sure they intend to remain in the community. Table 4d shows the relationship of this item to sensitivity to the community political environment. Once again, we find our expectations, based on Campbell's theory, disconfirmed. There is, if anything, a closer relationship between vote and environment among potential migrants than among those settled down to stay, though again this difference between *taus* of .15 and .23 is probably not significant.

It might be thought that emotional involvement in the outcome of local elections would indicate some degree of "community identification." Table 4e shows that there is a slight relationship in the expected direction between concern about local elections and sensitivity to the political environment. There are,

[6]Gresham Sykes, "The Differential Distribution of Community Knowledge," in Paul K. Hatt and Albert J. Reiss, Jr., *Cities and Society* (New York: Free Press, 1957), pp. 711-721. Sykes also found location of work in the local community to be an indicator of "localism," but we have no information on this for our respondents.

[7]Even clear positive results would be ambiguous since length of residence is also related to membership in community organizations, and, as we shall find later, such membership is clearly linked to community influence.

Table 4. Community Influence and "Community Identification"

	County Environment, in Terms of Democratic % of Two-Party Vote for President, 1952				Kendall's *tau c*
	18%–29%	30%–39%	40%–49%	50%–62%	
Table 4a:					
Homeowners	28%* (90)	29% (208)	46% (181)	38% (113)	.13 (N = 592)
Non-homeowners	30% (44)	40% (92)	41% (98)	58% (138)	.21 (N = 372)
Table 4b:					
Parents of school-children	27% (52)	40% (126)	55% (95)	48% (86)	.16 (N = 359)
Not parents of school-children	29% (82)	26% (171)	39% (184)	50% (165)	.20 (N = 602)
Table 4c:					
Resident of county five years or more	30% (118)	30% (263)	46% (248)	49% (223)	.18 (N = 852)
Resident of county less than five years	12% (16)	50% (34)	29% (31)	48% (27)	.12 (N = 108)
Table 4d:					
R "sure" he intends to stay in community	28% (87)	34% (232)	44% (216)	47% (189)	.15 (N = 724)
R *not* "sure" he intends to stay in community	32% (38)	28% (58)	47% (57)	55% (53)	.23 (N = 206)
Table 4e:					
R "cares" about local elections	28% (79)	28% (200)	45% (178)	48% (152)	.19 (N = 609)
R doesn't "care" about local elections	30% (50)	44% (87)	44% (89)	48% (85)	.11 (N = 311)
Table 4f:					
R "cares" about national elections	27% (86)	27% (227)	40% (193)	50% (188)	.21 (N = 694)
R doesn't "care" about national elections	30% (46)	51% (65)	54% (81)	44% (59)	.08 (N = 251)
Table 4g:					
R followed politics closely in press	21% (48)	27% (146)	36% (138)	42% (116)	.16 (N = 448)
R didn't follow politics closely in press	33% (86)	38% (152)	53% (142)	55% (135)	.20 (N = 515)

**Entries are percentage Democratic votes among respondents in the indicated category. Below each percentage is given the base on which it has been calculated, i.e., the total number of respondents in the indicated category.*

however, two problems in the interpretation of this finding. In the first place, it might be argued that the finding is spurious, because those voting with the majority in a community would naturally express more interest in local politics. A more basic problem in interpretation is raised by Table 4f, which shows that concern about national elections is more strongly related to community influence than is concern about local elections. This suggests that what is relevant to community influence is not concern about local elections, but rather concern about elections in general.[8]

At best, then, the relationship between community influence and various indicators of community identification is uncertain. Though each of these indicators can be plausibly linked to community identification, none segregates a group of respondents who are clearly and unambiguously more sensitive to the community political environment than are other respondents.

The second independent variable of Campbell's theory of community influence is perception of local political standards. If the community influence process involves awareness of community norms, then one might expect community influence to be related to exposure to local news media, since on the whole those individuals more highly exposed to the local media should be more aware of community politics and partisan norms. Table 4g shows, however, that there is no significant difference in the relative sensitivity of respondents who followed politics closely in the local newspapers and those who did not. We must conclude that the community influence process does not involve exposure to community standards, at least via the press.

We have been able to find no evidence relating community influence to either of the two explanatory variables isolated by Campbell. To be sure, none of the items we have examined taps *directly* the suggested dimensions—community identification and perception of community norms—and therefore, no single item would in itself be convincing evidence. On the other hand, the fact that none of these items is closely related to community influence does cast some doubt on the theory. We cannot reject it as confidently as we rejected the "party activity" theory, but we are forced to enter a verdict of "not proven."

The "Social Interaction" Theory

Thus far we have examined a variety of evidence tending to show that neither the "party activity" theory nor Campbell's "community identification" theory

[8]Another possible indicator of community identification was respondents' agreement or disagreement with the statement that "local elections are often unimportant." In the 1952 survey the *tau* for those respondents who disagreed (hypothetically, the "locals") was .18 (N = 833) and for those who agreed was .13 (N = 127). In the 1960 survey the comparable figures were .21 (N = 932) and .36 (N = 72). In other words, this item, too, fails to support the hypothesis linking community identification and community influence.

is an adequate explanation of the community influence process. The social interaction theory emphasizes the individual's social contacts as important media for the transmission of community influence. Let us now consider the relationships between susceptibility to community influence and various secondary and primary group memberships.

If the social interaction theory of community influence is correct, we would expect sensitivity to the community environment to be related to involvement in community associations, since such involvement presumably increases the respondent's interaction with other members of the community. (Our analysis of these membership effects is somewhat hampered by the fact that only a subsample of the national sample was queried about organizational involvement, so that N's tend to be low. Fortunately, however, most of the findings are quite distinct.) Consider, first of all, "claimed" membership, both nominal and active. Table 5a shows that among respondents who belong to no clubs or organizations, there is no tendency for vote to be related to the community environment. By comparison, respondents who claim membership in one group show considerable sensitivity to their political environment, and those who claim membership in two or more groups show substantially more sensitivity than single-group members. The differences among these categories are quite striking. Table 5b shows that parallel results obtain when only active membership is considered. Finally, Table 5c combines these results by comparing the relative sensitivity of nonmembers, nominal members, and active members. It appears that while even nominal membership in community associations increases one's susceptibility to community influence to some extent, active membership increases this susceptibility still further.

These results suggest that community influence is to a considerable extent mediated through community organizations. The social interaction theory implies something further about the sorts of groups likely to have this effect. Since, according to this theory, community influence depends on social interaction with other individuals who, on the whole, represent the dominant attitudes in the community, we would expect groups whose self-selection according to social and political attitudes is *greater* to be *less* effective mediators of community influence. Informal groups, for example, such as bridge clubs, are less likely to represent a cross-section of community sentiment than are formal groups, such as PTA's, and thus the informal groups should be less effective mediators of community influence. Tables 5d and 5e present the relevant data, which clearly confirm our theoretical expectations. Active members of informal groups are, at best, only slightly more susceptible to community influence than

Table 5. Community Influence and Membership in Secondary Associations

	County Environment, in Terms of Democratic % of Two-Party Vote for President, 1952				Kendall's *tau c*
	18%–29%	30%–39%	40%–49%	50%–62%	
Table 5a:					
Non-members	54%* (11)	46% (28)	41% (29)	52% (25)	.00 (N = 93)
Members of one association	33% (12)	43% (35)	48% (31)	57% (28)	.16 (N = 106)
Members of two or more associations	9% (22)	18% (40)	40% (30)	47% (36)	.33 (N = 128)
Table 5b:					
Not active members	39% (18)	44% (57)	40% (57)	52% (46)	.07 (N = 178)
Active members of one association	38% (13)	26% (19)	57% (21)	56% (23)	.23 (N = 76)
Active members of two or more associations	0% (13)	12% (24)	33% (12)	45% (20)	.38 (N = 69)
Table 5c:					
Non-members	54% (11)	46% (28)	41% (29)	52% (25)	.00 (N = 93)
Nominal members	14% (7)	41% (29)	39% (28)	52% (21)	.16 (N = 85)
Active members	19% (26)	19% (43)	48% (33)	51% (43)	.32 (N = 145)
Table 5d:					
Active members of informal associations	11% (9)	20% (20)	43% (7)	36% (14)	.22 (N = 50)
Not active members of informal associations	31% (36)	37% (83)	43% (83)	55% (75)	.18 (N = 277)
Table 5e:					
Active members of formal associations	17% (23)	15% (34)	47% (30)	54% (37)	.36 (N = 124)
Not active members of formal associations	36% (22)	42% (66)	42% (60)	50% (52)	.08 (N = 200)

**Entries are percentage Democratic votes among respondents in the indicated category. Below each percentage is given the base on which it has been calculated, i.e., the total number of respondents in the indicated category.*

non-members of such groups. Activity in formal groups, on the other hand, makes a major difference in community sensitivity.[9]

The evidence presented thus far demonstrates the importance of secondary associations in mediating community influence. What about the relationship between primary group contacts and community influence? There are two questions to be considered here. First, what is the effect of the community environment on the complexion of primary groups which are formed within it, and second, what impact, if any, does the community environment have on political attitudes apart from its effect on primary group composition?

Before examining the data on the first question, let us analyze the possible alternatives. Consider the partisan composition of five-member primary groups. On the one hand, there might be no influence of the community environment on the sorts of primary groups which form within it. This would be the case if all potential adherents of minority opinions were "able to" contain their friendships to like-minded community residents. In this case we would expect that, for example, in a community where the ratio of Democrats to Republicans is 1:3, the ratio of Democratic to Republican primary groups would also be 1:3. On the other hand, there might be no such tendency for like to attract like. That is, minority Democrats might draw their friends completely randomly (with respect to political opinions) from the community at large. In this case, we would expect the ratio of Democratic to Republican friendship groups to be 1:40.5. This somewhat surprising figure is simply the ratio of the probability of drawing 4 or 5 Democrats in 5 tries, from a population where there are 3 Republicans for every Democrat, to the probability of drawing 4 or 5 Republicans in 5 tries from the same population.

In fact, our evidence indicates that the partisanship of friendship groups is strongly associated with the partisanship of the county political environment.

[9]It is not surprising, in terms of the social interaction theory as explicated here, that members of labor unions are less, not more, susceptible to community influence than non-members. We would not expect union membership to involve social interaction with anything like a cross-section of community sentiment. For the 1952 survey *tau* for union members was .11 (N = 299) compared to a *tau* of .14 (N = 659) for non-members. The comparable figures for 1960 were .11 (N = 302) and .24 (N = 701). If community influence is to a considerable extent mediated through social interaction, then we might expect that minority groups would be less sensitive to the overall community environment, insofar as they are excluded from extensive interaction with much of the population. In 1952 the *tau* for Protestants was .14 (N = 619), and the *tau* for non-Protestants was .06 (N = 344). In 1952 the *tau* for whites was .16 (N = 930), while the *tau* for non-whites was –.21 [*sic*] (N = 36). These comparisons were confirmed in the replication using the 1960 survey.

Each respondent was asked about the party preferences of his five closest friends. In the most Republican communities (18%-29% Democratic) 57% of all respondents have all or mostly Republican friends, and only 5% have all or mostly Democratic friends. In the most Democratic communities (50%–62% Democratic) the comparable figures are 34% and 32%.[10] Though the existence of the phenomenon is not surprising, its extent perhaps is. Figure 1 compares the obtained ratio of Republican to Democratic friendship groups with two hypothetical ratios, one assuming complete "homophily," that is, restriction of friendships to one's fellow partisans, and the other assuming complete randomness in the selection of friends. This figure shows that while there is some "homophily," nevertheless potential minority voters have a disproportionately difficult time finding social support for their deviant views, especially in communities which are relatively one-sided. Thus, in the most Republican communities the ratio of Republican to Democratic *voters* is 2.5:1, while the ratio of Republican to Democratic *friendship groups* is 13:1.

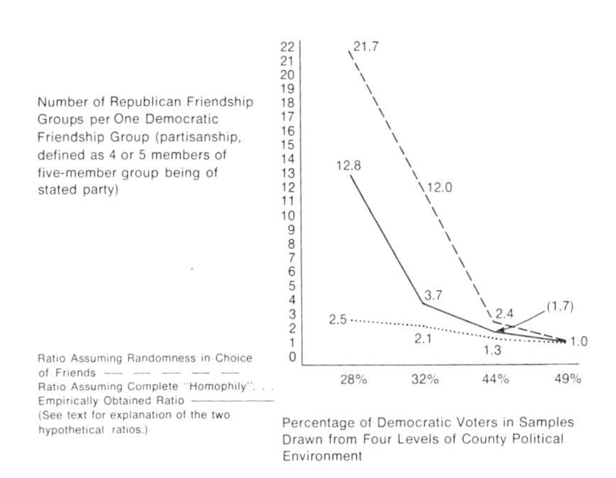

Figure 1. Partisanship of Friendship Groups as a Function of the County Political Environment

[10]Respondents with "mixed" or unknown friendship groups constitute a constant 34%–38% of the sample in all four partisan environments and are excluded from the present analysis. Their inclusion would complicate the analysis, but not alter the conclusions.

To be sure, this effect becomes less marked as the community approaches an even division between Republicans and Democrats. In the "moderately Democratic" communities in 1952 the ratio of Republican to Democratic voters was 1.3:1, while the ratio of Republican to Democratic friendship groups was 1.7:1. But empirically, many politically significant "climates of opinion" are quite one-sided. Most American communities, for example, are overwhelmingly favorably disposed to private enterprise, and the present analysis shows how difficult it would be for deviants from that viewpoint to maintain social support for their views. Or consider the case of party loyalties. The neighborhoods from which most Americans draw their closest friends are probably typically characterized by lop-sided distributions of party loyalties. The effect of these lop-sided distributions is, on the evidence presented here, to "smother" deviation from the dominant party. Much community influence is, then, mediated through the extended friendship group. A potential Democrat in a small Kansas town who must find most of his friends among Republicans, and who is eventually influenced by interaction with these friends to vote for Ike is clearly subject to this sort of community influence.

But what can we say about community influence apart from its impact on primary group composition? In Table 6 we find that when the partisanship of friendship groups is held constant, the remaining community influence is relatively slight, at least when "community" is defined at the county level. Berelson, Lazarsfeld, and McPhee have proposed what they term the "breakage effect" hypothesis, according to which community influence is most marked in its effects on individuals with mixed friendship groups. There is some weak confirmation for this hypothesis in the difference in sensitivity between respondents with mixed friendship groups on the one hand, and those with mostly Republican or mostly Democratic friends on the other.

Table 6. Community Influence and Membership in Primary Groups

	County Environment, in Terms of Democratic % of Two-Party Vote for President, 1952				Kendall's *tau c*
	18%–29%	30%–39%	40%–49%	50%–62%	
R's friends all or mostly Democratic	83%* (6)	81% (43)	82% (65)	83% (81)	.01 (N = 195)
R's friends all or mostly Republican	14% (77)	12% (157)	15% (109)	16% (85)	.03 (N = 428)
R's friends mixed or unknown in partisan terms	43% (51)	44% (100)	53% (100)	49% (85)	.07 (N = 336)

**Entries are percentage Democratic votes among respondents in the indicated category. Below each percentage is given the base on which it has been calculated, i.e., the total number of respondents in the indicated category.*

Thus, we have found, on the one hand, that community influence is to a considerable extent mediated through friendship groups and, on the other, that members of secondary associations are more susceptible to community influence than are non-members. We must now try to integrate these findings. There are three mutually compatible possibilities. First, it might be expected that associational membership opens up a broader spectrum of possible friendships, and that it thereby increases the likelihood of members having friends typical of the community at large. Looked at from the opposite point of view, non-members may be more likely to restrict their friendships to their more immediate social environment, which may differ substantially from the community environment. If this hypothesis is correct, we would expect the composition of friendship groups of associational members to show more sensitivity to differences in the overall community environment. In the second place, it might be that members of organizations not only are more likely to have friends typical of the community as a whole, but also are more sensitive to the opinions of their friends, whatever these opinions happen to be. Perhaps members of associations are more "other-directed." If this latter hypothesis were valid, it would magnify the effect of the greater "representativeness" of associational members' friends. Finally, it might also be true that the effect of organizational membership on susceptibility to community influence is not exhausted by these friendship-group phenomena. That is, it might be that even with friendship-group composition held constant, members of associations are still more sensitive to the community environment than are non-members. Each of these three possibilities can to some extent be tested with the present data.

To test the first hypothesis—that members of organizations have friends who are more "typical" of the community as a whole—we can examine the correlation between the county environment and friendship-group composition for organizational members and for non-members. Table 7 provides the relevant data. For members the correlation is .54, while for non-members it is .26, indicating that the composition of friendship groups of associational members is much more sensitive to differences in the community environment.[11] That is, one reason that associational members are more susceptible to community influence is that they are more likely to have friendship groups typical of the community as a whole.

The next hypothesis to be tested is that organizational members are generally more sensitive to their friends' opinions. The correlation between own vote and

[11]Note that if "homophily" were complete, the correlations in this table would be identical with the correlation between respondent's vote and county environment, *viz.*, *tau* = .18. The fact that the obtained *tau* for non-members is .24 indicates that even non-members are not able to insulate themselves from the general community environment completely.

Table 7. Composition of Friendship Groups and the Local Political Environment, by Activity in Secondary Associations

	County Environment, in Terms of Democratic % of Two-Party Vote for President, 1952				Kendall's *tau c*
	18%–29%	30%–39%	40%–49%	50%–62%	
Active members of secondary groups	5%* (20)	13% (30)	45% (20)	65% (34)	.54 (N = 104)
Not active members of secondary groups	0% (6)	32% (40)	33% (43)	59% (29)	.26 (N = 118)

**Entries are percentage of respondents with all or mostly Democratic friends. Below each percentage is given the base on which it has been calculated, i.e., the total number of respondents in the indicated category. Respondents with mixed or unknown friendship groups are excluded.*

friends' votes is .70 for group members, while the comparable figure for non-members is only .48. Thus, members of community associations are not only more likely to have friends typical of the community environment; they are also more sensitive to the opinions of those friends.

Finally, we can test tentatively the hypothesis that secondary group membership increases susceptibility to community influence even when we control for friendship-group effects. Table 8 shows that for each type of friendship group, members of associations do show a greater sensitivity to the community environment than do non-members. To be sure, both the *taus* and the N's are much too low to support any definite conclusion, but the pattern is quite consistent.[12]

Conclusion

We began this investigation in an effort to explain a widely-recognized phenomenon, the influence of the local political environment on the attitudes and behavior of community members. We found good evidence that this community influence is not mediated by the activity of party organizations. We were

[12]As in any cross-sectional analysis, the direction of causality is not definitely established by the above findings. That is, there may be a tendency for members of the political majority in an area to become more involved in secondary associations, rather than (or in addition to) a tendency for members of secondary associations to become more like the political majority. While this alternative cannot be excluded, its plausibility is reduced by the generally low salience of partisan politics for the average American. It is somewhat difficult to imagine that one's position in the political majority or minority in a locality has much to do with one's decision to become involved in nonpolitical associations in that locality. Moreover, the plausibility of the other alternative (that associations mediate community influence) is enhanced by the pattern of findings linking the secondary and primary group phenomena.

Table 8. Community Influence and Membership in Secondary Associations, with Partisanship of Friendship Group Held Constant

	County Environment, in Terms of Democratic % of Two-Party Vote for President, 1952				Kendall's *tau c*
	18%–29%	30%–39%	40%–49%	50%–62%	
Friends Democratic					
Association members	100%* (1)	85% (13)	76% (17)	86% (29)	.03 (N = 60)
Non-members	–	83% (6)	83% (6)	80% (10)	–.03 (N = 22)
Friends Republican					
Association members	5% (21)	7% (43)	18% (22)	6% (16)	.06 (N = 102)
Non-members	50% (4)	27% (11)	28% (18)	25% (8)	–.09 (N = 41)
Partisanship of friends mixed or unknown					
Association members	33% (12)	42% (19)	45% (20)	37% (19)	.01 (N = 70)
Non-members	57% (7)	46% (11)	40% (5)	43% (7)	–.12 (N = 30)

**Entries are percentage Democratic votes among respondents in the indicated category. Below each percentage is given the base on which it has been calculated, i.e., the total number of respondents in the indicated category.*

unable to find any evidence to support an explanation in terms of motivational conformity to perceived community norms. We turned to an explanation in terms of social interaction, and found clear evidence that community influence is mediated through primary and secondary groups in the community.[13] We found that the community political environment is an important determinant of the partisan complexion of friendship groups, that members of community

[13]Broadly speaking, we have examined three independent variables in this study: party contact, community identification, and social interaction. It may be of interest to note the intercorrelations among these three variables. There is virtually no relationship between party contact and any of the other variables (*tau* $\leq$.03). There are moderate positive relationships between social interaction and length of residence, home ownership, and parental status (*tau* = .09, .112, and .121, respectively). Thus, social interaction is far from perfectly correlated with our indicators of community identification. The overall effect of these findings is to strengthen our principal findings, for if we were to control for the spurious effect of organizational membership, the correlations between community influence and our indicators of community identification would be even weaker than those shown in Table 4.

organizations tend to have friends more representative of the community as a whole, and that they tend also to be especially sensitive to the opinion of their friends.

What is the relevance of these findings for understanding partisan community influence of the kinds mentioned at the beginning of this paper? Clearly, social interaction processes are important in accounting for the persistence of distinctive community partisan traditions, such as those investigated by Key, and in explaining the impact of suburban residence on political attitudes. The processes analyzed here are an important means of "socializing" newcomers into the partisan traditions of these areas. Similarly, these processes help to account for the difficulties the minority party faces in mobilizing its potential supporters. If our negative conclusions about Campbell's theory are valid, we can say that the political beliefs of one's community are probably *not* absorbed through deep roots long sunk in the local political soil. To vote like an Elmiran, it is not necessary that one "feel" like an Elmiran, that is, that one "identify" with Elmira. One need only be involved in the pattern of social relations through which the contagion of partisan sentiment passes.

The implications of our findings are, however, broader than the explication of some fraction of the remaining unexplained variance in American voting behavior. This study can be interpreted as an introductory exploration of the processes by which more general political beliefs and behavior are affected by the local community. Students of "political culture" and of "political ideology" have brought to our attention the significance of such orientations as tolerance, allegiance, and "subjective competence." It seems likely that one important determinant of these orientations is the community environment, but direct investigation of this relationship is both conceptually complex and operationally difficult. In this situation it is perhaps useful to begin by investigating analogous processes involving simpler kinds of attitudes, such as the partisan affiliations examined here. It seems likely that the processes here shown to account for the transmission of community partisan preferences also operate to spread and maintain community political culture. If so, this would have important implications for our interpretation of the relationship between political culture and the political system. Let us consider a few of these implications.

It has been repeatedly shown that social activity, and particularly membership in community organizations, is strongly linked to political participation. In New Haven, for example, Dahl found that "the more a voter participates in local political life, the more likely he is to participate in other forms of community organization, and conversely." Moreover, in Dahl's sample of political "subleaders" the median number of organizational affiliations was more than four. Our findings suggest, therefore, that political activists will be under especially strong (though perhaps imperceptible) influence to adopt those attitudes on which community opinion is relatively one-sided. Stated over-simply, our hypothesis would be that the more active a person is politically, the more conventional his beliefs will tend to become. In the case of partisan attitudes, this tendency will naturally be offset by the tendency for political activists to be strongly committed to a particular party. But in the case of non-partisan attitudes of the sort investigated by students of political culture, we would expect activists to adhere more strongly than non-activists to community conventions and norms. This, of course, is precisely what studies of this matter have revealed.

The importance of our findings for the comparative study of political culture depends on the generality of the processes uncovered here. It may not be that the transmission of all sorts of political beliefs in all sorts of communities follows this same pattern. But insofar as our findings are applicable, we would expect the transmission of political attitudes to be a function of the extent and intensity of formal and informal social interaction. We would expect, for example, the resistance of a closely-knit community to novel ideas to be greater than the resistance of an atomistic community, but once a new attitude had "caught on" in the former, we would expect its diffusion to be faster and more complete than in the latter. Furthermore, we would expect that the individuals most susceptible to novel or deviant ideas would be those most detached from the network of community social relations. This is, of course, a common finding of both anthropologists and political sociologists.

Theorists of democracy, at least since John Stuart Mill, have worried about the "tyranny" of public opinion. Our findings about the "smothering" effect of a lop-sided distribution of opinion reveal in some detail the nature and extent of this danger. Partisans in a three-to-one minority have much less than one chance in three of finding a supportive primary-group environment. In the case of presidential choice their chances are less than one in thirteen. To call this phenomenon "tyranny" is, however, to beg two important questions. In the first place, this "tyranny" is entirely unintentional—the majority does not plan to smother deviant views in this way. It is simply much more difficult for holders of minority views to find like-minded associates. Moreover, whether this effect should be called "tyrannical" or not depends on our assessment of the opinions which are "smothered." It is at least arguable that the "smothering" of racial prejudice or of anti-democratic attitudes is not contrary to those liberal democratic values which we share with Mill. On the other hand, in the case of attitudes less inimical to democracy itself, the "smothering" phenomenon is more alarming, and the need to counter its effects—by the enforcement of freedom of speech and (especially) freedom of association—is more pressing. The important point here, however, is not the evaluation of this phenomenon, but the understanding of it, so that we may better cope with whatever problems it raises for democracy.

Our investigation has also highlighted the political significance of community associations. Numerous social theorists, from de Tocqueville to Kornhauser, have suggested that such groups play an important role in "integrating" citizens into the life of the larger community. We have seen in the specific case of partisan attitudes how this "integration" process works. Group members are more exposed to dominant community opinions and are more sensitive to those opinions. Thus, in a community where sentiments favor democratic processes and values, group membership would tend to encourage the development of democratic attitudes, as de Tocqueville and his successors have argued. On the other hand, in communities where democratic attitudes are not widespread, group membership might have, at least in part, a contrary effect.[14] In a community where prejudice or antagonism to democracy was widespread, the network of community associations would tend to propagate these anti-democratic attitudes, and organizational membership would not have the effect of stimulating support for democratic norms. If this hypothesis is correct, it constitutes an important qualification of the "pluralist" thesis.

[14]To be sure, there are probably many other effects of group membership besides this sort of "integration" into community social relations, and some of these *other* effects might be supportive of democracy even in a community where anti-democratic attitudes were rampant. See William Kornhauser, *The Politics of Mass Society* (New York: Free Press, 1959), *passim.*

The Klan Revival[1]

James W. Vander Zanden

Since 1955 the nation's press has carried periodic reports of revived Ku Klux Klan activity in the South. Fiery crosses, motorcades, torchlight rallies, floggings, bomb terror, and the castration of a Negro have followed in its wake.[2] The hooded order, a reconstruction-era organization, had previously been revived in 1915, and again following World War II. The post-World War II revival, however, was short lived, and by 1952 the Klan had been suppressed through state and federal action.

Then came May 17, 1954, and the Supreme Court school desegregation ruling. Racial tensions slowly mounted during the year that followed. Nevertheless, even in the states of the Deep South, the belief was widespread that some desegregation would be inescapable. Delay was the major tactic of state officials. When, on May 31, 1955, the Supreme Court handed down its implementing decree, the NAACP quickly followed with at least forty-two petitions for immediate school desegregation in as many communities of Virginia and the Deep South. The result was an immediate and marked upsurge in counteractivity by the whites. Deep South states no longer were thinking in terms of buying time; compromise was being ruled out; die-hards' adamant opposition was the order of the day. In the rural Black Belt areas of the Deep South the citizens councils,

[1]The data for this paper were secured by field research in Georgia and South Carolina late in 1955 and in 1956 and from the extensive materials in the Library of the Southern Educational Reporting Service in Nashville, Tenn.

[2]At least three floggings have been linked with the Klan, one of which, near Travelers' Rest, S.C., resulted in the conviction of four Greenville, S.C., klansmen. Klansmen have been implicated in the Montgomery and Atlanta church bombings and in the attempted bombing of a Negro elementary school near Charlotte, N.C. Acquittals resulted in the former cases, but convictions were secured in the Charlotte case. Four klansmen were subsequently convicted of mayhem and sentenced to twenty years imprisonment for the Labor Day, 1957, castration of a Negro handyman near Birmingham, Ala. The act had been perpetrated, according to the courtroom testimony of the klansmen, as a test for one of their number to prove his worthiness "of becoming Assistant Exalted Cyclops."

Reprinted from James Vander Zanden, "The Klan Revival," American Journal of Sociology, *Vol. 65 (1960), pp. 456-462, by permission of The University of Chicago Press.*

until this time relatively small, isolated groups, gained momentum. Drastic, stringent punishment was meted out to Negro signers of integration petitions. In Deep South states politicians increasingly made segregation their chief campaign issue. In Mississippi fourteen-year-old Emmett Till was mutilated, murdered, and his body dumped into the Tallahatchie River. In Alabama a mob and the developments that followed in its wake successfully blocked the admittance of Autherine Lucy to the state university, where the Negro woman had enrolled under court order. Increasingly whites believed they could defeat integration.[3]

In this atmosphere of mounting tension and resistance the Klan made its reappearance. But, as contrasted with the citizens councils, its strength did not reside in the rural Black Belt areas of the South; on the contrary, it has been an urban phenomenon, with the preponderance of its strength located in the Piedmont of the Southeast.[4] In the last half of 1955 and the first half of 1956 came the zenith of citizens council activity throughout the Deep South. After this period organized council activity subsided: economic sanctions and pressures against Negroes became infrequent; attendance at mass meetings dropped sharply; chapters in wide areas became inactive; only a scattering of new chapters were formed; and renewals of membership and financial contributions dropped sharply. With the crushing of the integrationist movement in the Deep South, the citizens councils became, for the most part, inactive. The situation was summarized by Charles N. Plowden, banker, large landowner, and a prominent figure in the Summerton, South Carolina, council, the community from which had come one of the original cases before the Supreme Court. Speaking of the

[3]For a detailed account and analysis of the Southern resistance movement following in the wake of the Supreme Court school rulings, see James W. Vander Zanden, "The Southern White Resistance Movement to Integration," unpublished doctoral dissertation, University of North Carolina, 1958.

[4]Klan strength has resided in the following areas of the South. Alabama: Birmingham and vicinity (Jefferson, Shelby, Tuscaloosa, and St. Clair counties), the Montgomery-Prattville vicinity and Mobile; Florida: Jacksonville and vicinity (Duval and Nassau counties), Tampa, and Tallahassee, with a scattering of members in the north-central area of the state between these three urban centers; Georgia: Atlanta and vicinity (DeKalb, Fulton, and Cobb counties), Macon, Savannah, and Columbus, with a scattering of members in Americus, Warner-Robbins, Cochran, Vienna, Moultrie, Albany, Waycross, and Nashville; North Carolina: membership and activity centered in a triangular area with Reidsville on the north, Charlotte on the west, and Hamlet on the southeast; South Carolina: Greenville and vicinity (York, Cherokee, Spartanburg, and Greenville counties), Columbia and vicinity, and Florence, with a scattering of members in Darlington, Dillon, and Horry counties; and Tennessee: the Chattanooga-Rossville, Ga., vicinity, Maryville-Alcoa-Knoxville vicinity, and Nashville. Small chapters have also been reported in Baton Rouge, La., Waco, Tex., Little Rock, Ark., and southern Delaware.

Since fiery crosses, torchlight rallies, floggings, and bombings are the sort of activity that commands newspaper headlines, it is easy to exaggerate the size of Klan membership. Some estimates appear to be stimulated by the Klan's sensationalism and boasting. Although Klan membership figures are secret, the figure surely did not exceed 10,000 at the organization's zenith in late 1956 and 1957.

Summerton citizens council, Plowden remarked: "There's no need to meet. Everything's going along quiet." But the Klan exhibited a different course. It gathered slow momentum in 1955 and 1956 but did not reach its peak until late 1956, 1957, and early 1958, after which it, too, experienced a sharp tapering-off.

The growth and activity of the citizens council has been closely associated with the whites' perception of the imminence of desegregation. Robert Patterson, leader of the Mississippi councils, has repeatedly asserted in organizing speeches: "Organized aggression must be met with organized resistance." In short, movement begets countermovement. The corollary has also tended to hold true, namely, if movement subsides, so, too, does countermovement. The Klan development, on the other hand, has not followed a similar course. Nor, as has been noted, has its strength resided (with the exception of Tallahassee and Montgomery where the Negroes' movement for integration on buses was under way) in areas where the threat of integration was thought of by the general populace as immediate or especially threatening. This paper suggests that in part these incongruities can be explained and the appeal of the Klan understood by examining the position which klansmen occupy within the social structure.

The "mission" of the Klan is set forth in the handbook of the U.S. Klans, Knights of the Ku Klux Klan:

> We invite all men who can qualify to become citizens of the invisible Empire, to approach the portal of our beneficent domain, join us in our noble work of extending its boundaries, and in disseminating the gospel of our Klankraft, thereby encouraging, conserving, protecting and making vital the fraternal relationship in the practice of an honorable clannishness; to share with us the sacred duty of protecting womanhood; to maintain forever the God-given supremacy of the White Race; to commemorate the holy and chivalric achievement of our fathers; to safeguard the sacred rights, privileges and institutions of our civil government; to bless mankind and to keep eternally ablaze the sacred fire of a fervent devotion to a pure Americanism.

Since the Klan is a secret society, membership lists are not available. However, from a number of sources the names and occupational positions of 153 klansmen were identified.[5] They fall into four occupational groups: (1) skilled workers (e.g., garage mechanics, machinists, carpenters, and stonemasons); (2) marginal, small businessmen (e.g., small building-trade contractors and proprietors of food markets, grills, and gasoline stations); (3) marginal white-collar

[5]The names were obtained from those listed on charter applications for Klan incorporation in the several states, from police arrests for Klan activity, from a police-seized membership list in Charlotte, N.C., and from Klan spokesmen named in the press.

workers (e.g., grocery-store clerks, service-station attendants, policemen, and salesmen); and (4) transportation workers (primarily truck drivers) and unskilled and semiskilled workers in the textile, construction, automotive, aircraft, coal, and steel industries. This sample is of unknown representativeness and it is undoubtedly biased, yet it probably reflects the occupational breadth of the Klan's membership. Accordingly, caution should be taken into account in evaluating the following interpretations.

Of the 153 klansmen, 98 were in the first three occupational categories: skilled workers, 51; marginal businessmen, 11; and marginal white-collar workers, 36. These are commonly ranked in the upper rungs of the working class and the lower rungs of the middle class, that is, in an intermediate position between clear-cut "blue-collar" manual jobs and white-collar jobs, their status is insecure and they are anxious. At the same time, they generally lack the resources, skills, or education necessary to improve their life-chances.

The situation for the workers in the fourth category is different in that middle-class status is not teasingly and just immediately ahead of them. But the frustration may nevertheless be as acute, where the common success goals are internalized, yet they lack means of access to the approved goals. And their plight is made worse by the insecurity that has traditionally characterized employment in these industries (construction, automotive, textile, aircraft, steel, and coal). Furthermore, the automotive and aircraft industries are relatively recent arrivals on the Southern scene—part of a rapidly growing Southern industrial complex—which have drawn large numbers of workers from small towns and rural communities of the region. Often the workers have been uprooted from what are almost folk communities and propelled into an urban industrial world, with the consequent destruction of old rural values and life-ways, disruption of social ties, and isolation from durable personal ties and roots. Ambiguities regarding one's position, role, and status are the result. In a word, status disorientation occurs.

The picture has not been too different in the expanding Birmingham steel-coal complex. In the textile industry recent studies have pointed to the sharp undermining of the folk relationships that had characterized the mill villages. Increasingly, the mill hands are being engulfed in currents of social change. Traditional castelike barriers between the textile workers and "townspeople" are breaking down, and the mill villagers are becoming more heterogeneous in socioeconomic characteristics. Status, once predominantly ascribed, is becoming increasingly achieved. With the shift there has developed a growing disparity between the commonly extolled success goals of our society and the socially sanctioned means whereby they may be attained.

The klansman appears to have internalized *both* the success goals of American society and the institutionalized means for their realization. Thwarted in progressing toward the goals, he does not reject them, nor does he have recourse to socially prescribed means. Rather, he seizes upon the symbols of 100 per cent

Americanism and his membership in the superordinately defined white race—and elevates and magnifies these out of proportion. He overconforms to the institutionalized caste pattern of the South and to patriotic identification with America. Judged by white-group standards, his adherence to the dominant white-racial values and Americanism is excessive.[6] And this leads to conflict with other values, most particularly the sanctity of the individual and private property.

Tormented by his ambiguous status, the klansman, by emphasizing the difference between himself as a white and the Negro, may achieve, at least negatively, a sense of group identification. By conforming to the dominant white group, he gets some sense of identification and security. Nevertheless, insecurity and uncertainty lead to his compensating for his lacks through an exaggerated overconformity with the white-caste value system and exaggerated 100 per cent Americanism. For his props are not *any* props: they are props esteemed by society.

Secrecy plays a role similar to exaggerated conformity: the strongly emphasized exclusion of all outsiders makes for a feeling of possession. Klan secrets give the klansman a highly tangible and explicit group identification because they set him apart from the amorphous mass of humanity.

There are still other consequences. One's own weakness, inferiority, and amvibalence are not infrequently concealed from others and even from one's self, and the substitute often is compensatory self-aggrandizement, seen in the superpatriot and militant white supremacist and frequently expressed in Klan addresses:

> Our kind of whites were elected to rule the world and everything in it.[7]
>
> The Ku Klux Klan is the only white Christian Protestant 100 per cent American organization in America today. . . . Klansmen are the cleanest and most perfect people on earth.[8]

The exaggerated emphasis given by the Klan to symbols of status suggests a similar effort. The elaborate Klan regalia conspicuously establishes the individual's

[6]At times such excessiveness may be condoned if not actually wolcomed by the population at large, which sees it as a temporary expedient arising from a definition of the situation as unusual and frequently threatening. Means normally prescribed are seen as effective for accomplishing the task at hand, and their employment is justified by the atypical situation and its temporary character. At the same time, those more inhibited through a greater internalization of the prevailing societal norms are "saved" from violating the norms and from consequent anxiety. Thus the reaction among some Southern whites to Klan bombings and floggings has been: "I don't approve of violence. But they [Negroes] were asking for it. They had it coming to them." This situation is reminiscent of the reaction of many to Senator Joseph R. McCarthy.

[7]Klan speaker at a rally at Lakeland, Fla.; Memphis *Commercial Appeal*, July 22, 1956.

[8]Klan speaker at a rally at Pontiac, S.C.; Charlotte *Observer*, October 2, 1955.

membership in the "Invisible Empire" and sets him apart from the mass of humanity. The concern with status and individual aggrandizement is reflected in the organization's preoccupation with insignia, with the assignment of status-denoting colors for the robes of officials, and with the use of an exaggerated status-exalting nomenclature (e.g., Imperial Wizard, Grand Dragon, Grand Titan, Grand Giant, and Exalted Cyclops). Likewise, the respective authority and power of Klan officials have been major issues since the recent Klan revival and have also been crucial contributing factors in Klan factionalism and splintering.[9] In Birmingham a heated argument during a Klan meeting over "one-man rule" resulted in gunplay and the wounding of two klansmen. In Tampa the self-styled Grand Dragon of the Associated Florida Ku Klux Klans, W. J. Griffin, named six other Klans operating in the Tampa area and lamented to the press: "We have too many chiefs and not enough Indians to stage a war dance." Griffin asserted that "the old countersign and password won't work because all klansmen are strangers to each other." His answer: The Klan should adopt old Indian customs "and force grand dragons to wear tusks in their noses. . . . Members should be forced to be stamped with the branding iron or clip their ears with leather punches like farmers mark their livestock."

The excessive vehemence with which some klansmen extol their white status and disassociate themselves from Negro status suggests that basically they may feel themselves as weak, deprived, and helpless as they imagine the Negro to be. This appears reflected in statements such as these: "The Communists would have you believe that the nigger's blackness is only skin deep. All I gotta say to that is they ought to go skin one and find out for themselves. We are gonna stay white, we are gonna keep the nigger black, with the help of our Lord and Savior, Jesus Christ";[10] and "I've been a white man all my life and I always will be."[11] Such individuals may tend to equate their own lower status with the subordinate Negro-caste position, and their vehement dissociation from the Negro and their avowal of membership in the dominant group may be efforts to convince both themselves and others that they do not occupy an inferior position.

The Klan offers its members a chance to acquire importance, hope, and a sense of worthiness. It gives him a "cause," a sacred mission with meaningfulness and purposiveness. A strong sense of "mission" is a recurring theme in Klan speeches, e.g., "America was saved by the Knights of the Ku Klux Klan [at the time of the reconstruction] and if it is saved again, the Ku Klux Klan will do

[9]The largest of the Klans is the U.S. Klans, Knights of the Ku Klux Klan, chartered in Georgia. There have been at least fifteen splinter groups, six in addition to the U.S. Klans in South Carolina, Texas, and Louisiana, and at least two in Florida.

[10]Klan speaker at a Montgomery, Ala., rally; Montgomery *Advertiser,* November 25, 1956.

[11]Klan speaker at a Lakeland, Fla., rally; Memphis *Commercial Appeal,* July 22, 1956.

it."[12] A hooded klansman observed to the writer at a Klan rally outside of Orangeburg, South Carolina: "Believe me, mister—we ain't no hoodlum outfit. The reds and fools say we are, but we ain't. We're goin' to save this here country. You just watch and see!"

Finding his group identity ambiguous and/or his aspirations thwarted, the klansman can identify himself with something beyond and greater than himself—"The Invisible Empire." Since the organization lays claim to his whole person (not merely to a segment, as do most American voluntary associations),[13] his social being tends to become submerged within a greater whole. The success which was not forthcoming through normal channels promises to come through the organization and cause to which he has dedicated himself. At the same time, the Klan demands unconditional obedience to its rules and norms and enforces them. It is quite possible that individuals lacking stable or explicit group identification in the society-at-large find assurance, stability, and identification in such dogmatic and totalitarian commitments. By the same token, social change, as represented by integrationist and liberal movements, confronts him with indefiniteness, unconventionality, and loss of familiar anchorage.

But such inclusive commitment, by tying him with incomparable closeness to the group, makes him dependent. Severance from the group threatens him with a loss of substance and a part of his social being—with rootlessness and the loss of a stable life-feeling. The cohesion of the secret society is obtained in part by partially secluding the individual from other meaningful social relationships. This is reinforced through the definition of the klansman as a deviant by society-at-large, social sanctions not infrequently awaiting the "known" member. The result is that the individual tends to evaluate his behavior according to the norms of the Klan rather than of society-at-large.

Within this context the individual can legitimatize the use of violence, proscribed by society-at-large. Despite frequent disavowing of the use of violence, hardly veiled threats of violence are a repeated theme in Klan speeches. Examples include: "The way I feel about them niggers who want to integrate education is this—they don't want an education, they want a funeral."[14] "I'd shed every drop of my blood to keep kids from going to school with niggers."[15] "A Negro who

[12]A speaker at a Klan rally at Montgomery, Ala., September 9, 1956.

[13]As Simmel observes: ". . . [the secret society] quite characteristically claims to a greater extent the whole individual, connects its members in more of their totality, and mutually obligates them more closely, than does an open society of identical content. Through the symbolism of the ritual, which excites a whole range of vaguely delimited feelings beyond all particular, rational interests, the secret society synthesizes those interests into a total claim upon the individual" (Simmel, George. *The Sociology of George Simmel,* trans. Kurt H. Wolff [New York: Free Press, 1950], p. 360).

[14]Klan speaker at a Montgomery, Ala., rally; Montgomery *Advertiser,* November 25, 1956.

[15]Klan speaker at a Lakeland, Fla., rally; St. Petersburg *Times,* July 22, 1956.

tries to get into a white swimming pool [referring to a Negro who sought to enter a white pool at Durham, N.C.] is not looking for a bath, he's looking to get killed."[16]

Likewise, impulses toward aggressive behavior and violence deriving from thwarted aspirations can be justified by the standards of his group—or so he thinks. The Klan regalia hiding the individual's identity operates toward a similar end. Not alone does it protect the individual from recognition and possible social sanctions, but it obliterates the individual as a member of society-at-large while accentuating his Klan identification. And as an object of what the klansman frequently perceives to be unfair treatment from society-at-large, he can feel himself morally freed from the obligations that society would impose upon him. The use of symbols incrusted with emotional meaning, the performance of hallowed rituals, the singing of hymns—all these help in the breaking down of resistances that inhibit the responsiveness desired in the members of the fold.

Thwarted in realizing goals which society holds to be worthwhile and frequently occupying a precarious position within the social structure, the individual easily comes to see himself as the victim of inscrutable conspiracies and enemies. Time and again failing in his encounters with life, he develops a generalized feeling of inadequacy, but his "faults" appear to him as wholly outside of himself. It is he who is blameless, virtuous, more sinned against than sinning—and so his self-esteem is restored. All is reflected in the endless recurrence in Klan speeches of such words as *plot, conspiracy, hoax, corruption* and the like.

But the Klan, as contrasted with reformist or revolutionary movements, does not offer a program of basic social change. The source of discontent is not seen as the social system, social conditions, or the government. The difficulty is personified as an "enemy"—as "evil" persons, e.g., Eleanor Roosevelt, Richard Nixon, the justices of the Supreme Court, and Harry S. Truman; and "evil" groups, e.g., Jews, Communists, Catholics, foreigners, the "big-city" press, and "scalawags." Having internalized both the common success goals and the socially sanctioned norms for their achievement, he does not turn to attack the social system. On the other hand, members of reformist and revolutionary groups reject both the cultural goals and the institutionalized means, seeking to substitute others for them. By overidentifying himself with the existing order, the klansman seeks to realize success within the existing social structure: the obstacles barring success are, to him, merely the work of "evil" agents.

At times the obsession with "enemies" and "plots" reaches paranoid proportions; it appears as if everywhere there is a conspiracy afoot. This is reflected in the speech of a Klan leader at a Nashville rally who, in the course of his address, depicts as enemies Negroes, Communists, the press, the FBI, Russia, the Nashville

[16]A Klan speaker at a rally outside of Monroe, N.C.; Charlotte *Observer*, August 9, 1957.

school board, the Red Cross, the United Fund (the latter two for allegedly "using their money to transport Negroes around the country to break down segregation"), food dyes, the use of Salk polio vaccine (referred to as a "Communist plot"), and the fluoridation of water (referred to as "rat poison").[17] Because of their own insecure and weak position within the social structure and their neglible insight into their situation, the world about them seems hostile and evil.

Bibliographical Note

Much of the scholarly concern with interest group-individual relations is rooted in a theory of "mass society" and a concomitant emphasis on alienation, *anomie,* and apathy. One convenient summary of this theory is provided by William Kornhauser in *The Politics of Mass Society* (New York: Free Press, 1959). See, in addition, Daniel Bell, *The End of Ideology* (New York: Collier, 1961); and Erich Fromm, *The Sane Society* (New York: Rinehart, 1955).

For precise theoretical formulation and empirical studies on some of these concepts, see: Melvin Seeman, "On the Meaning of Alienation," *American Sociological Review,* Vol. 24 (December 1959), pp. 783-791; Wendell Bell, "Anomie, Social Isolation, and the Class Structure," *Sociometry,* Vol. 20 (June 1957), pp. 105-116; Dwight G. Dean, "Alienation and Political Apathy," *Social Forces,* Vol. 38 (March 1960); Murray B. Levin, *The Alienated Voter: Politics in Boston* (New York: Holt, 1960); Edward L. McDill and Jeanne C. Ridley, "Status, Anomie, Political Alienation and Political Participation," *American Journal of Sociology,* Vol. 68 (September 1962), pp. 205-213; and Samuel J. Surace and Melvin Seeman, "Some Correlates of Civil Rights Activism," *Social Forces,* Vol. 46 (December 1967), pp. 197-207.

For studies of differential participation in "group life" in America, which consider class, status, educational, and residential factors as well as psychological variables, see: Mirra Komarovsky, "The Voluntary Associations of Urban Dwellers," *American Sociological Review,* Vol. 11 (December 1946), pp. 686-698; C. Wright Mills, "The Middle Class in Middle-Sized Cities," *American Sociological Review,* Vol. 11 (October 1946); Morris Axelrod, "Urban Structure and Social Participation," *American Sociological Review,* Vol. 21 (February 1956), pp. 13-18; Wendell Bell and Maryanne T. Force, "Urban Neighborhood Types and Participation in Formal Associations," *American Sociological Review,* Vol. 21 (February 1956), pp. 25-34; Raymond Payne, "Some Comparisons of Participation in Rural Mississippi, Kentucky, Ohio, Illinois and New York," *Rural Sociology,* Vol. 18 (June 1953), pp. 171-172; Robert E. Anderson and Gallatin Anderson, "Voluntary Associations and Urbanization: A Diachronic Analysis," *American Journal of Sociology,* Vol. 65 (November 1958), pp. 265-273; Bennett

[17]Nashville *Tennessean,* June 9, 1957.

M. Berger, *Working Class Suburb: A Study of Auto Workers in Suburbia* (Berkeley, Calif.: Univ. California Press, 1960); Herbert J. Gans, *The Levittowners* (New York: Pantheon Books, 1967).

One major study of individual behavior and attitudes in relation to groups, parties, and, indeed, the political system in general is V. O. Key's *Public Opinion and American Democracy* (New York: Knopf, 1961). Key's book is another excellent example of "secondary analysis"—he utilizes data from the Michigan voting studies to focus on public opinion and public institutions.

Protest on both the right and the left deserves to be studied with considerably more care than it has received in the past, particularly by those who are not convinced that activism "outside the system" should be relegated to the periphery. Several excellent empirical studies have been published on the "radical right," including this collection: *The Radical Right,* ed. Daniel Bell (New York: Doubleday, 1963). See especially Seymour M. Lipset's "The Sources of the 'Radical Right.' "

It is unfortunate that as of mid-1968 no comparable full-scale account has yet been published on the various phases of the "New Left"—civil rights, student, or Vietnam activism. The most comprehensive account is Kenneth Keniston, *Young Radicals: Notes on Committed Youth* (New York: Harcourt, 1968); Keniston's book also includes a very thorough bibliography. One excellent sourcebook for documents and the organizational structure of SDS, SNCC, and various student movements exists: see Paul Jacobs and Saul Landau, *The New Radicals: A Report with Documents* (New York: Vintage Books, 1966). The best accounts of student protest movements are *The Berkeley Student Revolt,* ed. Seymour M. Lipset and Sheldon Wolin (New York: Doubleday, 1965); and Seymour M. Lipset and P. G. Altbach, "Student Politics and Higher Education in the United States," *Comparative Education Review,* Vol. 10 (June 1966), pp. 320-399. Howard Zinn summarizes the early history of SNCC in *SNCC: The Abolitionists* (Boston: Beacon Press, 1965).

In addition, the student may wish to peruse *Studies on the Left* (published since 1960); various "underground" papers (for example, *The Berkeley Barb; Avatar);* and such magazines as *Commentary, Dissent,* and *Ramparts* to get a feel for the values, debates, and organizational problems which exist in these new organizations.

The Comparative Study of Interest Groups

Students of comparative politics experienced the same professional soul-searching, during and after the behavioral revolution, that molded the study of American political institutions. Before World War II, a typical course in comparative government included little beyond historical studies of the formal institutions in a few Western nations. An occasional reference was made to the social and economic context, and considerable attention was paid to political parties, but no systematic attempt was made to link formal and informal structures. Non-Western nations were ignored, except by anthropologists.

With the appearance between 1955 and 1962 of a few landmark studies, a new trend became evident.[1] Attention was directed to the underdeveloped countries, and in that context the process of political socialization, communication, opinion formation, and demand articulation became central. An attempt was made to explore in some detail the relations between social, economic, and political patterns. The impact of this work has not been limited to studies of Africa, Asia, and the Middle East; it has also made itself felt in contemporary writing on American and Western European politics.[2]

There are strong arguments for including a comparative dimension in the study of political interest groups. First, there is an obvious need in all social inquiry to check major propositions in the broadest possible context in order to be sure that what is observed is not parochial or culture-bound. In addition, the American specialist can learn new research techniques by working in settings where access to public records or the cooperation of public officials is not always certain. Most important,

[1]These studies include David Apter, *The Gold Coast in Transition* (Princeton, N.J.: Princeton Univ. Press, 1955); Daniel Lerner, *The Passing of Traditional Society: Modernizing the Middle East* (New York: Free Press, 1958); Edward C. Banfield, *The Moral Basis of a Backward Society* (New York: Free Press, 1958); Gabriel A. Almond and James Coleman (eds.), *The Politics of the Developing Areas* (Princeton, N.J.: Princeton Univ. Press, 1960); and Lucian W. Pye, *Politics, Personality and Nation Building: Burma's Search for Identity* (New Haven, Conn.: Yale Univ. Press, 1962).

[2]The student can verify this point by comparing texts published before and after about 1955. The trend is particularly evident in the comparative field but can be seen in studies of American government as well.

however, is the opportunity for *theoretical* development which comparative studies afford.

If the student of comparative politics is to understand political institutions which differ widely from their American counterparts, he must learn to ask a broader set of questions than those appropriate, for example, to a study of four state legislatures. He may need to shift, for instance, from a survey of the activities of formal interest groups to a study of the process of "interest articulation" (the voicing of demands or claims on the political system). His point of departure may be a theoretical framework which asks, "What functions are performed by what structures and with what effect?"[3] instead of asking, "What impact do interest groups have, and why?" The new question may lead him to a study of the family, the army, or administrative officials rather than to a study of a union, a civil-rights group, or an organization called "Citizens for Civic Improvement." He will, through immersion in the comparative literature, learn to ask new questions about his own system. The formulation of new theoretical positions from which to approach such questions may, in turn, provide more satisfactory answers about emerging political trends in the United States.

Group theory and most past research on interest groups has been of minimal help in explaining why some sectors of American society remain politically unorganized, or, if organized, weak in relation to Congress or city hall. We lack the framework from which to analyze protest or mass-action movements, "confrontation" strategies, and civil disobedience and from which to assess their effectiveness in comparison with traditional techniques. We may be able to integrate traditional notions about group behavior with more recent developments in American politics by studying Latin American student movements, Japanese labor, or West African urbanization. This can only be accomplished, however, if the right questions, imbedded in a broad and meaningful framework, are asked.

Several major questions are raised and some alternative frameworks are discussed by the authors in this section. Almond and Verba are concerned with the idea of civic competence as a prerequisite for representative government. They inquire into the circumstances under which individuals attempt to influence their government, the methods employed, and the perceived effectiveness of those methods. Almond and Verba find that civic competence is markedly higher in all five countries which they studied in regard to the local government than it is to national affairs. They also find that *informal* channels of influence are more

[3]For a discussion of the structural-functional approach to the study of comparative politics, see Almond and Coleman, *op. cit.,* especially the Introduction; and Harry Eckstein, *Pressure Group Politics: The Case of the British Medical Association* (Stanford, Calif.: Stanford Univ. Press, 1960), especially the Conclusion.

important than interest groups or parties. But their most interesting data concern the relative importance of educational level and nationality. The student may want to compare Almond and Verba's findings and reasoning with that of Wright and Hyman in the previous section.

Verba uses information from the same survey to test one basic tenet of cross-pressure theory,[4] namely, that the tendency for individuals to belong to several different organizations mitigates political and social conflict. The article is important both because of the question it discusses and because of the analytical techniques employed. Verba's work is an example of "secondary analysis"—the use of data for purposes other than that for which it was originally collected.[5] In secondary analysis, it is often difficult to find *direct* evidence on questions not built into the original study. Verba displays considerable ingenuity in locating measures for his dependent variable, the existence of political polarization which could lead to sharp or unmanageable social conflict.

Samuel Beer raises a more traditional question: What is the relation between the structure of the formal political system and the strength of informal or "extra-legal" groups? He questions one common stereotype about American and British interest groups (American groups are strong because parties are weak; British groups are weak because parties are strong) and argues instead that *both* interest groups and parties must be understood in the context of the relative collectivism of the formal political and economic structures.

Little's article on voluntary associations in West Africa goes beyond the formal political group. He describes, instead, the organization and activities of four types of groups—tribal unions, friendly societies, occupational associations, and recreational groups. His central question is related to Kornhauser's:[6] What role do such groups play in aiding the individual to adjust to urbanization? He finds that these groups are "adaptive mechanisms" serving both the individual (by increasing self-esteem and by providing outlets for the energies of ambitious, educated youth) and the society (by substituting for traditional agencies of social control). Thus, quasi-judicial problems (for example, redress for seduction) are brought to the tribal unions and the occupational societies rather than to the official legal agencies.

[4]See the article by Kriesberg in Section 3 above and footnotes in Verba's article, in this section.
[5]Wright and Hyman's article in Section 5 of this volume is another example of secondary analysis.
[6]William Kornhauser, *The Politics of Mass Society* (New York: Free Press, 1959). See the discussion of Kornhauser in the Introduction to Section 5 of this volume.

Little himself notes the similarity of some of these institutions to their Western equivalents at different points in time (for example, the resemblance of occupational societies to medieval guilds). There are probably also similarities between the West African friendly societies and organizations currently operating among minorities in the United States. Perhaps interest-group theory should be broadened to cover the seemingly apolitical recreation and mutual-aid societies of the rural South and Midwest or the street and motorcycle gangs of urban America. If similarities between "mainstream" groups in one nation and "fringe" groups in another are to be analyzed and discussed meaningfully or if comparisons are to be made between the group universe in nations at *different points in their history* (for example, in nineteenth-century Britain and in twentieth-century Japan[7]), the need for an adequate common framework is imperative.

[7]See Richard Willey, "Pressure Group Politics: The Case of Sohyo," *Western Political Quarterly*, December 1964, pp. 703-723. Willey attempts to apply Eckstein's framework to the Japanese union movement and does not emphasize the parallels discussed here. However, students familiar with the history of British unionism will be struck by the similarities.

The Sense of Civic Competence

Gabriel A. Almond
Sidney Verba

Democracy is a political system in which ordinary citizens exercise control over elites; and such control is legitimate; that is, it is supported by norms that are accepted by elites and nonelites. In all societies, of course, the making of specific decisions is concentrated in the hands of very few people. Neither the ordinary citizen nor "public opinion" can make policy. If this is the case, the problem of assessing the degree of democracy in a nation becomes one of measuring the degree to which ordinary citizens control those who make the significant decisions for a society—in most cases, governmental elites.

From Gabriel A. Almond and Sidney Verba, The Civic Culture: Political Attitudes and Democracy in Five Nations *(Princeton, N.J.: Princeton University Press, 1963), pp. 180-213.*

Recent work on the theory of influence suggests that there are numerous means by which interpersonal influence can be exerted, and that it makes a difference which means are used. Here we shall be concerned with a particular type of influence that nonelites may exert on elites: a type that we label *political* influence. We shall roughly define the political influence of a group or individual over a governmental decision as equal to the degree to which governmental officials act to benefit that group or individual because the officials believe that they will risk some deprivation (they will risk their jobs, be criticized, lose votes) if they do not so act. Thus we define political influence as both the outcome of the decision and the motives of the decision makers. The outcome will benefit the influential groups or individuals more than it would if the influence were not exercised. And the decision makers act to benefit the groups or individuals because they believe they will suffer some deprivation or, what amounts to the same thing, fail to gain a reward. The latter criterion is important. Officials may act to benefit a particular group for a variety of reasons: out of a feeling of paternalism, for instance. But it is only when officials act because they fear the consequences of not acting that a group may be considered to be politically influential and a participant in the decision.[1] If the individual can exert such influence, we shall consider him to be *politically competent;* or if he *believes* he can exert such influence, we shall view him as subjectively competent.

So far we have defined political influence as the way in which governmental elites make decisions. Our study, however, concentrates upon the perceptions and behaviors, not of governmental elites, but of the ordinary citizen. We are concerned with the ordinary man's perception of his own influence. Thinking that one can influence the government or even attempting to influence government is not the same as actually influencing it. A citizen may think he has influence over decisions, or he may attempt to exert influence over decisions, and the government official may be unmoved. Conversely, a citizen may believe that all government decisions are made without any consideration of his needs and desires or of the needs and desires of his fellow citizens, when, in fact, government officials constantly try to calculate the way in which groups will react to their acts.

If the degree to which citizens believe they can influence the course of governmental decisions is not necessarily related to their actual level of influence, why study their subjective views of their competence? In the first place, we are interested

[1]This model represents, of course, a great oversimplification. If one were studying the "real" influence situation, rather than the ordinary man's perception of that situation, one would have to complicate things quite a bit. Government officials respond to many different groups for many different reasons. Furthermore, even where democratic political influence by the populace exists, the government official will have reciprocal influence, and this leads to a complex bargaining situation. Since we are not studying the "real" influence situation, however, such complications are not necessary; nor are we forced to ask which citizens exert influence over which officials in relation to which issues.

in the state of attitudes in a country. If democracy involves high levels of actual participation in decisions, then the attitudes of a democratic citizenry should include the perception that they in fact can participate. A democratic citizen speaks the language of demands. Government officials accede to his demands because they fear some loss otherwise—the loss of his vote perhaps—or because they consider it legitimate that he make such demands. The subject, too, may want and expect beneficial outputs from the government. But he does not expect these to be accorded him because he demands them. The government official who acts to benefit him responds, not to the subject's demands, but to some other force. In a traditional society with a highly developed set of norms as to what is due each member, the government official may be responding to these traditional rules when he acts in favor of an individual. Or in an authoritarian-legalistic political system in which the behavior of government officials is circumscribed by explicit rules, he may act as he does because the individual falls within a particular category, which, according to the rules, is to receive a certain type of treatment. In these situations the official is not acting capriciously. His decision to aid the individual is determined by a set of social or legal rules. And these rules may, of course, be enforced by an administrative hierarchy to which the subject may appeal. This kind of subject influence, or administrative competence, is more circumscribed, more passive than that of the citizen. It may set in motion an action that will affect the way in which a rule is interpreted or enforced against an individual. It is not a creative act of influence that can affect the content of the decisions themselves, except in an indirect way.

Second, the perception of the ability to exert political influence is significant even if individuals rarely try to use that influence, or are frequently unsuccessful when they do try. Much of the influence that our respondents believe they have over government probably represents a somewhat unrealistic belief in their opportunities to participate. It is likely that many who say they could influence the government would never attempt to exert such influence; and it is likely as well that if they tried they would not succeed. Yet such a belief in the ordinary man's ability to participate may have significant consequences for a political system. Though individuals' perceptions of their own political ability may not mirror the objective situation, it cannot be unrelated to that situation. If an individual believes he has influence, he is more likely to attempt to use it.[2] A subjectively competent citizen, therefore, is more likely to be an active citizen. And if government officials do not necessarily respond to active influence attempts, they are more likely to respond to them than to a passive citizenry that makes no demands. If the ordinary citizen, on the other hand, perceives that government policy is far outside his sphere of influence, he is unlikely to attempt to influence that policy,

[2]Evidence that those who believe they can influence are more likely to have actual experience in attempting to do so will be presented below, in Table 2.

and government officials are unlikely to worry about the potential pressure that can be brought to bear on them. Thus the extent to which citizens in a nation perceive themselves as competent to influence the government affects their political behavior.

Furthermore, the existence of a belief in the influence potential of citizens may affect the political system even if it does not affect the political activity of the ordinary man. If decision makers believe that the ordinary man *could* participate—and they certainly are not entirely cut off from the dominant social beliefs—they are likely to behave quite differently than if such a belief did not exist. Even if individuals do not act according to this belief, decision makers may act on the assumption that they can, and in this way be more responsive to the citizenry than they would be if the myth of participation did not exist. But whether myth or reality (and the statements we shall be talking about are probably a combination of both), the extent to which individuals think they can influence the government and the ways in which they believe they can do so are . . . important elements of the civic culture.

Here we are concerned with the perceptions that individuals have about the amount of influence they can exercise over governmental decisions. Several questions may be asked about their attempts to influence the government:

1. Under what circumstances will an individual make some conscious effort to influence the government? Direct political influence attempts are rare. For the ordinary citizen the activities of government—even local government—may seem quite distant. At the time that a decision is being made, the citizen is not aware that it is being made or of what its consequences for him are likely to be. It is probable, then, that only in situations of some stress, where a government activity is perceived to have a direct and serious impact upon the individual, will a direct influence attempt be stimulated.
2. What method will be used in the influence attempt? Some major dimensions in this respect include: the kinds of channels of influence that are used; whether the attempt is violent or non-violent; and whether the individual attempts to influence the government alone or attempts to enlist the support of others.
3. What is the effect of the influence attempt? The extent to which the government official changes his behavior in response to some influence attempt by a citizen is a problem beyond the scope of our study. However, since we are concentrating on the perspective of the citizen, we shall consider his view of the likelihood that an attempt made by him to influence the government will have any effect.

The Distribution of Subjective Competence

In developing our survey instrument, we took into account the fact that direct attempts to influence the government are more likely to arise in some stress situations, in which an individual perceives that an activity of the government is threatening injury to him. Our questions attempted to place the individual in such a hypothetical stress situation, so that we could ascertain how he thought he would react. We asked him to suppose that his local government or his national legislature was considering a law that he thought was very unjust and harmful. What did he think he could do about it? If the respondent thought he could do something, we probed to find out what it was. We then asked him how much effect he thought any action he took would have, and how likely it was that he actually would do something. A similar set of questions was asked about an unjust and harmful regulation being considered by the most local governmental unit.[3] These questions were about the political branches of the government, the elected governments on the national and local levels. Through these questions we hoped to get some notion of the respondent's views on the extent of his political competence and, more important, on the strategy of influence open to him.

The results for these questions on local and national subjective competence are reported in Table 1. Two points call for comment. First, in all five countries the sense of subjective competence occurs more frequently vis-à-vis the local government than the national government. This confirms widely held views of the closer relatedness of citizens to their local governments because of their greater immediacy, accessibility, and familiarity. American and British respondents most frequently say that there is something they can do about an unjust local regulation. More than three-quarters of those we interviewed in each of the two countries expressed the opinion that they have some recourse if they believe the local government is considering a law they think unjust; only 17 per cent say that there is nothing they can do. In the other three countries over 30 per cent of those interviewed report that there is nothing they can do in such a situation.[4]

[3]The exact wording of these questions was:

On the national government–

Suppose a law were being considered by [appropriate national legislature specified for each nation] that you considered to be unjust or harmful. What do you think you could do?

If you made an effort to change this law, how likely is it that you would succeed?

If such a case arose, how likely is it you *would actually* try to do something about it?

On the local government–

Suppose a regulation were being considered by [most local governmental unit: town? village? etc. specified] that you considered very unjust or harmful. What do you think you could do?

If you made an effort to change this regulation, how likely is it that you would succeed?

If such a case arose, how likely is it that you *would actually* do something about it?

[4]Many respondents make it quite clear that they believe there is nothing they can do, either because they consider themselves too powerless or because they consider government activities outside their sphere of competence. The following are some examples of these responses:

A German Housewife: "Nothing at all. The local council makes its decision, and there is nothing one can do about it."

*Table 1. Percentage Who Say They Can Do Something about an Unjust Local or National Regulation; by Nation**

Nation	Can Do Something about Local Regulation	Can Do Something about National Regulation
United States	77	75
Great Britain	78	62
Germany	62	38
Italy	51	28
Mexico	52	38

**Percentages in each case apply to the total sample.*

The second point brought out in Table 1 is that, although in all five countries the proportion that says it can influence the local government is higher than the proportion expressing national competence, this difference is relatively small in the American, British, and Mexican samples, and relatively large in Germany and Italy. Put briefly, three-fourths of the American respondents express local and national competence; more than three-fourths and a little less than two-thirds of the British respondents express local and national competence, respectively. In Germany almost two-thirds of the respondents express local competence, whereas only a little more than one-third express national competence. In Italy the proportion drops from one-half to less than one-third. And in Mexico the proportion declines from a little more than one-half to a little more than one-third. The generalization about the greater sense of competence vis-à-vis the local government holds up in our findings, but it is most apparent in Italy and Germany.

That an individual is subjectively competent does not mean that he will in fact try to change what he considers an unfair law. Ours was a hypothetical situation, and we do not really know what our respondents would do if they ever were actually faced with such a challenging situation. But we did ask them for their opinions on whether or not they thought they would act. In all countries many who say they can do something about an unjust regulation report that in fact they probably would do nothing. But the number who report that there is at least some likelihood that they would make an effort reflects the same national pattern reported above. If we consider the responses about the local government (the responses about the

---

A German Housewife: "I'd say nothing because I don't understand it, and I wouldn't do it right, anyway."

An American Semiretired: "Nothing. That's all because we put our trust in our elected people and we must feel they know more about these things than we do even though we don't always agree."

An American Housewife: "Not anything. No 'mam' not nothing . . . Nothing at all."

A British Retired Office Worker: "I wouldn't have much chance to do anything, being just one insignificant person."

An Italian Housewife: "What do you want me to do; I don't count for anything."

A Mexican Housewife: "Nothing. I have no one with whom to talk. I wouldn't know what to do in such a case."

national government form the same pattern), we find that 58 per cent of the American respondents and 50 per cent of those in Britain say there is some likelihood that they would actually make an effort to influence an unjust regulation. In Germany 44 per cent and in Italy 41 per cent make some such affirmation. (The question was, unfortunately, not asked in a comparable form in Mexico.)

Lastly, there is some evidence that the subjective estimate of one's propensity to act in this challenging political situation is closely related to actual attempts to influence the government. In all five nations a substantially larger proportion of those respondents who say there is something they can do about an unjust local regulation (let us, for convenience, call them "local competents") report some experience in attempting to influence the local government. (We find the same pattern in the national data.) These data are reported in Table 2. In all nations those who say they could influence the local government, in comparison with those who say they could not, are at least three times as likely to have attempted such influence.

Table 2. Percentage Who Say They Have Attempted to Influence the Local Government, by Local Competents and Local Noncompetents

Nation	Local Competents		Local Noncompetents	
	(%)	(No.)*	(%)	(No.)
United States	33	(745)	10	(225)
Great Britain	18	(748)	3	(215)
Germany	21	(590)	2	(365)
Italy	13	(508)	4	(487)
Mexico	9	(531)	2	(476)

**Numbers in parentheses refer to the bases upon which percentages are calculated.*

Thus the sense of local and national civic competence is widely distributed among the American and British populations. In Germany and Italy local competence is widely distributed, national competence is much less widely distributed. In Mexico, though the general level of civic competence is lower than in the United States and Britain, the discrepancy between the local and national level (as reported in Table 1) is less great than in Germany and Italy. It also appears that there is a relation between subjective competence and political action.

Local competence and national competence are, as one would expect, fairly closely related. The man who believes he can influence the national government is more likely to think he can influence the local government than is the man who does not feel competent on the national level. Conversely, the man who feels competent locally is also more likely to believe he can influence the national government than is the man who does not have a sense of local competence. Earlier it was pointed out that local competence is more widespread than national competence. Furthermore, local competence is most widely distributed in nations in which local government autonomy and the accessibility of local government officials to ordinary citizens is most firmly institutionalized. . . . Adding these three facts together—local and national competence are related, local competence is more widespread than national, and local competence is related to the institutional availability of opportunities to participate on the local level—one has an argument in favor of the classic position that political participation on the local level plays a major role in the development of a competent citizenry. As many writers have argued, local government may act as a training ground for political competence. Where local government allows participation, it may foster a sense of competence that then spreads to the national level—a sense of competence that would have had a harder time developing had the individual's only involvement with government been with the more distant and inaccessible structures of the national government. To argue this point is to speculate beyond our data on national and local competence. But . . . the individual's belief in his ability to affect the government derives, at least in part, from opportunities to be influential within smaller authority structures such as the family, the school, and the place of work.

The Strategy of Influence

Another aspect of political competence is the strategy an individual would use in attempting to influence the government. The *way* in which those who report that they could influence the government say they could exert this influence is, of course, important. It makes a difference whether someone has only the vaguest notion of what he can do, or a clear view of the channels open to him for expressing his point of view. It also makes a difference what resources he believes he has available to use. Furthermore, the strategy that an individual would use will naturally affect the extent to which his subjective view of his ability to influence represents real influence potential—that is, it represents the sort of activity that has some chance of changing the behavior of the government officials. We shall deal primarily with those who think they have influence, the "competents," and ask how they would exert that influence.

The strategies of influence that individuals report they would use in connection with the local government are summarized in Table 3. (Comparable data on the national government will be presented below.) Let us look first at the question of what social resources the individual feels he has available to him. This is highly significant for understanding the nature of his perceived relationship to his government. Government organizations are large and powerful, especially when compared to the individual. This is especially true of the national government, but even local government represents an institution whose resources are much greater than those of the ordinary man. Looking at the individual and his government, one is tempted to see him as lonely, powerless, and somewhat frightened by the immensity of the powers he faces. This is in fact one of the most frequent descriptions of the average man in modern political societies. In the theory of the "mass society" the individual is described as related directly as individual to the state. He has no other social resources to support him in this relationship and naturally feels ineffective and anxious.[5] However valid this theory may be concerning the actual amount of power the average man has and the social resources available to him, our data suggest that a large number of our respondents do not view themselves as the model of mass society describes them. In their relationship to their government they think of themselves as neither powerless nor, what is more important, alone.

This fact is reflected in the data reported in Table 3. A number of our respondents believe that they can enlist the support of others in their attempts to influence the government. What is most striking is the variation from country to country in the numbers who feel they can call on others to aid them. In the United States 59 per cent of our respondents indicated that they could attempt to enlist the support of others if they wished to change a regulation they considered unjust. At the other extreme, only 9 per cent of the Italians mentioned the use of this social resource. In the other countries the proportions reporting that they would try to enlist the support of others varied from 36 per cent in Britain, to 28 per cent in Mexico, to 21 per cent in Germany.[6]

Whom would citizens enlist to support them? Individuals as we know are members of a large number of social groups. They are not merely citizens of their nations; they are members of families, communities, churches, voluntary associations, trade unions, and a great variety of other groups and organizations. Basically these associations can be divided into two classes: formal organizations and informal face-to-face groups.

Much has been written about the important role of formal organizations in the political process—especially the role of political parties and associational interest groups. Both play major intervening roles between the individual and his government. They aggregate the demands of citizens and communicate these to government officials. Recently there has been growing interest in the informal face-to-face network of social groups to which an individual belongs—family, friends, work group, and neighbors. Here the main emphasis has been upon the impact of these groups on the political attitudes of their members, and on the process of communication downward; that is, to the individuals from such formal institutions as government, political parties, and the mass media.[7] Little has been

[5]On this general topic see William Kornhauser, *The Politics of Mass Society* (New York, 1959).

[6]Since question wording can seriously affect the response received, it is important to note here that the notion that one could enlist the support of others was in no way suggested by the question or by the interviewer's probing of the question. Interviewers were carefully instructed not to ask such questions as: "Is there anyone you could get to help you?" or "Would you attempt to do this alone or with other people?"

[7]On the subject of the political functions of informal groups, see Sidney Verba, *Small Groups and Political Behavior* (Princeton, N.J., 1961), Chap. 2.

Table 3. What Citizens Would Do to Try to Influence Their Local Government; by Nation

What Citizens Would Do	U.S.	U.K.	Germany	Italy	Mexico
Try to enlist aid of others					
Organize an informal group; arouse friends and neighbors, get them to write letters of protest or to sign a petition	56	34	13	7	26
Work through a political party	1	1	3	1	—
Work through a formal group (union, church, professional) to which they belong	4	3	5	1	2
Total percentage who would enlist others' aid*	59	36	21	9	28
Act alone					
Directly contact political leaders (elected officials) or the press; write a letter to or visit a local political leader	20	45	15	12	15
Directly contact administrative (nonelected) officials	1	3	31	12	18
Consult a lawyer; appeal through courts	2	1	3	2	2
Vote against offending officials at next election	14	4	1	1	—
Take some violent action	1	1	1	1	1
Just protest	—	—	—	12	—
Other	1	2	—	3	5
Total percentage who would act alone+	18	41	41	43	24
Total percentage who would act with others or alone	77	78	62	51	53
Total number of respondents	970	963	955	995	1,007

**Total percentages are less than the total of the individual cells, since some respondents gave more than one answer.*

+This row includes only the respondents who replied that they could do something but did not mention working with others. Hence the total is less than the sum of the individual cells, which contain respondents who may have mentioned both group and individual activity.

said about the role of such informal associations in what we might call the "influence-upward" process: the process by which citizens in a democracy influence the attitudes and behavior of government officials. But our findings show most strikingly that, when it comes to the support that individuals believe they could enlist in a challenging political situation, they think much more often of enlisting support from the informal face-to-face groups of which they are members than from the formal organizations to which they belong or with which they are affiliated. In all countries except Germany, less than 1 per cent of the respondents indicate that they would work through their political party if they were attempting to counteract some unjust regulation being considered by the local government; the German figure is about 3 per cent. Clearly, no matter how important the role of political parties may be in democratic societies, relatively few citizens think of them first as the place where support may be enlisted for attempts to influence the government.[8]

In all countries more individuals report that they would attempt to work through other formal organized groups than through political parties. But when one considers the entire range of formal organizations to which people may belong, the number who report they would enlist their support is small: no more than 3 per cent of the respondents in any country. Of course, not all respondents have some formal organization at their disposal; such organizations are more frequent in some nations than in others. And the percentage who report membership differs substantially from country to country. Furthermore, not all formal organizations are equally politically relevant.

But even among those respondents who belong to a formal organization that they report is involved in politics, the number who would invoke such membership in a stress situation is much smaller than the number who are members. In the United States, where such memberships are most frequent, 228 respondents report membership in this kind of organization, but only 35 of these Americans report that they would work through that organization if they were trying to influence a local regulation. In Italy, where such memberships are least frequent, we find the same pattern. Fifty-six Italians belong to some organization they believe is involved in political affairs, but only thirteen of those members would work through it if they were trying to influence a local regulation. The aid of a formal organization would be called upon most frequently in Germany, but only half as frequently as the occurrence of membership in a politically relevant organization.

That formal organizations rarely would be invoked by individuals who were trying to influence the government does not mean, however, that these organizations are politically unimportant. They still may affect an individual's political influence, for he may have more influence over government officials merely by being a member of such a group, even if he makes no overt attempt to influence the government. And this sort of influence is of great significance—probably of greater overall significance than the overt influence attempts that ordinary citizens make from time to time. Furthermore, though an individual would not use

[8]To some extent the infrequent mention of a political party in this context probably understates the role of parties in this influence process. Many more respondents mentioned contacting government officials. If they explicitly mentioned that the partisan affiliation of the official was relevant in their attaining access to him, they would be coded as working through a party. But many may have considered this affiliation relevant even if they did not mention it.

his formal organization as the means to influence the government directly, his membership in itself enhances the prospects that he will believe himself capable of influencing the government and will actually make some such attempt. Thus he may for a variety of reasons . . . develop greater self-confidence in his own political competence.

Cooperative political behavior. As Table 3 indicates, in all nations respondents less frequently mention enlisting the support of formal groups than informal groups–arousing their neighbors, getting friends and acquaintances to support their position, circulating a petition. This in itself is striking, though it ought not, for reasons given above, to be taken to imply that these informal groups play a more significant role in the political process than do formal organizations. What is most striking is not the frequency with which informal groups are mentioned in all countries, but the sharp differences in frequency among the nations.

Thus Table 4 shows that 56 per cent of the American respondents, 34 per cent of the British, and 26 per cent of the Mexicans reported that they would use this informal group strategy, as compared with 13 per cent of the Germans and 7 per cent of the Italians. If we consider the proportion of local competents who say they would cooperate with their fellow citizens in attempting to influence the government,[9] we find that 74 per cent of American local competents would use informal groups, whereas only 13 per cent of Italian local competents and 22 per cent of the Germans would do so. In Mexico, though the proportion of local competents is relatively low, the proportion of those local competents

Table 4. Those Who Would Enlist the Aid of an Informal Group to Influence an Unjust Local Regulation

Nation	Percentage of Total Sample (%)	(No.)*	Percentage of Local Competents (%)	(No.)
United States	56	(970)	74	(745)
Great Britain	34	(963)	43	(748)
Germany	13	(955)	22	(590)
Italy	7	(995)	13	(508)
Mexico	26	(1,007)	50	(531)

**Numbers in parentheses refer to the bases upon which percentages are calculated.*

[9]The percentage of respondents mentioning a particular strategy of influence can be computed either as a percentage of the entire population or as a percentage of the local competents only. Both figures are important. The first figure reflects the propensity for certain types of political behavior in a nation. But if we are interested in how nations differ in the strategies their citizens will use, we must use the second figure; for if we did not, the national differences in the percentage choosing a particular strategy might reflect merely that there are more in one country than in another who report that there is nothing they could do. In the following tables the percentages will be reported in both forms.

who would work through informal groups is quite high—50 per cent. And in Britain the proportion of local competents who say they would seek the cooperation of others is about as great—43 per cent.

The notions that one can cooperate with one's fellow citizens in attempting to influence the government and that such cooperation is an effective means of increasing one's own influence dominate the bulk of the responses of the local competents in the United States and play an important role in responses in Britain and Mexico. In all five countries, however, there are individuals who would work with others in attempting to influence the government. A few illustrations may help to convey that attitude:

> *An American Office Manager:* "You can't do anything individually. You'd have to get a group and all get together and go to the proper authorities to complain."
> *An American Salesman:* "Get up a petition. Get together with people who have the same objection. Taking it up with the responsible person like the mayor or police commissioner."
> *An American Housemaid:* "I could discuss it with others and see how many others felt the same about it as I did. We could then write a letter each to some government person in charge and let him know how we felt, or we could write one letter and get a lot of people to sign it."
> *An English Dispatch Clerk:* "Contact neighbors and friends and make a protest to the councillors. . . ."
> *An English Foreman Gardener:* "First thing—get a petition going. Take it up to the Council offices and make yourself spokesman of a group. You could try the local M.P."
> *An English House Painter:* "You could more or less get a petition up and show the feeling. You could discuss it with your workmates and your wife."
> *A Mexican Shoemaker:* "Protest, join a group of citizens, and personally go to the office where it was issued and talk about it to the authorities."
> *A Mexican Housewife:* "I would get together all the people and send a petition to the president or the governor of the state signed by all."

In a democratic political system, the belief that cooperation with one's fellow citizens is both a possible and an effective political action represents, we suggest, a highly significant orientation. The diffusion of influence over political decisions, by which we define democracy, implies some cooperative ability among the citizenry. This cooperation seems to be necessary, in terms of both the amount of influence the ordinary man can expect to have and the results of his influence on governmental decisions. By definition, the "average" man's influence over the government must be small. Compared with the forces of government—and this would apply to local as well as national government—he is a frail creature indeed. If the ordinary man is to have any political influence, it must be in concert with his fellows. Second, from the point of view of the output of a democratic government, noncooperative and completely individualistic influence attempts could lead only to dysfunctional results. Every individual demand cannot be met, or the result will be chaos. If the government is to be responsive to the demands of the ordinary man, these demands must be aggregated, and the aggregation of interests implies cooperation among men. The aggregation of interests involved in the cooperation of groups of like-minded individuals is aggregation on a rather low level, but it does suggest a propensity to work together with one's fellows, which is relevant for larger political structures as well. In any case, we may suggest that the citizen who believes he can work cooperatively with others in his environment if he wants to engage in political activity has quite a different perspective on politics from the individual who thinks of himself as a lone political actor.

Furthermore, the notion that one can affect a government decision by bringing one's peers into the dispute is a highly political notion. It represents a fairly clear attempt to use political influence in one's relations with government officials. The threat that *many* make—whether it is the threatened loss of votes or of support, or the threat of public criticism—is, other things being equal, greater than the threat that *one* can make. Thus the individual who mentions getting others to join him in his dispute with the government is more likely to see himself as a citizen able to influence his government than as a subject who lacks such influence. And the variations among the five nations in the frequency with which such groups are mentioned reflect variations in such citizen competence.

It is particularly important to note what sorts of groups are involved here. The informal groups our respondents talk of forming do not exist, at least in a politically relevant sense, before the political stress situation arises. The individual perceives himself as able to create structures for the purpose of influencing the government. These structures represent a form of influence that had not been committed to politics before the politically challenging situation arose. In this sense, the ability of the individual to create structures to aid him in his disputes with the government represents a reserve of influence on his part. He has not committed his complete support to some larger social system, as has the individual in the so-called mass society; nor is he cut off from contact with the government, as is the parochial.

That a large proportion of people in a country perceive that the informal face-to-face groups of which they are members can be rallied to their support in time of political stress represents a significant aspect of the political culture of that nation. It means that some of the most basic building blocks of the social structure have been incorporated into the political system. An individual's role as citizen, particularly as a democratic, influential citizen, fuses with his other social roles. The type of political activity sparking this fusion of informal group membership and political citizenship is also highly significant. The fusion takes place because of political demands being made by citizens upon their government. They invoke their friends and neighbors in an attempt to influence their government. Thus the fusion occurs at the heart of the democratic process—the process by which the ordinary citizen exercises some control over his government. This is profoundly different from the fusion between face-to-face groups and government that has been attempted within totalitarian states. Here the government has attempted to influence the individual: family and friendship groups are penetrated by the state to support its attempts to propagandize and control. The state attempts to control these informal groups. In the countries we studied the invocation of informal groups has a contrary meaning. It is an attempt to penetrate and control government. It represents a meshing together of polity and community, rather than an assimilation of community into the polity.

Lastly, we have stressed the importance of this propensity toward cooperation with one's fellow citizens, not merely because we believe that it has significant consequences for the political system, but because we feel it is a type of behavior that can best be understood and explained by the type of study contained in this book. In the first place, the frequency with which individuals talk of cooperating with their fellow citizens to influence the government is not as dependent upon the structure of government as is the frequency with which they say they can influence the government. Whether or not someone feels he can affect the course of government action obviously depends to a large extent upon the structure of government—the extent to which it provides citizen access. But the difference between the individual who responds that he would write a letter to the local council and the one who responds that he would write a letter to the local council *and try to induce his friends to do likewise* cannot be explained by national differences in the structure and powers of their respective local councils.[10] As we shall see shortly, these differing levels of social and economic development,

[10]This is not completely true. Governmental structure may be more amenable to group influence in some countries than in others. But this is more likely to occur because of the government's past experience with such groups than because of the government's formal structure. On the other hand, there is no doubt that certain structures of government foster such "banding together" protests more than do others. Structures where power is diffused among a large number of autonomous or semi-autonomous boards and councils and the like (especially elected boards and councils) are more likely to foster such protest than are structures dominated by a centrally appointed official whose domain includes a larger area (as with the Italian prefect system). But this is an example of the general proposition that interaction will occur between political orientation and political structure. In this case, however, to explain the origins of this group-forming attitude according to formal political structure alone would be unconvincing. One has to look beyond the structure of the local government.

There is, however, another way in which governmental structure may foster or inhibit the group forming propensities of a population. The legal systems of nations differ in the extent to which they ban, regulate, or in other ways make difficult the formation of non-governmental associations. Legal systems on the European continent have been more hostile to such groups than has the Anglo-American legal system. And though these regulations refer largely to formal organizations . . . they might have an effect on informal groups as well. See on this point, Arnold Rose, "On Individualism and Social Responsibility," *Archives Européennes de Sociologie,* Vol. 2 (1961), pp. 163-169.

while they can explain many of the political differences among the nations, cannot explain the propensity to cooperate politically. The origin of this propensity must be sought elsewhere. It can be traced to social values and attitudes and to the degree of partisan fragmentation in society.[11]

Though the use of primary groups as a resource for influence is most common in the United States, Britain, and Mexico, there are several interesting differences between the United States and Britain on the one hand and Mexico on the other. The notion that one can mobilize an informal group as an aid in attempting to influence the government appears to be of greater significance for the actual exercise of influence in the former two countries. Earlier it was pointed out that those who report they can do something about an unjust local law (the local competents), compared with those who report the opposite, are much more likely to report some experience in attempting to influence the government. If we look only at the local competents and ask how those who would work through groups and those who would act alone differ in the extent of their experience in attempted local influence, we find that in the United States and Britain those who would work through groups are more likely to have had experience in these endeavors. In the United States 36 per cent of those who report they would work through informal groups (n: 547) also report that they have at some time actually attempted to influence the government, whereas only 25 per cent of those local competents who would use some other strategy (n: 198) report such experience. In Britain the parallel figures are 23 per cent for those who mention informal groups (n: 315) and 15 per cent for other local competents (n: 414). In Mexico, on the other hand, those who mention informal groups are a bit less likely to be the experienced respondents: 7 per cent of those who mention informal groups (n: 264) report experience, as against 10 per cent of the other local competents (n: 267).[12]

Furthermore, in the former two countries the use of informal groups as a means of influencing the government is seen, not only as a means to protest, but as the key to effective protest. In order to test the extent to which individuals felt they could influence their local government, we asked another question after asking what respondents thought they could do about an unjust local law: "If you made an effort to change this regulation, how likely is it that you would

[11]The relationship between social and economic development and the propensity to form groups will be discussed at the end of the chapter.

[12]In Germany those local competents who mention informal groups are somewhat less likely to have had actual influence experience. Seventeen per cent of those who mention informal groups (n: 126) report past experience, as against 23 per cent of local competents who do not mention them (n: 460). In Italy those local competents who mention groups are somewhat more likely to be experienced: 16 per cent (n: 67), as against 13 per cent (n: 438) of those who do not mention groups.

succeed?" Of interest to us here is that a large number of American and British local competents volunteered the statement that their protest would have some likelihood of success only if others joined with them. (The percentages were 30 in the United States and 20 in Britain.) In Mexico, though a good percentage felt there was some likelihood that they would succeed if they attempted to influence their local government, fewer than one per cent of the respondents suggested that this would be the case only if they had the support of others. Though the use of informal groups is perceived as a means of influence in Mexico, it is not yet perceived as the key to effective influence.[13]

One further difference deserves mention. In the United States and Britain the use of informal groups as a means of influencing a governmental decision is considered much more appropriate on the local than on the national level. In Mexico, on the other hand, the proportion who would use informal groups is about the same on the local and national levels. The fact that in Britain and the United States, more than in Mexico, the use of such groups is closely related both to experience and to expectations of success, coupled with the fact that such strategy is considered more appropriate in connection with the local government in the former two countries, suggests that informal group strategy is based on a more realistic appraisal of the potentialities of such a strategy—a realistic appraisal deriving from actual experience with such groups on the local level. In Mexico this influence strategy is less well grounded in actual local experience. It appears to be another instance of the aspirational character of the Mexican political culture.

Individual action. The respondents who spoke of themselves as acting alone in their attempt to influence the government show some variation, as Table 4 indicates, in the strategies they mention. In the United States and Britain respondents are more likely to say they would approach an elected government official rather than an appointed official of the bureaucracy. In Mexico and Italy respondents are as likely to say they would direct their protest toward one type of official as toward the other. In Germany, however, more respondents mention appointed officials than elected officials as the target of their protest. It is tempting to consider these results to be a reflection of a more highly developed political competence in the United States and Britain. A protest to an elected official seems to be inherently more of a political protest, in the sense of involving an implied threat of deprivation to the official if he does not comply—for the loss of the vote is the most usual deprivation with which the individual can threaten an offending official. This may partly explain the differences among the nations in the chosen targets of influence attempts; but it is more likely that these differences

[13]In Germany the percentage of local competents who mentioned that they would succeed only if others joined them was 12; in Italy it was 5.

merely reflect national differences in the relative position and importance of elected and appointed officials within the structures of local government.

Lastly, not all of those who say they could do something about an unjust local regulation had any clear strategy in mind. As Table 3 indicates, 12 per cent of the Italian respondents said that they could protest if faced with a regulation they considered unjust, but when asked how or to whom they could protest, gave no more specific reply. The 12 per cent who would protest represent about one-fourth of all Italian local competents. While this answer shows a higher level of subjective competence than the answer that one could do nothing, it reflects little awareness of the political channels through which one might effectively approach the government.

National Competence

We saw in Table 1 that in all nations fewer respondents say they could influence the national legislature than the local government and more say there is nothing they could do. In Table 5 we report the strategies respondents say they would use vis-à-vis the national government. In all nations formal organizations are somewhat more often mentioned as a resource for influencing the national government than the local government. (And if one calculated the percentage as a proportion of "national competents" rather than as a proportion of the entire sample, the difference would be sharper.) Conversely, in all nations fewer respondents mention using informal groups in connection with the national government than mentioned them in connection with the local government, though the pattern is the same; these groups are mentioned most frequently in the United States, followed by Britain and Mexico, then Germany and Italy. Generally, national influence strategies tend to rely more on the organized structures of politics, such as interest groups, political parties, and the press, or on individual approaches to elected political leaders. As we have already pointed out, this probably reflects realistic calculations. It takes a larger group and greater and greater political skill to bring influence to bear on the national than on the local government. However, our evidence suggests that informal group competence persists significantly at the national level in the United States and Britain, even if it does not bulk as large as it does at the local level.

Social Groups and Subjective Competence

Clearly the five nations differ in the extent to which their citizens believe themselves capable of doing something should government threaten their interests; they differ, too, in the strategies the citizens would use. Why are there such differences? The causes are many and we do not claim to deal with them all in this study. We shall concern ourselves with the more limited question of whether the differences observed are general differences among the political cultures of our five countries, or are differences that vary sharply and in the same way among

Table 5. What Citizens Would Do to Try to Influence Their National Government; by Nation

What Citizens Would Do	U.S.	U.K.	Germany	Italy	Mexico
Try to enlist aid of others					
Organize an informal group; arouse friends and neighbors, get them to write letters of protest or to sign a petition	29	18	7	6	18
Work through a political party	1	2	6	2	—
Work through a formal group (union, church, professional) to which they belong	4	3	7	2	3
Total percentage who would enlist others' aid*	32	22	19	10	20
Act alone					
Directly contact political leaders (elected officials) or the press; write a letter to or visit a local political leader	57	44	12	7	8
Directly contact administrative (nonelected) officials	—	1	4	4	6
Consult a lawyer; appeal through courts	—	—	1	1	4
Vote against offending officials at next election	7	3	4	1	—
Take some violent action	—	—	2	1	4
Just protest	—	—	—	3	—
Other	—	2	—	2	3
Total percentage who would act alone+	42	40	18	18	18
Nothing	21	32	56	50	50
Don't know	4	6	7	22	12
Total percentage‡	123	111	106	101	108
Total number of respondents	970	963	955	995	1,007

**Total percentages are less than the total of the individual cells since some respondents gave more than one answer.*

+This row includes only the respondents who said they could do something but did not mention working with others. Hence the total is less than the sum of the individual cells, which contain respondents who may have mentioned both group and individual activity.

‡Percentages exceed 100 because of multiple responses.

subgroups themselves, whatever the country. If the former is true, one would expect most Italians to respond in the same way, no matter what their social position, and to differ from Americans of all social groups. If the latter is true, one would expect upper-status Italians to differ significantly from Italians of lower status, and to resemble Americans of similar status. There are many difficulties in making such comparisons—not the least of which is the difficulty of getting equivalent status measures across societies; but by using roughly equivalent subgroups for comparisons, we shall attempt to make them. Furthermore, by using different measures to compare these results, one can begin to distinguish those patterns that seem to depend more upon the distribution of other social characteristics within a society. If the differences among the nations disappear when one considers only social groups that are roughly matched, one has an aspect of political culture that is less specific to the particular culture. On the other hand, if the nationals in a particular social grouping of one country still differ significantly from those of a similar social group in other countries, though they resemble closely their fellow nationals of diverse social backgrounds, one is probably dealing with an aspect of political culture whose roots are in the unique experiences of that country, and not in the experiences common to all our countries.

Let us look first at the relationship between citizen competence and education. We choose education as the first variable to consider, because of its close relationship with the factors that would tend to make a man feel subjectively competent. . . . As Figure 1 clearly points out, in all countries the more education an individual has, the more likely he is to consider himself capable of influencing the local government; that is, to be what we have called a local competent. (The percentage of individuals who say they could affect a local law is measured on the vertical axis; the level of education on the horizontal.) In the United States 60 per cent of those who did not get beyond primary school and 95 per cent of those with some college education are local competents. And the pattern repeats itself in each country. This then is a clear uniformity across national lines. No matter what the frequency of local competence within a nation, the incidence of this competence is greater among those with higher education.

What about the differences among and within nations? The question is a bit harder to answer, for differences exist both among educational groups within the same country (as the slopes of the lines indicate) and within similar educational groups among nations (as the different heights of the lines indicate). Some differences among nations diminish significantly within similar educational groups. For instance, though the American and German national totals for local competents are quite different, the differences between the two countries almost disappear when similar educational groups are compared. The greatest similarity in national totals occurs between the United States and Britain, on the one hand, and Mexico and Italy, on the other; yet in each pair the members differ somewhat more from each other between similar educational groups than they do on the national level. When the primary educated of America and Britain are

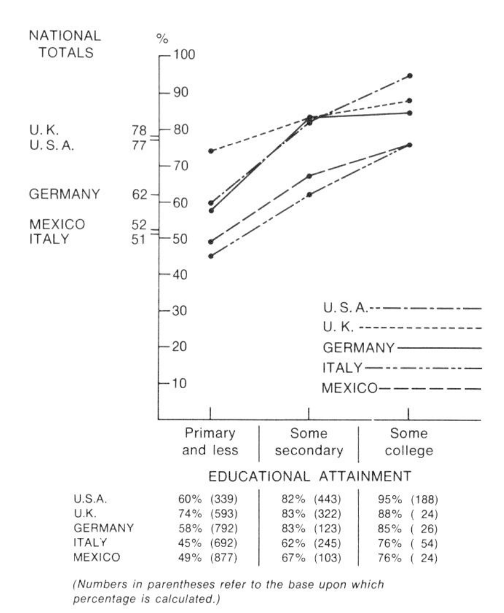

	Primary and less	Some secondary	Some college
U.S.A.	60% (339)	82% (443)	95% (188)
U.K.	74% (593)	83% (322)	88% (24)
GERMANY	58% (792)	83% (123)	85% (26)
ITALY	45% (692)	62% (245)	76% (54)
MEXICO	49% (877)	67% (103)	76% (24)

(Numbers in parentheses refer to the base upon which percentage is calculated.)

Figure 1. Percentage of Respondents Who Say That They Can Do Something about a Local Regulation That They Consider Unjust or Unfair (by Nation and Education)

compared, those in Britain show a higher rate of citizen competence; and when the lower educational groups of Italy and Mexico are compared, those in Mexico show a somewhat higher competence on the lower two levels.

Thus education has a mixed effect on the differences among nations. But the following general statements can be made on the basis of Figure 1. On all levels of education Mexican and Italian respondents are less frequently local competents than are respondents on similar levels in the other three countries (though on the university level the difference becomes quite slight.) Second, the higher the educational level, the less difference there is among nations. This fact comes out clearly if one looks at the range among the nations on each level of education. On the elementary school level the range between the nation with the greatest frequency of local competents (Britain) and the nation with the least frequency (Italy) is 29 percentage points; on the secondary school level there are 21 percentage points between the nations that have the greatest frequency (Britain and Germany) and the one with the least (Italy); and on the university level 19 percentage points separate the United States, on the one hand, from Italy and Mexico, on the other.

Which are greater, national or educational differences? The measure of these is rough, but if one compares the ranges between the highest and lowest nation

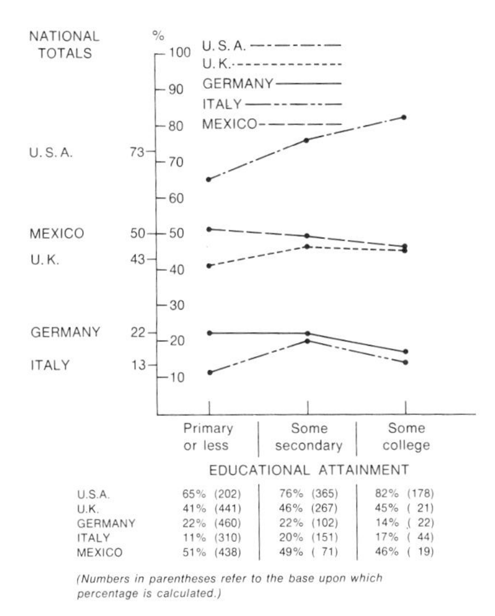

	Primary or less	Some secondary	Some college
U.S.A.	65% (202)	76% (365)	82% (178)
U.K.	41% (441)	46% (267)	45% (21)
GERMANY	22% (460)	22% (102)	14% (22)
ITALY	11% (310)	20% (151)	17% (44)
MEXICO	51% (438)	49% (71)	46% (19)

(Numbers in parentheses refer to the base upon which percentage is calculated.)

Figure 2. Percentage of Local Competents Who Would Enlist the Support of an Informal Group in Order to Influence a Local Regulation They Thought Was Unjust (by Nation and Education)

within each educational group (as reported in the previous paragraph) with the ranges between the highest and lowest educational group within each nation, the results suggest that there is certainly as much–if not, on the average, more–variation among educational groups within a single nation than among individuals with similar educational attainment in different nations. In the frequency with which respondents believe themselves competent to influence the government, there is within each nation about as much, if not more, difference among the educational levels as there is cross-nationally on each educational level. The ranges between the educational group that most frequently reports itself competent to influence the government (those with some university education in each nation) and the group that least frequently reports such competence (those with only primary education or no education in each country) are: United States, 35 percentage points; Britain, 14 percentage points; Germany, 27 percentage points; Italy, 31 percentage points, and Mexico, 27 percentage points. These figures are rough, since they compare the extreme cases as to education and as to nation. But they do suggest that in overall local competence, similar educational groups compared cross-nationally resemble one another at least as much as, and perhaps more than do different educational groups within the same nation.

So far we have considered the extent to which individuals believe they can influence an unjust local regulation. But the strategy an individual would use may be more important than the simple distinction of whether or not he thinks he can do anything. In particular, the belief that one can cooperate with one's fellow citizens as a means of influencing the government appears to be important. Does this political strategy depend to as large an extent upon educational attainment as does the existence of local competence? The data in Figure 2 suggest that it does not.

The percentage of local competents who would work through informal groups varies sharply from country to country even within each educational group, but varies very little among educational groups within the individual countries.[14] Only in the United States does the frequency with which such activity is mentioned vary directly with educational attainment, and even here the relationship is not as strong as that between educational levels and local competence in general. Consider again the contrast between the United States and Germany. Within similar educational groups, German and American respondents hardly differ in the frequency with which they say that there is something they can do about an unjust local regulation. But if we compare the percentage of these local competents who would cooperate with their fellow citizens, we see that on each educational level German respondents are much less likely to mention such activity. Furthermore, well-educated German respondents are no more likely to talk of such activity than are less-educated ones. Unlike the situation in relation to overall local competence, where the range of difference among nations was no greater and perhaps a little less than the range of variation among one nation's educational groups, the variation among nations in the frequency with which political cooperation is mentioned is generally much greater on all educational levels than among educational groups within a nation. Here, then, may be a pattern of political culture the existence of which is independent of the educational attainment of an individual or the educational level in a nation. Education, our data suggest, may lead individuals to believe that they can influence their government, *no matter what country they live in* (providing, of course, that there is at least some institutional structure to support this attitude). Our data also suggest that as the overall educational level of nations rises, they will become more similar in this respect. But education does not necessarily increase the potentiality that individuals will create

[14]The percentage is calculated as a percentage of local competents, not of the total population. This is to isolate the political strategy that competents would use from the fact that the frequency of competents differs from country to country.

groups to support them. The ability to create political structures through cooperation with one's fellow citizens in time of stress seems to be typical of some nations and not of others. It is an element of political style, not a result of educational attainment.

Our discussion suggests that local competence varies with social grouping, while the use of informal groups as the strategy of influence is much more dependent upon national political style. Figures 1 and 2 compared respondents on differing educational levels, but the same pattern emerges if one compares respondents by occupation and by sex. But there is little variation among these groups in the frequency with which a group-oriented strategy is selected.

The data on educational, occupational, and sex differences in subjective competence suggest that whether or not one believes himself capable of influencing a local or national regulation depends a lot on who he is within his own country.[15] If he has more education, higher status, or is male, he is clearly more likely to consider himself competent. One's self-perceptions of his role as a citizen vary greatly with one's social position within a nation. But whether or not the local competent believes that his friends and neighbors are available to help him in a stress situation depends relatively little on his social position within a nation; more important is the nation he happens to live in. Political competence thus grows with higher education or occupational status, but cooperative competence seems to be rooted in specific national political cultures.

[15]The questions on "national competence" produce a similar pattern of response.

Organizational Membership and Democratic Consensus

Sidney Verba

The role of private, non-governmental organizations in democratic government has been dealt with from a variety of points of view. Three of the most important are: pressure group politics, mass politics, and theories of cross-pressures. The concern of pressure group theorists has been largely with the problem of the allocation of goods and services in a society—with the classic question of who gets what, when and how. The concern of "mass politics" theorists has been with the role of such organizations as mediators between rulers and ruled. The "cross-pressures" focus involves the role of non-governmental organizations in structuring political competition, in particular in mitigating the intensity of such competition.[1] Non-governmental organizations, thus, have been dealt with in relation to three of the most important theoretical problems that arise in democratic politics: the problem of the allocation of values among competing groups; the problem of citizen participation in politics; and the problem of the structuring of patterns of conflict among competing groups. And these organizations may become especially important at a time when other institutions are operating less effectively in these areas. With

[1]The classic works are, of course, Arthur F. Bentley, *The Process of Government* (1908); and David Truman, *The Governmental Process* (New York: Knopf, 1959). Most relevant from the point of view of theoretical analysis and comparative politics are Gabriel A. Almond, "A Comparative Study of Interest Groups and the Political Process," *American Political Science Review,* Vol. 52 (1958), pp. 270-282; Harry Eckstein, *Pressure Group Politics* (Stanford, Calif.: Stanford Univ. Press, 1960), Chapter 1; and Joseph LaPalombara, "The Utility and Limitations of Interest Group Theory in Non-American Field Situations," *Journal of Politics,* Vol. 22 (1960), pp. 29-49. There have been numerous recent critiques of the pressure-group approach. The one that is most relevant to the concern of this paper is by William C. Mitchell. In an unpublished manuscript entitled *Some Recent Theories of American Politics,* he stresses both the limitations of group theory as an allocational theory as well as the paucity of data that exists to support it. On the mass society approach, see William Kornhauser, *The Politics of Mass Society* (New York: Free Press, 1959).

Sidney Verba, "Organizational Membership and Democratic Consensus," Journal of Politics, *Vol. 27 (August 1965). Reprinted with permission.*

the decline of ideology, the waning of parliamentary opposition, the inability of political parties to structure meaningful electoral issues, and the inability of parliaments to control major policy decisions (all characteristics of politics in many contemporary democracies), the locus of politics may move out of the political party-electoral system-parliamentary nexus into a realm where interest groups and other associations play a major role.

This paper will deal with the third theoretical problem discussed above—cross-pressures and the structuring of patterns of conflict within political systems. It will try to test some of the hypotheses about the effects of multiple group affiliation on the intensity of political conflict using data from a cross-national survey of attitudes towards politics.[2] That the data come from several different political systems—the United States, Britain, Germany, Italy and Mexico—is important. The multiple membership theories have been developed in an American context and applied to American politics. The cross-national validation of the hypotheses or the specification of the conditions under which the hypotheses hold or do not hold should do much to illuminate the theory. Furthermore, though the theory developed within the American context, there has been relatively little empirical work done to test it even within that context.[3] There is often a danger that useful suggestions—especially when they are as interesting and compelling as the multiple membership theories—will be taken as fully validated conclusions about politics. Though the data presented here will be far from adequate to support or refute the hypothesis that multiple group affiliation tends to mitigate political conflict, it should make some contribution to that task.

Multiple, overlapping memberships in organizations, according to cross-pressure theories, prevent the polarization of political conflict. This takes place in two ways. On the elite level, organizational leaders reduce the intensity of their claims on other social groups because of the diversity of membership in their organization. On the level of the organizational rank and file, so the argument goes, the individual shares membership—and consequently shares some goals as well as perhaps has personal contact—with people with whom he differs politically. And this exposure tends to lower the level of opposition to political opponents. William Kornhauser aptly characterizes the pluralist system of affiliation. "Cross-cutting solidarities . . . help prevent one line of social cleavage from becoming dominant, and they

[2]The data is based upon a cross-national survey conducted in five nations—the United States, Great Britain, Germany, Italy, and Mexico. Approximately 1,000 interviews were conducted in each country using a stratified, multistage probability sample. The interviews were conducted in early summer 1959, with the exception of those in the United States, which were in March 1960. For a fuller discussion of the data and for some other results based upon this survey, see Gabriel A. Almond and Sidney Verba, *The Civic Culture: Political Attitudes and Democracy in Five Nations* (Princeton, N.J.: Princeton Univ. Press, 1963). The samples are described in Appendix A.

[3]See Mitchell, *op. cit.*

constrain associations to respect the various affiliations of their members lest they alienate them. . . . They may be contrasted with situations in which religious and class lines tend to closely correspond, as in France where anti-clericalism is largely a working-class phenomenon."[4] An overlapping pattern of organizational affiliation, it should be noted, is a way of *managing* the strains that arise from patterns of cleavage in a society, not a way of *eliminating* cleavage. The latter is not a meaningful possibility in a modern democratic state. To manage cleavage implies that the intensity of competition among political opponents remains low enough to make the alternation of power from one group to another acceptable to the competitors. This means that differences in policy preferences must be kept in bounds: they must be negotiable, and the differences must not be so severe as to make the accession to power of one's political opponents a matter of severe danger to one's own interests. Policy controversies have to be kept from escalating to controversies over total ways of life or among irreconcilable groups.

In this connection it is possible to distinguish two types of partisanship: one involves the positive commitment of an individual or group to a particular political party; on the individual level it involves identification with and willingness to support a party; while on the group level it involves the extent to which a particular social group supports the party that is closest to its interests. The other type of partisanship is more negative, and involves the extent to which supporters of one party are hostile to the opposition. The two types of partisanship are closely related, but the existence of the former does not necessarily imply the latter. And the two types of partisanship have different social consequences.[5] Indeed, a general problem in democratic politics is how to prevent a politicized electorate organized around the support of competing parties from becoming a deeply divided electorate organized into two hostile camps. Here voluntary associations may play an important role. There is evidence that organizational membership—in particular, union membership—is related to an increase in what we have called positive partisanship.[6] Multiple-membership theories would suggest that such affiliation would also be related to a reduction in negative partisanship. It is this latter relationship we shall explore in this paper.

[4]Kornhauser, *op. cit.*, pp. 80-81. See also Talcott Parsons, " 'Voting' and the Equilibrium of the American Political System," in *American Voting Behavior*, ed. Eugene Burdick and Arthur J. Brodbeck (New York: Free Press, 1959), p. 102; and Bernard Berelson and Gary A. Steiner, *Human Behavior: An Inventory of Scientific Findings* (New York: Harcourt, 1964), p. 620.

[5]On the different forms of partisanship and their different consequences, see Almond and Verba, *op. cit.*, pp. 288-295.

[6]See, for instance, Bernard Berelson, Paul F. Lazarsfeld, and William N. McPhee, *Voting* (Chicago: Univ. Chicago Press, 1954), pp. 51-52; Angus Campbell *et al.*, *The American Voter* (New York: Wiley, 1960), pp. 379-380. Linz reports similar findings for Germany. See Juan J. Linz, *The Social Bases of West German Politics*, unpublished Ph.D. dissertation, Columbia University, 1959, Chapter 26.

Overlapping memberships should reduce conflict by changing the social level at which conflict is resolved. One can conceive of a political system made up of two closed camps with no overlapping of membership. The only channels of communication between the two camps would be at the highest level—say when the leaders of the two camps meet in the governing chambers—and all conflict would have to be resolved at this highest level. Politics comes to resemble negotiations between rival states; and war or a breakdown of negotiations is always possible. At the other extreme is the system with many cross-cutting solidarities. Conflict is resolved not on the highest but on the lowest level—within the mind of the individual as he tries to balance off his commitment to several sides at once. The result, if the works on cross-pressures are correct, is for the individual to take a less intense political stance and for partisanship in general to be less negative.

Conflict resolution at an intermediary level is also consistent with the cross-pressures approach. Ordinary organization members may not modify their political views if exposed to cross-cutting solidarities, but organizational leaders, who are more sensitive to such matters, may take less extreme positions because of their multiple clientele.

Thus a network of non-governmental organizations with overlapping memberships does not reduce the overall amount of conflict in a society; rather it takes it out of the realm of *political* conflict. Conflict is resolved within the individual or, on a somewhat higher level, within the organizations themselves. "The essential fact here is that most structurally important groupings in the society will contain considerable proportions of adherents of *both* parties. To an important degree, therefore, the structural ties that bind them together on non-political bases cut across their political allegiances. Hence the tendency to political cleavage will tend to be checked by a set of mechanisms that operate *below* the level of party division. . . ."[7]

Conflict reduction, according to the theories of multiple membership, depends on *overlapping* membership. Multiple membership in organizations might indeed have the opposite effect if memberships were cumulative rather than overlapping. The multiple membership hypotheses assume a chain of relations something like this: (1) organizational membership, (2) exposure to or identification with others of opposing political views, (3) cross pressures, (4) reduction in intensity of political competitiveness. The second step is crucial. If organizations were homogeneous in membership from the point of view of the major lines of social and political cleavage—e.g. drawing all members from one political party, one religion, one region, one social class—individuals would be placed in situations where their political views would be reinforced and levels of conflict would increase. In that case the chain of connection would be as follows: (1) organizational membership, (2) exposure to or identification with others of like background or

[7] Parsons, *op. cit.*, p. 102.

political views, (3) reinforcement of views, (4) increase in intensity of political competitiveness. Overlapping membership should result in lower intensity of political commitment, indecision about political commitment, indecision about political choices, increased tolerance of political opponents, withdrawal from political conflict situations, and so forth. Cumulative memberships should result in increased political involvement, increased commitment to a particular point of view, increased hostility to political opponents, and so forth. Thus the social composition of organizations is a crucial variable as are their communications structures. The latter affects awareness of and interaction with others in the organization. Furthermore, it is not the number of organizations involved that is crucial but the number of psychologically meaningful affiliations. The role of membership in formal organizations is to increase the chance of being placed in either a psychologically meaningful cross-pressured situation or a situation of cumulative social contacts. But membership in even a single organization could have either of these opposing effects, depending upon whether the membership exposed the individual to others of similar or different social background and political inclination.

Most of the evidence on the effects of multiple memberships relates to what are considered above to be intervening variables.[8] Thus it has been shown that individuals who do experience some psychological cross-pressures—say prefer the candidate of one party and the policies of the other—are likely to be less interested in politics, to delay in making decisions, and to withdraw from the decision by not voting. Or individuals whose social affiliations are inconsistent—that is, the majority of those in one social group with which they are affiliated have political leanings different from the majority in some other group with which they are affiliated—are also likely to be somewhat less intensely politically committed.[9] Conversely, there is evidence that those who come from homogeneous and isolated political environments are more likely to be intense in their political commitment. Thus workers living in working class districts are more likely to be politically active than workers living in middle class districts (and vice versa for the middle class),

[8]The work of the Survey Research Center at Michigan has concentrated on what is to us the intervening variable of attitudinal cross-pressures and their impact on political attitudes. As they put it, they " . . . proceed without inquiring into what has led to attitudinal cross-pressures. It is the effect, rather than the cause, of conflict that is of primary interest." Angus Campbell *et al., op. cit.,* pp. 80-81.

[9]See Paul F. Lazarsfeld, Bernard Berelson, and Hazel Gaudet, *The People's Choice* (New York: Duell, Sloan and Pearce, 1944), pp. 53 ff.; Bernard Berelson, Paul F. Lazarsfeld, and William N. McPhee, *op. cit.,* pp. 128 ff.; Campbell *et al., op. cit.,* pp. 87-88; V. O. Key, *Public Opinion and American Democracy* (New York: Knopf, 1961), p. 69; Martin Kriesberg, "Cross-Pressures and Attitudes: A Study of the Influence of Conflicting Propaganda on Opinions regarding American-Soviet Relations," *Public Opinion Quarterly,* Vol. 12 (Spring 1949), pp. 5-16. For a critique of many of these studies, see H. Daudet, *Floating Voters and the Floating Vote* (Leiden: Stenfert Kroese N.V., 1961).

and political radicalism is more often found among groups isolated from the rest of society—miners, lumberjacks, and other isolated professions.[10]

The role of formal organizations in this process has been less frequently directly studied. But this deserves direct consideration as well. Such organizations grow in importance with economic and social modernization, and the implications of this growth for democratic politics would be greatly illuminated by evidence on the relationship between formal associational membership and political conflict. This is especially the case since the mere growth in the number of affiliations would have opposite effects depending on whether the intervening process was one of overlapping memberships or of cumulative memberships. In this respect our ability to test some of these hypotheses with data from several nations is important. The hypothesis would be that in the United States, from whose politics the cross pressures hypotheses have been derived, organizational membership would be related to a reduction of intergroup hostility. On the other hand, organizational affiliation in Italy should be of the cumulative kind and produce an increase in intergroup hostility. As Joseph LaPalombara has pointed out, "formal interest groups in Italy frequently organize *within* . . . sub-cultures; very few of them cut across sub-cultural lines, even when the logic of a common economic interest would appear to compel such unification. . . . Even within each of the sub-cultures, the groups are further fragmented. It is not uncommon, for example, to find Communist, Catholic, Socialist, Republican, and Neo-Fascist rough equivalents of the League of Women Voters."[11] The pattern of organizational composition that one would expect in the other three nations is somewhat more ambiguous. In Britain one might expect a pattern something like that in the United States but probably more homogeneous in class terms. In Germany one might expect a similar pattern. Though pre-Nazi organizational life was very much like the fragmented picture we have for Italy, the structure of organizational life has become less fragmented—as evidenced best by the non-partisan DGB, the German trade union organization.[12] The expectations in Mexico are even more ambiguous because of the lack of a firm structure of political competitiveness (due to the essentially one-party system). For this reason we shall concentrate largely on the comparison between the United States and Italy, the two countries where our expectations are clearest.

This paper will deal with individualistic hypotheses about conflict resolution —that is with those hypotheses about the impact of overlapping membership on

[10]See Kornhauser, *op. cit.,* Chapter 13; and Seymour M. Lipset, *Political Man* (Garden City: Doubleday, 1959), Chapter 4.

[11]LaPalombara, *op. cit.,* p. 43. See also his *Interest Groups in Italian Politics* (Princeton, N.J.: Princeton Univ. Press, 1964).

[12]See, for instance, Joseph Kaiser, *Die Repräsentction Organisierter Interessen* (Berlin, 1956); and Rupert Breitling, *Die Verbände in der Bundesrepublik* (Meisenheim am Glan, 1955).

systems of conflict that relate such memberships to the attitudes of the individual members of organizations. To confirm the individualistic hypotheses as to the effects of multiple organizational membership on political conflict, one would have to be able to demonstrate, at minimum, that such memberships expose individuals either to cross-pressures or reinforcement of their political beliefs; and that the cross-pressures of the heterogeneous environment result in a reduction in the intensity of political conflict among individuals while a homogeneous environment increases that intensity. Thus for the individual one would have to know whether or not he belongs to any organization, the social composition of the organization, whether the individual is in fact exposed to the presumed social pressures, and whether these exposures are related to differences in political attitudes. Even such information would allow us to confirm these hypotheses only on the individual level—that is, we could show that individuals modified their political views under such conditions, but would not be able to show that this resulted in a reduction of political tension for the system as a whole. Such a confirmation on the individual level would be useful nevertheless given the paucity of data to support the hypotheses so far.

But even the individual level confirmation of the multiple membership hypotheses in the full sense spelled out above will not be possible with the data to be presented in this paper. The data were gathered in the course of a survey study of individual attitudes, a survey conducted for other purposes than the direct testing of these hypotheses. The data are therefore somewhat indirect. We do know the number of organizations to which an individual belongs. What we do not know, and what could not be ascertained in individual interviews, is the composition of these organizations, in particular the extent to which they involve either overlapping or cumulative memberships. This means that the crucial intervening variable remains unmeasured. But since we do have clear expectations as to these intervening organizational compositions in at least two of the nations, we can at least ask if the results in terms of political attitude change are what one would expect.

The Political Attitudes of Organization Members

There is much evidence that organizational membership is associated with political participation and involvement. The cross-national survey whose results are reported in *The Civic Culture* found that in all five nations studied, the associational member is more likely to be politically active, to be informed about politics, to be involved and care about political affairs, to believe himself to be a competent citizen, and to express support for democratic norms. Furthermore, the type of organization to which an individual belongs, the number to which he belongs, and the extent of his activity within the organization are all related to his political activity and involvement. Members of organizations that are somewhat involved in politics, members of more than one organization, and active members tend to be more politically involved. But more important, perhaps, is the finding that *any* membership—even if the individual is but a passive member of his organization, or the organization has no political content–is associated with higher levels of political activity and involvement.[13]

These data clearly suggest that voluntary organization membership plays an important role in the maintenance of a participatory political system. This is relevant to the problem of the relationship between organizational membership and political conflict. For one thing, the results cited above suggest that the measure of organizational membership is a powerful one; it does differentiate similarly among political actors in all five countries in terms of some important political attributes. Furthermore, since organizational members are likely to be heavily concentrated in the politically active strata, the relationship between organizational membership and attitudes toward political conflict takes on increased importance in terms of the overall level of political conflict in the society.

A relationship between organizational affiliation and the extent of political conflict in a nation would be hard to sustain if there were no variation in the frequency of such membership from nation to nation. As Table 1 indicates, however, there is substantial variation in the frequency of organizational membership and in the frequency of multiple membership. In the United States over one-third of the total sample are members of more than one organization, while 16 per cent in Britain, 12 per cent in Germany, 6 per cent in Italy and 2 per cent in Mexico are multiple members.[14]

As we have pointed out, where memberships overlap, the individual with multiple affiliations should have a greater tolerance of political opposition. One would

[13]See Almond and Verba, *op. cit.,* Chapter 11. Similar data are reported in Key, *op. cit.,* pp. 504-506; and Linz, *op. cit.,* Chapter 25.

[14]The figures reported are for the response to a question, "Are you a member of any organization now (trade or labor union, business organization, social group, professional or farm organization, cooperative, fraternal or veterans' group, athletic club, political, charitable, religious or civic organization) or any other organized groups?" The absolute amount of memberships reported varies somewhat from other studies of the subject, largely due to the inclusion of trade unions within the question. Membership in political or religious organizations did not include party or religious affiliation itself but includes organizations that are politically related or church related. For a discussion of the distribution of these memberships within the nations studied and of the kinds of memberships these entail, see Almond and Verba, *op. cit.,* pp. 301-307 and 320.

One of the objections to the multiple membership theory that can be made is that the system on which the theory is originally based, the United States, is one in which the rate of organizational membership is not as high as folklore suggests. Everyone is not a member of some organization, and fewer are members of more than one. But the theory of multiple memberships does not require that every citizen be a member of more than one organization, but merely that sufficient number are members to make an impact on politics. How many is a sufficient number is hard to define. But the comparative evidence suggests that though it is true that not every American is a member of some such organization, there is sufficient variation among nations in the frequency of such membership–with the frequency of such membership being quite a bit larger in the United States–that it is plausible to consider these differences as significant factors having effects on political systems.

Table 1. Respondents Who Belong to One or More Organizations, by Nation (in Per Cent)

Per Cent Who	U.S.	U.K.	Germany	Italy	Mexico
Belong to one organization	25	31	32	24	23
Belong to two organizations	14	10	9	5	2
Belong to three organizations	9	4	2	1	0
Belong to four or more organizations	9	2	1	—	—
Total per cent multiple members	32	16	12	6	2
Total per cent members	57 (970)*	47 (963)	44 (955)	30 (995)	5 (1007)
Per cent of members who are multiple members	55	34	27	20	8

**Numbers in parentheses refer to the bases upon which percentages are calculated.*

expect that the intensity of political differences will be tempered and that even if the extent of *political* difference is held constant, common identification will reduce the general hostility to political opponents. On the other hand, where memberships cumulate, one would assume greater hostility to political opponents among organization members.

Thus, based on our assumptions as to the nature of the associational systems in the United States and Italy, we would expect that organizational membership is associated with a more tolerant and open view of political opponents in the United States and a more hostile view in Italy. A measure of hostility to political opponents might be a question asked of respondents as to whether or not they would approve of the marriage of a son or daughter to a supporter of the opposition political party.[15] This question deals essentially with the limits of politics—how far are political criteria allowed to penetrate into personal life. The individual who considers such criteria irrelevant is saying, as it were, that there are limits to politics, and that in certain circumstances other values are more important than political ones. On the other hand, the individual who would reject someone for admission to the primary group on the basis of political criteria takes a more hostile view of political opponents. The latter tendency is, thus, an indicator of the

[15]The question read, "Suppose a son or daughter of yours were getting married. How would you feel if he or she married a supporter of the ——— Party? Would you be pleased, would you be displeased, or would it make no difference?" The question was asked about all the major parties in each of the nations studied. See *ibid.*, pp. 132-160, for a discussion of this question and a report of the responses to it. The data that will be reported in Table 2 below refer to the attitudes of the supporters of the major parties in each nation toward marriage of a child to the supporter of the major opposition: in the United States, Republican attitudes toward marriage of a child to a Democrat; in Britain, Conservative attitudes toward Labour; in Germany, CDU attitudes toward SPD; in Mexico, PRI attitudes toward PAN; and vice versa in each case. In Italy three parties are involved. Table 2 reports the attitudes of Christian Democratic supporters toward the marriage of a child to a Communist supporter and the attitudes of both supporters of the PCI and PSI toward marriage with a Christian Democrat. In Table 2, education is controlled. The use of other socio-economic variables would make little difference in the results.

degree of fragmentation of a political system into closed and competing political groups. Evidence of such fragmentation was found most frequently in Italy, and with intermediate frequency in Germany and Mexico. On the other hand, the great frequency with which American and British respondents reported that partisan affiliation was an irrelevant criterion for admission to the primary group was taken to be an indicator of a less fragmented political system in which partisan disputes were "kept in their place" by not being considered proper criteria for more intimate social relationships.[16] But we are not interested here in the relative frequency with which such hostility to political opponents is expressed, but with the relationship between this and organizational affiliation. If cross-pressures mechanisms are at work, a "closed" attitude toward those of opposing political views would be *less* likely among those with many memberships. If reinforcement mechanisms are at work, a "closed" attitude would be *more* likely.

The data in Table 2 offer little evidence to support the hypothesis that cross-pressures mechanisms are at work. The expectation would be that in the United States at least and perhaps elsewhere those respondents who are members of more than one organization would be more likely than the members of one organization to say that partisan affiliation is irrelevant for admission to close personal relationships, and that the members of one organization would in turn be more likely to be "open" to political opponents than would those who are unaffiliated. But in the United States, Britain, and Germany frequency of organizational affiliation appears to be unrelated to one's views on the admission of a political opponent into the primary group. And this pattern appears on both educational levels.

There is some tendency for the relationship expected from a cross-pressure situation to appear in the Mexican data. Non-members are somewhat more likely than members, and members of one organization somewhat more likely than multiple members to express hostility toward political opponents. But the tendency is not very strong and appears only among Mexican respondents on the lower educational level; among those with secondary education or better there is a slight opposite tendency. And the few respondents with more than one membership makes the comparison between multiple members and single-members not very reliable.

The only nation in which there is a definite relationship between group affiliation and inter-party hostility is Italy. And here we find confirmation of the alternate hypothesis to the cross-pressures one. As we predicted for Italy, members of more than one organization are *more* likely to oppose entry into the primary group of a political opponent than are members of one organization, and members of one organization in turn express inter-party hostility more frequently than do respondents who report no organizational affiliation. Sixty-four per cent of the multiple-members would be displeased if a son or daughter married the supporter

[16]See *ibid.*, pp. 288-299, for a discussion of this subject.

Table 2. Organizational Membership and Attitude toward Marriage of a Child to a Supporter of the Opposition Party (Supporters of Major Parties Only)

Attitude toward Marriage of Child to Supporter of Opposition Party	U.S.			U.K.			Germany			Italy			Mexico		
	Non-memb.	Sing. memb.	Mult. memb.	Non-memb.	Sing. memb.	Mult. memb.	Non-memb.	Sing. memb.	Mult. memb.	Non-memb.	Sing. memb.	Mult. memb.	Non-memb.	Sing. memb.	Mult. memb.
Total															
Displeased	4%	3%	4%	7%	8%	7%	14%	17%	13%	43%	54%	64%	26%	22%	6%
Indifferent	93	91	95	91	90	91	73	68	76	39	35	32	60	68	84
Other	3	5	3	1	1	–	2	6	5	12	6	3	9	7	11
Don't know	–	1	–	–	–	1	10	9	1	5	4	–	4	4	–
Total number	299	196	267	375	223	136	314	192	63	296	124	31	405	167	17
Primary Education or Less															
Displeased	5%	4%	6%	8%	6%	6%	13%	15%	13%	41%	55%	[56] %	26%	20%	*
Indifferent	91	88	89	91	94	94	76	70	80	41	34	[44]	63	68	*
Other	4	6	4	–	–	–	1	7	4	12	8	–	9	9	*
Don't know	1	2	–	–	–	–	10	8	2	7	4	–	3	2	*
Total number	194	122	193	272	137	68	275	158	46	229	84	18	352	124	7
Secondary Education or Above															
Displeased	3%	1%	2%	4%	13%	9%	24%	23%	[13] %	48%	53%	[77] %	25%	28%	*
Indifferent	96	95	96	95	85	89	64	59	[67]	35	42	[15]	51	64	*
Other	1	3	2	1	2	0	9	3	[13]	15	3	[8]	12	2	*
Don't know	0	0	0	0	0	1	3	15	[7]	1	3	[0]	12	7	*
Total number	105	74	183	98	79	64	33	34	15	66	38	13	53	43	10

*Too few cases.

of an opposition party, in contrast with 54 per cent of the single-members, and 43 per cent of those with no organizational affiliation.

A quite similar pattern is apparent if we use as an index of inter-party hostility the type of terms the respondent chooses to describe political opponents. Respondents were asked to characterize the supporters of the various political parties.[17] For our purposes, we are interested in respondents who choose negative terms ("ignorant people," "selfish people," etc.) to describe the supporters of opposition parties. Table 3 reports the relationship between number of organizational memberships and the selection of negative terms to describe one's political opponents. The findings parallel those in Table 2, and again offer little evidence that organizational affiliation is related to a reduction in the extent of partisan hostility. In the United States, Britain, Germany and Mexico there is little apparent relationship between frequency of organizational membership and the use of negative terms to describe one's political opponents.

Again, the only relationship between group membership and opinions of opposition party supporters is found in Italy. And again, the reinforcement hypothesis is confirmed, for it is precisely among those respondents with the greatest number of group affiliations that hostility toward the opposition party is most frequently expressed; and among the organizationally unaffiliated respondents that negative terms to describe one's political opponents are least frequently employed. It is, of course, not unexpected that such negative views or so frequent opposition to marriage with a political opponent is expressed in Italy. We are, after all, asking supporters of the Christian Democratic party how they feel about the Communists, and the Communists and Socialists (the interviewing took place in 1959, long before the "opening to the left") how they feel about the Christian Democrats. But what is of interest here is not the absolute level of such hostility, but the fact that the organizational system reinforces this hostility. Here is an example then of a situation in which organizational membership (and we assume that the intervening process involves cumulative, not overlapping, memberships) acts to increase social tension and fragmentation.

The Italian results are expected. It is more surprising that one does not find evidence for the conflict-reducing effects of an overlapping pattern of membership elsewhere, particularly in the United States and perhaps in Britain. Organizational

[17]The question read, "We're interested in what sorts of people support and vote for the different parties. If you had to generalize, which expressions on this list come closest to describing the kinds of people who vote for the ——— Party?" The list contained the following items: people interested in national strength and welfare; selfish people, interested in their own welfare at the expense of others; intelligent people; religious people; betrayers of freedom and the country's welfare; ignorant and misguided people; Fascists, militarists; people interested in the welfare of humanity; atheists, godless people. The first two responses were recorded. Other answers not on the list (in particular, the answer that "all sorts of people" support a particular party) were recorded as well. The question was asked about each of the major parties. The data in Table 3 refer to the same parties as in Table 2. (See footnote 15.)

Table 3. Percentage of Respondents Who Choose Negative Terms to Characterize Supporters of the Opposition Party, by Organizational Membership (Supporters of Major Parties Only)

Nation	Total			Primary or Less			Secondary or Above		
	Non-members	Members of One Organization	Members of More Than One Organization	Non-members	Members of One Organization	Members of More Than One Organization	Non-members	Members of One Organization	Members of More Than One Organization
U.S.	12% (299)*	14% (197)	13% (276)	15% (194)	17% (122)	21% (93)	6% (105)	8% (75)	9% (183)
U.K.	41 (377)	45 (222)	41 (134)	42 (277)	48 (134)	48 (67)	38 (96)	43 (81)	36 (64)
Germany	14 (314)	16 (192)	9 (63)	12 (275)	15 (158)	9 (46)	24 (33)	12 (34)	13 (15)
Italy	43 (296)	56 (124)	71 (31)	41 (229)	50 (84)	61 (18)	51 (66)	67 (39)	85 (13)
Mexico	20 (405)	20 (167)	6 (17)	20 (352)	25 (124)	+	18 (53)	9 (43)	+

(Number in parentheses refers to the base upon which percentage is calculated.)

**i.e., 12 per cent of non-members use negative terms to characterize the supporters of the opposition party.*

+Too few cases.

membership has been shown to have an important relationship with other political attitudes and behaviors—those relevant to the degree of participation and involvement—and this makes the lack of pattern in connection with inter-party hostility even more surprising. The situation is highlighted if we look more closely at the effect of the number of organizational affiliations on attitudes toward those who support political parties other than one's own. In Tables 2 and 3 we compared non-members and single-members with multiple members.

Table 4 breaks down the multiple member groups more finely. Yet, even when we compare respondents who belong to three or four or more organizations with those who belong to one or no organization, we find that the degree of hostility toward supporters of the opposition party—as measured by the use of negative terms—does not decline. In the United States, those with most memberships (four or more) are somewhat less likely to choose hostile terms to describe political opponents than are those with fewer memberships, but there is

Table 4.

No. of Organizations	U.S.		No. of Organizations	U.K.		Germany	
None	12%	(299)	None	41%	(377)	14%	(314)
One	14	(197)	One	45	(222)	16	(192)
Two	15	(117)	Two	39	(86)	8	(49)
Three	14	(79)	Three or more	45	(49)	[14	(14)]
Four or more	9	(80)					

(Number in parentheses refers to base upon which percentage is calculated.)

little difference among those with one, two or three memberships—and those who belong to one, two or three groups are *more likely* to choose hostile terms than are those respondents who are non-members. And in Britain and Germany, the group of respondents with most memberships (three or more) are as likely or more likely than those with no memberships to choose hostile terms. And the situation is similar with regard to inter-party marriage. Unless we are to assume that the member of three, four, or more organizations in these countries is no more likely to mingle with those of opposing parties than is the man who belongs to no organization—a situation that is not impossible, though unlikely if the assumptions, at least about American organizations, are true—we must also call into question the assumption that such common memberships lead to a reduction in the intensity of political antagonism.

A similar measure of inter-party conflict reveals a similar pattern for the supporters of the various political parties in the nations studied. One way in which a sense of confidence in one's political opponents facilitates democratic politics is that it makes the losers in political contests more willing to turn the reins of government over to the winners. Table 5 reports the views of the supporters of

Table 5. Index of Trust in Opposition Party and Organization Membership (Proportion of Respondents Saying the Opposition Party Would Probably Not Harm Nation minus the Proportion Saying It Would)*

Nation	Party	Non-member		Single Member		Multiple Member	
U.S.	Republican view of Democrats	51%	(111)	51%	(69)	62%	(127)
	Democrats' view of Republicans	53	(186)	41	(128)	45	(148)
U.K.	Conservative view of Labour	−7	(175)	−11	(104)	−6	(79)
	Labour view of Conservatives	51	(200)	37	(119)	33	(57)
Germany	CDU view of SPD	16	(188)	10	(107)	31	(39)
	SPD view of CDU	25	(126)	22	(85)	[54	(24)]
Italy	DC view of PCI	−47	(227)	−63	(101)	−68	(25)
	PCI/PSI view of DC	−10	(67)	−22 (32)+			
Mexico	PRI view of PAN	16	(356)	13	(145)	†	
	PAN view of PRI	8	(50)	−21	(22)	†	

(Numbers in parentheses refer to base on which percentage is calculated.)
**"Opposition" refers to the party the respondent opposes.*
+"One" and "multi" combined because too few cases in either separately.
†Too few cases.

the party in power in the five nations as to whether they believe that the accession to power of the leading opposition party would be likely to "seriously endanger the country's welfare," as well as the views of the supporters of the leading opposition party as to whether the actions of the incumbent party might involve a similar danger.[18] The figures reported refer to the difference between the percentage saying that such serious danger "probably wouldn't" occur and the percentage saying it "probably would"—the higher the figure the more frequently the particular groups expressed confidence in their political opponents. If organization membership was acting to increase cross-pressures and to reduce interparty hostility,

[18] The question read, "The ——— Party now controls the national government. Do you think that its policies and activities would ever seriously endanger the country's welfare? Do you think this probably would happen, that it might happen, or that it probably wouldn't happen?" "Let me ask you about some other parties that might someday take control of the government. If the ——— Party were to take control of the government, how likely is it that it would seriously endanger the country's welfare? Do you think that this would probably happen, that it might happen, or that it probably wouldn't happen?" The name of the party in control of the government in the respective nation was inserted in the first question, while the follow-up questions were asked about all of the leading opposition parties.

one would assume that expressions of serious concern over the activities of one's political opponents would decline as one moved from non-members, to members, to multiple-members. Conversely, if the organizations were cumulative in impact, one would expect the opposite. In Italy, as expected, organization members are less likely to trust their political opponents. For the other nations, the data in Table 5 are far from unambiguous, but they do suggest that organizational membership is as likely to be associated with greater concern about the activities of one's political opponents as it is with less. In the United States, no clear pattern exists as to the views of Democrats about Republicans, while there is some evidence that Republicans who are members of more than one organization would be less fearful about a Democratic accession to power. In Britain one finds no pattern for Conservatives and a tendency for Labour Party supporters to be more fearful if they belong to organizations. In Germany, the supporters of both major parties appear somewhat less fearful of the opposition if they are organization members, though among the CDU supporters the tendency is far from clear. And in Mexico, organization members are somewhat more fearful of their political opponents.

The Organizational Leaders

The lack of confirmation of the overlapping membership hypotheses calls into question the extent to which cross-pressures mechanisms operate to reduce the intensity of political conflict on the level of the ordinary organization member. But this does not mean necessarily that the system of organizational affiliations plays no role in conflict reduction. As was pointed out earlier, even if conflict reduction does not take place on the lowest level—i.e., within the mind of the ordinary citizen—cross-pressures may operate and conflict resolution take place on the level of the organizational leaders.

There are a number of reasons why one would expect the impact of the organizational system on patterns of conflict to be greater on the level of the organizational leadership. The commitment of many members of voluntary associations to their association is often minimal, and such minimal commitment would serve to reduce the impact of membership on their political attitudes. On the other hand, leaders of organizations are in the center of communications networks and are more likely to be aware of and sensitive to the views of their memberships. Thus, though we do not find evidence to support the overlapping membership hypotheses on the level of the ordinary group member, perhaps we shall find it on the level of organizational leadership. And the pattern of intensification of conflict associated with organizational membership in Italy will perhaps be stronger on the level of the organizational leadership.

Table 6 distinguishes between organizational members who have ever held a position as an officer in one of the organizations to which they belong and those who have not. In cases where overlapping membership mechanisms were operating,

Table 6. Leaders and Followers

Percentage Opposed to Interparty Marriage (in Per Cent)

Nation	Non-members		Officers: One Organization		Officers: More Than One Organization		Ordinary Members: One Organization		Ordinary Members: More Than One Organization	
U.S.	4	(299)	2	(44)	3	(182)	3	(149)	4	(92)
U.K.	7	(375)	18	(40)	10	(70)	6	(180)	5	(66)
Germany	14	(314)	18	(17)	16	(19)	17	(175)	11	(44)
Italy	43	(296)	65	(26)	[73	(11)]	51	(96)	58	(19)
Mexico	26	(405)		19	(95) *			31	(148) *	

Percentage Choosing Negative Terms to Characterize Opponents

Nation	Non-members		Officers: One Organization		Officers: More Than One Organization		Ordinary Members: One Organization		Ordinary Members: More Than One Organization	
U.S.	12	(299)	16	(45)	14	(182)	13	(149)	13	(92)
U.K.	41	(377)	46	(37)	35	(69)	45	(182)	47	(66)
Germany	14	(314)	18	(17)	10	(19)	14	(175)	9	(44)
Italy	43	(296)	77	(26)	[82	(11)]	51	(96)	63	(19)
Mexico	20	(405)		15	(95) *			22	(148) *	

(Number in parentheses refers to the base upon which the percentage is calculated.)
**Single and multiple memberships combined in Mexico due to small number of Mexican multiple members.*

we would expect that officers of organizations would manifest less hostility to political opponents than would rank and file members, whereas they would manifest more hostility where cumulative membership mechanisms were at work. Similarly, the differences between members of one organization and members of more than one would be greater among those who hold some leadership position than among those who are more passive members.[19]

The data in Table 6 do not support the hypothesis that overlapping membership mechanisms leading to a reduction in political hostility are operating on organizational elite levels in the United States. As the pattern of responses to the questions on inter-party marriage and on the characteristics of political opponents indicate,

[19]In Table 6, "ordinary members" are those respondents who report that they have never held a position as an officer in any of the organizations with which they are affiliated. Officers are those who have held such a position in at least one of the organizations with which they are affiliated. Thus those listed as "Officers, more than one" are respondents who are members of more than one organization, but who may have been officers in either one of these organizations or in more than one.

there is little difference between officers of organizations and rank and file members, or, indeed, between officers and non-members. And just as the members of a single organization are little different from the members of more than one organization, so the officers with a single affiliation are quite like the officers with multiple affiliations. If anything, there is some slight tendency for officers to manifest somewhat greater hostility to opponents than do non-members or rank and file members—using the question of the terms used to describe opponents as the indicator of this. Thus there is no more support in the American data for the proposition that conflict reduction mechanisms are operating on the organizational elite level than there is for such a process on the rank and file level.

In the British data, there is some evidence on the elite level for the pattern one would associate with cross-pressures mechanisms. Though officers are not less hostile to political opponents than members—and, indeed, on the intermarriage question they are somewhat more hostile—officers with multiple affiliations are less hostile than officers with a single affiliation, a difference that does not appear when we compare multiple and single members on the rank and file level. In Germany and Mexico, however, there is little difference between officers and rank and file members.

In Italy, on the other hand, there is confirmation of the hypothesis of the greater impact of a cumulative system of memberships on the organizational elite level than on the rank and file level. Officers of organizations are more hostile to their political opponents on both of the measures of such hostility, though the effect of the number of organizations is roughly the same for both officers and rank and file members.

In general, the pattern found for organizational elites is similar to that found for members in general. The cumulative membership hypotheses are confirmed in Italy. The overlapping membership hypotheses are not confirmed elsewhere. It is true that the measure of organizational elite status is a relatively weak one—the official positions held within the organization can be quite minor for someone to be considered an officer by our measure. It is possible that if one had a sample of top organization leaders the overlapping membership hypotheses would be confirmed. But the elite data presented in Table 6 gives little indication of such confirmation.

Type of Organization

In the data that have been presented so far we have been lumping together a wide range of organizations, and this might have something to do with the fact that the expected pattern does not emerge in the American data. Ideally we should be able to separate out those organizations with heterogeneous memberships from those with homogeneous memberships, but our data do not allow that. We can, however separate out one type of affiliation that should be closely related to the heterogeneous-homogeneous distinction—union membership. We would assume that union membership would involve a more homogeneous environment than other organizations. But when we compare those who are union members, either as their only affiliation or in conjunction with some other affiliation, with respondents who are affiliated with other types of organizations, we find little systematic difference among these groups in terms of the particular dimensions with which we have been dealing. There is little regular relationship between union affiliation and the expression of inter-party hostility. More important, if we consider only those single and multiple members whose associational affiliation does not include union affiliation, we still find no evidence for the conflict reducing effects of organizational affiliation that we expected to find.[20] Similarly, if we separate out politically involved organizations from politically uninvolved ones (using the respondent's estimate as our measure) we find it makes no difference.

Communications Patterns

Much of the hypothesized connection between organizational membership and political attitudes involves the intervening effect of the communications patterns to which the individual is exposed within his organization. If shared membership is to affect one's political views, the views of fellow members must be communicated. Explicit political discussion may not be necessary; but at minimum the individual concerned has to receive some communication about the political characteristics of his fellow members as well as other relevant characteristics—their social characteristics, their religious views, and so forth—if his contact with them is to have any effect. Though we do not know the social composition of the various organizations, we do know something about the communications activities of those who are organizational members, and this may help us to explain the nature of the impact of these organizations.

Organizational members are more likely to report that they discuss politics than are non-members. Whether this is due to the opportunities presented by the social contacts that organizations afford, or to the interest in political matters that may be aroused in organizational participation, or just to the fact that those

[20]One would have expected, furthermore, that unions would play a reinforcement role for the supporters of the left party and a cross-pressures role for the supporters of the right party. When one breaks down the sample this way, there are too few cases to make many reliable comparisons, but the comparisons that can be made offer little support for this. In Germany the hypothesis received partial support. Among CDU supporters, union members are less hostile to the SPD than are the members of a non-union organization; while among SPD supporters there is no difference between union members and members of other kinds of organizations in their interparty hostility. In Britain we find, contrary to expectations, that Conservative supporters who are in unions express more hostility toward Labour Party supporters than do Conservatives who belong to some other kind of organization (as measured by the frequency with which they select negative descriptive terms to describe them), though on other measures of inter-party hostility there is no difference. And there is little pattern among Labour supporters. In the United States, there is little pattern. But again, in most instances the number of cases is too few for more than tentative comparison.

who are more interested in politics are also more likely to be joiners, is not relevant at this point. What these data indicate is that those who are in organizations are more likely to be exposed to discussion about political matters. But what kind? This is the crucial question for understanding the role of such organizations in relation to the conflict system within a nation.

Some indication of the effects of organizational membership on the nature of political communications can be seen if we consider the responses to another set of questions about political discussion. Respondents were asked about the number of people with whom they avoided political discussion. Did they avoid all political discussion, did they restrict political discussion to certain people, or did they feel free to discuss politics with anyone?[21] Thus respondents could give what might be called a "closed" response, that they discuss politics with no one; a "cautionary" response, that they discuss politics only with certain people; or an "open" response, that they feel free to discuss politics with anyone. What is of interest here is the way in which organization members differ from non-members in their reported freedom to discuss politics. One would assume that this freedom would be affected by both the homogeneity and the tolerance of the groups to which they belong. If an organization is politically homogeneous, one would assume that there would be little need for restrictions on political discussion. Not that everyone would discuss politics, but if one wanted to do so there would be no reason for caution since all members would agree. On the other hand, if the organization were heterogeneous in its political composition, the freedom to discuss politics might depend upon the degree of tolerance one found for disparate political views. And since even in the most tolerant societies, informal and formal pressures exist for conformity to group norms, one would assume that in heterogeneous organizations, some caution would be appropriate.

The responses of non-members and members as to their freedom to discuss politics are reported in Table 7. Some generalizations are possible from the table. In all nations (and on both educational levels) organizational members—and multiple members even more so—are not likely to be political isolates, that is, to say they avoid all discussions. In all nations cautionary responses (i.e., that there are some or many people with whom they avoid discussion) increase as one moves from non-members to members to multiple members. But the most interesting response category in the table is that referring to those who report themselves completely open in political discussion; who say they feel free to discuss politics with anyone. Here the contrast between the United States and Britain on the one hand and Italy on the other is particularly striking. In the former two nations,

[21]The question reads, "If you wanted to discuss political and governmental affairs, are there some people you definitely wouldn't turn to, that is, people with whom you feel it better *not* to discuss such topics? About how many people would you say there are with whom you would *avoid* discussing politics?"

Table 7. Freedom to Discuss Politics and Organization Membership (By Nation and Education)

Reported Freedom to Discuss Politics	U.S. Non-memb.	U.S. Sing. Memb.	U.S. Mult. Memb.	U.K. Non-memb.	U.K. Sing. Memb.	U.K. Mult. Memb.	Germany Non-memb.	Germany Sing. Memb.	Germany Mult. Memb.	Italy Non-memb.	Italy Sing. Memb.	Italy Mult. Memb.	Mexico Non-memb.	Mexico Sing. Memb.	Mexico Mult. Memb.
Total															
Open	31	25	27	30	28	27	19	29	28	20	23	36	19	20	8
Some restrictions	27	35	43	30	38	43	11	17	21	12	22	29	20	30	46
Many restrictions	17	19	21	18	19	23	18	26	36	15	21	14	20	27	33
Closed	24	21	9	15	11	4	42	21	14	38	28	16	23	14	8
Other, don't know	0	0	—	7	3	3	10	7	1	12	5	4	17	8	4
Total cases	414	242	314	509	294	160	536	308	111	201	239	55	765	220	22
Primary or Less															
Open	28	19	23	26	29	26	17	28	30	17	20	27	19	22	+
Some restrictions	24	32	39	30	32	37	11	15	17	9	18	23	18	24	+
Many restrictions	18	18	23	19	29	30	18	26	35	12	22	19	18	31	+
Closed	30	30	13	16	13	4	44	23	16	45	33	31	24	16	+
Other, don't know	0	0	—	8	4	3	10	7	1	17	7	0	21	8	+
Total cases	261	149	107	352	168	73	471	239	82	516	150	26	697	169	11
Secondary or Above															
Open	37	34	29	38	28	29	36	35	18	29	28	46	15	13	+
Some restrictions	34	40	44	30	47	48	16	23	30	19	28	32	33	47	+
Many restrictions	15	19	29	16	15	17	20	25	41	24	20	11	31	18	+
Closed	14	6	6	13	9	3	22	12	11	19	19	4	14	8	+
Other, don't know	—	—	—	4	2	2	5	4	0	8	3	7	6	13	+
Total cases	153	93	207	157	126	87	55	68	27	183	88	28	67	50	10

Reported Freedom to Discuss Politics	U.S.			U.K.			Germany			Italy			Mexico		
	Non-memb.	Sing. Memb.	Mult. Memb.	Non-memb.	Sing. Memb.	Mult. Memb.	Non-memb.	Sing. Memb.	Mult. Memb.	Non-memb.	Sing. Memb.	Mult. Memb.	Non-memb.	Sing. Memb.	Mult. Memb.
Party in Power															
	(Republican)			(Conservatives)			(CDU)			(DC)			(PRI)		
Open	30	25	30	26	21	23	18	27	26	17	22	36	15	24	+
Some restrictions	29	42	42	33	41	42	11	21	33	14	24	32	23	32	+
Many restrictions	16	19	20	22	24	30	18	27	28	18	24	24	24	30	+
Closed	25	14	8	15	11	4	42	20	10	36	25	8	19	10	+
Other, don't know	—	—	—	4	1	1	11	6	3	15	6	—	18	7	+
Total cases	111	69	127	175	104	79	188	107	39	227	105	25	356	145	13
Party out of Power															
	(Democrats)			(Labour)			(SPD)			(PCI/PSI)			(PAN)		
Open	32	25	28	31	30	30	24	32	[12]	36	31	*	27	28	+
Some restrictions	30	34	40	30	39	46	9	15	[25]	10	22	*	22	24	+
Many restrictions	18	19	24	16	17	17	29	26	[54]	13	12	*	16	24	+
Closed	20	21	8	14	9	3	29	18	[8]	31	31	*	21	21	+
Other, don't know				8	5	3	8	9		9	3	*	14	3	+
Total cases	186	128	148	200	119	57	126	85	[24]	67	32*	*	50	22	3

*"One" and "multi" combined because of too few cases in either separately.

+Too few cases.

members are not more likely than non-members to report that they feel free to discuss politics with anyone. If anything, they are slightly less likely to report such freedom. In these two nations organizational membership is associated with a sharp reduction of political isolation; but this isolation is replaced by a sense of caution in political discussion. In Italy, in contrast, organization members and especially multiple members are more likely to report that they feel free to discuss politics with anyone. The data would then support the hypothesis that organizations in Italy tend to be homogeneous in political composition.

In Mexico, the pattern is as in the United States and Britain in that the frequency of completely "open" responses does not change (if one ignores the multiple members who are few in number) while in Germany the pattern is between that of Italy and the United States and Britain.

Table 7 also reports the percentages of respondents who said they feel free to discuss politics with anyone for the supporters of the leading political parties in the five nations. The results are suggestive in terms of our interest in homogeneous versus heterogeneous organizations. For the supporters of the two American and the two British parties, organizational membership is not associated with a greater sense of freedom in political communications. With the Italian Christian Democrats, the German Social Democrats, and (to a lesser extent) the CDU supporters, and the supporters of the Mexican PRI, organizational membership is associated with a greater sense of freedom of discussion and, inferentially, a more homogeneous political environment. The contrast between the CDU and the SPD is instructive, for though both exhibit a pattern of somewhat greater freedom to communicate among organization members, the more homogeneous SPD exhibits a somewhat greater degree of such freedom. The PRI data may not be comparable to that from the other nations due to the relative lack of competitiveness of the party system. Thus in a system in which the leading party receives the support of close to 90 per cent of the voters, supporters of that party are likely to find a homogeneous environment as they enter organizations.

In general then, the data suggest that organizational membership in the United States and Britain (and to a lesser extent in Germany and Mexico) is related to a reduction of the isolation of the individual. Members are open to at least some political discussion. But they are not placed in an environment where indiscriminate political discussion is warranted. Rather they are placed in heterogeneous environments where they must use some caution in choosing with whom they discuss politics. On the other hand, in Italy, organizational members find themselves in a much more homogeneous and therefore permissive political atmosphere; one in which they can feel free to discuss politics with anyone. These data might help explain why our hypothesis was not confirmed in the United States and Britain, but the alternate hypothesis was confirmed in Italy. In the heterogeneous organization in which cross-pressures mechanisms operate there may be informal inhibitions to political discussion, and this may in turn dampen the effects of the increased contact. Where memberships are cumulative, on the other hand, such inhibition on communication may be less frequent.[22] In this sense, cumulative membership patterns may have a greater impact than overlapping ones.

Conclusion

Earlier in this paper two possible models of the relationship between organizational affiliation and political conflict were presented–the cumulative and the cross-pressures model. Our hypothesis was that the relationship between organizational membership and conflict in Italy would approximate the cumulative model; while that in the United States would approximate the cross-pressures model. In the other three nations we expected an intermediate pattern. The data presented for Italy fit our hypothesis. Both the data on attitudes towards political opponents and on communications patterns within organizations support the hypothesis that Italian organization members are exposed to cumulative social and political contacts and that these contacts reinforce the political views that were originally held, thus exacerbating political conflict in the society.

The data for the United States, however, do not support our hypothesis that organizational members become exposed to more heterogeneous political environments due to their organizational membership, and that the resulting cross-pressures lead to a reduction in the intensity of political opposition. When contrasted with the results as to the strong relationship between organizational membership and other attitudinal and behavioral measures, this failure to confirm the hypothesis is surprising.

There are a number of possible reasons why this expected pattern did not appear. Any one of the links in the chain of relationships that was posited earlier may be weak. In the first place organizational membership may not expose individuals to as varied a set of social contacts as assumed. After all, organizational members are not selected on a purely random basis. Though organizational membership may not be as stratified politically as our data suggest is the case in Italy, it is likely that memberships tend to cluster politically thereby eliminating much

[22]These inhibitions to communication may not be severe, and the sanctions for engaging in political discussion with those of opposing views may not be great. It may be rather a tendency to avoid disharmonious interpersonal contact. When those who reported some limitation on their freedom to discuss politics were asked why they avoided such discussions, the most frequent answer in the United States, Britain, and Germany was that such discussions can be unpleasant and can disturb interpersonal relations. (The percentages so answering were 35 per cent in the United States, 43 per cent in Britain, and 25 per cent in Germany.) In Italy, this type of inhibition appeared less frequently–the most frequent reason for avoidance of political discussion being that the respondent feels too ignorant and the second most frequent that others are too biased. But 17 per cent of the Italian respondents who avoid political discussion did say that it was because such discussions can be unpleasant and disturb personal relations. In Mexico, only 4 per cent gave this latter response. The most frequent reason for avoiding political discussions in Mexico was that people are biased and dogmatic and that, therefore, such discussions are useless.

of the "expansive" character associated with such memberships. Secondly, even if membership in organizations results in contact with others of differing political views, the effects of such contact may be dampened by informal inhibitions on communications within these organizations. Our communications data suggest that this may be the case. Lastly, it is possible that organizational membership does lead to exposure to a more varied social group and that this does lead to cross-pressures, but that cross-pressures do not result in a reduction of hostility to political opponents. This is the least likely explanation, since there is substantial evidence to support this last link in our chain. Where cross-pressures have been observed–between attitudes, or between one's own views and those of one's friends–the results have been usually as predicted. Perhaps, then, the linkages between organizational affiliation and the development of cross-pressures situations are the weak ones in the argument.

These results, it may be repeated, cast doubt on the hypotheses about organizational affiliation and the reduction of political conflict only insofar as these hypotheses are about the effects of multiple memberships on the political attitudes of the individual member as individual. It may be that the effect of overlapping membership is greatest on the level of the organization itself. Top leaders may be more sensitive to multiple pressures and, *in their organizational roles,* may take less intensely partisan political positions. Thus conflict resolution will be moved to the level of the organizational elites, and the system of overlapping memberships will still play a major role in reducing the intensity of such conflict. Our data on organizational leaders do not support this point, but it may be that we were not dealing with a high enough level of leadership. Furthermore, we related organizational leadership to the personal political views of the leader. It is possible that these views would be unaffected by the nature of the organization led, but that the leaders when acting in their formal leadership roles may take less intense positions. This needs further research.

In terms of the more interesting set of hypotheses dealt with in this paper–about systems of overlapping memberships–the results reported here are negative. In a discipline with well established theoretical underpinnings, such findings are of course most exciting because they cause one to reconsider accepted theories. In a discipline such as political science where we have few generally accepted hypotheses and fewer tested ones, such negative findings are often the cause of disappointment. The bottom file drawers of political scientists are probably filled with such negative findings. But this is unfortunate, for the major reason for collecting empirical data is to test our hypotheses or notions about political reality.

The negative findings in this case are particularly interesting because of the widespread use of the overlapping membership theory and the paucity of empirical testing of it. The data are a bit too indirect to challenge this theory too strongly. The data do not support the hypotheses, but it would be going too far to say that they refute them. Yet in the absence of better data supporting the overlapping membership hypotheses, these data give one pause. And such a pause would be useful if it led to further, more direct attempts to test these hypotheses. If they are to be central to theories of functioning democracy, they deserve that testing.

Group Representation in Britain and the United States

Samuel H. Beer

We usually think of Great Britain as a country of strong parties and weak pressure groups; the United States as a country of weak parties and strong pressure groups. I wish to suggest some contrary views: that not only are British parties strong, but so also are British pressure groups; that in comparison both American parties and pressure groups are weak. The terms "strong" and "weak" cry out to be defined. The meanings I give them derive from a historical development—the rise of "collectivism"—that has similarly affected both parties and pressure groups.

What are the consequences for policy? Strong parties can more readily resist pressure groups. They can also more readily yield them what they want. On the other hand, the dispersion of power may simply produce a self-defeating war of all against all in which even the special interests suffer. Centralized power at least creates the possibility of deliberate and orderly solutions.

The Collectivist Economy

The virtue of centralized power is worth examining if for no other reason than that the opposite doctrine holds so high a place in liberal democratic thought. Liberals and Radicals in both Britain and America have applied the doctrine of dispersed power to both the economy and the polity. In the Smithian model of the economy, for instance, the wealth of the nation and the satisfaction of consumers' wants will be maximized if the market is free. No unit, not even government, is to exercise "market power." Once power is removed, rational and

Samuel H. Beer, "Group Representation in Britain and the United States," Annals of the American Academy of Political and Social Science, *Vol. 319 (1958). Reprinted with permission.*

voluntary exchange will result and along with it other desirable consequences in the allocation of resources and the satisfaction of the consumer.

Very similar is the Liberal-Radical model of the polity. Remove Burke's "established" aristocracy and all other agents of power that had historically guided the political process; reduce society to its individual, rational atoms; then power removed, reason will reign. A free, competitive marketplace of ideas, automatic and self-regulating like the marketplace of the laissez-faire economy, will test the truth of opinions. Upon opinions so tested, popular government will base public policy.

In both the British and American economies in the nineteenth century, the market conditions required by the self-regulating model did actually exist in very great degree. And in both, to no inconsiderable extent, these conditions still exist. But in the past two generations or so, certain structural changes have taken place —reaching a further point of development in Britain than in the United States— that depart radically from this model. These developments, which we may call "collectivism," can be summarized under four headings. One is the tendency to a concentration of economic power among a few large buyers or sellers in a particular industry or complex of industries. Along with the increase in size of units has gone a change in internal structure that is referred to by terms such as bureaucracy and managerialism. Moreover, where such large units have grown up, they tend to deal with one another by a process of "bargaining"—or perhaps it is better to say, "collective bargaining." Finally, while bargaining tends to be confined to the relations of producers—whether business firms or trade unions—in their dealings with the mass of ultimate consumers, large units have learned to shape, even to create, the very "wants" that presumably they have come into existence to satisfy.

Collectivist Parties

In the polity as in the economy, there have been similar tendencies toward collectivism. By this I do not mean the increase in government intervention—the rise of the welfare state and the controlled economy. I mean rather that in the political structure have occurred certain changes analogous to those changes in economic structure summarized above. Starting from these contrasting models of the polity, the self-regulating and the collectivist, we may compare the distribution of power in Britain and the United States. It would appear that, as economic collectivism has proceeded farther in Britain than in the United States, so also has political collectivism.

We may look first at the relative number of units and their internal structure. Examined in the light of these criteria, both British parties and pressure groups present striking contrasts with the American models. While in both polities there are two major parties, the loose and sprawling parties of American politics make the British appear highly concentrated. In the American party, power is dispersed among many units—for example, personal followings or state and local machines—with the result that only occasionally and for limited purposes, such as nominating a Presidential candidate, does the national party act as a unit. In terms of density—that is, the per cent of eligibles organized as party members—American parties exceed British. But if we apply a measure of intensity, such as payment of dues, it is clear that British parties have mobilized the electorate far more highly than have American. In the British party, moreover, this membership is brought together for unified action by an elaborate and effective system of articulation, in particular active representative bodies extending from bottom to top and a bureaucratic staff running from top to bottom. There are still semiautonomous centers within the party that a perfected merger would obliterate. But to an American, a British party is a highly unified social body, remarkably well equipped for coordinated action: we think, for instance, of the fact that all candidates must be approved by a central-party agency and that they will all run on the same platform. No doubt, the most striking expression of this power of united action is the extent of party voting in the House of Commons. Judged even by Lowell's strict criteria, party voting has been on the increase for a hundred years and today reaches nearly one hundred per cent.[1]

Along with such concentration, and perhaps making it possible, goes a high measure of political homogeneity. (I do not mean social homogeneity, for, measured by nonpolitical criteria, the British are a very heterogeneous people.) This political homogeneity in the electorate as a whole is reflected in what students of voting behavior call the "nationalizing" of British politics. When political opinion moves, it moves in unison throughout the country: in a general election the "swing" from one party to the other is much the same in every constituency. In the United States, as Schattschneider and Paul David have shown, voting has also tended in this direction.[2] Sectionalism and the number of one-party states are on the decline. But—as 1956 illustrates—nothing like the uniformity of swing in British voting has been reached.

In spite of mass membership and representative bodies, however, the internal structure of the British party gives great power to central party leaders—far more, of course, than that possessed by American leaders. It is rather as if the Congressional caucus of post-Federalist days had been imposed upon the Jacksonian party system. In both British parties, as R. T. McKenzie has shown, the leaders of the

[1]Lowell counted as a party vote a division in which at least 90 per cent of one party voted in favor and at least 90 per cent of the other party voted against. A. L. Lowell, "The Influence of Party upon Legislation in England and America," *Annual Report of the American Historical Association for 1901,* Vol. 1 (Washington, 1902), pp. 319-542.

[2]E. E. Schattschneider, "The United States: The Functional Approach to Party Government," in *Modern Political Parties,* ed. Sigmund Neumann (Chicago: Univ. Chicago Press, 1956), pp. 194-215. Paul David, "Intensity of Inter-Party Competition and the Problem of Party Realignment," a paper presented at the meeting of the American Political Science Association, September 5-7, 1957.

parliamentary party, and especially the Leader, are dominant.[3] That is a loose description and needs must be, since the Leader's power is complex and certainly far from dictatorial. He must continually practice "the art of management," appeasing a dissident faction, finding a formula, keeping up party morale. Indeed, he is a "manager"—a modern-day manager committed to party principle, of course, but by his function compelled above all to think of the continuation of the organization.

Collectivist Pressure Groups

Turning from parties to pressure groups, we find that in Britain as in the United States, the center of the stage is occupied by organizations based on the great economic interest groups of modern society, especially the big three of business, labor, and agriculture. Given the nature of public policy, which affects these interests so often and so intimately, pressure groups claiming to speak for them are bound in turn to influence policy making more frequently and on the whole more effectively than pressure groups of other types.

In Britain as well as the United States, in addition to such "self-oriented" pressure groups, we must also deal with what S. E. Finer calls "promotional" groups.[4] Among the former we may classify such organization as the Federation of British Industries, the Trades Union Congress, the National Farmers Union, the British Medical Association, the National Union of Teachers, the British Legion, the National and Local Government Officers' Association. The "promotional" groups include the Howard League for Penal Reform, the National Council for Civil Liberties, the Peace Pledge Union, the Campaign for the Limitation of Secret Police Powers. As compared with the self-oriented groups, writes Finer, the latter "do not represent 'interests' in the same sense at all. They represent a cause, not a social or economic 'stake' in society."[5]

Such a broad distinction in the character of goals tends to have important consequences for structure and behavior. The promotional group, for instance, tends to be open to all like-minded persons, while the self-oriented group has, so to speak, a fixed clientele. By and large the self-oriented group can more readily extract money and work from its members on a continuing and regularized basis. It may also be less subject to splintering and more capable of continuous, unified action. At least in part for such reasons, the more powerful pressure groups of the British polity are self-oriented groups, based on a vocational interest, bureaucratic in structure, and continuing over a long period of time. While some form of group politics has long flourished in the British as in other polities, this modern,

[3]R. T. McKenzie, *British Political Parties* (New York: St. Martin's Press, 1955), *passim.*

[4]S. E. Finer, *Anonymous Empire: A Study of the Lobby in Great Britain* (London: Pall Mall Press, 1958), p. 3.

[5]*Ibid.*

collectivist type has emerged only in recent generations.[6] There is some sense in saying that one line of development in the history of British pressure groups has been from the promotional to the self-oriented, vocational type. Possibly a similar development has taken place in the United States, although here the third party has often played the role of the promotional group in Britain. We might also find that the promotional group remains a more important feature of the American polity than of the British.

Farm, labor, and business organizations. Concentration and bureaucracy characterize British pressure groups as well as parties. Hardly without exception the big vocational pressure groups in Britain have a higher index of density and concentration. There, for instance, the National Farmers Union is the only significant organization of farmers and includes 90 per cent of its potential membership. In the United States, of course, only a fraction—no more than 30 per cent—of all farmers are organized and these are divided among three main groups and various minor ones. While absolute numbers are much smaller in Britain, we must remember that British agriculture is highly diversified as to crops, size of farms, and location. Yet through the NFU British farmers speak with one voice to a degree rarely achieved by farmers in the United States. No doubt this is true because to no small extent the organization is run from the top. In Bedford Square is a large and able bureaucracy and at its head stands one of the ablest managers in modern Britain, Sir James Turner—sometimes known as the "Sacred Bull of British Agriculture."

In the field of trade unions, just a little less than half the total working force has been organized, while in the United States the figure is around a quarter. To one peak organization, the TUC, nearly all unions are affiliated and it has been the undisputed spokesman for organized labor for generations. Its permanent secretary, even when Walter Citrine held the post, has never occupied the position of, say, a Gompers. The heads of the Big Three,[7] however, have as prominent a political role as our Reuther, Meany, and Lewis. The British labor leaders of this generation are more likely to have worked their way up the bureaucratic ladder by long and able management than to have emerged from heroic struggles for the right to organize or for better contracts. Contrary to popular impression and in strong contrast with American experience, the strike has almost ceased to be an instrument of labor-management relations in Britain since as far back as

[6]S. H. Beer, "The Representation of Interests in British Government: Historical Background," *American Political Science Review,* Vol. 51, No. 3 (September 1957), pp. 635-645; "Pressure Groups and Parties in Britain," *American Political Science Review,* Vol. 50, No. 1 (March 1956), p. 4.

[7]The Transport and General Workers' Union; the National Union of General and Municipal Workers; the Amalgamated Engineering Union—which among them include 30 per cent of all unionists affiliated with the TUC.

1932.[8] If by bureaucracy, however, we mean full-time paid staff, then British unions generally are far less well endowed than American. The reluctance of the rank and file to pay dues sufficient to employ such staff–and to pay substantial salaries to any permanent official–seriously handicaps British unions.[9]

In the field of business, in Britain as in the United States the basic unit of political action is the trade association. Comparison is made a little easier if we consider only national manufacturing trade associations.[10] Of these there are 1,300 in Britain and some 950 in the United States. Density is high: a sample survey showed that 90 per cent of larger firms and 76 per cent of smaller firms in Britain belong to such associations. Concentration among manufacturing trade associations is considerably greater in Britain. The peak association is the Federation of British Industries (FBI) which represents, through its affiliated trade associations and directly through member firms, some 85 per cent of all manufacturing concerns employing ten or more workers.[11] In the United States, on the other hand, the National Association of Manufacturers has never represented more than 6 per cent of all manufacturing concerns.[12] If the same base as that used for the FBI were taken, however, there is reason to think that the NAM figure would be more like 20 per cent to 25 per cent. The contrast would still be striking.

Bargaining in the Polity

So much for the briefest sort of sketch of collectivism in the structure of the British polity. Let us turn to the modes of interaction of these massive unit actors, in particular the political party and the pressure group.

What we have called bargaining is a principal trait of the relationships of large producers in the collectivist economy. Its essence is that each of the negotiating units is highly dependent on the other as a seller or as a buyer. In a free market, on the other hand, each seller can turn to other buyers and each buyer to other sellers and none have significant market power. In bargaining, however, each unit has substantial market power; hence, the ultimate decision is made as a result of negotiations in which each gauges his offers in the light of expectations about the possible offers of the other.[13]

[8]Hugh A. Clegg, "Strikes," *Political Quarterly,* Vol. 27, No. 1 (January-March 1956), pp. 31-35.

[9]John A. Mack, "Trade Union Leadership," *Political Quarterly,* Vol. 27, No. 1 (January-March 1956), p. 77.

[10]Data on British associations are from P.E.P., *Industrial Trade Associations; Activities and Organization* (London, 1957).

[11]S. E. Finer, "The Federation of British Industries," *Political Studies,* Vol. 4, No. 1 (February 1956), p. 62.

[12]R. W. Gable, "N.A.M.: Influential Lobby or Kiss of Death?", *Journal of Politics,* Vol. 15 (May 1953), p. 257.

[13]See Thomas C. Schelling, "An Essay on Bargaining," *American Economic Review,* Vol. 45, No. 3 (June 1956), pp. 281-283.

A similar kind of decision making occurs where a party enjoys large power over the authority of government, while a pressure group with which it deals enjoys similar power over something—such as votes—that the party wants. Such a situation is very different from one in which government authority is dispersed among many elected officeholders and voting power among an unorganized electorate. In the latter situation, there is a kind of bidding for votes on one side and for promises or policies on the other that has a limited, but real, analogy with the economic free market. Where the centralized party in office confronts the massively organized pressure group, decisions are made quite differently. Indeed, some who have sat in on the Annual Price Review between the National Farmers Union in Britain and the Ministry of Agriculture have reported that the proceedings and the way in which a settlement is reached resemble nothing so much as collective bargaining. For both the farmers and the ministry there is a range of outcomes that would be better than no agreement at all. Each opponent pretty well knows what this range is. No wonder it has sometimes taken four months for a decision to be reached!

Consultation with interests is a feature of all modern Western democratic governments. Some years ago Leiserson, writing of representative advisory committees, traced their origin to "the delegation of discretionary rule-making powers under legislative standards to administrative agencies executing various types of social legislation."[14] Leiserson's statement, broadened somewhat, is a generalization valid for not only American, but also for Western European government: increasing government intervention for such purposes as social reform, economic stability, and national defense has led to the grant of rule-making power to administrative agencies and to increasing participation of interested groups in decision making at that level.

Different stages in this development, however, can be distinguished, depending upon how far the scope of policy has been expanded and the polity has become collectivist. The extent to which power has been mobilized and unified on each side—on the side of the party in power and on the side of the pressure group with which it deals—will determine whether bargaining predominates in the relationship. In the United States, we find administrative consultation on a vast scale both in Washington and in the state capitals. In Britain, a more collectivist polity, the situation is better described as "quasi-corporatism."

It is against the background of this power pattern that we must examine the emphasis that British pressure groups give to the various points in the process of decision making. The formal structure of authority—British parliamentary government as compared with the American separation of powers—will play its role. But we must recall that a hundred years ago Britain also had parliamentary

[14]Avery Leiserson, *Administrative Regulation: A Study in Representation of Interests* (Chicago: Univ. Chicago Press, 1942), p. 162.

government, yet pressure groups then gave far more attention to the legislature than they do now.

Administrative Consultation

In each polity we may distinguish four main phases of policy making: at elections, in the legislature, within the party, and at the administrative level. British pressure groups exert their major influence at the administrative level, taking this to include both ministerial and official contacts. Perhaps their second most important point of influence is within the party. In contrast American pressure groups, by and large, concentrate on the first two points: the electorate and the legislature.

There are, of course, many variations within these two broad patterns. A very important difference may result from the character of the power base of a group. There is a kind of power–and this is particularly important in Britain–that is created by the expansion of policy itself. "The greater the degree of detailed and technical control the government seeks to exert over industrial and commercial interests," E. P. Herring wrote, "the greater must be their degree of consent and active participation in the very process of regulation, if regulation is to be effective or successful."[15] This generalization, I should think, holds for most Western democracies and surely for Britain. There, certain types of control exercised in recent years–price control, materials allocation, tariffs, import control, and the encouragement of exports and productivity are only some of the more striking examples–simply could not be enforced effectively without the substantial co-operation of the groups concerned. The group's technical advice is often well-nigh indispensable. But co-operation–something more than grudging consent to "the law"–is a further necessity. Our farm programs with their referenda and farmer-elected committees recognize this necessity. But in Britain the far wider scope of regulation and planning–even after the various "bonfires of controls"–gives this power factor far greater weight.

A few examples: The farmers–meaning in effect the NFU–are represented on a set of local committees that have had important administrative duties under various agricultural programs, and the chance that the NFU might encourage these farmer representatives to withdraw from the committees has been a force in the annual price reviews. When the Conservatives in denationalizing part of the transport industry in 1946 dismantled the government haulage (that is, trucking) system, a standby scheme was organized by the industry itself. The Labour government's limitation of advertising expenditure was policed by the organized advertisers, and its important anti-inflationary effort to restrain both dividends and wage increases was carried out–and with remarkable success–on a voluntary basis by organized business and labor.

[15]E. Pendleton Herring, *Public Administration and the Public Interest* (New York: McGraw-Hill, 1936), p. 192.

Neither the British nor the American system of consultation between government and pressure groups has been fully described.[16] Some rough impressions, modestly intended, may be in order. In both countries the central device is the representative advisory committee. British examples range from high level bodies such as the Economic Planning Board, the National Joint Advisory Council of the Ministry of Labour, the National Production Advisory Council on Industry, on which the relevant peak organizations, the FBI, BEC and TUC, are represented, to the multitude of advisory committees of the main economic departments to which trade associations send representatives. The latter are connected with the system of "sponsoring" departments which grew up during and after World War II and which means today that every industry and every branch of it, no matter how small, has a sponsoring department or section of one, somewhere in the government machine. Apart from such committees, although often around them, a regular system of informal consultation has grown up. Private and public bureaucrats continually call one another on the telephone or meet for luncheon and discuss a problem on a first-name basis. Often several departments and several groups are concerned.

On the American side, the immense documentation on advisory committees in the federal government that was assembled by a subcommittee of the Government Operations Committee in 1957 has not yet been analyzed by political scientists.[17] But it is clear that from the time of the National Recovery Administration, the use of this device, from being relatively rare, has immensely increased. The number of advisory committees associated with government departments at the center–and in addition to many more at the local or regional level–runs into the hundreds. One major set established by statute are in the Department of Agriculture–for instance, the Commodity Stabilization Committees. Of the remainder, the vast majority it seems are associated principally with the defense effort–procurement, development, standards, stockpiling, and so on–and consist of industry advisory committees. In comparison with similar British industry advisory committees, the American appear to depend less on trade associations, the result at least in part of the Defense Production Act of 1950 that requires that nonmembers as well as members of trade associations be included. The peak associations–the NAM and United States Chamber of Commerce–also play a much less prominent role than their British counterparts not being represented, as such, on even the Business Advisory Council. Certainly trade unions are not called in for advice so frequently or on so broad a front in the United States as in Britain. The TUC

[16]For a brief sketch of important aspects of American practice, see *Consultation with Industry,* a history of the Office of Industry Advisory Committees of the N.P.A. (Washington, D.C.: U.S. Dept. of Commerce, 1953).

[17]*Advisory Committees* (Parts I-V), subcommittee of the House Committee on Government Operations, 84th Congress, 2nd Session (1956); hearings before the same subcommittee on H.R. 3378, 85th Congress, 1st Session (1957); H.R. Report 576 on H.R. 7390, 85th Congress, 1st Session (1957).

alone, for instance, is represented on some 60 committees touching all aspects of social and economic problems.

Of the broad character of the power relationship we can speak with confidence: the American executive possesses far less actual power than the British. Quite apart from the degree of delegated powers in this country, the political independence of Congress and the exercise of administrative oversight by Congressional Committees mean that the group interested in influencing policy must give great attention to the legislature. Some years ago Blaisdell found that pressure groups, while concerned with the administration, focused their attention principally upon Congress.[18] Broadly this must still be the case, although it would be interesting to know how far the defense effort may have shifted the balance.

Pressure on Parties

At the Democratic National Convention in 1956 the number of trade-union officials sitting as delegates ran into the hundreds, while at the Republican convention there was no more than a scattering. Generally, however, in both national and state parties in the United States, the connection of pressure groups and parties is less close than in Britain. We do not have the formal affiliation of the trade union movement with one party. But the more important difference arises from the fact that American parties are so poorly unified that they do not provide an effective channel for influencing the use of government authority. In Britain, on the other hand, the party ranks second–although perhaps a poor second–to the administration as an object of pressure.

Where the power is, there the pressure will be applied. Where we see the pressure being applied, therefore, we shall probably find the seat of power. Judged by this rule, the central organs of the British party, especially the parliamentary party, are far more powerful than the party's representative assemblies. Pressure groups do not openly descend on a British party conference as they do on the platform hearings of an American party convention. Their representatives, however, may be present and spokesmen for various special interests–farmers, trade unionists, veterans, teachers, old-age pensioners, advertising men with a concern for commercial broadcasting–will take up a good deal of time at a party conference.

The important point of influence, however, is the parliamentary party–its regular, full meetings and its specialized committees–and to a lesser extent the party's central office. We are familiar with the way leaders of the Labour party while in power or in opposition will frequently consult with the trade unions on pending decisions. There is also an active alignment, if not formal affiliation, of organized

[18]Donald C. Blaisdell, *Economic Power and Political Pressures,* Monograph 26, T.N.E.C., Investigation of Concentration of Economic Power, 76th Congress, 3rd Session (Washington, 1941), pp. 57 and 70.

business with the Conservatives. During the passage of the bill nationalizing transport in 1946-47, for instance, the Conservative opposition tabled several hundred amendments. Where had they come from? In practice the party's Parliamentary Secretariat–a body of party employees, not MPs–acted as intermediary between the transport committee of the parliamentary party and the various pressure groups, especially the General Council of British Shipping, the Dock and Harbors Association, and a joint committee of the Federation of British Industries, National Union of Manufacturers, and the Association of British Chambers of Commerce.[19]

Inseparable from these channels of influence is one of the, to an American, most curious phenomena of British politics. He is the "interested MP"–that is, the member who is connected with an outside interest group by direct personal involvement, such as occupation or ownership of property, or by membership or office holding in an outside organization speaking for an interest group. Today and for generations the House of Commons through the personal involvement of its members has represented a far wider range of interests than has the American Congress, notoriously inhabited by lawyers.

In Britain such personal involvement was a principal way in which interest groups of the nineteenth century made themselves heard in government. Of more importance in today's collectivist polity is the member connected with an outside organization. The MPs sponsored and subsidized by the trade unions are the best-known examples. But there is also a host of others: a joint Honorary Secretary of the Association of British Chambers of Commerce, the Chairman of the Howard League for Penal Reform, a Director of the Society of Motor Manufacturers and Traders, the President of the British Legion, the Secretary of the National Tyre Distributors Association–there seems to be hardly a member who fails to note some such connection in his biography in the *Times' House of Commons.* Perhaps some Congressmen also have similar connections. Amid their wide membership in churches, fraternal organizations, and "patriotic" groups as recorded in the *Congressional Directory,* however, they fail to mention them.

Perhaps, as S. E. Finer has suggested, the absence of such interested members from the Congress is one reason why American pressure groups must make up the deficiency by hiring lobbyists in such large numbers. For the interested MP is an active lobbyist within the legislature. His principal role is played within the parliamentary party, but his activity in the House itself is more observable. He may speak openly as the representative of a group, as the President of the British Legion often does in forwarding the Legion's campaign to increase disability pensions.[20] He is more likely to be effective at the amendment stage of a finance or

[19]Finer, *op. cit.* (note 3 *supra*), pp. 67-68. For other examples of pressure group activity in the House of Commons, see J. D. Stewart, *British Pressure Groups: Their Role in Relation to the House of Commons* (Oxford: Oxford Univ. Press, 1958).

[20]J. H. Millett, "British Interest Group Tactics: A Case Study," *Political Science Quarterly* (March 1957).

other bill when, briefed by his association, he suggests changes, which perhaps at the same time are being urged on the Minister and civil servants by officers or staff of the pressure group.

Influencing Public Opinion

Herring long ago observed how American pressure groups direct great attention to influencing public opinion: not only to win support for some immediate objective, but also to build up generally favorable attitudes. This he found to be a trait of the "new" lobby, and it is not irrelevant that this technique arose along with the development of modern mass-advertising methods and media. A major difference in Britain is that the big vocational pressure groups rarely mount such public campaigns. In the nineteenth century, this was not so. Beginning late in the century, however, this propagandist function seems more and more to have passed to political parties. Today and for many years now, the parties, in contrast with the pressure groups, have virtually monopolized communication with the voters as such—that is with the general public as distinguished from communication by a pressure group with its clientele.

This differentiation of function in political communication has gone very much farther in Britain than in the United States. A striking feature of nearly all the vocational pressure groups there is the extent to which they urge their demands simply and frankly as special interests. There is a significant contrast, I think, with American pressure groups which tend to base their claims on some large principle of social philosophy or national policy—as, for example, in the vast public-relations program of the NAM.

Yet the public campaign has sometimes been used by the big pressure groups of British politics and its use may be on the increase. Examples are the antinationalization campaign launched by the Road Haulage Association in 1946-47; Tate and Lyle's famous "Mr. Cube" campaign against the nationalization of sugar refining in 1949-50; and in general the growing use of Aims of Industry, a public-relations agency founded to defend and advocate free enterprise. Lesser efforts have been pressed by the National Union of Teachers and the British Legion. If this practice grows greatly, one might well expect it to weaken the position of the parties.

Such a development—which I do not expect—could have great consequences for the British polity. For without in any degree being cynical, one must acknowledge the large part played by British parties in creating the present political homogeneity of the British electorate—the national market for their brand-name goods. The British party battle is continuous and highly organized and so also is the stream of propaganda directed at the voter. Through it the party voter is strengthened, if not created, and the tight party majority in the legislature prepared. Even more important, the framework of public thinking about policy, the voter's sense of the alternatives, is fixed from above. Popular sovereignty in the polity has been qualified by the same means that have qualified consumers' sovereignty in the economy.

In this Americans are not likely to find much cause for self-congratulation. We will hardly say that we are more free of political propaganda. As in other aspects of the American power pattern, the difference is that the centers from which this weighty influence emanates are far more dispersed and unco-ordinated. Is this necessarily to our advantage? Some words of E. P. Herring's suggest an answer:

> A democracy inclines toward chaos rather than toward order. The representative principle, if logically followed, leads to infinite diversity rather than ultimate unity. . . . Since the "voice of the people" is a pleasant fancy and not a present fact, the impulse for positive political action must be deliberately imposed at some strategic point, if democracy is to succeed as a form of government.[21]

[21] Herring, *op. cit.* (note 15 *supra*), p. 377.

The Role of Voluntary Associations in West African Urbanization

Kenneth Little

Introduction

Taken as a whole, the West African region was relatively unaffected by the modern world until the end of the 19th century. Modern development of the hinterland began with the British and French realization that these territories constituted an expanding market for imported goods as well as important sources of mineral and raw materials needed by the metropolitan country. The French were also concerned with the question of military manpower. These factors were finally crystallized by World War II and the events following it. The

Kenneth Little, "The Role of Voluntary Associations in West African Urbanization." Reproduced by permission of the American Anthropological Association from the American Anthropologist, *Vol. 59 (August 1957).*

British war effort demanded greatly increased supplies of palm kernels, cotton, cocoa, and other locally grown products as well as hides, tin, iron ore, etc., which the colonial governments concerned were required to stimulate (cf. Fortes 1945: 205-219). Since the War there have been resettlement schemes, new industries and constructional projects have been instituted, and there has been a general improvement in communications by road, rail, and air. With the strategic implications of West Africa in the struggle against Communism also becoming manifest, political development has also gone on very rapidly, and there has been a corresponding expansion of education and the social services.

The consequence of all these technical and other changes is that there are now many more different modes of life and ways of earning a living than existed in West Africa some fifty years ago. It also goes without saying that its inhabitants have acquired a taste for the material elements of Western civilization, including consumer goods of every possible kind. In addition to new economic incentives, Western interests ranging from Christianity and nationalism to football and ballroom dancing have also been generated on a wide scale. In short, there has been produced the kind of phenomenon which anthropologists have customarily studied under the heading of culture contact, or acculturation. This term, however, is not precise enough for purposes of present analysis. First, many of the principal agents of cultural change nowadays are Africans themselves, and second, many Western ideas, practices, and procedures have already been fully assimilated to African culture. Africans became important as "acculturative agents" about the middle of the 19th century when Western-educated Creoles from Sierra Leone went off evangelizing and trading down the Coast. All the way from the Gambia in the west to the Congo in the south they constituted, in many cases, little oases of westernized culture. Consequently, although much of the traditional life has disintegrated, new forms of social organization have arisen out of the older structure. There are, moreover, considerable differences in the extent to which given peoples and groups of Africans have undergone so-called detribalization, and it is rare to find whole communities which have completely severed all traditional loyalties and obligations. More often is it the case, as I propose to show, that the African individual moving out of the tribal area continues to be influenced by tribal culture. In other words, instead of viewing the contemporary West African situation in terms of the juxtaposition of two entirely different cultures, we shall do better to conceive it as a process of adaptation to new circumstances and conditions. Cultural contacts still go on, but between westernized Africans and other Africans, as well as between Westerners and Africans; so that the changes occurring are no different in kind from those within a single society (cf. Little 1953:4).

The Urbanization of West Africa

What, in effect, this transformation of West Africa involves is a social process somewhat analogous to the social changes that resulted in the urbanization of

Western Europe during the 19th century. Western contact with Africa, like the Industrial Revolution in Europe, has created new social and psychological needs which life in the countryside is rarely able to satisfy. The consequence is a tremendous migration of men and women to the towns, and to places where money can be earned to pay taxes, to provide bridewealth, and to buy manufactured goods and appliances.

Many of these people are in search of a higher standard of living in the shape of the more up-to-date amenities and better housing as well as the higher income that the town can offer. But this is not the only motivation. A large number of the younger men are looking for further educational opportunities, or are hoping to start a fresh career. Others move as a means of escaping from the restrictions of village life, and some of the younger girls, as well as the boys, out of love of adventure and desire for fresh experiences (cf. Balandier 1955a). As Fortes has written in reference to the Gold Coast: "Labour, enterprise, and skill are now marketable in their own right anywhere in the country. . . . People feel that there is little risk in moving about, especially if, as appears to be the case with most mobile elements, their earning capacity is low. A clerk getting £2.10 a month feels that he cannot go much lower if he moves" (Fortes 1947:149-179). The development of motor transport, in the shape of the ubiquitous lorry, is an important factor in these respects. Not only has it greatly increased local mobility between town and town, and between town and surrounding countryside, but it has created a new and influential social role—that of the lorry-driver, as a go-between between the urban labor market and the rural village.

Most of this migration is in the direction of towns already established as large centers of Western commerce and administration, of the rapidly growing ports, and of places where mining and other industries are being developed. Its effect has been to swell the population of such places far beyond their previous size, as well as to convert a good many villages into urban areas. For example, the principal towns of Senegal in French West Africa increased their populations by 100 percent between 1942 and 1952 and those of the French Ivory Coast by 109 percent during the same decade. In the Gold Coast there was an increase of 98 percent in the populations of the five largest towns between 1931 and 1948 (Balandier 1955b). Cotonou in Dahomey grew from 1100 in 1905 to 35,000 in 1952 and Lunsar, in Sierra Leone, which was a village of 30 inhabitants in 1929, has a population today of nearly 17,000 (Lombard 1954:3, 4; Littlejohn n.d.).

Although urbanism in terms of "a relatively large, dense, and permanent settlement of socially heterogeneous individuals" (Wirth 1938) is not a general characteristic of traditional life, it is far from being a unique phenomenon in West Africa. In 1931, some 28 percent of the Yoruba population of Western Nigeria lived in 9 cities of over 45,000 inhabitants, while a further 34 percent lived in cities of over 20,000 inhabitants (Bascom 1955). However, what distinguishes the "new" African city—"new" in the sense, as Georges Balandier points out, that they were built by European colonists—from traditional urbanism is that a large part of its population is industrial, depending upon the labor market for a living. This is particularly evident in the case of towns of recent growth. In Cotonou, for example, some 10,000 persons out of a population of some 35,000 are in wage employment (Lombard 1954).

A further point is that the modern town is much more heterogeneous. It has groups of professionals, office workers, municipal employees, artisans, etc., and in addition to its indigenous political and social segmentation, it also accommodates a large proportion of "strangers." Not only do the latter frequently outnumber the native inhabitants of the town, but they include a wide diversity of tribes. For example, Kumasi, although the capital of Ashantiland, contains as many non-Ashantis as Ashantis; Takoradi-Sekondi contains representatives of more than 60 different tribes (Busia 1950); and less than 10 percent of the inhabitants of Poto-Poto, one of the three African towns of Brazzaville, were born in that city (Balandier 1955a). In the Gold Coast, as a whole, more than two-thirds of the inhabitants of the big towns have been there for less than five years. A further significant characteristic of these urban populations is the numerical preponderance of young people over old and, to a less appreciable extent, the preponderance of men over women. For example, only 2.4 percent of the population of Cotonou are over 60 years of age. In 1921, men considerably outnumbered women, but by 1952 the masculinity rate had dropped to 111. In an area of Poto-Poto, on the other hand, where the average age of the population is about 25, there are only 515 females to every 1000 males (Balandier 1955a).

Voluntary Associations

1. Tribal unions. From the point of view of social organization one of the most striking characteristics of these modern towns is the very large number and variety of voluntary associations.[1] These include a host of new political, religious, recreational, and occupational associations as well as the more traditional mutual aid groups and secret societies out of which some of these more recent organizations have developed. What generally distinguishes the latter kind of association is its more formal constitution and the fact that it has been formed to meet certain needs arising specifically out of the urban environment of its members. It is also more "modern" both in respect to its aims and the methods employed to attain

[1]Michael P. Banton (n.d.) estimates that some 130 registered societies were in existence in Freetown in 1952. The number of unregistered societies is unknown. Pierre Clement (1956: 470-471) reports some 62 "authorized" and "unauthorized" societies from Stanleyville, Belgian Congo. There are very few data concerning individual participation, although J. Lombard reports of Cotonou that out of 35 persons who belonged to one or more associations, 20 belonged to regional groups, 17 to professional associations, 13 to political groups, 3 to musical societies, 1 to an athletic club.

them. One of the best illustrations of these points is provided by certain tribal associations of an extraterritorial kind, known in Nigeria and the Gold Coast as Tribal Unions.

These tribal unions range from little unions, consisting of a few members of the same extended family or clan (Aloba 1954), to much larger bodies like the Ibo State Union which is a collection of village and clan unions. In Nigeria, these associations were originally formed by Ibo and other migrants from Eastern Nigeria to protect themselves from the hostile way in which they were received when they took jobs as policemen, traders, and laborers in the towns of the West and the North. Their aim is to provide members with mutual aid, including support, while out of work, sympathy and financial assistance in the case of illness, and the responsibility for the funeral and the repatriation of the family of the deceased in the case of death. The main raison d'être, however, is that of fostering and keeping alive an interest in tribal song, history, language, and moral beliefs, and thus maintaining a person's attachment to his native town or village and to his lineage there. In furtherance of this sentiment, money is collected for the purpose of improving amenities in the union's home town and to provide its younger people with education. Social activities include the organization of dances on festival days and of sports meetings and games for their young people. Some of these unions also produce an annual magazine, called an Almanac, in which their members' activities are recorded (Offodile 1947:937, 939, 941).

Associations based upon membership of the same ethnic group also exist in French and Belgian Africa where they perform somewhat similar functions. In Cotonou, for example, such groups welcome and look after persons newly arrived from the country. They provide a means whereby both the old people and the "evolue" can keep in touch with their rural relatives and friends. Each such association has an annual feast and celebration which brings together everyone from the same region. It is also a means of helping the needy and aged members of the group (Lombard 1954).

In Nigeria there have also been developed home branches of the tribal union abroad; and as a final step, State unions have been created, comprising every union of members of the same tribe. It is not surprising, therefore, that these Nigerian tribal unions have obtained a power and influence far beyond their original objectives. The larger unions have played an important part in the expansion of education. They offer scholarships for deserving boys and girls and run their own schools. In some places, the monthly contributions of members for education are invested in some form of commercial enterprise, and appeals for money to build schools seem to meet with a particularly ready response. One observer claims that he saw an up-country union raise in six hours and in a single meeting over £16,000 for such purposes. Some higher education overseas has also been provided, and several leading members of the Nigerian Eastern House of Assembly owe their training in British universities to State union money

(Aloba 1954). Even more ambitious plans have included the building of a national bank where people can obtain loans for industrial and commercial purposes. In this connection, some unions have economic advisers who survey trade reports for the benefit of members (Offodile 1947). These tribal unions also serve a number of important political purposes and are recognized as units for purposes of tax collection. In addition to pressing local authorities for better roads, dispensaries and hospitals, and other public amenities, they have been a powerful force in the democratizing of traditional councils; in the multitribal centers they were for many years the recognized basis for representation on Township Advisory Boards or Native Authority Councils. They have also provided a forum for the expression of national politics and for the rise to positions of leadership of the younger educated element (Coleman 1952).

2. *Friendly societies.* In addition to the tribal union, there are also a large number of tribal societies where objectives are limited to mutual aid and benefit. One of the most complicated of these organizations is run by the wives of Kru immigrants in Freetown. This kind of society is divided into three classes. A member pays an admission fee of one guinea and enters the class of least importance. He or she may subsequently be promoted to a higher class and in this event will be expected to make members of that class a present of several pounds. On his or her death, the relatives receive a sum of money commensurate with the deceased person's status. These societies endeavor to develop a high esprit de corps and have been known to impose fines of as much as £20 on members guilty of unfriendly conduct toward each other (Banton 1956).

Kru men go to sea for a living and so the members of their societies are divided into "ships," named after various recent additions to Messrs. Elder Dempster's fleet, instead of classes. The Kru also have so-called "family societies" comprising the migrant members of a particular class, or *dako* (a small local federation of patriclans). These groups also provide bereavement benefits. In Freetown there are also a number of traditional organizations, including so-called secret societies and dancing groups, which provide funeral expenses, presents, and entertainment for members when they marry. The congregations of mosques, too, usually have what is loosely called a *Jama Compin* (Compin = Krio, "Company") whose members help each other over funerals. Up country, another Moslem group, composed of women, endeavors to intervene in domestic quarrels and to reconcile man and wife. In this case, a sixpenny subscription is collected every Sunday, and persons joining as new members have to pay the equivalent of what a foundation member has already paid in subscriptions. Some of this money is disbursed as alms, but most of it is used to provide sickness and funeral benefits (Little 1955).

A different kind of mutual aid group is the *esusu,* which is of Yoruba origin. Members of the group pay in at regular intervals a fixed sum and the total is given each time to one of the members. This is an important method for buying trading stock, expensive clothing, etc. (Banton 1956; Bascom 1952). In southeastern Nigeria, a somewhat similar kind of "contribution club" is divided into seven sections, each under a headman. Each member pays one or more weekly subscriptions. The headmen are responsible for collecting the shares from their members, and when the shares have all been collected, the money is handed over to a member nominated by the headman in turn. The recipient has a number of obligations, including that of supplying a quantity of palm wine for the refreshment of club members (Ardener 1953:128-142).

A further organization serves all three functions–providing funeral benefits, charity, and helping its members to save. This is the *Nanamei Akpee,* or "mutual help" society. It has its headquarters in Accra and branches in several other Gold Coast towns, including Keta. The Keta branch has well over 400 members, the great majority of whom are educated or semiliterate women traders. There is a monthly subscription of one shilling and when a member dies, the surviving relatives are given at least £10 towards the cost of funeral expenses. Money for loans is raised at weekly collections which begin with community singing. All the women present give as much money as they feel they can afford, and their contributions are written down in a book which also contains a list of the society's members, in order of seniority. When the collection is finished, all the money is given to the member whose name takes first place; the following week it is given to the second, then to the third, and so on. Eventually, all members will in this way receive a contribution, though the process as a whole naturally takes a very long time. However, the man or woman receiving a collection is also given a list showing the amount of money contributed by other members. This determines, during later weeks, the amounts he must contribute himself. For example, if A has given B two shillings then B must raise the same amount when eventually A's turn arrives to receive a weekly collection. In effect, this arrangement means that senior members, i.e., those who have joined early, receive an interest-free loan, which they repay weekly by small contributions; those on the bottom of the list, on the other hand, are saving in a small way, for their own ultimate benefit. In a period of rising prices, those at the top of the list naturally have the advantage, but on the other hand those who wait longer may receive more because the society's membership will in the meantime have increased. There is an element of chance in all this which adds spice to the normally dull business of saving, and this partly explains the society's popularity. Finally, when a member falls ill he is visited in the hospital, given small gifts of money, and so on. At times the society also gives presents and small sums of money to old and sick people even if they are not members (Carey n.d.).

3. Occupational associations. In addition to raising loans through such organizations as *Nanamei Akpee,* African market women also form associations in order to control the supply or price of commodities in which their members trade. Some of the larger markets have a woman in charge, and each of the various sections which women monopolize, such as the sale of yams, gari, cloth, etc. is also headed by a woman, who represents them in relation to customers and the market authorities. In Lagos market each such section has its own union, which discourages competition between women trading in that particular commodity (Comhaire-Sylvain 1951). Another women's association is the Fish Sellers Union at Takoradi-Sekondi. The members of this association may club together to raise money to buy fishing nets. The group then sells the nets to fishermen on agreed terms. A fisherman who receives a net sells his catches during the fishing season to the creditor group, and the value of the fish is reckoned against the net. In this way, the members are able to obtain the fish on which their livelihood depends (Busia 1950). Women also associate for industrial purposes. In southern Nigeria, for example, there are women's societies which run a bakery, a laundry, a calabash manufactory, and a gari mill. One of the most interesting of these associations, the Egba Women's Union in Abeokuta, claims a membership of 80,000 women, paying subscriptions of 13 shillings a year. It operates as a weaving co-operative, and runs a maternity and a child welfare clinic as well as conducting classes for illiterate women.

Other occupational and professional associations are concerned with the status and remuneration of their members as workers. Such groups include modern crafts such as goldsmiths, tinkers, gunsmiths, tailors, and barbers, as well as certain trade unions which, unlike Government sponsored trade unions, have come spontaneously into being. One example of these is the Motor Drivers Union at Keta which is now a branch of a nationwide union which negotiates freight rates, working conditions, and so on. Unlike European trade unions, this Motor Drivers Union is an association of small entrepreneurs owning their own vehicles rather than an association of employees. Its main purpose is to look after the interests of drivers generally and in particular to offer them legal assistance and insurance. When a driver is convicted, the Union tries as far as possible to pay his fine; and when a driver dies the Union provides part of the funeral expenses. There are also smaller sickness and accident benefits. The entrance fee is 14 shillings and there is a monthly subscription of one shilling. In addition, the Union organizes meetings and dances (Carey n.d.).

The organization of modern crafts, on the other hand, takes on the form of guilds resembling those of medieval Europe. The first rule of all these guilds in Yoruba towns, where many of them have developed, is that every craftsman, whether master, journeyman or apprentice, must be registered with the guild, must attend meetings, and must pay his dues. One of the guild's prime functions is to maintain a reasonable standard of work in the craft. It determines the rules of apprenticeship; fixes prices of workmanship; and settles disputes, whether between master and apprentice or between craftsman and customer. On the other hand, the guild does not undertake to care for its members in sickness or old age; neither does it function as a bank, lending money to members for tools. Most forms of social security are still organized by the lineage—in which the guild members still retain full membership—and not by the guild (Lloyd 1953).

Unions of a different kind which are also concerned with the status and remuneration of their members are associations of prostitutes. These have been reported from Takoradi and also from Brazzaville. In the latter city, the members of such organizations try to improve their own social and economic position by insisting on a high standard of dress and deportment, and by ostracizing other women who are too casual or too free with their sexual favors. Each group has its own name, such as *La Rose, Diamant,* etc. and is under a leader, an elderly woman, who can set a pattern of elegance and sophistication. Membership is limited and is regulated by a committee. There is also a common fund out of which members in financial straits are helped and their funeral expenses paid should they die. In the latter event, the association behaves as if it were the family of the deceased. Every girl goes into mourning, giving up her jewelry and finer clothes for six months, at the end of which there is a night-long celebration in some "bar-dancing" establishment hired for the occasion (Balandier 1955a: 145-148).

4. *Entertainment and recreational associations.* A large number of associations are concerned with dancing and musical forms of entertainment. Many of these, such as the drumming companies found in Ewe villages in the Gold Coast, still retain much of their traditional character. A number of groups in Brazzaville also perform traditional music, but on a commercial basis. These societies consist of young men who have formed themselves into an orchestra under the presidency of an older man whose compound they use for the purpose of staging an evening's "social" on Saturdays and Sundays. The public is charged for admission on these occasions and the "band," which goes by such appropriate titles as *Etoile, Jeunesse, Record de la Gaieté,* etc. undertakes outside engagements. The receipts are divided among the members according to their position in the society and anything left over goes toward the purchase of new instruments and the provision of further conviviality (cf. Balandier 1955a:143-144). Other such associations, which began as simple dancing societies, have developed under urban conditions into a relatively complex organization and set of modern objectives. A striking example of this kind of phenomenon is the dancing *compin* of Sierra Leone. This is a group of young men and women concerned with the performance of "plays" of traditional music and dancing and with the raising of money for mutual benefit. The music is provided mainly by native drums, xylophones, and calabash rattles, and is accompanied by singing. The dancing which, like the drumming, shows signs of Western influence, is somewhat reminiscent of English country dancing. A "play" is generally given in connection with some important event, such as the close of Ramadan, or as part of the ceremonies celebrating a wedding or a funeral. The general public as well as the persons honored by the performance are expected

to donate money to the compin on these occasions. Money is also collected in the form of weekly subscriptions from the members (Banton 1956; Little 1955).

In one of these organizations, which are particularly numerous among Temne and Mandinka immigrants in Freetown, this amount goes into a general fund to cover corporate expenses of the society's activities–rent of yard, provision of lamps, replacement of drum skins, etc. Then, when any member is bereaved, a collection is held to which all must contribute. However, quite an elaborate procedure is necessary before the money can be paid. The bereaved person must first notify the Reporter with a reporting fee. This is passed on to the company's Doctor, who investigates the circumstances of death, for the company will fine any member who has not notified them of a relative's illness so that they can see that the sick person receives attention. The Doctor washes the body and sends the Prevoe (Provost) round to the other members, telling them to gather that evening when they must pay their contributions. When anyone avoids payment without good cause, the Bailiff may seize an item of his property of equal value. The evening's meeting is organized by the Manager. He will bring the company's lamps, for members are under an obligation to take part in a wake which will last into the early hours. At the wake the bereaved person will provide cigarettes, kola nuts, bread, and coffee, and will employ a singer. Another duty of the Doctor is to examine members before admission, and to attend them if sick. The Commissioner or Inspector is the disciplinary officer and he can arrest or eject trouble makers, the Prevoe acting on his orders. The Clerk or Secretary keeps accounts and writes letters, and the Cashier receives from the Sultan for safe keeping any money accruing to the society. The Sultan is the chief executive; his female counterpart, who has charge of the women members, is the Mammy Queen. For the dancing there is a leader who directs it, and a Conductor who supervises the band. There is also a Sister in charge of the Nurses, young girls who bring round refreshments at dances, often in white dresses with a red cross on the breast and the appropriate headgear. If there is no woman Doctor, an older Nurse or Sister may assist the Doctor with the invalids, or the washing of the corpse. There may also be further officials, such as an Overseer, an M. C., a Solicitor, a Lawyer, Sick Visitor, etc. Many of these titles involve no work, but they can be given to honor even the least deserving member and to strengthen his identification with the group's company (Banton n.d.).

Other groups concerned with recreation range from Improvement Leagues and Women's Institutes to cricket and football clubs. Some of the latter are characterized by such colorful titles as Mighty Poisons, Hearts of Oak, Heroes, etc. (Hodgkin 1956). Football teams are also run by associations of the former pupils of certain schools, known as Old Boys Associations, which also organize receptions and "send-offs" and sometimes hold evening classes. Most organizations of the latter kind are modeled rather closely on European lines, particularly the so-called "social club." This is constituted for dining and drinking purposes as well as for tennis, whist, billiards, ballroom dancing, amateur dramatics, and other European recreational and cultural activities. For the latter reasons, "social clubs" are mainly confined to the most Westernized section of the population, including well-to-do professionals and businessmen as well as teachers, clerks, and other white collar workers. Such clubs are open to persons of any tribe, but members are expected to conform to European patterns of social etiquette. Europeans themselves are frequently admitted either as members or as guests. Examples of this kind of institution are the Rodgers Club in Accra, the Island Club in Lagos, and the Bo African Club in Sierra Leone. In the latter association, all official business and proceedings, including lectures, debates etc., are conducted in English. At the weekly dance, which is one of the club's principal activities, the general rule is for the women to wear print or silk dresses (without the head tie), and the men open-necked shirts with a blazer or sports jacket. On special occasions evening dress is worn by both sexes. In addition to its ordinary activities, this club undertakes a number of public functions, including special dances to honor visiting notables. It also entertains the teams of visiting football clubs, and its premises are used for such purposes as political meetings and adult education classes (Little 1955).

Women, too, have their social clubs which broadly complement those under the control of men. These are very often known as Ladies' Clubs and Women's Institutes. Many of the latter have been formed under the auspices of churches. A large number of literate husbands have nonliterate wives, and some of these women's clubs reflect the sociological situation in that they are divided into "literate" and "illiterate" sections which hold separate meetings. "Literate" activities consist mainly in sewing and crochet work, in practicing the cooking of European and native dishes, and in listening to talks about household economy. Individual literate women given instruction in these arts to the "illiterate" meeting, and in return nonliterate women sometimes teach the literate group native methods of dyeing, spinning, basketry, and traditional songs and dances (Little 1955).

Women's Institutes are primarily the result of the initiative of educated women. For example, the President and leading officers of the Keta Women's Institute in the Gold Coast are teachers, although the bulk of its membership consists of market women. It is principally a social club, but it has certain other more important interests. For example, it has acted as a "pressure group," intervening with the Urban Council in support of a plan for improving amenities at the local markets. Among other local changes, the women achieved the provision of ambulance services, and the employment of a larger number of female nurses at the Keta hospital (Carey n.d.).

The Organization of Voluntary Associations

Before we attempt to generalize about these voluntary associations, it is necessary to distinguish between three rather different types. The first is still basically concerned with traditional activities, although with some slight modification; in the second type, traditional activities have been deliberately modified or expanded to suit modern purposes; and the third type is wholly modern in organization and objectives. It will be convenient to term these three types respectively "traditional," "traditional-modernized" and "modern."

The function of the "traditional" association is generally limited to the organization of some particular religious, occupational, or recreational interest, such as a cult, a trade, or some form of dancing or drumming. Space unfortunately prevents description of religious associations in general. These exist alongside Islam and the ancestral cult, and according to Hofstra (1955) they may be divided into four categories: (1) Christian churches organized by missionaries, (2) so-called African churches, (3) looser, smaller groups of a syncretistic character, (4) irregularly organized movements of a messianic or prophetic kind. In the traditional type of association some provision may be made for mutual benefit, but this is incidental to the main purpose of the society. Membership in the group is usually confined to persons belonging to the same village or ward of a town and is often related to other traditional institutions, such as an age set. For example, drumming companies among the Ewe are organized on a ward basis, and usually there are three in every ward. The first comprises children up to the age of about fifteen; the second consists of the so-called "young men," ranging in age from about fifteen to thirty; and the third comprises "elders," i.e. the male population over thirty or so. The senior companies usually give themselves names such as "Patience" or "U.A.C." (abbreviation for United Africa Company), and some of these are, in effect, associations of semiprofessional entertainers who travel about the country in search of engagements (Cary, n.d.). Although the organization of such "traditional" associations is generally quite simple and informal, a number of them have adapted to modern conditions by incorporating literate persons as officials and by widening the scope of their function. In the traditional economy of the Gold Coast, for example, each trade or occupation normally had a chief-practitioner who settled disputes and represented his associates in relation to outsiders. This is largely true today, but in addition some of these groups have turned themselves into local branches of a nationwide union. In the case of the goldsmiths, this involved appointing its chief-practitioner as Life-Chairman of the association, while an educated man who could deal adequately with its business affairs was elected President. Similarly, the semiliterate president of the Carpenters Union now has a literate secretary and treasurer to help him (Carey n.d.).

It goes without saying that the great majority of people who belong to "traditional" associations are unlettered. The number of persons who can read and write or speak a European language is larger in the "traditional-modernized" association, but what mainly distinguishes the latter is its syncretistic character, its relatively formal organization, and the variety of its functions. A particularly striking example of the latter point is *La Goumbé*, a Moslem and predominantly

Dioula youth organization for both sexes in the Ivory Coast. This combines the functions of emancipating young women from family influence; assisting the process of marital selection; providing, on a contributory basis, marriage and maternity benefits (including perfume and layettes for the newborn); preserving the Dioula tribal spirit; running an orchestra; and acting as the local propaganda agent for *Rassemblement Democratique Africain.* It also maintains its own police force (cited by Hodgkin from Holas 1953:116-131). In addition to a written constitution which embodies the declared aims and rules of the society, this kind of association sometimes has its own name and a special uniform of its own, and generally follows such Western practices as the holding of regular meetings, keeping of minutes, accounts, etc. The wearing of a uniform type of dress is probably more characteristic of women's societies than those formed by men. The women members of *Nanemei Akpee,* for example, all dress in white for meetings, and the practice of appearing in the same kind of dress, including head-tie, necklace, and sandals, is followed by other women's groups on formal occasions. Finance plays an important part in its affairs, and there is a regular tariff of entrance fees; weekly or monthly dues are collected and fines are sometimes levied. These funds are administered by a Treasurer or Financial Secretary, sometimes supervised by a committee which also conducts the everyday business of the association, including the sifting of fresh applications for membership, settlement of disputes, etc. Related partly to the wide diversity of functions performed is the large number of persons holding official positions in some of these societies. Many of these office-bearers, as exemplified by the dancing compin, have European titles, or, as in the case of the Kru women's societies, are known by the native equivalents of such titles.[2] This enactment of European roles, as in the dancing compin, is a fairly common feature of associations of the "traditional-modernized" type. It has been termed "vicarious participation in the European social structure" by J. Clyde Mitchell, but as Michael Banton points out (1956), this possibly places too much emphasis on the process of westernization and too little on the independent process of change in the tribal group. An assistant official sometimes has the duty of conveying information about the society's activities to the general public as well as to members. *La Goumbé,* for example, has a number of town criers, members of the *griot* caste, to carry news through the town (Holas 1953).

The organization of the "traditional-modernized" association is also rendered more elaborate by a tendency toward affiliation. This ranges all the way from a fully centralized organization of individual branches to a loose fraternal arrangement between entirely autonomous branches of the same movement. Affiliation of individual branches sometimes seems to be the result of traditional conditions. Thus, the "village-group union" of the Afikpo Ibo of Nigeria is apparently modelled largely upon the indigenous age-set structure of the people concerned (cf.

[2]For example, *Chelenyoh,* Secretary; *Weititunyon,* Treasurer (Banton n.d.).

Ottenberg 1955:i-28). The *Goumbé* movement comprises a number of local "cells" co-ordinated by a central committee, which settles disputes between them and lays down general policy (Holas 1953). The dancing compin movement, on the other hand, consists of a large number of separate societies which occasionally exchange visits and information and extend hospitality to each other's members, but are otherwise entirely independent. Finally, although membership of these associations tends to be tribally or regionally circumscribed, this is not invariably so. Even tribal unions sometimes have persons from more than one tribe among their members. The Benin Nation Club (Nigeria), for example, provides facilities for all natives of the Benin Province (Comhaire-Sylvain 1950:246 ff.). Several occupational and other groups recruit their members on an intertribal basis, and this also applies to some of the societies run by women.

The "modern" association has already been briefly described in terms of the "social club," and so it will suffice merely to add that its organization is broadly the same as that of any European association of a comparable kind. Like its European counterpart, it is often a medium for social prestige.

Despite their wide variety, one objective common to all types of voluntary association is that of sociability and fraternity. Not only is the serving of refreshments, including such beverages as tea, palm wine, beer, or stronger drink, an integral part of any formal gathering of members, but the latter are expected and encouraged to visit each others' homes, especially in the event of illness or bereavement. Again, although some groups, including certain guilds and occupations, are confined to persons of the same sex, it seems to be a fairly common practice for women to be admitted into associations under the control of men, and for men to be members of certain associations in which women predominate. Some associations organized by men deliberately encourage the recruitment of female members but have them under a more or less separate administration, with the women's leader responsible to the head of the society. A further fairly common feature of all kinds of voluntary associations is the fact that most of their personnel are young people. Indeed, some societies expect their members to retire at the age of thirty (Holas 1953), and it is rare for persons over middle age to play an active part in their affairs. This, however, is less typical of the "traditional" organizations that it is of the other types of association which, nevertheless, quite often like to have an elderly man or woman as an honorary president. The role of such a person is to uphold the associations's reputation for respectability and to help its relations with the wider community. The fact that he is not infrequently a person of importance in tribal society is indicative of the desire of such associations to keep on good terms with the traditional authorities. The size of membership is a more variable factor. It ranges from a mere handful of individuals to several hundred or even thousands, in the case of the larger tribal associations. In the smaller societies, which are often very ephemeral, the amount of support given is probably bound up as much with the personality and personal influence of the leader as it is with the popularity of the institution.

Voluntary Associations as an Adaptive Mechanism

It was suggested earlier that the social changes resulting from culture contact may be seen as an historical process of adaptation to new conditions. Adaptation in the present context implies not only the modification of African institutions, but their development to meet the demands of an industrial economy and urban way of life. In effect, as Banton has shown in reference to Temne immigrants in Freetown, this sometimes amounts to a virtual resuscitation of the tribal system in the interests of the modernist ambitions and social prestige of the younger educated element concerned (Banton 1956:354-368). The unpublished findings of Jean Rouch seem to give even greater emphasis to this kind of phenomenon, which he has labelled "super-tribalization." Some of the immigrants into the Gold Coast, whom he has studied, have gained sufficient solidarity through their associations and cults to dominate over the local population, achieving monopolies in various trades (cf. Forde 1956:389). A further important effect of this kind of development, as both Busia (1950) and Banton (n.d.) have pointed out, is to inhibit the growth of civic loyalty or responsibility for the town concerned. Modern urbanism, in other words, is the conditioning factor in contemporary African society as well as the culmination of so-called acculturation. West African urbanism of course differs from comparable Western situations in being less advanced, although it is probably more dynamic. It involves a particularly rapid diffusion of entirely new ideas, habits, and technical procedures, and a considerable restructuring of social relationships as a consequence of the new technical roles and groups created.

Voluntary associations play their part in both these processes through the fresh criteria of social achievement that they set up and through the scope that they offer, in particular, to women and to the younger age groups. Women, and younger people in general, possess a new status in the urban economy, and this is reflected in the various functions which these associations perform as political pressure groups, in serving as a forum for political expression, and in providing both groups with training in modern methods of business. Equally significant is the fact that women's participation in societies with a mixed membership involves them in a new kind of social relationship with men, including companionship and the opportunity of selecting a spouse for oneself. In particular, voluntary associations provide an outlet for the energies and ambitions of the rising class of young men with a tribal background who have been to school. The individuals concerned are debarred by their "Western" occupations as clerks, school teachers, artisans, etc. and by their youth from playing a prominent part in traditional society proper; but they are the natural leaders of other young people less

Westernized and sophisticated than themselves. This is largely because of their ability to interpret the "progressive" ideas they have gained through their work and travel, and through reading newspapers and books, in terms that are meaningful to the illiterate rank and file of the movement.

It is, in fact, in relation to the latter group, particularly the urban immigrant, that the significance of voluntary associations as an adaptive mechanism is most apparent. The newly arrived immigrant from the rural areas has been used to living and working as a member of a compact group of kinsmen and neighbors on a highly personal basis of relationship and mutuality. He knows of no other way of community living than this, and his natural reaction is to make a similar adjustment to urban conditions.

This adjustment the association facilitates by substituting for the extended group of kinsmen a grouping based upon common interest which is capable of serving many of the same needs as the traditional family or lineage. In other words, the migrant's participation in some organization such as a tribal union or a dancing compin not only replaces much of what he has lost in terms of moral assurance in removing from his native village, but offers him companionship and an opportunity of sharing joys as well as sorrows with others in the same position as himself. (Probably an important point in this regard is the large number of offices available in some associations, enabling even the most humble member to feel that he "matters.") Such an association also substitutes for the extended family in providing counsel and protection, in terms of legal aid; and by placing him in the company of women members, it also helps to find him a wife. It also substitutes for some of the economic support available at home by supplying him with sickness and funeral benefits, thereby enabling him to continue his most important kinship obligations. Further, it introduces him to a number of economically useful habits and practices, such as punctuality and thrift, and it aids his social reorientation by inculcating new standards of dress, etiquette, and personal hygiene. Above all, by encouraging him to mix with persons outside his own lineage and sometimes tribe, the voluntary association helps him to adjust to the more cosmopolitan ethos of the city (Banton 1956; Offodile 1947:937, 939, 941). Equally significant, too, is the syncretistic character of associations of the "traditional-modernized" type. Their combination of modern and traditional traits constitutes a cultural bridge which conveys, metaphorically speaking, the tribal individual from one kind of sociological universe to another.

The latter point is also indicative of various ways in which these voluntary associations substitute for traditional agencies of social control. Not only are positive injunctions to friendly and fraternal conduct embodied in the constitution by which members agree to bind themselves,[3] but many associations have

[3]"Added . . . is the internal discipline which is often maintained among members of well organized tribal unions. Where there is perfect control of extraneous activities of the members,

rules proscribing particular misdemeanors and what they regard as antisocial behavior. In this respect, the frequent inclusion of sexual offenses, such as the seduction of the wife or the daughter of a fellow member, is very significant. The association also sets new moral standards and attempts to control the personal conduct of its members in a number of ways. For example, the Lagos branch of *Awo Omama* Patriotic Union resolved not to marry any girl of their town so long as the prevailing amount of money asked for bridewealth was not reduced (Comhaire-Sylvain 1950). The dancing compin will withhold its legal aid from a member unless the company's officials examining the case feel that he is in the right. Also, there are women's groups concerning themselves specifically with the settlement of domestic quarrels, which expel members who are constant troublemakers in the home and among other women. More frequently, punishment takes the form of a fine, but the strongest sanction probably lies in the fact that every reputable association is at pains to check fresh applications for membership (Offodile 1947:939, 941). In other words, a person who has earned a bad name for himself in one organization may find it difficult to get into another; and this form of ostracism may in some cases be as painful as exile from the tribe.

A final important point is the extent to which disputes of a private or domestic nature, which would formerly have been heard by some traditional authority such as the head of a lineage, are now frequently taken to the head of an association, even when the matter is quite unconcerned with the life of that particular body (Kurankyi-Taylor n.d.; Offodile 1947:28).

Conclusion

Theorists of Western urbanism have stressed the importance of voluntary associations as a distinctive feature of contemporary social organization. Wirth, in particular, has emphasized the impersonality of the modern city, arguing that its psychological effect is to cause the individual urbanite to exert himself by joining with others of similar interests into organized groups to obtain his ends. "This," wrote Wirth (1938) "results in an enormous multiplication of voluntary organizations directed towards as great a variety of objectives as are human needs and interests." However, this thesis has not been strongly supported by empirical enquiry. According to Komarovsky (1946:686-698), who studied voluntary associations in New York, the old neighborhood, the larger kin group, might have broken down, but they have not been replaced by the specialized voluntary

---

it is hard to see two litigants in court being members of the same tribal unions. I remember at Makurdi the Ibo Federal Union there had a strict regulation, which was observed to the letter . . . that no Ibo man shall send another to court under any pretext without first bringing the matter to the union for trial and advice. The result of this was that in that town the Ibo deserted the courts, except if drawn there by members of different tribes or by disloyal members of their own union, but this latter case is rare" (Offodile 1947).

groups to the extent usually assumed. Floyd Dotson, who conducted a similar investigation in Detroit, also failed to find a wholesale displacement of primary by secondary groups. He concludes that the majority of urban working class people do not participate in formally organized voluntary associations (Dotson 1951:687-693). Perhaps more significant for the present context is the fact that the same writer found even less participation in voluntary organizations among the working class population of Guadalajara, the second largest city of Mexico (Dotson 1953:380-386).

The quantitative methods used in obtaining the latter results have not as yet been employed in African towns, so it is impossible to make exact comparisons. Also, the investigations concerned appear to have been made among relatively stable populations. Further study is therefore needed of the two factors which seem to be largely instrumental in the growth of these African voluntary associations. The first of these factors is the existence of an urban population which is largely immigrant, unstable, and socially heterogeneous. The second is the adaptability of traditional institutions to urban conditions. Possibly, it is the existence and interrelationship of these two factors rather than "anomie" which creates the essential conditions for the "fictional kinship groups," which, according to Wirth, substitute for actual kinship ties within the urban environment.[4]

References Cited

Aloba, Abiodun
1954 *Tribal Unions in Party Politics.* West Africa, July 10.

Ardener, Shirley G.
1953 *The Social and Economic Significance of the Contribution Club among a Section of the Southern Ibo.* Annual Conference, West African Institute of Social and Economic Research. Ibadan.

Balandier, Georges
1955a *Sociologie des Brazzavilles Noires.* Paris, Colin.
1955b "Social Changes and Problems in Negro Africa." In *Africa in the Modern World,* edited by Calvin W. Stillman. Chicago, Univ. Chicago Press.

Banton, Michael
1956 "Adaptation and Integration in the Social System of Temne Immigrants in Freetown." *Africa,* Vol. 26, No. 4.
1957 *West-African City: A Study of Tribal Life in Freetown.* O. U. P.

Bascom, William
1952 "The Esusu: A Credit Institution of the Yoruba." *Journal of the Royal Anthropological Institute,* Vol. 82.

[4]It has been noted in this connection that voluntary associations among Mexican immigrants in Chicago are participated in by only a small minority. Nevertheless, they play an important role which directly and indirectly affects the life of the entire colony (Taylor 1928: 131-142).

1955 "Urbanization among the Yoruba." *American Journal of Sociology,* Vol. 60, No. 5.

Busia, K. A.
1950 *Social Survey of Sekondi-Takoradi.* Accra, Gold Coast Government Printer.

Carey, A. T.
N.D. Unpublished study of Keta, Gold Coast. Department of Social Anthropology, Edinburgh University.

Clément, Pierre
1956 In *Social Implications of Urbanization and Industrialization in Africa South of the Sahara.* Edited by Daryll Forde. (Prepared by the International African Institute, London.) Paris, UNESCO.

Coleman, J. S.
1952 *The Role of Tribal Associations in Nigeria.* Annual Conference, West African Institute of Social and Economic Research. Ibadan.

Comhaire-Sylvain, Suzanne
1950 "Associations on the Basis of Origin in Lagos, Nigeria." *American Catholic Sociological Review,* Vol. 11.
1951 "Le Travail des Femmes à Lagos." *Zaire,* Vol. 5, Nos. 2 and 5.

Dotson, Floyd
1951 "Patterns of Voluntary Association among Urban Working-Class Families." *American Sociological Review,* Vol. 16, pp. 687-693.
1953 "Voluntary Associations in a Mexican City." *American Sociological Review,* Vol. 18, pp. 380-386.

Forde, Daryll
1956 "Introduction." *Social Implications of Urbanization and Industrialization in Africa South of the Sahara.* Daryll Forde, ed.

Fortes, M.
1945 "The Impact of the War on British West Africa." *International Affairs,* Vol. 21, No. 2.
1947 "Ashanti Survey, 1945-46: An Experiment in Social Research." *Geographical Journal,* Vol. 110.

Hodgkin, Thomas
1956 *Nationalism in Colonial Africa.* London, Muller.

Hofstra, S.
1955 "De Betekenis van Enkele Niewere Groepsverschijnselen voor de Sociale Integratie van Veranderent Afrika." Medelingen der Koninklijke Nederlandse Akademie van Wetenschappen, ofd. Letterkunde, *Nieuwe Reeks,* Deel 18, No. 14.

Holas, B.
1953 "La Goumbé." *Kongo-Overzee,* Vol. 19.

Komarovsky, Mirra
1946 "The Voluntary Associations of Urban Dwellers." *American Sociological Review,* Vol. 11, No. 6.

Kurankyi-Taylor, E. E.
N.D. *Ashanti Indigenous Legal Institutions and Their Present Role.* Ph.D. dissertation, Cambridge University.

Little, Kenneth
1950 "The Significance of the West African Creole for Africanist and Afro-American Studies. *African Affairs,* Vol. 49.
1953 "The Study of 'Social Change' in British West Africa." *Africa,* Vol. 23, No. 4.
1955 "Structural Change in the Sierra Leone Protectorate." *Africa,* Vol. 25, No. 3.

Littlejohn, James
N.D. Unpublished pilot study of Lunsar, Sierra Leone Protectorate. Department of Social Anthropology, Edinburgh University.

Lloyd, Peter
1953 "Craft Organization in Yoruba Towns." *Africa,* Vol. 23, No. 4.

Lombard, J.
1954 *Cotonou: Ville Africaine.* de I'Institut Français Afrique Noire (Dakar), Vol. 16, Nos. 3 and 4.

Offodile, E. P. Oyeaka
1947 "Growth and Influence of Tribal Unions." *West African Review,* Vol. 18, No. 239.

Ottenberg, S.
1955 "Improvement Associations among the Afikpo Iko." *Africa,* Vol. 25, No. 1.

Taylor, Paul S.
1928 *Mexican Labor in the United States.* University of California Publications in Economics, Vols. 6 and 7.

Wirth, L.
1938 "Urbanism as a Way of Life." *American Journal of Sociology,*Vol. 44, No. 8.

Biographical Note

Few genuinely cross-national studies of interest groups exist; occasionally, however, a framework developed in one context is applied to another setting. Thus, except for the items listed under "General Discussions," only a sampling of the empirical work on interest groups done in single countries can be listed. Additional information on interest groups can be found in some general works on comparative political systems—where the focus is not always the group—if the student is willing to search through the relevant sections.

General Discussions

Specifically on interest groups: Gabriel Almond, "A Comparative Study of Interest Groups and the Political Process," *American Political Science Review,* Vol. 52 (March 1958), pp. 270-282; Roy C. Macridis, "Interest Groups in

Comparative Analysis," *Journal of Politics,* Vol. 23 (February 1961), pp. 25-45; Joseph La Palombara, "The Utility and Limitations of Interest Group Theory in Non-American Field Situations," *Journal of Politics,* Vol. 22 (February 1960), pp. 29-49; and Henry W. Ehrmann, "The Comparative Study of Interest Groups," in *Interest Groups on Four Continents,* ed. Henry W. Ehrmann (Pittsburgh: Univ. Pittsburgh Press, 1958). This book includes several excellent contributions on interest groups abroad and several round-table discussions which draw many common threads together.

Not on interest groups but containing excellent material: Harold D. Lasswell and Daniel Lerner, *World Revolutionary Elites: Studies in Coercive Ideological Movements* (Cambridge, Mass.: M.I.T. Press, 1965); and D. W. Brogan and Douglas V. Verney, *Political Patterns in Today's World* (New York: Harcourt, 1968), which contrasts liberal democracy with the Communist system. (Chapters 2 and 7 are especially relevant to the study of interest groups.)

Single Country and Area Analysis

Great Britain: Harry Eckstein, *Pressure Group Politics: The Case of the British Medical Association* (Stanford, Calif.: Stanford Univ. Press, 1960); S. E. Finer, *Anonymous Empire: A Study of the Lobby in Great Britain* (London: Pall Mall Press, 1958); and J. D. Stewart, *British Pressure Groups: Their Role in Relation to the House of Commons* (Oxford: Oxford Univ. Press, 1958).

France: James M. Clark, *Teachers and Politics in France: A Pressure Group Study of the Fédération de l'Education Nationale* (New York: Syracuse Univ. Press, 1967); Jean Meynaud, *Les Groupes de Pression en France* (Paris: Colin, 1967); and Henry W. Ehrmann, "Pressure Groups in France," *Annals,* Vol. 319 (September 1958), pp. 141-148.

Germany: Ralf Dahrendorf, *Society and Democracy in Germany* (New York: Doubleday, 1967), Chapters 14-18.

Other areas: Nobutaka Ike, *Japanese Politics: An Introductory Survey* (New York: Knopf, 1957); Richard Willey, "Pressure Group Politics: The Case of Sohyo," *Western Political Quarterly,* Vol. 17 (December 1964), pp. 703-723 (an application of Eckstein's framework to the Japanese labor movement); George Blanksten, "Political Groups in Latin America," *American Political Science Review,* Vol. 53 (March 1959), pp. 106-127; Monroe Berger, *The Arab World Today* (New York: Doubleday, 1962), Part 2 (on social groups and on the social basis of political institutions); Aristide R. Zohlberg, "The Structure of Political Conflict in the New States of Tropical Africa," *American Political Science Review,* Vol. 62 (March 1968), pp. 70-87; Leonard M. Thompson, *The Republic of South Africa* (Boston: Little-Brown, 1966), pp. 133-163. (This volume, like most of those in the Little-Brown series on comparative politics, edited by Almond, Coleman, and Pye, contains an excellent section on interest articulation.)

The Communist World: H. Gordon Skilling, "Interest Groups and Communist Politics," *World Politics,* Vol. 18 (April 1966), pp. 435-451; A. Doak Barnett, *Cadres, Bureaucracy and Political Power in Communist China* (New York: Columbia Univ. Press, 1967); and Wlodzimierz Weselowski, "Class Domination and the Power of Interest Groups," *The Polish Sociological Journal,* No. 3-4 (1962), pp. 53-64.

An Introduction to Political Gaming

Political and military games have been used as training devices and research instruments for some years. Long before the outbreak of World War II, for example, high-ranking members of the German foreign office used a war game to explore German defense alternatives in the event of a Polish attack. The Japanese and the Allies also used games for predicting the outcome of various military operations.[1] During the decade of the fifties, military-political simulations flowered at the Rand Corporation, at Northwestern University, at MIT, and elsewhere. By the late 1960s, educational games covering almost every aspect of historical and contemporary political life were in wide use in secondary schools and universities, as well as in industrial and military settings. Formal parlor games combining the simulation concept with the visual appeal of a *Monopoly* board are now available for home entertainment.

A distinction should be made between "games" and "simulations." A formal body of literature, called game theory, dates back to von Neumann's work in 1928.[2] (The interested student may want to consult the brief bibliography at the end of this section and browse through some of the current work.) "Games," as the term is used in the literature, are governed by fixed mathematical principles. The classical model is the two-person zero-sum game. It is constructed in such a way that one player battles the other for a finite and known amount of resources; the total losses are always equal to the total gains of the two parties. (If I lose two points and win three, my opponent loses three points and wins two.) The outcome of such a game, assuming that both players are rational, is

[1]See H. Goldhamer and Hans Speier, "The Role of Operational Gaming in Operations Research," *Journal of the Operations Research Society of America,* Vol. 5 (February 1957), pp. 1-27, and Harold Guetzkow, "The Use of Simulation in the Study of International Relations," *Behavioral Science,* Vol. 4 (July 1959), pp. 183-191, for a discussion of the historical use of games and simulations.

[2]See J. von Neumann, "Zur Theorie der Gesellschatspiele," *Mathematische Annalen,* Vol. 100 (1928), pp. 295-320; and J. von Neumann and O. Morgenstern, *Theory of Games and Economic Behavior*, 2nd ed. (Princeton, N.J.: Princeton Univ. Press, 1947).

predictable through logical means. Many war games and political games follow game-theory logic, although the outcome is not as neatly measured when the number of players is increased beyond the initial pair of opponents.

Other contemporary "games," including the one presented below, are not properly games but are *simulations.* They are efforts to approximate problem situations in the real or historical world, under conditions which do not always permit *exact* calculations of outcomes, and where the total losses and gains do not always add up to zero. In *Urbos,* for example, no two players have exactly opposed goals, and the passage or defeat of a legislative proposal cannot be said to benefit one player five "utiles" while costing the other four players a total of five "utiles." The lack of precision does not make such a simulation useless; it simply means that the tenets of formal game theory cannot be applied in evaluating the strategies of different players or the outcome of several playing periods. It might even be argued that the loss in research precision of simulation models is offset by their closer approximation to real life conditions. The game-theoretical model, in contrast, often requires drastic simplification of real problems.

Simulations have been used for two different purposes: as research tools and as teaching devices. When simulation is employed for research, the particular problem under consideration (for example, the probable effect of nuclear proliferation on the stability of international coalitions) is usually repeated dozens of times by several different teams of players under two or three experimental conditions. Every effort is made to account for the effect of personality differences, physical conditions, outside events, and the like on the outcome of the game. Messages, position papers, and other written materials produced by the players are meticulously analyzed during and after the game. The purpose of such an endeavor is to provide relatively precise answers to problems of theoretical or immediate political significance.

Urbos, in contrast, has been designed as a teaching device. Although it is likely that a great deal of insight about the world of city politics could be gained by analyzing the outcome of repeated plays, particularly if a specific problem were the repeated focus (for example; the relative effectiveness of conciliation versus confrontation tactics of the "Have-Nots"), the primary goal is increased student insight into the political bargaining process. Even those students who have attended public hearings or followed newspaper accounts of the kinds of problems included in *Urbos* have learned a great deal through actual *participation* in this simulation. Those who have railed at the impotence of city hall have been quite sobered by their own experience in handling the reins of power; those who have charged that most civil-rights bills are merely pious mouthings have found themselves composing the same "mouthings" after repeated failure to gain support for stronger proposals.

The success of the simulation and the degree to which it will approximate "reality," hinge above all on the ability of the students to play their roles in a consistent fashion. Short of constructing their own game—an undertaking strongly recommended if class time permits—the students' *successful* experience in taking the role of an urban educator or a businessman (an experience in empathy) is probably the most rewarding aspect of the effort.

Urbos: *A Simulation of the Urban Political Process*

Edward Berger
Harvey Boulay
Betty H. Zisk

Urbos: *Participants' Instructions*

Urbos is a simulation of the group process within an urban political system. As a player you will be a member of one of five groups: Business, Government, Have-Nots, Humanists, and Educators. Each group has a set of goals which reflects the interests of similar groups in real life. The object of the game for each group is to maximize its own set of goals. This is accomplished by securing the adoption of proposals which affect the political life of the community in ways which are favorable to your group, and by opposing the adoption of proposals which are unfavorable.

Urbos *was constructed specifically for this book. It was developed from the game* Sitte, *originally created by Hall T. Sprague and associates, Western Behavioral Sciences Institute, La Jolla, California.*

Each group has a certain number of "influence points" which it can use to support or oppose proposals up for adoption. Proposals are considered "passed" when they have accumulated a predetermined number of positive influence points and "defeated" when they have accumulated a predetermined number of negative influence points. You will not be told how many points are needed for passage, but this should become clear to you after a few periods.

The passage of proposals not only affects the goals of specific groups but may also alter certain general "indicators" of the political health of Urbos. The indicators are Financial Health, Level of Public Services, Civic Order, Equality, Educational and Cultural Offerings, and Civic Pride. These will be more fully explained later. Some of these indicators may have special importance to certain groups. The Have-Not group, for example, should have a special interest in the indicator for Equality.

In a sense, long-range success or failure for a group is reflected in the status of these indicators at the game's end rather than in the sheer number of proposals that the group has successfully supported. In other words, unless the adoption of proposals affects the status of indicators in meaningful ways, such "victories" will be hollow ones. You will also find that success in playing *Urbos,* like success in real-life political situations, depends on the ability of your group to interact with other groups. To a certain extent such interactions are "formalized" by the rules of the game, but there is still plenty of room for bargaining, logrolling, *quid pro quo*, and even possibly deception. The successful playing of the game also depends to a large extent on the ability of the participants to "play their parts." Businessmen, for example, must try to act like businessmen if the simulation is to be realistic.

The play of the game. At the end of these instructions, you will find a "Rating in Brief" analysis, which depicts the political health of Urbos in terms of the indicators as the game begins. This is supplemented by the short essay "Urbos in June 197_." You will also find a set of goals for Urbos interest groups and an explanation of the various status indicators. Before the game begins, you should be familiar with this material.

The game is divided into five (or more) playing periods. Each playing period except the final one has two sections. During the first section of each playing period, groups are allowed to communicate with other groups only by written messages. Your primary concern during this first section is to decide how your group will allocate its influence points for that period. Each section of each playing period should be about 15 minutes long. At the end of the first section of each playing period, each group must record its allocations of influence points for that period on its decision form. These forms are sent to Control for tabulation. The final period of the game ends at the point when the last allocation report is filed with Control.

The groups may allocate their points as follows:

1. Each group has 50 influence points which it may expend during the five periods of the game (60 for a six-period game and so on).
2. In the first period, you must allocate exactly 10 points—no more, no less.
3. In all succeeding periods, each group must allocate at least five but no more than 15 influence points.
4. Points may be allocated positively or negatively for any given proposal.
5. In reckoning the total number of points you have allocated, ignore plus and minus signs; for example, six "plus" points and four "minus" points means 10 points allocated.
6. When Control tabulates the allocation of points on proposals, of course, these positive and negative signs are not ignored. Moreover, influence points will accumulate on a given proposal over the entire game, although these are reduced by a predetermined correction factor from period to period.

There is space on your decision form to keep a running tally of the total number of influence points your group has allocated. In the event that a group runs out of influence points before the final period, it will be allowed to continue in other phases of play (bargaining and so forth). Control may use its judgment in publicizing the fact that a team is in this position. A group may not elect to "pass" in a period so long as it has points left to allocate.

During the second section of each playing period, the groups may move about and confer with other groups. The groups will find it helpful during this section if they plan their activities and try to practice division of labor wherever possible. The game requires that each group elect a chairman at the start of the game. You may also want to divide up other functions—for example, someone to take care of paperwork throughout the game.

At the end of the second section of each playing period, Control will return your group's Status-Report/Decision Form, so that you will be able to see how the indicators have changed. Allocation of points for a proposal will not change the status indicators until the proposal has been adopted. Some indicators, however, will change regardless of proposal adoption due to the effect of certain "natural trends" which are built into the game. When Control returns these forms to you, the first section of the next playing period will begin.

The special role of Government. It is obvious that Government is more than just one group among many in the political process of an urban system. In order to take this into account in the game, all proposals which involve Government action or participation will be sent to the Government team when they have received the normal number of points necessary for adoption. They will not be considered adopted unless they have been signed by the chairman of the Government team or receive an extraordinary amount of support (to be determined by Control). Control shall also determine which proposals require this special approval from Government. There is no time limit for Government to pass on any proposals it receives. There need be no official announcement that a proposal has been submitted to Government by Control for final approval. Groups may continue to allocate points for such a proposal (this might be necessary, of course, if Government should choose to exercise a "pocket veto" over a proposal which would otherwise be adopted). Because of this special function, the Government team should be slightly larger than the others.

Introduction of new proposals. As the game progresses, your group will probably want to introduce new proposals to augment the six with which the game started. Your group has been supplied with forms to help you in drawing up these proposals. All portions of this form must be filled out as specifically as possible. A new proposal must be signed by the chairmen of three groups before it can be submitted to Control. The signature of the chairman of Government on a new proposal does not automatically indicate the assent of Government should the proposal gain enough points for adoption, nor does sponsorship of a new proposal commit a group to allocation of points for it at any time. New proposals may be sent to Control at any time during the game; however, a proposal will not appear on the agenda of proposals up for adoption until the first section of the period *after* its receipt by Control. Control reserves the right to refuse any new proposal which is poorly (that is, ambiguously, vaguely) written or which is impossible to implement in the context of the game.

*Urbos in June 197_*

Urbos is an old, established city, and one of the nation's major commercial and industrial centers. Like most metropolitan centers, Urbos faces middle class emigration to the suburbs, growing minority problems and unrest, transportation snags, and increasing evidence of inadequate schools, housing, recreational facilities, and other major amenities. Urbos also has a highly developed patronage system which, despite civil service, controls the hiring policies for many local administrative agencies. Most city employees (including police, fire, educational, recreational and service workers) are hired on the basis of recommendations from the local political party elite. The city's downtown commercial area is now in the process of being redeveloped, partly with state and federal funds.

Urbos has a well-deserved reputation as an educational, cultural, and financial center; at the same time much of this reputation is based on past glories. Urbos' institutions of higher learning remain relatively sound, and civic opera, orchestra, chamber groups, and museums are strong. Secondary education in Urbos, however, leaves much to be desired, and the children of Urbos' elites seem to be leaving the city to search for better elite-cultural opportunities. A major reason for this exodus is the vicious circle of high taxes, high cost of living, and low level of public services. Increasingly, however, the majority of Urbos' population couldn't care less about the state of the arts or the way the old things seem to be running down.

Unemployment rates are relatively high, if compared to the national average. School dropout rates are also high. Minority problems have been dealt with, at least on a temporary basis, by state legislative fiat, but little progress has been made to resolve the issues which underlie the race problem. Demands for equal opportunities by the Have-Nots of Urbos, for years quiescent, are now very much on the rise.

Urbos' Rating in Brief

1. Financial health. (2).[1] Urbos' tax rate for both residential and business property is so high that further increases will drive residents and businessmen elsewhere. New (and badly needed) services and capital expenditures thus cannot be undertaken without cutting existing expenditures; any gain for schools or parks, for example, must be at the expense of transportation, public housing, or some other service.

2. Educational and cultural offerings. (3). This is a mixed score. Outsiders who come into Urbos and elites who remain in the city can take advantage of excellent elite-oriented arts and education. Non-elites, however, must contend with inadequate public education and cultural services. Aesthetically, the same mixed situation exists. In the city itself, the newly developed core area would rate highly; the remainder of Urbos is a vast stretch of unaesthetic squalor.

3. Public services. (2). On the whole, transportation, housing, and general services (sanitation, health, and so on) are poor and have been ignored. Until recently, most business and government effort has gone into redevelopment of the downtown commercial area. A degree of caprice is built into Urbos' long-range planning efforts because much depends on administration, largely carried out by patronage appointees.

4. Civic order. (3). Rumbles of dissatisfaction among minority groups are increasing because of the inequalities in the city. The citizens of Urbos have feared outbreaks during the past several summers, but no violence has occurred on a major scale. Yet parts of the downtown commercial area are "unsafe" at night, and the crime rate is climbing slowly but steadily.

[1]This initial status of (2) refers to an eight-point scale ranging from 1 (poor) to 8 (excellent). See the "Status Report Form" for details.

5. *Equality.* (1). Great disparities continue to exist because of discrimination in the private sector, a perpetuation of the old power structures in the public sector, and the existence of old inequalities in available housing, education, and economic opportunities.

6. *Civic pride.* (5). High but unjustified.

Goals for Interest Groups

(Note: each group's goals are listed in approximate order of the priority of that group.)

Government

1. Maintenance of civic order.
2. Balanced budget. This means, given the present financial health of Urbos, that there can be no increase in expenditures unless:

    a. current expenditures are cut *or*
    b. new revenue sources are found.

3. Maintenance of maximum level of government control over the economic, social, and political structures.
4. Enhancement of civic pride in order to retain present residents of Urbos and to attract new residents.

Business

1. Lowest possible tax rate. This implies a balanced budget, if not decreased expenditures. A balanced budget implies, given the present financial health of Urbos:

    a. no increase in spending unless current expenditures are cut *or*
    b. a search for new revenue sources.

2. Attraction of new industry to Urbos and expansion of present consumer base.
3. Independence from government control and from control of all non-business groups.
4. Maintenance of civic order. Business cannot flourish in an atmosphere of fear and possible violence.
5. Maintenance of adequate levels of education and public services so that potential employees and consumers are available.
6. Enhancement of civic pride so that businesses will remain in Urbos and new business will come in.

Education

1. An increase in the level of public expenditures for educational purposes in order to raise the quality of educational offerings in Urbos.

2. Independence of educational authorities from political control.

3. Maintenance of civic order and public services at levels adequate to carry on a superior educational system.

4. Enhancement of civic pride in order to retain high quality teachers and to attract new teachers to Urbos.

Have-Nots

1. Equality for all men.

2. A larger share of the Urbos budget for services, education, and business opportunities which will improve the lot of the Have-Nots. This goal includes:

a. better housing
b. better schools
c. better transportation
d. job opportunities
e. "vacations with pay–take your wife and kids to the seashore."

3. A stronger voice in running Urbos affairs.

Humanists

1. Preservation and enhancement of aesthetic and cultural values with increased expenditures, where necessary, on conservation, historical and cultural activities and programs; opposition to programs which hamper those goals.

2. Maintenance of civic order. Culture is unimportant in a chaotic environment.

3. Increased equality, brotherhood, and love, with an increase in expenditures which will further these ends.

4. Enhancement of Urbos' civic pride as a cultural and humanitarian oasis in order to bring a halt to the present population exodus and to attract new residents. Humanists cannot afford to lose elite population; these are the bulwark of cultural and educational activities.

Six Proposals for Action

Public Proposals (Government Approval Required)

1. Jobs. Public hiring in Urbos should be undertaken in the future with no consideration for race, color, or religion; no city contracts shall be granted in the future to any private firm which discriminates in hiring. A legal apparatus shall be set up to deal with charges of infringement of this policy in both the public and private sectors. Staffing costs are to be met from the regular Urbos budget with funds diverted from other enforcement operations.

2. *Transportation.* The Urbos government shall construct more off-street and underground parking facilities near the central business district and shall improve major arterial highways into Urbos. This will aid consumer-shoppers and encourage prospective employers in the financial and commercial area. These facilities are to be financed by a 2 percent sales tax on all products except medical supplies and educational materials sold within Urbos city limits. As presently constituted, the highway construction plan entails destroying a number of historical landmarks.

3. *Schools.* A significantly larger proportion of the Urbos budget shall be devoted to a crash program to improve the quality of college-preparation schooling for exceptionally intelligent children. In addition to taking a larger slice of the Urbos budget, the hiring of additional personnel and the revamping of facilities for the new program will require an estimated 2 percent increase in property taxes.

4. *Parks.* The size of the Urbos central park, which borders on the central business district, shall be increased by setting aside up to 5 percent of city land as it becomes available and by taking land by eminent domain if necessary. This enlarged central park is to be the first step in a program of establishing green-belt areas (parks and recreational facilities) within the Urbos limits. The program is to be financed by a 20-year bond issue, which will necessitate a 2 percent increase in property taxes.

5. *Promotion.* In order to attract new industry to Urbos, a 40 percent property tax rebate shall be in effect for new industry investing more than $50 million within the city. The rebate shall run for a period of 10 years from the date of relocation. This may result in a short-run loss of revenue, but the long-range effects should be a net increase in taxable property and a consequent lowering of the tax rate.

Private Proposals (Government Approval Not Required)

6. *Opportunities.* The three major universities in the Urbos area agree, in cooperation with the Urbos Association of Manufacturers (UAM), to provide a total of 200 scholarships for the education of black students who would not otherwise meet normal educational standards for admission to the universities. Business also agrees to hire, on a preferential basis, the students so trained. The universities agree to train them to the point where they are qualified to meet normal

hiring standards. Two-thirds of the funds are to be contributed by business directly to the university program, and one-third are to be provided by the universities by diverting funds from normal scholarship programs. It is estimated that the yearly cost of the program will be upwards of $600,000. The enforcement of the program will be voluntary, but public statements will force a moral commitment.

Name of Group

Status Report: The Condition of Urbos by Periods

Instructions to Group: This form must be turned in with your decision form at the appropriate time in each period. Control will calculate the effects of group activity and translate these effects into changes in the six indicators below. The indicators are weighted along the following lines:

1	2	3	4	5	6	7	8
Poor			Fair				Excellent

The Status of All Indicators for Each Period Is

Beginning of Period No. ___	Financial Health	Educ. Cult.	Public Services	Civic Order	Equality	Civic Pride
1 (Start of Game)						
2						
3						
4						
5						
6						
7						
Final Status at Game's End						

Decision Form (Point Allocations for Each Period)

Instructions to Group: When your group has decided how it is to allocate its influence points, you must enter your decision in the appropriate spaces below. This form must be submitted to Control when allocations are called for at the midpoint in each game period. This form, together with the Status Report Form, will be returned at the start of the next period.

Proposal No. and Short Title	Period Number 1	2	3	4	5	6	7
1							
2							
3							
4							
5							
6							
7							
8							
9							
10							
11							
12							
13							
14							
15							
16							
17							
Total Points Allocated This Period							
Total Points Allocated So Far in the Game							

For This Game You Have a Total of ____ Points to Expend over ____ Periods

For Control Only
Per. No.
Prop. No.
Sh. title

New Proposal Form

Instructions to group: Make proposals as specific and clear as possible. Make sure that financing and enforcement provisions (if necessary) are within the bounds of possibility. New proposals may be submitted to Control whenever they have the signatures of *three* group chairmen.

Substance of proposal

Financing (dollar amounts not necessary, just a general idea of how the new proposal is to be financed)

Enforcement (if necessary, some proposals may be seen as self-enforcing; others will require institutional arrangements of some sort)

Authorized signatures: (1) ____________________ Group: ________

(2) ____________________ Group: ________

(3) ____________________ Group: ________

Urbos Form for Control Use

For Government Only

The following proposal has received sufficient influence point allocations for adoption. Actual adoption, however, is dependent on its receiving approval from your group in the form of a signature of the chairman of Government or upon its receiving an extraordinary number of influence points.

If you wish to give your approval to this proposal, sign this form and return it to Control. You may hold this form as long as you wish, or you may refuse to sign it. You may use your own discretion about whether you wish to make it known to other groups that the proposal is in your hands. Keep in mind, however, the fact that the proposal may be enacted simply by further accumulation of influence points.

Proposal No.: ____

Short Title.: ______________

Signature ________________________

Chairman of Government Group

Period No.

INDICATOR STATUS SUMMARY FORM (FOR CONTROL ONLY)

INDICATOR	POTENTIAL EFFECT OF PROPOSAL NO.:														Total Indicator Effect of Bills Passed:
	1	2	3	4	5	6	7	8	9	10	11	12	13	14	
Financial Health															
Educ. and Cult.															
Public Services															
Civic Order															
Equality															
Civic Pride															

INDICATOR	Value at Start of Period	Effect of "Natural Trends"	Subtotal	Effect of Proposal Adoptions	New Value (for Status Report to Each Group)
Financial Health					
Educ. and Cult.					
Public Services					
Civic Order					
Equality					
Civic Pride					

PERIOD ANALYSIS FORM (POINT ALLOCATION AND PROPOSAL STATUS), FOR CONTROL ONLY

End of Period No. ____

Proposal No.	Urbos Interest Groups					TOTAL (+ or −) This Period	Previous Total Divided by 2	NEW TOTAL
	Busi-ness	Have-Nots	Educa-tion	Govern-ment	Human-ists			
1								
2								
3								
4								
5								
6								
7								
8								
9								
10								
11								
12								
13								
14								
15								
Total Points Allocated This Period						List of Bills Passed This Period		
Total Points Used So Far in the Game								

Postgame Evaluation

Players of *Urbos* will want to discuss the results of this simulation at some length. In evaluating *your* success as a member of a specific team, you should remember that the best measure of your success is not the sheer volume of bills passed through your support (or defeated because of your opposition), but rather the *trends shown in the indicators* which are most intimately connected with your group's goals. Thus, a Business team is most interested in Economic Health and Civic Order; a Have-Not team is primarily concerned with Equality, and to some extent with Services and Education.

In evaluating your game, you will want to try to compare your results with "reality" in the outside world. Each player should ask himself:

1. If I were in fact a spokesman for X Group, would my members continue to support me in the light of my behavior in *Urbos*? Did I accomplish enough to satisfy them? Did I behave in the way that they would expect?

   (Some simulations include an internal evaluator on each team. His job is to determine whether the team's decisions are in line with the wishes of the team's constituency. Would such an internal evaluator have approved of your actions?)
2. How closely did my behavior approximate the "real" behavior of businessmen, educators, or whomever I was representing? Did I find it necessary to depart from "normal" behavior in order to cope with the demands of other players? Why? Did I find that my personal feelings sometimes conflicted with the demands of my role? Why? Did these conflicts affect the course of the game?
3. If I felt that this simulation did not lead to an accurate reflection of "reality," can I pinpoint the reasons for the problem? Were there any rules, playing conditions, or arrangements concerning the relative power of the players which struck me as naive or unrealistic? How would I change these rules or other arrangements if I were writing my own game?
4. What major trends did I notice in the course of the game? Did government become more or less effective? Did some groups begin and end in a relatively ineffective position? Were some groups hopelessly naive? Did some behave too cynically? Why? Did these trends differ from the "real life" situation I would have predicted? Why?
5. Did any of these trends show real promise of casting some light on "real" situations? Why or why not?
6. What, if anything, do I believe that I have learned from playing *Urbos*? In answering this question, try to distinguish between results of unique events or personality problems, problems arising from game rules which are not reflections of reality, and trends which may be characteristic of the "real world."

Urbos in the Classroom

The following commentary is based on pretesting *Urbos* in the classroom at Boston University. It is meant to be suggestive rather than prescriptive; there probably are an infinite number of fruitful variations on the format described here. Any communications from those who try this simulation under different conditions would be welcomed.

General Comments. *Urbos* can be played by as few as 13 people[2] or by as many players as space and acoustical conditions (things tend to get rather loud) will allow—about 20 to 30 seems to be the optimal size. With about 20 to 25 people, we would recommend that three work as Control, three work as messengers, five work on the Government group, and three or four work on each other group. (The Government group should be slightly larger because of its special responsibility on all legislative proposals.) Because the success of the game depends on the student's ability to play his role consistently, we suggest that students be assigned (or allowed to volunteer for) roles which are comfortable or "natural" in terms of their own values; at the same time, there may be some merit in urging a few students to adopt unfamiliar roles.

We have played *Urbos* under both classroom and seminar-in-the-home conditions. We found that the sense of continuity and resultant student ability to maintain consistent roles were greatest when the game could be played in a single session; the chance to spread groups over several rooms was also helpful. The game can be played, however, in three one-hour classroom periods, if a moderately large room is available. Students should be warned, however, to maintain jury conditions under this arrangement—that is, not to discuss the game between periods.

About five playing periods, each half an hour long, seem to work well. The first period should be somewhat longer to give players a chance to become familiar with the game and to give each group a chance to iron out some of its internal differences. This is particularly important if the groups are large and a variety of opposing views is represented. We suspect that a shorter game will prevent the full flowering of alliance formation and the effort to seek workable compromises; a game of six to eight periods, in contrast, should be very fruitful but may require two evenings or a full day for playing.

Supplies and advance preparation. Players should study the instructions and especially the "Group Goals" and "Proposals for Action" well in advance of the game. The professor should duplicate the necessary forms in the following quantities for a five-period game:

[2]Two on each team, two for Control, and one messenger.

150 message forms, in triplicate
5 "Decision Forms" (one for each group)
5 "Status Reports" (one for each group)
5-30 "Participants' Instructions," as reproduced above

"Participants' Instructions" should include the following: "Instructions," "Goals for Urbos Interest Groups," "Urbos in June 197_," and "Six Proposals for Action." (One copy for each player is helpful and will accelerate the process of mastering the game materials; if each player owns a copy of this book, no problem will arise.)

Message forms can follow a simple format—a space for the name of the group sending the message, a space for the name of the recipient group, and a space for the game period and time of message. Information on the sequential order of messages is vital for a post-game analysis. Message forms should be stapled together in triplicate, and a supply of carbon paper should be furnished to each group.

The Control group should have a typewriter and a supply of paper and carbons for special bulletins and reports. A blackboard can be used if the game is played in a single room. Name tags designating team membership for each player are helpful.

The Control group should assemble a basic packet of materials for each group and distribute it at the beginning of the game. If the game is played over a number of class periods, these should be collected and redistributed at the beginning of each session.

Tips for Control group. The Control group has four major tasks. The first of these is *maintenance of a communication system* between groups and between groups and Control. This task includes facilitating a smooth flow of messages during playing periods and issuing statements on the status of proposals, new proposals, and changes in indicators as a result of decisions made.

The second task is *general supervision of the tempo of the game.* If one or two periods of inaction occur, it is up to Control to "get things moving" via bulletins, news conferences, warnings to individual groups. If frenzied activity with little substantive output occurs, Control should use its judgment on appropriate action. Warnings and injunctions to action may be in order; in other cases, "waiting it out" is advisable.

Control may also decide to "leak" some messages for a variety of reasons—for example, one group may be slow in starting while others are busily undercutting its goals. On the basis of pretest experience, however, we would warn against excessive meddling by Control. Such leaks may backfire.

Control's third task is *dealing with special problem situations.* All the following problems arose during the extensive pretesting of *Urbos*; we cannot, of course, predict the problems you may encounter in addition to the ones below.

1. One or two groups appeared to be totally ignoring their goals (beyond reasonable strategic limits).
2. Proposals were made, and were supported by a majority of groups, which were beyond the constitutional powers of Urbos agencies to promulgate, finance, or enforce.
3. Proposals were vague, ambiguous, or unenforceable as written.
4. Messages were stolen, and false or forged messages were sent.
5. Private communications systems (hand signaling, paper airplanes, or other acts which short-circuited the Control system) were employed.
6. One or more players threatened to quit the game; other actions outside the simulation were threatened or taken; nongame payoffs were invoked (for example, "I won't go home with you!" from a husband to wife).

No rules can be laid down to cover every possible problem, but we have found that these three guidelines are useful:

1. Control has the obligation as well as the authority to reject or to demand revision of proposals which are vague or unconstitutional within the limits of the game. It also should warn groups which are departing from group goals that they are not acting within the role-situation required in *Urbos.*
2. Control should use its own judgment in adjudicating problems such as irreconcilable splits within groups. Control may insist that a group continue to function as a unit, or it may allow a split with a prorated apportionment of influence points.
3. Any group behavior which is clearly "outside the system" of *Urbos* should be stopped on the spot. Stolen messages, forgeries, nongame payoffs, and threats to leave the game cannot be tolerated. Control's main dilemma in cases of this sort will be to distinguish between problems which arise under adjudication (2, above) and outside-the-game threats (3).

Control's last major task is the *maintenance of records. Keeping in touch with conferences and conversations throughout the game* is desirable both for the sake of postgame evaluations and a final detailed analysis of the game. If possible, a member of Control should be free to wander about, to listen to both intragroup and intergroup conferences, and to keep in touch with events. Players should be assured that such observation is neutral and that no breach of confidence will occur.

Variations in Urbos. The "Group Goals," "Status of Urbos," and "Proposals for Action" for Urbos were written in mid-1968. If real-world political events between that period and the time in which you play the game are unusual enough to render some of these statements obsolete, you should not hesitate to modify them. The general guiding principle of *Urbos*—the idea for a framework for collective bargaining among relevant groups—is the focal point of this simulation; the specific city profile, goals, and proposals are secondary. In addition, if you believe that a modification of parts of *Urbos* would make the simulation more relevant to your students' interests in terms of economic or geographical background, you should make the necessary changes.

Point requirements for passage of proposals and effects of passage of proposals on indicators. We have left these measures unspecified in our instructions because we believe that you will not want to release these figures to participants in *Urbos* in advance; the number of influence points needed to pass a proposal should be inferred by students as the game progresses. You may want to determine your own indices on these issues. If, however, you would like further information on these points, or have any other questions about the playing of *Urbos*, you should contact Betty H. Zisk, Department of Government, College of Liberal Arts, Boston University, Boston, Massachusetts.

Bibliographical Note

The best general works for the nonmathematical student are Anatol Rapoport, *Fights, Games and Debates* (Ann Arbor, Mich.: Univ. Michigan Press, 1960); *Readings in Game Theory and Political Behavior*, ed. Martin Shubik (New York: Doubleday, 1954); or a more recent book of readings, *Game Theory and Related Approaches to Social Behavior* (New York: Wiley, 1964).

Early classics by von Neumann have been cited above. The student may also want to consult the following: Jessie Bernard, "The Theory of Games of Strategy as a Modern Sociology of Conflict," *American Journal of Sociology*, Vol. 59 (March 1954), pp. 411-424; R. Duncan Luce and Howard Raiffa, *Games and Decisions* (New York: Wiley, 1957); R. Duncan Luce and A. A. Rogow, "A Game Theoretical Analysis of Congressional Power Distributions for a Stable Two-Party System," *Behavioral Science*, Vol. 1 (1956), pp. 83-96; Anatol Rapoport, "Critiques of Game Theory," *Behavioral Science*, Vol 4 (January 1959), pp. 49-66; and Richard Snyder, "Game Theory and the Analysis of Political Behavior," in *Research Frontiers in Politics and Government*, ed. Stephen K. Bailey *et al.* (Washington, D.C.: Brookings Institute, 1955).

Many simulations of interest to the student of international politics are reported in *The Journal of Conflict Resolution*.